Welcome to Hospitality

...an Introduction

3rd Edition

Join us on the web at

culinary.delmar.com

Welcome to Hospitality

...an Introduction

3rd Edition

KAYE (KYE-SUNG) CHON, PH.D., CHE
Dean
School of Hotel and Tourism Management
The Hong Kong Polytechnic University

THOMAS A. MAIER, PH.D
Asst. Professor Leadership and Revenue Analytics
DePaul University

Australia • Brazil • Japan • Korea • Mexico • Singapore • Spain • United Kingdom • United States

Welcome to Hospitality . . . an Introduction, 3rd Edition
Kaye (Kye-Sung) Chon and Thomas A. Maier

Vice President, Career and Professional Editorial: Dave Garza

Director of Learning Solutions: Sandy Clark

Acquisitions Editor: James Gish

Managing Editor: Larry Main

Product Manager: Anne Orgren

Editorial Assistant: Sarah Timm

Vice President, Career and Professional Marketing: Jennifer McAvey

Marketing Director: Wendy Mapstone

Marketing Manager: Kristin McNary

Marketing Coordinator: Scott Chrysler

Production Director: Wendy Troeger

Senior Content Project Manager: Nina Tucciarelli

Art Director: Bethany Casey

Library of Congress Control Number: 2009920753

ISBN-13: 978-1-4283-2148-9

ISBN-10: 1-4283-2148-9

Delmar
5 Maxwell Drive
Clifton Park, NY 12065-2919
USA

Cengage Learning is a leading provider of customized learning solutions with office locations around the globe, including Singapore, the United Kingdom, Australia, Mexico, Brazil, and Japan. Locate your local office at: **international.cengage.com/region**

Cengage Learning products are represented in Canada by Nelson Education, Ltd.

To learn more about Delmar, visit **www.cengage.com/delmar**

Purchase any of our products at your local college store or at our preferred online store **www.ichapters.com**

Printed in China
3 4 5 6 7 17 16 15 14

Contents

APPENDICES

Preface

Welcome to Hospitality: An Introduction, 3rd Edition explores the fascinating worlds of lodging, foodservice, meeting planning, travel and tourism, gaming, sports management, revenue management principles, and the related businesses that make up the hospitality industry. This edition identifies the latest trends found throughout the industry and addresses what the industry is doing to adapt to modern technology.

Perhaps you are considering a career in hospitality. If so, this book will help you decide. Alternatively, you may have already decided to pursue a career in hospitality but want to broaden your understanding of the industry. If so, this book will help you understand how all parts of the industry are related.

Welcome to Hospitality is designed to:

- Arouse your interest in the many career opportunities available in the industry.
- Help prepare you for the challenges faced by professionals in hospitality management.
- Explore trends that will have an impact on your future in the industry.
- Provide a global perspective on present and future industry issues.
- Suggest directions for educational and professional development.
- Share the enthusiasm and excitement that are part of the hospitality spirit.

Background

While hospitality is an "industry," its roots lie in social and cultural life. Throughout history, the industry has been shaped by the societies and cultures in which it has grown. Societal and cultural issues continue to shape the industry—issues like environmental concerns, economic changes, the increase in women business travelers, and legislation affecting smoking in restaurants.

Today, leadership in the hospitality industry goes far beyond traditional skills in operations. Leaders must be able to understand and predict how hospitality will be affected by the changing world. *Welcome to Hospitality* describes the industry in relation to social trends and cultural patterns. It will help you develop the leadership skills that are so important in this dynamic industry.

Perhaps the most striking contemporary trend affecting the hospitality industry is "globalization." Nations no longer exist in quiet independence but in growing interdependence. As a result, Western countries and cultures have begun to recognize the strength, vitality, and complexity of other nations and cultures. The third edition of *Welcome to Hospitality* has been revised with a deep appreciation of other traditions and cultures. But it is not an "international" book in the sense that all cultural and historical forms of hospitality are represented. The authors acknowledge that their own cultural heritages and industry experiences are limited.

Through history, the spirit of hospitality embodied the obligations to treat strangers with dignity, to feed them and provide them with drink, and to protect their safety. As the world becomes increasingly smaller and more aware of its vast diversity, this "spirit of hospitality" seems especially important. *Welcome to Hospitality* invites you to share in this spirit.

Supplements

Instructor's Manual

An Instructor's Manual is available to accompany this text. Included in the Instructor's Manual are correlations of chapter objectives and end-of-chapter exercises and activities to the SCANS (Secretary's Commission on Achieving Necessary Skills) competencies. The Instructor's Manual also contains chapter outlines, answers or suggested solutions to all end-of-chapter exercises, chapter tests and answers, and transparency masters.

Instructor Resources CD

New to this edition, an Instructor Resources CD is available to accompany this text. In addition to the Instructor's Manual contents, the Instructor Resources CD contains an ExamView® computerized test bank and PowerPoint© lecture slides to accompany each chapter.

Organization and Content

Welcome to Hospitality...An Introduction, 3rd Edition is organized into five parts and thirteen chapters.

Part 1, The Spirit of Hospitality, includes two introductory chapters.

- Chapter 1, Welcome to the Hospitality Industry, defines hospitality from the perspective of the guest. It introduces the various segments of the industry as well as important themes that are presented throughout the text.
- Chapter 2, Travel and Tourism: Partners with Hospitality, helps you understand the relationship between travel and tourism on one hand and lodging and related hospitality businesses on the other.

Part 2, Lodging, explores the lodging industry, past and present.

- Chapter 3, Dynamics of the Lodging Industry, explores the evolution of the lodging industry and classifications of various lodging properties and prototypes.
- Chapter 4, Hotel Development, introduces you to hotel development, including the planning, forecasting, design, construction, and opening processes.
- Chapter 5, Hotel Management and Operations, provides an overview of the management and operation of a hotel. Management structure, human resources, and the function of each department are discussed.

Part 3, Foodservice, covers the foodservice industry.

- Chapter 6, Hospitality and the Foodservice Industry, presents the variety of commercial and on-site foodservice types. You win learn to analyze a foodservice operation in terms of its market, concept, and menu.
- Chapter 7, Introduction to Culinary Arts, outlines the traditions of culinary arts, the organization of the kitchen, and the production cycle.
- Chapter 8, Beverage Management, introduces you to the variety of beverages that have traditionally been part of foodservice. You will learn about winemaking, brewing, and distilling. This chapter also emphasizes the responsibility hospitality operations have toward guests concerning alcohol consumption.

Part 4, Specialized Segments of the Hospitality Industry, introduces industry segments that cater to business travelers and long-term guests and that manage leisure and recreation activities for guests. Although these segments are not necessarily related to each other, foodservice and lodging play a vital role in their operations.

- Chapter 9, Meetings, Conventions, and Special Events, introduces you to the rapidly growing meeting, convention, exposition, sports management, and long-term health-care industries.
- Chapter 10, Recreation and Leisure Industry, presents recreation management and theme parks, resorts, and related segments of the hospitality industry.
- Chapter 11, Global Gaming and Casino Operations, presents the major players in the industry and the pros and cons of gambling. The casino customer is profiled, along with career opportunities in the fast-growing gaming industry.

Part 5, The Future and You, looks at the impact of the twenty-first century on hospitality and tourism.

- Chapter 12, Globalization and the Future of Hospitality, explores the future of the hospitality industry in terms of demographic, global, and technological trends.

- Chapter 13, Building for Success, looks to your future in the hospitality industry and suggests ways that you can plan for success.

New to This Edition

The third edition of *Welcome to Hospitality: An Introduction* has been updated by unique industry perspectives and professional profiles, comprehensive career opportunities in the hospitality and tourism network, practical industry applications, new-graduate glimpses, new references, and an extensive chapter on gaming. A truly exhaustive revision, the third edition features the following chapter-by-chapter enhancements:

Chapter 1: Welcome to the Hospitality Industry

This chapter has added new introductory sections on special events management, sports management, and gaming with updated business profiles reflecting current trends within the hospitality and tourism network.

Chapter 2: Travel and Tourism: Partners with Hospitality

Includes updated statistical data related to international tourism expenditures and world tourism growth overall.

Chapter 3: Dynamics of the Lodging Industry

Has expanded coverage of the growing lodging sector, featuring hotel product types that are new to the industry. Also presents the world's largest lodging/management companies, with insight into the idiosyncrasies of third-party managerial contracts.

Chapter 4: Hotel Development

Offers extensive coverage of specific hotel development criteria and building econometrics. Presents and discusses financial pro forma feasibility studies that include cost estimates of new hotel prototype development. Provides a breakdown of the top hotel brands among management companies.

Chapter 5: Hotel Management and Operations

This chapter has been substantially expanded and updated because of growing interest in operations management and financial performance. We have added new material on revenue management and its importance in yielding higher profit margins. Also discussed is the latest in organizational structure, reflecting current salary ranges found in the lodging sector.

Chapter 6: Hospitality and the Foodservice industry

Includes new material on the top ten independent restaurants in the United States, as well as statistical data on sales volumes, average checks, and meals served. There is also new information on consumer choice top selected chain restaurant winners, and industry perspectives on franchise strategy and cost-benefit analysis of independent versus owned restaurants.

Chapter 7: Introduction to Culinary Arts

Offers updated information and material on culinary certification programs, including master chef, executive chef, and pastry chef positions.

Chapter 8: Beverage Management

New discussions have been included on the trends and new products in the beverage industry. Top beverage brands are highlighted by market share and new information is included on emerging international wine regions.

Chapter 9: Meetings, Conventions, and Special Events

This chapter provides a new section identifying the growing trends in event planning and management. Career opportunities are identified in the club and sports management fields, with specific careers in event planning presented. Updated figures and tables help to break down revenues and expenditures associated with the convention, exhibition, and meetings industry.

Chapter 10: Recreation and Leisure Industry

Presents new coverage of market profiles and career opportunities associated with the burgeoning cruise ship industry, There are also new statistics on the top ten luxury resorts in the world, plus an expanded section on sustainable tourism.

Chapter 11: Global Gaming and Casino Operations

This chapter examines the legalization of casinos and the history of gambling worldwide. The chapter shows how American casinos are different from other global ventures and who the major casino companies are today. It discusses the pros and cons of allowing casinos to open, as the establishment of new gaming jurisdictions slows down in America following a series of industry mergers. The chapter closes by discussing the details of gaming operations and the career opportunities they offer.

Chapter 12: Globalization and the Future of Hospitality

Presents updated statistical information on the world's fifty largest hotel chains, consumer satisfaction indexes, and trends in changing hospitality workforce demographics. Included is in-depth coverage and discussion of the future of technology and its importance to online travel planning, revenue management systems, and video conference capabilities.

Chapter 13: Building for Success

This chapter has been updated to reflect current statistical data on the projected growth of food service and lodging industry managerial occupations, as well as current reference sources for travel industry and hospitality related jobs.

Learning Tools

The revised edition of *Welcome to Hospitality* provides a number of tools to help you learn.

Overview and Objectives

Each chapter begins with an overview that outlines what you should learn. The objectives that follow help you focus on the main points and see the sequence of information that will be covered.

Key Terms

As you work through this book, you will notice that we have set important industry terms in boldface and have defined them in context when introduced. Also, we have spelled out acronyms the first time they appear in the text. All key terms are listed in the Glossary, and Appendix A provides an alphabetical listing of the most commonly used acronyms for terms and organizations in the industry.

Feature Pages

Throughout the chapters, you will find a variety of interesting feature articles.

- *Professional Profiles* present the lives, achievements, and contributions to the industry of individuals such as Barry Sternlicht, Thomas Cook, and J. Willard Marriott.
- *A Day in the Life of...* features give an inside look at various careers in the industry. They provide background information on job responsibilities, daily tasks, and attributes needed to be successful on the job.
- *Business Profiles* provide an historical perspective on leading companies including Disney Theme Parks, Hyatt Hotels and Resorts, and Roy's Restaurants.
- *Graduate Glimpses* convey current information and peer advice from successful hospitality graduates.
- *Industry Insights* provide interesting facts and trivia on history, law and ethics, culture, technology, business innovations, and the environment.

Chapter Summary

Each chapter ends with a summary of the topics and issues covered in the chapter to help reinforce its learning objectives and prepare you for the exercises and critical thinking activities that follow.

End-of-Chapter Exercises

Check Your Knowledge questions test your recall on topics discussed throughout the chapter. *Apply Your Skills* activities focus your knowledge on industry problems. *What Do You Think?* questions challenge your critical thinking skills on issues relevant to the material in each chapter. *Case Studies* provide scenarios for further discussion and activities. The *Internet Exercises*, new to this edition, encourage investigation of a variety of topics on the World Wide Web.

Biographical Information

Kaye (Kye-Sung) Chon, Ph.D., is a former Professor and Director of the Tourism Industry Institute at Conrad N. Hilton College at the University of Houston in Houston, Texas. Currently, Dr. Chon is the Chair Professor and Director of Hotel and Tourism Management at the Hong Kong Polytechnic University. He has published over two hundred articles on hospitality industry issues. Dr. Chon is the executive editor of the *Journal of Hospitality and Tourism Research* as well as editor-in-chief of the *Journal of Travel and Tourism Marketing* and the *Asia Pacific Journal of Tourism Research.* In 1993, Dr. Chon received the prestigious John Wiley & Sons Award from the Council on Hotel, Restaurant, and Institutional Education for his lifetime achievement in scholarship and research.

Thomas A. Maier, Ph.D., is an International Professor of Service Leadership and Innovation at the Rochester Institute of Technology in Dubai. He is also the president of TAM—Global Services Inc. He has acquired a wide range of hospitality, development, and practical business experience over the past twenty-five years working for the Starwood and Red Lion Hotel brands. Most recently, he served as vice president of hotel operations for the Red Lion Hotel Corporation from 2001 until 2008, having held various management positions within that corporation since 1992. Dr. Maier was recently named the recipient of the RIT—2008 Dr. Paul Kazmierski Memorial Award from the School of Hospitality and Service Management for his achievements in and commitment to the field of human resource development.

Kathryn Hashimoto, Ph.D., author of the Global Gaming and Casino Operations chapter, is associate professor in the Department of Hospitality Management at East Carolina University. She received a PhD in Marketing from Century University, and a PhD in Curriculum and Instruction from the University of New Orleans. Her research interests are international consumer behavior, advertising, service management, and gaming. She is a renowned author and researcher and her articles have appeared in gaming and hospitality industry publications.

Reviewers

JOHN N. MELLON
Misericordia University
Dallas, PA

RICHARD J. MILLS, JR.
Robert Morris University
Moon Township, PA

KEN MYERS
University of Minnesota, Crookston
Crookston, MN

DENIS P. RUDD
Robert Morris University
Moon Township, PA

JAN VAN HARSSEL
Niagara University
Niagara, NY

The Spirit of Hospitality

A universal symbol for hospitality is the pineapple. While the exact origin of this symbol is unknown, many believe the idea was borrowed from the people—most likely inhabitants of Brazil—who first domesticated the pineapple.[1] These people placed pineapples outside their homes to signify that visitors were welcome. European explorers introduced the fruit to Europe and the American colonies in the seventeenth century. As the exotic fruit was rarer and more costly than caviar, it symbolized the very best in hospitality. It was used to welcome and honor royal and wealthy guests.

The idea of hospitality, of course, dates back much further—from historical evidence found at the first centers of civilization (such as Mesopotamia in present-day Iraq), to Biblical references of the washing of guests' feet, to later accounts of English innkeepers receiving weary travelers over a mug of ale. The core concept of hospitality, however, has remained the same: to satisfy and serve guests.

In this text you are offered the proverbial pineapple as you embark on a journey to explore the world of managing guest service. Welcome to the hospitality industry!

ch1

Welcome to the Hospitality Industry

OVERVIEW

What is hospitality? Ask this of fifty people and you are likely to receive fifty different answers. "Receiving guests in a generous and cordial manner." "Creating a pleasant or sustaining environment." "Satisfying a guest's needs." "Anticipating a guest's desires." "Generating a friendly and safe atmosphere." Each speaker has an intuitive (and correct) expectation of what hospitality is and isn't.

What is the hospitality industry? Finding one all-encompassing description of hospitality as an industry is as difficult as defining hospitality. The **hospitality industry**—comprising businesses that serve guests away from home—can be defined by its scope, mission, and providers. As you work through this book, your definition of *hospitality industry* will be continually updated and refined, expanded and honed. In these pages, you will become familiar with the industry's past, present and future, consistently building upon your understanding of what hospitality—and the industry surrounding it—are. This chapter introduces the industry by (1) outlining its scope, (2) examining its mission, and (3) describing ways to pursue its many career opportunities.

OBJECTIVES

When you have completed this chapter, you should be able to:

1. Define *hospitality industry* and provide at least one specific example of both successful and unsuccessful hospitality that you have experienced.
2. Identify the basic components of the hospitality industry.
3. Explain the relationship between guest satisfaction and employee responses during a service encounter.
4. Compare the benefits of obtaining a formal education and acquiring experience.
5. Recommend ways to ensure learning and growth throughout a hospitality career.

KEY TERMS

amenities
cuisines
entrepreneur
fusion cuisines
Gen-Xers
Gestalt evaluation
hospitality and tourism network
hospitality industry
labor-intensive
millennial generation
on-line distribution
service encounter
tourism
trends

The Scope of the Hospitality Industry

Historians have traced the development of the hospitality industry through thousands of years and many cultures. Viewing the industry through the lens of history is helpful because it reveals the strong relationship between the shape of hospitality and the needs and expectations of different societies. Because societies will continue to change in what they need and want, the hospitality industry will also continue to change. Future leaders within the industry will need to be focused on the ever-changing workforce and the evolving expectations of the traveling consumer.

The hospitality industry encompasses a wide range of businesses, each of which is dedicated to the service of people away from home. Today, career opportunities are available in many facets of the hospitality and tourism field. They include the tourism management, human resource management, special events management, sports management, club management, and gaming sectors.

An Age-Old Industry

Historians speculate that the first overnight lodging structures were erected along Middle Eastern trade and caravan routes around four thousand years ago. These structures, the *caravanserai*, were at eight-mile intervals and operated much like the present-day Middle Eastern *kahns* in that they provided shelter (for both humans and beasts) but nothing else. Provisions—food, water, and bedding—were supplied by the traveler. Early accounts of these establishments reveal physical conditions that would be considered harsh by today's standards. However, the spirit of hospitality was strong, perhaps especially so in the Middle East. A traditional Middle Eastern saying illustrates devotion to hospitality: "I am never a slave—except to my guest."[2] (More on the history of lodging facilities is found in Chapter 3.)

In many countries, the quality of hospitality services varied according to the fees paid and the location of an establishment. Some early accounts tell of vermin-infested inns and poor-quality food, but not all were bad. For example, *lesches*, social gathering places in ancient Greece, had a reputation for good

Photo courtesy of Radisson Hotels International

Guests being greeted at the Radisson in Chennai, India. A warm welcome creates an inviting environment and makes a good first impression.

food. Guests could choose from a variety of delicacies, including goat's milk cheese, barley bread, peas, fish, figs, olives, lamb, and honey.[3] Guests also had their choice of *lesches* to frequent—Athens alone had 360![4] (More food and beverage history is found in Chapter 7.) As mentioned earlier, the word hospitality has religious, social, and cultural significance. For instance, in the New Testament of the Bible (New International Version), the word hospitality appears in five instances. Romans 12:1, for example, says "Share with God's people who are in need and practice hospitality." Implied here is that genuine hospitality comes only when you have the spirit of "sharing" with care, concern, and love for the other people's well-being.

Fine service could also be found in ancient Rome, circa A.D. 43: "There were hotels on all main roads and in the cities, the better ones having a restaurant, a lavatory, bedrooms with keys or bolts...and also a yard and stabling. An inn at Pompeii had six bedrooms round two sides of an inner courtyard, with a kitchen on the third side. Its large bar and restaurant were a little ways away, on the main street."[5]

Roman society had a singular influence on the hospitality industry. Many of Rome's citizens were wealthy enough to travel for pleasure, and well-built Roman roads gave them easy access to most of the known world. As soldiers conquered new areas, Roman citizens could visit exotic places in comfort. Communication between guest and host presented no problems, as Latin had become a universal language. (In fact, much hospitality terminology springs from Latin: *hospe* means host or guest; *hospitium* means a guest chamber, inn,

Industry Insights

LAW AND ETHICS

Early Regulation of the Hospitality Industry

The earliest known regulation of the hospitality industry is found in the Code of Hammurabi. During Hammurabi's rule over the Old Babylonian Empire from 1792 to 1750 B.C., he developed what was considered a wise and fair set of laws The code required the landlady of a tavern to report any guest who planned crimes. The code also forbade adding water to drinks or giving false measures. The penalty for these "crimes" was death by drowning.[1]

By the time of the Roman Empire, regulations had changed. For example, the wife of an innkeeper could not be punished for disobeying the laws against adultery; innkeepers were not allowed to serve in the military because the military was an honorable service; and innkeepers were not allowed to act as guardians for minor children.[2]

Sometimes regulations were set forth by tavern owners. In sixteenth-century England, rules such as the following were common: No more than five people in one bed; no boots to be worn in bed; no razor grinders or tinkers to be taken in; no dogs allowed in the kitchen; organ grinders must sleep in the wash house.[3]

Although some of these old regulations seem preposterous, early regulations helped further the development of the industry, and some still are on the books today.

---

[1] W.C. Firebaugh, *The Inns of Greece and Rome; And a History of Hospitality from the Dawn of Time to the Middle Ages* (Chicago: F.M. Morris Company, 1923).

[2] Ibid.

[3] Fernand Braudel, *The Structures of Everyday Life*, Volume I (New York: Harper & Row, 1982).

or quarters. Other related words with this root include "hospice," "hostel," "hospital," and "hotel."[6])

With the fall of the Roman Empire, travel declined and inns became almost nonexistent. From the fourth through the eleventh centuries, the Roman Catholic Church kept the hospitality industry alive by encouraging religious pilgrimages between monasteries and cathedrals throughout Europe. Roads were built and maintained by clergy from the local monasteries. Hostels built on church grounds offered places to eat and sleep. Churches did not charge for these accommodations, although travelers were expected to make a contribution to the Church. When travel and trade gradually increased in Europe, the monasteries remained a major hospitality provider for both the business and recreational traveler.

Besides priests and missionaries, other travelers, including traders, merchants, diplomats, and military personnel, traveled the expanding Mediterranean and European roadways. Not all these wayfarers were taken care of by the Church; independent innkeepers also welcomed travelers on their journeys. When a group of Italian innkeepers incorporated in the year 1282, hospitality evolved from an act of charity to a full-fledged business.

Private ownership in England flourished less quickly. In 1539, as part of his dispute with the Roman Catholic Church, England's King Henry VIII declared that all lands owned by the Church were to be given away or sold. This decree inadvertently caused the growth of innkeeping because it required that churches give up their hostels. The Church lost its role as host and innkeeper, and private inns multiplied. (We discuss contemporary political influence on the hospitality industry in Chapter 12.)

Hospitality and the Tourism Network

From its simple origins as a collection of privately owned, independently operated businesses, the hospitality industry has grown in complexity and size. Today's hospitality businesses interact with one another on a global basis, and must stay aware of what is happening around them. For example, hotel investment companies, developers, joint ventures, management companies, and hotel chains now spread across the world. Economic conditions in Asia may affect a company's holdings either there or in its home country. An American hotel company may be a joint venture partner with an Asian company that builds hotel projects all over the world.

Hospitality businesses are also closely intertwined with those in the travel and tourism industry. **Tourism** is travel for recreation or the promotion and arrangement of such travel. Tourism and the hospitality industry so strongly affect one another that some associations and industry leaders, including the Council on Hotel, Restaurant and Institutional Education (CHRIE), consider the combined industries of hospitality and tourism as one large industry—the hospitality and tourism industry. The components of this large industry include (1) food and beverage services, (2) lodging services and ski resorts, (3) recreation services, (4) campgrounds and theme parks, (5) travel-related (tourism) services, (6) the gaming industry, and (7) products provided with personal services in conjunction with the first four components. Because these components are separate and often competing industries, this group of industries will be referred to in this text as the **hospitality and tourism network**. We use "network" in the sense of an interconnected set of parts or components.[7] (See Figure 1.1 for an overview of the hospitality and tourism network.) Sometimes this large network is referred to simply as the hospitality industry, especially because it emphasizes the responsibility of industry personnel to be hospitable hosts and managers of all services offered.[8]

This chapter focuses on the two major components of the hospitality portion of the network: lodging services and food and beverage services. But first we will discuss the interrelatedness of the network's components and the global forces that can affect them all.

Industry Connections and Global Forces

In Chapter 2 you will learn how the various components of the loosely knit global network of tourism and hospitality interrelate. Throughout the remaining chapters, but especially in Chapter 12, we will discuss how global forces affect

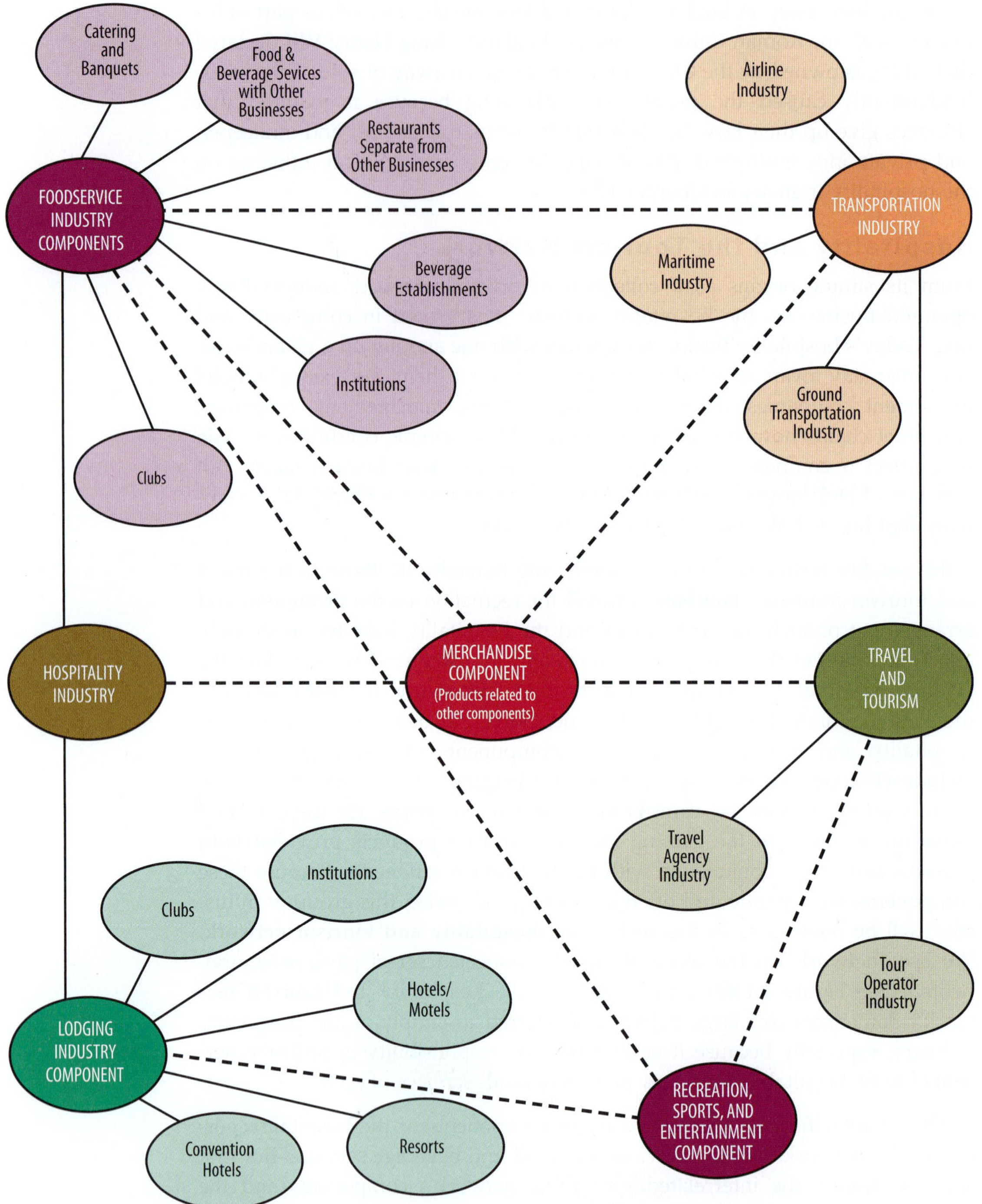

FIGURE 1.1 Hospitality and Tourism Network

Business Profile

POST HOTEL AND SPA

Luxury Ski Resort Positioned as a Destination Resort

Hotel and resorts may be positioned to offer services in many different market segments. The Post Hotel and Spa offers a product specifically targeted to recreational skiers. The hotel is situated in a majestic resort location in the Canadian Rockies. The Post Hotel and Spa offers luxurious accommodations, fine dining, and wellness/spa services. The distinguishing feature of the Post Hotel and Spa is its reputation as a rustic resort in proximity to Banff National Park and Lake Louise Ski Area. Since 1942, the Post Hotel and Spa has been recognized as a gourmet dining destination as well. The wine cellar at the Post Hotel and Spa is said to feature more than 28,000 bottles of wine. Guests can enjoy a long, hard day skiing and relax with a spa treatment and gourmet meal, while enjoying picture-perfect mountain scenery.

Source: http://www.posthotel.com

this complex network. Those forces are analyzed to discover **trends** (prevailing tendencies or general movements), which may be sociocultural, economic, technological, or geopolitical. These changes are dramatically affecting the exchange of goods and services worldwide, challenging industry leaders to find new ways to compete while creating new and exciting opportunities. They also illustrate the dynamic nature and ever-increasing globalization of the industry.

Photo courtesy of Radisson Hotels International

The senior citizen population continues to expand, providing additional workforce as well as career opportunities in health-care facilities and retirement communities.

Workforce Issues For the first time in the history of the modern workforce, hospitality employees are working closely with people who are as young as their children and as old as their parents. Managers are realizing that age has just as much to do with employees' hopes, learning styles, and expectations as do culture, gender and other characteristics. By understanding each generation and by giving employees what they need to thrive, leaders can do more to increase productivity, morale, and employee retention. Merit is overcoming longevity as the deciding factor that contributes to promotion. People from very distinct generations are competing for leadership positions in the workplace. Baby boomers, **Gen-Xers**, and **millennial generation** employees compete for the same jobs, and often younger workers get them. Sometimes, because of the post-industrial info-centered work world, the person in charge may be younger than those he or she manages. As both Generation X and millennial generation workers bring skills that some baby boomers may not possess, they may end up finding themselves supervising either older or younger employees.

The entrance of the baby boom generation into middle age has contributed to the trend known as the aging of America. Chapter 12 shows how such a trend affects opportunity. Experts predict that more senior citizens will be in the workforce, particularly in the food and beverage component of the industry. In addition, as the senior population expands, institutions such as health care facilities and retirement centers will need a larger supply of workers to satisfy the increase in customers.

Consequently, although the components of the hospitality and tourism network are continually changing with respect to labor, opportunity, and growth, the network will continue to dominate as a global industry.

Lodging Industry Component

Lodging best typifies the hospitality industry, because it involves providing overnight or longer-term services to guests. In the United States, the lodging industry employed 1.16 million people full time and part time and generated $85.6 billion in 1997.[9] Today, hospitality is a growth industry that generates nearly $90 billion annually and employs nearly 18.5 million nationwide, a number that is expected to increase about 10 percent between now and 2012. For many people, lodging is simply a place to sleep. For others, lodging facilities are all-in-one operations that extend beyond providing a bed and include entertainment and recreation facilities. For this reason, the lodging industry has evolved to accommodate varying customer preferences—from budget motels to luxury hotels to all-inclusive resorts.

In Chapter 3, you will learn about the specifics of lodging, including types of lodging facilities, owning and managing lodging operations, and marketing. You will learn about hotel development and operations in Chapters 4 and 5, conference and convention centers in Chapter 9, and resorts and casino hotels in Chapters 10 and 11.

Professional Profile

IAN SCHRAGER

Boutique Hotel Creator and Hotelier

Ian Schrager is known as a pioneer in the nightclub and hospitality industry. He is best known for his creation of Studio54 in New York City in the 1970s. He has a keen talent for creating business concepts and the ability to capture the imagination of his clientele with his one-of-a-kind hotel venues. His unusual professional expertise lies in his ability to combine the elements of art, fashion, and culture in his hotel projects. He is best known for his exceptionally entrepreneurial mindset and his ability to create arresting design and decor and fashionable hospitality concepts.

Schrager's career began in the seventies with pioneering hospitality concepts such as the "boutique hotel," which featured signature artwork and creative decor, indoor/outdoor atrium lobbies, and metropolitan spa destinations. In 1964 he opened the first such property, Morgans Hotel, with Studio 54 partner Steve Rubell.

Schrager went on to create urban boutique hotels in other highly visible, affluent cities, including London, Miami, and San Francisco. He is recognized as the creator of "urban chic," which connotes affordable luxury in the metropolitan setting. Instrumental to Schrager's success has been his ability to collaborate with artists, entertainers, and culinary experts. He has a keen sense of how to pair unusual, creative concepts with exceptional quality and service delivery. His latest partnership is with J.W. Marriott and the Marriott hotel brand.

Source: Ian Schrager Companies, http://www.ianschragercompany.com

Food and Beverage Industry Component

The food and beverage component of the industry employed more than 10.2 million people in 1998. In 2005, the restaurant and accommodation industries employed 12.2 million people, or about 9 percent of all employed U.S. workers. This far-reaching industry, with nearly 799,000 facilities throughout the United States, ranges in scope from street vendors to four-star restaurants to institutions (colleges and hospitals, for example).

Patrons enjoy a variety of **cuisines**, including food cooked and served in styles from around the world such as Chinese, Indian, Malaysian, Thai, French, Italian, Cajun, Japanese, American, and Mexican, as well as a variety of ethnic **fusion cuisines**. This variety is evident in all types of foodservice facilities and concepts. You might buy a tamale from a vendor on a street corner, get sushi at a take-out bar, or have tea and scones at a British tearoom. Settings also include diners, twenty-four-hour coffee shops, French farmhouses, noodle shops, and other facilities with clever themes to draw the public. Generally, food and beverage establishments can be categorized in relation to the market served, concept, and menu. These will be discussed in more detail in Chapters 6, 7, and 8.

In Chapter 6, you will explore the diversity of the foodservice component of the industry, including the many kinds of commercial restaurants and institutional food services. Chapter 7 presents foodservice careers, operations, social issues, and the art of food preparation. Chapter 8 examines the beverage component of the industry, including trends in beverage consumption, types of beverages, risk management, and liquor liability.

Service—The Mission and Product of Hospitality

When friends and relatives come to your home, you want them to feel comfortable. You go out of your way to greet, serve, and entertain your guests. When you visit someone else's home, perhaps you are treated to food, drink, and maybe even a comfortable bed. These **amenities** (features that add material comfort, convenience, or smoothness to social interactions) help define the behavior known as hospitality. This behavior is also a service. And service is the most important product of the hospitality industry.

The Nature of the Product

The intangibility of service makes it a little difficult for many people to see hospitality as an industry. Often, when people think of industries, they

Business Profile

STARBUCKS

Neighborhood Locations Serving Coffee for the World

Coffee for the world

The Starbucks coffee empire began in Seattle in 1971. It was founded by three partners and later expanded under the leadership of Howard Schultz. The linchpins of the Starbucks business model are its neighborhood locations and its gourmet coffee blends. Typically, Starbucks stores are found on busy pedestrian corners in urban centers. Starbucks' practice of making it easy for customers to have a gourmet coffee blend, coffee drink, or espresso in the vicinity of their office or neighborhood created a worldwide phenomenon.

The entrepreneurial spirit of Howard Schultz led Starbucks to worldwide prominence. Its identity and marketing message are well received by customers. Starbucks takes pride in its earthy store design concepts, concern for the environment, and strong sense of community. The founder's creative energy was not only exhibited in the décor and marketing messages, but also in the various types of coffees and espresso drinks available. The combination of personalized flavor combinations and gourmet coffee beans from around the world helped create an international brand identity second to none.

As of February 2007, Starbucks had 7,521 company-operated outlets worldwide: 6,010 of them in the United States and 1,511 in other countries and U.S. territories. In addition, the company had 5,647 joint-venture and licensed outlets, 3,391 of them in the United States and 2,256 in other countries and U.S. territories. This brought the total number of locations (as of February 2007) to 13,168 worldwide. Starbucks kiosks can be found in many popular grocery chains in the United States and Canada, as well as in many airports. In some cities, such as Los Angeles, there are actually two Starbucks stores located across the street from each other. In 2008, Starbucks announced the closure of over 50 stores worldwide as a result of the slowing US economy.

Source: http://www.starbucks.com

picture large manufacturing complexes with towering smokestacks and noisy production lines. These industries produce tangible products that usually can be handled, stored for future use, and uniformly produced. Service, on the other hand, is an intangible product. Respect shown to a guest cannot be held in the hands; pulling out a chair for a guest cannot be stored for future use; and acceptable practices in one culture may be considered rude in another, rendering uniformity in service impractical.

Some businesses related to hospitality also produce tangible products, such as special kitchen equipment used in commercial restaurants. But for most hospitality businesses, the main business is creating memorable experiences by furnishing services. Their shared mission is to provide services while also making a profit. James C. Penney, the retail store magnate, described this double-barreled task when he said, "If we satisfy our customers, but fail to satisfy our business, we'll soon be out of business. If we get the profit, but fail to satisfy our customers, we'll soon be out of customers."[10]

Restaurants and hotels have a twofold purpose: to satisfy both the physical and psychological expectations of guests. They accomplish this through providing a good product (the meal or the room) and a good service (delivering the meal or room appropriately).

Issues Arising from Product Delivery

Delivery of an intangible product leaves room for conflicting perceptions of its quality. Not only might people within the industry disagree on some theoretical points, but customers and employees may view the service delivery from quite different perspectives. A once-in-a-lifetime experience for the guest is often a routine occurrence for the employee. The guest is investing time, money, and emotions in the hope of receiving a pleasurable experience. All these are lost if the service fails to meet that expectation. The employee, however, can merely resolve to do better with the next guest.

Perception of Value

Service does not run on a continuum from good to poor. Such a scale is impossible because the variables involved in determining good or poor service—guest expectations and the firm's image—are not fixed. Even the concept of value (also called relative worth) is based upon guest perception. It is fair to say, however, that most guests want quality service at a fair price.

Guests perceive good service on the basis of their own expectations of the hospitality staff and their overall experience of the property. Their perception of value is based on the customers' expectations in relation to how much they spend for the service and how much they would spend for a similar service elsewhere. Certainly, people do not expect the same services from a low-priced hotel as they do from a high-priced hotel. However, what they do expect are the same or better services at the hotel or restaurant where they are guests (and at the same or better prices) than at the competition (the hotels or restaurants they didn't choose to visit this time).

Good service is often equated with the number of amenities, the degree of personal attention/interaction, and/or the speed of service delivery.

While these factors are related to service, equating them with service quality is misleading. Service, and service quality, are contextually defined by the guest's expectations as well as the organization's image. Good service at an Applebee's neighborhood restaurant is entirely different from good service at a Wolfgang Puck venue, yet both can provide quality service.

The Service Encounter.

The period of time in which a customer directly interacts with a service is known as the **service encounter**. That interaction may take place with either personnel or with physical facilities and other visible elements. If the hospitality establishment's advertising leads a guest to expect valet parking, the presence or absence of such service affects the guest's perception of the firm. In human interactions, both guests and employees bring to the encounter certain expectations and personality traits.

What do guests expect of hospitality establishments? The specific answer may vary, but will always include this: guests want, expect, and demand service, and that service must be delivered in a courteous, efficient manner.

Guests measure the quality of service by comparing the services received with what they expected to receive, given the type of establishment offering the service. Five general elements comprise the scale by which service may be judged: (1) price-value, (2) reliability, (3) responsiveness, (4) assurance, and (5) empathy.[11] Since a majority of these are an assessment of human interaction, how an employee performs during a service encounter contributes heavily to the perception of quality service.

Photo by Corbis/Joseph Sohm; ChromoSohm Inc.

A customer's expectations of service and quality vary based on appearance.

Most employee-guest interactions that significantly influence the guest's perception of satisfactory or unsatisfactory service fall into one of three general categories:[12]

1. Employee response to service delivery system failure, commonly known as service recovery. When services that are normally available are lacking or absent (such as when a reservation is lost), when service is unreasonably slow, or when other failures occur in the core service system, the employee's response plays a crucial role in the customer's perception. Ideally, genuineness in response and flexibility exhibited by the server, followed by immediate corrective action, may save the customer experience and preserve future loyalty. An offer of monetary or in-kind relief may (or may not) be part of the genuine response to customer displeasure. As compensation, an upgraded room or free drink may be offered, and the encounter is usually perceived as satisfactory. But compensation is not the only solution. Plausible explanations and assistance in solving the problem are often enough to assuage the guest. On the other hand, if the employee offers no compensation, explanation, or solution, the encounter is usually perceived as unsatisfactory. The employee's response can turn a negative experience into a positive memory or magnify the original problem by creating "two wrongs."
2. Employee response to customer needs and requests. When the customer wants the service delivery system altered to meet unique needs, the employee's response often means more than whether or not the need was met. Special needs include emergency situations, medical or language difficulties, customer preferences, specific dietary requirements, customer error, and dealing with the disruptive behavior of other customers. Once again, if the employee acknowledges the request and at least attempts to fulfill it (or explains why it cannot be fulfilled), the customer is usually satisfied. On the other hand, employee disinterest or unwillingness to consider resolving the service encounter leaves the customer dissatisfied.
3. Unprompted and unsolicited employee actions. The amount of attention or lack thereof given the customers will leave them feeling either pampered or frustrated. Taking extra time, providing additional information, or showing interest in the customer's comfort are all employee responses that leave the customer satisfied. Truly out-of-the-ordinary behaviors also belong in this group, as do behaviors in the context of cultural norms, exemplary performance under adverse circumstances, and Gestalt evaluations.

In the **Gestalt evaluation**, the service encounter is evaluated holistically—"everything went right." Also in this category are the cases where a customer has a series of encounters with one provider, and subsequently becomes a loyal patron or vows never to return.

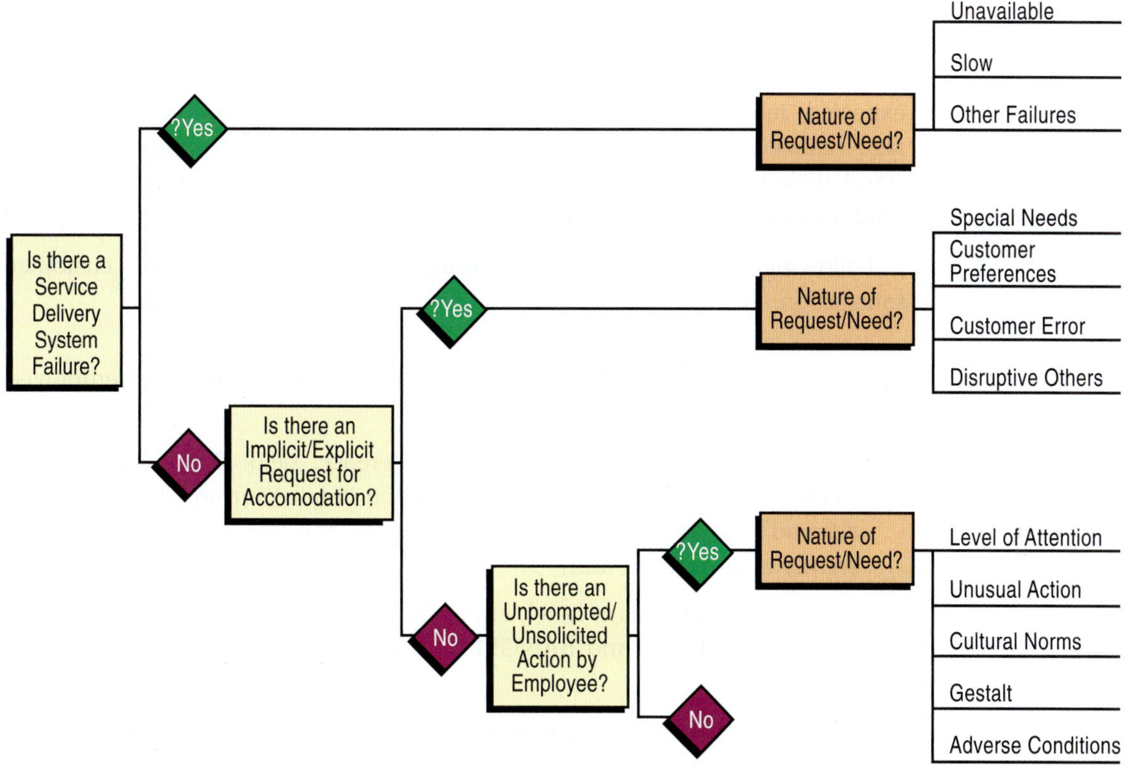

FIGURE 1.2 Incident Sorting Process of Service Encounters

Source: Adapted from Mary Jo Bitner, Bernard H. Booms, and Mary Stanfield Tetreault, "The Service Encounter: Diagnosing Favorable and Unfavorable Incidents," *Journal of Marketing* (January 1990): 76.

Analyzing the Service Encounter

The foundation of "good service" is not found in an abstract philosophy or set of rules. It certainly goes beyond saying "have a nice day" or answering the phone before the third ring. Rather, it emerges from interactive processes in which people respond with sensitivity and genuineness to serve in their specific role(s). The employee begins by actively listening to discover the guest's expectations. (See the problem-solving flowchart illustrated in Figure 1.2, Incident Sorting Process of Service Encounters.)

Guest: Every time I stay at ABC Hotel, I miss room service hours. Seems like it's never available.

Employee: Sounds like you could use a bite to eat. Can I help you by having dinner delivered to your room?

As you've learned, guest expectations help define what service is. Consequently, there is no universal situation that can illustrate good service. For example, you and a friend stop at a downtown eatery for a bite. You are in the middle of a shopping excursion and want to "eat and run." However, the waitress has timed your meal to be a leisurely, hour-long lunch. Is this poor service? In your mind it might be, since your expectation is to get in and get out of the restaurant as quickly as possible. For someone else, however, such a pace might be just what they wanted and expected, meaning they received good service. The key competitive advantage realized by successful hospitality operators is their ability to understand their targeted customers' expectations and exceed those expectations time and time again.

Following are examples of varying degrees of guest or customer satisfaction.

Taste of Success Pete Stevens relates an incident of unprompted employee action.

> I was an attendee at a three-day conference, held at the Marriott Copley Place in Boston. I arrived in Boston in late morning, borrowed a friend's car to handle some other business, and headed for the hotel shortly after dark (in rain).
>
> I couldn't find the darn hotel. I'm circling the block—looking, looking, swearing, looking—and BANG! I hit a median curb; flattened the left front tire.
>
> I got out of the car, and ran across traffic in the rain toward a covered building entranceway where I encountered a red-, white-, and gold–uniformed doorman. I was at the Marriott.
>
> Brad came toward me and asked if he could help. I explained my car trouble, told him I was checking in, and asked where I might find a phone to call for assistance.
>
> Brad went with me to the car, held traffic while I made a U-turn, told me that he'd fix the tire, and directed me to the front desk. Later in my room, I received a call from Brad, letting me know that the tire was fixed and the car was in the garage.
>
> Three days later, when I was leaving for the airport, there was Brad again. He waved and said, "Hope you enjoyed the conference, Dr. Stevens. Have a safe trip [home]."[13]

Service does not need to be "spectacular" to be considered good. In some settings, good service is almost unnoticeable, because everything goes along according to the guest's expectations. Generally, it is only when the service falls outside the limits of the guest's expectations that it is deemed satisfactory or unsatisfactory.

A Disappointing Experience In an article published in the *Cornell Hotel and Restaurant Administration Quarterly*, Bonnie J. Knutson, a faculty member at the School of Hotel, Restaurant, and Institutional Management at Michigan State University, stresses how meeting or exceeding guest expectations is paramount in generating guest satisfaction. Following is Knutson's personal account of how not to serve a guest.

> Having spent the morning giving a seminar on this very topic of customer satisfaction, I was tired, hungry, and on a tight time schedule. So I stopped at a nearby deli-type restaurant that featured "New York Dogs." When I saw both chili and hot dogs on the menu, I knew exactly what I wanted—no, what I needed—for lunch: a nice, long, juicy coney dog covered with chili and onions. I love coney dogs.
>
> Stepping up to the counter, I was greeted by a friendly order taker. The conversation went something like this:
>
> **Order Taker:** "Hi, can I help you?"
>
> **Me:** "Yes. I'd like a coney dog and black coffee."
>
> **Order Taker (looking perplexed):** "We don't have coney dogs."
>
> **Me:** "I know they're not on the menu. Just put some chili and onions on your hot dog and we'll call it a coney dog."
>
> **Order Taker:** "But, ma'am, we don't have coney dogs."
>
> **Me (determined):** "You have hot dogs, don't you?"
>
> **Order Taker:** "Yes."
>
> **Me:** "You have chili, don't you?"
>
> **Order Taker:** "Yes."
>
> **Me (beaming):** "Then there's no problem. Just put some chili on the hot dog and some onions on the chili, and I'll have my coney dog."
>
> **Order Taker:** "But we do not have coney dogs."
>
> You get the picture. The conversation went on in this vein for another three minutes before I learned that the reason she couldn't sell me a coney dog was that she didn't know what to charge me. It wasn't in the manual, and company policy didn't give anyone at the unit level the authority to create a menu item or change a price. I didn't care. All I wanted was a coney dog.[14]

Obviously, this encounter fell outside the guest's expectations. And not meeting guest expectations about service often prevents the desired result—a repeat customer.

Led Astray Service perception and guest expectation are also influenced by the physical facilities and other visible elements. Take, for example, the true story of a family traveling by car from Pennsylvania to California. They stopped for an overnight stay in Arizona, where all they wanted was a good night's rest and a hot meal. Noticing a sign for Asian cuisine nearby, the family decided a Chinese dinner would be just the ticket for their evening meal. It would be

The Fujiya Hotel, established in 1878, is one of the oldest Western-style hotels in Japan. The hotel's success is based on meeting guest expectations.

Photo by Kaye (Kye-Sung) Chon

convenient, nutritious, and a nice change from the American cuisine they had thus far been served. All set for dim sum and Peking duck, they opened the door and entered the restaurant. There before them lay the furnishings of an American steak house, replete with a high-hanging wall menu that listed typical steak-house fare. A quick family conference determined that their hunger was more urgent than their present desire for Asian food, and they decided to stay where they were. Unfortunately, even though every member of the family liked steak and the prices were reasonable, the meal (and experience) was less than satisfactory because it didn't deliver what they had been led to expect.

Principles for Achieving Guest Satisfaction

Guest satisfaction is the fulfillment of a guest's wants and needs. In the hospitality industry, market share dominance is exceeding guests' expectations on a regular basis. A hotel guest expects a safe, clean, comfortable sleeping room.

A restaurant patron anticipates a tasty meal in a clean, pleasant atmosphere with a balanced price–value relationship. Meeting these expectations is the hospitality professional's priority. The job is done only when the customer is satisfied.

Although quality service is contextually defined by guests' expectations, some approaches to service apply almost universally. Knutson proposes these ten principles for satisfying and keeping customers.

1. Recognize your guest. Personalizing interactions by using the guest's name is not always possible, but a sincere and warm interaction goes a long way.
2. Make a positive first impression. The initial greeting and warm welcome are essential elements of creating a positive exchange. Guests judge your advertising claims against beliefs they already hold and accept only new information that matches those beliefs. Changing a negative first impression is challenging, if not impossible.
3. Fulfill your guests' expectations. Guests expect a trouble-free environment. All they want is to have their needs met without aggravation. Those organizations that can exceed customer expectations will have a leg up on the competition.
4. Reduce the effort required of the customer. Guests want to exert as little effort as possible in purchasing your service. Remember, they are there to relax, so own your product and educate your customer about your product in order to align expectation with optimal satisfaction.
5. Facilitate customer decision making. The guest may not be familiar with all you have to offer. Guest decisions can be facilitated in subtle ways, such as carrying a flaming dessert that is sure to attract attention high on a tray. Engage the customer in dialogue about the food and beverage offerings to enhance their experience and narrow the uncertainty of satisfaction they may have.
6. Focus on the customer's perception. Whether or not the guest's perception is an accurate one, for her or him it is reality.
7. Avoid violating the customer's unspoken time limits. Time spent waiting always seems four times longer than it really is. Anticipate the next sequence in the service delivery and time the service accordingly.
8. Create memories the customer will want to recapture within the context of his or her expected experience from the service encounter. Good times and memories of good times are what we really sell. When customers leave establishments, all they take with them are the memories … and it is good memories that keep them coming back.
9. Expect your customer to remember bad experiences. Also expect your customer to tell about those bad experiences, embellishing with each retelling. The result can be an unfavorable impression on people who haven't yet patronized your establishment.
10. Put the customer in your debt. Your goal is to have your guests leave your property feeling as though they have received so much value for their expenditure that they owe you another visit.[15]

A Day in the Life of...

A FRONT DESK CLERK

Photo by Michael Dzaman

Usually I am the first and last contact with our guests. I represent the hotel to the guest throughout all stages of the guest's stay. My job involves customer service, answering the telephone, securing payment for services rendered, and resolving problems. I must possess a working knowledge of the reservations process and room pricing strategies. I take same-day reservations and future reservations and often need to be able to sell features of the hotel along with the necessary pricing strategy guidelines.

In addition, I am responsible for checking guests in and out of their rooms. When a guest arrives with a reservation, I pull the reservation from a computer; confirm the name, address, and length of stay; and ask for a method of payment. If a credit card is to be used, I process the payment in my computer and have the guest sign the registration card or folio acknowledging the rates and length of stay. At check-in I can also take cash deposits as necessary to cover any phone or other charges that may be incurred. After check-in, I give the guest the room key and directions to the room, and offer to summon a bellhop to help with the luggage. I then place the information about the guest and room in the appropriate front desk racks and communicate the information to the appropriate hotel personnel.

For guests who are walk-ins, or those who don't have reservations, I find out each guest's name, address, and the expected length of stay. If a room is available, I quote the rate and ask about preferences for a smoking or nonsmoking room, location, and room size. I also try to "sell up" by suggesting that the guest spend a little extra money to obtain a larger room, one with a better view, or one with more amenities. The rest of the check-in process is the same as for guests with reservations.

At check-out, I take the guest's key, look up the account on the computer, and inform the guest how much is owed. I inquire whether or not everything was satisfactory. Then, I ask the guest if I might book another stay with us or one of our affiliated hotel properties. If the guest needs transportation from the hotel, I explain how to get a shuttle or taxi.

At the start of each day, I print a report of special requests of incoming guests. Requests are recorded in the computer station at the desk and entered into a logbook, and they become part of a guest's history in the computer system. The history is used each time the guest returns for a visit in order to personalize the guest's experience. Another report lists any groups that will be arriving. Using it, I can prepare a materials packet, which includes a room key, for each guest to speed up check-in.

Between check-ins and check-outs, I handle the mail and messages and the placement of items in safe deposit boxes for the guests. I post and file all charges to the proper accounts. In addition, I work closely with the housekeeping department in keeping room status reports up to date and in coordinating requests for maintenance and repair work. I must know all safety and emergency procedures and be aware of accident prevention policies as well.

Another important task is solving guest problems. I am the liaison or contact between the guest and the hotel. When guests have problems, they call me or come to the front desk. My job is to solve the problems—or quickly find someone who can.

The bottom line is this: Keep your guests happy by keeping everything easy for them. In turn, a satisfied guest is a repeat guest and that makes "dollars and sense" for the hospitality professional.

Pursuing Opportunities in Hospitality

As a service-oriented industry, hospitality depends on people with interpersonal skills—both natural and developed. The previous section illustrates how every encounter is centered on the employee's ability to communicate effectively with the guest. Even so, many other skills and abilities are involved in the broad range of opportunities available. These vital skills can be honed through classroom and work experiences.

Opportunities Abound

As today's largest industry, the hospitality and tourism network employs 200 million individuals, or one in nine workers worldwide, and generates $3.4 trillion in annual revenues worldwide.[16] In the United States alone, it employs over 7.3 million people. Total revenue generated by the industry in the United States represents almost $100 billion.[17]

Career opportunities abound in the hospitality and tourism network. Each facet of the hospitality and tourism network offers different positions and career growth opportunities.

Tour and Travel Management—Marketing consultant, marketing manager, travel planner, tour operator, tour escort, sales manager, meeting and convention planner, convention and visitors bureau manager, travel agent, **on-line distribution** agent, corporate travel consultant,

land transportation coordinator, transportation consultant, airline agent.

Human Resources Management—Director of training, training manager, human resources manager, vice president of human resources, benefits program manager, labor relations manager

Special Events Management—Wedding planner, decor specialist, entertainment coordinator, pastry chef, menu planner, theme coordinator

Sports Management—Sports marketing professional, ticket sales manager, public relations officer, event manager, facility manager, agent, concessionaire, liaison with sports governing bodies

Club Management—General manager, director of sales and marketing, dining room manager, golf pro, special events coordinator, catering manager, controller, engineer

Gaming—Executive level positions include: Vice President of Gaming Operations, Director of Gaming Sales and Marketing, and Vice President of Casino Operations. Operational positions include: pit boss, black jack dealer, slot machine supervisor, cocktail waitress, and gaming machine service technicians.

Hospitality, besides being a service industry, is a **labor-intensive** industry. This means that it relies on a large workforce to meet the needs of its guests. Many resort hotels can be likened to small cities, employing thousands of people in their restaurants, parking lots, laundry rooms, gaming areas, ski slopes, beach operations, spa services, lounges, and offices. Even small businesses require enough employees to staff three shifts a day and keep the operations going seven days a week, fifty-two weeks a year.

Of all possible industries to choose from, hospitality is one of the most exciting and accessible. Entry-level positions beckon employees to the thousands of hotels, motels, restaurants, country clubs, resorts, casino and gaming operations, cruise lines, and other components of hospitality. (You'll learn about leisure-time or recreation-oriented hospitality components in Chapter 10.) And hard-working individuals have many opportunities for quick advancement. A junior manager in some restaurant operations can assume full operating duties in as little as twelve to eighteen months. Employees of chain hotels may be moved to other locations and higher positions as new hotels are added to the chain and experienced employees are needed to operate them.

The hospitality industry also affords a vast array of entrepreneurial opportunities. An **entrepreneur** is an individual who creates, organizes, manages, and assumes the risks of a business or enterprise. Stories about successful entrepreneurs—such as Colonel Harlan Sanders, Cesar Ritz, or Thomas Cook—permeate the industry.

Identifying Required Skills and Abilities

Of course, knowing there are opportunities is very different from pursuing them, and in selected components of the industry some jobs are tough to get.

Professional Profile

MICHAEL MURPHY

Senior Vice President of Sales— Marriott International

Photo courtesy of Michael Murphy

Michael Murphy—Senior Vice President Sales, Marriott International

Michael Murphy graduated from Rochester Institute of Technology in Rochester, New York in 1984 with a bachelor's degree in hotel and service management He is now senior vice president of worldwide sales for Marriott International.

"A typical day for me is such that there are no two days alike. Each and every day I need to ask myself, what did I do today to contribute to the revenue growth of Marriott International? In a typical day I can have up to eight back-to-back meetings in which we are designing the sales strategy for Marriott. The best part of my job is spending time with our global account managers and their customers. To have the opportunity to listen to our customers and respond to their business needs is thrilling."

I have achieved success in my career because I have the ability to surround myself with great leaders. I need high energy and the ability to focus on excelling today with a long-term lens. It is important for me to surround myself with great mentors and have an outstanding family who understands and provides support.

The challenges I have faced in my career have been dealing with poor performers on my team and being able to identify their needs and issues fast enough. I have learned over the years the importance of knowing when to ask for help and being humble. Balancing work and life is essential, with life always coming first!

My career plan has always been excelling today and keeping an eye on the possibilities of tomorrow. Possibilities can amount to anything. The job I am in today can last for the balance of my career. We have huge goals ahead of us that require laser focus. Once we succeed we can do anything. This has always been my approach to my career. I have been promoted fourteen times in twenty-four years. If you excel today...tomorrow will come.

The U.S. Department of Labor established a commission in 1990 to examine the demands of the workplace and to determine whether the current and future workforce is capable of meeting those demands. The commission, under the Secretary of Labor, was asked to define the skills needed for employment and to propose acceptable levels of achievement in those skills. The Secretary's Commission on Achieving Necessary Skills (SCANS) identified two types of skills: competencies and foundations. Competencies are the skills necessary for success in the workplace, and foundations are skills and qualities that underlie the

TABLE 1.1 SCANS Competencies

Resources	Allocates time
	Allocates money
	Allocates material and facility resources
	Allocates human resources
Information	Acquires and evaluates information
	Organizes and maintains information
	Interprets and communicates information
	Uses computers to process information
Interpersonal	Participates as a member of a team
	Teaches others
	Serves clients and customers
	Exercises leadership
	Negotiates to arrive at a decision
	Works with cultural diversity
Systems	Understands systems
	Monitors and corrects performance
	Improves and designs systems
Technology	Selects technology
	Applies technology to task
	Maintains and troubleshoots technology

competencies. (See Tables 1.1 and 1.2.) The SCANS competencies and foundations are skills and abilities required for most jobs across the spectrum of different industries. The commission also undertook to rate the skills as to their importance for specific tasks within specific jobs. A five-step rating system placed skills on a continuum that ranged from "not critical" to "extremely critical."

In response to the recommendations issued by the SCANS and the goals outlined in the resulting America 2000 Program, the Convocation of National Hospitality and Tourism Industry Associations (the Convocation), which included CHRIE and other U.S. associations, developed model position descriptions for hospitality and tourism occupations. The model descriptions serve as organizers to help managers develop customized descriptions of individual positions in their own businesses. The position descriptions also help students understand the requirements of potential jobs and assist instructors in education and training programs that prepare students for the hospitality workplace.

The model descriptions build on the SCANS list of skills but also include information regarding the education, experience, and physical requirements of the position.

TABLE 1.2 SCANS Foundation Skills

Basic Skills	Reading
	Writing
	Arithmetic
	Mathematics
	Listening
	Speaking
Thinking Skills	Creative thinking
	Decision making
	Problem solving
	Seeing things in the mind's eye
	Knowing how to learn
	Reasoning
Personal Qualities	Responsibility
	Self-esteem
	Social
	Self-management
	Integrity/honesty

As an example, consider the position of hotel front desk clerk, discussed earlier in this chapter. The SCANS job description lists tasks in terms of skills and shows that sixteen foundation skills and abilities and twenty-one competencies are required to do the job satisfactorily. The skills that are rated "highly critical" and "extremely critical" for the job include speaking, social, listening, cooperation (working in teams), conscientiousness (individual responsibility), working with cultural diversity, and understanding how systems work. The Convocation model description lists twenty-two specific tasks along with the competencies required. In addition, this model description states that a high school diploma or equivalent is required. The applicant should be able to speak, read, write, and understand the primary language(s) used in the workplace and by the guests who visit the workplace. Also, previous hotel-related experience is desired. Physical requirements of the job include writing, standing, sitting, walking, repetitive motions, hearing, visual acuity, and, on occasion, being able to lift and carry up to forty pounds.

In contrast, consider the position of restaurant manager. Only nine tasks, mostly supervisory, are listed. Twenty competencies are listed, and range from serving customers to allocating money. Included in the foundation skills are creative thinking, knowing how to learn, and seeing with the mind's eye. An associate or bachelor's degree is preferred, along with a minimum of three years experience as a food server, host/hostess, or dining room manager. One

Industry Insights

CULTURE

Language Classes

"Мы забронировали два номера на сегодня."*

Upon hearing these words, a Russian-speaking hotelier would realize new guests had just arrived, and would welcome them appropriately. The hotelier without this skill would realize a problem had just presented itself, and would play the "charades version" of the checking-in process.

The globalization of businesses and the increase in world travel have enhanced the importance of foreign-language competency. Many hospitality companies require their executives to acquire a second (and even third) language. With the emergence of the Asian market, many international companies now provide second-language and cultural diversity training to help their executives stay current with foreign counterparts. For many, launching a second-language program is worth any cost, resulting in boosted employee morale, improved business relations, and enhanced customer service. At a minimum, hospitality workers will need to learn and be in command of basic greeting and directional phrases in both the host and guest languages as a result of the expansion of global tourism.

Employees at any level benefit from second-language skills. Although expecting your staff to acquire several languages is perhaps impractical, expecting them to understand basic phrases in common languages is not. Most people already recognize many foreign phrases: *buenos dias, auf wiedersehen, bon voyage, grazie, sayonara, l'hôtel, il ristorante.*** Adding a few common phrases in several major languages should be fairly easy, fun, and a definite guest-pleaser.

* Russian—"We reserved two rooms for today."

** Spanish—"Good morning"; German—"Goodbye"; French—"Have a good journey"; Italian—"Thanks"; Japanese—"Goodbye"; French—"The hotel"; Italian—"The restaurant."

physical requirement is the stamina to work a minimum of fifty to sixty hours a week. Having hands-on experience in each of the positions within a restaurant or food and beverage operation combined with an educational foundation ensures a powerful background and improves marketability of prospective career entrants.

Meeting the Requirements

The information that follows gives an overview of the various means of acquiring the skills and knowledge needed to take advantage of opportunities in the hospitality and tourism network: formal and informal education, industry associations, and lifelong learning.

Formal Education

There are many who break into the hospitality industry with the equivalent of (or less than) a high school diploma. However, higher education generally leads to better entry-level jobs, quicker advancement, higher wages, and sharper strategic thinking skills. Hundreds of undergraduate programs in hospitality administration and hotel, restaurant, and institutional management are available throughout the United States, Canada, and other countries. In addition, graduate-level programs are offered by approximately sixty universities in North America. Several universities (such as Virginia Tech; Cornell, in upstate New York; and Purdue, in Indiana) now offer Ph.Ds in hospitality administration. Table 1.3 identifies levels of programs available, as well as curriculum and length of time necessary to complete a specific program.[18]

Hospitality programs are very diverse. In the past two to three decades, the number of programs available in the United States has risen from approximately forty four-year programs to more than 170. In addition, there are more than seven hundred programs which offer associate's degrees, certificates, or diplomas.[19] There is no "typical" program, and finding the "right" program is simply a matter of personal choice. Many programs offer a well-rounded education in science, English, mathematics, marketing, human resources, and the humanities, as well as specialization in areas such as nutrition, hotel engineering, or management. The important thing to remember is that whether you choose a vocational program, a two- or four-year hospitality

TABLE 1.3 Key Attributes of Hospitality and Tourism Programs by Program Type or Level

Program Type	*Institutional Settings*	*Curriculum Objectives*	*Completion Time*	*Faculty*
Certificate and Diploma Programs	Business, Technical, and Career Institutes	To provide students with specialized skills for specific hospitality and tourism jobs.	1-3 years	Primarily industry experience and training. Many also have baccalaureate degrees and some have graduate degrees.
Associate and Diploma* Programs	Community Colleges and Technical Institutes	To provide training and education necessary for hospitality and tourism management careers. Emphasis is on career education and technical skills, but curricula include general education components. Some degrees can be transferred to baccalaureate programs.	2 years	Combination of industry skills and experience with combined undergraduate and, in many cases, graduate training.
Baccalaureate Degree Granting Programs	Four-year Colleges and Universities	To provide career education in combination with a broad general studies component and advanced learning skills. Emphasis on developing conceptual abilities and integrating knowledge of hospitality and tourism with other disciplines.	4 years	Combination of industry experience and graduate education. Heavy emphasis on graduate education.
Graduate Degree Granting Programs	Universities	To provide advanced education for specialized industry positions or for future educators. Emphasis on creating an interdisciplinary base for applied research, policy analysis, planning, and theoretical education.	1-2 years (Masters) 3-5 years (Doctorate)	Doctoral education with some industry experience. Industry experience not always required.

*Diplomas at some Canadian community colleges and European technical colleges are awarded for completion of a course of study that meets or exceeds requirements for an Associate Degree in the United States.

Source: Guide to College Programs in Hospitality, Tourism and Culinary Arts, 9th ed., © 2006 by International Council on Hotel, Restaurant and Institutional Education.

program, or a liberal arts degree coupled with industry experience, additional education is almost always imperative for the career-oriented professional.

Formal education has increased in importance as business organization has become more complex. National and international corporations dominate the industry. Hospitality firms with high levels of organization expect their manager trainees to hold college degrees; indeed, specific qualifications for all hospitality jobs are becoming more important.

For other entry-level, skilled-level, and managerial positions, education not only enables the hospitality professional to keep up with rapid changes in management techniques, technology, and finance, but also enhances opportunities for future advancement because education teaches critical thinking and conceptual thinking skills. A look at Figure 1.3 shows four sample career ladders with the period of time and level of experience needed to reach the top.

Informal Education

The importance of formal education has not lessened the importance of acquiring knowledge through work experience. Even with a degree, you'll probably need experience before a large company will consider you for its higher management positions. It is not enough to understand the inner mechanisms of a business as shown in a textbook, because most day-to-day experiences are not "straight from the book." Your potential employer will want to feel confident that you will be able to apply your knowledge—knowledge acquired formally and on-the-job—to real situations. Work experience supplies that evidence.

If your goal is upper-level management, work experience in the different types of jobs that managers oversee is very important. For example, hotel managers must be knowledgeable about maintenance operations, foodservice, housekeeping, accounting, and every other function they are responsible for managing. Since managers help others do their jobs well, this task is made easier by knowing the specifics of those particular jobs. Additionally, experience in specific jobs offers managers and supervisors a higher degree of credibility and compassion for those they are leading because they have a deeper understanding of the issues at the front-line level.

Hotel, Restaurant, and Tourism Associations

Industry associations and organizations offer certificates and diplomas upon completion of one to three-year programs. For example, the American Hotel and Lodging Association (AH&LA) Educational Institute has established a program that leads to a certificate as a certified hotel administrator (CHA). The American Culinary Federation (ACF) offers cook or pastry/baker certificates, and the National Tour Association (NTA) offers a certified tour professional (CTP) certificate. Certificates or diplomas are offered by other associations as well: the Educational Foundation of National Restaurant Association, the

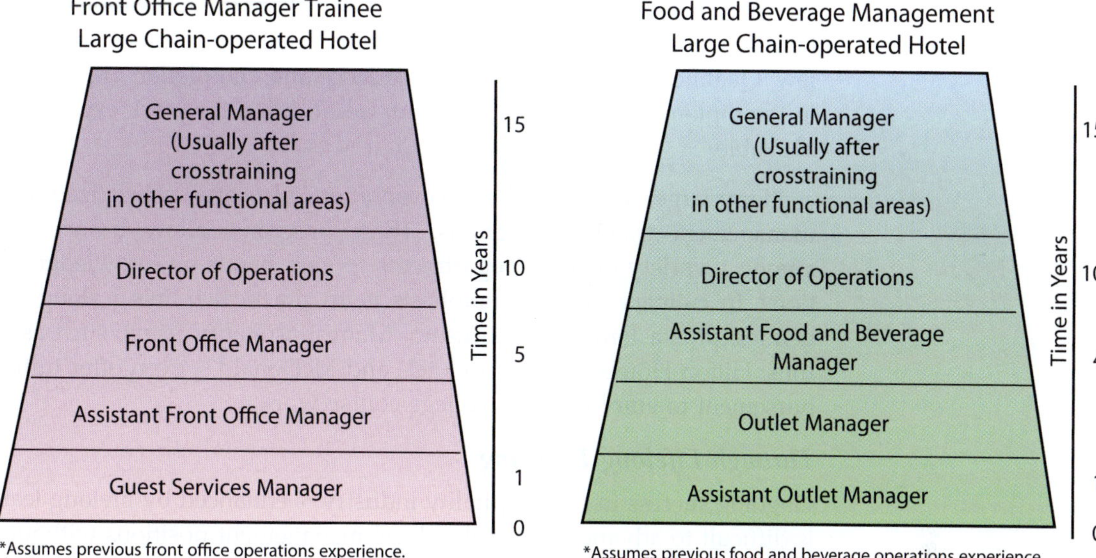

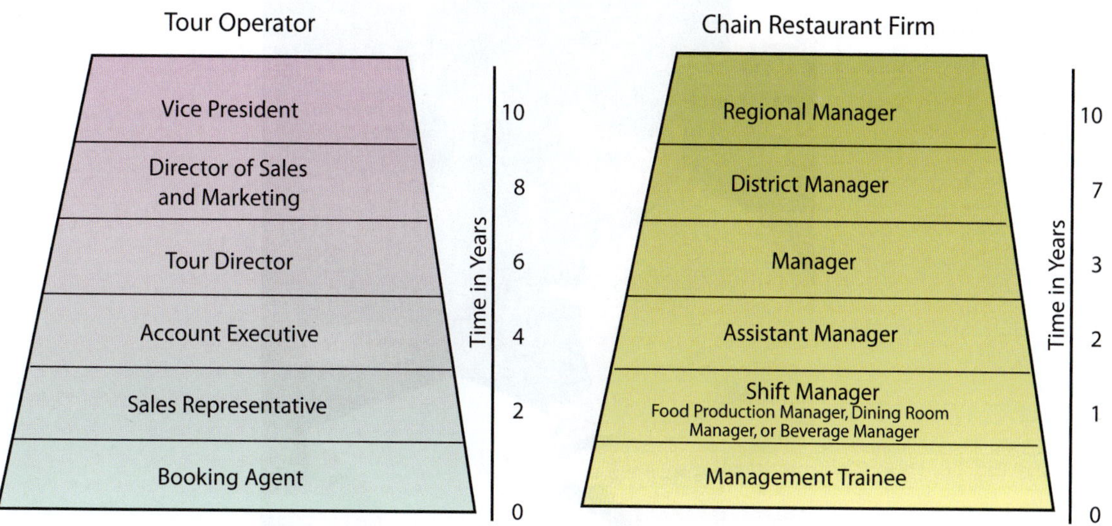

FIGURE 1.3 Sample Career Ladder
Source: Guide to College Programs in Hospitality, Tourism and Culinary Arts, 9th ed., © 2006 by International Council on Hotel, Restaurant and Institutional Education.

International Executive Housekeepers Association, the Professional Convention Management Association, and the Dietary Managers Association, to name a few. Qualifications include work experience and completion of specific courses in the diploma or certificate program. Certification for work experience is also available.

Many large hotels and hotel corporations also offer specialized, on-the-job management training programs. These programs allow trainees to rotate among a variety of hotel departments to gain hands-on knowledge of operations. In culinary arts, the emphasis is on practical training along with academics, plus a long apprenticeship. Many hospitality firms, such as Holiday Inns, Hilton Hotels, Red Lion Hotels and McDonald's, even offer tuition reimbursement to employees for college course work.

Through Lifelong Learning

Ongoing success in the hospitality industry is enhanced by lifelong learning. It is difficult to advance into higher-level management positions without staying current through continuing education. In years past, physical labor was the focus of many jobs. In years to come, mental labor and leadership acumen

Courtesy of Photodisc

Associations and organizations offer programs that combine coursework with work experience.

will take its place. Those individuals with curiosity, creativity, and a willingness to embrace constant change will be tomorrow's successful leaders in the hospitality industry.

With increased competition, multigenerational blending in the workplace, cultural diversity, globalization of the hospitality industry, and the rising costs of doing business, the concept of lifelong learning applies to all levels of the hospitality workforce, from marketing executives to front desk clerks. Adaptability is vital. How can you stay on top of a changing industry and ensure lifelong learning? Here is a five-step plan that may help:

1. Review your resumé regularly. Are your skills up to date? Have you demonstrated or improved a specific skill in the last year? Does your experience level mirror your personal strategic development?
2. Write down specific goals and your intended methods to achieve them. Since industry knowledge is constantly broadening, you might choose an educational goal such as taking one class every six months on a subject related to your career. Many community colleges offer short, low-cost professional courses year-round. Many companies offer continuing education benefits designed to stimulate internal learning and career development. Research those companies that partner with leading hospitality institutions for further information.
3. Your career is a marathon, not a sprint. Remember the tortoise and the hare: The greatest rewards do not necessarily go to the fastest, but rather to those who keep learning and gaining experience. Build a strong foundation of both practical and educational experience.
4. Associating with others who share your professional interests and goals will give you a chance to exchange ideas and build on the shared enthusiasm of a support group. Joining a professional organization or subscribing to a trade journal will help you keep up to date on national and global issues affecting the hospitality industry. Seek and cultivate mentoring relationships in order to gain knowledge from those who have blazed the trail before you.
5. Rely on yourself to advance. While many people will give you invaluable assistance in learning the ropes, ultimately, your career is your responsibility.

Summary

- The hospitality industry is part of a large network that includes food services, lodging services, recreation services, travel-related services, gaming/casino services, and products provided with personal services in conjunction with the above industries.

- The history of the hospitality industry reveals how other forces have contributed to its current status and will continue to influence it in the future.
- The combined businesses of hospitality and tourism compose the world's largest industry, sometimes referred to as the hospitality and tourism network.
- Service is both the mission and the product of the hospitality industry. Since it is an intangible product, not everyone's perception of it is the same. Its importance to the industry is second to none.
- Employees and guests bring to the service encounter certain personality traits and expectations, which may differ. This characteristic of an encounter prevents service from being contained in a set of rules or a philosophy. Those organizations that harness the essence of service and consistently deliver something that goes beyond service promises and customer expectations may be afforded greater market share and customer loyalty.
- The broad scope of the hospitality industry offers many career opportunities, including management and entrepreneurship. Career advancement may be accelerated through obtaining a solid education and gaining meaningful practical experience.
- A successful career-minded hospitality professional never stops learning. In this rapidly changing business, dedication to lifelong learning is a must.

ENDNOTES

[1] David Attenborough et al., *The Atlas of the Living World* (Boston: Houghton Mifflin Co., 1989): 138.

[2] Elizabeth Devine and Nancy L. Braganti, *The Travelers' Guide to Middle Eastern and North African Customs and Manners* (New York: St. Martin's Press, 1991): 15.

[3] W.C. Firebaugh, *The Inns of Greece and Rome: and a History of Hospitality from the Dawn of Time to the Middle Ages* (Chicago: F.M. Morris Company, 1923): 25.

[4] Ibid., 35.

[5] J.P.V.D. Balsdon, *Life and Leisure in Ancient Rome* (England: McGraw-Hill Book Company, 1969): 215.

[6] *Webster's New Twentieth Century Dictionary*, Unabridged (New York: Simon & Schuster, 1979).

[7] Theodore M. Bernstein, *Reverse Dictionary* (New York: New York Times Books, 1975): 116.

[8] Charles J. Metelka, ed., *The Dictionary of Tourism* (Wheaton, IL: Merton House Publishing Company, 1981): 36.

[9] American Hotel and Lodging Association (AH&LA), Lodging Industry Profile in 2008, http://www.ahla.com/

[10] National Restaurant Association (NRA), National Restaurant Association 1998 Restaurant Industry Pocket Factbook, http://www.restaurant.org/.

[11] Mary Jo Bitner, Bernard H. Booms, and Mary Stanfield Tetreault, "The Service Encounter: Diagnosing Favorable and Unfavorable Incidents," *Journal of Marketing* (January 1990): 72.

[12] Ibid.

[13] Pete Stevens, "Winning!!! Getting Customers, Keeping Customers, and Making Money," *Hospitality Resources Ink* (1989): 163.

[14] Bonnie J. Knutson, "Ten Laws of Customer Satisfaction," *Cornell Hotel and Restaurant Administration Quarterly* (November 1988): 15–16.

[15] Ibid., 14–17.

[16] http://www.ibanet.org/.
[17] http://www.wvtourism.com/.
[18] U.S. Department of Labor, Secretary's Commission on Achieving Necessary Skills (SCANS) (Washington, D.C.: U.S. Government Printing Office, 1992): 24.
[19] Riegel, "Introduction to Career Opportunities," 6.

CHECK YOUR KNOWLEDGE

1. What factor created a need for hospitality as an industry? What connects the hospitality industry to the tourism industry?
2. List the major components of the hospitality and tourism network.
3. Give one example each of successful and unsuccessful hospitality you have experienced. Describe the most meaningful service exchange you have encountered.
4. Why is guest satisfaction so important? How does it play a role in the success of the business enterprise where you work or have worked?
5. List three ways to achieve lifelong learning.

APPLY YOUR SKILLS

The following table shows the results of a survey of guests receiving satisfactory or dissatisfactory service delivery from a hotel, restaurant, or airline. Review the table below and the service encounter categories in Figure 1.2, then answer the questions that follow.

1. The total number of survey respondents was 699. How many responses were due to service delivery system failures? Special requests? Unsolicited employee actions? What might be inferred from comparing the subtotals for groups 2 and 3?
2. Customer dissatisfaction in group 1 encounters is almost twice as great as satisfactory encounters of the same type in group 1. The reverse is true for group 2. What does this suggest?
3. What might explain the balance of group 3–type encounters?

TABLE 1.4 Service Encounter Statistics

	Outcome		
Group	*Satisfactory*	*Unsatisfactory*	*Total %*
1. Employee Response to Service Delivery System Failures	23.3%	42.9%	33.2%
2. Employee Response to Customer Needs and Requests	32.9%	15.6%	24.2%
3. Unprompted and Unsolicited Employee Actions	43.8%	41.5%	42.6%

Source: Adapted from Mary Jo Bitner, Bernard H. Booms, and Mary Stanfield Tetreault, "The Service Encounter: Diagnosing Favorable and Unfavorable Incidents," *Journal of Marketing* (January 1990).

WHAT DO YOU THINK?

1. If you want to move into an upper-level management position with a major hotel chain, would you pursue education? Explain.
2. Assume that you work in a restaurant as a server. One evening, table number two is occupied by a couple with a young child. During the meal, the child fusses and cries so loudly that another guest begins to complain. What would you do?
3. Imagine two restaurant managers. One is hired from outside a company and has extensive budgeting, management, and marketing experience, but no direct food service experience. The other works up through the ranks to arrive at the restaurant manager position. What are the possible strengths each manager could bring to the job?
4. Since "the guest is always right," what would you do in the following situation? A guest checks into her room and immediately calls you, the front desk clerk, to request a nonsmoking room. In checking the reservation, you note that her request has already been fulfilled. The guest, however, insists that the room smells of smoke.
5. Based on some of the things you have learned so far about hospitality, what do you plan to apply to your own career path?

CASE STUDY

Yuki Shinoda manages her hotel's marketing department. Recently the sales staff has noticed a drop in return guests. Careful inspection of the newly renovated property showed no evidence of any problems there, and interviews with members of the sales staff have not produced any good leads toward solving the problem. At the suggestion of the general manager, Yuki began observing staff members who dealt directly with the customers. Soon the problems became evident. Even though the front desk staff was operating efficiently and each staff member was performing his or her job as required, the customers checking in and out seemed uncomfortable and hurried. More observation in other areas of the hotel confirmed her suspicions that guests were not really feeling at home among staff members. Although subtle, the interactions between guests and customers seemed strained. Further observation and conversations with the personnel director convinced Yuki that the drop in repeat sales was in part due to the poor interactions between the staff and guests.

1. How could Yuki and the personnel director approach solving this problem?
2. What other factors might be involved in the drop in return guests?
3. How could the hotel reach those guests who had stopped returning? What message should it give them?
4. How might Yuki benefit from having both a formal education in hospitality and work experience when solving this problem?

Travel and Tourism: Partners with Hospitality

OVERVIEW

Hospitality, travel, and tourism compose the world's largest industry and contribute greatly to global economic development. The industry worldwide generated more than $3.4 trillion in gross output in 2004. In the United States, it generated more than $1.3 trillion in 2004.[1] Countries leading in hospitality and tourism revenues are the United States, France, Germany, Mexico, the United Kingdom, and Japan.

In this chapter you will learn how hospitality, travel, and tourism interrelate, how tourist destinations and hospitality facilities are keys to the reasons people travel, how destinations are promoted and distributed, and what some of the effects of the industry are on society.

OBJECTIVES

When you have completed this chapter, you should be able to:

1 Describe the relationship between the hospitality industry and travel and tourism management.

2 List major components of business travel.

3 Name and describe ways tourism is promoted.

4 Define *destination image* and explain how such images affect where people choose to travel.

5 Discuss the positive and negative effects of tourism.

KEY TERMS

carrying capacity
charter operator
congress
convention
convention and visitors bureaus (CVBs)
corporate travel manager
demonstration effect
destination
destination marketing organizations
direct spending
ecotourism
elastic
excursionists
expositions
familiarization trip
frequent flyer
frequent guest
functional image
gross domestic product (GDP)
inbound operators
incentive travel
indirect spending
infrastructure
kiosk
leakage
marketing
meeting planner
middlemen
multiplier effect
necessary leakage
opportunity cost
retail travel agent
symbolic image
tour operators
tour package
tour wholesaler
tourism industry
tourism office
tourists
trade shows
travel intermediaries
yuan

The Relationship of Hospitality to Travel and Tourism

The components of the hospitality network may be independent and competitive businesses, yet they share an interdependency that has evolved over the centuries. This relationship can be seen in the roles that destinations and hospitality facilities play in motivating people to travel.

Although travel encompasses all movement or displacement of people, not all travel involves tourism. Refugees, migrants, explorers, nomads, soldiers, and commuters certainly travel, but they are not tourists.[2] Tourism-related travel involves the movement of visitors to a place to enjoy its attractions, special events, hospitality, lodging, food, and entertainment. People who take trips of one hundred miles or more and who stay at least one night away from home are **tourists**. People who travel to a site and return home the same day are **excursionists**.[3] The **tourism industry** is concerned with attractions and events that draw tourists and excursionists to an area.

Interdependence in the Hospitality and Tourism Network

The Hawaiian Islands in the Pacific Ocean are a popular tourist site; indeed, tourism accounts for 70 percent of Hawaii's economy. In 2005, over 7.5 million visitors traveled to Hawaii. The state average is close to 185,000 visitors on average per day. The average length of stay is 9.1 days, with each visitor

Pali Mountain range—Oahu, Hawaii

spending roughly $174 per day, totaling 11.9 billion dollars annually. Not all visitors arrive by air; in 2005, cruise ship arrivals averaged close to 321,000 visitors.[4]

Being a desirable destination, however, isn't enough to create a successful tourism trade. A means to get to the destination must also exist. Since there is no land passage between Hawaii and the mainland, tourists must travel by air or sea. The more people who are attracted to Hawaii's shores, the more travel tickets are sold by the airlines and cruise ships to transport them there.

If Hawaii had nothing to offer the traveler, the airlines and cruise ships would have less trade. The converse is also true: If there were no convenient or comfortable means of transportation, fewer people would visit Hawaii, and the state's tourism trade would decline. The success of each component contributes to the overall success of Hawaii's tourism industry, and vice versa. This interdependence of the many products and services making up the network is an important aspect of hospitality, travel, and tourism.

The intertwinings within the network may already be familiar to you through personal experience. Recall the last time you and your family took a vacation trip. First, you selected a destination. A **destination** is a location where travelers choose to visit and spend time, no matter what their motivations, needs, or expectations. Perhaps you researched your vacation options on one of the many on-line sites, consulted a local travel agency to help select a destination, or contacted the convention and tourism bureau of an area you wanted to visit for information on attractions and available activities. When the time came to go, you needed some form of transportation, either your own vehicle or one from a hired source. During the vacation, you probably purchased food and lodging accommodations. You may have purchased souvenirs or other items from gift shops or boutiques.

All these components of hospitality and tourism are interrelated. Without attractions and hospitality establishments, there is usually no popular destination; without a popular destination, there may be no need for an airport; without an airport, there may be less need for a travel agent. The interdependence among the components of hospitality, travel, and tourism is strong, especially in those countries that rely on hospitality and tourism for a major portion of their economic base. Bermuda, for example, monitors the standards of all its hotels, foodservice businesses, and attractions. The people of Bermuda work to satisfy vacationers in every aspect of their visits, thinking that customer dissatisfaction with even one meal or hotel room will color the entire trip with an overall sense of dissatisfaction.

Tour and Travel Packages

The hospitality, travel, and tourism industry has recognized the advantage of putting various components together and selling them as a tour package. A tour package is a composite of related services offered at a single price. A package might include more than one form of transportation. For example, the price of a Caribbean cruise usually includes airfare to and from the point of departure. Or a package might include a day of sightseeing by chartered bus, with lunch at a popular restaurant. Another example might be an airline that offers reduced rates at certain hotels if a traveler decides to use its service. Tour packages usually save people money, and many people like having all of the arrangements made for them when they travel. A typical tour of the Rocky Mountains in the western United States would include air travel, motor coach transfers, hotel accommodations, meals, and admission fees to National Park system locations and other attractions on the itinerary.

Frequent Flyer/Frequent Guest Programs

Hospitality and travel businesses compete to capture a larger share of business travel. One innovative program introduced by airlines is the **frequent flyer** program. Later, hotel chains adopted the idea, calling it the **frequent guest** program. These programs are promotions designed to gain customer brand loyalty. By flying a certain number of miles on the same airline or by continuing to stay at the same brand of hotel, travelers earn free trips or free (or upgraded) lodging. Recent studies indicate that the frequent flyer programs and frequent guest programs are not as profitable as in the past, primarily due to the relatively high cost of the award to the airlines and hotels. However, since travelers have accepted and now expect the frequent flyer programs, they are still offered. Frequent traveler programs have integrated services reaching far into retail services. Airlines offer Visa credit cards with points matched per dollar purchased. Airlines have also created members-only executive-style boardrooms that offer personalized services and travel arrangments. Frequent flyer privileges now include first-class seats, preferential boarding, fast-track security lines, and standby upgrading privileges. Major hotel companies have integrated both points-based awards and travel vouchers redeemable with affiliated airline partners as exchange mechanisms to retain and reward frequent users.

Familiarization Trips

Typical marketing and promotional activities by tourism organizations include familiarization trips, or "fam trips," and trade shows. A **familiarization trip** is a free or reduced-price trip given to travel agents, travel writers, and others in the travel trade, who will then promote the destination. A fam trip is an excellent promotional tool, giving the individual firsthand experience with the facilities, services, and attractions available at a destination. Several travel associations hold annual trade shows where suppliers, carriers, destination marketing groups, and intermediaries exhibit. Some of the major trade shows in North America include the annual trade shows of the National Tour Association (NTA), the American Bus Association (ABA), and the American Society of Travel Agents (ASTA). Often hotel companies or individual properties will conduct their own fam trips in order to concentrate their marketing and promotional efforts on a particular new product offering or announcement to their targeted customer base. Hosting a fam trip enables travel and tourism partners to collaborate and focus on a specific destination in order to intensify the marketing message.

High-Tech Amenities

Part of the marketing task is deciding what services to offer. Those businesses that target business travelers offer extra services that facilitate business transactions. Technological advances in air travel are making it possible for business travelers to conduct business while in flight. Onboard fax machines, credit card–operated phones at every seat, and business radio and video services help business people stay in touch with their offices and the rest of

Business Profile

ALASKA AIRLINES

Industry Leader in Frequent Traveler Mileage Program

Alaska Airlines' frequent traveler program has been recognized as a leading customer loyalty program. They offer mileage credits for partner trips on over a dozen domestic and international carriers. The Alaska Airlines loyalty program offers one-for-one mileage credits for purchases on their signature Visa credit and debit cards and has aligned with several major retail vendors to offer the same bonus mileage credits for purchases of goods and services. Included in the alternative product offerings are leading hotel and rental car brands. Frequent customers using Alaska Airlines benefits are able to pre-board airplanes, are eligible for complimentary first-class seating accommodations, and receive priority seat availability on standby status. Most importantly, **Alaska Airlines gold members-or top level elite travelers with their airline based on number of miles flown each year** receive VIP customer service and are treated with exceptional care and professionalism.

the country while thirty thousand feet in the air. Just as laptop computers are becoming a common sight in the business world, airlines are taking other steps to keep their passengers up to date while airborne. In September 1991, Singapore Airlines became the first carrier to offer international telephone service from the sky. On the ground, some airlines provide remote office centers

Photo by Michael Dzaman

Many large hotels provide office centers with fax machines, computer hookups, and copying services for business travelers.

located in their terminals, which may offer a variety of businees traveler support services.

Technological advances are not limited to in-flight services, airlines now enable customers to purchase tickets, pre-check flight status, and print their own boarding passes from remote locations. The majority of airports offer check-in via automated **kiosk** hardware in lieu of traditional person-to-person check-in.

All components of the tourism and travel network benefit from technological advances. From quick-service restaurants with customer-access computers for ordering to remote office centers in hotels, high-tech amenities remain a popular customer draw.

Female Business Travelers Another marketing task is deciding who is the customer. As a rapidly growing segment of the U.S. business travel market, female business travelers are gaining more attention from marketers. Today more than one-third of all business travelers are women. This growth is a direct reflection of the changing role of women in today's economy. Women now make up over 46 percent of the total workforce. By the year 2014, women will account for more than 47 percent of the total workforce, and 61 percent of all working-age women will be employed. Many now fill top management positions. This influx of businesswomen means there are more women business travelers.

When this market segment first began expanding in the 1970s, industry professionals weren't sure how to handle it. Attempting to answer the question, "What do businesswomen want," some hotels instituted women-only floors with pastel-colored rooms. Others provided magazines such as *Glamour* or *Cosmopolitan* for their female guests. This strategy proved to be a major blunder. Women don't want to receive *Glamour* magazine when the *Wall Street*

Industry Insights

CULTURE

Geographical Names of Places

A successful travel or tour professional planning international trips for clients must take into account differences in geographical names. For example, if an Italian guide asked if you wanted to see the beautiful city of Venezia, you probably could guess the destination was Venice. However, if asked to visit Magyarország, would you equate it with Hungary, land of the Magyars? An American tourist visiting France, Norway, and Germany may be surprised, when checking railway and flight schedules, that the French refer to Germany as Allemagne, while it is known in Norway as Tyskland and as Deutschland in Germany. Since the Danube River flows through several countries, your clients may find themselves cruising down the Danube, Dunarea, Duna, Dunav, or Dunaj River, depending on where they embark.

So, before you send your clients off to "parts unknown," make sure they'll know when they get there.

Journal is delivered to their male counterparts staying in the same hotel. Overall, female business travelers need the same basic services as their male counterparts.

Hotels that stress service and security were the favorites of women travelers. The services demanded most were business centers with faxes, copiers, and personal computers; limosine service; 24-hour room service; and two-line telephones. Suggested safety and security measures included not calling out the room number of a person checking in, providing valet parking and well-lit parking lots, and having visible security guards.[5] Most of these services have become industry standards and are still in place today.

Distribution through Travel Intermediaries

Travelers can purchase their own tickets and reserve their own hotel rooms on many different e-commerce distribution channels, but a travel distribution system typically includes middlemen. **Middlemen** are business firms that distribute products from the producers to the clients. Travel middlemen are called **travel intermediaries**. The most common travel intermediaries are retail travel agents and wholesale tour operators. Increasingly, however, other types of travel intermediaries, such as corporate travel managers, incentive houses, and meeting planners, and most importantly, on-line travel agencies are becoming more dominant. (Table 2.1 lists a number of positions available in travel-services businesses.)

Retail Travel Agents

A **retail travel agent** is a retailer in travel services who receives income directly from suppliers (airlines, hotels, car rental companies) and other intermediaries in the form of commissions (typically 10 percent for airlines

TABLE 2.1 Positions Available in Tourism- and Travel-Services Businesses

Airline Pilot	Foreign Food Specialty Cook	Receptionist
Auto/Recreational Vehicle Rental Agency Manager	Front Desk Clerk	Recreation/Social Director
Baggage Porter	Guest-History Clerk	Reservation Agent
Baker	Guest House/Hostel Manager	Resort Caretaker
Banquet Captain	Guide	Retail Store Manager
Bellman	Hotel Manager	Ski Instructor
Business Travel Specialist	Incentive Travel Specialist	Souvenir Shop Owner
Campground Manager	Industry Training Specialist	Ticket Taker
Chef de Cuisine	Inspector	Tour Broker
Club or Lounge Manager	Kitchen Supervisor	Tour Leader
Concession Operator	Lifeguard	Tour Operator
Convention Manager	Marina Manager	Tour Wholesaler
Craftsperson/Artisan	Meeting/Conference Planner	Tourist Bureau Manager
Cruise Director	Motor Coach Operator	Translator
Destination Development Specialist	Museum Curator	Travel Agency Manager
Director of Engineering	Park Ranger	Travel Agent
Doorkeeper	Parlor Chaperone	Travel Counselor/Sales Manager
Entertainer	Pastry Chef	Travel Journalist/Writer
Exhibition Carver	Promotion/Public Relations	Waiter/Waitress
Food and Beverage Analyst	Specialist	Wine Cellar Stock Clerk

Source: Adapted from U. S. Department of Labor, Occupational Titles Arranged by Industry Designation (Washington, D.C.: U.S. Government Printing Office, 1991).

and lodging reservations). A customer purchasing a $500 airline ticket, for example, would not pay extra for a travel agent's services; the airline would pay the agent 10 percent ($50) for booking the flight. A retail travel agent also serves as a counselor, advising travelers on and recommending destinations, hotels, and carriers. Travel agents used to book many of the arrangements for international travel and tourism consumers, however, today individual leisure and business travelers are able to book their own air travel, accomodations, and transportation needs via third party travel company intermediaries though the internet.

Tour Wholesalers and Operators

A **tour wholesaler** is a company or an individual who designs and packages tours. A **tour package** to Mexico City, for example, may include airline seats, hotel rooms, meals, ground transportation or car rental, and visits to tourist attractions. Instead of buying each of these items separately, the tourist purchases them all in one package, usually for far less money than they would cost if purchased one by one. Once a tour package is designed, a tour

A Day in the Life of...

A TRAVEL AGENCY MANAGER

A travel agency manager's top priority is service. A manager's duties include office work and general management responsibilities as well as travel consultation and planning.

Managerial duties include the same tasks associated with most businesses. The manager must train new office personnel, supervise and assist employees as needed, and monitor and evaluate staff performance. Responsibilities include operating the agency efficiently, which includes selecting and maintaining new technology and allocating resources to finance it. Successful travel agencies must keep abreast of technological advances that help staff serve clients more effectively.

In today's technologically advanced world, it is not surprising that the use of computers is central to a manager's business. Using computer-based sources and on-line services, a manager and staff can quickly access and share information about international events and backgrounds as well as up-to-date currency exchange rates. Computers provide current information on crises such as a sudden or unexpected political or military upheaval, weather catastrophes, an airline strike, or a resort shutdown. Electronic services even help agency personnel obtain travel documents such as passports and visas for clients traveling abroad.

Scheduling flights, reserving room accommodations, and making out itineraries are details that must be attended to and double-checked to ensure a smooth trip for a client. The corporate or business traveler often needs specific travel and lodging arrangements that are convenient to their schedule and to their business contacts in the destination area. They may also require arrangements for car rentals and sometimes even special tours or recreation. The travel agency manager must make sure staff is providing each client with personal needs economically.

Sometimes managers are solicited by airline sales officials regarding sales and package offers. Many times airlines, cruise lines, or resorts offer packages that are more affordable than a personally planned trip, and the manager must stay familiar with what is being offered in order to provide her clients with the best choices. To implement these tasks effectively, travel agencies must maintain a thorough knowledge of current events and world geography.

Consulting with clients and planning leisure trips is a fascinating challenge for a manager and staff. By asking a few leading questions, you can determine where to start. If a couple is planning a honeymoon, for example, you might ask if the honeymooners prefer a warm or a cold climate. Do they like to fish or ski? Do they prefer modern or historic settings? What is their expected budget for the trip? Opening conversations usually reveal whether the clients already know what they want or are unsure and would appreciate professional input.

Travel agency managers also encourage clients to come back after their trip to share their experiences. This feedback lets the agency know what works and what doesn't, which helps the staff plan future trips for all clients.

wholesaler sells the packaged tour either directly to clients, through retail travel agents, or on their own e-commerce Web site.

There are three types of tour wholesalers. The **charter operator** assembles a package tour and sells it to the public or tour operators. **Tour operators** may then resell the package to groups of tourists. The packages usually include an escort or guide with the tour. **Inbound operators** specialize in providing tour packages to international travelers visiting the United States.

Corporate Travel Managers

Many large corporations have in-house travel departments headed by a **corporate travel manager**. The corporate travel manager handles all aspects of travel arrangements for employees of the corporation. Many corporations think that an in-house manager can reduce their travel costs and increase their bargaining power in negotiating prices for hotels, carriers, and other types of travel services. The clients of the corporate travel manager are employees of the company, and most of the travel arrangements are for business purposes.

Incentive Houses

An incentive house manages incentive travel. **Incentive travel** is a marketing and management tool currently used by many North American corporations to motivate clients, salespeople, and other employees to meet sales objectives. Case studies show that incentive travel can be a powerful management and marketing tool. One example is the Northeast Division of Sherwin-Williams, a manufacturer and retailer of paint. The company implemented an incentive travel program to boost sales: for every gallon of paint purchased by commercial painters, the company offered bonus points. After earning a certain number of bonus points, the a painter could take a free vacation trip. Currently, many North American corporations use this type of program to motivate salespeople in retail outlets, such as automobile dealerships, to reach and exceed sales goals. The most frequent users of travel incentives in North America are insurance companies and home appliance manufacturers. Usually, incentive travel redemption occurs at exotic destinations. Destination promoters and marketers are well aware of this phenomenon and position their product accordingly.

Meeting Planners

The increasing number of conventions and meetings has led to the creation of the position of professional meeting planner. A **meeting planner**, whether independent or an employee of an association or corporation, coordinates every detail of meetings and conventions, which can be complicated affairs. Imagine how many details would be involved in planning a meeting for a thousand or more people—booking all the rooms, making sure meeting rooms have proper seating and presentation equipment, arranging air travel and ground transportation, planning meals and activities, and making sure attendees have their tickets and the necessary information on time. Meeting planners need specialized

Professional Profile

THOMAS COOK

Travel Agency Pioneer

Thomas Cook, founder of the world's first travel agency, was a successful and innovative entrepreneur. As a young boy growing up in England in the early 1800s, he left school at the age of ten to pursue various money-making ventures. Some of his professional endeavors included farming and selling books. Finally, at the age of twenty, he settled on a career as a Baptist missionary.

Within three years of organizing his first travel package, Cook left the ministry to begin his own travel agency. He continued to organize many temperance-related tours, and expanded the business to include tours for other travelers as well. At first, all the trips were contained within the boundaries of the British Isles. In 1855, that changed.

Seeing an excellent business opportunity, Cook arranged for a travel excursion from Leicester, England to Calais, France, for the Paris Exposition of 1855. Encouraged by its success, the next year he organized a tour of the European continent. Because so many people registered for this tour, Cook was able to schedule a second tour only a few weeks later for the overflow.

As Thomas Cook's business increased, he used his buying clout to procure discounts for his clients. Many hotels and railways honored his system of "accommodation cards" or coupons because Cook handled such a large share of the tourism market.

Thomas Cook was a pioneer of the travel agency business. His temperance tours and innovative ideas led the way to mass tourism. In fact, the phrase "Cook's tour" is still used today to refer to a tour that goes to many places and stops briefly at each one. Cook died in 1892 but his business is still thriving. Branches of the business, today called Thomas Cook Group plc, are found all over the world.

knowledge and skills to handle all these details for an event efficiently. As a result, many associations and corporations have found that hiring a meeting planner is a must for successful meetings or conventions.

Today travel agencies are both traditional and e-commerce based. Significant travel and travel-related services can be assembled on-line. Indeed, often the best pricing is available through on-line sources.

Choosing Destinations Today

Travelers today avail themselves of hospitality services for many of the same reasons as in the past. The two main reasons for travel are business and leisure-time activities. (See Figure 2.1 for a comparison of selected characteristics of business and pleasure travelers.)

Business Activities

Business travel has become an important part of the hospitality and tourism industry. The airline, rental car, and lodging industries are particularly interested in this segment because it is not as variable as pleasure travel.

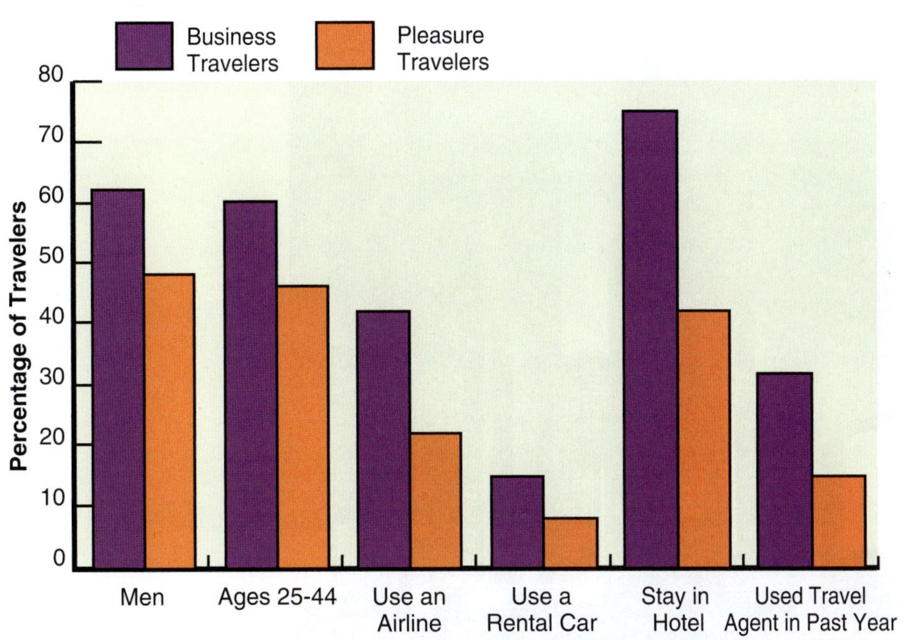

FIGURE 2.1 Comparison of Business Travelers and Pleasure Travelers

Destination choice for the business traveler is rarely a matter of personal taste or preference. If you work in the home office of a company based in New York, and you have a meeting with a plant manager in Texas, whether or not you'd prefer to go to Texas rather than another destination is largely irrelevant. That's where the meeting is, and that's where you need to go.

Although demand for business travel is **elastic**, meaning demand changes with economic conditions, it is not as elastic as the demand for pleasure travel. Pleasure trips can be postponed when the economy is poor. Whether the economy is good or bad, certain types of business travel must still take place. (Economic forces affecting the hospitality and tourism network are further discussed in Chapter 12.)

Business travel is also less seasonal than pleasure travel. Whereas most vacation travel occurs during warm weather months (between spring and early fall in most places), business travel occurs continually throughout the year. This less-elastic demand of business travel allows hotels and other hospitality organizations to attract revenue that balances out the peaks and troughs of leisure-time travel. However, business traveler competition is fierce. Hospitality organizations and brand-affiliated organizations compete aggressively with one another to solidify business customer loyalty and the steady stream of business it represents.

Meetings and conventions account for a large segment of business travel. Originally a **convention** referred to a meeting with large numbers of people in attendance. Today it is a generic term referring to virtually any size of business or professional meeting held in one specific location. Conventions are held by large corporations, government agencies, and other organizations

The Renaissance business and convention center in Detroit, Michigan, can accommodate any size meeting.

Photo courtesy of Hines Interests Limited

known as SMERF (social, military, educational, religious, and fraternal) groups. Outside the United States, the term **congress** is often used instead of *convention*. **Trade shows** and **expositions**, held mainly for informational exchanges among tradespeople, also account for a large portion of business travel throughout the world.

Business and professional people travel to meetings and conventions for a variety of reasons: to learn about the latest trends in an industry, to take part in training programs, to see demonstrations of new technology, to meet contacts, and to find out about the competition. Meetings, conventions, and expositions are discussed further in Chapter 9.

Leisure-Time Activities

Leisure-time destination choices and motivations for travel can be grouped into common categories. Generally, people evaluate more than one category when they make the decision to travel. You'll learn more about these specialized components of the hospitality and tourism network in Chapter 10 and 11.

Visiting Friends and Relatives One of the strongest factors in choosing a destination is the desire to visit family and friends. Although people visiting other people often do not need commercial lodging, they probably will take advantage of other hospitality and tourism services such as transportation, recreation, food, museums, entertainment, and products during their trip.

Education Some people choose a destination because of the opportunity it offers to further their studies. Elderhostel—a nonprofit that offers educational tours for mature adults—often organizes groups to study the language, art, culture, nature, or history of a place. College students may choose a summer study-abroad program in order to gain fluency in a foreign language or to acquaint themselves with another culture. Science or history buffs can join expeditions or archaeological digs to further their knowledge of a specific subject.

Culture Cultural attractions are very popular with tourists. Art museums, natural history museums, historical villages, and icons such as the Great Wall of China and the Eiffel Tower attract sightseers from the world over. Architectural masterpieces such as the Taj Mahal in India also draw tourists. Another form of cultural destination travel focuses on the people at a site, such as Native Americans or aboriginal Australians.

People of different cultures also have different motivations for leisure-time travel. For example, people who live in Singapore travel to many northern destinations to see snow. For them, the snow itself is an attraction. Motivations such as seeing snow can be either a primary or secondary reason for travel, depending on one's cultural orientation.

Nature Visiting natural landmarks as a destination is largely a nineteenth-century U.S. creation. Since the United States had fewer historically significant places than Europe, many Americans traveled throughout the United States to see natural wonders. Today natural wonders around the world, such as the Grand Canyon in Arizona, Angel Falls in Venezuela, or the wild animal preserves in Kenya attract many tourists. The accommodations at nature sites may be on the rustic side and some tourists may rely on camping gear and stay at campsites.

Recreation Destinations that offer visitors the opportunity to participate in a variety of sports or activities, such as hiking, golf, fishing, or gaming, draw large crowds. Large theme parks, such as Disney World in Florida, Kings Island in Ohio, and Cove Atlantis in the Bahamas, offer recreation and entertainment activities. Some resorts make a concerted effort to cater to families by providing organized, adult-supervised activities for children.

Historically Significant Places A serious side to leisure-time travel involves memorials and monuments. Many tourists visit monuments that have been erected to honor an individual or a group of people in remembrance of lives lost or for patriotic tribute. For example, the Vietnam Veterans Memorial in Washington, D.C., draws thousands of visitors daily.

Some memorials, such as the U.S. Holocaust Memorial Museum and Manzanar War Relocation Center, have been established not only to honor

Families and friends travel to the Vietnam War Memorial Wall in Washington, D.C. to honor those who were killed or declared missing in that war.

Courtesy of Photodisc

the dead but also to keep alive the concepts of freedom and the rights of citizens. These memorials serve to remind people of past injustices.

Events Sometimes people arrange their vacation travel around specific events. The events may involve sports, such as the Olympic Games, the Super Bowl, or the World Cup soccer finals. The events may be world's fairs, Carnaval in Rio de Janeiro, Brazil, the Calgary Stampede in Alberta, Canada, or Broadway plays. Usually the event is more important than the location, but people often avail themselves of hospitality and tourism services on the trip.

Religion Religious holidays, pilgrimages, and pageants have long motivated people to travel. For example, every ten years since 1634, tourists have been drawn to a Bavarian village southwest of Munich to see the Oberammergau Passion Play. The religious drama is an entirely local production, and villagers spend ten years preparing for their roles. Much of Oberammergau's income comes from tourist trade.

Health Spas are as popular today as they were during the Roman era. People travel to places that will help them shape up, trim down, or feel better physically. Sometimes a destination is chosen because of its climate. For example, many sinus sufferers in the eastern United States find relief in the dry, hot climate of the West.

Other Factors Other factors also affect the choice of destination. These include ease of access, price, attractive advertising, and level of satisfaction in previous experiences. Another factor is the attitude of the local residents. Vacationers are more likely to return to a destination where they feel welcome than to one where they feel unwanted.

Multiple Motivations

Obviously, these categories are very general. Any one destination may be chosen for a number of reasons. One person might visit Washington, D.C. to study documents at the National Archives. Another visitor might travel there to honor a loved one at the Vietnam Veterans Memorial. A business trip might be planned to coincide with the blooming of the cherry blossoms, a thrilling sight that draws people to the city year after year.

In addition, one destination may offer different motivations to the same visitor. A traveler might visit the National Cathedral in Washington, D.C., both to attend religious services and to study its architecture.

Marketing and Promoting Tourism and Travel

Marketing is a related group of business activities that have the purpose of satisfying demand for goods and services for consumers, businesses, and government. The marketing process includes estimating the demand, producing the product (the destination), pricing the product to satisfy profit criteria, and promoting and distributing the product.[6] (Marketing is discussed further in Chapter 3.)

While hospitality and tourism have evolved over the centuries, the industry as we know it today took shape in the 1950s through an increase of marketing efforts. Before 1950, only a few states in the United States had agencies that promoted tourism. Today all fifty states are involved in such activities. The combined efforts of the various components of the network—hospitality businesses; the airlines, railroads, and bus companies; and national, state, and private associations—began developing destinations through various marketing strategies.

Destination Development

Destination development begins with an idea and the selection of a site. Some sites are natural and some are constructed. Some sites have existed for millennia, such as the Egyptian pyramids and the Grand Canyon. But they need facilities or access roads before the sites have the potential to attract and handle large numbers of visitors. In the cases of the Grand Canyon and the Egyptian pyramids, the U.S. and Egyptian governments, respectively, own the sites. They regulate how hospitality and tourism businesses will operate.

Some privately owned destinations are developed for reasons other than making a profit. Nonprofit groups may develop an area in order to preserve it. Concern for the environment prompted the organization of the Pink River Dolphin Preserve, highlighted in the Industry Insights feature later in this chapter.

Other sites, such as Disney World and The Cove Atlantis beach resort in the Bahamas, are developed by entrepreneurs who invest in the destination to make a profit. Private developers may work with government agencies during

Business Profile

THE COVE ATLANTIS RESORT HOTEL

Successful Destination Resort Concept

Many international resort destinations strive to create lasting impressions, previously unseen concepts, or uniquely designed facilities. The Cove Atlantis Resort in the Bahamas offers a uniquely designed, water-centered destination resort, large enough to be considered a city in itself.

The Cove's architecture reflects a tropical, open-air feeling with high ceilings. Central to the theme at the Atlantis resort destination are the Cove lagoon pool and varied water features within the hotel. The resort features two exclusive beaches among its landscaped gardens and tropically appointed ambience. But perhaps the Cove is most celebrated for its spectacular views of the sea and tropical palm tree–lined horizon.

Source: http://www.thecoveatlantis.com/home.aspx

the planning, funding and building stages. The **infrastructure**, or underlying economic foundation, must be considered. This basic framework includes transportation and communication systems, power facilities, and other public services.[7]

Government's Role in Tour and Travel Development

Because of the economic gains that tourism can bring to an economy, all levels of government make an effort to develop and promote tourist destinations. One way governments do this, as described earlier, is by providing facilities and capital investment upkeep at government-owned destinations, such as national parks, monuments, and historical attractions.

Governments are also involved in planning and promoting sites that are developed through the private sector. They often raise money through bonds and taxes to help build convention centers or stadiums. And they help the hospitality and tourism industry by reducing or waiving taxes on establishments to attract businesses to a site. This allows a company to use more of its financial resources in the actual development of the site. It may even make financially feasible a new development that, before tax benefits, was marginal at best.

Government funds are used to develop and operate mass transit systems, airports, shipping docks, and highways. Water, sewage, and electrical systems also make up the infrastructure of an area, and all must be able to handle the needs of an increased population brought about by tourism.

Another role of government related to tourism is to control of the flow of people across national borders. Most governments issue passports to identify citizens who are traveling or living in another country. When two nations have extended diplomatic recognition to each other and have negotiated travel

Courtesy of Photodisc

The Sphinx, operated by the Egyptian government, attracts large numbers of foreign visitors each year.

and commercial agreements, they determine the requirements for the citizens in each country to travel or work in the other. A traveler receives a *passport* from his or her home country, while a *visa* is issued by the country into which the traveler is entering.

Today so many people are traveling to so many different places, often within short time frames, that it has become increasingly difficult for customs and immigration officials to identify people who are traveling illegally. In addition, technology is enabling many of these illegal travelers to obtain and use authentic-appearing but nevertheless false documents. The most significant recent development in international travel has been the heightening of government-imposed security measures. In light of the 9-11 terrorist attacks on the United States and the overall terror threat worldwide, more rigid country entry requirements, i.e., finger printing and eye scanning, coupled with tighter security measures, now cause prospective international travelers some inconvenience and require more thorough trip planning.

Organizations that Promote Tourism and Travel

The following is a brief look at the government agencies and professional and trade associations that promote hospitality and tourism. Appendix B contains an extended list of such organizations and associations, including travel associations and chambers of commerce. Promotion takes place at various levels—international, national, state, regional, and local.

International Level

The World Tourism Organization (WTO) is headquartered in Madrid, Spain, and serves as a consulting agency for the United Nations. The WTO's main

Industry Insights

TECHNOLOGY

Antifraud Passports

The U.S. Department of State has developed a new passport to combat growing fraud and infiltration of unwanted visitors such as political "undesirables" and criminals. In the past, identifying a citizen leaving the country was fairly easy. Recognizing that same person trying to reenter—especially if the traveler's passport had been lost or stolen—was a chore for officials and an inconvenience for the traveler. In an effort to discourage forgeries, designers used special inks and graphics on the inside pages of the improved passports. Also inside is another forgery deterrent, a *kinegram*. Similar to the holograms common on many charge cards, the color-changing kinegram depicts the letters *U.S.A.* and a likeness of Benjamin Franklin's face. The new passports, which began to replace the old models in 1993, sport a bar code that enables customs and immigration officials to use scanners to detect fraudulent documents. Using the new passports will speed up the reentry process for legitimate travelers and increase officials' ability to identify and apprehend clandestine travelers. Additonally, there is now an international "no-fly list" utilized by both the airlines and governments to determine the presence of high-profile terror suspects. The United States has implemented eye scanning and fingerprinting requirements that all inbound international travelers must comply with upon arrival in the country.

objectives are to promote and develop tourism in the interest of economic, social, and cultural progress of all nations; to seek to foster peace, health, and prosperity throughout the world; and to facilitate people's access to education and culture through travel.

The WTO provides a forum for addressing problems that affect tourists everywhere, such as the problem of international terrorism. It conducts research to find possible solutions to problems and to identify worldwide trends in the industry. The results of this research enable the WTO to provide valuable information to tourism promotion agencies in individual countries.[8]

Two other noteworthy international organizations are the Organization for Economic Cooperation and Development (OECD) and the Pacific Asia Travel Association (PATA). The OECD is a multinational organization that was created in 1960. It fosters the planned development of tourism as a form of world trade. PATA is a membership organization of government and private business representatives that promotes and monitors travel among countries within the Pacific Rim.

National Level

At the national level, governments promote their countries in the international tourist market through national tourist organizations (NTOs). The United States Travel and Tourism Administration (USTTA), under the jurisdiction of the Department of Commerce, is the NTO for the United States. Established by

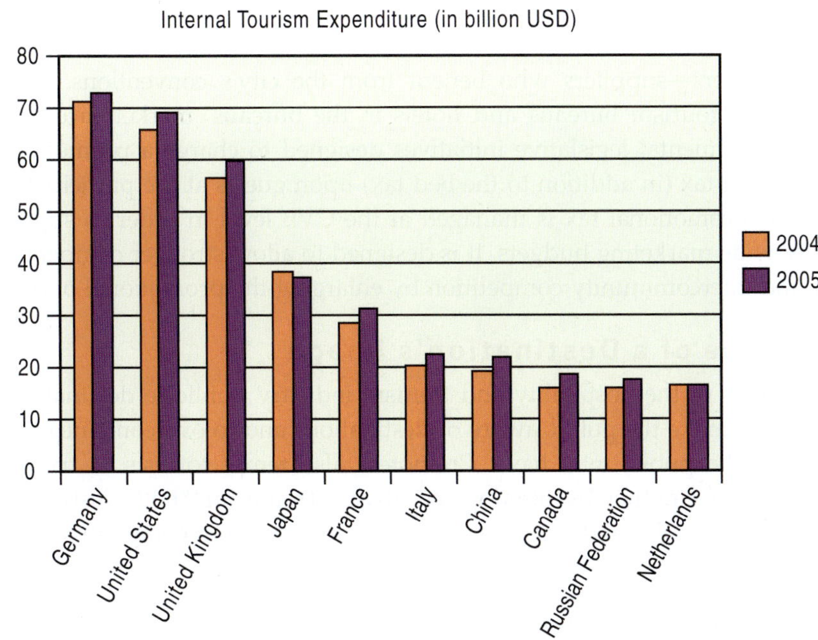

FIGURE 2.2 International Tourism Expenditure (in billions of US$)
Source: World Tourism Organization, October, 2006.

the National Tourism Policy Act of 1981, it has the major governmental responsibility for the promotion of the United States as an international destination. As a part of the Department of Commerce, USTTA is headed by an undersecretary of commerce. Figure 2.2 shows the top international tourism expenditures of 2004 and 2005.

In some countries, such as Mexico, government leaders have recognized the importance of tourism to the nation's economy and have elevated the status of the NTO to the cabinet level, instituting a ministry of tourism. Regardless of their position in their respective governments, NTOs have similar objectives. They promote their countries through publicity campaigns, conduct research, and develop plans for destinations.

State Level

In the United States, each of the fifty states has a **tourism office** that is typically part of the state's agency for economic development. Also referred to as **destination marketing organizations** (DMOs), these organizations are in charge of developing and implementing tourism programs for individual states. They produce and distribute literature on destinations and promote convention sites.

Regional and Local Level

At the regional and local level, **convention and visitors bureaus (CVBs)** are the organizations typically responsible for promoting tourism. Their job is to promote the entire region or city as either a business or pleasure destination.

A CVB may be an independent organization, or a department within a municipal government or a chamber of commerce. All CVB activities are funded by bureau members—suppliers who benefit from the city's conventions. Some regional/local tourism bureaus and hotels in the bureaus' marketplace have enacted supplemental legislative initiatives designed to charge a promotional and marketing tax (in addition to the bed tax) upon guests at the participating hotels. This promotional tax is managed at the CVB level in order to supplement city-wide marketing budgets. It is designed to allow stronger competitive thrusts and intercommunity competition by enlarging the promotional budget.

Importance of a Destination's Image

The promoters of the hospitality and tourism industry publicize destinations. They work to make the public aware of destinations and to overcome negative images that the public may have. Promoters also tempt tourists to try one destination over another by offering incentives. Trendy or "hot" destination imaging is a valuable marketing advantage in an ever more competitive marketplace for destination resorts and urban centers.

The Role of Destination Images

The image people have of a destination is a major factor in determining where a family or an individual goes for vacation or where a business entity holds a meeting or convention. Tourists don't often have firsthand knowledge of destinations and, therefore, may choose a specific destination based on images. A college student's decision to go to Daytona Beach for spring break may be based on images of the area—hot, sandy beaches; noisy crowds of fun-loving students; salty sea breezes; and rhythmic ocean waves.

Every destination has an image. For example, many people probably have an image of Spain, whether they've been there or not. Perhaps they picture bullfights and flamenco dancers, or open-air cafes. Likewise, people may have images of China—perhaps the Great Wall, Tiananmen Square, or people riding bicycles to work. One person's image of a particular place may differ from the images others have, but highly publicized images may be commonly held.

When asking a sampling of Koreans what images immediately come to mind when they hear the words *United States*, the most frequent responses included "the Statue of Liberty, it's a big, strong country, democracy and liberty, the U.S. flag, the White House, big cities, the Wild West, Disneyland, blue jeans, hamburgers and Coca-Cola, Niagara Falls, the Golden Gate Bridge, George Washington, John F. Kennedy, King Kong, and (unfortunately) drugs and violence."

The Source of Destination Images Every time someone is exposed to anything related to a destination, it helps to form an image of that place. Books, movies, television, postcards, songs, photographs, news stories, and advertising all contribute to images of various destinations. Austria became a popular vacation destination for many Americans as a result of the favorable images portrayed in the movie *The Sound of Music*.

Courtesy of Photodisc

The Great Wall of China is a common destination for travelers to China.

Individuals who have never been to the western part of the United States may have an image of sagebrush-lined roads, endless desert, and bronco-bustin' cowhands. These are common images in movies, books, and postcards. Of course, not everyone's image will be the same. Some people will think of the skyscrapers, snowcapped mountains, or Air Force bases that are also a part of the West. Individual images depend on the whole range of things one has been exposed to about the West.

What about a negative image? One of the difficulties in promoting India as a tourist destination is the image of poverty people associate with the country. The scenic beauty and many cultural attractions in the country are overshadowed by negative scenes of starving people and squalor. This negative image makes it a challenge for India's tourism marketers to promote the country's tourism overseas.

Images of a destination are so important that states and countries spend millions of dollars to build positive images of their destinations. One good example is the "Find yourself here" campaign by the state of California. Additionally, the state of California utilized world-famous Hollywood actor and current governor Arnold Schwarzenegger as a pitchman in video ads promoting the state as a tourism destination. As a result of this campaign, tourism in the state increased dramatically.[9]

Images and Tourist Satisfaction A tourist's overall travel experience can be examined through the process of destination image modification. This image modification process can have significant implications for tourist areas. The following example illustrates why.

State license plates are sometimes used as a form of state tourism promotion.

Shinichi is a 19-year-old college student who decides to take a vacation over spring break and reads brochures for spring travel packages to Daytona Beach. He has never been to Florida and is excited about the idea of going to Daytona Beach. At this point, Shinichi's image of Daytona Beach is based mainly on two things—the written information from the tour package brochure and his previous knowledge about Florida, acquired through books, mass media, and friends. Shinichi's image of the destination is most important here because his expectations of Daytona Beach are based on his images of the area.

Spring break comes, and Shinichi travels to Daytona Beach. He swims and meets new friends. When he returns home, he goes through a "recollection" stage. In the recollection stage, Shinichi evaluates his overall experience of Daytona Beach. The evaluation process includes a comparison of his expectations and his actual experiences. When the actual experiences live up to the expectations (based on images of the destination), there is satisfaction. If the actual experiences do not live up to expectations, there is dissatisfaction. Depending on his level of satisfaction or dissatisfaction, Shinichi will decide whether to return to Daytona Beach in the future. More important, he'll talk about his experiences with his friends. Shinichi's descriptions to his friends will in turn help his friends form images of Daytona Beach. The primary images of a destination as perceived by a tourist have a lot to do with the tourist's ultimate satisfaction or dissatisfaction. Everything that happens, good or bad, is ultimately based on the original image.

Functional and Symbolic Images Research shows that a tourist destination's image can be described in both functional and symbolic terms. A **functional image** of a destination is associated with specific activities and attractions at the destination. Therefore, functional images of Daytona Beach are things such as sandy beaches, swimming and other water activities, shopping, an atmosphere for rest and relaxation, local cuisine, and hotel accommodations. Conversely, an area's **symbolic image** is related to the "personality" of the area as perceived by the visitor. Like many consumer products, different destinations have different personalities. Whereas tourists consider some destinations family-oriented, they also strongly associate other places with the image of singles and college students. The symbolic or personality image of Daytona Beach is young and lively, whereas the symbolic image of Disney World is family-oriented.

Studies show that both functional and symbolic images of a destination area are highly correlated with choice. That is, depending on the tourist's perception of symbolic images associated with the destination, the tourist will or will not select the place as a travel destination. In choosing a particular area for vacation, a tourist considers not only what specific interests and activities are available, but also whether the destination is "my type of place" to go.

Business Profile

DISNEY THEME PARKS

Destination Image Exemplified

Photo used by permission of Disney Enterprises, Inc.

The Walt Disney Company was founded in 1923 and has long been committed to leading the hospitality industry in entertainment, customer service, and excellence in resort destination management. Today, Disney is a multifaceted global enterprise with business divisions including movie and studio production, theme parks, hotels and resorts, and television media programming. Each of these business divisions reflects a well-integrated business model based on the founding principles of creativity, quality, and excellence in customer service.

The company's founder was Walter Elias Disney (1901–1966) and he was best known for his ability to capture the imagination of kids and create family entertainment. Walt Disney is credited with the birth of the theme park. He used his popular animated characters as the core theme and offered complete family entertainment, lodging, and meals, but it was a learn-as-you-go venture.

Disneyland Park, which opened in the 1950s in Anaheim, California, was designed to provide family-oriented entertainment activities. But provisions made for meals and other tourist necessities were not adequate. Consequently, independent businesses sprang up around Disneyland to address these lucrative service areas. In 1955, the Disneyland Hotel opened; it remains the park's only lodging facility.

The Walt Disney Company then redefined its hospitality design to include self-contained destination areas for the entire family. Walt Disney World Resort, near Orlando, Florida, offers over thirty-two resorts plus over 190 restaurants and snack bars. Monorail trains, ferryboats, and shuttle services transport guests from one location to another within the resort. Guest services include ATMs, camera rentals, baby services, personal lockers, lost and found offices, and first aid stations.

Four Disney resorts were opened by 1993–Disneyland in California, Walt Disney World in Florida, Tokyo Disneyland in Japan, and

continues...

continued...

Disneyland Resort Paris in France. Hong Kong Disneyland Resort was opened in 2005. The parks feature colorful animal characters, reproductions of historical buildings, rides, elaborate stage shows, and immaculate landscaping. The Magic Kingdom park contains areas with more specific themes, including Main Street U.S.A., Adventureland, Frontierland, Fantasyland, and Tomorrowland.

Walt Disney World Resort covers forty-seven square miles (making it twice the size of Manhattan) and hosts more than 20 million visitors a year. The Magic Kingdom alone spans one hundred acres, with forty-five rides, shows, and adventures. Epcot, with its showcase of future technology and world cultures, extends over 260 acres. One of the newest attractions is Animal Kingdom, a high-adventure authentic African safari on five hundred acres of deep jungles, forests, and vast savannahs. Throughout every park, young, friendly, enthusiastic workers greet and serve visitors and maintain the spotlessly clean and well-manicured grounds that foster the "magic" image created by the park's developers.

Virtually every amusement park in the United States is measured against Disney's theme parks. Walt Disney spent his life creating images to entertain, and now the parks that bear his name create the image to which park developers must aspire if they want to be successful. In 2006 revenue at Disney hit an all-time high of $34 billion, a 7 percent increase over the previous year. In addition, earnings per share for the year increased 34 percent to $1.64, reflecting growth in each of Disney's businesses—media networks, parks and resorts, studio entertainment and consumer products.

Source: http://www.disney.com

The Effects Of Hospitality, Tourism, and Travel

Many countries and destination areas seek the advantages that make tourism attractive. A healthy tourism trade benefits countries economically, socioculturally, and environmentally. Figure 2.3 shows how international tourist arrivals have increased. Of course, some disadvantages also exist. Careful planning and management can help lessen negative impact.

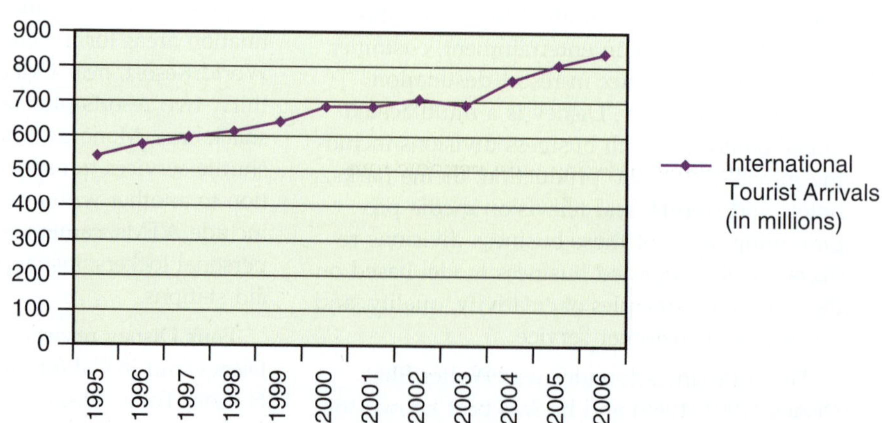

FIGURE 2.3 World Tourism Growth *Source:* World Tourism Organization, January 2007.

Economic Gains and Costs

When a destination is developed for tourism, the wave of tourists coming in has a tremendous impact on the local and national economy. Sometimes the local economy reaps the benefits; at other times, it bears the costs and outsiders take home the gains.

Economic Gains

Almost all destinations require facilities and services nearby to satisfy the needs of visitors. Regardless of their reasons for traveling, tourists usually spend money during their stay at a destination. Visitor spending provides income and profit for many businesses, including hotels, campgrounds, restaurants, service stations, golf courses, grocery stores, and souvenir shops.

Business travel to a destination for conventions and meetings directly benefits transportation businesses, hotels, and restaurants. Almost everyone living in the destination area receives some economic benefits directly from business travel. Write-ups in professional journals and trade magazines about conventions and the destination itself help establish a positive image for an area. If the area has a solid business image, other businesses are likely to locate there. Destinations (usually local municipalities) invest in convention centers to attract conventions, meetings, trade shows, and expositions. Although expensive to build, a facility that is successful at bringing in business groups will

Graduate Glimpse

NANDITA SHARMA

As an assistant controller at Marriott International in Washington, D.C., Nandita Sharma is responsible for attending operations meetings, reconciling asset and liability accounts, communicating with operations managers, ensuring proper control procedures are in place and enforced, auditing, assisting with periodic forecasts, helping managers understand their budgets, reviewing service and product contracts, monitoring licenses to ensure they are valid, and special projects to enhance hotel profits.

Sharma graduated from the Pennsylvania State University in fall 2005. While a student there, she worked in teams with her classmates. This background enables her to appreciate differences among co-workers, and to facilitate productive meetings. She credits the Pennsylvania State University hospitality program for her success today. "It exposed me to many meetings, seminars with alumni and other professionals." She says a great handshake is the first opportunity to impress people. The basic techniques she gained in her writing classes also benefit her in her everyday work.

She is confident that she can become a senior assistant controller, and then a director of finance in Marriott International in the next five years.

Developing countries use tourism as a vehicle for economic development.

Photo of the Royal Palace of Phnom Penh, Cambodia by Kye-Sung Chon

generate employment, and the entire community can benefit from the subsequent economic windfall.

Tourism also generates government revenue from direct taxation of tourism businesses and tourists. Local, state, and national governments receive revenues from sales taxes, room taxes, alcohol and gasoline taxes, and user fees for campgrounds, parks, tollroads, and other amenities. Increased government revenue that may be used to improve the area's infrastructure can elevate the quality of life for local residents.[10]

The flow of tourism dollars into a local economy involves direct and indirect spending. **Direct spending** is money that goes directly from the traveler into the economy. This money includes payments for hotel rooms, restaurant meals, rental cars, recreation, entertainment, souvenirs, and miscellaneous items.

Once the money has reached the owners of the tourist facilities, it is respent. The respending, which is called **indirect spending**, generates more income and further employment. For example, foodservice establishments ideally buy food and beverages from local suppliers. The suppliers make purchases from local farmers. Part of the money also supports employees who work in the hotels, restaurants, and other tourist businesses. The workers in turn pay for housing, buy groceries, and so forth. This respending, which expands the economy, is called the **multiplier effect**. The greater the multiplier effect, the more advantageous tourist spending is to the local economy.

Economic Costs

Tourism can also have a negative impact. One concern is the **opportunity cost**, or the benefit that will be sacrificed by using a resource one way rather than another. The opportunity cost of tourism is the cost of developing tourism rather than some other industry. For example, a community might have to decide between expanding an airport to bring in more tourists or allowing a manufacturer to locate on a particular piece of real estate. The community cannot do both, so people must project the total profit from both ventures and choose the one that will have the greatest long-term benefit. If they choose the airport expansion rather than the manufacturer, they will pay an "opportunity cost" by not having the manufacturer, losing potential manufacturing jobs and other local profits. However, the opportunity cost of not having the airport expansion could be far greater.

Leakage Another economic cost is **leakage**, or money that flows out of the local economy to purchase outside resources. Many of the goods and services that are needed to satisfy tourist desires have to be imported. Thus, not all of the direct and indirect tourist expenditure money will stay in the local economy. The more imports that are necessary, the higher the leakage will be, Sometimes a large part of the income from tourism has to be used to pay for imported materials and equipment. Construction materials may not be available in a large enough quantity in the destination area. If not, they will have to be purchased elsewhere. For example, hotel beds, bathroom fixtures, elevators, and air conditioners may have to be imported. If a country has a small domestic automobile industry, it may have to import cars or buses to satisfy transportation needs of tourists. When an area has the resources to produce all the necessary goods and services, on the other hand, the full amount of tourist spending will remain there. In such an economy, it is possible for each dollar spent directly for hospitality services to generate three additional dollars. The more developed the local economy, the higher the multiplier effect; conversely, the greater the leakage, the less the multiplier effect on the local economy.

Globalization of Tourism and Travel Business As cultural attitudes and lifestyle changes contribute to longer lifespans, travelers are brand-wise, travel more, and desire new experiences in both cultural and event-based tourism experiences. Research indicates that by the year 2050, the world's population will grow to 9 billion, with less than 6 percent coming from developed countries. The percentage of population aged sixty-five and older will increase from 15 percent to over 25 percent by 2015. This increased travel by the "silver" segment will keep Europe the number-one tourism exporting region, delivering 730 million travelers by 2020. Not only will travel increase exponentially, but shifts will occur in travel patterns from north to south and west to east. The emergence of China and India means they will capture 15 percent of the total global passenger growth. This increasing interest in global travel has prompted development by large, multinational hospitality entities as well as smaller, locally based tourism operations geared towards the tourist market in developing countries. These smaller operations include ecotourism, community-developed projects. and authentic travel experiences.[11]

More importantly, the emergence of multinational corporations has also affected tourism income in destination areas. International hotel and restaurant chains have opened properties throughout the world. Much of the profit from these businesses returns to the home countries. The payment of airfares to foreign-owned airlines is another way in which countries lose tourist income. Some developing nations, such as China, are working to establish their own airlines to capture this income.

Income earned by outside investors is another factor that reduces a country's tourism revenues. Because destination development takes a huge investment of capital, some countries cannot afford to finance large-scale projects. They may seek financial assistance abroad. Without outside help, the destinations might not be developed for tourism. But the price to these developing countries is high. They often spend years repaying loans and paying interest on the investments.

Money may also be spent abroad for management fees. Local hotels that are not part of a chain, for example, may be managed by foreign corporations to which a fee is paid for their services. If the local labor force is not big enough, workers may have to be imported to fill jobs in lodging, foodservice, and other tourist-related businesses. The imported workers may invest or save some of their earnings in their home countries.

Some aspects of leakage are considered necessary. **Necessary leakage** refers to the cost of promoting the destination abroad. If a destination wants to attract tourists, it must advertise to convince potential customers that it is more appealing than other destinations. National tourist organizations promote their destinations by advertising in media abroad and by offering fam trips to travel agents and travel writers.

Minimizing Leakage

Developing countries can minimize the loss of tourist income. For example, through trade negotiations, they can reduce imports of tourism-related materials and support local industries instead. Many nations also limit foreign ownership to 49 percent or less. Outside control of the hospitality industry might be further reduced by incentives offered to local hotel and restaurant owners. The number of imported managers and professionals might be reduced if education and training programs are offered to local employees. These measures may help ensure that a greater percentage of tourist money will stay in a destination area. Thus, the economic benefits of destination development can outweigh possible negative impact.

Sociocultural Impact

The effects of increased hospitality and tourism activities on the ways individuals interact with other members of their society also may be positive or negative. Changing family lifestyles and cross-cultural contacts may result in either positive or negative influences. However, most concern surrounds the social ills that can result from tourism.

Changing Family Lifestyles

Many local residents find their lives changed when they obtain tourism-related employment. Young people may enter the job market for the first time when tourism development occurs. On the positive side, this may contribute to increased family income, allowing families to buy products that were previously beyond their means. The change in lifestyle may also lead to demands for better housing and changes in dress and eating habits. When local people adopt practices from tourists, this is known as the **demonstration effect**. The demonstration effect can have a negative outcome, though, if local residents come to realize that, even with their increased income, they cannot afford to live like the tourists. A feeling of envy or resentment toward affluent visitors may result. This situation tends to occur most in those destinations where the economy is based primarily on tourism.

Traditional relationships between the young and the old may change as young people take jobs in tourist businesses. Established local trades or industries may suffer as workers are drawn toward tourism. A young man whose father and grandfather both farmed for a living may decide that instead of following the family tradition he would rather work toward managing a hotel. People who once made their living from the land or sea may come to prefer the steady paycheck of an amusement park employee. On the other hand, if tourists should stop coming to the destination, employees will have to either return to their traditional occupations or look for equivalent work elsewhere.

Cultural Awareness and Preservation

Integrating host culture values and perspectives with those of inbound tourists may prove to be complex and require mitigation efforts to bridge the divergent cultural perspectives. However, one positive effect of tourism is an increased understanding among people of different nations. Tourism is a vital force for peace in this regard. Our stereotypic view of people in another country can change with a single visit. A study of U.S. students visiting Russia for the first time showed that tourism resulted in positive changes in the attitudes of the tourists.[12] Likewise, a study of first-time American visitors to South Korea showed a big difference between pre-visit and post-visit perceptions; after they returned home, visitors showed a more favorable attitude toward the country and its people.[13]

Tourism can also help preserve historical sites and culture. Colonial Williamsburg in Virginia is one example. The historic homes, styles of dress, and traditions of the area are not only preserved but also attract tourists from all over the country and the world. Wise County, a coal-mining community in rural Virginia, successfully preserves its coal-mining heritage by promoting museums and local culture for tourists. The Polynesian Cultural Center in

Photo by Kye-Sung Chon

Thai dancers in Erawan, Bangkok are an example of cultural tourism. Thailand proudly displays its tradition and culture to tourists.

Hawaii offers visitors the chance to see traditional Polynesian dances, learn about the Pacific Islander culture, and hear island music. In these examples, tourism combines preservation with business; without tourist dollars, many areas such as these could not afford to preserve their culture.

Tourism has also been credited with helping traditional arts and crafts survive. In the southwestern United States, for example, tourist exposure to Native American cultures has greatly increased the demand for indigenous arts and crafts, such as pottery, jewelry, and weaving. A similar picture emerges among the Inuit people in parts of Northern Canada, where tourist demands for souvenirs have promoted their soapstone carvings.

A wave of tourists from other cultures may have less desirable consequences. For example, the Pennsylvania Amish had lived quietly for hundreds of years until they became a tourist attraction. Tourism businesses built motels, restaurants, and souvenir shops to serve the growing numbers of tourists. Farmland became less plentiful and more expensive, forcing many Amish to move outside the area.

Tourism can contribute to the undermining of social standards and to the commercialization of a culture. Some people say that local artistic standards suffer when reproductions of native crafts are mass-produced for tourist consumption. They also claim that commercialization has a negative effect on local religious and social customs. In some places, for example, ceremonial dances that were once performed for religious purposes are now staged to entertain tourists. Because of a concern that foreign influences might affect its culture, China was closed to outside visitors until the late 1970s. No country wants its cultural heritage turned into a sideshow, but generally the benefits of tourism (especially the economic benefits) outweigh other concerns. Currently,

China is the world's sixth-largest tourist destination and the World Tourism Organization has predicted that China will be the world's largest tourist market and destination by 2020. China hosted the 2008 Olympics in Beijing, and will host the Shanghai World Expo in 2010. A twenty-year tourism plan developed by China estimates that by 2020 the country's tourism revenue will exceed 3.3 trillion **yuan**.[14] Furthermore, China is expected to rise as one of the world's top four tourist generating countries along with the United States, Germany and United Kingdom. According to some industry estimates, about 5 percent of China's 1.3 billion population will be able to travel overseas by year 2015, which would mean about 65 million outbound tourists from country. Considering that slightly less than 18 million Japanese are traveling abroad each year, this would mean that the world will soon see as many as four Chinese tourists for each Japanese tourist traveling around the world.

Social Ills

Social ills include such problems as crime, displacement, and discrimination. Organized crime and prostitution are sometimes associated with tourism. Indeed, research studies show a correlation between the growth of tourism and increased crime. Promoters, law enforcement officers, and other stakeholders may have to deal with the fact that tourists who do not know their way around a city may be targets for criminals. The negative publicity from such attacks may be difficult to overcome.

Tourism can cause displacement if local residents find they can no longer live in their community after it has been newly developed as a destination. An increased demand for land for tourist facilities can cause property values to soar. Small businesses may fail if they cannot afford to pay increased rents. Local residents may find their rental properties being torn down to make way for luxury hotels. Such effects can be particularly hard on low-income families or older people who live on fixed incomes. When gambling was legalized in Atlantic City, New Jersey, for example, working-class residents were faced with the choice of paying high rents, real estate prices, and property taxes or moving out of the area.

The negative effects of tourism may include discrimination. Hiring and promotion practices of corporations new to an area may be discriminatory against local employees. A community may discriminate against transplanted corporate employees. When there are not enough local workers to build and manage the tourist businesses, workers may be brought in from outside the area or even the country. A sudden wave of large numbers of outside workers may cause resentment in local workers. This may be especially true if the incoming employees occupy managerial positions that earn high salaries while leaving the low-paying menial jobs to local workers. If local workers see a higher standard of living for the newcomers, they may actively discriminate against them. On the other side, if the culture and lifestyle of the local residents is very different from that of the newcomers, the newcomers may be uncomfortable in their new situation.

Industry Insights

ENVIRONMENT

Sustainable Tourism and Environmental Impact

When appropriately planned and managed, tourism can contribute to the preservation and protection of the environment. By designating national parks and state parks, a country's natural environment can be preserved and protected. Also, many communities pass laws and establish guidelines for such things as architectural design and waste disposal to maintain the beauty of an area.

However, too much tourism, or poorly planned tourism and tourism-related development, can result in pollution and damage to the natural environment. Tourism is often seasonal and generates mostly part-time, unskilled jobs for local people, with specialist and management positions occupied by expatriates. By far the greatest benefits flow to developers and investors (often multinational companies, hotel chains, and international airlines) rather than to local communities. Those communities can be exploited and their resources taken over by outside interests for tourism. Tourism can destroy natural environments by filling them with large-scale resorts, golf courses, marinas, and other facilities, and the tourism industry is a major polluter through sewage and other waste discharge.

Source: Sofield, Trevor, H., B. (n.d.) Re-thinking and Re-conceptualising Social and Cultural Issues of Tourism Development in South and Southeast Asia. Case Study; Institute for Sustainability and Technology policy.

Furthermore, the impacts of tourism on the local environment can cause harm to sensitive heritage sites, for example, the Lascaux Cave in France had to be closed to the public because the tourists' breath and body heat were destroying the pictures left on its walls by Paleolithic artists. The mere presence of the visitors warmed the air around them, which caused condensation on the cooler cave walls. When the droplets fell, they took with them pigments from the 17,000-year-old paintings. Authorities realized that, over time, none of the original paintings would survive.[15]

Another example of the need for further planning is the Hol Chan Marine Reserve in Belize. In 1987, the government set up the reserve to protect fish and coral from fishers and divers. The reserve has proved very successful—the fish and coral are thriving. But how long will it last? The increase in fish has attracted more tourists, and the resort town nearby has reached its **carrying capacity**, meaning the maximum number of people who can use the destination without causing the environment to deteriorate and the quality of the visitors' experience to decrease. By exceeding the carrying capacity, the destination's water and sanitation systems have been strained. Increased sewage in the bay is adding nutrients that disturb the fragile balance of the coral reefs.[16] On the other hand, promoters of tourism point out that without tourism, efforts to protect beautiful sites and exotic animals and plants might not have been undertaken.

Industry Insights

TOURISM, TRAVEL AND THE ENVIRONMENT

Pink River Dolphin Preserve

Photo courtesy of Roxanne Kremer

Peru's Pink River Dolphin Reserve, officially known as the Cumaceba National and Regional Communal Reserve, is an example of ecotourism.

The preserve sits near the confluence of the Yarapa and Cumaceba rivers in the headwaters of the Amazon River. It was established by Roxanne Kremer, founder of the International Society for the Preservation of the Tropical Rainforest, a growing nonprofit organization.

Visitors' fees and private contributions enable Kremer's group to preserve rain forest areas. The group acquires land and then funds local people who take care of the camps and patrol the area against illegal poaching, logging, and commercial fishing activities. Careful planning and strict controls of water use and waste management help protect the preserve from negative effects of increased human presence. All fieldwork is designed to preserve the natural environment as well as the natural behavior patterns of the dolphins and the other wildlife in the area.

Hospitality and tourism leaders have become more focused in the last few years on issues related to "quality of life" for citizens. Heritage Interpretation International (HII) was created in 1991 to promote and preserve the world's cultural and natural heritages. The organization held a conference in Honolulu, Hawaii, under the theme of "Joining Hands for Quality Tourism." This conference sought ways to maintain a balance between the preservation of our natural and cultural heritages and tourism development. This balance is often called **ecotourism**, meaning ecologically sound tourism.

The American Society of Travel Agents (ASTA) and related organizations in the hospitality and tourism industry also encourage the growth of peaceful tourism and environmentally responsible tourism. ASTA established environmental guidelines related to air, land, and sea travel. The agents encourage energy and environmental conservation, efforts to improve water and air quality, recycling, safe management of waste and toxic materials, noise abatement, and community involvement in these efforts.

ASTA also suggests that hospitality and tourism employees be well-trained in the principles of conservation. It recommends that hospitality and tourism organizations adopt their own environmental codes to cover special sites and ecosystems.[17]

Summary

- Listed here are some of the professional opportunities open to those holding tourism degrees and higher education credentials:
  - In the travel industry: travel agencies, tour operators, charter companies.
  - In the hotel and catering industry: hotels and hotel chains; tourist resorts (alpine, coastal, rural); convention centers; vacation centers.
  - In tourist attractions and related businesses: artistic and cultural heritage sites; nature parks; amusement and theme parks; fairs, conferences and expositions; shops; recreational and athletic facilities.
  - In the transportation sector: airlines; car and bus rental agencies; railway companies; ferries and cruise ships.
  - Tourist information providers, promoters, and consultants: tourist agencies; local, regional, and national organizations; consumer organizations; media organizations; providers of tourism information technology products; consultancies and research groups.
- The components of the hospitality and tourism network usually operate independently and often compete with each other, yet they share a mutual interdependency.
- Common reasons for business travel include attendance at meetings, conventions, trade shows, and expositions.
- Nine major categories of destination choice and motivation for leisure-time travel include friends and relatives, education, culture, nature, recreation, historical sites, events, religion, and health.
- Destination development begins with an idea and the selection of a site. Some sites are natural and some are constructed. Sites that are millenia-old have facilities built to accommodate tourists. Some destinations are created to be tourist attractions.
- Governments work with private developers to plan and promote tourism. They provide facilities at government-owned destinations, raise money through bonds and taxes, reduce or waive taxes to attract businesses to a site, and build and operate the infrastructure that allows a site to handle incoming tourists.
- Governments market tourism through the World Tourism Organization (WTO), national tourism organizations (NTOs), destination marketing organizations (DMOs), and local convention and visitors bureaus (CVBs).
- Every destination has an image. The functional image of an area is determined by the tourist's perception of its specific activities and functions. The symbolic image represents the relationship between one's self-concept and the destination's image.
- Promoters entice travelers to use a service or visit a location by offering incentives such as travel packages, frequent flyer/frequent guest

programs, and high-tech amenities, and by responding to particular segments of society such as women business travelers.

- Tourism products and services are distributed through intermediaries such as retail travel agents and wholesale tour operators. Other channels of distribution include corporate travel managers, incentive houses, and meeting planners.
- Tourism has economic, sociocultural, and environmental effects that can be positive and negative. Careful planning and management can increase the benefits of tourism.

ENDNOTES

[1] http://www.ibanet.org, http://wvtourism.com.

[2] Zbigniew Ted Mieczkowski, "Some Notes on the Geography of Tourism: A Comment," *Canadian Geographer* XXV (1981): 189–190.

[3] Metelka, Charles J., ed., *The Dictionary of Tourism* (Wheaton, Ill.: Merton House Publishing, 1981):76.

[4] http://www.hawaii.gov.

[5] Anita Gates, "The Best Hotels for Women," *Working Woman* (April 1993): 77–81.

[6] Douglas Greenwald, *The McGraw-Hill Dictionary of Modern Economics*, 3rd ed. (New York: McGraw-Hill Book Company, 1983): 288.

[7] Ibid., 235.

[8] David W. Howell, *Passport: An Introduction to the Travel and Tourism Industry* (Cincinnati, Ohio: South-Western Publishing Co., 1993): 197–198.

[9] http://www.visitcalifornia.com.

[10] Kale H. Sudhir and Katherine M. Weir, "Marketing Third World Countries to the Western Traveler: The Case of India," *Journal of Travel Research* (Fall 1986): 2–7.

[11] Deloitte. *Hospitality 2010: A Five-Year Wake-Up Call*. Author, 2006. (Available from the Preston Robert Tisch Center for Hospitality, Tourism and Sports Management, New York University)

[12] Abraham Pizam, Jafar Jafari, and Ady Milman, "Influence of Tourism on Attitudes: U.S. Students Visiting USSR," *Tourism Management* (March 1991): 47–54.

[13] Kye-Sung Chon, "Tourism Destination Image Modification Process: Marketing Implications," *Tourism Management* (March 1991): 68–71; Kye-Sung Chon, "Perceptual Differences of Korea as a Tourist Destination between Pre-visit and Post-visit American Tourists" (Master's thesis, University of Nevada, Las Vegas, 1985).

[14] http://www.atimes.com.

[15] Jean-Phillipe Rigaud, "Art Treasures from the Ice Age: Lascaux Cave." *National Geographic* (October 1998): 488–489.

[16] Alston Chase, "The Reluctant Ecotourist," *Modern Maturity* (April–May 1993): 60–62.

[17] *Putting the Pieces Together* (Alexandria, Va.: American Society of Travel Agents, 1991): 14.

CHECK YOUR KNOWLEDGE

1. How are the hospitality industry and travel and tourism related?
2. What motivated people to travel in ancient times? Compare their reasons with the reasons of today's travelers.
3. What are the major reasons for business travel?
4. List the types of organizations that promote the hospitality and tourism industry at various political levels.
5. List three positive and three negative effects of tourism in either economic, sociocultural, or environmental terms.

APPLY YOUR SKILLS

Table 2.2 gives an example of selected international tourism receipts for ten countries. It also shows the **gross domestic product (GDP)**—the total value of goods and services produced within a country, minus the net payments on foreign investments—of those countries. Study the table and then complete the following questions.

1. For each country, compute the percent of the GDP provided by international tourism receipts.
2. Using your answers to question 1, rank the top five countries in international tourist receipts.
3. List the four countries on the chart that have the highest percentage of GDP from international tourism.
4. To which countries is international tourism more important, those with the top receipts or those in which international tourism makes up the largest percentage of GDP? Explain your answer.

TABLE 2.2 International Tourism Receipts in Relationship to Gross Domestic Product

Rank	*Country*	*International Tourism Receipts*	*Gross Domestic Product*
1.	France	74.7	77.9
2.	Spain	54.7	57.3
3.	United States	48.0	52.3
4.	China	45.7	48.4
5.	Italy	35.3	39.9
6.	United Kingdom	26.8	29.5
7.	Germany	20.3	22.4
8.	Mexico	20.7	20.2
9.	Austria	18.8	19.1
10.	Russian Federation	18.7	19.0

Source: Word Tourism Organization (WTO) www.world-tourism.org

WHAT DO YOU THINK?

1. Provide two recent examples of interdependency among components of the hospitality and tourism network.
2. Why might governments offer lower tax rates to large businesses rather than small businesses to encourage their participation in destination development?
3. What advantages do tourists gain by using the services of travel agencies or tour operators?

4. If you were to develop a new tourist destination, what types of information would you need to collect and study before you started to plan?

5. What marketing strategies would you use to attract both male and female business travelers?

CASE STUDY

You have just been hired as marketing director of the convention and visitors bureau in Elderville, a small but prosperous southern community. Because of its name, the town has an image of being a retirement community. The business leaders in town want to build a convention center to attract more businesspeople to Elderville. However, the retirement image doesn't appeal to many businesspeople, who are looking for a meeting and convention area that offers a variety of entertainment as well as up-to-date meeting facilities.

After a few weeks in Elderville, you find out that it's an ideal spot for business. It's close to a major city, but still quiet. There are three golf courses, two lakes, an attractive country club, excellent schools, an airport within twenty-five miles, and lots of specialty shops and restaurants. Plus, Elderville is named after the kind of trees in the area, not an older population.

1. What is the first thing you would do to change the image of the community?

2. How could you establish Elderville as an exclusive, classy destination rather than a retirement community?

3. Why would business leaders want to attract businesspeople rather than vacationers? Could you do both successfully in Elderville? Explain.

Lodging

They are not all known by the same name: throughout time, inns, taverns, coaching inns, public houses, hotels, motels, resorts, lodges, and conference centers have offered travelers places to stay. They do not offer the same services: the Peninsula Hotel in Hong Kong serves high tea, and the Plaza Hotel in New York offers guests a special creme brulée. The Wynn Hotel in Las Vegas features its own on-site golf course. The Royal Hawaiian Hotel in Waikiki Beach offers guests a lush pink bathrobe in their room and all its guests are greeted with a fresh-smelling floral lei upon arrival. Moreover, they certainly do not have the same ambiance: travelers may find historic architecture, "medieval" inns, or ultra-chic urban high-rises. Haute-country decor, lush gardens, and eighteenth-century cobblestone streets provide the serenity of a bygone era at the Chewton Glen Hotel in Chewton, England; the Cove Atlantis in the Bahamas offers an all-inclusive ocean resort experience and swimming pools where guests mingle with dolphins. Boutique spa destination resorts in Thailand present their guests with the option of indigenous facial treatments and **"hot rock" massages**. The Lodge in Aspen, Colorado, provides activities and accommodations for skiers in the winter and music lovers in the summer; while the Convention Hotel provides meeting rooms and accommodations for convention groups.

Each has its own identity, operating style, goals, and loyal following. But from Eastern Hemisphere to Western, from luxury to budget, there is one thing they all have in common—extending the spirit of hospitality to overnight guests.

ch3

Dynamics of the Lodging Industry

OVERVIEW

If there is one constant in the lodging industry, it is that everything changes. Chapter 2 gave you an overview of the internal and external forces that bring about change in the hospitality network as a whole, a subject we will elaborate on in Chapter 12. Each of these forces also influences the hotel component of the network specifically. For example, changes in transportation technology brought about an increase in both hotel supply (number of rooms available to rent) and demand (people who want to rent rooms or use services). More people began traveling more frequently than ever before. With the rise in demand came an influx of new supply: hotels judiciously located and designed to serve guests. The economic boom of the 1980s made hotel development so desirable that an overabundance of supply soon developed. Although the favorable economic climate also increased demand by giving travelers greater financial freedom, the demand did not grow as quickly or as widely as the supply. The industry entered the 1990s with a glut—more rooms than could be filled. Efforts to boost demand have resulted in greater complexity of lodging classification, ownership, and marketing. The cyclical nature of the lodging industry creates rapidly changing

OBJECTIVES

When you have completed this chapter, you should be able to:

1. **Identify influences affecting the hotel industry over the years.**
2. **Explain how lodging properties can be classified.**
3. **Discuss the advantages and disadvantages of operating independent and chain properties.**
4. **Compare the company-owned, franchise-licensed, and management contract forms of chain ownership.**
5. **Identify the eight Ps of hospitality marketing.**

KEY TERMS

all-suite hotels
bellhop
concierge
franchise agreements
franchisee
franchisor
"hot rock" massages
hotelier
management contracts
market pricelevels
market segments
marketing
occupancy rate
positioning
profit-sharing lease
return on investment
suites
vacation ownership
VIP

conditions that increase the complexity of facility operations. As of this writing, lodging industry economics were highly favorable, having rebounded from the post–9-11 economic downturn. Industry leaders and forecasters have reported record levels of revenue and demand trending since early 2004. In 2008, severe economic conditions have materialized causing contractions within major industries around the world, including the Hospitality and Tourism sector of the United States.

The Evolution of Lodging Facilities

Lodging continually changes to accommodate its guests. Often these changes have come through the forces you will read about in Chapter 12—political, psychological, socioeconomic, technological, and economic—forces that have always influenced lodging efforts. For instance, in England lodging took a leap forward during the Tudor period of the sixteenth century. Political stability, technological improvements in transportation, and changing social conditions were all factors. Historian A. E. Richardson mentioned this in *The Old Inns of England*:

> "The inn now began to fulfill a definite function in social life, half public and half domestic; and the passage of the century witnessed an astonishing increase in its numbers … there is no doubt that the new type of hostelry throve chiefly because it accorded so perfectly with the changing social system."[1]

No records reveal the exact increase, but tax-related records show that in 1577 there were 480 inns, alehouses, and taverns throughout the English county of Norfolk, as well as 876 in Middlesex (now part of Greater London).

By the mid-1600s, lodging supply and demand had received another boost from a new service—the stagecoach. Since the industry depends on the ability of its guests to travel from their homes to lodging facilities, changing methods of transportation have always had a direct impact on the lodging component of the hospitality network. In the new millennium, diversification of brands and targeted specialty segments have emerged in the form of mega-resorts, spas, vacation ownership condo-hotels, and environmentally friendly concepts throughout the world.

The Influence of Transportation Technology

When stagecoach routes were established in the 1600s, coaching inns soon developed. At these inns, travelers were fed and lodged overnight, and tired horses were exchanged for rested ones. Large coaching inns kept hundreds of horses on hand to supply fresh animals to the mail and passenger coaches that stopped there. Exchanging horses took around thirty minutes, giving passengers enough time to eat. Since the stage usually arrived at a specified time, the innkeeper had everything prepared to serve the passengers upon their arrival. Customer care was the focus as servers stood at the door to take each guest's hat and coat. The landlord or landlady then ushered the guest to a table laden with sparkling dishes and spotless linens.

Along with the coaching inns existed "public houses"—private homes that were opened to feed and house guests. The first building designed specifically as a hotel is thought to be New York's City Hotel, erected in 1794. For two dollars, guests received lodging in one of the hotel's seventy-three rooms, along with room service and meals—8:00 A.M. breakfast, 3:00 P.M. dinner, 6:00 P.M. tea, and 9:00 P.M. supper.

The invention of the railroad in 1825 brought about more changes in lodging choices. Train travel decreased journey time and enhanced comfort—a 110-mile trip that previously took eleven hours by stagecoach took only two and a half hours by train. The result was that travel between substantial distances became practical for many more people. Naturally, new inns, taverns, and restaurants flourished close to railway stations, beginning a trend that would continue for almost a century. In parts of the developing American frontier, hotels, taverns, and restaurants were built even before the railroad arrived, in hopes of attracting the railroads and other new businesses. Quite a few American resorts, including several in New York's Catskill Mountains and in Florida, were built along major rail lines. Henry Flagler, builder of the Ponce de Leon Hotel in St. Augustine, Florida, went so far as to buy up the region's railways to ensure his guests convenient transportation to the hotel's doors. Conversely, railroad companies took part in hotel development. The Greenbrier Resort in West Virginia was built and developed by the Chesapeake & Ohio Railway company, and is still served by it today. The expansion of rail travel stimulated the trek west and gave rise to the grand lodges in America's national parks, such as Yosemite in California and Yellowstone, in Idaho, Wyoming, and Montana. These parks, as well as Glacier National Park, located in northern Montana, became must-see destinations and inspired many to journey across the country to witness glacial beauty and experience alpine suroundings. Hotels and lodges were constructed of massive timber beams and featured gabled roofs with rock fireplaces and slate flooring and interior finishes. Guests could walk among the scenery, then relax in a grand lodge where they were served and pampered with Western hospitality.

It was during the launching of the railroads that the first of the truly grand urban hotels was built in America. The Tremont House was erected in 1828 in Boston. This begat a new kind of hospitality professional—the **hotelier**, who was the keeper, owner, or manager of the property. The Tremont House was designed specifically to welcome and serve guests. Isaiah Roger's neoclassical hotel featured 170 private rooms, a rotunda lobby, large meeting rooms, a two-hundred-seat dining room serving French cuisine, and a reading room full of newspapers from countries worldwide. Because the hotel was three stories tall (and elevators had not yet been invented), Tremont's management created the position of **bellhop** to help guests carry luggage upstairs.

With its many innovations, the Tremont set the standard for America's grand hotels and inspired a luxury revolution in Europe. In America, the age of grand hotels had begun—among them the Astor House, New York (1836); the original Parker House, Boston (1856); the Palace Hotel, San Francisco (1875); the Ponce de Leon Hotel, St. Augustine (1888); and, of course, the Waldorf-Astoria in New York (1893, 1931).

The speed and nature of travel changed once again with the introduction of commercial jets in 1958. Center city hotels declined as the airport became the new drawing card for hotel, motel, and restaurant development. New resorts were built in places easily accessible by air. Jet airline service so decreased the time and inconvenience of international travel that globalization of business became the norm. In 2005, there were more than 4.4 million rooms in approximately 48,000 facilities throughout the United States alone, grossing over $122.7 billion.[2]

The Influence of Economic Fluctuations

Generally, throughout history, when economies have expanded, so have supply and demand. The healthy economy at the beginning of the twentieth century ushered in the Golden Age of hotels, during which time a number of large hotels were constructed in the United States. On its heels came the Great Depression, a time when banks failed, unemployment skyrocketed, and travel sharply decreased. Many of the hotels that survived the depression are now highly familiar brands—Statler, Ritz-Carlton, and Hilton, to name a few. Another major economic boom occurred in the 1980s. Tax incentives for investors, expectations of higher demand, and a growing economy helped fuel extensive hotel development. In the late 1980s and early 1990s, however, further development was curtailed and the industry was seriously hurt by excessive room supply, economic recession, elimination of tax incentives, the dot-com bust in California's Silicon Valley, and the 9-11 terrorist attacks.

In recent years, there have been more guests than hotel rooms. This ratio of guests to rooms helps analysts track the overall health of the industry. Called the **occupancy rate**, this ratio is a percentage derived by dividing the total number of rooms occupied during a given period (night, week, or year) by the total number of rooms available for occupancy during that period.[3] In the 1990s, the industry-wide average occupancy rate reached a thirty-year low.[4] In the 1960s, the average occupancy rate for hotels and motels in the United States was nearly 70 percent. In 1991, the average was 60 to 65 percent.[5] In 1993, it was estimated that nearly 40 percent of all U.S. hotel rooms were vacant nightly.[6] However, 1998 profited from the slow but steady rise in the industry, pushing the average occupancy rate back up to 64 percent.

The supply of hotel rooms has grown about 1.4 percent per year since 1965, with the biggest growth spurts occurring in 1972–1973 and 1985–1989. Demand, however, expanded at a rate of 1.4 percent per year from the mid-1960s to the mid-1980s and at a rate of 4.3 percent per year in the mid-to-late 1980s.[7] The economic recession that followed the great boom of the late 1980s dramatically—and negatively—affected the industry. Changing tax laws eliminated tax shelters and low-interest loans, foreign investment slowed, lenders required greater equity investment and personal guarantees, and fewer people traveled, a response to economically hard times. In 2005, the average U.S hotel's occupancy rate was 63.1 percent; however, the standard price per room was $90.88. Average rate or pricing elasticity has been strong since early 2000, when the average room rate was $78.62. The current industry benchmark utilized to track the synergistic relationship between occupancy (volume) and average rate (pricing) is referred to as revenue per available room or REVPAR. It is derived from a calculation that measures total revenue dollars generated per available room per hotel.[8]

Classifying Lodging Properties

Because of constant changes, staying current with just who is offering what and where can be difficult for the guest. The necessity of classifying hotels came about when hotels began to differ from one another enough to appeal to different groups of people. Long gone are the days when the guest had two choices—luxury hotels or budget hotels. Hotel entrepreneurs such as Kemmons Wilson, the founder of the Holiday Inn chain, created a third option when they built facilities intended to serve middle-class families. Luxury, midpriced, and and budget property classes had clear-cut boundaries in the beginning. Potential guests knew they could expect more services at a luxury hotel than at a budget motel, and something in between at a midpriced hotel.

As the economy in general boomed and room supply increased, hoteliers focused on setting themselves apart from the crowd by offering specialized accommodations. No longer just a place to sleep, hotels were appealing to conventioneers, business groups, special-interest groups, and resort-based

Industry Insights

HISTORY

Origin of the Motel

In the 1920s and 1930s, automobiles began to be priced within the reach of average families, and this helped expand a segment of the lodging market. Many Americans took to the road for vacations and opted to spend the night at some of the first motels. Configured as a series of separate cabins, they were called auto courts or tourist cabins.

After World War II, the availability of automobiles and the new interstate freeway system enabled unprecedented numbers to travel easily. These people generally wanted little more than a place to bathe and sleep, and to eat if no restaurant facilities were nearby. A combination of the words motor and hotel—*motel*—identified the new breed of lodging facilities that developed to meet the needs of these travelers.

Eventually, motels—also called motor inns, motor courts, or motor lodges—sprang up along all major highways, near airports and convention centers, and close to interstate highway interchanges. Today, motels serve much the same purpose as in yesteryear: providing simple overnight accommodations convenient to destinations or routes. These independent roadside motels and motor inns have experienced severe losses of market share because of the proliferation and expansion of major lodging brands. New prototypical properties have emerged on the U.S. lodging landscape. However, motels offering budget accomodations still occupy a niche position in the marketplace inasmuch as they appeal to the budget traveler, who typically drives from market to market and seeks the simplest of accommodations at the lowest of rates.

incentive travelers. Descriptive hotel classifications helped potential guests locate suitable lodgings and, as such, became a valuable marketing tool.

As this diversity flourished, so did competition for customers and brand loyalty. Because properties continually upgraded their services, boundaries between descriptive labels blended into one another. Old systems of classification were not as useful. For instance, the Marriott brand, once recognizable as a midpriced hotel chain, began to include hotels classified as economy (Fairfield Inns), business (Courtyard), extended stay (Residence Inns), all suite

Photo courtesy of Bass Hotels & Resorts, Inc.

Newer lodging facilities, like this Holiday Inn in Atlanta, Georgia, offer full-service and extended-stay facilities to attract business travelers.

(Marriott Suites), and upscale (Marriott Hotels and Resorts). Other chains also began to cater to a myriad of guests—from business to pleasure travelers and from individuals to groups. Consequently, lodging classification became more complex. Facilities are now grouped according to size, amenities, price, type of guest (business or pleasure), or type of hotel (luxury, full-service, economy, or extended stay, to name a few). Many facilities fit into two or more categories, and do so in order to attract multiple types of guests.

In the pages that follow you will learn about types of lodging facilities and the descriptive labels that help guests choose accommodations that fit their needs. You'll also learn about market price levels, which provide a helpful tool for analyzing the industry, and general levels of service categories, based on the hotels' purposes and the guests they target. This chapter focuses on hotels, motels, and all-suite hotels.

Descriptive Labels

Hotels, resorts, vacation ownership properties, and boutique hotels are the most widely recognized forms of lodging.They can be found almost anywhere—in the center of a huge metropolis, at an exotic beach location, or even on the streets of a small town (where one might find a charming bed-and-breakfast inn). For the most part, hotels and lodging facilities attract transient guests who need a place to stay for a night or two while traveling for business or pleasure. Guests looking for more permanent lodging are served by hotels that specialize in residential or extended-stay accommodations. The extended-stay lodging concept has emerged as a viable alternative to traditional business and vacation hotel accomodations. The extended-stay product competes strongly in the midpriced segment.

Professional Profile

BARRY STERNLICHT

Hospitality Industry CEO, Investor, and Developer

Barry Sternlicht may be best known as a successful hotel industry leader with experience in finance, development, and organizational leadership. Mr. Sternlicht has held positions as chairman of the board and chief executive officer at Starwood Hotels. Under his leadership, he successfully expanded the company, acquiring worldwide hotel brands like Westin, Sheraton Hotels, and The St. Regis Collection. He has been a member of the Presidential Tourism and Travel Advisory Board, the Young Presidents Organization, the World Travel and Tourism Council, and the Urban Land Institute.

Sternlicht's organizational leadership and business acumen have enabled him and his company to execute a multitude of financial transactions, mergers, and acquisitions. These transactions have ranged in size from $1 million to $14 billion. Sternlicht's latest venture primarily reflects investment activities under the aegis of the Starwood Capital Group. Starwood Capital Group recently acquired a large European hotel network with a mixture of luxury hotels and related companies. Perhaps Barry Sternlicht's most significant attributes are his visionary role in global enterprises and the keen investment expertise that allows him to execute large financial transactions within the hospitality network.

Source: Starwood Capital Group, http://www.prnewswire.com

Hotels

From the age of grand hotels to the troubled late nineteenth century, the hotel has been the most fabled type of lodging. It has been commemorated in movies and musicals, and some of the country's most important business has been conducted within hotel walls. Where other countries saw fit to build castles for their royalty, Americans built hotel palaces for the people—places where anyone able to pay could rent a room for the night. Varying greatly in style and service, most hotels share a similar structure. They generally have more than two stories, with guest rooms located along common hallways. Guest rooms usually have a bed, bathroom, telephone, and television. In addition to housekeeping, services may include luggage assistance, a business center with computers, Internet access, and a photocopier or fax machine, a spa, recreation facilities, restaurants, or bars. Hotels are most often located in or near business districts, travel destinations, and airports. Hotels may be classified as full service or limited service. Full-service hotels typically offer room service and three-meal-a-day dining, and often offer banquet, meeting, and convention services as well.

Motels

Although the advent of the automobile stirred the lodging industry in the 1920s, the Great Depression was a major setback, causing many hotels to fail. Financial institutions turned away from the lodging industry after hotels defaulted on their mortgages during the 1930s, and the industry did not begin

to recover until well into World War II, when hotels were built to house Americans aiding the war effort. Motels offered fewer amenities and were less expensive to build and operate than downtown hotels. Their lower rates, basic accommodations, roadway locations, and lack of a central lobby were well-suited to the new overnight automobile traveler.

Motels are generally less formal than hotels. Guests usually carry their own luggage, and free parking is available, often adjacent to the guest's room. Many motels provide swimming pools and restaurant service, which may be within the motel or in detached, leased, or third-party operated facilities. Where competition for lodging dollars is keen, motels may offer services similar to those at area hotels. Guests who prefer to save money may opt for a budget motel that has smaller rooms, no pool, and fewer amenities.

All-Suite Hotels

Unlike regular hotels, **all-suite hotels** rent only **suites**, often combining living space with kitchen facilities, or a bedroom section with an attached parlor. To keep rates competitive with other hotels, many all-suite hotels have small lobbies and no public meeting rooms. Some do not offer restaurant or bar facilities. As the market has expanded, however, some all-suite hotels have reintroduced public areas and limited foodservice, creating a unique hybrid concept with market positioning somewhere in between limited and full service. These hybrid concepts are often referred to as select service products. All-suite properties have targeted business travelers for steady weekday business, especially longer stays of multiple room nights, while offering weekend family leisure travelers a recreational service in the local marketplace by featuring a water or amusement park connection. Amenities such as free breakfast, cocktail hour, and access to an on-premises health club keep these lodging properties competitive with the hotel lodging segment overall.

Convention Hotels

Convention hotels provide meeting and banquet facilities for large groups (usually five hundred or more individuals) who book overnight accommodation in their guest rooms. Because they target groups, these hotels need large lobbies to accommodate group arrivals. They also have a high percentage of double-occupancy rooms and emphasize food and beverage services. Convention hotels may offer **concierge** floors to cater to individual guests' needs. Convention group business is heavily reliant on municipal and civic facilities, which in turn are supported by economic development agencies and infrastructure in the community. Many urban locations and secondary markets have funded expansive facilities with tax dollars in order to attract and compete for large-group and convention business. Close alignment of facility capacity and room inventory in a particular marketplace is essential. Some of the premier metropolitan convention destinations in the world can accommodate more than fifty thousand attendees at a time.

Resorts

With the expansion of both domestic and international travel, leisure and resort tourist destinations have emerged. Resorts ranging from themed amusement experiences (Disney Resorts) to the exotic Atlantis complex and other oceanfront properties have become more prominent in the lodging industry landscape. Resorts of today offer all-inclusive experiences that capture the imagination and fantasy of the traveler. Activities range from golf to spa treatments, aquatics, skiing, hiking, and nature interaction.

Vacation Ownership Hotels Recent trends within the lodging industry have replaced some typical hotel and lodging products with mixed-use destination accommodations where travelers can purchase fractional ownership interests in their lodging facility of choice. This phenomenon has emerged as the **vacation ownership** industry. Initially, resort locations were the primary market, but more recently these properties began to appear in urban developments and fractional ownership investment solidified its place in the lodging industry. Many vacation ownership lodging destinations offer similar services as full-service hotels and resorts; however, they expand the residential feel of the product. The biggest differences between vacation ownership resorts and traditional lodging are (1) the real estate ownership interest in the product and (2) the ability of owners to rent their interest in the time-share unit to someone else or trade their vacation interval with another owner for a stay somewhere else in the network of participating time-share products. All of the major brands, including Hyatt, Hilton, Marriott, and Starwood Hotels, offer lucrative and highly competitive vacation ownership experiences. Not only has the vacation ownership segment created new demand in the industry, but it has also created a new opportunity for hotel brands to garner stronger market share and brand loyalty by marketing to their in-house, captive customers with additional product offerings.

Other Lodging Types There are as many types of lodging establishments as there are guest interests. Young travelers may opt for the inexpensive rooms and community kitchen privileges offered at hostels. Guests looking for personal service and charming locations are often interested in bed-and-breakfast establishments and guest houses, both of which are private homes opened to overnight guests. The main difference between the two is that breakfast is included in the rate at bed-and-breakfasts, but not at guest houses. Lodges provide accommodations and housekeeping for those interested in a specific activity, such as hunting or skiing. Residential hotels cater to long-term guests, such as a family relocating to another region. Offerings are similar to those at regular hotels, with daily maid service, food and beverage facilities, and so forth; but the decor is more homelike, with kitchen, living area, and bedroom.

Other types of lodging, such as resorts, spas, and casino hotels, will be discussed in Chapters 10 and 11, and we will also provide more information on convention hotels, bed-and-breakfasts, and other lodging facilities. Table 3.1 lists samples of descriptive labels used to help guests choose appropriate accommodations.

Levels of Service

At one time, hotels differed distinctly in the services they offered. Recognizing that all guests do not expect the same services nor have the same amount to spend on lodging, the hotel industry offered a variety of services at different prices, aimed at particular markets (groups whose members have similar expectations and budgets). During the 1980s, hotel companies divided these markets into ever-smaller segments in an attempt to broaden their overall market appeal. Then they tried to offer specific services to each target group or segment. As competition grew, hoteliers began upgrading their services, and by the early 1990s, service categories were no longer clear-cut. In the twenty-first century, economic vitality has created a more densely segmented stratification. Major brands have maximized their positioning and have been successful in creating new market share through the creation of new brand names and concepts. For instance, Starwood Hotels has recently introduced Aloft, Hyatt Hotels has recently introduced Hyatt Place, and IHG has recently introduced Hotel Indigo. As a result, the industry is more competitive than ever before. Classifying hotels

TABLE 3.1 Sample of Lodging Descriptive Labels

Label	Description
All-Suite Hotel	Apartment-style accommodations that may include breakfast and/or complimentary drinks in the room rate. Large in size, brand and corporate-operated.
American Plan (AP)	Hotel accommodations with three meals daily included in the price of the room. Also see Full Pension. Large in size, brand and corporate operated.
Bed-and-Breakfasts (B&Bs)	Lodging provided in private homes; breakfast usually provided, sometimes other meals; often in historic homes. Small in size, independent operation.
Casino Hotel	Hotel that provides gaming facilities. Usually massive in size, brand and corporate operated.
Conference Center	Facility designed to provide the space and services needed for groups holding meetings. Some are resorts and some may be affiliated with colleges, universities, or religious organizations. Very large in size. May or may not be branded.
Elderhostel™	Network of several hundred universities and colleges in the United States and Canada that offer persons age sixty or older programs of educational courses and adventure. Most often, accommodations are provided in campus dormitories.
European Plan (EP)	Hotel accommodations with no meals included in the price of the room.
Full Pension or Pensione	Term used in Europe to indicate hotel accommodations that include three meals daily.
Half Pension	Hotel accommodations that include bed, breakfast, and one other meal. Also see Modified American Plan.
Hostel	Dormitory-style accommodations, often for specific groups, such as youth, where facilities are basic, shared, and supervised.
Modified American Plan (MAP)	Hotel accommodations that include breakfast and either lunch or dinner in the price of the room.
Rental Condominium	Furnished apartments found mostly in resort areas, usually rented by the weekend, week, month, or season.
Residential Hotel	Accommodations that provide services for guests who wish to stay for an extended period of time—a month, a season, or longer.
Resort Hotel	Accommodations that provide recreational and entertainment facilities.
Spa	Accommodations built around natural resources and providing health promotion amenities such as mineral waters, sun, air, special diets, and exercise. Offer wellness cuisine and health-conscious experiences.
Transient Hotel	Accommodations that provide basic room amenities only.
Vacation Ownership Hotel	Furnished residences found mostly in resort and urban revitalization areas, usually rented by the weekend, week, month, or season.

by service uses four main categories: luxury, full-service upscale, limited-service mid-scale, and economy.

Luxury Hotels and Resorts

Traditionally, independent hotels have offered the finest accommodations money can buy. Luxury properties are descendants of the grand hotels, featuring expensive, lavishly decorated public areas and the highest levels of customer service. They offer the finest cuisine and a full range of amenities, from shampoos and hair dryers to private Jacuzzis and fireplaces. Whether parking your car, carrying your luggage, or delivering room service, staff members—including concierges, bellpersons, front desk attendants, and waitstaff—are well-trained and efficient. Luxury resorts offer the finest entertainment and recreational facilities available. A part of luxury properties' attraction is their ability to perpetuate an exclusive image by charging high rates. Hotels in the category include Four Seasons and Ritz-Carlton properties throughout the United States, and the Waldorf-Astoria, and the Trump Plaza in New York. The Royal Sonesta, a deluxe hotel in New Orleans, Louisiana, spends an estimated $1.5 million annually on guest service. Their guests must find such service pleasing—with an average occupancy of 75 percent in 1992, the hotel grossed $15.6 million in sales in 2006.

Full-Service Properties

Featuring properties operated by Hilton, Hyatt, Westin, and Marriott, this category of hotels attempts to offer a wide range of services at lower rates than luxury hotels. Full-service hotels generally offer clean, well-decorated spaces with meeting and restaurant facilities, a limited room-service menu, and a variety of recreational activities. Although not as extravagant as the luxury

Industry Insights

CULTURE

Japanese Abeku Hotels

The Japanese have combined efficiency and ingenuity into an enticing proposition—*abeku*, also called fashion hotels or love hotels. The *abeku* often resemble European castles or Alpine chalets and provide garden settings. Nearly all offer 360-channel television, videos, stereo, sauna, and in-room refreshments.

But what the *abeku* really offers is a private sanctuary. Japan's high population density and traditional use of lightweight walls (for safety in earthquakes) result in close living arrangements. Privacy in an *abeku* is preserved with a touch-screen reservation system and state-of-the-art automation. Guests can check in and out and pay their bills without being seen by anyone else.

Business is booming for these hotels, with Sunday being an especially busy day. Length of stay can range from several hours to several days. *Abeku* hotels comprise twenty thousand of Japan's lodging facilities.[1]

[1] T.R. Reid, "Japan's No-Tell Hotels," Washington Post, August 13, 1990, sec. A.

Image copyright olly, 2008. Used under license from Shutterstock.com.

properties, full-service hotels generally have large, attractive public areas. The services of the concierge or other staff may be limited to designated **VIP** floors.

Some all-suite and extended-stay hotels with good-sized public areas also fit into the full-service category, with amenities like in-room coffeemakers, microwave ovens, and refrigerators.

Limited-Service Properties

Lodging establishments like Days Inn, Hampton Inn, and Quality Suites & Inns were once considered limited-service facilities. Usual offerings included simple, clean rooms with telephones, free cable television, swimming pools, and an adjacent restaurant. Staff services, other than housekeeping, were limited, but some offered a few extra amenities, such as complimentary shampoo and lotion, to distinguish themselves from the economy properties. The remaining all-suite hotels fit into this category because of their limited services and amenities and small public areas.

Economy Properties

Once offering only basic bed and bath facilities, economy properties now focus on "more value for the dollar" and provide clean, low-priced lodging. Typical economy properties did not offer meeting and recreational facilities or food and beverage services, with the possible exception of a vending area featuring prepackaged snacks and video games. Staff roles were limited to providing basic front-office services, security, and housekeeping services. Generally, the smaller guest rooms of the economy hotels offered one or two double beds and a separate bathroom equipped with no more than towels and soap.

A CONCIERGE

However you define it, a concierge's job is not an easy one: in a single day, he or she may act as tour guide, travel agent, weather reporter, restaurant reviewer, secretary, reporter, and more. The most common guest requests a concierge responds to are making dinner reservations, confirming and reissuing airline tickets, making limousine arrangements or car rentals, obtaining theater tickets, and providing maps and directions to local attractions.

Since many of the requests a concierge responds to are last minute, being able to handle pressure graciously is an important quality.

While details of how the job of concierge came into being are sketchy, many believe the profession dates back to the Middle Ages when the doorkeeper of the castle was also keeper of the keys, responsible for locking the royal family and guests safely in for the night. (Hence, the international symbol for a concierge is a pair of crossed golden keys worn on each lapel.) It was not until centuries later, in the mid-1970s, that several San Francisco hotels brought the concierge concept to America. In the beginning, the concierge would leave messages on guests' pillows informing them of various services. Now, of course, computers facilitate many of the requests, although personal service is the hallmark of the profession. The concept of a concierge is now a very familiar one to international travelers from all parts of the world. Today, most major hotels have at least one concierge on staff.

Since every day is different and every guest request has the potential to be unique, training as a concierge is not clear-cut. However, the professional trade organization Les Clefs d'Or (The Golden Keys), which boasts an international membership of more than four thousand, does set some standards for membership, including a minimum of five years in the hotel industry (three as a concierge) and letters of recommendation from current association members.

Properties in this category include EconoLodge, Motel 6, and Daystop. The Economy Lodging Systems management company has positioned Knights Inn as "the lodging choice of Middle America." According to former president of Knights Inn, Gregory P. Terrel, "The target is traveling salesmen, senior citizens, and people with a family income of $30,000 a year."

Market Price Levels

In August of 1993, a new general classification system called **market price levels** was created. Smith Travel Research, an independent research firm that counts the AH&LA among its clients, currently uses this system to slot lodging properties into the following categories based on room rate:

Luxury Properties	Properties with actual room rates above the 85th percentile in their geographic market. Typical luxury segment pricing rates average upwards of $350 per night. In 2005, U.S. occupancy in the luxury segment was 70.5 percent with an average room rate of $325.
Upscale	Properties with actual room rates above the 70th percentile and below the 85th percentile in their geographic market. In 2005, U.S. occupancy in full-service upscale properties was 67.5 percent with an average room rate of $122.
Midpriced	Properties with actual room rates above the 40th percentile and below the 70th percentile in their geographic market. In 2005, U.S. occupancy in the limited-service midpriced segment occupany was 65.3 percent with an average room rate of $86.38.
Economy	Properties with actual room rates above the 20th percentile and below the 40th percentile in their geographic market. In 2005, U.S. occupancy rates in the economy segment were 63.1 percent and average room rates were $53.82.
Budget	Properties with actual room rates below the 20th percentile in their geographic market. In 2005, U.S. occupancy rates in the budget segment were 73.3 percent, with an average room rate of $36.53.

Classifications in this system are not industry-wide; definitions depend upon the market area, such as a city or particular geographic region. Some segments will not be found at all in some market areas. And although some chains may be found in different segments depending on the geographic area, on the whole, traditional labels still apply. Hotels that were considered luxury properties under the service level scheme are still found in the luxury segment or the adjacent upscale segment.

While the market price levels will be easier for researchers to use in their analysis of the lodging industry, hoteliers will no doubt continue to use general categories that convey to guests certain levels of service based on amenities.

Types of Lodging Ownership

When the lodging industry was in its infancy, individuals and companies owned and operated their own hotels. As the industry grew and diversified, another ownership structure emerged to meet lodging's new goals. Both of these structures—independent and chain, respectively—offer distinct advantages and disadvantages for the hotelier. Yet another common form of ownership in today's marketplace is referred to as a joint venture or JV. A joint venture is a partnership agreement among two or more entities or individuals that governs management oversight, investment criteria, ownership, and expected **return on investment**. Long-term lease arrangements are actually another a type of ownership whereby an individual or enterprise makes a ground lease payment for a hotel and keeps the net proceeds after lease payment. Viable lease arrangements need to be long term and often are fifty to one hundred years in length.

Independent Ownership

Originally, the only option was independent ownership. An individual or company opened a hotel and managed it, taking complete responsibility for the hotel's success or failure. If you have always dreamed of running your own business, independent ownership is probably what you have in mind.

Advantages

Independent owners have complete control over every aspect of their business—from selecting the brand of towels guests use to deciding how to comply with government regulations. Often, independent hoteliers can have an unusual bond with their communities. As community members, independent hotel owners and employees may make use of their firsthand knowledge of the community to attract guests, obtain investors, garner community support for new ventures, and negotiate discounts from suppliers. Such relationships keep independent hoteliers in touch with their communities, enabling them to sense new trends and adopt appropriate policies.

Another advantage of independent ownership is operating freedom. Owners have the freedom to implement and test their own ideas, and may make changes at any time. These factors combine to give the independent hotel a local feel, encouraging guests to see the hotel as an integral community asset—a distinct advantage when competition is tight due to a poor economy. Another major advantage of an independent hotel is the absence of franchise licensing fees and brand marketing overhead expenses. Furthermore, major brands impose certain brand standards for operation and product consistency. These brand standards may require the owner to make certain levels of capital investment in order to stay active in the brand.

Disadvantages

Despite their operating freedom and generally small scale, independents confront more difficult financial challenges than chain hotels. They faced the highest failure rate in the recession of the early 1990s. In order to get off the ground, they usually must raise large amounts of capital and show a very early profit, despite limited advertising and sales budgets. Independent hoteliers develop all of their own operations systems, so they succeed or fail based on the effectiveness of these systems. These systems are often very expensive and require significant debt service. Alternatively, independents may turn to third-party intermediaries that offer systems such as reservation services. However, such intermediaries lack the overall marketing reach and power of established brands. Additionally, the intermediaries charge a commission that can be as high as 10 or 15 percent of the room rate.

Chain Ownership

Chain properties fall into three main groups: (1) parent company-owned and operated by the brand; (2) franchises licensed by investors and operated by management who contract to use the name and systems of a brand; or (3) management contract properties owned by an investor or investors and operated under contract by the brand. In addition, there are referral groups in which the operators of a property own and operate their own hotel but participate in a group reservation system. Table 3.2 ranks the twenty-five largest hotel chains in the United States, while Table 3.3 ranks the fifteen largest international management companies.

Industry Insights

BUSINESS INNOVATION

Consortia

As independent hotels struggle in difficult economic times, they are increasingly turning to marketing and reservation consortia to compete against chains and franchises. Consortia are organizations of independent hotels that offer their members the same types of centralized reservation systems and/or large-scale marketing campaigns as do franchisors. "A consortium does cut costs for the property," says Kirk Kindles, Holiday Inn Worldwide vice president, "but it doesn't replace brand image and marketing power."[1]

Yet consortia do fill an important marketing niche for independent hotels who want to compete with corporations without joining them. Paris's Inter Hotels International is a nonprofit organization comprising independent groups in several European countries. Members pay a fee, receive a plaque, and are listed in a directory. They are represented at sixty travel trade shows and partner with one hundred tour operators around the world.

Historically more prevalent in Europe than in the United States, consortia are looking to expand into the U.S. marketplace. In January 1992, Inter Hotels International launched itself as a U.S. franchisor and consortium. Other American consortia include Leading Hotels of the World, Preferred Hotels and Resorts, and Grand Tradition Hotels.

[1] Chris Baum, "Franchising Evolves Worldwide As Technology, Competition Grow," Hotels, (February 1993): 48–52.

TABLE 3.2 World's 25 Largest Corporate Chains

Rank			Rooms		Hotels	
2005	*2004*	*Company Headquarters*	*2005*	*2004*	*2005*	*2004*
1	1	**Utell/Unirez-Pegasus Solutions Rep. Services** Dallas, TX USA	**1,161,467**	1,050,091	**7,684**	7,487
2	2	**SynXis Corp.** Southlake, TX USA	**808,920**	720,000	**6,741**	6,500
3	4	**Supranational Hotels** London, England	**250,000**	257,000	**1,500**	1,692
4	6	**Hotusa-Eurostars-Familia Hotels** Barcelona, Spain	**157,789**	118,861	**1,763**	1,439
5	5	**InnPoints Worldwide** Albuquerque, NM USA	**154,418**	145,936	**1,367**	1,066
6	8	**Keytel S.A.** Barcelona, Spain	**130,000**	92,000	**1,300**	1,150
7	7	**Worldhotels** Frankfurt am Main, Germany	**102,000**	100,000	**525**	500
8	9	**Leading Hotels of the World** New York, NY USA	**83,000**	83,000	**430**	420
9	12	**Associated Luxury Hotels** Washington, DC USA	**68,000**	48,280	**87**	86
10	11	**Preferred Hotel Group** Chicago, IL USA	**66,670**	56,726	**316**	285
11	10	**Logis de France** Paris, France	**65,019**	66,881	**3,399**	3,517
12	14	**AHMI** Paris, France	**39,000**	34,308	**237**	178
13	16	**Great Hotels Organization** London, England	**35,699**	27,252	**235**	168
14	13	**Historic Hotels of America** Washington, DC USA	**34,014**	37,745	**209**	213
15	15	**Sceptre Hospitality Resources (SWAN)** Englewood, CO USA	**23,147**	30,732	**159**	140
16	24	**Luxe Worldwide Hotels** Los Angeles, CA USA	**20,000**	10,000	**200**	185
17	18	**Small Luxury Hotels of the World** Surrey, England	**18,000**	17,250	**359**	329
18	20	**ILA-Chateaux & Hotels de Charme** Brussels, Belgium	**15,652**	15,253	**286**	324
19	17	**Minitel International** Lausanne, Switzerland	**15,000**	25,500	**253**	591
20	25	**Epoque Hotels** Miami, FL USA	**13,654**	7,362	**223**	103

Continues . . .

TABLE 3.2 World's 25 Largest Corporate Chains (*continued*)

Rank			Rooms		Hotels	
2005	2004	Company Headquarters	2005	2004	2005	2004
21	23	**Chateaux & Hotels de France** Paris, France	**13,412**	10,608	**540**	514
22	—	**The Charming Hotels of the World** Rome, Italy	**11,664**	—	**159**	—
23	21	**Design Hotels** Berlin, Germany	**11,000**	11,682	**143**	137
24	22	**Relais & Châteaux** Paris, France	**10,583**	10,688	**453**	440
25	—	**Distinguished Hotels International** New York, NY USA	**6,477**	—	**109**	—

Source: Hotels (2006).

Advantages

One of the most important advantages of chain ownership is the strong national brand identity shared by chain hotels. This identity is maintained through advertising campaigns financed by the chain company from the profits of each of the hotels. In addition, most hotels are connected to the chain's centralized reservation system, which allows guests to call one number to reserve a room at any of the brand's locations. Because of a chain's size, it may have greater access to capital, as well as bulk purchasing power, centralized control and information systems, and personnel training programs. Each member of the chain has access to the common expertise of the company, including site-selection proficiency. Additionally, brand loyalty and rewards programs have become signature programs of each brand. Many brands have linked their guest rewards programs with airlines, banking services, and other major retail brand names to solidy their customer loyalty and brand strength. Chain-wide, these companies offer high levels of consistency in product offerings and service levels marketed specifically to their targeted customers.

Disadvantages

Perhaps the biggest disadvantage to chain ownership is the need to establish brand loyalty among potential guests and to diversify property offerings. Trying to be all things to all types of guests has put chains at a distinct disadvantage. Many are scrambling to compete not only with other hotels but within other segments of their own chain, which may operate a number of properties including full-service, all-suite, or economy hotels. Chain-imposed

TABLE 3.3 World's 15 Largest Management Companies

Rank			Rooms Managed		Propeties Managed	
2005	*2004*	*Company Name*	*2005*	*2004*	*2005*	*2004*
1	2	Interstate Hotels & Resorts	63,980	71,789	282	315
2	4	Ocean Hospitalities	20,060	19,572	129	123
3	5	John Q. Hammons Hotels and Resorts LLC	15,465	14,499	65	59
4	6	White Lodging Services Corp.	4,493	12,526	105	90
5	7	American Property Management Corp.	12,450	11,550	45	42
6	-	Innkeepers Hospitality Management	10,383	9,971	78	75
7	16	Crestline Hotels & Resorts	9,905	7,419	41	34
8	10	Janus Hotels and Resorts	9,900	9,914	47	48
9	11	Outrigger Enterprises Group	9,481	10,834	45	55
10	14	Sage Hospitality Resources	9,241	8,845	47	47
11	20	Merritt Hospitality LLC	8,366	7,320	28	23
12	12	Remington Hotels LP	8,141	9,339	35	45
13	18	Driftwood Hospitality Management	7,666	6,410	34	26
14	17	Destination Hotels & Resorts	7,623	8,401	30	33
15	21	GF Management	7,574	6,754	39	33

Source: Hotel & Motel Management (June 5, 2006).

requirements for capital improvements, while necessary to stay competitive within the marketplace, may be prohibitively expensive.

Company-Owned and -Operated

Few chains remain that are not franchisors or under management contract. The industry's economic problems in the early 1990s resulted in mergers, resellings, new forms of ownership, and new types of operating organizations. Most companies simply could not survive without franchising their brands or hiring management companies. One organization that did not franchise, Red Roof Inns, believes that staying company-owned and operated gives them more consistency chain-wide than other form of ownership. This type of ownership structure shares many of the advantages and disadvantages of independent ownership.

Franchise-Licensed

Some chains offer franchise opportunities. **Franchise agreements** are contracts in which the **franchisor** (the brand owner) grants the **franchisee**, or buyer, the right to use the franchisor's name and proven method of doing business. The franchisee must build the hotel, buy any equipment required to run the business, and pay a number of fees including a franchise fee, advertising fees, reservation fees, and royalty fees based on room revenues. Fees range anywhere from 4 to 8 percent of gross revenues. For this the franchisor generally provides operating instructions, personnel training programs, access to a centralized reservation system, and cooperative purchasing and advertising. For the parent company, franchising is a way to generate substantial revenue.

Franchises offer individuals the opportunity to buy an established brand name, along with its marketing concept, business format, and products for use in the franchisee's facility. Compared to independent owners, franchisees face diminished risks when operating hotels because they can rely on franchisors' tested business practices. Franchising enables an owner to enjoy operating a hotel while still benefiting from the well-known name and reputation associated with a large lodging chain. Access to the franchisor's central reservation system, business planning, market research, personnel training programs, and site-selection expertise also provides franchise hotels with a competitive edge.

While franchisees may have access to many of the same programs as chains, they may also have to pay for them, often with large fees. Franchise fees range from 3 to 5 percent of gross room revenues and are in addition to marketing fees for reservation connectivity and processing costs. Franchisees also may experience inflexibility, including dependence on the franchisor to make important decisions. The franchisor may impose changes in operations, higher quality standards, and new marketing requirements. Investors who want control over their own businesses will be disappointed by the lack of power offered them under a franchise agreement.

Management Contracts

Until World War II, hotel companies and individuals owned and managed their own properties. After the war, when financing was hard to obtain in the United States, hotel companies looked offshore for opportunities. For example, the Puerto Rican government, trying to attract tourism and industry, approached hotel mogul Conrad Hilton about developing a hotel in Puerto Rico. The government offered to build, furnish, and equip the hotel, then lease it to Hilton for two-thirds of the profit. Hilton provided preopening expenses and working capital as well as management expertise in what was called a **profit-sharing lease**. Other countries, including Cuba, soon wanted Hilton hotels as well. However, the Cuban revolution caused Hilton to lose a great deal of money. Believing such leases were too risky, Hilton decided the governments, or owners, should take full ownership responsibility, including payment of operating costs, debt service, and working capital. These new arrangements were called **management contracts**.[9]

Under a management contract, the owner maintains financial responsibility for the property itself, and the management company is responsible for operating the property, using the owner's money. In addition, the management company is usually required to provide the owner with financial reports and notice of any policy changes affecting the hotel. The length of the contract and the fees paid to the management company for its services are negotiable. Contract length is determined by the balance of power between the management company and the owner, but the average length is twenty-five years. Recently, the balance of power has shifted to the owners, and newer management contracts usually are only five to ten years in length, with renewals at the discretion of the owner. Also, contracts often have clauses that afford owners the opportunity to cancel agreements based on performance. The basic fee structure is more complicated, but stems from a base-fee or incentive-fee arrangement.

Generally, owners prefer incentive fees based on the hotel's gross operating profit (its revenue minus its operating costs before taxes), because incentive fees require that the management company take some risk in the hotel's operation. Management companies prefer base fees determined by the gross operating revenue (the total payments received for goods and services) because it assures them of a payout even if the hotel does not generate profits. Some management contracts include a combination of the two types of fees.[10]

Marketing

The shared purpose of all lodging facilities, regardless of classification or ownership type, is meeting a guest's needs. This lofty ideal can be a challenge to fulfill, because guest needs and desires are constantly shifting. The hotel marketing department conducts research to stay current with the needs and desires of potential guests, and to plan and implement ways to meet those needs. But knowing and understanding guest needs is only one of the goals of marketing. **Marketing** is the process of planning the hotel's concept (type of facility, services offered, and location), what rates to charge, and how to reach potential customers, all in a way that satisfies individual and organizational objectives.[11] Fierce competition, growing market complexity, and guest sophistication have all heightened the importance of successful marketing. The result has been ever-expanding budgets for marketing and special recognition of marketing staff.

Marketing may soon be the hospitality manager's first priority. Specialized training (and perhaps even degree programs) for hospitality professionals may soon be required, since the field is becoming so complex. The Educational Institute of the AH&LA headed in this direction when it instituted the Certified Hospitality Sales Professional Program in 1993. The program is open only to those employees whose work responsibilities are at least 50 percent sales.

Graduates must renew their certification every five years by participating in professional development activities. Programs such as this help the sales professional develop the necessary skills to define—and target—specific market groups. Today, a wide variety of certification programs now exist within the Educational Institute of the AH&LA, which provides training for working professionals. Areas of certification include operations, engineering, sales and marketing, accounting, and administration.

Market Segmentation

The lodging industry's target market is all the potential guests of lodging properties—whether they are visiting relatives, conducting business, or relaxing on vacation. Because the total market is so vast, marketers break it into **market segments**—smaller, identifiable groups with common characteristics. These segments can be defined using any set of characteristics, such as those found in geographic, demographic, or psychographic information. Often, information from different sources is combined. For example, one hotel may first narrow its target segments by focusing on one geographic area (all people living in Taiwan). The segments may then be further narrowed by financial status (all people living in Taiwan whose income is above $20,000 a year and below $50,000). By continuing this process, marketers can find increasingly more precise targets. Marketing to narrow targets is a more efficient use of marketing dollars but is also the most expensive form of marketing, because most companies must target several segments at once.

Broad Segments

The most common marketing segment is defined by trip purpose—either business or leisure. In an effort to maximize their occupancy rates, most lodging facilities attempt to attract members of both groups, because their differences are sometimes complementary. For instance, business guests are more likely to need lodging from Monday through Thursday, and hoteliers can lessen the weekend slack by planning specials for leisure guests who are more likely to travel on weekends. Not all of the differences balance one another so nicely, however. Since many of the needs of each groups are specific to that group, different marketing strategies are necessary.

Business Guests Business travel is the most important source of guests for 80 percent of all hotels.[12] For this reason, recognizing and catering to the special needs of the business traveler is vital to the success of the lodging industry. Traditionally, business travel is high on weekdays and low on weekends, with the average trip lasting approximately three and a half days. During their stay, business travelers usually spend the majority of their time working. This means their needs are specific: well-lighted workspaces; a telephone; and access to equipment like personal computers, modems, high-speed Internet (ideally wireless), and comprehensive business services.

The business segment can be further defined by socioeconomic and psychographic factors. Some business travelers are on limited budgets, while others spare no expense for their accommodations. This latter group often expects VIP treatment and luxury accommodations. In some cases, business travelers need lodging for extended periods. For conferences, business guests may need access to meeting and banquet facilities. The business traveler segment is highly competitive among chain-affiliated brands as well as independent operators. Chain-affiliated brands have a distinct advantage over independent operators in attracting business travelers because of their loyalty and incentive travel programs. Hilton Honors encourages guests to accumulate points and redeem them for prizes, future travel, accommodations, vacation ownership, and other incentives. The business traveler is the bread-and-butter foundation of many urban hotels' occupancy. Retaining loyal business travelers is a key operating component of today's lodging sector.

Leisure Guests Personal and leisure travel accounts for 50 percent of all hotel stays. Discriminating and extremely conscious of price and value relationships, leisure travelers' desires may vary widely—from one night's stay in basic accommodations to several weeks at a resort with extensive recreation, entertainment, and food and beverage facilities. In the past, leisure trips were lengthy. Today, however, the increase in dual-income families has influenced the trend toward shorter, more frequent trips close to home. Weekend

Photo by Michael Dzaman

Some hotels depend on business travelers staying on weeknights for a majority of their income.

getaways, as these trips are often called, have been spurred by the difficulties of coordinating vacation time. Still, families with two working parents (76 percent) are more likely to vacation than those with one (64 percent).

Advantages of Segmentation

A clearer understanding of guest needs helps the marketer select appropriate marketing methods, which in turn allows the company to "get the most bang for its buck." A clearer guest image also helps keep management costs at the most efficient level, since hotel design and operations depend on who the potential guests will be. Certainly a luxury hotel has higher building and operating costs than a budget hotel. The luxury hotel could no more afford to accommodate a $70-a-night guest with no need for extra staff services than could a budget motel dedicate its staff to serving one guest's extravagant requests for personal services and amenities. Obviously, knowing the preferences of intended guests and then promoting the company to them is necessary to planning all aspects of hotel operations. Targeting those guests and achieving full market-share performance is essential to obtaining an adequate return on investment.

Segmentation also allows companies to place more than one brand on a single reservation system. For example, Choice Hotels' reservation system serves Quality Inns, Hotels, and Suites; Clarion Hotels, Suites, and Resorts; Comfort Inns and Suites; EconoLodges; Sleep Inns; Rodeway Inns; and Friendship Inns. They are able to do this by highlighting the differences between each of their brands' service offerings and facilities.

Disadvantages of Segmentation

Industry experts do not all agree on the advantages of dividing the market so narrowly, in part because many travelers may not want, need, or be able to distinguish between lodging concepts. Also, identifying segments and knowing how finely or broadly to define those segments can be a time and money-consuming endeavor. If the segmenting choices are sound, the marketing process will probably pay for itself. Unfortunately, the final results are not always particularly useful, and some companies may find themselves appealing to a nonviable segment. To prevent this, a marketing plan is devised, using a mix of methods.

The Marketing Plan

Generally, two marketing plans are used. A short-term plan determines the marketing strategies for a year or less; a long-term plan covers five years or more. The plans will contain a lot of the same material, although the short-term plan includes more details. A major benefit of using a plan is goal consistency. Strategies outlined in a plan include budgets and time schedules

Business Profile

HYATT HOTELS AND RESORTS

An Industry Leader

Photo courtesy of Hyatt Regency Grand Cypress

The first Hyatt hotel—a motor hotel outside Los Angeles International Airport—opened in 1957. By 2007, Hyatt Hotels Corporation (a subsidiary of Chicago-based Global Hyatt Corporation) managed, franchised, or operated 123 hotels in the United States, Canada, and the Caribbean. Another subsidiary of Global Hyatt Corporation, Hyatt International Corporation, operated 217 hotels and resorts with more than 90,000 rooms in forty-four countries around the world. Hyatt specializes in deluxe accommodations and meeting facilities. Hyatt is also known for the quality of its food and beverage product—in many cities, Hyatt restaurants are considered the best in the market.

Hyatt pioneered many concepts that are now industry standards. Hyatt Regency Atlanta, the world's first contemporary atrium hotel, revolutionized the lodging industry when it opened in 1967. Its twenty-one–story atrium lobby was an overwhelming success, inspiring hotel architects to include grand, wide-open spaces in their designs. Hyatt also was the first chain to introduce the VIP/concierge floor concept, which Hyatt calls Regency Club. Guests enjoy rooms with extra amenities in a restricted-access area of the hotel, as well as continental breakfast and evening hors d'oeuvres in the Regency Club lounge.

Hyatt also offers a children's program. The Camp Hyatt program offers supervised activities for children ages three to twelve. The activities reflect the culture, geography, and history of the resort's location. Other children's incentives are popular at Hyatt hotels and resorts in the United States, Canada, and the Caribbean.

Hyatt's Business Plan program offers business travelers rooms in a special area of the hotel. These rooms include a printer/copier/fax machine and an expanded work area. Business Plan also provides a continental breakfast, morning newspaper, and waived telephone access fees.

Travel awards, available through Hyatt's Gold Passport program, include not only exclusive guest rooms, but also airfare, car rental, and cruise savings.

Hyatt ranked in the top ten in the category "Highest in Guest Satisfaction Among Upscale Hotel Chains" in the J.D. Power and Associates 2006 Domestic Hotel Guest Satisfaction Study. Corporate travel managers ranked Hyatt number one in the upscale category in the Business Travel News 1999 Hotel Chain Survey.

Internet usage for travel planning and booking has blossomed, and Hyatt has been at the forefront of hotel industry e-commerce. Hyatt's Web site provides ease in making reservations, detailed hotel information, meeting planning resources, and graphics.

For many years, Hyatt has had several initiatives in place to increase diversity in the company and industry. In addition to supporting hospitality students with scholarship money and internships, Hyatt created a Diversity Council in 1999 to examine a host of diversity issues and initiate programs to increase diversity. Hyatt was recognized in 1999 and 2000 as one of Fortune magazine's "Top 50 Companies for Asians, Blacks, and Hispanics." Hyatt Hotel was also one of the "50 Best Companies for Minorities" in 2004.

for each goal, market analysis, and the company's intended image or market standing.

Without a plan, marketing budgets can be exhausted on trips down "blind alleys" and fail to show adequate return on advertising dollars.The marketing staff must keep the guest's perception of the hotel's image in the forefront. The guest's viewpoint is extremely important—she must be able to clearly see the advantages of one hotel over a competitor's, or she may decide to stay elsewhere. Proper marketing of a hotel's advantages and brand identity is critical. Hoteliers must keep in mind that people are generally looking for appropriate service and value.

The process of marketing services is different from processes used for marketing goods. In goods-producing industries, the product is tangible. For instance, in retailing, the product may be clothes, furniture, or appliances. Hospitality's product, on the other hand, is largely intangible. The product is the service a guest receives from the hospitality firm and its staff (although tangible items such as a sleeping room, lobby, architecture, design feel, recreational services, or food and beverages may also be involved). The successful marketer uses a variety of methods to promote the lodging industry, including direct or personal sales, advertising, public relations, promotions, and packaging.

Graduate Glimpse

RYAN EDDY

As a senior account executive responsible for group sales for the New York Marriott at the Brooklyn Bridge, there is no typical day for Ryan Eddy. Each day he faces an ever-changing environment. Eddy is responsible for expanding the hotel's large-group business and driving market share for the financial, insurance, retail, manufacturing, sports, and entertainment markets within the downtown Brooklyn area. His daily tasks may include qualifying new group inquiries by following the standard sales processes, quoting availability to customers based on their request for proposal (RFP) specs, following up with customers regarding outstanding bids, and soliciting prospective and repeat customers for new business.

Eddy graduated from the University of Delaware with a bachelor's degree in hotel, restaurant, and institutional management and minors in economics and hospitality management information systems. He was offered the position of sales manager in Marriott's New York regional sales office upon graduation in 2004, after completing several Marriott summer internships in various locations and specialties, in addition to working as a front desk agent during school semesters. He views both education and work experience as important contributors to his current role. He also attributes his success after graduation to good mentorship from upper management. He advises, "Be aggressive and willing to do what it takes to win business." In the next five years, Eddy plans to achieve a director-level position in sales or cross back into operations to work toward becoming a general manager.

Elements of Marketing Methods

Alastair Morrison, author, marketing consultant, and associate professor, has categorized these methods into what he calls the eight Ps of marketing: product, people, packaging, programming, place, partnership, pricing, and promotion.[13] Each of these methods is controllable by the hospitality firm and is used to attract guests based on guest needs.

Each element may be used alone or as part of a mix. Generally, in a mix, one element is given priority. For example, luxury hotels use product marketing extensively, as it emphasizes their services, ambiance, and luxurious accommodations. A sample ad may read, "Outstanding new facility with superb amenities. Features pools, tennis, Jacuzzi, sauna, and exercise equipment." Of course, other types of hotels also use product marketing. A bed-and-breakfast might advertise its "beautiful scenery by day and comfort at night; private baths, central air, craft shop." This type of ad appeals to the guest who is looking for specific amenities and services.

An example of the people element might be an advertisement featuring a chef holding an apple pie in her outstretched arms and the caption "Just like Mom used to make." The Flora-Dale Resort, Mears, Michigan, also used the people element in an ad: "Where The Wife Gets a Vacation, Too! Where families build happy memories, on sand dunes, at the pool or beach, playing together, enjoying two delicious meals daily." This type of ad may appeal to a guest who selects a lodging facility based on comfort and familiarity.

Packaging is defined as offering more than one product or service to the consumer for one total price. For example, a limited-service hotel may offer a "Weekend Getaway Package" that offers two nights' lodging accommodations, limousine service to and from the hotel, and a Sunday buffet breakfast for a single price. The Gatlinburg Royal Townhouse Motel in Tennessee advertised the inclusion of tickets to Dollywood as part of its fall special. Packaging often appeals to the value-conscious guest.

Programs are tailor-made offerings for groups sharing a special interest. Hotels can cater to many different segments by developing special activities, events, and short-term educational programs. Mohonk Mountain House, a national historic landmark in New Paltz, New York, offers more than thirty programs including Smoke Enders clinics, foreign language instruction, music, and Entrepreneur School. (See Table 3.4.)

The success of *place* marketing depends, of course, upon the desirability of a location. Hotels located at popular destination sites, such as Disney World, use the popularity of the site to attract guests. Their ads generally mention the attraction first, such as "Only ten minutes to Disney World." Another example of the place element is an advertisement featuring a beach scene with a couple strolling arm in arm and a caption that reads, "Three's Company—You, Her, and the Ocean." Guests desiring a romantic getaway may be attracted by such an appeal.

TABLE 3.4 Partial 2007 Program Listing for Mohonk Mountain House

Program	Dates
Classics on the Mountain Music Festival	June 12–17
Summer Nature Week	June 18–22
Festival of the Arts	July 6–August 24
Summer of Discovery—Children Stay Half Price (midweek)	July 8–26
Garden Holiday	August 26–31
Artist's Inspiration Week	September 16–21
Hudson Valley Harvest	September 21–23
Halloween Haunts and Happenings	October 26–28
A Guide to Ageless Aging (November)	November 2–4
Couples' Romantic Getaway	November 16–18
Home for the Holidays	December 7–9
Mars and the Marvelous Meteors with Bob Berman	December 13
Mohonk's Holiday Gala (Children Stay Free)	December 14–20

Source: http://www.mohonk.com/theme_programs/theme_programs.cfm

Partnership requires the cooperative efforts of several industry groups. One classic example is the cooperative marketing efforts of Diner's Club International, which combines five hotel companies, five airlines, and one credit card company. "So dine with the Diner's Club Card. Sleep on it. Rent with it. And watch your frequent flyer miles soar."

Budget hotels often use a combination of *price* and location elements in their marketing mix. Inexpensive yet clean and comfortable lodging located along travel routes appeals to many people on a long trip.

Promotions are activities, other than those that fit into the above categories, which stimulate and create consumer interest in a product or service. For hotels, these activities may include special events, offers, exhibits, or discounts. Such an example would be a hotel's sponsorship of a community festival. Not only would the festival attract out-of-town guests, but it would be an avenue for creating a positive public image for the hotel. Promotions make use of advertising, sales, and public relations.

Sales is the method most often identified with promoting the industry. It involves direct, personal attempts to sell the product to potential guests. For example, when resorts contact convention planners, their job is to persuade the planners to schedule their next meeting at the resort. Sales requires one-on-one contact and affords the salesperson the opportunity to tailor his or her message to each client.

The least personal promotional technique, advertising, is making a product known through the media. The advantages of advertising compared to sales

Photo by Michael Dzaman

Billboards attract attention by advertising incentives like Jacuzzis and indoor pools.

are (1) many people can be reached at once; (2) an ad can "reach behind closed doors"; and (3) a large sales staff is not necessary, because advertising does not require personal contact. Examples of advertising are found almost everywhere, from television to radio to print to outdoor billboards and internet media. However, effective return on advertising dollars is not automatic. The advertiser must understand how to allocate resources so that profit objectives are satisfied. In other words; one should ask, "Is this advertising campaign going to generate enough revenue to cover its costs and contribute incremental profit to the bottom line?"

Public relations is the process of positively manipulating the public's perception of a company. This may be done not only through public relations campaigns and advertisements, but also through press releases, special events, and company policies that relate to timely topics like financial disclosure, the environment, affirmative action, and other areas of public concern. Strong and active public relations activities can afford lodging operations a significant competitive advantage.

The Evolution Continues

The process of establishing a distinctive place in the market (and in the minds of potential guests) is called **positioning**.[15] It may be the most important step in lodging marketing, for if a hotel is positioned incorrectly, it will not reach its profit potential, no matter how appropriate its pricing or how well it is promoted. With constantly changing industry conditions, positioning is not a one-time event; repositioning is also necessary to keep properties operating at their highest potential. Repositioning was the task given to the marketers of the Delta Chelsea Inn of Toronto. In 1988, the Chelsea began an $80 million renovation program and marketers began mapping out a plan to reposition the hotel from a 3.5-star property to a 4.5-star one while maintaining some of its previous image as a familiar, comfortable, and trustworthy hotel. Nancy H. Arab, director of public relations for the Chelsea, explains the process:

> The Chelsea was to be positioned as the quintessential hotel of good taste and good manners, offering above-average accommodations, service, food, drink, and entertainment, at eminently reasonable rates ... The Chelsea's original good taste, high value, and Edwardian English persona was strengthened and broadened to satisfy the higher expectations of today's mid-market prospect.

Many economy chains are now using incentives or value-added perks as a way to stay competitive by adding to a guest's perceived value. For example, in late 1993, Howard Johnson's began offering the use of a Sega portable video game as part of the room package.

In other examples, Courtyard by Marriott threw in complimentary telephone calls and faxes for its guests; and Ramada Inns gave free disposable cameras to families.

The VIP amenities offered at the Hyatt Regency O'Hare in Chicago are tailored to fit the seasons. During election time, guest rooms sport a red, white, and blue Uncle Sam hat filled with popcorn and cookies shaped like elephants and donkeys. Basketball season brings a basket filled with peanuts, beer, beer mugs, and Chicago Bulls trading cards. While such perks may seem trivial, they're a relatively inexpensive marketing ploy for hotels to attract—and keep—guests.

Summary

- The strong economy of the 1800s resulted in the development of modern hotels and ushered in the Golden Age of hotels.
- The lodging industry faced a severe upset in supply and demand in the 1980s. Excessive supply forced hoteliers to find new methods for classifying, owning, and marketing their properties. The 1990s saw moderate economic returns, but 9-11 and the dot-com bust caused unprecedentedly low returns and economic hemorrhaging in the industry. Until 2008,the industry enjoyed strong performance in occupancy and high average rate and pricing elasticity due to expanded travel patterns and relatively strong economic conditions in the macroeconomic landscape.
- Lodging facilities may be classified according to different criteria, including price and description of services. These flexible classifications are useful to both potential guests and the industry itself. New and emerging classifications include vacation ownership, spa resorts, mega-resorts and boutique hotels.
- While independent hotel companies have considerable flexibility, independent hoteliers also bear the most difficult financial challenges.

- Franchise agreements are contracts in which the franchisor grants the franchisee the right to use the franchisor's brand name and its proven method of doing business in exchange for a franchise fee.
- A management company operates the owner's property in exchange for a percentage of the profits.
- Marketing is the process of developing, pricing, promoting, and distributing goods or services. Methods of marketing include sales, advertising, public relations, promotions, and packaging.
- Positioning and repositioning are the keys to successful lodging marketing.

ENDNOTES

1 A.E. Richardson, *The Old Inns of England* (New York: Charles Scribner's Sons, 1935), 6.

2 The 1998 Lodging Industry Profile, American Hotel & Motel Association, http://www.ahma.com.

3 Charles J. Metelka, ed., *The Dictionary of Tourism* (Wheaton, Ill.: Merton House Publishing Company, 1981), 53.

4 Annetta Miller, "Sega, Kitty, and Breakfast, Too," *Newsweek* (September 6, 1993): 58.

5 Waters, The Big Picture, 154. Retrieved online September 10, 2008 from www.ks3curriculum.files.wordpress.com

6 M.O. "Bus" Ryan, "Business Travel in '93: You Won't Pay a Lot for a Room," *Business Travel Management* (January 1993): 36.

7 Patrick E. Culligan, "Looking Up: Lodging Supply and Demand," *Cornell Hotel and Restaurant Association Quarterly* (August 1990): 32.

8 Smith Travel Research, Retreived online August 15, 2008 from www.smithtravelresearch.com/

9 Charles A. Bell, "Agreements with Chain-Hotel Companies," *Cornell Hotel and Restaurant Association Quarterly* (February 1993): 27–28.

10 "The Concierge Explained," *Business Week* (November 26, 1990): 169.

11 John M. Tarras, *A Practical Guide to Hospitality Finance* (New York: Van Nostrand Reinhold, 1991), 168–170.

12 "AMA Board Approves New Marketing Definition," *Marketing Educator* (Spring 1985): 1.

13 Christopher H. Lovelock, *Services Marketing* (Englewood Cliffs, N.J.: Prentice-Hall, 1984), 134.

CHECK YOUR KNOWLEDGE

1. What provoked the dramatic increase in lodging facilities after World War II?
2. Why did occupancy rates reach a thirty-year low in the early 1990s?
3. If you were to invest in a new lodging venture, would you select a hotel, motel, resort or vacation ownership product?
4. Why is marketing position important?
5. If you were attempting to negotiate a hotel management contract, what fee basis would you prefer if you were the management company? Why? Answer the same question from the perspective of the property owner.

APPLY YOUR SKILLS

Calculate the occupancy rates for the following hotels based on the information given and by using this formula: Divide the total number of rooms occupied during the year by the total number of rooms available and multiply by 100.

1. Hotel A: 120 rooms available; average number of rooms rented per day = 80; average occupancy rate per year = ?
2. Hotel B: 560 rooms available: average number of rooms rented per day = 320; average occupancy rate per year = ?
3. Hotel C: 1,000 rooms available: average number of rooms rented per day = 630: average occupancy rate per year = ?

WHAT DO YOU THINK?

1. Do you think the demand for lodging will catch up to supply? If so, when? If not, why?
2. If you were going to operate a hotel, would you want it to be independent, franchised, or chain? Why?
3. If you were the owner of an independent hotel and had limited funds, how would you spend your marketing budget?
4. What do you think is the most important concept of marketing for the hospitality industry?
5. What can the lodging industry do to catch up with goods-producing industries in the marketing arena?

CASE STUDY

One full-page magazine ad for Holiday Inn shows a smiling, professional-looking woman checking into a Holiday Inn. The copy says, "Who would know better how to make you feel welcome wherever you travel? Any day you may be one of the 15 million people who set out on a journey. Over the years, we've welcomed more of you to more places in the world than anyone else. And all that experience has shown us how to make you feel perfectly at home. Even in a place where the only familiar sight may be our friendly sign. Holiday Inn. Stay with someone you know."

1. What phrases in this ad might appeal to travelers?
2. How does this ad try to convince you that Holiday Inn is the place to stay if you want to feel welcome?
3. If you were writing an ad for a hotel you work at or have worked at what would you say to welcome your guests?

Hotel Development

OVERVIEW

Why develop a hotel? The reasons are as plentiful as the number of proposed developments. Financial reasons—such as to make a return on investment or to increase the value of surrounding properties—usually are at the forefront. Some developers build for personal satisfaction. Pride in ownership, the satisfaction of putting together a deal such as a joint-venture arrangement, real estate investment trust, or exchange-traded equity investment fund, a corporate expansion strategy, a new hotel brand launch, and the desire for notoriety are just a few motives for hotel development. In addition, people who enjoy combining the risk of real estate development with the gratification of a career in a service industry often build for the sense of accomplishment.

Regardless of their reasons for building, all hotel developers face the same processes on their way to achieving their goals. Although all the steps play a part in an orderly development process, they do not occur in a fixed order. One developer may first decide what type of hotel to build and then select an appropriate site. Another may first identify a good location, and decide later what type of hotel to build on it. All developers must set into motion and accomplish the same phases of development activity: (1) conceptualization, (2) feasibility analysis, (3) financial commitment and deliverablility, (4) design and construction, and (5) management and operation. You will read about these steps in this chapter and Chapter 5.

OBJECTIVES

When you have completed this chapter, you should be able to:

1. Identify the steps of hotel development from conceptualization to grand opening.
2. Explain how location influences the success of a hotel.
3. Evaluate the importance of completing a feasibility study and interpreting the results before building a new lodging facility.
4. Outline the factors involved in obtaining financial backing for hotel development and operation.
5. Identify the basic design requirements of a hotel.
6. Explain the concept of ambiance and its role in guest satisfaction.

KEY TERMS

ambiance
back of the house
concept
debt service
expansion
forecasting
franchise agreements
front of the house
management contracts
preopening expenses
resorts
securitization

An Overview of the Process

As with most processes, hotel development begins when a person or firm perceives an opportunity for building a hotel. Generally, these individuals or firms are property owners, investors, or developers looking to invest in real estate. A hotel development or management company may be looking to expand, a municipality may be trying to reverse economic blight, or a developer may be looking to revitalize an area through the addition of a hotel. Regardless of their reasons, these individuals or firms are interested in investing in the lodging industry. Before doing so, they need to consider the basics of hotel development from conception to construction and operation and assess potential financial returns.

Conceptualization

There is an old saying that "ideas are a dime a dozen," but making ideas a reality takes time, commitment, and large amounts of money. Adequate time

and effort must be allotted in the beginning of a project to clarifying the original idea and planning how it is to be executed. To sharpen the initial concept, a hotel developer needs to examine it from different angles. He or she should ask, "What is my source of capital, and how is the financial model going to provide return on investment? What is the required or expected return on investment? What are the macro market conditions affecting the lodging industry? Who is my target audience? What needs am I trying to satisfy? What are the micro market conditions in the surrounding area? Is there a large enough market? What size facility do I need? What can this hotel offer its guests as a uniquely positioned product that its competitors don't or can't? What are the currrent and projected demands for hotel room nights in the marketplace?" From the start, these and other questions must be studied. Once the preliminary development concept is clarified, ideas and goals can be formalized into concrete objectives and the development team can be assembled.

Feasibility Analysis

One task for the development team is to determine whether the project is feasible (capable of being carried out successfully). This determination is based on a detailed study of the factors involved in opening and operating a successful hotel. The team looks for evidence that supports or rejects the likely success of the concept. Success is measured financially, because hotel investors expect repayment of, as well as interest on, the money they invest. The feasibility study answers the question "Will the proposed hotel generate enough profit to meet the expectations of its investors?" Different investors expect different levels of return. Usually, investors prefer to see cash-on-cash returns in excess of 10 percent. Not only does the feasibility study project the hotel's rates and occupancy levels, and estimate its operating expenses; it also determines the necessary capital investment needed for acquisition, construction, and ongoing operations. If these projections predict an acceptable return, preliminary design and development schedules are generated, and the project proceeds to the next stage—commitment.

Commitment

This stage is a critical turning point for the project. It is here that the developers must secure funding and begin negotiations with architects, designers, and construction and management companies. If the project is to be developed in-house and not by a separate company, this is when the key members of the in-house team are assembled and brought into the development process. If the development project is to be handled externally, then competitive bid processes are entered into to determine the best fit for the project in terms of cost and expertise. Funding must cover more than the cost of construction; it must also cover the expense of operating until the hotel reaches viability, commonly referred to as stabilization. The operating margins and construction budgets must be decided on during this phase so they can be included in the design stage.

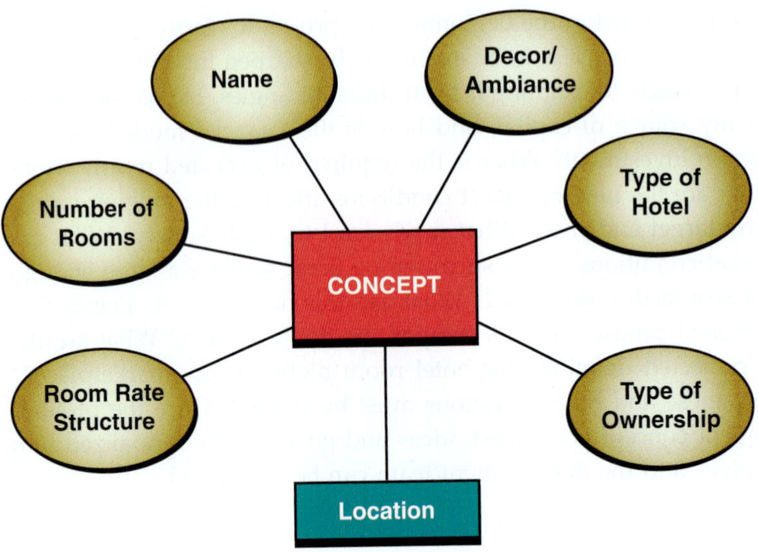

FIGURE 4.1 First, the idea...

Design and Construction

Once the project team is fully committed and funding has been obtained, the actual design and construction of the hotel begins. The project is designed, built, and equipped according to the expected finished product identified in the feasibility study and the goals of the developers. The development team works to keep the project on schedule and within the established budget guidelines so that financial troubles don't stall the project before opening. During the design and construction phase, management or **franchise agreements** are formalized and the management and operating staffs are mobilized. Preliminary marketing and personnel training usually begin during this stage.

The Opening

The final stage in hotel development is the actual opening. The new hotel staff must have the project up and running by the scheduled opening date. By this time, the marketing and sales staff are fully operational and have been working to ensure that the hotel will have guests from the first day. All front- and back-of-the-house staff have been trained and are prepared to welcome guests. When all last-minute adjustments to the facility and operating programs have been made, the facility opens for business.

Choosing the Right Location

The hotel's **concept** includes such things as its name, market positioning, decor and theme, star rating, type of service, and location. All of these factors contribute to the hotel's potential success, but the location is the most influential. Even a superb concept probably will not survive in the wrong location. Location factors include: ingress and egress, major arterial roadways, parking availability, visibility to the street, proximity to major traffic routes, and proximity to major attractions or tourist destinations (such as theme parks).

Business Profile

FOUR SEASONS HOTEL

Successful Concept

In 1961, four friends-turned-business partners with no experience in hotel management built and opened the Four Seasons Motor Hotel in Toronto, Canada. The Four Seasons was designed around the concept of "quality first." Today, understated elegance and attention to the little details give the hotel an opulent ambiance.

Guests are pampered: they receive twice-a-day maid service, free shoeshines, complimentary umbrellas, monogrammed terrycloth robes if they are repeat customers, and milk and cookies for children. An incident at Toronto's Four Seasons hotel provides an example of the sort of guest relations and customer service that are the company's hallmark. Long-time bellhop Roy Dyment received a phone call from a guest in Washington, D.C., who had left behind two suitcases. Since the guest needed the contents urgently, Dyment boarded a plane—on his own time and at his own expense—and flew to Washington, personally delivering the luggage. "This," says Four Seasons president Isadore Sharp, "is the kind of devotion and loyalty money can't buy."[1]

While the Four Seasons hotels are not large by industry standards—the number of rooms averages 325 per hotel—they do have an excellent international reputation. In 1972, the Four Seasons found they could not compromise this reputation. Although they once formed a partnership with another hotel to build an enormous 1,450-room hotel across from Toronto's city hall, the Four Seasons eventually pulled out. "Never again would we try to be all things to all people," said Sharp.[2]

Commitment to excellence puts the Four Seasons in a class by itself. It thrives on providing the finest in service and accommodations and catering to the rich and famous. With some of the highest room rates in the industry, the Four Seasons is a home-away-from-home for world leaders, rock stars, Arab sheiks, and royalty. In 1999, the Four Seasons hotel chain became the world's leading operator of luxury hotels, managing seventy-three properties in thirty-one countries under the Four Seasons and Regent names.[3] Today, Four Seasons Hotels continues to target expansion by opening hotels in international metropolitan markets and resort destinations around the world.

---

1 Gerald Clark, "The Inns That Issy Built," *Reader's Digest* (August 1991): 73.

2 John DeMont, "Sharp's Luxury Empire," *MacLean's* (June 5, 1989): 32.

3 www.fourseasons.com/press/releases

This formula for success is supported by studies showing that most guests rate proximity high on their list of deciding factors when choosing a place to stay. Business travelers especially prefer hotels close to their destinations and transportation routes. History has shown that when upward economic trends bring new supply into the marketplace, the value of a good location rises sharply. A developer's choice of location helps determine the mix of business and leisure travelers and the types of facilities and amenities offered.

Lodging facilities may even be classified according to their location—airport, downtown, suburban, highway, or resort. This section describes the features of these sites, their limitations, and the types of hotels and motels typically built at each location to attract particular groups of guests.

Airport Properties

Developed alongside the growing airline industry, airport properties were originally built to house airline flight crews and those travelers whose flights were postponed, canceled, or delayed overnight. They also provided food and beverage services to passengers waiting for flights. Such airport properties average a minimum of 100 guest rooms. Over time, airport hoteliers realized they did not have to rely exclusively on providing lower-rated low priced rooms; instead they strived to reach larger markets and began adding guest rooms as well as banquet and meeting facilities. They targeted local business groups and large organizations hosting regional conventions, and today they offer good-sized, quality facilities that save participants travel time between the airport and a convention facility. Such marketing puts airport facilities in direct competition with downtown convention hotels. In addition to their convention facilities, airport properties offer quick and easy transportation to and from the airport, ranging from underground moving sidewalks to shuttle services.

Downtown Properties

Because of their ability to help stimulate revitalization, downtown properties consist of both the oldest and newest lodging properties in an area. Due to the limited availability of land in the inner city and the high cost of developing in densely populated areas, downtown hotels usually are high-rise structures. Usually, downtown hotels need to build above- or below-ground parking structures. These properties tend to have higher average room rates than all

Business Profile

LAS VEGAS (NEVADA) CITY CENTER

Las Vegas City Center Development—Innovative Mixed-Use Hotel, Retail and Commercial Complex

Large scale urban mixed use development projects are emerging aound the globe in major cities. Although they are usually not as dense as the Las Vegas project, more and more international mixed-use urban developments are under construction in Dubai, Shanghai, and Singapore. However, the Las Vegas City Center project, with upwards of a million square feet of store, residential, hotel and commercial services. will have a post office, medical services, entertainment, and a myriad of lodging and residential living alternatives. The complex will be a self-contained community and one of the largest development sites in the world.

Source: http://www.citycenterlasvegas.com

other types of hotels except destination, all-inclusive resorts, because of the expense of real estate and the high cost of doing business in a city.

Serving predominantly business travelers and conventioneers, downtown hotels tend to have higher occupancy rates on weekdays and lower occupancy

Professional Profile

STEVE WYNN

Visionary Hotelier and Developer

Steve Wynn began his career as chairman of the board, president and chief executive officer of Mirage Resorts, Inc. He is best known for his hotel, resort, and gaming operations, which personify ultimate luxury. He has created a worldwide brand of luxury projects serving international jet setters. He has been the creative talent behind some of the world's finest and most distinctive hotel/gaming development projects.

Steve Wynn grew up in upstate New York and began his hospitality career by making investments in outdated hotel/casino properties. He was successful in developing and controlling real estate in Las Vegas, Nevada, ultimately building a multi–billion-dollar organization. His projects are often associated with the highest quality and excellence in product offering and service delivery. Most recently, Wynn has expanded his hotel/gaming holdings into Macau, China. He continues to be viewed as "the man at the top" of hotel/gaming development in the United States.

Source: http://www.investorrelations@wynnresorts.com

on weekends. To meet the needs of their business guests and to attract other groups—including tourists in town for sports and cultural events—specialized types of downtown properties have developed in both large and small cities. For example, in some cities, extended-stay and all-suite properties have emerged on the landscape in order to provide services to long-stay hotel users. Recently, urban revitalization trends have incorporated the mixed-use development concept, in which a high-rise building may have condominium residences on the upper floors, hotel rooms on the middle floors, and office and retail uses on the ground floor.

Suburban Properties

In the 1950s, the U.S. population began to move away from the core city into outlying areas where housing and land were less expensive. Business soon followed, creating a demand for lodging in the suburbs. Suburban properties originally provided lodging for travelers who wanted quick access to the downtown area for sports and cultural events and meetings, but who did not want to spend the night there. These day trips provided one source of transient guests, but not enough guests to fill the facilities. Thus, suburban hoteliers marketed restaurants, lounges, banquet facilities, and meeting spaces to nearby suburban businesses and local residents.

Although suburban properties may benefit from lower taxes and land costs, they are frequently restricted by other regulations, including height and size zoning guidelines. As a result of these regulations, most suburban hotels are mid-rise structures with two hundred to five hundred rooms.

Industry Insights

LAW AND ETHICS

Zoning

Zoning, a procedure to regulate land use, helps city planners bring about orderly growth and change for an area. Zoning boards delineate areas as residential, commercial, or manufacturing (industrial) zones. In order to preserve the characteristics of each area, only certain activities are allowed within its boundaries. Permission to operate a business at a specific site must first be granted by the local zoning board. Most jurisdictions have established zoning areas. In some jurisdictions, unzoned areas exist, which may be developed with few or no restrictions. If a developer needs to get a variance or rezoning (an exception or change to current zoning regulations to allow an alternative use), he or she must go through a cumbersome approval process, so sufficient time and money needs to be allocated. Often, developers hire third-party engineering, environmental, and legal consultants to assist with this process.

In skyscraper-filled New York City, zoning laws protect even the air space above an area. The empty space above an elite men's club became the focus of a zoning dispute between the club and a real estate firm that wanted to build an office tower behind the club. The firm coveted the prestige of the club's Park Avenue address, an identity that would significantly increase rental fees. But the club refused the firm's plan to run an arcade from the desired street, through the club, and into the new building, allowing the tower to use the address its planners sought. The tower developers next offered several thousand dollars for the club's air rights—its ownership interest in the space above the club. But the financially ailing club held out for more money.

When the tower developers obtained the desired address through a special proclamation by the presiding officer of the New York City Council, they no longer needed the club's cooperation. The zoning board granted the developers the right to make the tower taller than originally planned, and it was redesigned so that all rentable office space would look out over the clubhouse and onto Park Avenue. But club members had plans of their own. They decided to build a 475-foot-high hotel on top of their clubhouse, reducing the tremendous view the tower planners were counting on to a view of brick and mortar.

Another round of intense negotiations finally resolved the issue. The club sold its air space to the real estate firm for $5 million.

Highway Motels

Like airport properties, highway motels developed with the growth of transportation. During the 1950s and early 1960s, the interstate highway system was built. Its interchanges provided numerous sites for motel development to meet the lodging needs of vacation and business travelers. Serving transient guests who stay an average of one night, these facilities are generally very simple one or two-story, exterior-corridor structures with fewer than two hundred rooms. They provide free surface parking and outdoor or enclosed recreational facilities for both business and leisure travelers. Unlike other types of properties, these facilities may have more than one building. Public space and registration areas may be separate from guest rooms. Usually breakfast and workout facilities are provided without charge.

The average stay for highway motels, which provide easy access to rest for travelers, is one night.

Photo by Michael Dzaman

Resorts and Attractions

Resorts are either located near a particular attraction or are attractions in and of themselves. Location is more essential to their success than it is to other types of properties. Their ability to attract guests is based on their ability to create a site where people want to go. Unlike other types of properties, resorts are often built away from population centers and transportation routes.

Although they may benefit from low land costs, government sponsorship, and/or a unique physical environment, resorts often must compensate for a lack of infrastructure. Mackinac Island, a resort area in Michigan, prohibits automobiles. Large resort hotels on the island receive food and other products by a horse-drawn cart. More typically, roads and utility systems may need to be developed, as well as transportation from airports and train and bus stations. Usually site development costs are significantly higher for a resort that needs to bring utilities and infrastucture to the building area than for a property located in an established municipality with power, gas, sewer, street, and utility connections. Some resorts may have to construct their own water treatment and sewer plants. Additionally, resorts may have to be relatively self-sufficient, so they need large storage areas for supplies and support areas for laundry, food and beverage, and maintenance services. Some resorts even provide employee housing and off-duty employee recreational facilities.

Originally designed for the upper middle class and very rich, resorts—including those located at constructed attractions like Walt Disney World and at natural attractions like the Rocky Mountains—are growing in popularity among the working middle class. Just as malls offer one-stop shopping, resorts create destinations for one-stop vacationing. Tourists usually stay a minimum of two or three days, but often stay for their entire vacation. Despite this growing tourist base, in order to stay profitable year-round, resorts have turned toward convention and incentive business to generate added demand. The

business market requires that resort hotels provide meeting and banquet facilities, which creates one more source of competition for downtown hotels.

Assessing Feasibility

Historically, location has been considered the key to a hotel's success, but today's market has made the success equation much more complicated. Investors and developers appraise the possible success of a project before committing large amounts of time and money. To determine whether a development project is feasible, developers need the results of a detailed analysis of all the factors involved in making a hotel successful. A preliminary feasibility study may be conducted internally by experienced members of the development team, but a more detailed study by a hotel consulting firm, although expensive, may prove more accurate and is usually preferred by lenders. Table 4.1 lists common report sections of feasibility studies along with specific information found in each section.

Market Area

This phase of a feasibility study is conducted to determine demographic and socioeconomic data, customer demand by segment, competitive market supply, and overall occupied room production for the area surrounding the site. Such information helps determine what market the new facility will attempt to reach and whether the surrounding area can support the new facility. This section of the feasibility study should answer specific questions about level of demand in relation to supply (room inventory—customer demand), pricing considerations, and future growth projections for the chosen location.

TABLE 4.1 Feasibility Study

Report Section	*Information*
Market Area	Geographic and economic: available market and workforce, channels of distribution, existing attractions
Competition	Competitors: brands in the market, competition's concept, current operations, future goals
Site	Geographic and legal: infrastructure, zoning regulations, environmental measures, title insurance
Demand	Target market and demographics: market share, market segmentation trends, pricing strategies
Facilities and Services	Hotel type and design: layout, construction, efficiency and cost of equipment, availability and cost of raw materials
Financial Estimates	Economic feasibility: proposed budget, start-up costs, projected revenues, projected return on investment

Who lives in or visits the area? Demographic data answers this question. The relative size and importance of various market segments, such as leisure, business, and convention travelers, is measured, as well as the size, availability, and wage costs of the potential workforce. The developer needs assurance that the hotel can attract enough guests to make the enterprise profitable enough to operate. She or he also need assurance that there will be enough workers in the area to staff the operation. Working habits and employment/unemployment rates are studied in order to predict possible labor problems that the hotel might encounter.

Does this area already attract the desired market segment? Interviews with representatives of major travel generators, transportation authorities, tourist and convention bureaus, comparable lodging properties, and development and redevelopment programs provide information on likely future guests. Tax rolls provide concrete data specifying bed tax collections and can help determine occupied room activity for the marketplace under consideration. Other important market considerations are the locations and target markets of competitors, the proximity of target markets to the proposed facility, the travel patterns of visitors to the area, and the spending patterns of those travelers.

Can this area support a new facility? Information is gathered about an area's legal limitations, the status of the infrastructure, and natural and constructed attractions.

Once gathered, all of these factors help the development team make decisions about whether to continue with the project and, if so, in which directions to take it.

Competition

The next step in analyzing the feasibility of a project is to evaluate the competition. Key to a project's success is its position in the market. To determine this position, developers must know and understand each competitor's brand, current market share, customer base, loyalty, occupancy rates, average room rates, and strengths and weaknesses, as well as its services, amenities, and whether or not it is a franchise or management affiliate. Comparisons with competitors help developers define the factors involved in lodging success in the region. A thorough search of records needs to take place in order to determine any and all new construction activity that may be bringing new inventory on line in the market. Also important is an evaluation of all proposed facility designs.

Site

Once developers have determined that a market exists and that there is an open niche among the competitors, they must determine whether their chosen site is suitable for building a lodging facility. They must evaluate factors such as the distance to the proposed site from major attractions, including business centers and recreational areas; the geographic characteristics of the site itself, including the amount of preparation needed to build; the capacity for future expansion; and the regulatory, environmental, and legal issues that would affect the proposed facility. Making an appropriate judgment about the site also requires research into any plans for the area around the proposed site and an analysis of the current and proposed infrastructure.

Once these inquiries are complete, a thorough search is undertaken to examine the conditions of the site soil and seismic activity. In addition, a complete title search is performed for any reservations or easements recorded against the property, liens, or other problems that would prevent the developer from acquiring the land "free and clear" of encumbrances.

Demand

When an appropriate site is located, the developers should again focus on the proposed facility's target market. This time the goal is to determine the proposed facility's projected occupancy rate and, eventually, its average room rate so that the developers can find out if the project is economically feasible. It is important at this stage to document the current and projected travel and expenditure patterns of visitors to the area, probable future lodging supply, seasonal variations, average length of stay for different travel groups, and modes of transportation. A complete pro forma financial statement is compiled projecting five to ten years of operating results. The pro forma is usually assembled market segment by market segment in order to identify targeted customers and the appropriate level of pricing per segment. Not only is the room demand computed at this stage of the development model, but other income sources such as food and beverage are also identified.

Facilities and Services

After figuring the projected demand and occupancy, the developers can decide what type and size of lodging facility to build. For the project to be economically feasible, occupancy rates usually need to be about 60 percent or higher. If the hotel is built too large for the projected demand, its occupancy will be low. If the hotel is built too small, it may not be able to accommodate large groups and thus lose a prospective source of business. In the same way, if a developer builds a small residential hotel aimed at executive business travelers in an area with a high percentage of transient leisure travelers who tend toward shorter average stays, the residential hotel's occupancy rates will be low. The facility must be built to meet the needs of its target market. Studies of this target market should indicate which amenities and services are most appropriate for the expected mix of business and leisure travelers.

Financial Estimates

The purpose of the feasibility study, as mentioned earlier, is to determine the hotel's economic feasibility. Financial estimates not only help developers make final decisions about whether to commit to a project, they also help developers obtain financing for the hotel, and determine the most reasonable expected return on investment. Using the projected occupancy rates and estimated room rates by segment for that particular type of facility, developers may project revenues for the various departments within the hotel. Projections allow for variations in demand as well as inflation rates.

In order to model financial trends into the future, **forecasting** that includes macroeconomic trends in concert with local market variables must be undertaken. National, regional, and local economic information is necessary in order to determine accurate projections. Third-party travel research providers offer industry-wide trending and reporting mechanisms that identify demand and supply changes. These tools generate data that may or may not affect the specific investment location and marketplace. Travel research providers can also create customized reporting tools that identify occupancy and average room rate trends for any given marketplace based on the desired location and grouping of competitor sets.

After determining the projected revenue, developers estimate costs of constructing, opening, and operating the facility. Construction costs include items such as land acquisition, architectual planning, interior design, construction management oversight, building foundation, utility hookups, fire and life safety systems, building envelope, parking lot paving, compliance with accessibility mandates, roofing, interior finishes, furniture, bathrooms, plumbing, heating and air-conditioning systems, restaurant and bar fixtures, meeting space sound systems and airwalls, and kitchen equipment.

Once the construction and furniture, fixtures and equipment costs are estimated it is then necessary to estimate the operating costs. Operating costs include signage, supplies and equipment, uniforms, payroll, management fees, initial and ongoing staff training, employee turnover expenses, maintenance of food and beverage facilities, opening and ongoing inventory, in-room entertainment, laundry facilities, and computer access systems.

The total cost must also include expenses related to the general maintenance of the facility, capital reserves (4 percent of annual revenues) for ongoing upgrades, and any fees relating to franchise licensing or national marketing.

From projected costs and revenues, developers and potential investors can determine estimated profits and, thus, the project's feasibility. This step is crucial because feasibility is directly related to obtaining financing. Regardless of the property's potential, if developers cannot obtain the necessary financing in a timely fashion, the project may be delayed permanently or cancelled.

Fiscal Commitment to the New Hotel

Deciding to enter the hotel business is a big step involving the commitment of large amounts of time, money, energy, and other resources. Developers turn toward investors for part or all of the financial backing needed. Investors expect fixed returns on their investments. The fixed returns must be factored into the financial pro forma in order to illustrate projected return on investment. Commitment of development, preopening, and operating costs is necessary before construction can begin.

Finding Investors

To begin our discussion of how developers search for investors to provide the capital for such an undertaking, we shall discuss how investment has been influenced by past economic events. Investment practices change with the economic tide. Constructing new facilities was a good investment practice in the 1980s; buying and renovating an existing structure was a better option for the 1990s. Even in 2007, the cost of buying and repositioning an existing hotel was less than that of building from the ground up. Building new involves the cost of land acquisition, which is not a component of the cost of purchasing existing facilities. Although existing facilities have fixed prices that are inclusive of land, the majority of new build projects have realized a retirement of debt. Today, the average cost of a new build hotel (for example, a Hilton Garden Inn with 120 rooms) averages $125,000–150,000 dollars per key, whereas the purchase of an existing hotel, such as a twenty-five-year-old Radisson Hotel, may be as low as $50,000–75,000 per key, with an estimated $20,000–$30,000-per-key renovation plan. The difference in cost is a function of time frame: renovating an existing hotel takes twelve to fourteen months, while a start-to-finish new construction project can take eighteen to thirty-six months, with entitlements, or governmental approvals, included in the timeline. The shorter turnaround time for renovation means investors get their return on investment sooner, because the ongoing operations of the hotel keep cash flow coming in, whereas there is zero cash flow until opening in the case of a new construction project.

Investment Practices During the Hotel Boom

Many investors and lending institutions were eager to associate themselves with the lodging industry in the boom times. The flourishing economy and expanding hospitality industry motivated practically everyone, it seemed, to jump onto the growth bandwagon. Lending institutions not only granted loans, but also bought into hotels as part owners in order to share in the industry's profits. As the trend continued, some institutions so eagerly craved a share of the lodging industry's profits that they relaxed their standards for lending. In their excitement about possible growth, they took risks that they probably would not have taken if lodging had not been prospering so much.

Investors React to Economy's Slowdown

As a result, the industry growth went too far too quickly, and investors who had jumped in to share the profits instead found themselves sharing unexpected loses. Excessive supply diluted the market. Investors, lending institutions, and lodging businesses bore the burden of an overbuilt industry and reckless investment. Not only were investors and lending institutions stuck with the unprofitable hotels they had bought into, they were swamped with foreclosed hotels that had been unable to make good on their loans. When hotel investors suddenly wanted out of the hotel business, they could find few other investors to buy their failed or unprofitable properties. Hundreds of hotel properties were auctioned off in the early 1990s by the federally appointed savings and loan cleanup agency known as the Resolution Trust Corporation. Some investors and lending institutions held onto failing properties and hired management companies to keep them open, hoping to recover some of their money. Others, trying to distance themselves from lodging, sold their hotels for whatever prices they could get and wrote off the losses.

A Day in the Life of...

A MARKET ANALYST

The business of hospitality is just that—a business—with all of the financial considerations and property evaluations that come with running an enterprise. It is for this reason that the job of market analyst is so important.

A market analyst is used any time a hotel or restaurant is involved with such transactions as buying, selling, developing, financing, or refinancing. A thorough analysis of the property's condition can determine its potential revenue as well as its expenses and market value.

The following four-phase process is typically employed by the market analyst:[1]

1. *Defining the objectives.* Working with the property manager, the market analyst outlines the task at hand by compiling information on the property. This may include the location of the property and the types of facilities it offers, as well as historical financial details including debt, equity, and operating results and trends. In addition, the market analyst must determine the purpose of the study.

Continues...

Continued...

2. *Collecting data.* Using a data collection checklist to ensure that important information is not overlooked, the market analyst begins compiling data from such references as the property owner, previous market research, competitive analysis, in-house documents, and other available data sources.
3. *Analyzing data.* Using the data collected, along with sophisticated computer analysis programs, the market analyst begins to formulate conclusions. Software programs such as the Fixed and Variable Income and Expense Forecasting Model predict a hotel's net income before debt service by identifying which revenues or expenses are fixed and which are variable. Other programs, like Room Night Analysis, measure hotel demand in a certain area over a period of time to forecast the hotel's probable occupancy percentage. Both types of programs allow the market analyst to manipulate data and simulate actual market conditions. The final product will usually include a cash-on-cash return percentage and an IRR (internal rate of return) on the initial investment in the range of 16–20 percent.
4. *Making conclusions.* Finally, the market analyst formulates final conclusions. These conclusions can include, but are not limited to, such things as local economic and demographic conditions, projected operating expenses, trends in lodging demand, and suitability of improvements and amenities. In this step, the analyst presents pros and cons of the investment scenario considered.

Remember, a market analyst is only as good as the data he or she collects. In fact, accurate data collection is the most important component of this four-phase process.

---

[1] Stephen Rushmore, *The Computerized Income Approach to Hotel—Motel Market Studies and Valuations* (Chicago: Appraisal Institute, 1990), xii–xiii.

Courtesy of Photodisc

Effects on Investment of the 1990s Recession

The economic climate of the early 1990s had a significant impact on the availability of hotel financing from credit companies, savings and loans, commercial banks, insurance companies, and pension funds. Where the basis for lending in the 1980s had been real estate value, in the 1990s it became cash flow. Reputable brand names and unblemished management credentials became necessary to make deals work. Some municipalities, trying to encourage economic development, were forced to tax the industry to raise capital to support convention center and hotel development. In the face of these problems, the financial plans of most firms were directed at solidifying their niche in the market. Where internal funds were limited, most financial plans reflected strategic alliances or joint ventures designed to gain market share.[1]

During this tight period, hotel companies and developers found creative ways of financing their hotels. Some of these included **securitization**, which is a process of issuing bonds to finance or refinance a loan; leasing land instead of buying it; and obtaining loans through the Small Business Administration, an independent federal agency committed to supporting small businesses. Those investors able to obtain hotel acquisition financing were finding the United States a buyer's market as financial institutions sold off foreclosed hotels to reduce the number of hotels in their investment portfolios. The softening U.S. lodging market saw an influx of foreign investment from Asia, Europe, Canada and the Middle East geared towards acquisition and repositioning of hotels.

Hotel Industry Investment Today Economic recovery soon followed the turbulent times of the late 1990s. Stabilization in the hotel and lodging sector occurred in the latter portion of 2005. Strong consumer confidence afforded lodging industry operators the opportunity to reinvest deferred maintenance dollars into their hotels while raising room rates in response to increased customer demand. Improved financial performance spurred values in both the real estate and cash flow calculations of hotel properties. As a result, many operators were able to refinance their debt and capture significant equity from their original investments at the top of the valuation curve. However, the influx of capital into the marketplace soon began to overinflate the values of lodging properties, thus beginning the next cycle of overvalued assets. In 2007, the hospitality industry was still going strong, with solid demand and consumer confidence. However, the development pipeline had new supply and expanded inventory coming on line, coupled with diversification in brand names. The increased supply may have an adverse affect on the industry overall. The effects of the overvalued assets and increased supply were not directly known since the onset of the sever economic downturn in 2008.

In 2008, the American economy suffered a dramatic contraction in value. The government had to bail out many major financial institutions, the marketplace froze credit availability, and housing values plummeted. The majority of hotel stocks lost over 50 percent in value, while the airline industry implemented fuel surcharges, luggage tariffs, additional fees for meals and beverages on flights, and significant fare increases.

Difficult economic conditions impact the hospitality industry unfavorably because when discretionary income evaporates, consumers travel less and spend less money on vacations. This trickle-down effect causes hotels, airlines, travel companies, and theme parks to lay off workers as a result of declining revenues. Declining employment and rising costs of goods and services drive inflation upward. Inflationary growth constricts economic **expansion**, causing companies to operate leanly until economic recovery occurs.

With the volatility of the lodging sector and tightening lending practices, **management contracts** have become increasingly popular, because lending institutions require them as a condition of financing. Lending institutions expect management companies to provide some equity to help finance these new hotels. Another trend is toward limited-service properties, which fare better than other types of hotels and motels when money is tight. And, just as foreign investors turn toward the United States when the hotel market is down, U.S. companies turn toward investments in Hotel projects overseas. In the future, more multinational strategic alliances in the hospitality industry may be seen.

Renovation Financing Options

The lack of available financing has led to an upsurge in hotel renovations. Many owners have decided that they can earn a fair return by reinvesting operating income in their hotels, because the renovated properties will increase in value.[2] In response to an oversupplied marketplace, hotel owners and operators renovate to recapture lost market share or reposition to reach a new group of clients. The ITT Sheraton Corporation spent $47 million to transform the Sheraton City Squire in New York from a hotel whose main clientele was leisure and tour groups to a hotel that now attracts corporate business travelers. The renovated 650-room property, now called the Sheraton Manhattan, reopened in February, 1992.[3]

Today, the Sheraton Manhattan charges between $350–$500 for a one night stay and a meal in the restaurant may run as high as $48 per person for dinner.

At this point, you should see that the choice to pursue new development rather than focusing on acquisition and repositioning requires consideration of many factors. Rising building and construction costs, in concert with greater code and regulatory requirements (such as accessibility, life safety, and fire sprinklers), must be taken into account when deciding to invest in the lodging industry. In some instances renovations are unavoidable, as in the cases of those hotels in southern Florida, Kauai, Hawaii, and New Orleans, Louisiana, which were damaged by devastating hurricanes.

Increased interest in environmental issues, and sustainable construction and development expectations that hazardous construction materials found in older buildings should be removed, add to the cost of renovating. Asbestos insulating materials and lead pipes head the list of hazardous substances. Looking for ways to reduce energy costs and waste, some hotels are replacing outdated boilers and furnaces, installing water conservation devices, and using recyclable products wherever possible.

The Renaissance Vinoy Resort's renovations brought it into compliance with safety regulations while preserving its original ambiance.

Photo courtesy of Renaissance Vinoy Resort

Development and Preopening Costs

Examining the types of expenses incurred during the development process helps explain the cash outlays involved in development. (Of course, these costs will vary according to the type of lodging facility planned.) In addition to the actual cost of acquiring land and constructing the facility, money must be set aside for **debt service** (interest on loans) due diligence, legal fees, brokerage commisions, permitting, pre-design and architectural fees, code requirements, procurement of long–lead-time items, and preopening expenses.

Preopening expenses occur during the construction of the property, when key personnel are employed to plan the hotel's operation and an advertising and/or public relations firm is enlisted. The preopening team needs to plan for the parties and events that make up the opening ceremonies, and hire and train personnel for each of the hotel's departments. Those employees will also need office supplies and equipment, such as fax machines, photocopiers, and computers.

These costs, plus the costs of furnishing and decorating the hotel, landscaping the grounds, and stocking up on supplies like irons, ironing boards, coffee makers, TVs, microwaves, ice buckets, stationery, luggage carts, cleaning supplies, linens, uniforms, and glassware, may add up to 50 to 75 percent of the actual construction costs.

Operating Costs

In addition to the expenses just listed, the working capital needed to pay salaries and operate the property before it begins to turn a profit makes developing a hotel a considerable investment from its inception. Hotels need a constant supply of working capital beyond the development phase. Often the

Industry Insights

ENVIRONMENT

The hotel industry is no different from any other inasmuch as the concern for global warming is evident. Buildings can and will have an impact on climate change.

In the lifetime of an average building, the construction phase is not when most energy is consumed. Rather, this occurs when the building is in use and energy is used for heating, cooling, lighting, cooking, ventilation, and so on. Typically, more than 80 percent of the total energy consumption takes place during the use of a building, and less than 20 percent during its construction.

Recognizing this, hotels are making greater use of existing technologies like thermal insulation, solar shading, and more efficient lighting and electrical appliances, and are implementing educational and awareness campaigns. To achieve improved energy efficiency in buildings, you do not always need to use expensive high-tech solutions. Simple solutions exist, such as smart design, flexible energy solutions, and providing appropriate information to the building users. Specific examples of simple solutions are sun shading and natural ventilation, improved insulation of the building envelope, use of recycled building materials, and smart adoption of the size and form of the building to its intended use.

A key element in successful environmental programming in hotel development is the inclusion of building-sector stakeholders, including investors, architects, property developers, construction companies, tenants, etc. They all need to understand and support such policies in order for the policies to function effectively.

In developed countries, the main challenge will be to achieve emission reduction among existing buildings. The main way to do this is to reduce the use of energy. In other parts of the world, especially places like China, where almost 2 billion square meters of new building space are added every year, the challenge is to leapfrog directly to more energy-efficient building solutions.[1]

Environmental awareness is not limited to construction and building design. The typical hotel operation offers reuse of bath linens and bed sheets as an optional daily service based on guests' desire to participate in sustainability efforts.

Hotels also have undergone efforts to convert guest rooms to nonsmoking rooms. The thought behind this is simple: Take a smoking room and designate it as a nonsmoking room. The act itself, however, is not so simple. Converting a smoking room into a nonsmoking room can cost upwards of six hundred dollars.[2] The conversion involves such things as shampooing carpets, replacing linens, cleaning drapes, and even painting walls and ceilings.

In spite of the costs, many hotels have jumped on the nonsmoking bandwagon and made the switch. Traditionally, hoteliers set aside the majority of rooms for smokers. Twenty-six percent of all U.S. adults still smoke, and international travelers, who comprise 10 percent of all U.S. hotel guests, smoke even more than Americans. Even so, the conversions have primarily been the result of customer pressure. By 1993, Marriott had converted 60 percent of its rooms to nonsmoking—a 22 percent increase from just three years earlier. By September 2006, all of its hotels in the United States and Canada were smoke free. And Hilton, from 1987 to 1993, increased its nonsmoking rooms by 10 percent, making 50 percent of its rooms nonsmoking. Now, all of its rooms are smoke free. This trend is likely to continue as smokers—and hoteliers—kick the smoking habit.

---

1 www.unepsbci.org

2 Julie Schmit, "Hotels Kick the Habit," *USA Today*, April 13, 1993, E1.

most significant expenses of hotel operation are wages, salaries, and employee benefits. Hotel operators must also be ready to pay maintenance costs of buildings, utilities, insurance, interest on debt, taxes, and the cost of supplies such as linens, cleaning and office supplies, uniforms, food and beverage inventory, kitchen equipment and extra lamps and furniture. Other expenses include advertising and marketing, plus costs of running any additional services such as recreational facilities and restaurants.

Controlling Costs

Throughout the development of any lodging facility, owners and management teams should be aware of ways to eliminate unnecessary costs. Even more important, managers and designers must plan for cost controls once a property is open. Two major areas for cutting costs are (1) efficient engineering systems and (2) efficient use of space and technology, with labor considerations and workforce productivity taken into account.

Energy Efficiency

Given the current rise in energy costs, energy efficiency is getting a heightened level of attention. Whether for new construction or current operations, hotel and lodging energy costs are a critical operational expense line item. Green and sustainable construction, along with high initial investment costs in new energy-efficient equipment, contribute to ever-increasing new build construction costs. Engineering innovation is now taking hold of every aspect of hotel design. Fixtures, lighting, plumbing, and major boiler units, along with heating and cooling systems, incorporate energy-efficient specifications. Modern digital controls, which are standard features of the latest technology found in energy systems, conserve power and drive down energy costs.

Green hotels and sustainable development are the buzzwords in today's development circles. Standards of green and sustainable construction follow a mutually accepted protocol known as Leadership in Energy and Environmental Design (LEED). LEED is the nationally accepted green building rating system of the U.S. Green Building Council. There are two components of green building—hotel or otherwise. One is the physical aspects of the building and site, such as water savings, energy efficiency, and materials selection, and the other is indoor environmental quality.[4]

Today, movements towards sustaninable, energy-efficient engineering systems are at the forefront of new hotel construction and development. Other principles found in LEED-certified projects are solar energy, reusable water, reduction of emissions, fluorescent lighting, use of organic products and detergents, and clever use of green space.[5]

Security and Loss Prevention

Theft of any kind significantly raises the cost of operating a hotel property. When it affects guests, theft can irrevocably damage a hotel's reputation.

When it affects the hotel, theft adds to the cost of doing business. Thus hotel security takes several forms, regardless of the size of the facility or the security staff.

If planned correctly, a hotel should have a built-in security system, especially in the **back of the house**. Hotel design should allow for a tightly controlled flow of supplies from the receiving area to the storage area to the end user's area. This may be accomplished with electronic key access and video surveillance technology. In addition, employee training should provide awareness of the effects of loss.

Another area of security is safety and protection. Guest protection programs can range from brochures mentioning the availability of safe-deposit boxes to verbal warnings about not opening doors to strangers. Preventative measures may include providing well-lit parking lots and corridors, locking entrance doors at a certain time, and screening visitors.

Screening visitors does not require armed guards to check guests' identification at each entrance. The CLS Video Guardian from Computerized Lodging Systems Inc. helps increase guest safety. This videophone system enables a guest to screen visitors—even in the dark—before opening the door. In addition, the system can automatically record a digital snapshot of visitors to the room while the guest is away from the room or sleeping.

Design of the New Hotel

Once financing for construction has been obtained and all involved parties have committed to the project, construction planning begins. Using the information obtained in the feasibility study and the decisions made about the appropriate size and type of facility for the chosen site, architects devise a pre-design plan with the principals of the project to determine scope and concept understanding of the desired end product for the hotel. The pre-design plan involves careful review of expected positioning in the marketplace. A key element to consider is the identification with a brand or naming convention of the property.

Based upon the pre-design dialogue, more detailed planning and design activities take place. They include the work of interior designers, who specify every aspect of the hotel's design including the locations of guest rooms, fabric selection, furniture finishes, carpet and wall selections, bathroom layout, design and finishes, lighting design, artwork, uniform styles, telecommunication systems, restaurant and bar service concepts and decor, and the number of electrical outlets in each meeting room. Owners and managers must be involved in this planning process because they are most familiar with guests' needs, and because they will be the ones charged with making the facility profitable once it opens. Owners and designer/architectual teams must work cohesively and understand each other's areas of expertise and vision for the project. Owners may know the targeted customer audience, but the designers and architects know how to create the feel and experience desired.

The hotel's design must satisfy two essential needs simultaneously: providing guests with a comfortable, safe environment in which they can enjoy their stay, and allowing hotel staff to keep the hotel operating efficiently so it will achieve the expected return on investment for the owner(s).

Basic Lodging Design

Although each type of lodging facility has particular characteristics designed to meet the needs of its guests, most lodging properties share a basic structure. One common element is the division between the front and the back of the house. The **front of the house** comprises all the areas the guests will contact, including the lobby, corridors, elevators, guest rooms, restaurants and bars, meeting rooms, and restrooms. The other areas of the property are considered the back of the house. These are the support areas. The duality of hotel design reflects the complex relationship between the two areas. Depending on the available space, the back of the house is typically the first area where changes affecting budgets occur. Careful consideration must be given to the importance of back-of-the-house workspace and employee production environments. The front of the house is completely dependent upon the smooth operation of the back of the house, yet the guest should never be aware of the action "behind the scenes." Up front, the atmosphere should be calm, collected, and efficient, satisfying guests' every desire. The back of the house should be arranged to achieve maximum efficiency from each employee without allowing the guest to feel the drive for efficiency.The following sections discuss other elements of basic lodging design for the front and back of the house.

Front of the House

Because the front of the house is the area all guests see, it must be designed to sell the hotel to potential customers. The designers' tools include space, shape, texture, color, and light—elements that affect guests' impressions of a particular area. Light, especially, can make these areas look inviting, yet relaxed. Each area must be designed for the convenience and comfort of the guest.

Because the lobby is the first and last part of the hotel a guest sees, it plays an important role in the design of a hotel. As it is where the initial impression and sense of arrival is created, the lobby is the hotel showcase, featuring fine art, elegant finishes, and comfortable furnishings. The lobby must also be functional. The registration area must be immediately apparent to incoming guests and should provide enough room to serve a number of guests checking in and out at the same time. The lobby also serves as the gathering place for guests coming and going or meeting others.

"The architecture of the lobby may grab their initial interest and set the tone for the quality and feel of the overall property, but it's the guest room that keeps them coming back," according to a former design director and vice president for Sheraton, Ramada, Inter-Continental, and Holiday Inns.[6] It is upon this theory that most guest rooms are designed, making them the focus of a hotel's design.

Throughout the industry, designers have found a variety of ways to arrange traditional bed and bath facilities to serve a wide range of guests. Plans range from the standard double-double (two double beds) to luxurious suites set up to resemble apartments. Recent developments in room design include upgraded pillow-top mattresses as standard features, higher–thread count bed linens, triple-sheeted beds, in-room entertainment and wireless technology options, rainmaker shower heads, and brand-name retail amenity products such as shampoo, soap, and conditioner. Furniture offerings include built-in microwaves and refrigerator units, flat-panel TV sets, and ergonomic workstations.

Other areas in the front of the house must be just as well planned. One indication of the quality of hotel restaurant planning is the popularity of the restaurant with customers outside the hotel. Today, many chain-operated restaurants choose to build next to hotels in order to compete for hotel guests' business. For this reason, restaurant and bar services in hotel properties need to present a compelling story in order to compete with external services. National branding and leasing options exist for lodging operators; this allows them to liven up hotel projects by featuring name-brand chefs and chain-operated tenants within the property. Hotel meeting facilities must also be carefully designed to meet conventioneers' needs for audiovisual equipment, large exhibition spaces, and a variety of meeting rooms with privacy capability and sound separation. Flexibility in space use is critical in this area, as it maximizes simultaneous event scheduling.

Guest Room Floor Plans

When planning a hotel, architects are charged with the task of designing an original facility with the maximum possible guest room (revenue-producing) area. Careful planning over time has yielded various workable configurations, some more efficient than others. These configurations fall into two main categories: slab plans and tower plans.

Slab plans are primarily horizontal, with single- or double-loaded corridors that may be stacked one upon another or arranged in a variety of patterns to create L shapes and courtyards. In a slab layout, architects must consider where to place the elevators, fire stairs, and service areas for each floor. In tower plans, the layout is vertically oriented, with guest rooms and corridors surrounding a central core. The main variable is the tower's shape, which may be either rectangular, circular, or triangular. Within the core, the elevators, storage area, and stairway must be organized. The architects must also determine how to make the corridor reach corner rooms and how many guest rooms will surround the core on each floor. Careful planning is necessary in order to have efficient use of space and optimize engineering systems to provide guest comfort in terms of heating, cooling, and ventilation requirements.

Back of the House

Although invisible to the guest, the back of the house is an important part of the hotel's structure. Efficiency and control are the main objectives for the back of the house. Architects must plan for the smooth operation of the hotel without revealing its workings to the guest. This planning must allow for the flow of supplies from the receiving area to storage areas, and eventually to their respective end users, whether they be guests or employees. The plan must also enable employees to enter and exit the building, as well as to perform their work out of sight of hotel guests.

Among the departments in the back of the house is housekeeping, which requires storage areas on each floor for linens and cleaning carts. In addition, the chief housekeeper needs an office that contains a larger storage area for excess supplies, including extra lamps and small furnishings . Unless all laundry is sent to a laundry service, the hotel will need areas for laundering linens and towels. In larger hotels, space may be designed for additional cleaning equipment, including dry cleaning equipment and pressing machines. One critical item often overlooked in the back-of-the-house design is the employee rest and meal break area. Changing demands in the marketplace and workforce challenges now require hotel operators to maximize employee comfort in order to attract and retain quality workers.

Regardless of size, all lodging properties must also have areas designed for engineering. This is where the heating and cooling systems and other environmental controls are located. This area also contains storage space for spare parts and equipment.

Accomodation must be made in the back-of-the-house design for systems and technological equipment; phone towers, property mangement systems, Internet connectivity, office space, and security surveillance equipment. Properties that offer food and beverage services need the additional storage areas and kitchens found in any free-standing restaurant or bar. (More about restaurants appears in Chapters 6, 7, and 8.)

Accessibility

Most of us assume that a chosen hotel will be accessible to all users. The facility must be accessible both in terms of its location and its design.

Accessibility Design

Many design considerations for persons who are physically challenged are just extensions of good design principles that apply to the needs of all guests. These needs include security, independence, safety, and comfort. All guests want to feel a sense of security when staying in a hotel, fostered by measures like guest-room lock systems. Hoteliers need to be sensitive to the needs of all guests because they will ultimately stay where they feel most secure.

Guests also want to feel independent. Simple amenities like easy-to-turn door handles and lowered light switches may help youngsters and guests with limited mobility operate more independently.

Safety is essential for both guests and employees. Providing a barrier-free environment, nonslip bathing facilities, fire safety equipment, seamless

Industry Insights

TECHNOLOGY

Rating Hotels for Accessibility

For the physically challenged guest, a hotel's accessibility is a key factor in his or her decision whether or not to return to a given property. The Americans with Disabilities Act of 1990 requires public institutions such as hotels to make accommodations for people with disabilities. Most hotels now satisfy minimum requirements for features such as grab bars in bathtubs and Braille plates on hotel elevator panels.[1] Thorough accessibility includes such items as curb cuts, doors that swing out instead of in, wide doors and hallways, and furniture and amenities within reach of a person confined to a wheelchair; wide parking stalls; lowered front desks for check-in, roll-in showers in the bathroom; and specialized TTY phones for deaf and hard-of-hearing guests. Guests with disabilities must be able to experience the essence of the property. This means they should be able to use the pool, exercise room, bar, and meeting rooms, and have the opportunity to stay in and around most parts of the hotel like any other guest.

According to one frequent guest, the Omni International Crowne Plaza and Stouffer's hotel chains rank highly in terms of accessibility. "They've done an outstanding job," says David Burdett, "The doors are wide and the hallway is big enough to turn a wheelchair around in... There's a king-size bed with room to roll a chair between it and the wall."[2]

---

[1] Brooke Stauffer, "Traveler Criticizes Hotels' Accessibility," *USA Today*, April 13, 1993, 9F.

[2] Ibid.

sidewalk-to-curb entry points, and a well-maintained property aid in the safety of all persons in the hotel. Some guests will need additional help in dealing with emergencies, especially in large or multistory facilities. Hotel plans should take into account what to do in an emergency, whether natural or constructed.

Finally, all guests expect to be comfortable. "Comfort" is really a combination of design elements and hospitality services, and care must be taken to ensure that all guests are extended such comforts equally. Comfort considerations might include easy-to-reach adjustable room thermostats (placed low on walls), wheelchair-accessible swimming pools and spas, remote-controlled televisions, wireless Internet connectivity, remotely controlled window blinds, voice-recognition phone and messaging products, and multimedia connectivity to personal operating systems.

The Americans with Disabilities Act of 1990

America's first federal accessibility legislation was the Architectural Barriers Act of 1968. It mandated that all buildings constructed, altered, or financed by the federal government after 1969 be accessible and usable by persons with physical disabilities.[7] In 1973, Congress established by statute the Architectural and Transportation Barriers Compliance Board to develop and enforce

Hotels are required to provide reasonable accessibility and safety to guests with disabilities, as was done in this bathroom.

Photo by Michael Dzaman

accessibility standards, which took effect in 1982.[8] But this legislation had little impact on the hospitality industry, since it affected only those buildings constructed or financed through the federal government.

More comprehensive legislation, the Americans with Disabilities Act of 1990, was signed into law on July 26, 1990, by President George H.W. Bush. A prominent hospitality publication called the act "the most sweeping piece of legislation since the... Civil Rights Act of 1964, which forbids discrimination on the basis of race, sex or national origin." The ADA combines the Civil Rights Act and the Rehabilitation Act of 1973 to extend equal employment opportunities to qualified persons with disabilities and to provide for equal access to public accommodations.[9]

Who are "persons with disabilities"? ADA legislation defines this group as persons who have physical or mental impairments that substantially limit one or more of their major life activities, have records of such impairments, or are regarded as having such impairments. Although the estimate cited in the ADA legislation was 51.2 million Americans with disabilities, experts seem to agree that the broad definition probably encompasses a greater number of Americans than originally estimated.

Regardless of the actual figures, the ADA has had broad implications for the lodging industry. All public facilities were required to comply with this legislation by January 26, 1992. This compliance meant public facilities had to make reasonable modifications in policies, practices, and procedures unless those modifications would fundamentally alter the nature of the services provided to the public. For example, adding brighter lights to accommodate the needs of persons with vision impairments would be a reasonable accommodation in a guest room. Yet this change would not be reasonable in a hotel's nightclub, where dim lighting is generally considered an integral part of the atmosphere. Compliance also meant making reasonable modifications to facility designs and equipment for both guests and employees. The ADA is currently under modification and is expected to be enhanced in 2007 with coverage expanded to include almost all areas of the hotel facility. (Other implications of the ADA, including modifications to employment practices, are discussed in the next chapter.)

Ambiance

The most elusive element of lodging design is **ambiance**—the complete impression and personality that a lodging facility presents to its guests. When planning a hotel or its renovation, designers create an image that carries out the initial conceptualization. From the choice of building materials to the color of the carpeting or tile, this image becomes the theme of the entire property. Whether a tropical paradise, historic country inn, or futuristic convention center, the theme should relate to the hotel's target market. Today, a key element of ambiance that is being incorporated into hotel design is sensory perception. Sensory perception deals with the sights, sounds, and smells of the customer experience. Smell is being introduced in the form of both artificial and natural aromas. Vanilla scents may be introduced into a lobby for sense-of-arrival impact, or freshly baked cookies may be placed at the front desk and given to guests at check-in. "Natural-smelling" landscape and floral treatments may

be strategically placed in high guest traffic areas. Mood-altering music is carefully coordinated with the target audience's level of sophistication to enhance the sound-generated ambiance of the hotel while deepening the conceptual feel of the property in public areas.

Architecture and interior design play important roles in creating a guest's perception of a particular facility. Ambiance tells guests whether they are in an economy or luxury property; it makes them feel at home or uncomfortable in new surroundings; and it can determine whether a guest returns to the property or stays somewhere else. The importance of ambiance can be seen in the increase in renovations and in the trend toward more residential-style furnishings in both new and renovated properties.

Summary

- Hotel development is a five-step process: conceptualization, feasibility analysis, commitment, design and construction, and management/ operation.
- Location is a key factor in a hotel's success, helping to determine its target markets, facilities, services, and probability of success.
- Feasibility studies are essential to determining the economic potential of a project. Studying the market area and sources of demand helps developers decide what type of facility to build, what types of amenities and services to offer, and whether or not the investment can provide a desirable return.
- The decrease in money available through traditional lending institutions in the early 1990s has led to creative financing efforts on the part of developers. An upsurge in hotel renovation to increase market share, followed by a strong lodging market performance, have been the results.
- Engineers control operating costs by installing the latest in energy conservation features. Sustainable development is catching on and emerging as a must-have in future new build projects.
- Cost control in a hotel includes efficient labor productivity, back-of-the-house design, theft prevention, and other security measures.
- All hotels share a basic design pattern. The pattern is divided into two distinct areas—the front of the house and the back of the house.
- The front of the house includes all of the areas a guest sees while staying in a hotel, and should create an appealing ambiance that signifies the intended feel and personality of the project.
- The back of the house includes all of the areas behind the scenes. These areas must be planned to maximize the efficiency and contentment of hotel employees.
- Accessibility is a key factor in a hotel's design. Title III of the Americans with Disabilities Act of 1990 requires the lodging industry to ensure that physically challenged guests have equal access to lodging and hospitality services. This statute has had a significant cost impact on new construction estimates.

ENDNOTES

[1] Center for Hospitality Research and Service and Michael D. Olsen, "Trends," *Hotel & Motel Management* (February 4, 1991): 41.
[2] Chris Baum and Sally Wolchuk, "Problem: Losing Market Share? Solution: Renovate," *Hotels* (November 1992): 104.
[3] Baum and Wolchuk, 104.
[4] Ibid., 95.
[5] *The Wall Street Journal Smart Money Magazine*. September 2007, 109.
[6] Regina Baraban, "Designing Women," *Lodging Hospitality* (July 1991): 33.
[7] Vernon Mays, "P/A Inquiry: Inside The Hotel Guest Room," *Progressive Architecture* (June 1988): 111.
[8] U.S. Department of Justice, Civil Rights Division, Americans with Disabilities Act Handbook (Washington, D.C.: U.S. Government Printing Office, 1992), Appendix.
[9] Robert H, Woods and Raphael R. Kavanaugh, "Here Comes the ADA—Are You Ready? (Part I), *Cornell Hotel and Restaurant Association Quarterly* (February 1992): 25.

CHECK YOUR KNOWLEDGE

1. What are the steps of hotel development?
2. What role does location play in a hotel's development?
3. What role does return on investment play in the location decision?
4. Why should developers commission a feasibility study before building a hotel?
5. Why has hotel financing become scarce, and how are hotel companies dealing with this problem?
6. What special design considerations are required for front-of-the-house and back-of-the-house areas?

APPLY YOUR SKILLS

Using the sample statement of income in Table 4.2, determine L'Grand's profit and loss margin in the following situations.

1. If there was no increase in revenue but the annual operating expenses increased by 10 percent, what would be the net income or loss before taxes?
2. In its second year L'Grand Hotel's net revenue and operating expenses differed from the previous year's in these items: room sales increased 4 percent, utilities were 25 percent higher, food and beverage costs were 3 percent lower, and maintenance was 12 percent higher. What were L'Grand's net revenue and total operating expenses for its second year of operation? What was the net income or loss?
3. What percent of L'Grand's net revenue comes from room sales? From food and beverage sales? From other departments?

WHAT DO YOU THINK?

1. If you could build a hotel anywhere in the world, where would you build it? What would be the particular limitations of that site?
2. Should a feasibility report be expanded to include an environmental impact study? Support your answer.

TABLE 4.2 Sample Statement of Income

L'Grand *Hotel Statement of Income* *for the Period Ending December 31, 20XX*	
NET REVENUE	
Room Sales	$850,000
Food and Beverage	$600,000
Other Departments	$50,000
Total Revenue	$1,500,000
OPERATING EXPENSES (Divisional and Overhead Expenses)	
Rooms	$170,000
Food and Beverage	$300,000
Salaries and Benefits	$90,000
Supplies	$30,000
Laundry	$40,000
Other	$90,000
Utilities	$70,000
Maintenance	$40,000
Total Operating Expenses	$830,000
FIXED CHARGES	
Property Taxes	$44,000
Insurance	$36,000
Interest Expense	$150,000
Depreciation	$100,000
Total Fixed Charges	$330,000
TOTAL EXPENSES	$1,160,000
NET INCOME BEFORE TAXES	$340,000

3. The history of the lodging industry seems to imply a cyclical pattern. If this theory is true, what types of changes would you expect in hotel development in the next twenty years? In hotel financing?
4. How can sustainable practices be used to create a competitive advantage in the market?

CASE STUDY

Angelica and Tomas Garcia recently purchased real estate near a popular seashore. Despite public concerns that the area is overdeveloped and that developers are destroying the coastline, the Garcias plan to build an all-suite resort hotel.A preliminary feasibility analysis has determined that there is sufficient demand to justify building the hotel at this location if the facility can attract some of its competitors' guests. The two major competitors focus on attracting conventions to large, modern facilities. One features a world-renowned chef to attract banquets, while the other has an internationally recognized management company and brand name.

1. What types of services could the Garcias offer to attract their competitors' convention guests?
2. What types of design considerations could appease the local environmental concerns?
3. What other studies might the Garcias commission before seeking financing?

ch5

Hotel Management and Operations

OVERVIEW

The management and operation of a hotel or resort can be a monumental undertaking. Hundreds of employees may work for a particular facility in jobs requiring all levels of skill and knowledge. In this chapter you will look at the major departments within the typical hospitality operation and their basic functions. You will examine how these departments are affected by human resources issues, including personnel needs, unions, immigration issues, and legal concerns regarding the workforce. You will also learn about financial issues regarding hotel operations—finding the break-even point, managing revenue generation activities, food and beverage contributions, minor operating departments' profit contribution, and using ratings and referrals to enhance profitability.

OBJECTIVES

When you have completed this chapter, you should be able to:

1 **Describe the basic organizational structure of a hotel or resort operation, including the types of positions available and the responsibilities of each.**

2 **Describe ways the hotel industry can reduce its turnover rate and build employee morale.**

3 **Identify major pieces of equal opportunity legislation and analyze their effect on hotel management and employees.**

4 **Understand the scope and importance of revenue management processes and their contribution to profit. Analyze strategies for determining break-even points, other services, and room rates.**

5 **Analyze strategies for producing positive net operating margins.**

KEY TERMS

assistant housekeepers
back-of-the-house
bell captain
bellhops
break-even point
catastrophe plans
chief engineer
collectively bargains
computerized reservation systems (CRSs)
controller
credit manager
electronic voice-mail systems
employee assistance programs (EAPs)
executive housekeeper
floor supervisors
front-desk manager
front-of-the-house
general manager
green card
grievance
human resources manager
illegal aliens
immigrants overall
iPods
job coach
laundry manager
laundry room attendants
overbooking
paymaster
plant manager
property management system
quid pro quo
refugees
return on investment
room attendants
room clerk
room rack
room service manager
room service operators
rooms division manager
servers
sexual harassment
sexually offensive or hostile work environment
stipend
total yearly expenses
turnover rate
undocumented workers
wake-up call
wireless Internet
yield management

Basic Management Structure

Hotels and resorts, regardless of size, are organized to provide lodging and related services to guests. All share some organizational similarities as they strive to fulfill this mission. In Chapter 4 you were introduced to the terms **front-of-the-house** and **back-of-the-house** as they relate to the design and layout of a hotel or resort facility. These same terms refer to the staff and departments within a lodging establishment. The front-of-the-house staff comprises those individuals or departments who have direct contact with the guests. The back-of-the-house staff are those individuals who operate behind the scenes to make a guest's stay pleasant and safe. (See the hotel organizational chart in Figure 5.1 and a list of typical positions in Table 5.1.)

Administrative Departments

The positions involved in hotel administration are classified as back-of-the-house. These administrative areas include general management, accounting, human resources, and marketing and sales.

General Management

The **general manager** is the chief operating officer of the hotel, with responsibilities in four main areas: (1) relating to guests and employees; (2) overseeing

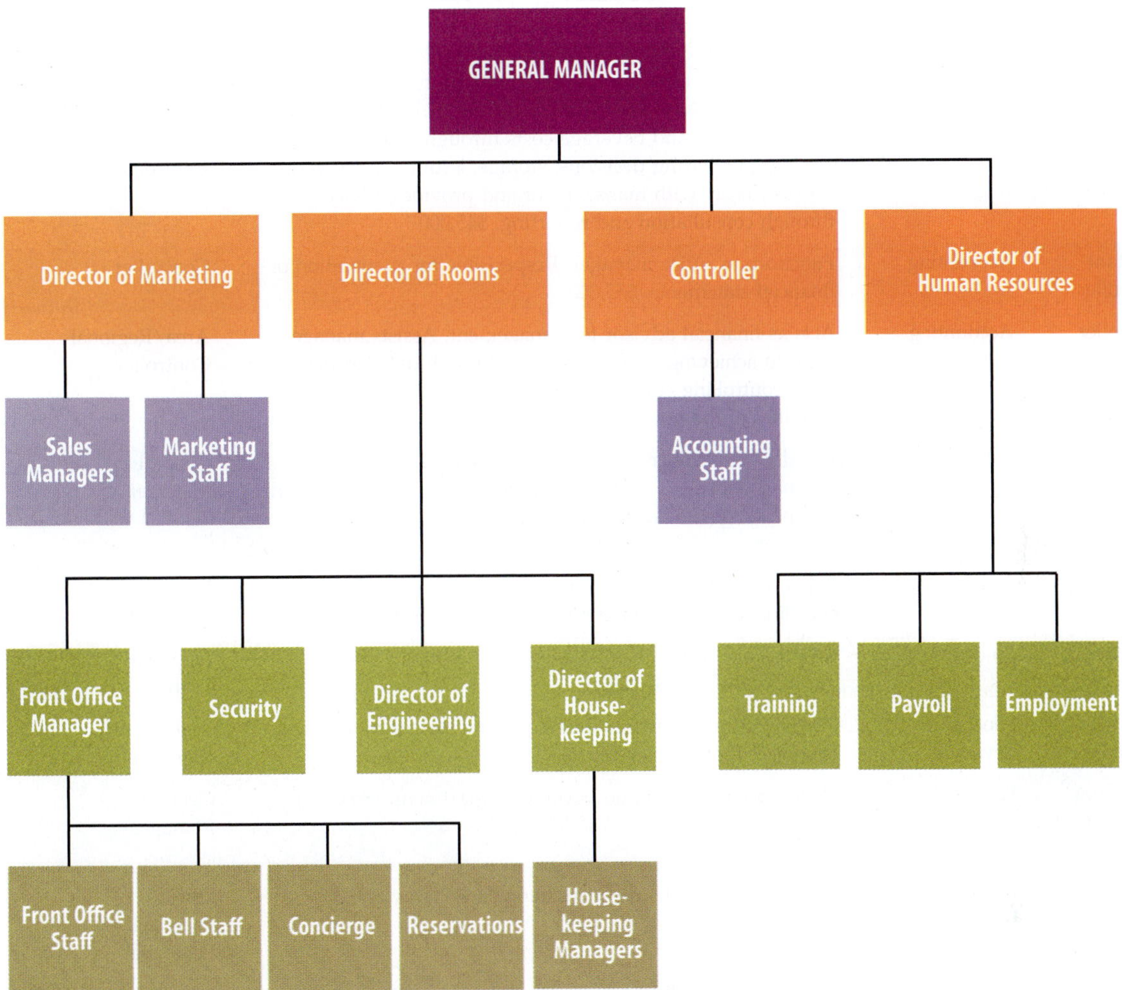

FIGURE 5.1 Sample Organizational Chart for a Limited Service Hotel Property
Source: Guide to College Programs in Hospitality, Tourism and Culinary Arts, 9th Ed. © 2006 by International Council on Hotel, Restaurant and Institutional Education

operations; (3) increasing profitability; and (4) facility maintenance and appearance. The general manager is charged with promoting guest satisfaction. This is sometimes done through direct interaction with guests, but is more frequently accomplished by promoting smooth operations and ongoing training and development of service personnel.

The general manager supervises and organizes all other departments within the hotel and, therefore, must be familiar with the operations of each area. Most general managers have at least three to five years of work experience in various hotel positions, learning at first hand the skills required by and functions of each department. The majority of general managers hold a bachelor's degree in hotel management or a related field. Armed with a thorough knowledge of management principles, they lead through effective delegation of responsibility and emphasize a team approach to problem solving and service.

TABLE 5.1 Key Hotel Management Positions-Typical Salary

Title	*Department*	*Description/Salary*	*Advancement Opportunity*
Food and Beverage Controller	Accounting	Regulates food and beverage costs through menu planning, pricing/purchasing decisions, storage, issuing of dry goods. Works closely with management and provides advice through consultation and reporting. $45,000	Assistant Controller
Assistant Controller	Accounting	Functions as office manager. Responsible for preparation of financial statements. $55,000	Controller
Controller	Accounting	Acts as financial advisor to management. Assists management in achieving profit objectives through detailed planning, controlling costs, and effectively managing assets and liabilities of the hotel. $65,000–85,000	Area/Regional Controller
Director of Operations	Administration	Usually the number-two manager in a hotel. Responsible for the management of all operating departments, such as food and beverage, housekeeping, etc. $65,000	General Manager
General Manager	Administration	Supervises all activities within the hotel. Responsible for the coordination of all departments. $85,000–$150,000	Regional and Corporate
Director of Engineering	Engineering	Responsible for the maintenance of the physical and mechanical plant. $50,000	Regional Team
Steward	Food and Beverage	Purchases and supervises the receipt and storage of food and beverages for the hotel. $45,000	Restaurant Manager
Director of Food and Beverage	Food and Beverage	Oversees entire food and beverage department. $65,000	General Manager
Catering Manager	Food and Beverage	Sells banquets and supervises banquet services. $50,000	Director of Food and Beverage
Convention Services	Food and Beverage	Acts as liaison between meeting planners and the hotel. Responsible for execution of major functions. $45,000	Catering Manager/ Director of Food and Beverage
Front Office Manager	Front Office	Acts as a liaison between the guest and the hotel for reservations, registration, and information. $45,000	Cross-training in other divisions/ Director of Operations
Reservations Manager	Front Office or Marketing	Oversees reservations functions, plans for reservations and yield management and supervises guest check-in and departure transactions. $45,000	Front Office, Manager/Director of Marketing
Director of Human Resources	Administration	Responsible for all employee programs and employment practices, inclusive of regulatory requirements and employment compliance issues. $55,000	General Manager
Housekeeping Manager	Housekeeping	Supervises the work of room attendants and housepersons in assigned areas. $45,000	Director of Housekeeping
Director of Housekeeping	Housekeeping	Supervises all housekeeping personnel. In charge of all renovation and purchase of housekeeping supplies. $55,000	Cross-training in other divisions/ Director of Operations

Continues. . .

TABLE 5.1 *(Continued)*

Title	*Department*	*Description/Salary*	*Advancement Opportunity*
Director of Marketing	Marketing	Oversees all marketing and sales functions, develops marketing and sales plans. $55,000–$60,000	Director of Operations with cross-training in other divisions
Director of Sales	Sales	Sells convention facilities for meetings, banquets and receptions. Sells rooms to volume purchasers such as corporate travel directors of large companies. $50,000	Director of Marketing

Source: Guide to College Programs in Hospitality, Tourism and Culinary Arts, 9th Ed. © 2006 by International Council on Hotel, Restaurant and Institutional Education.

Image copyright Dmitriy Shironosov, 2009. Used under license from Shutterstock.com

A general manager must have good communication skills.

The manager must possess the motivational and communication skills necessary to maintain and enhance employee satisfaction and productivity, which in turn increases guest satisfaction.

Numerous managerial duties are carried out by department heads and other managers who report directly to the general manager. Depending on the size of the property, the **rooms division manager** may supervise front office operations and reservations as well as housekeeping. Large hotels distribute the rooms division manager's responsibilities among an executive assistant manager, who manages the functions that deal directly with front office operations and revenue management; a revenue manager, who oversees the reservations and yield management functions; and an executive housekeeper, who manages the housekeeping department.

In todays typical hotel operating unit the Marketing and Sales functions have separate functions and associated personnel. Many hotel companies have come to the realization that appropriate resources need to be dedicated to both of these disciplines. In a hotel operating unit with both Sales and Marketing functions as separate divisons, the work is typically assigned as follows:

Sales: managing sales personnel, budgeting and forecasting top line revenues, defining sales segmentation assignments and execution of sales related activities, on-going customer relationship strategies, new account acquisition, customer satisfaction, pricing modeling, yield mangement, and group rooms coordination.

Marketing: development of overall marketing plan, creation of hotel brand imaging and market positioning, development of advertising theme and execution of advertising plan, responsible for all print materials and collateral brochures, interfacing with public relations firm(s) and or public relations planning, creation and execution of internal merchandising plan, responsible for community relations and liason for the socially responsible programming.

Graduate Glimpse

JEREMY ASHBY

Executive chef and owner of Azur Restaurant and Patio in Lexington, Kentucky, Jeremy Ashby believes that procuring the freshest ingredients is the way to start every day. When he finds what he needs, he transforms it with the aid of his greatest tools—ideas and the people he works with—to fit into the events of the day. Leveraging his coworkers' strengths and helping them to develop in areas that need improvement are major priorities for him. Each day he strives to set new benchmarks for himself and his staff so they will achieve and grow.

To Ashby, a successful day is one on which he has extended hospitality on many different levels and in various situations. He has discovered that treating his staff with the same level of respect and courtesy he expects them to use with guests is the best way to get them to provide the highest level of service to their clients. Ashby explains, "Complete participation by everyone involved in our company, from the employees to the suppliers, is necessary to create a memorable experience each time we have a customer."

Ashby attributes his success to his education, which helped in building up his confidence and his ability to stay excited and passionate about his chosen profession. After graduating summa cum laude from Johnson & Wales University with an associate's degree, he refined his expertise of culinary arts by pursuing a bachelor's degree in hospitality management at the University of Kentucky, and was inducted into the honorary society Chaine des Rotisseurs. He added, "The quote from Joseph Campbell about 'following your bliss' is crucial in this profession. You must love what you are doing." And he is practicing that—continuing to develop his skills as a chef, owner, and manager of a fine establishment.

Accounting

Hotel accounting functions come under the supervision of the **controller**, or head accountant. The controller manages the accounting department and all the financial dealings of the hotel. She participates in long-term financial planning and projections, capital budgeting, and forecasting. The controller is also accountable for effective control procedures and governance issues related to financial performance.

The accounting department handles accounts payable, accounts receivable, and the payroll. The accounts payable department is responsible for verifying and paying bills incurred for the purchase of materials and services. The accounts receivable department records all money received by the hotel and may oversee credit, billing, and cashiering functions.

Career positions within a hotel's accounting department vary significantly based on the size of the operation. The job of comptroller is a highly specialized one, generally filled by an accountant with a college degree who has qualified as a certified public accountant (CPA). The comptroller needs significant prior experience in both accounting and the hotel industry. Large hotels may also employ a **credit manager**, whose responsibilities include validating and authorizing guest credits and collecting overdue accounts. A **paymaster** may head a large payroll division within a hotel. Under the supervision of these individuals are numerous clerks and cashiers who post sales, issue checks, keep records, and compute salaries and wages. Most of these jobs require some bookkeeping or accounting background, as well as computer literacy. Recent developments in corporate governance require accounting staff to acquire skills in financial reporting and comply with regulatory standards.

Human Resources

All hotels must interview, hire, and train their workforce. Within larger hotels, these activities may be performed by a separate human resources department. This department manages the hotel's employee benefits program and training and development activities. It also monitors compliance with laws that relate to equal opportunity in hiring and promotion. Usually a college-educated **human resources manager** heads the human resources department.

Marketing/Sales

Regardless of size, all hotels market their rooms and services. In the hospitality industry, most employees, regardless of position, are marketers of sorts, since the guest comes into contact with so many different individuals within the organization.

Specific responsibilities of the marketing department within any hotel may include

- sales of hotel rooms and facilities to individuals and groups
- advertising in print and media sources
- managing public relations to maximize the image of the hotel

Larger hotels sometimes hire Human Resource Managers to interview, hire, and train staff.

Courtesy of Photodisc

- establishing contacts with travel agents and tour guides
- managing electronic distribution channels

In chain and franchise properties, marketing functions are fulfilled by the chain's or franchisor's central management. A large marketing department may coordinate the efforts of various professionals, including those of director of advertising, director of public relations, director of sales, and various sales representatives. It is not uncommon for large global brands to employ sophisticated advertising and public relations firms to help them develop and carry out an effective market positioning strategy. It is safe to say that in today's lodging environment, niche positioning and service delivery require targeted programming in order to effectively target their customer base. Thereafter, the delivery of effective service promises designed to garner market share and customer loyalty can asist in improving the financial performance of the hotel asset.

Service Departments

To provide lodging to guests, all hotels are organized around five basic functions: (1) front desk operation/guest services (concierge), (2) housekeeping, (3) building maintenance/engineering, (4) food and beverage, and (5) security.

Beyond these common services, hotels and their departments can vary tremendously. For example, most luxury hotels include a restaurant and beverage department, while most budget facilities do not. The performance of these functions can also vary widely among different types of hotels. Business guests of a convention center hotel may expect high-tech front desk operations, and guests at a resort may prefer a more personal approach.

Front-Desk Operations

Front-desk, or, more accurately, front-office, operations are the heart of any hotel business. The front office staff oversees room availability, registers guests, processes reservations, supervises check-out, and assigns rooms and keys. It also answers guest questions about hotel activities and resources and provides information about nearby restaurants and attractions. The front desk is critical because it usually sets the tone for the guest's whole experience at the hotel or resort. First impressions can make or break a guest's stay.

The number of individuals involved in front-desk operations, and the specificity of their jobs, varies with the size of the lodging establishment. The smallest hotels or motels may have one individual per shift handling all functions of the front office, including the night audit function. More often, a **front-desk manager** or lead hourly supervisor oversees a team of workers. A description of common duties performed by these workers follows.

Reservations Reservations can be booked through a local reservations clerk, via the sales or marketing department, or through a nationally or even internationally centralized reservation system. The art of revenue management has become highly specialized and sophisticated; therefore, reservations and pricing strategies are highly complex. Many hotels use a computerized property management system to store information about reservations, room availability, and room rate. Often, this system includes inventory allocation and pricing. In some cases, front-desk agents and/or reservations personnel may be solely responsible for coordinating and executing the arrival and departure of guests, using a property-level computerized reservation system. Most lodging establishments know through experience that they will incur some no-show reservations. To combat this loss of income, **overbooking** of rooms is a relatively common practice. Many hotels book 10 to 15 percent more reservations than they have rooms available. Usually this causes no problem, but when it does, the hotel uses a cooperating hotel nearby to accommodate overflow.

Check-in At smaller lodging properties, the **room clerk** is the individual at the front desk who greets and registers hotel guests. If the guest has booked a reservation in advance, the room clerk first verifies the reservation information. If no advance reservation has been made, the clerk provides details of room rate and availability. This information must be immediately available to the clerk so that she can sell an available room to the prospective guest. As mentioned above, many hotels use a computerized **property management system** to store this information. Smaller establishments may maintain this information on a **room rack** that posts cards showing the status of all guest rooms. Hotels and motels usually require guests to pay for their room in cash at check-in or to guarantee payment with a credit card.

After registration, the room clerk makes a room assignment and provides a key or key card to the guest. Electronic key cards offer higher levels of security than conventional keys, and can track room entry so the hotel can, if necessary, reconstruct activities involving all assigned keys within the system. Key cards have magnetic strips that hold electronically encoded information. This information is readable by an electronic card-reading unit attached to the guest-room door. Key cards are programmed to expire at the date and time of the guest's scheduled departure.

Check-out The check-out procedure is managed by the front office staff, and often is the duty of the same people who handle registration. Since most hotels require advance payment for rooms, or at least advance credit card verification, check-out is usually a simple process. Ever greater numbers of hotels use their property management computer program to record all guest charges and issue the final statement at check-out. In some hotels, a guests can view her account, verify the charges, and authorize a credit card payment without leaving her room. A copy of the itemized statement is placed under the room door, made available for pickup in the lobby at departure, or sent in the mail. Check-out is the hotel's final chance to make a lasting impression on the guest, solidify customer loyalty, and cultivate future return visits.

Greeting The **bell captain**, a position found in most medium to large hotels, is an individual of great importance to the reputation of a lodging establishment. The bell captain or one of her staff is often the first individual a guest meets upon arrival. The bell captain trains and supervises all **bellhops**, those individuals who usher arriving guests to their rooms and carry their luggage. The bell captain is responsible for orchestration of arrivals and departures, and often makes the critical first and last impression of a guest's stay.

Photo by Corbis

Bell captains and bellhops play the important role of presenting first impressions to guests.

Bell captains supervise the hotel's door attendants and valet parking crew. Bell captains, bellhops, and door and valet parking attendants depend on tips for a large portion of their income. It is considered customary to tip a bellhop about $2 to $3 for each bag carried. A hotel door attendant can expect, on average, a $3 to $5 tip for hailing a cab.[1]

Communication Traditionally, telephone messages, mail, and faxes were held at the front desk until they could be delivered to guests. Technology is modifying this practice, however, as more hotels install **electronic voice-mail systems**. Voice mail allows a caller to leave a message for delivery to a guest room phone. By dialing a coded number, guests can retrieve their messages at any time, sometimes from either within or outside the hotel. Voice mail dramatically reduces the need for telephone assistance at the hotel's main switchboard. Voice-mail systems enable callers to leave messages in any language without concern about translation or misunderstanding. This can be a real benefit for international travelers and callers. Using voice mail, hotels can provide guests with information about hotel restaurant and shop hours, as well as any special events or activities of note.

At New York City's Rihga Royal Hotel, telephone service is even more sophisticated.[2] Each room guest is issued a cellular phone, and when the room phone is unanswered, the call automatically forwards to the cellular phone. Only if the cellular phone is unanswered does the call reroute to the hotel's telephone operator. At present, this service is found in only a few luxury hotels.

Some hotels transmit guest messages via television. A blinking light on the telephone alerts the guest to check a special message channel on the guest room television. Messaging systems, videoconferencing, mobile technology, and e-commerce have advanced to the point where the flat-panel television in the guest room serves as the anchor for high-tech gadgetry, housing integrated communication systems with sophisticated internal merchandising capabilities. At many properties, **wireless Internet** service is available. Most hotels and resorts charge for Internet connectivity, and it has replaced telephone fees as a minor operating department income stream.

Hotel guests can make both long-distance and local calls directly from room phones without using the hotel's telephone operator. Telephone charges are electronically calculated and added to the guest's account. Many hotels offer dual-line phones that allow the guest to place one caller on hold while answering a second call. However, advances in mobile technology have diminished hotels' telephone income and demand for employee services in this area.

Another telephone service that has undergone change is the traditional hotel **wake-up call**. In earlier years, hotel telephone operators called a guest's room to wake her at a set time. This system was time consuming and inefficient, particularly when hundreds of guests requested wake-up calls at the same hour. Now, computers place the wake-up calls. Hotels that do not use a computerized wake-up system may place alarm clocks in the rooms so guests can set their own wake-up signal.

Information Services Most large hotels provide a concierge who answers questions, solves problems, and performs the services of a private secretary for the hotel's guests. Positioned in the front lobby area or on a luxury floor, this individual may furnish information about a city's restaurants, theaters, and tourist attractions, book restaurant reservations, or obtain theater tickets for guests. The ever-resourceful concierge may serve guests by hailing taxis and limousines or arranging for the purchase and delivery of flowers, candy, or other gifts.

In the smaller hotel, the front-desk clerk, manager, bell captain, or bellhop should be prepared to provide directions and information about restaurants and attractions in the surrounding area.

Housekeeping

Housekeeping, often the largest department within the hotel, is one of the most crucial in terms of guest satisfaction. Guests routinely list facility cleanliness as one of the key components of a satisfactory hotel stay. Poor housekeeping can quickly ruin a hotel's reputation and business.

The overriding responsibility of all who work in housekeeping is to keep guest rooms and other facilities clean, well stocked, and in good repair. The housekeeping department is headed by the **executive housekeeper**. The executive housekeeper handles hiring, training, and supervising of staff, as well as the purchasing of cleaning supplies and equipment. This person also sets cleaning priorities, such as cleaning. Typically, cleaning schedules are based on productivity standards and room occupancy forecasts.

Room Preparation Cleaning guest rooms involves changing bed and bath linens, making beds, dusting, vacuuming, and scrubbing bathroom surfaces and fixtures. In addition, trash cans are emptied; supplies of toilet paper, soap, shampoo, and tissue are replenished; and lights, televisions, and radios are checked to be sure they are working. In-room bars and refrigerators are restocked as well. Usually, in-room amenities and bar products are provided and replenished by the food and beverage department.

Individuals who perform the daily room cleaning are called **room attendants**. Duties of the room attendant vary considerably from one property to another, but the average room attendant cleans about fifteen rooms per day. Room attendants in luxury hotels may have more extensive duties, so they are expected to clean fewer rooms.

Entry-level positions for room attendants pay only minimum wage, but require little or no experience. There are advancement opportunities within the housekeeping department, because larger hotels usually have **floor supervisors** and **assistant housekeepers** who supervise the day-to-day work of room attendants. Typically, housekeeping supervisors advance to executive housekeeper roles and may advance further into overall rooms division management, which encompasses the housekeeping and front-office departments.

Hotel Laundry Providing clean linens for guest rooms and baths is a major part of the housekeeping function. Some hotels operate their own laundry facilities. The **laundry manager** supervises **laundry room attendants** who wash, dry, iron, and fold the laundry. Other lodging facilities own their own linens but pay to have the washing, ironing, and folding done by a commercial laundry service. Commercial linen services rent clean towels and sheets to lodging establishments. Renting linens usually is the most expensive method of the three, but is practical for small establishments. Uniforms worn by hotel staff are sometimes cleaned and maintained by hotel laundry departments. Financial analysis that takes market conditions into account must be performed to determine the most cost-effective way to meet the hotel's linen needs.

Laundry and Dry Cleaning for Guests Hotels have long been expected to offer laundry and dry cleaning service for their guests. Many hotels contract with commercial laundries and dry cleaners off the premises to clean and press guest clothes. Larger hotels may operate these services in house. Providing clean laundry for guests is rarely a moneymaker for the lodging establishment and is often expensive for the guest, but it is a service that many business travelers, in particular, demand. Lodging establishments that cater to family recreation or extended-stay travelers often provide self-service coin-operated washers and dryers.

Building Maintenance/Engineering Maintenance and engineering tasks may be the responsibility of the housekeeping department in smaller hotels. In these establishments, private contractors are brought in to make repairs and improvements. Large hotels may have their own staff of painters, plumbers, electricians, and carpenters, who perform repairs as well as preventive maintenance. Often, housekeeping and engineering work together to plan and implement the long-term upkeep of guest rooms. The executive housekeeper may have considerable say in the selection of color schemes, carpet, wallpaper, furniture, and other interior decorating items. Paint, furniture, and fixtures in guest rooms cannot be allowed to deteriorate or become dated if a hotel is to maintain its reputation. Most hotels redecorate guest rooms every few years on a planned schedule. Ongoing repair and maintenance of the physical plant is essential if the property is to retain its asset value and competitiveness. Preventive maintenance software is available that tracks all major pieces of equipment that require periodic service. This helps prevent major mechanical failures and costly replacement.

The engineering department, along with the housekeeping department, must pay close attention to the sensory experiences a guest will have at the hotel. More and more facilities engineers are acquiring advanced design and decor skills in order to keep pace with industry innovations.

A Day in the Life of...

THE CHIEF ENGINEER

Photo by Michael Dzaman

The chief engineer,[1] or plant manager, in a hospitality firm is first and foremost a supervisor. It is the job of the chief engineer to plan and organize the tasks that will be carried out by the crew. The objective of those tasks is to ensure that all equipment and mechanical and electrical systems throughout the facility operate properly and safely.

Because the chief engineer is a manager, a typical day includes coordinating staff and directing the upkeep of major mechanical systems in the building. In addition to these mechanical responsibilities, the chief engineer's administrative responsibilities include hiring, firing, and training employees as well as budgeting. This can account for as much as 60 percent of the chief engineer's ten- to twelve-hour day. Maintaining communication among departments and with supervisors is also an important function of the chief engineer. Most days are spent planning, coordinating, and supervising fulfillment of repair and maintenance orders, dealing with staffing situations, and teaching managers of other areas how to keep their departments and employees from damaging the equipment and physical plant. Another important responsibility of the chief engineer is energy management and conservation.

In addition to assuring that crew members are doing quality work, the chief engineer may work as a technician, maintaining or upgrading various systems such as heating, venting, cooling, water, and electrical. (In large facilities, the chief engineer will likely delegate such technical duties to a staff member.) Specifically, most chief engineers should

- Have an electrical license and know how to do wiring.
- Understand how to install and repair plumbing equipment.
- Know how motors work and how to repair them, or know whom to call to repair them.
- Be able to offer advice during renovation or construction of facilities.

Other responsibilities of the chief engineer are negotiating contracts with and getting bids from vendors and obtaining insurance certificates. Weekly or daily meetings with people outside of the organization are not uncommon. Again, the chief engineer wants to ensure the proper maintenance of the facility while controlling costs.

To become a chief engineer, a high school diploma is important. So is further education that focuses on heating and air-conditioning systems, plumbing, and electrical repair. Having several years of work experience in the field is a must. In addition to technical expertise, experience in management, especially in budgeting, is necessary. Most chief engineers must have industry certifications in electrical and mechanical systems in order to supervise associated trade employees in various repair and maintenance roles.

---

[1] John Palmer, *Principles of Hospitality Engineering* (New York: Van Nostrand Reinhold, 1990), 180.

The engineering department is supervised by a **chief engineer**, sometimes called the **plant manager**. An important function of the chief engineer of a large property is to implement and maintain water and energy conservation measures for the hotel. Conservation measures may take the form of modifying existing operations and equipment, educating guests and staff about sustainable practices, and installing more energy-efficient equipment.

Security

Providing guest protection and loss prevention is essential for any lodging establishment, regardless of size. Travelers are likely targets for thieves because they often carry large quantities of cash and valuables. Violent crime is a growing problem, and protecting guests from bodily harm has been defined by the courts as a reasonable expectation for hotels. In all hotels and motels, security must be the shared responsibility of all employees. The cost of loss due to theft or injury can be tremendous. First, a hotel's reputation can be significantly damaged, which results in a direct loss in bookings. Second, the hotel may have to pay considerable amounts to replace goods that are stolen or damaged by guests, employees, or professional thieves.

Today, most hotels have at least one professionally trained security officer, and larger hotels have a security department headed by a chief of security. The chief of security has extensive training in law enforcement and advanced first aid, as well as civil and criminal law. In addition, many hotels hire private third-party security firms, either to assist during peak business periods or to provide primary security functions within the facility.

Advances in technology help the security officer perform her regular duties. Two-way radios are fairly standard, as are closed-circuit television cameras for use in out-of-the-way corridors and doorways, as well as in food, liquor, and equipment storage rooms. Smoke detectors and fire alarms increase guest and staff safety.

Fire alarm systems are typically connected directly to the local fire department to improve initial response times in case of fire emergency.

Electronic key cards, discussed earlier in this chapter, offer superior room security for hotels and their guests.[3] Key cards typically do not list the name of the hotel or the guest's room number, so if a card is lost or stolen it is not easily traceable. Lost key cards can easily be rekeyed and replaced. In addition, most key card systems record entries into the guest room as a security measure. This provides important information if theft or damage is noted at a later date.

These technologies deter theft by employees as well as outsiders. The security department usually works with the hotel's human resources director to minimize employee theft. Recruitment and hiring guidelines typically require screening prospective employees by checking references, and often include criminal background checks and drug tests as well. Employee theft is known to be worse in organizations where morale is low, and when employees feel frustrated or taken advantage of. Hoteliers often remark that when one employee is known to be stealing, others tend to follow.[4] Hotels that work to build a sense of organizational commitment among staff have fewer problems with employee theft.

Security staff develop **catastrophe plans** to ensure staff and guest safety and to minimize direct and indirect costs from disaster. The catastrophe plan reviews insurance policies, analyzes physical facilities, and evaluates possible disaster scenarios to determine whether they have a high or low probability.[5] Possible disaster scenarios might include fire, bomb threat, earthquake, flood, hurricane, or blizzard. The well-prepared hotel has formal policies in place to deal with any possible scenario and trains employees to implement emergency procedures should they become necessary.

Formalized risk managment divisions exist in larger corporations. They coordinate regular audits to determine compliance with security objectives. Often insurance companies collaborate with hotels to minimize safety and security-related costs, and may participate in staff training as well as inspecting facilities.

Food and Beverage Operations

Beyond the four basic functions of front desk, housekeeping, maintenance/engineering, and security, hotels can offer an endless array of additional guest services such as pools, spas, and business services. The most common additional services involve food and beverage operations. The primary components of the foodservice operation in a large property include banquets, catering, restaurants, and room service. Since foodservice is covered in other chapters of this book, we will not discuss it in detail here. However, room service is one facet of the food and beverage industry that is unique to the hotel and motel industry.

Room Service A survey, in the nineties, of the American Hotel & Lodging Association (AH&LA) showed that 75 percent of all airport lodging facilities and 56 percent of all lodging properties in general offer room service.[6] Hotel general managers agree that room service is a highly desired service, but one that rarely adds to the profitability of the hotel. In fact, room service operations often run at a loss. Staff needs are greater in room service than in restaurant dining rooms, since it takes longer to transport a meal from a hotel kitchen to a guest room several floors above. Volume of room service sales is typically lower and the hours of service are often extended beyond those of the hotel dining room.

Even though room service itself may lose money, it is offered because hotel guests want and use it. Hotels cover their losses through room revenues or other high-margin departments. Active business travelers often prefer the convenience that room service provides, because they can eat and work at the same time. Tired hotel guests may want the comfort and informality of eating in their room, where they do not have to dress up for meals. And some unaccompanied travelers feel more relaxed eating in their own rooms. Competitive market forces make it important for a property to provide room service of a quality that is consistent with the hotel's overall standards.

The room service department is headed by a **room service manager. Room service operators** take orders over the telephone. Phone greeters often use the guest's name several times during the course of the conversation to personalize the service experience. **Servers** transport the food from the kitchen to guest rooms.

Breakfast is the most commonly ordered room service meal, and during the work week many hotel patrons order breakfast at the same time. This can create massive supply and delivery problems for the room service department. To increase room service efficiency, some hotels provide doorknob order forms that allow guests to order from a limited breakfast menu the night before, and specify (within a 30-minute time window) when they want the meal to be delivered. Pre-staging and rolling room service tables with heat boxes are used to minimize set-up time. This allows linens, condiments, and utensils to be pre-set and ready to go. Designated elevators may be reserved for use only by room service staff in the morning, so that deliveries can be made quickly. Other hotels use "flying pantries,"[7] which are service elevators stocked with prepared continental breakfast trays that can be quickly delivered to guest rooms.

Vending Machines The vending machine has always offered an alternative to restaurant meals and room service. Some hotels upgrade the quality and selection of vending machine offerings by stocking fresh fruits, yogurt, and prepared sandwiches in addition to the standard vending machine fare. Sophisticated vending machines now exist that offer gourmet meals, **iPods**, and other trendy high-tech items for guest consumption, effectively replacing gift shops. Hyatt has introduced a concept called "Raid The Pantry" in properties that lack twenty-four–hour room service. A room key enables guests to enter and help themselves in a "pantry" area stocked with sandwiches, soft drinks, and cookies.[8]

Human Resources Management Issues

Attracting and retaining a competent workforce has always been a challenge for the hospitality industry, but today the challenge is even greater. In the growing hospitality industry there is always more hiring to be done. Hotels are changing hiring procedures and benefits to appeal to workers and reduce the high **turnover rate** in the industry.

Personnel Needs

In 1998, the lodging industry in the United States employed about 1.16 million people. By 2008, there were approximately 3.85 million hospitality jobs.[9] The hotel and restaurant industries, as well as the travel and health care sectors, are growing more rapidly than the general population. Many businesses in these industries are staffed all day, every day of the week. This means that there is tremendous competition among service industries to attract and retain good employees.

Turnover Rate

The lodging industry has one of the country's highest employee turnover rates. An area of concern within the hospitality industry is the high rate of employee turnover and the increased costs of training and developing new personnel. Employee turnover does more than reduce service quality and damage employee morale—it hits a hotel's bottom line. Therefore, a critical component of increasing long-term retention of employees is for leaders to create a work environment that contributes to high employee satisfaction and morale.

A turnover rate is calculated by dividing the number of workers replaced in a given time period by the average number of employees needed to run the business. Some hotels report as much as 100 percent turnover in the course of a year. Turnover may be especially high in this industry because of inadequate methods of recruiting, screening, and hiring new employees; inadequate training and supervision of all employees; the high number of jobs requiring relatively low levels of skill; poor wages and benefits; increased inventory of hotel rooms in the marketplace; and the perception that there are few opportunities for advancement. The cost for a hotel to fill each hourly position job in 2006 was estimated to be between $2,600 and $14,000. The cost of turnover for each managerial employees was an estimated $20,000.[10]

Addressing the Turnover Issue

In the hospitality industry, the strength of an organization lies in its employees' motivation level and dedication to serving customers. This service mentality needs to be grounded in the work satisfaction and morale of line-level associates, or those that directly interface with guests . In the hospitality industry, retention and morale issues are intimately linked to guest satisfaction. Therefore, employee training, development, and growth are essential elements of human resource management programs at the property level. Creating a work environment that fosters employee satisfaction is key to providing market-leading customer service and sustaining profitablilty.

Faced with tough competition in the labor pool and the high cost of employee replacement, hotels have begun implementing programs that reduce employee turnover. Many helpful methods for reducing turnover exist. Accurate job descriptions help set clear performance standards. A good description details how, where, and when tasks are performed. Clear evaluation standards need to be set, and hours, wages, and benefits need to be spelled out.

Business Profile

RED ROOF INNS

A Consistent Leader in Economy Lodging

Photo courtesy of Accor Economy Lodging

As the lodging industry stumbled into the 1990s, economy properties played an increasingly important role in relation to their more expensive counterparts. In 1993, Red Roof Inns, a consistent leader in the economy segment, was the largest privately owned and operated economy lodging chain in the United States, possessing 210 properties with 23,438 rooms.

Red Roof's focus on building a repeat guest clientele appears to be the key to its success. To ensure guest satisfaction, the company instituted several programs. One is the employee empowerment training program, which teaches employees to solve guests' problems on the spot. Another program is the Red Check satisfaction guarantee, which urges guests not to unpack unless they are completely satisfied with their accommodations. Specialized Business King rooms offer well-lit work stations, modem jacks, and access to fax and photocopy machines, in addition to king-size beds, thus providing guests with business amenities at a budget price.

In compliance with the Americans with Disabilities Act of 1990, Red Roof had made all of its properties accessible by 1994.[1] Design features include hand-held shower wands; unobstructed, wheel-under sinks; lowered coat hooks, towel bars, and door peepholes; maneuverability space (minimum of three feet of clearance through room passageways); fire alarms with red strobe lights and louder alarms; and telecommunications devices for the hearing impaired.

Founder James R. Trueman and former chairperson of the board Barbara Trueman named the chain after the Red Roof Tavern steak house in Kalamazoo, Michigan—the place where they conceived the idea to start the economy hotel chain. Red Roof Inn opened its first motel in Grove City, Ohio, in February 1973. In 1984, Red Roof Inns became the first economy lodging company to computerize all property management systems, interconnecting them with the corporate office.

Sold in 1993 to Morgan Stanley Real Estate Limited Partnership, Red Roof Inns planned to expand its chain, not only in its original markets, but on the West Coast as well. In 2007 it was sold for $1.32 billion, this time to U.S. Citi Global Special Situations Group and the Westbridge Hospitality Fund. The company introduced franchising in 1996 to accelerate expansion during the booming economy. By 1999, there were forty franchises across the United States.

---

[1] http://www.red roof.com

Empowering employees to make routine decisions and to change procedures when warranted allows employees to carry out their jobs with greater ease. When a hotel guest questions a bill, a front desk employee usually asks her supervisor to review the situation before making adjustments. This is time consuming and frustrating to employee and guest alike. Instead, hotels should train and encourage employees to use their own judgment to make such decisions. The results of empowerment are positive, and hotels report that both employee and guest satisfaction improve.[11]

Because benefits are important to most employees, establishing incentive programs increases employee satisfaction. Many hospitality companies offer bonuses, guaranteed raises, and paid vacations to employees who remain on the job for pre-established periods of time. Hotels also operate incentive programs to reward desired behaviors. For instance, a room-cleaning contest might run for one month. Room attendants are awarded points for successful cleaning of each room. The attendant with the most points wins a cash bonus, time off with pay, or free meals at the hotel. Incentive programs can be used to increase sales at the front desk, reward regular attendance, encourage prompt sign-in for work, or promote any other goal identified by management or employees.

Perhaps the most important factor in keeping employees happy is simply knowing the employees' needs. Employees sometimes quit because of personal or family problems. Familiarity with the lives and challenges of employees enables managers to offer more attractive benefits packages that include contingencies for family emergencies.

Benefits Packages

Most companies understand that benefits attract and keep employees. Unfortunately, benefits are expensive, and some companies provide them only to those who work thirty or more hours per week. Medical and life insurance programs are frequently limited to full-time employees. Some benefits are assumed to be available to all employees, such as the Social Security pension program. Other benefits, such as child or elder care and employee assistance programs, were instituted as a response to socioeconomic trends. Challenges within the lodging industry reflect a frantic competition for workers. In order to meet hiring needs, industry leaders have had to reevaluate their benefit packages in order to remain financially competitive while attracting and retaining competent workers. Additionally, multigenerational mixing of the workforce is becoming increasingly complex. The need to manage both cultural diversity and generational differences will challenge future leaders entering the hospitality marketplace to create a cohesive workplace geared toward guest satisfaction.

Pension Programs Social Security, administered by the U.S. government, is the largest pension program in the country. Employees and their employers are required to contribute a certain percentage of income to Social Security. Social Security contributions are made even by those who work part time.

Eligible retired employees can begin receiving full Social Security benefits after age sixty-five. Many companies also contribute to a private pension program; however, most companies restrict participation to full-time employees.

Child Care With so many working mothers in the hospitality industry, some hotel organizations operate their own child-care programs. The Opryland Hotel in Nashville provides an on-site day-care center for its employees with rates determined on a sliding scale tied to employee income. The Buena Vista Palace in Walt Disney World Resort offers on-site day care. Marriott also provides on-site day care at its corporate headquarters. Establishments operating on-site child care report reduced employee turnover and increased productivity.

Many more hotels offer a **stipend**, or allowance, toward child care in a facility or home of the employee's choice. Sometimes, if a hotel can guarantee a certain number of children for a day-care center, it can negotiate lower employee-only rates.

Elder Care As the population continues to mature, care of aging parents will become another concern for working families. Again, forward-looking establishments may offer stipends or services for elder care.

Employee Assistance Programs **Employee assistance programs (EAPs)** are services offered to employees for the management of personal problems. EAPs most frequently provide employees with access to counseling and substance abuse treatment services. The EAP may allow each employee's family to make a certain number of free visits to a psychologist per year, and make subsequent visits at a somewhat reduced fee. Some EAPs also offer legal or financial services at reduced rates.

Human Resources Legislation

Hotels and motels, like all employers in the country, are subject to federal, state, and local laws that govern hiring and employment. The Equal Employment Opportunity Commission (EEOC) is the agency of the U.S. government charged with ensuring fair and equitable treatment in employment. The U.S. Immigration and Naturalization Service (INS) monitors the employment of the foreign born. Ongoing debate surrounds guest and foreign worker programs that may adversely affect the hospitality industry in the global marketplace. Increased demand for hospitality workers means industry will continue to pressure government officials to address the exchange and free flow of hospitality workers across the globe.

Family and Medical Leave Act of 1993

On February 5, 1993, President William J. Clinton signed into law the Family and Medical Leave Act. This law requires companies with fifty or more employees, including part-time or seasonal workers, to grant leave for up to twelve weeks each year. Any male or female employee who has worked for the employer for at least twelve months, and for at least 1,250 hours during the last twelve months, can apply for the leave. Leave can be used for the care of a newborn, a newly placed adopted or foster child, or a seriously ill immediate family member. The employee may also use the leave for convalescence.

The employer is not required to pay the employee during the leave, but medical insurance must be continued under the same terms and conditions as were in force before the leave. Usually the employee must use any and all accrued vacation and sick leave benefits while on leave, commensurate with the number of days out of work, until the earned benefits are exhausted. The employee is guaranteed employment in the same position, or at the same level and salary, when she returns to work. Studies have shown that the cost of placing a worker on leave is much less than the cost of replacing the employee.[12]

Equal Pay Act of 1963

Discrimination in pay rates on the basis of gender is prohibited by this act. Basically, this law directs that an employer cannot pay a worker of one gender less than it pays a worker of the other gender if the jobs involve equal skills, effort, and responsibility, and are performed under similar working conditions.

Title VII of the Civil Rights Act of 1964

The most all-inclusive equal employment opportunity legislation in the United States, Title VII prohibits discrimination in employment on the basis of an individual's race, color, religion, sex, or national origin. Several other important federal laws and court cases clarify and strengthen Title VII.

Protection from Sexual Harassment

Since the passage of the Civil Rights Act of 1964, workplace discrimination on the basis of gender has been illegal. However, it took the involvement of the Supreme Court to define and outlaw the practice of **sexual harassment**. The Supreme Court ruled that sexual harassment occurs whenever any unwanted sexually oriented behavior changes an employee's working conditions and/or creates a hostile or abusive work environment.[13]

Two basic categories of sexual harassment are defined. The first is called **quid pro quo**. This could be a situation where a supervisor demands sexual favors in exchange for tangible job benefits, like a promotion or raise. The second form of sexual harassment is the **sexually offensive or hostile work environment**. In this situation, the employee might be subjected to sexual comments, pictures, or actions that are deemed offensive, even though they may not threaten the person's job or possibilities for promotion. The Civil Rights Act of 1991, signed by President George H. W. Bush, allows an employee who wins a sexual harassment case to recover financial damages.

Employers cannot discriminate on the basis of age, sex, or race when hiring employees for any position in the hospitality industry.

Corporate lawyers recommend that lodging establishments develop a written company policy prohibiting sexual harassment in the workplace. Since there is no uniform definition of sexual harassment, it is recommended that the hotel policy spell out the specific conduct that is prohibited. The policy should require that employees report sexual harassment incidents within a specified time period, and the policy should define several channels through which complaints can be made. Additionally, it is recommended that all employees complete (and sign a document verifying completion of) training on company policies related to sexual harassment and hostile work environment. This strategy may lessen the company's liability in the event an employee violates company policy and is found to be the cause of harassment or a hostile work environment.

The courts have held business managers liable in cases of sexual harassment where managers knew about the charges but failed to take appropriate action. Consequently, a company's sexual harassment policy should spell out how an investigation will be conducted, as well as identifying the punishments or courses of remediation the offender will face if the charges are substantiated.[14]

The Age Discrimination in Employment Act of 1967

The federal Age Discrimination in Employment Act of 1967 (ADEA) prohibits discrimination in employment on the basis of age. The act requires equal treatment of employees and job applicants, regardless of age, and prohibits discharge of any individual because of age. A 1990 amendment to the ADEA

Industry Insights

CULTURE

Breaking Down Barriers

The term "open door policy" has taken on a new meaning. In today's hospitality market the majority of new employees will be women, minorities, and/or immigrants. Consequently, the hospitality industry must continue to open doors and break down barriers for women and minorities.

According to Ron Wilkinson, former vice chairman of the American Hotel & Lodging Association Diversity Task Force, "We spend all this time adjusting to foreign guests' needs without looking to the cultural needs of employees."[1] Within the last several years, the industry has made a concerted effort to practice what is known as "diversity management." Diversity management is a simple concept which, according to *Lodging* magazine, "allows for differences in values—arising from gender, socioeconomic level, age, and ethnicity—to coexist in the work environment."[2] Diversity management includes such things as a closer look at promotional opportunities for women and minorities, facility changes for a barrier-free environment, and even a revision of job descriptions.

But diversity training programs are not without their pitfalls.[3] Because of the relative newness of such programs, the issue can get complicated. Employees and managers can take opposing sides. Sometimes, if programs lose focus, reverse discrimination can result. Still, experts contend that nearly any program is better than none at all.

Many hotels are taking steps to break down barriers. They do this by surveying the current workforce, holding focus groups to find out what level of cultural diversity exists at their property, and adding a diversity training program to their agendas. As cross-cultural breakthroughs are made, these first steps may very well lead to open doors and open minds for everyone.

---

1 Christine O'Dwyer, "Opening Doors and Minds," *Lodging* (May 1992): 12.

2 Ibid., 13.

3 Kathleen Murray, "The Unfortunate Side Effects of Training,'" *New York Times*, August 1, 1993.

specifically outlawed age discrimination in employee benefit programs. Employees within a certain age classification are considered a protected class and warrant careful and consistent due process in terms of unfavorable performance reviews and dismissal consideration.

Title 1 of the Americans with Disabilities Act

Employers cannot discriminate on the basis of a worker's disabilities. In [1988] the President's Committee on Employment of the disabled estimated that 49 million Americans are disabled in some way, including those with "hidden disabilities" such as learning disabilities, diabetes, illiteracy, and AIDS. Since the passage of the Americans with Disabilities Act, employers have been prohibited from asking job applicants about past or current medical conditions. Employers cannot require job applicants to take pre-employment physicals. In addition, Title 1 defines an applicant as being qualified for a job as long as he or she can perform the "essential functions" of the job with or without reasonable accommodation. The term *essential functions* refers to the job tasks that are fundamental to the performance of the job. For example, an essential function for a bellhop would be the ability to carry heavy luggage or push a full luggage cart. If an individual's disability made this impossible, she would not have to be hired.

The employer is required to provide "reasonable accommodations" to make the workplace accessible to the disabled. Reasonable accommodations may include making facilities wheelchair accessible, providing readers or interpreters for those who cannot read or are visually impaired, and modifying or acquiring equipment to allow a disabled person to perform essential job functions. The federal Equal Employment Opportunity Commission (EEOC) estimates that about half of all persons with disabilities require no workplace accommodation in order to perform essential job functions. Of the remaining 50 percent who need accommodation, 20 percent of those accommodations will cost less than $50; and most other accommodations will cost less than $500.[15]

Marriott, Hyatt, and Radisson are three hotel companies that have established aggressive recruitment and training programs for mentally and physically challenged workers. These programs operate under the assumption that given proper job matches, training, and support, both employees and employers benefit greatly.

Often, a **job coach** is used to train and supervise the mentally or physically challenged worker, particularly if this is the person's first employment experience. The job coach helps the individual master all elements involved in holding and performing the job, including communicating effectively with

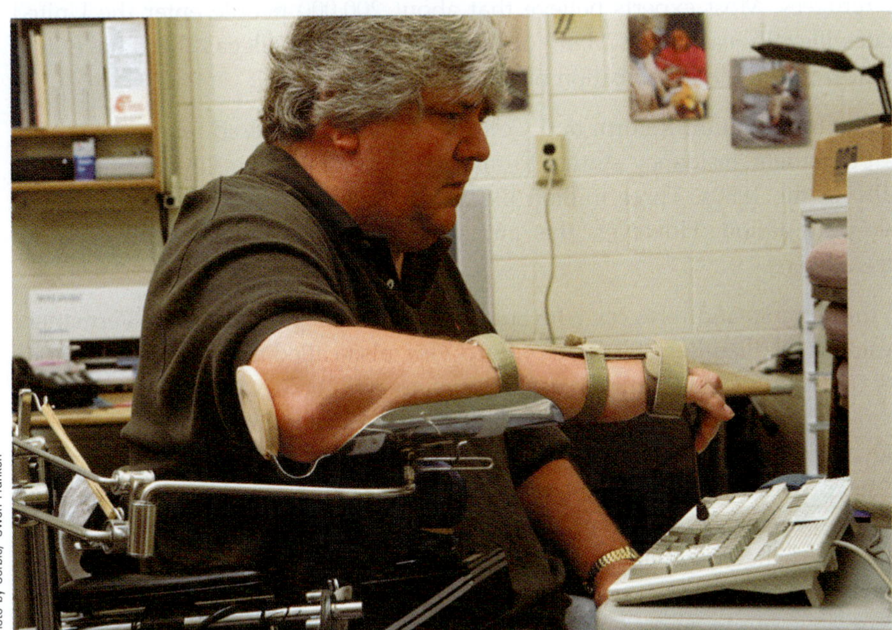

Photo by Corbis/ Owen Franken

Hotels must accommodate the needs of physically challenged employees and guests.

customers; developing appropriate relationships with supervisors and fellow workers; maintaining personal hygiene; and being punctual.

Most organizations find the initial cost of training a physically or mentally challenged worker to be greater than that of training a traditional employee. Sometimes government funding pays for part of the cost. Nevertheless, most businesses value their workers with disabilities very highly. These businesses generally agree that employees with disabilities are very conscientious and have significantly lower turnover rates.[16]

Immigration Issues

An estimated one million foreign-born people move to the United States each year. An immigration quota set by Congress limits the number of **immigrants overall** admitted for permanent residency each year. Individuals are given permission to move to the United States based on a system that gives preference to those who have families in this country, desirable job skills, or wealth. Currently, about 7.9 million immigrants are allowed into the United States each year.

Refugees are individuals who are escaping from persecution in their home country attributable to their ethnic group or race, religion, belief, or group membership. The U.S. Department of State determines the number of refugees who can legally establish permanent residence in the United States each year. In 2007, the United States admitted 48,217 refugees for permanent resettlement. Since 1980, 1.7 million refugees have been admitted to the United States.[17]

Undocumented workers, sometimes called **illegal aliens**, are people who move to the United States without permission to enter as either immigrants or refugees. Most experts believe that about 200,000 people enter the United States illegally each year. Many of those who enter as illegal aliens have little money and minimal education or job training.

The Immigration Reform and Control Act of 1986 offered amnesty, as well as permanent residency status, to aliens who entered the United States illegally in the 1980s. Three million illegal aliens applied for amnesty during a two-year period. However, this amnesty provision is no longer offered to illegal aliens.

Immigrants and refugees who enter the country legally receive a Permanent Resident or Alien Register Receipt Card visa, also called a **green card**. Employers can legally hire immigrants and refugees who hold valid green cards and who complete an employment eligibility form. (See Figure 5.2.) Still, some employers knowingly hire illegal aliens, pay them less than the legal minimum wage, provide no insurance benefits, and fail to make Social Security contributions on their behalf. If caught by the government, these employers can be fined, and the illegal alien may be deported. Proposed legislation to update the 1996 law is under consideration; debate surrounds the issues of border security, amnesty, guest worker programs, and eligibility for full citizenship.

U.S. Department of Justice
Immigration and Naturalization Service

OMB No. 1115-0136
Employment Eligibility Verification

Please read instructions carefully before completing this form. The instructions must be available during completion of this form. ANTI-DISCRIMINATION NOTICE. It is illegal to discriminate against work eligible individuals. Employers CANNOT specify which document(s) they will accept from an employee. The refusal to hire an individual because of a future expiration date may also constitute illegal discrimination.

Section 1. Employee Information and Verification. To be completed and signed by employee at the time employment begins

Print Name: Last | First | Middle Initial | Maiden Name

Address *(Street Name and Number)* | Apt. # | Date of Birth *(month/day/year)*

City | State | Zip Code | Social Security #

I am aware that federal law provides for imprisonment and/or fines for false statements or use of false documents in connection with the completion of this form.

I attest, under penalty of perjury, that I am (check one of the following):
- ☐ A citizen or national of the United States
- ☐ A Lawful Permanent Resident (Alien # A__________________
- ☐ An alien authorized to work until____/____/____
  (Alien # or Admission #________________________________

Employee's Signature | Date *(month/day/year)*

Preparer and/or Translator Certification. *(To be completed and signed if Section 1 is prepared by a person other than the employee.) I attest, under penalty of perjury, that I have assisted in the completion of this form and that to the best of my knowledge the information is true and correct.*

Preparer's/Translator's Signature | Print Name

Address *(Street Name and Number, City, State, Zip Code)* | Date *(month/day/year)*

Section 2. Employer Review and Verification. To be completed and signed by employer. **Examine one document from List A OR examine one document from List B and one from List C** as listed on the reverse of this form and record the title, number and expiration date, if any, of the document(s)

	List A	OR	List B	AND	List C
Document title:	________		________		________
Issuing authority:	________		________		________
Document #:	________		________		________
Expiration Date *(if any)*:	___/___/___		___/___/___		___/___/___
Document #:	________				
Expiration Date *(if any)*:	___/___/___				

CERTIFICATION - I attest, under penalty of perjury, that I have examined the document(s) presented by the above-named employee, that the above-listed document(s) appear to be genuine and to relate to the employee named, that the employee began employment on *(month/day/year)* ____/____/____ **and that to the best of my knowledge the employee is eligible to work in the United States. (State employment agencies may omit the date the employee began employment).**

Signature of Employer or Authorized Representative | Print Name | Title

Business or Organization Name | Address *(Street Name and Number, City, State, Zip Code)* | Date *(month/day/year)*

Section 3. Updating and Reverification. To be completed and signed by employer

A. New Name *(if applicable)* | B. Date of rehire *(month/day/year) (if applicable)*

C. If employee's previous grant of work authorization has expired, provide the information below for the document that establishes current employment eligibility.
Document Title:________________ Document #:________________ Expiration Date (if any):___/___/___

I attest, under penalty of perjury, that to the best of my knowledge, this employee is eligible to work in the United States, and if the employee presented document(s), the document(s) I have examined appear to be genuine and to relate to the individual.

Signature of Employer or Authorized Representative | Date *(month/day/year)*

Form I-9 (Rev. 11-21-91) N

FIGURE 5.2 Employment Eligibility Verification Form

Unions

In some areas of the country, it is common for hotel employees to join labor unions. The most widespread labor union in the industry is the Hotel Employees and Restaurant Employees International Union, which has a national membership of about 440,000. Other hotel workers are represented by the Teamsters or the Service Employees International Union.

The main goal of a union is to improve the hours, wages, benefits, and working conditions of its members. Once employees become members of the union, the union **collectively bargains** with the hotel management to establish conditions and wages acceptable to union members and hotel management. If an employee has a complaint against the employer, a **grievance** may be filed. In accordance with a predefined grievance procedure, a union representative, the employee, and hotel management work to settle the dispute. Union members must pay monthly dues in order to stay employed and remain a member of the union in good standing.

The union contract may require that new employees be hired solely from a pool of unemployed union workers, and may have strict rules about the number of full- and part-time union workers a hotel may keep on staff. The union contract may also restrict or strive to limit the variety of duties that employees can perform. From an employee's point of view, a union contract may offer superior job security, well-regulated hours and wages, and clearly defined responsibilities and benefits. But a union contract may also keep out the inexperienced, particularly those who want to work part time.

From the employer's point of view, the union contract may limit flexibility in hiring and staffing. A union operation may be saddled with too many employees on days when occupancy rates are down. On other days, there may be too few employees, because some contracts restrict temporary hiring. It will be interesting to see if competition for workers forces employers to voluntarily offer more of the benefits that unions bargain for without the rigidity that sometimes ensues under a union contract. Unionization offers third-party representation for employees working in organizations that they feel have not treated them fairly with regard to working conditions and compensation.

Producing an Efficient and Profitable Operation

Operating a lodging establishment profitably is the ultimate goal for those who own and manage the facility. Many publicly traded lodging corporations need to make a positive **return on investment** for their shareholders. A facility's income must be sufficient to cover departmental operating expenses such as payroll, supplies, uniforms, and employee salaries. Additionally, there are departmental overhead expenses such as utility bills, taxes, insurance, and sales and marketing expenses. By measuring occupancy rates and room rates, the successful hotelier can increase the likelihood of profitability. Room sales drive primary revenue and profitability, while food and beverage can either be a loss leader or contribute significant income and profit to the operation. In every case, the hotelier hopes that income will exceed expenses, and thereby generate profit.

As the lodging industry grew and developed, it became necessary for industry members to compare and contrast financial data. To do so, they needed to establish a financial "language," or system of accounts, in which to communicate figures and statistics.

Uniform System of Accounts for Hotels

In the mid-1920s, the Uniform System of Accounts for Hotels was developed for the Hotel Association of New York City, and in 1926 it was adopted by the AH&MA's forerunner, the American Hotel Association of the United States and Canada. Its development was of major significance to the industry, because it created both a common financial language for use among hoteliers and a formal organizational structure.

The implications of this structure are considerable. The Uniform System divides hotel operations into structural categories and departments. For example, the broad category of marketing would include several departments such as advertising, sales, promotions, and public or customer relations. Thus, employees and expenses can be grouped in ways to determine the exact costs of each part of the hotel's operation. In addition to the division of costs, the structure also establishes a hierarchy or chain of command for the hotel. To a certain extent, the Uniform System also establishes the basis for job classifications, allowing for continuity when employees move from one position to another.

Break-Even Analysis

Hotels and motels perform a break-even analysis to determine the business's break-even point. This is the point at which costs equal revenue—where there is neither a profit nor a loss. Before determining the **break-even point**, a hotel must first calculate **total yearly expenses**. All costs for the year are recorded, including

- property, automobile, and liability insurance
- real estate taxes
- depreciation on equipment
- interest on borrowed money
- salaries, wages, and benefits
- payments for property
- payments for furniture, equipment, and automobiles
- water, gas, electricity, and phone
- supplies
- other operating expenses

Industry Insights

BUSINESS INNOVATION

Break-Even Occupancy

Many industry experts agree that there is no single way of determining a hotel operation's break-even point. Complex sales structures—which may include room, catering, telephone, and club revenues—have in the past hindered the ability of senior management to simplify the process of determining break-even occupancy. Meeting investors' objectives also complicates the procedure.

The primary difficulty in calculating a hotel's break-even point is that profit margins of the many components of a hotel vary. For example, a menu item offered at a hotel's upscale restaurant will have a higher profit margin than, say, a similar menu item offered at the hotel's deli or café. These differing sales figures have made it almost impossible to predict accurately the break-even occupancy.

A twenty-year veteran of the industry, B.S. Wijeysinghe, has developed a method of calculating break-even room occupancy using a common, fixed item—the number of rooms available in a hotel.[1] Dubbed the GITHE (general indicator to hotel efficiency), Wijeysinghe's concept is said to be a simple and accurate calculation of break-even occupancy for hotel operations.

In addition, the GITHE method works as a system of efficiency management, giving management better control of the business. The GITHE calculation process allows a "what if" look at what can be done to reduce or eliminate losses and increase profit.

[1] "Break-even Occupancy for a Hotel Operation," *Management Accounting* (February 1993): 32.

Once yearly expenses have been totaled, it is necessary to perform a series of calculations based on such factors as room rate. Many hoteliers find that determining break-even occupancy is difficult at best, because complicated sales and cost structures make the calculation variables anything but fixed.

A general rule of thumb for calculating the break-even point is to determine total daily expenses and divide this figure by the average room rate. This merely yields an estimate of the number of rooms that must be rented in order to cover costs. Of course, anything in excess of the break-even occupancy contributes to the hotel's profit. The higher the occupancy rate, the greater the profitability of the facility. In the United States, the average occupancy rate for hotels and motels was about 66.4 percent in 2006.[18]

Setting Room Rates

Performing break-even calculations involves using a hotel's average room rate. But how is the room rate determined? Ideally, the room rate should be high enough to generate a healthy profit for the company, but not so high as to discourage guests from staying at or returning to the hotel. Optimal revenue managment practices determine the relationship between occupancy and average rate positioning. Often management must decide whether or not to take lower-rated business in order to increase occupancy. Typical rooms division gross operating profit margins range from 68 percent to 75 percent, compared to food and beverage departmental profit margins of 10 to 18 percent.

Let's say that a 100-room hotel has an average occupancy rate of 65 percent. Annual expenses are $1,500,000. The owner wants to earn a profit equal to 15 percent of total expenses. Fifteen percent of $1,500,000 is $225,000. The total amount of money needed for the year is $1,725,000, so the daily total is $4,726. At 65 percent occupancy, the average room rate needs to be $72.71 to meet expenses and hit the profit target. ($4,726 ÷ 65 = $72.71.)

Most hotels charge different rates at different times for the same room, depending on specific conditions in the marketplace. Hotels that cater to the business traveler usually offer lower rates on weekends to attract visitors and local residents for getaway weekends. Rates vary by the season in areas where recreational travel is weather dependent. Length of stay and prepayment may also influence room rate. Groups who book many rooms at the same time may negotiate special rates because they bring substantial food and beverage revenues. Airlines and car rental companies frequently offer special hotel room rates as part of a travel package. In addition, most hotels offer discounts to seniors, members of travel clubs like AAA, members of the military, and employees of the federal government. Rates may differ by between $25 and $30 per night depending on the time of year and day of the week. In the example of the 100-room hotel, the hotel could charge various rates for the room, as long as the average over the year remained $72.71 per day.

The practice of varying the room rate as the occupancy varies is called **yield management**. Yield management involves analyzing past reservation patterns, room rates, cancellations, and no-shows in an attempt to maximize profits and occupancy rates and to set the most competitive room rates. For example, a hotel that is nearly fully booked on a particular night will charge its highest rate for any remaining rooms. On the other hand, a relatively empty hotel will offer discounted prices for its rooms, since it is important to sell some rooms (even at discounted prices) rather than none at all. Like the airline industry, hotels set rates on a day-to-day basis to yield maximum profits. Sophisticated computer programs use the hotel's history of demand to help hotel managers arrive at these figures.

Referrals and Ratings Systems

In their effort to improve overall occupancy rates, hotels and motels are always interested in boosting advance room reservations. Ways to accomplish this include joining a referral association, using a toll-free reservation system, and being evaluated by an influential rating service.

Referral Associations

Referral associations offer some of the same benefits as franchises, but at much lower costs. A referral association may provide an independent hotel with increased visibility, marketing, and buying power, without the necessity of giving up control or ownership. Hotels and motels within a referral association share a centralized reservation system and a common image, logo, or advertising slogan. The referral association publishes a membership directory, usually given away free or for a small fee to interested guests. In addition, the referral association may offer group buying discounts to members, as well as management training and continuing education programs.

Hotels and motels pay an initial fee to join the referral association and an annual membership fee. Generally, this fee is much less than that paid to become a member of a hotel franchise system. Size and appearance standards for member establishments within the referral association are less stringent than those found in a franchise agreement, so guests may find more variation among these facilities than among franchise members.

The largest referral association is Best Western, which has more than 4,200 hotels in eighty countries. Budget Host and Flags Inn are other large referral associations. Some referral associations appeal to particular specialty hotel properties, such as the 127-member Historic Hotels of America Association. This association lists hotels that are at least fifty years old, are recognized as having historical significance, and have maintained their historic architecture.[19]

Reservation Systems

Since the 1980s, comprehensive **computerized reservation systems (CRSs)** have gained importance in the travel industry. A computerized reservation system is a complex database that provides information about many travel options, including airline flights, car rentals, and hotel, motel, and resort rentals. SABRE and DATAS II are two of the most well-known computerized reservation systems. One of the primary benefits to membership in a referral association or franchise is the link to its toll-free reservations system and e-commerce portal. Since the 1960s, toll-free telephone reservation systems have grown in popularity. Today, when a prospective guest calls the reservations center of a franchise or referral organization, an operator (also called a reservationist) uses an on-line system to obtain information about hotel or motel locations, room rates, and availability. The system can also supply information about hotel amenities, such as restaurants, swimming pools, and fitness centers. The reservation operator can immediately book a reservation by keying in the relevant guest information and credit card number.

Interested participants purchase access to a CRS program, which allows a travel agent or clerk to receive information directly over the computer without talking to a telephone reservationist. The CRS is an interactive system that allows the agent to obtain up-to-the-minute hotel availability and rate information and book the reservation electronically, if desired. The travel agent can compare rates and information from many competing hotels or motels in a particular city. Some CRSs will even transmit a computer graphic of the hotel facilities and room layout, so the travel agent or prospective guest can evaluate a picture of the facility before making a reservation.

CRS bookings save money and time because numerous telephone calls to reservationists are not necessary. In addition, the CRS can provide instant confirmation of a reservation by immediately printing a copy of the booking. The best of these centralized reservation systems can communicate room availability and rate information instantaneously around the world. Today CRS technology and reservation management systems are significant component of overall hotel and resort financial peformance. Career opportunities exist in call center managment, reservation supervisory positions, IT support services and management, and property-level reservation management positions.

Rating Systems

In the years before the growth of franchises and referral chains, travelers depended on rating guides to direct them to hotels or motels. Now, the name of a franchise or chain implies a certain level of quality in service, price, and accommodations, and travelers in the United States do not rely so heavily on ratings. Nevertheless, hotel ratings are still important. Domestically, the American Automobile Association (AAA) and Mobil are among the most influential rating services. And in international travel, hotel guides and ratings remain very important.

The AAA is one of the most widely recognized rating services in the United States. It publishes a series of Tour Books that rate hotels using a system ranging from one diamond, representing a good basic facility, to a high of five diamonds, designating an exceptional establishment. Accommodations that do not meet AAA's minimum standards are not listed in the books.

Photo courtesy of American Automobile Association)

The American Automobile Association (AAA) operates one of the most widely recognized lodging rating systems in the United States.

Industry Insights

HISTORY

Hotel Rating Systems

Although half of the European countries and Australia do not have an official hotel rating system, France and Italy can be credited with setting the standards for such a system. However, both the French and the Italians keep their rating systems closely guarded secrets. One thing is certain: each is a government-sanctioned system that checks and measures properties against a defined standard, and the higher the rating, the higher the room rate.[1]

Various symbols, including but not limited to stars, are used to rank hotels. The AAA provides its diamond ranking system as a service to its clients. The Michelin guides (published by the French tire manufacturer) use an elaborate ranking system of symbols and icons—seven pages' worth. The English Tourist Board inspects hotels and rates their level of quality using crowns.

A rating system, whether government run, as in France and Italy, or customer driven, as in the United States, is a means by which hotels justify the rates they set for their rooms.

---

[1] Coleman Lollar, "The Hotel Rating Game." *Travel & Leisure* (July 1990): 65.

Mobil Travel Guides, like the AAA Tour Books, are revised and published annually. Mobil uses a five-star rating for its highest-ranking hotels or motels, and one star to designate hotels that are "good, better than average."[20]

Numerous other publishers rate hotels and motels around the world. Two of the more widely known travel guide series are Frommer's and Fodor's. In addition, many specialty guides are written to appeal to particular audiences such as business travelers, the budget-minded, or those traveling with children.

Travel professionals, in particular, refer to the Hotel & Travel Index, which provides information on thousands of hotels, resorts, lodges, and motels around the world. The Hotel & Travel Index is updated four times per year. Travel agents may use the index to find basic information before accessing a CRS for specific hotel availability and reservations.

Summary

- Many career opportunities exist in the hotel and resort segment of the tourism industry. Advanced corporate-level positions include corporate directors of finance, operations, marketing, and information systems, and e-commerce analysts. Mid-level and operating field postions include general manager, controller, director of sales, revenue manager, food and beverage manager, executive chef, and executive housekeeper. Entry level positions include front office supervisor, restaurant manager, and sous chef. Some positions and organizational features are common to all hotels, regardless of size or type.

- Every hotel provides at least four basic functions: front desk, housekeeping, building maintenance, and engineering, and security.
- The hospitality industry has a very high turnover rate. Recruitment and retention of good employees is a major focus for hotels and resorts. Successful leaders of hotels and resorts will need to take actions necessary to address the growing shortage of and demand for quality hospitality workers.
- Federal, state, and local laws govern hiring and employment practices. Discrimination on the basis of age, sex, race, religion, or disability is illegal.
- Both average room rate and occupancy rate determine a hotel's profitability. One measure of profitability is revenue per available room (REVPAR). To make a profit, a hotel must collect more money from room rentals than it needs to cover its expenses.
- Hotels join referral associations to gain increased visibility and to be listed in an association's reservation system.
- Computerized reservation systems supply current information on room rates and availability, and enable a reservation to be made electronically. The emergence of sophisticated electronic distribution channels and reservation technology make computers, and computer skills, an important part of yield management in hotel and resort operations.
- The American Automobile Association and Mobil are two major hotel rating services in the United States. Travel professionals often use the Hotel & Travel Index. Many other tour guides and facilities rating books are published each year.

ENDNOTES

1 New York City Bound? "Tipping Facts," *Hotels* (April 1993): 6.

2 "Rihga Royal Goes Cellular: Guests Take Calls Anywhere," *Cornell Hotel and Restaurant Administration Quarterly* (December 1992): 92.

3 R. Dan Reid and Melvin Sandler, "The Use of Technology to Improve Service Quality," *Cornell Hotel and Restaurant Administration Quarterly* (June 1992): 68–73.

4 Nelson R. Bean, "Planning for Catastrophe: The Fast Track to Recovery," *Cornell Hotel and Restaurant Administration Quarterly* (April 1992): 64–69.

5 Anne Spiselman, "Speed & Quality in Roomservice," *Hotels* (April 1993): 58–60.

6 Ibid., 58.

7 Ibid., 60.

8 Personalized Management Associates, http://www.pmasearch.com/.

9 Bruce Tracey and Timothy R. Hinkin, "The Costs of Employee Turnover: When the Devil is in the Details," *Cornell University School of Hotel Administration.* The Center for Hospitality Research Reports (December 2006): 8.

10 John J. Hogan, "Turnover and What To Do About It," *Cornell Hotel and Restaurant Administration Quarterly* (February 1992): 40.

11 Lawrence E. Sternberg, "Empower vs. Control," *Cornell Hotel and Restaurant Administration Quarterly* (February 1992): 69–73.

12 Gerald L. Uslander, "From Companies That Have Family Leave: How Costly and Disruptive Is It Really?" *Employment Relations Today* (Spring 1993): 5.

13 Dan Lacey, *Your Rights in the Workplace* (Berkeley: Nolo Press, 1991), 6/2.

[14] Titus Aaron and Edward Dry, "Sexual Harassment in the Hospitality Industry," *Cornell Hotel and Restaurant Administration Quarterly* (April 1992): 93–95. This article presents and extends the major recommendations summarized in this paragraph.
[15] Hotel & Motel Management, March 17, 1997.
[16] Ibid.
[17] U.S. Department of State, http://www.state.gov, 1998.
[18] Hotel News Resource, http://www.hotelnewsresource.com, 2006.
[19] Historic Hotels of America, http://www.lakeside-inn.com, 1998.
[20] www.aaa.com/Diamond

CHECK YOUR KNOWLEDGE

1. Explain the difference between the terms *front-of-the-house* and *back-of-the-house* and name two job titles in each area.
2. Describe the five basic functions around which all hotel and motel services are organized.
3. Explain why room service can be an expensive operation, and describe methods hotels use to speed service and increase efficiency.
4. Identify methods hotels use to reduce their turnover rate.
5. Explain the major legal mandates that relate to hiring and employment.

APPLY YOUR SKILLS

Review this hotel's simplified list of expenses and revenues for the past three years and use this data to answer the questions below.

Year 1 Expenses: $1,475,000
No. of Rooms for Rent: 115
Average Room Rate: $65
Average Occupancy: 65%

Year 2 Expenses: $1,525,000
No. of Rooms for Rent: 115
Average Room Rate: $65
Average Occupancy: 70%

Year 3 expenses: $1,700,000
No. of Rooms for Rent: 115
Average Room Rate: $75
Average Occupancy: 60%

1. How much money was collected in each of these years from room rental?
2. Calculate the net profit (before taxes and loan interest) earned in each of the three years. Which year was most profitable?
3. If the average room rate remains at $75 in Year 3, what does the occupancy rate need to be in order to increase net profits to 25 percent of total expenses?

INTERNET EXERCISES

The U.S. government provides information about job prospects in a publication entitled "Occupational Outlook Handbook." Visit the Department of Labor's Web site and search for data on three hospitality-related occupations. Then answer the following questions for each of the three occupations you selected.

1. What are the typical working conditions for the position?
2. What are the primary qualifications for the position?

3. What is the job outlook for the position?
4. What are the average earnings for the position?

WHAT DO YOU THINK?

1. What do you think would be some of the benefits and difficulties of employing mentally challenged individuals in a hotel operation? Explain.
2. Your hotel employs many foreign-born individuals. What benefits or modifications do you think might be important to offer in order to maximize the productivity and satisfaction of these employees? What could you do to maximize communication and cooperation between immigrants and native-born employees?
3. You own a small independent central-city hotel that appeals to business travelers. You have the opportunity to become a franchisee of a major brand. What factors should you consider before deciding whether to align with a franchise company or remain independent?
4. What are some methods you would employ to discourage employee theft at a hotel?
5. Which technological innovation do you think has changed the nature of the hotel business the most in the last ten to fifteen years? Explain.

CASE STUDY

You have recently become the general manager of a large hotel facility in the southeastern United States. The annual turnover rate among housekeeping staff has steadily increased to more than 150 percent. Your housekeeping staff includes 575 hourly employees. You know that the hotel wastes thousands of dollars replacing hourly workers.

You have decided that one of your major goals for the next year will be to develop methods that decrease turnover. Your goal for the first year is to decrease turnover to 100 percent.

1. Using the industry average of $2,000 per hourly employee, what is the cost of turnover for the year? If turnover is reduced to 100 percent, how much will the hotel save in one year?
2. What changes could you make in recruitment and hiring that might reduce turnover?
3. How could you calculate the costs and the benefits of operating an on-site child-care center? How could you calculate the costs and the benefits of reimbursing employees for part of their child-care expenses?

Foodservice

Supplying food and drink to hungry customers is a time-honored practice that dates back over the centuries. A wonderful twelfth-century Chinese painting on silk depicts a vendor in a bamboo stall selling sweetmeats (candied fruits and cakes). Restaurants unearthed from the tons of ashes from Mt. Vesuvius that buried Pompeii in AD 62 show not only that restaurants existed, but that they catered to different budgets and needs. Some were set in amiable surroundings; others were in dim little rooms.

Travel and the growth of cities gave rise to the need for commercial food establishments. As the world's population has continued to grow, as economic circumstances have continued to change, and as technology and improvements in communications have brought the cultures of the world closer together, that need has kept pace. Today, the variety of foods and beverages available, the different foodservice operations that offer them, and the many ways to cook and serve them would be mind-boggling to the food and beverage providers of the past. This variety offers a cornucopia of food for thought to hospitality students of the present.

ch6

Hospitality and the Foodservice Industry

OVERVIEW

The U.S. foodservice industry is gigantic. More than 12.8 million workers—about 9 percent of the total workforce—are employed in foodservice. Over 935,000 foodservice facilities operate in the United States, ranging in scope from street-corner hot dog vendors to elegant full-service restaurants. The average adult eats out 192 times each year and spends 44 cents of each food dollar on meals purchased away from home. On any given day about 46 percent of the population are foodservice patrons.[1]

In this chapter, you will learn some different ways to classify foodservice establishments according to type of business and level of service, and you will learn the difference between commercial and institutional (on-site) foodservice.

OBJECTIVES

When you have completed this chapter, you should be able to:

1 Describe the relationship between market, concept, and menu in commercial and retail foodservice.

2 Identify the primary characteristics of fine dining, theme, ethnic, casual, family, and cafeteria/buffet restaurants.

3 Describe the key differences among independent, chain, and franchise foodservice operations.

4 Describe the differences between commercial and institutional (on-site) foodservices.

5 Identify the primary characteristics of the segments of the institutional foodservice market.

KEY TERMS

commercial foodservice
concept
cook-chill
exponential
franchisee
franchisor
market segments
menu engineering
on-site foodservice
price-value relationship

The Relationship of Market, Concept, and Menu

In this chapter, market, concept, and menu are the basic tools used in describing foodservice operations. Every operation, from small "mom and pop" stores to large chain restaurant organizations, serves a particular segment of the overall market for foodservice. Each foodservice operation responds to the needs and expectations of its market through its concept and menu. Proper alignment of market, concept and menu is essential in achieving a successful foodservice enterprise.

Market Segments

It is a basic truth in the hospitality business that meeting the needs and expectations of guests is necessary for success. Failure to meet the guests' expectations and needs means they will not return, and the business will inevitably close. Every foodservice operation depends upon its ability to respond to the demands of its customers.

Not all potential customers have identical needs and expectations for foodservice. Some people enjoy and are able to afford fine dining at relatively expensive restaurants, while others prefer the company of other regulars in a neighborhood restaurant. Some people prefer the adventure of ethnic dining and others the predictability of a steak and a baked potato. Individuals experience different needs and expectations of foodservice at different times. Special occasions, such as birthdays or anniversaries, may call for celebratory meals. For more ordinary occasions, such as traveling across town to a business meeting, the best course of action might be to grab a burger at a quick-service restaurant on the way.

Market segments is a term used to describe subgroups of consumers who share a specific set of needs and expectations. In foodservice, for example, businesspeople seeking to impress prospective clients constitute a market segment, just as do families traveling the interstate highway seeking an inexpensive and convenient place to stop. Each segment has decidedly different needs and expectations for its dining experiences. The restaurant that satisfies the needs of the traveling family is not as likely to draw the businessperson for a power lunch.

When thinking about market segments, it is helpful to imagine actual people with real needs and expectations for dining. However, it is important to remember that the same people may occupy several market segments, depending on their needs and expectations for foodservice at any given moment. The businessperson seeking a dramatic and impressive dining experience on Friday may, on Saturday, become part of a traveling family looking for a quick-service meal. An individual can be, and often is, part of two or more market segments. Consequently, while market segments often seem to describe distinct groups of individuals, they actually focus on sets of needs and expectations.

Market segmentation is based on the principle that it is very difficult, if not impossible, to be all things to all people. A single restaurant cannot serve the needs of all people at all times. Focusing on a specific set of related needs and expectations for foodservice makes it possible for a restaurant to excel in particular ways, thus drawing the attention—and business—of those who seek that particular dining experience.

Market segmentation helps a restaurant define and target groups of customers within its marketplace. If a restaurant understands and knows how to evaluate market segment performance, it will be able to analyze predicted customer volume, including niche opportunities. Determining the ideal segment to target requires a restaurant to perform significant market analysis before it arrives at a final concept and menu. However, doing this will help it achieve optimal competitive positioning.

Think of the foodservice market like a pie—one that is sliced into segments. However, it is not always easy to tell where in the market to make the first cut or how big a slice to take. The foodservice market can be divided in many different ways, and not all yield consistent results. The key for any successful foodservice venture is to identify which opportunities exist in a specific marketplace. Dividing the market into various segments gives investors the opportunity to determine which market segment offers the best chance for success. "Success" in this context means achieving the best possible alignment of concept, talent, opportunity, and customer wants and needs. Consider the following examples of how the foodservice industry can be segmented.

Geographic Location

For some foodservice operations, a convenient location is essential for success. Most quick-service restaurants have multiple locations because few people are inclined to drive two hours for a hamburger and fries. However, some other restaurants, known as *destination restaurants*, which have earned their reputation for, say, serving wonderful steaks and huge portions, may draw their clientele from relatively great distances.

Age

Among the fast-food restaurant chains, McDonald's has achieved a considerable competitive advantage by targeting children. The Ronald McDonald character, playgrounds, and specialized decor, as well as a tradition of making corporate gifts to children's charities, all function to strengthen McDonald's appeal to the younger set—and its parents. Many of these children remain loyal to McDonald's even after becoming adults. They then introduce their own children to McDonald's. This has resulted in generation-to-generation brand loyalty within McDonald's market segment.

Ethnicity

Ethnicity can be a powerful draw in terms of customer loyalty and community development. Restaurants identified as purveyors of ethnic foods may appeal to members of a cuisine's ethnic group as well as to others who are interested in enjoying foods from different cultures. Ethnically based foodservice offers comfort and familiarity by providing foods that are considered to be part of a culture.

Social Class

Certain kinds of restaurants confirm their customers' social class—or, at least, their customers' social aspirations. Such restaurants may be places where it is possible to see the famous, or where it is fashionable for the famous to be seen. Customers expect these venues to provide high quality in both concept and execution. For instance, an upscale restaurant would probably not last very long if it served meals on placemats set with plastic flatware, because customers expect linen tablecloths and polished silverware.

Price

Some restaurants are known for being expensive, others are known for being inexpensive. Typically, the criterion is not so much the actual dollars spent but the cost in relation to the value received. Marketing specialists refer to this phenomenon as the **price-value relationship**. Customers expect to receive greater value for higher prices, or at least to get value or quality that is in line with the price paid.

Market segments are very fluid in the foodservice industry. Customers' needs and expectations may vary widely depending on the circumstances of the moment. In addition, their needs and expectations defy neat categorization along one or two easily identified dimensions. The decor may be critical in fulfilling some guests' expectations, whereas for other guests the decor is irrelevant. Foodservice operations that understand the needs and expectations of their guests, and are effective at meeting them, are far more likely to succeed than those that do not. Equally important is not overreaching customer needs and thereby wasting valuable resources on components of the operation that are unimportant to the consumer.

Concept

Overall concept is one of the primary ways an establishment responds to its market segment. **Concept** refers to the many elements in a foodservice operation that contribute to its function as a complete and organized system that serves the needs and expectations of its guests. Some of the most basic elements in a foodservice operation's concept include the size of the facility, its location, its feel and personality, and its hours of operation.

Facility Size

The size of a foodservice facility is usually described in terms of its annual dollar volume or number of seats, although overall square footage or number of meals served also describes size. The number of seats is directly related to the volume of business conducted by the operation, except where take-out, delivery, or drive-through windows are a significant part of the business. Other than restaurants that offer take-out and delivery, operations with more seats have the potential to do more business than comparable, smaller ones that charge equal prices.

In theory, there is a best size for every foodservice operation. An operation can be too small, so it loses business; too large, so it is expensive to maintain; or just right. There is only one hard-and-fast rule pertaining to the size of an operation: the facility should have sufficient capacity to meet the needs of the market as profitably as possible. A six-hundred-seat restaurant may have a difficult time surviving in a small town on the eastern edge of Montana because it cannot generate enough business to pay for the space and the utilities needed to keep it warm and lighted. Similarly, a sixty-seat fine dining operation in a major urban area may turn customers away or have lines stretching down the block, and would thus do better financially if it had one hundred seats. Of course, most foodservice operators would rather deal with the problem of too many customers than too few. Smaller restaurants can perform adequately as long as their turnover rate is high. Turnover (the rate at which guests move through a restaurant) is a significant factor in operating a successful restuarant. A restaurant with frequent turnover may have fewer seats than its competition, but do a greater volume of business. A high turnover rate per meal period would be three times the number of seats in the entire restaurant.

Construction and development costs have a significant impact on a foodservice establishment's success or failure. If the initial overhead costs associated with acquiring land and building a facility are prohibitive, it places more pressure on the operational performance of the restaurant to succeed financially. If fixed overhead costs are disproportionate to income, viability becomes a problem.

Location

Location is a critical factor in many foodservice concepts. A great product at a great price is of no value if it is too far away from its intended market. For this reason, most chain restaurants prepare a careful site analysis before locating a new unit to ensure it is convenient to the target market. Location must be viewed holistically when developing the concept for a new foodservice operation. A restaurant with a dramatic and unusual theme may be able to draw its clientele from a far greater area than an ordinary operation. Similarly, some locations seem destined for restaurant success because of external factors, such as proximity to major tourist attractions.

Sometimes it is said that the three key elements in any restaurant's success are, in order, "location, location, location." This statement, while partly true, is misleading without further explanation. Different market segments require different locations. A good location for one concept may be horrible for another. Some restaurants thrive far off the beaten path; some fail on a busy street corner. But good visibility and street access are a factor in location quality. If a foodservice establishment is located inside a mall and customers have to make a left turn across six lanes of traffic at an intersection without a traffic light to enter the mall parking lot, the establishment may be doomed because it has neither good visibility nor ease of access.

Hours of Operation

Hours of operation may seem like a rather mundane element of a foodservice operation's concept, but deciding when to be open for business is extremely important. The cost of labor needs to be balanced against customer demand. A truck stop restaurant that is not open around the clock does not understand the needs of its primary clientele. Similarly, restaurants in urban areas may thrive by serving only the lunch trade. Again, the key is to determine customer needs and expectations and then strive to meet them.

Theme and Design

For a number of contemporary foodservice operations, theme is the central element in the concept. Difficult to describe with precision, theme can be thought of as the collective effect of a number of factors that, when joined, create a distinctive total dining experience. Restaurants with strong themes give their guests the sense of being transported to another time or place, capturing the imagination by projecting a specific atmosphere and personality.

Often a theme is derived from another culture. For example, Polynesian-themed restaurants, popular in the 1970s, created an atmosphere of the tropical islands. Cane furnishings, fishing nets, flower-print uniforms, and special appetizers and entrees transported guests from cold city winters to an imagined warm tropical paradise.

Rather than borrowing from another culture or time, a theme may intensify the characteristics of local culture for the amusement of tourists. A popular trend in Texas some years ago was the "western experience." Northerners dressed in western garb frequented huge restaurants on the outskirts of cities, where they sat at picnic tables, ate barbecue, drank Texas beer, listened to country music, and rode (at least for a moment) the mechanical bucking bronco.

Themes also may reflect special interests: rock music (Hard Rock Café), automobiles (Studebaker's), or sports celebrities (Michael Jordan's), to name a few. Several cities are witnessing a resurgence of diners, perhaps driven by nostalgia for a simpler past. Some restaurants even parody the past, such as Ed Debevic's, a restaurant built to imitate a classic diner of the 1950s.

Design is important to virtually all foodservice operations, and is particularly vital to themed operations. Through design—the arrangement of space, the finishes, the furnishings, the table settings (plates, glasses, and flatware), the lighting, the sound, and the choice of colors—the theme of a restaurant is made visually apparent to the guest.

Industry Insights

RAINFOREST CAFÉ

Themed Restaurant Concept

The Rainforest Café is positioned to attract families with children and adults seeking to have an adventure during their dining experience. The Rainforest Café is innovatively designed to recreate a forest atmosphere with automated gorillas, singing parrots, rain showers, and waterfalls. The servers dress in colorful floral, jungle print outfits. One of the most interactive features that accentuate the rain forest theme is a simulated thunderstorm, followed by a rain sprinkle. The menu is themed to match the décor, and specialty exotic drinks are served in souvenir glasses. Each outlet is designed with a gift shop in the front of the building, so guests waiting for tables can shop for retail products with the rain forest motif.[1]

In restaurants that have no explicit theme, design is still important. Design creates the subtle quality known as atmosphere. It conveys to the guests in powerful, but often subconscious, ways the nature of the establishment. Different lighting approaches can, for example, create a sense of excitement and action or delineate intimate spaces.

Design is a critical element in the guest's experience of value. Through design the guest receives subtle cues. How far apart are the tables? Are the walls painted or papered? Are they made of solid mahogany? Are the tablecloths white linen? Red and white checkerboard oilcloth? Brown butcher paper? Some restaurants serve crab on fine china and others serve it on plastic dinnerware. Still others slice a cardboard beer case in half lengthwise, put a dozen crabs steamed in spices in the box, haul it to the table, and serve it to the guest with a bib and a wooden mallet. Each way speaks differently of value and targets a different market segment.

Quality in design speaks subtly of value. However, this is not to say that expensive design is necessary for success. Everything depends upon the needs and expectations of the market. An inexpensive restaurant with great food may be a success even though it is obvious that the dining room was, until a month ago, a coin-operated laundromat. Similarly, many restaurants dare not invest in obvious efforts at "design" for fear of driving away the regulars who would never consider eating or drinking at a place with pretensions. But these are exceptions that prove the rule. A fine dining establishment expecting the average customer to spend $150 per meal should not serve caviar on a paper plate or a fine Cabernet Sauvignon in a plastic cup.

---

[1] http://www.rainforestcafe.com

Forms of Service

Form of service refers to the way food and beverages are presented to the guest. Different forms of service address the varying needs of different market segments and also contribute to the guest's perception of value. Service forms range from formalized tableside cooking to self-service buffets with a cashier at the end of the counter.

Table Service

Table service is positioned at the higher end of the market and targeted to the middle to upper demographic segment. Guests are seated by a host or hostess. Orders are taken by servers at the table, and food and beverages are brought to the table. Usually, several courses are offered on the menu, which is accompanied by a wine list or a listing of specialty drinks. Soiled dishes are cleared by servers or buspersons.

Buffet Service

Buffet service is positioned at the low to middle level of the market and targets the value-conscious and family segments. Buffet service is also associated with catered events or special events where guests come to a "buffet table" to obtain food and beverages. Wedding receptions, church potlucks, and Sunday brunches at restaurants and clubs often use buffet service. The distinguishing factor is that the guest must come to the buffet table for food.

Banquet Table Service

Banquet table service is common at large group events, such as special events and conventions. It can be targeted to the family, social, or business market. Banquet service is very similar to ordinary table service in that a server brings food to the guests' table. However, banquet service often requires transportation of food from a central kitchen. Food may be "plated" in the central kitchen and moved in special heated carriers to the dining area, or it may be transported in bulk to a small serving kitchen adjacent to the dining area and plated there.

Cafeteria Service

Cafeteria service is targeted at low-end and institutional markets. It is found in student and corporate dining halls and fast food venues such as ballparks. In cafeteria service, like buffet service, guests pick up their own food and take it to their table. The difference between the two is that cafeteria-style service typically has employees "dishing up" food for customers, whereas buffets are usually self service. Cafeterias also have permanent serving counters, whereas many buffet serving areas are temporary. Cafeteria service originally required guests to form a single line that passed by counters with beverages, desserts, entrees, etc. Contemporary cafeteria service designs are far more free flowing, allowing customers to circulate from counter to counter at will. Some cafeterias are very similar to food courts—open spaces with multiple food outlets and selections of of cuisine with a common seating area: guests can choose among "shops" specializing in a particular type of food item or style of cuisine.

Family-Style Service

Family-style service is positioned as a value concept in the market and is often used at summer camps, as well as in a small number of commercial restaurants, particularly ethnic restaurants. Family-style service involves bringing various food items in sufficient quantities for tables of six, eight, twelve, or more diners. Food is passed from person to person, as at a traditional family dinner. In some forms of family service, one person at the table is designated to go to a counter where bowls and platters of food are available. In another form, the food is brought to the table by servers. In Basque restaurants, such as those found in Winnemuca, Nevada, diners are seated with strangers at long picnic-style tables. The menu is fixed—guests eat what the server brings to the table.

Room Service

Room service is associated with hotels, where guests can order a meal from a menu and have it brought to their room. Similar systems characterize contemporary hospital foodservice, where patients order from a menu and their selections are brought to their rooms. Hospitals, however, tend to provide meals at scheduled times, whereas hotel room service may be available twenty-four hours a day. Typical room service menus are derived from the hotel restaurant's menu offerings, with a significant surcharge added.

Quick Counter Service

Quick counter service establishments are positioned at the low end of the market and target the value-conscious and fast-food segments. At quick counter service operations, the customer stands at a counter, places an order, pays, waits while the order is assembled, and then receives the order. Fast-food restaurants such as McDonald's and Burger King utilize quick counter service. Food materials are delivered to outlets in packaged and/or processed form for quick preparation and service.

Traditional Counter Service

Traditional counter service represents an earlier form of ordering and receiving food more quickly than is found in restaurants with table service. Customers, particularly single customers, who do not want to take a table and wait for a server can sit on a stool at the counter. There they are served by a counter person, often a short-order cook. A number of coffee shop chains (Denny's) as well as lunch counters in discount stores such as WalMart provide traditional counter service.

Industry Insights

HISTORY

The Diner

They're all the same. They're all different. Located in Anywhere, USA, the diner is an American tradition. It's a place where the coffee and the gossip are hot and the server knows your name (perhaps "Hon" or "Sugar" if you aren't from the area). It's a place where the day's tasks are done fast and efficiently, where the grill sizzles and the refrigerator hums—all within view of the customer, who perches on a traditional chrome stool.

When Walter "Scotty" Scott opened his horse-drawn lunch wagon in Providence, Rhode Island in 1872, the diner began an era that has ebbed and flowed—yet endured—over the years. During the time just before and after World War II, the American landscape was sprinkled with diners—six thousand of them. Today, fewer than one-third of that number exist, although the number is growing again.

Early diners were manufactured in factories, built on wheels, and streamlined for efficiency. (Traditionally, a counter divides the diner in half—one half for the kitchen, one half for the customers.) Over the years, diners have undergone many transformations, including the addition of booths and tables to expand customer seating and the introduction of a myriad of interior designs, ranging from sanitized white Formica to Art Moderne.

And with its revival in recent years, the diner is popping up again not only in the United States, but also in Canada and Europe, pushing an American icon higher on its chrome pedestal.

Take-out Service

The term "take-out" is generally applied to table-service restaurants that offer food to customers who prefer to take it home and eat it there. Some contemporary restaurants, like Pizza Hut's delivery-and-take-out-only units, offer take-out service but do not have tables. Today, many full-service restaurants offer take-out service as a normal component of day-to-day operations in order to significantly increase their market share and revenues.

Delivery Service

Delivery service, where prepared food is brought to the customer's home, was popularized for today's consumers by Domino's Pizza. But delivery service also characterizes meals on wheels programs for seniors, as well as urban restaurants that deliver within neighborhoods. Some delivery services are not

Photo copyright © Papa John's Corporation

Pizza is often delivered directly to the customer.

connected with a particular restaurant. Instead, they offer a limited menu of items from various participating neighborhood restaurants. The customer places an order with the delivery service, which in turn places the order with the restaurant, picks up the order, and delivers it to the customer.

Carhop Service

Carhop service originated with the "drive-in" restaurants made popular in southern California in the 1940s and 1950s. Customers drive into the restaurant parking lot but remain in their cars. Orders are called into an intercom or are given directly to a carhop (a server) who comes to the driver's side window. The carhop returns with the food, presents the check, and collects payment. In some instances, the fifties drive-in concept is reinforced by service personnel who, like carhops of the past, wear roller skates to serve patrons.

Drive-Through Service

Drive-through service is the contemporary counterpart to carhop service. Drive-through service is commonly found in quick-service restaurants. Customers place an order through a microphone, drive forward to a window, pay, and receive their order. A variation on the system uses two windows, one to receive payment and the next to deliver food. Today, new drive-through coffee establishments are popping up all over the world. Many small vacant lots have been developed with two-sided drive-through coffee and breakfast outlets that target commuters on their way to work.

Quality of Service

Quality of service is a relative term that depends on the form of service, price point, market position, and concept involved. Each type of service is characterized by different criteria. Speed of service is critical in quick counter service, but not as critical in fine dining table service, where guests do not want to be rushed through an expensive meal. Similarly, a server who confuses who ordered what at a table is more quickly forgiven than a drive-through restaurant worker who mixes up orders and gives the double hamburger to the Chevy and the fish sandwich to the Honda, instead of the other way around.

One helpful way to view quality of service is through the idea of "service scripts." A service script is a sequence of interactions implicitly anticipated by both the service person and the guest. The script lays out what each party is to say and do and contains the expectations for the service encounter.

Different foodservice operations have different scripts. Guests at fine dining restaurants expect to be seated and served. However, table service is not part of the script at quick-service restaurants.

The server and the guest may have different expectations; if so, they may be acting out different scripts. When expectations go unfulfilled, problems can emerge. For example, a guest whose experience is not going according to the script—"Why hasn't that server come to pick up the check?"—may interpret the experience as poor service. He or she may not be aware that, in this establishment, guests pay the cashier. Regardless of level of service, efficient and knowledgable service personnel are essential. The server should be able to answer questions about menu offerings and specials. The service script may be helpful in establishing a flow of communication, but nothing beats an accurate description of menu items and an informed approach to selling the establishment's food and beverage products.

Ideally, a foodservice operation's concept is closely related to the needs and expectations of its target market, and in some ways they are inseparable. However, the elements of a foodservice concept, like market segments, are best thought of as fluid. For a given concept, some elements may be essential whereas others may be less important or irrelevant. A restaurant such as a coffee shop that seeks the breakfast trade, but whose hours of operation are from 11:00 A.M. until 10:00 P.M., is a contradiction in terms and can hardly be expected to succeed. Another example is a hot dog stand in a baseball stadium: it will not stand or fall on the attractiveness of its decor.

Menu

Many people who frequent restaurants believe the menu is a list of what the chef prefers to cook. Even some restaurateurs believe that they are the food experts and thus their menus should reflect what they believe is best for the customer.

Only the most renowned chefs are able to develop a menu that both expresses their culinary artistry and succeeds in the marketplace. Most restaurateurs understand that the customer is the final—and most important—judge of the menu. If customers cannot find what they expect on the menu, the choice is simple: Go elsewhere.

The menu is the foodservice operation's plan for meeting the needs and expectations of its guests. It is perhaps the most significant element in the execution of the foodservice enterprise. It lists those items that customers will desire and appreciate. It dictates staffing, equipment, space layout, and investment requirements. The menu, therefore, is the product plan for a restaurant and, as such, is the biggest determinant of whether it will achieve a profitable return on investment.

Conventional wisdom holds that the more items listed on the menu, the more customer needs and expectations can be satisfied. Therefore, an extensive menu is ideal. In fact, the opposite is true in most cases. A limited menu frequently is more profitable than an extensive menu. A limited menu is far easier than an extensive menu to "position" in the mind of the potential customer. Doing a few menu items exceptionally well is usually more effective than trying to do everything moderately well. Trying to do everything often results in being known for doing nothing in particular very well. **Menu engineering** is a valuable tool. A restaurant can use its menu strategically to market signature items, thus differentiating its concept while minimizing the number of items on the menu.

One market advantage of a limited menu is that customers know what they will be served. Certainly, take-out services like Domino's Pizza and Pizza Hut Delivery benefit from this advantage. These companies know that the customers who call have already narrowed their choices. A smaller menu refines the operation's focus so it can operate in a disciplined, efficient manner.

No hard and fast rules define what constitutes a limited or extensive menu. Much depends on the foodservice operation's concept and market. For example, twelve entrees (main items) would be a rather extensive menu for a drive-through-only hamburger stand. However, twelve entrees would constitute a relatively limited menu in a casual dining restaurant such as a Bennigan's or a T.G.I. Friday's, where the concept dictates that there be a broad variety of menu offerings. The goal of menu limitation is not to reduce every menu to six items or less. Rather, it is to find the optimal number of menu items necessary to meet the needs and expectations of the market segment, operate a profitable establishment, and give the operation a well-defined position in the minds of potential customers.

Menus typically state prices for food and beverage items. Pricing, like menu item selection, should demonstrate a clear understanding of the market segment served by the foodservice operation. Prices that are too high will not generate perceived value in the eyes of customers. But pricing has an effect on profits, and prices that are too low will threaten the operation's financial survival. Setting prices for menu items is thus a balancing act. Specific strategies for pricing go beyond the scope of this text. But it is important to emphasize that menu pricing, like menu item selection, ultimately will be judged by the customer.

The menu and the concept of a foodservice operation are closely related. Ideally, the menu items and prices closely fit the concept. Ed Debevic's, a restaurant designed to resemble a 1950s-style diner, serves hamburgers, meat loaf, and fried chicken. Salmon ceviche or foie gras would clearly be out of place.

Contemporary Commercial Foodservice Concepts

Market, concept, and menu are helpful tools for understanding similarities and differences among foodservice operations. These tools bring into focus key elements in foodservice that can then be used to identify trends and developments in the industry. Market, concept, and menu can also be used to classify foodservice operations, both commercial and institutional. Commercial foodservice operations range from fine dining establishments to quick-service restaurants. (Institutional foodservice concepts are discussed in a subsequent section.)

Fine Dining

The fine dining restaurant is characterized by a high level of attentive table service, expensive-looking furnishings and decor, and fine cuisine. This category of restaurant sometimes is referred to as "white tablecloth," as tables in such establishments are often covered in white linen and set with fine china and flatware and crystal glasses. Prices lie at the high end of the spectrum, with guests paying $100 or more to enjoy an appetizer, entree, and dessert. The addition of liquor or wine can drive the average customer check over $150 per person.

Business Profile

ROY'S RESTAURANTS

Contemporary Dining Concept—Fusion Cuisine

Roy Yamaguchi is a chef known for his fusion cuisine, which originated in the Hawaiian Islands. He was born in Japan and grew up in Hawaii, where he learned to blend the two cultures. Yamaguchi gained national and international recognition for his excellence in culinary creativity when he introduced "Hawaiian fusion cuisine." He has a master chef accreditation from the Culinary Institute of America in New York, and has built his name and culinary skills into a worldwide brand.

Yamaguchi is now regarded as a pioneer who mastered a distinctive style that brought his cooking to the forefront of contemporary gastronomy. As testimony to his success, there are now thirty-five Roy's restaurants, including twenty-five in the continental United States, seven in Hawaii, two in Japan, and one in Guam.[1]

---

[1] http://roysrestaurant.com

Historically, fine dining establishments tend to flourish during periods of economic growth.

The fine dining category can be further divided into smaller segments. Some fine dining restaurants draw a clientele of culinary adventurers who choose a restaurant because of the reputation of the chef. Such restaurants are termed "celebrity chef" operations. Examples include Danny Meyers' restaurants in New York City, Michael Mina's restaurants in Las Vegas, Wolfgang Puck's restaurants in southern California, and Charlie Trotter's restaurants in Chicago and Las Vegas.

Other fine dining restaurants may depend on their landmark location to attract an upscale tourist trade. These operations are often found atop the tallest buildings in major cities or adjacent to tourist destinations. Indeed, some restaurants are destinations in their own right.

Through cuisine, landmark location, or other factors, white tablecloth restaurants make every effort to create a dining experience that communicates elegance, refinement, and attentiveness to each guest's spoken and unspoken needs. In the context of culture and society, fine dining restaurants may serve as a means for individuals of wealth to express their status or entertain like-minded and socially connected individuals. An invitation to dine at a white tablecloth restaurant can be a subtle (or even overt) attempt to impress or influence. The finer the restaurant, the finer the experience and the greater the opportunity to create a lasting impression.

Because of their relatively high position on the price scale, fine dining restaurants thrive in periods of economic prosperity but suffer during economic downturns. Their success also has been affected by societal factors, such as changes in tax laws that reduce the deduction for business meals, and troublesome economic conditions. However, as of this writing the popularity of fine dining and celebrity chef–sponsored restaurants was at an all-time high. The establishment of additional high-end dining venues and the development of distinctive food products have created an unprecedented opportunity for consumers to experience the best of the best in culinary talent. Uncertainty surrounding the economic recession in 2008, could hamper the economic growth and viability of many new restaurant start-up projects and threaten the on-going viability of these high-end dining concepts.

A number of organizations have diversified their clientele while maintaining brand identity by offering fine dining at a less expensive prices. They have done this by opening "sister" restaurants that offer the cachet of the original establishment at a lower price. For example, Chicago's Brasserie Jo is a sister restaurant to Everest, generally regarded as one of the top fine dining establishments in the city. Brasserie Jo is named after Jean Joho, the renowned chef at Everest, and offers similar Alsatian (eastern French) fare at a substantially lower price.

Theme Restaurants

Theme restaurants take a different approach to providing a distinctive dining experience. Whereas fine dining establishments tend to create a sense of elegant dining, theme restaurants seek to provide diners with an experience that evokes other times or places. Some themes are relatively mild in execution, such as restaurants that have visual touches drawn from English pubs, sports bars with memorabilia from local teams, or seafood restaurants with porthole-shaped windows. Other restaurants are far more dramatic in the enactment of their themes, such as Medieval Times, where guests watch jousting matches between knights on horseback. Price, cuisine, atmosphere, and service vary widely among theme restaurants. However, with respect to price, most fall within the middle range, charging $15 to $30 for appetizer, entree, and dessert. Similarly, most have table service. The atmosphere and design depend on the theme. Pricing may vary according to location; for instance, restaurants in urban centers often have prices at the higher end of the spectrum, while those in secondary or tertiary markets are at moderate or lower price points.

The theme of a restaurant has little to do with the quality of the food or the service, but it often helps the restaurant secure a position within the customer's mind as memorable, different, and fun. Themes thus help restaurants stand out from the crowd of everyday dining establishments. The risk of a theme restaurant is that the concept will not be attractive to a substantial number of people or will be just a fad and soon lose its appeal.

Casual Dinnerhouses

Closely related to theme restaurants are casual dinnerhouses such as Bennigan's, T.G.I. Friday's, and Chili's. Casual dinnerhouses seek to attract middle-income individuals who enjoy dining out yet wish to avoid high prices and the formality of fine dining restaurants. Thus their prices fall in the midrange, their atmosphere is comfortable, and their mood is relaxed. Alcohol is frequently served at casual dinnerhouses. They are often viewed as good price-value experiences.

Distinguishing between theme restaurants and casual dinnerhouses is not always possible. Many theme restaurants have a relaxed atmosphere, and many casual dinnerhouses have themes. The difference between the two is often a matter of interpretation. For many purposes, the two can be collapsed into one category. To complicate the categorization process further, some casual dinnerhouses have themes built around ethnicity or culture. Over the last few decades, a number of chain restaurant companies have developed casual dinnerhouse concepts with ethnic themes to attract the baby boom generation. Chi-Chi's (Mexican) and the Olive Garden (Italian) are prime examples.

Ethnic Restaurants

While a number of casual dinnerhouses have ethnic themes, true ethnic restaurants—whose origins and target markets are quite different—also exist. A separate category for ethnic restaurants is necessary to highlight these differences.

The ethnic restaurant category includes establishments closely tied to the cultures from which they originate. Such restaurants are often located in areas where large numbers of people of the culture live. The cuisine tends to be authentic rather than derivative, decor reflects the tastes of a particular culture, and the menus may be in the native language.

Ethnic restaurants represent a category of the commercial foodservice industry that is likely to experience significant growth in coming years. In part, this growth will be the result of globalization and the changing demographic composition of the United States. Also, the proliferation of ethnic restaurants serving authentic cuisine is likely to attract increasing numbers of guests who enjoy novel dining experiences and want to experience other cultures.

Ethnic restaurants reflect the variety and diversity of their native cultures. An ethnic restaurant may be expensive or inexpensive, elegant or casual. It may offer take-out with limited table service, like the typical Mexican *taqueria*, a restaurant that serves different kinds of tacos and *antojitos*, snacks made with corn tortillas. Rather than offering full-course meals, it may emphasize snack-size portions such as those served in a *tapas* bar, a restaurant that specializes in serving a variety of Spanish appetizers. It may be an Ethiopian restaurant that encourages guests to eat with their fingers or a Japanese restaurant where guests sit on the floor on padded mats.

Family Restaurants

Family restaurants, which in earlier years were classified as coffee shops, offer table and counter service, a somewhat limited menu, and a family-friendly atmosphere. The difference between casual/theme restaurants and family

A cook serving up orders at a small family restaurant.

Courtesy of Photodisc

restaurants is not always distinct, but the family restaurants are usually less sophisticated in theme and ambiance and alcohol is rarely sold. Children's menus and food choices that appeal to the younger palate are standard features, as are "comfort" foods such as mashed potatoes, biscuits and gravy, and macaroni dishes. It is not uncommon for a family restaurant to have breakfast items available all day. Complete meal prices fall in the $7 to $15 range. Shoney's, Bob Evans', and Denny's are family restaurants, as are many smaller locally owned and run operations.

Grill/Buffet

The grill/buffet category includes steakhouse chains that use buffet service as well as cafeterias. Steakhouses in this category include Golden Corral, Bonanza, Ponderosa, and Ryan's Family Steakhouse. Cafeterias include Home Town Buffet and Old Country Buffet (both divisions of Buffet, Inc.), Furr's/Bishop's, and Picadilly's. Both types of restaurants use a self-service format, and the buffet frequently offers all you can eat for one price. Grill and buffet restaurants traditionally serve segments of that market that seek high value for a relatively low price. Families seeking inexpensive meals and seniors on fixed incomes are important markets for these restaurants. These operations need a high volume of business to be profitable. The buffet concept often enables customers to consume larger-than-average quantities of food and therefore raises the restaurant's cost of food. However, because these restaurants have the ability to do a high volume of business with little waste, they have lower operating costs than those in other segments, allowing them to produce a viable incremental return on investment.

Cafeterias (now called buffets) were a popular concept in the early decades of the twentieth century, when they served inexpensive meals to working people. Some were extensive operations even by today's standards. The Ontrá Cafeteria in Chicago, for example, had seats for 1,226 patrons. Although the popularity of cafeterias has waned in many parts of the country, they remain strong in the southeastern area of the United States.

Industry experts agree that steakhouses and grill/buffets compete for the same customers. The grill/buffet category holds a relatively small share of the overall foodservice market (less than 3 percent), and struggled to maintain sales levels during the late 1990s. Today, cafeteria and quick-service concepts are sometimes offered in concert with one another. Stadiums and other special event venues may offer a combination of buffet, cafeteria, and quick-serve choices for diners. Hybrid buffet/cafeteria restaurants are not uncommon. They comingle themes and cuisine styles, offering customers a wide variety of food options.

Quick Service

The quick-service category, sometimes called fast food, is by far the largest in the foodservice industry. In fact, quick-service chains in the United States alone produced over $173 billion in sales in 2005, grossing additional billions in Europe and Asia.

While the "quick service" or "fast food" concept is usually identified with large, U.S.-based chains, quick food has long been part of many societies. Cities throughout the world have street vendors who proffer their wares—everything from tostadas near the waterfront in Veracruz to *gluay habn* (something like banana smoothies) in Thailand's markets. Similarly, fast food was available in the United States long before it became an institution through the expansion of major chains. During the late nineteenth century, lunch wagons served the needs of factory workers. Later, lunchrooms offered relatively speedy counter service thanks to short-order cooks who were highly skilled at preparing multiple orders. In the early decades of the twentieth century, Horn and Hardart pioneered the first vending machine chain, the "Automat," which required "only that patrons pump coins into slots beside the food of their choice, visible behind sparkling little windows."[2]

The quick-service category today is characterized by relatively low prices, limited menu offerings, utilitarian decor, and modified counter service. Factory-like food production processes make it possible to prepare of large quantities of menu items to exacting standards of quality and consistency.

This category is dominated by large chains. McDonald's is the largest chain in the world. In 2005 it had revenues over $20.4 billion and operated more than thirty-one thousand restaurants worldwide. Yum! Brands Inc., which owns Pizza Hut, KFC, Long John Silver's, and Taco Bell, is the second largest quick-service restaurant organization. Other large quick-service chains include

Foodservice operators are joining forces with large retailers.

Photo by Kaye (Kye-Sung) Chon

Burger King ($11.3 billion in 2002 sales) and Wendy's ($2.45 billion in 2006 sales). Many believe that this segment of the restaurant industry has reached the saturation point. Today the primary opportunities for growth in quick-service restaurants lie outside of the United States. For example, in 1992 McDonald's operated 8,959 restaurants in the United States and 4,134 restaurants (32 percent) in other countries. In 1997, the number of U.S. McDonald's outlets grew to 12,380, while its restaurants outside the United States numbered 10,752 (46 percent). From 1988 through 1997, McDonald's growth rate in net income from domestic operations was 3 percent; from non-U.S. operations, it was 19.4 percent, clearly indicating the importance of international expansion to the chain's continued growth. Today, there are over thirty thousand McDonald's outlets worldwide.

The quick-service market today includes themed, ethnically oriented eateries serving Chinese, Indian, Japanese, and Mexican food. Another growing trend in the quick-service market is the use of kiosks and carts to reach customers in high-volume, nontraditional sites. Kiosks require a much lower capital investment than freestanding restaurants, since the square footage needed for a kiosk operation is greatly less. Express restaurant kiosks now appear in airports, strip shopping centers, hospitals, and office buildings.

Neighborhood/Third Places

A valuable contemporary perspective on a particular kind of restaurant was presented by Ray Oldenburg in his book *The Great Good Place*. For Oldenburg, some hospitality establishments function for people as a "third place." People in modern society have a first place—their home. Their second place is where they work. The third place is where people congregate for informal public interaction away from home or work.[3]

Oldenburg argues that American society has been increasingly focused on the first two places—home and work. Suburbanization has uprooted families from traditional neighborhood ties and relationships, increasing the focus on the home. The demands of work have increased, and people find themselves both working more and spending more time getting to and from work. Little time is left for informal social interaction. And even when the time is available, the opportunity is not. Increasingly, Oldenburg says, Americans "...are encouraged to find their relaxation, entertainment, even safety, almost entirely within the privacy of homes that have become more a retreat from society than a connection to it."[4]

As Oldenburg sees it, the problem with the American emphasis on home and work is that neither is sufficient to provide a sense of community. Without a time and place for relief from the demands of work and the confines of home, Americans become impatient, bored, lonely, and alienated. The third place offers an alternative to the demands of work and the loneliness of suburban life. But the third place is more than a retreat or an escape. Third places offer what first and second places cannot: the informal social interaction that leads to genuine community.

Third places may include coffee shops, neighborhood taverns, and lunch counters. In Europe, the English pub, the French sidewalk café, and the German beer garden often function as third places. What sets third places apart from other commercial establishments are the following:

- Neutral ground. Third places are places where people can interact without the social pressures of being hosts or guests in a home. A third place is one where "individuals may come and go as they please, in which none are required to play host, and in which all feel at home and comfortable."[5]
- A leveler. Third places are inclusive and democratic. Contact with others is not based on similarities in social status, class, or rank. Rather, "the charm of one's personality, irrespective of his or her station in life, is what counts."[6]
- Conversation. Taverns where strangers watch a wall of large-screened televisions in sullen silence are not third places. Third places are characterized not only by conversation, but by good conversation—an art which many Americans lack, for want of practice.[7]
- Accessibility and accommodation. A third place is easily reached by people who live in the local area, and is available to them during most hours of the day and night. Third places "stand ready to serve people's needs for sociability and relaxation in the intervals before, between, and after their mandatory appearances elsewhere."[8]

- The regulars. Third places, by their very nature, are supported by a core of regulars. Regulars are the people who make the place come alive. As Oldenburg pointedly observes, the regular visitor does not go to the third place because of the quality of food or the happy-hour drink specials. Instead, "what attracts the regular visitor to a third place is supplied…by the fellow customers."[9]
- A low profile. Third places are not fancy or well decorated. Thus they "discourage pretension" and encourage regulars to "come as they are."[10]
- Home away from home. Third places are not homes, but they are like them in several key ways. They offer a sense of possession without ownership—although it is not clear whether the third place belongs to the regulars or vice versa! By facilitating interaction among friends, they regenerate people in an atmosphere where they can be themselves. Third places provide a warmth that "emerges out of friendliness, support, and mutual concern."[11]

The kinds of hospitality establishments that qualify as third places offer an interesting contrast to the kinds of restaurants often held up as models for success in the hospitality industry today. Seldom are third places highlighted on the front page of *Nation's Restaurant News*. In fact, by many commercial and financial measures of sound management, third places are examples of what not to do. One could easily point out that regulars who spend lots of time but little money are poor customers, that an attractive decor would entice more customers than a plain one, that better food would improve business, and that closing during slow periods makes good business sense. All of these criticisms of third places are valid. However, they all miss the important point. The kinds of business strategies and management practices that make for commercially successful bars and restaurants are not as effective in the third place. They may even destroy its nature as a social gathering place for regulars. Today, the most common seen and readily available third place, both in and out of the United States, is Starbucks. A chain based in Seattle, Washington, Starbucks has fast emerged on both the domestic and international scene as a neighborhood gathering place with relaxed seating, quick-service food and beverage products, music, entertainment, and Internet connectivity.

Oldenburg's concept of the third place provides a helpful perspective on the social and cultural dimensions of hospitality, often overlooked by those who see only its "business" aspects.

Coffeehouses

Coffeehouses are among the fastest growing foodservice concepts largely because of the dynamic growth of Starbucks, which expanded from fewer than two hundred stores in 1992 to over three thousand stores in 2007. Just as the explosive growth of Pizza Hut several decades ago created a market in which competitors found a place, so has Starbucks made it possible for numerous other coffeehouses to succeed. Many coffeehouses in urban and suburban

Many coffee shops offer a wide variety of coffees and a place to relax.

areas provide a contemporary version of a third place, where patrons gather to talk, read the newspaper, and enjoy a latte or cappuccino. In cyber-cafés, patrons log on to the Internet rather than reading the morning paper.

Catering

Today catering and special event planning continues to grow both in dollars and in its share of the foodservice industry, however, when the overall food and beverage industry declines during uncertain economic times the catering and events segment constricts proportiantely. Changes in the business, including mobile kitchens, box lunches, thematic stage productions, props, decor treatments and the growth of supermarket catering services, have transformed catering into a highly profitable segment of the foodservice industry. Today's highly competitive, state-of-the-art special event catering services offer gourmet foods, high-fashion tent decor, elegant and ethnically attuned service delivery, and innovative beverage services that include carved ice and specialty glassware for beverage products.

Creativity has had much to do with catering's success. As budgets grew smaller for both business and social occasions, creative menu options, menu substitutions, self-serve formats, and smaller portions helped caterers to retain and even add business. Caterers have a special advantage, because they know in advance about how many people they must prepare for and what the menu will be. This lets them estimate fairly accurately how much food to order and cook, eliminating waste.

Catering has become so appealing that everyone with a kitchen seems to be getting into the act. Destination restaurants and image-conscious chefs are providing their signature dishes and restaurant staff for special events, thus creating an additional revenue stream. Hospitals and schools are beginning to leverage their foodservice facilities and staff to increase revenues, especially during downtime. For the last few years, the Detroit public school system has catered meals for local private schools. The catering revenues have allowed the school system to upgrade its kitchen equipment and add more fresh produce to its menus.

While catering's rewards may be great, it has its drawbacks. Increased competition in an already pressure-packed industry is more than some can handle. Also, restaurants that cater have to guard against devoting too much time to catering at the expense of their on-site business.

Restaurant Ownership

Owning a restaurant is a dream shared by many. But the restaurant business is tremendously competitive. About half of all individually owned restaurants fail within their first year; 85 percent close within five years.[12] Most restaurants are small businesses with annual sales under $500,000.[13]

The three most common restaurant ownership structures are independents, chains, and franchises. Multiunit foodservice firms represent a fourth ownership structure that combines some of the features of independents and chains.

Independents

Independent restaurants have one or more owners, and they are usually involved in the day-to-day operation of the business. Even if the owners have more than one property, each property operates independently, and usually has no formal identity or marketing relationship with the others. These restaurants are not affiliated with any national brand or name, and consequently offer their owners the greatest independence, creativity, and flexibility, as well as the greatest risk. To succeed, they need to identify an unmet need in their marketplace, build a product image, and develop a local or regional following.

An independent restaurant is not necessarily small. Each year, *Restaurants & Institutions* ranks the top one hundred independent restaurants according to gross sales. Table 6.1 shows its 2007 rankings.

Chain Restaurants

Chain restaurants represent an important source of growth in the commercial foodservice industry. Chain foodservice operations captured an increasing share of the total market for foodservice in the latter half of the twentieth century. Favorite chain restaurants are listed in Table 6.2. Across all menu categories, these chains received the highest overall scores from their customers. These restaurants were rated on the following criteria, including menu variety, quality, value, and service.

Professional Profile

GUY AND FRANCK SAVOY

Generations of Excellence in the Culinary Profession

Famous Parisian culinary genius and pioneer Guy Savoy and his protégé and son, Franck Savoy, operate some of the finest restaurants in the world. Guy Savoy, a renowned chef who's restaurants have earned three Michelin stars, was born in the French town of Bourgogne to a gardener and a tavern owner. He is a recipient of the prestigious Legion d'Honneur, awarded by the French government. His roots in the culinary tradition began when he apprenticed with chocolatiers. Today, he has successfully created the world's finest French cuisine and fine dining enterprises.

His son Franck is following his example. He has brought sophistication and market-leading ingenuity to the United States, delivering luxurious culinary experiences in the family's Las Vegas operations. Both father and son have a commitment to high style, excellence, and perfection in the variety of gastronomic components they integrate into their worldwide brand. These components include cuisine, viticulture, service etiquette, marketing and branding, conceptual development, and culinary authorship.

The Savoy legacy is an interesting phenomenon in the leadership field. Successful parent-child culinary dynasties are quite rare, given today's global environment and generational diversity. Guy and Franck Savoy share a commitment to excellence, and it shows in their approach to today's highly competitive epicurean industry.[1]

[1] http://www.caesarspalace.com.

A chain foodservice operation is one in which all of the individual restaurants are virtually identical in market, concept, design, and name. Consistency is the core competency of restaurant chains. A successful chain features an established product and a national marketing support mechanism.

Part of the marketing strategy of a chain restaurant is to remove uncertainty from the dining experience. The same menu, food quality, level of service, and atmosphere can be found in any one of the restaurants, regardless of location. Customers thus do not face the "risk" of entering a strange restaurant, selecting from unfamiliar menu items, or worrying about the cleanliness of the kitchen.

McDonald's, Wendy's, Burger King, Taco Bell, and all of the other major quick-service restaurant concepts are examples of chain restaurant operations. With few exceptions, each restaurant is visually and functionally identical. But quick-service restaurants are not the only examples of chains. The casual dinnerhouse concept was also made popular by chain operators. Examples of chain casual dinnerhouses include Bennigan's, Chili's, Olive Garden, Chi-Chi's, and Red Lobster.

A chain may be owned by an individual, a family, a publicly held corporation, a franchise company, or a management company. Managers and

TABLE 6.1 The Top 10 Independent Restaurants in 2007

		2007 Sales	Avg. Dinner Check	Meals Served	Seats	Square Footage
1.	Tao Las Vegas Restaurant & Nightclub, Las Vegas, NV	$66,636,546	$70.00	750,000	400 dining; 100 bar	62,000
2.	Tavern on the Green, New York, NY	$37,636,999	$63.36	531,792	1,500 dining	27,000
3.	Joe's Stone Crab, Miami Beach, FL	$29,680,810	$65.00	347,423	450 dining; 30 bar	N/A
4.	Smith & Wollensky, New York, NY (Third Avenue outlet)	$28,702,000	$86.00	394,000	390 dining	N/A
5.	Tao Asian Bistro, New York, NY	$26,842,734	$74.00	427,000	300 dining; 35 bar	10,500
6.	Old Ebbitt Grill, Washington, DC	$22,851,237	$24.00	800,000	430 dining; 75 bar	18,000
7.	Gibsons Bar and Steakhouse, Chicago, IL	$20,846,253	$35.95	344,404	170 dining; 60 bar	8,725
8.	Fulton's Crab House, Lake Buena Vista, FL	$20,673,932	$44.05	469,329	500 dining; 40 bar	40,064
9.	SW Steakhouse, Las Vegas, NV	$20,500,000	$100.00	190,000	284 dining	N/A
10.	Bob Chinn's Crab House, Wheeling, IL	$20,449,151	$35.77	724,678	650 dining; 100 bar	19,969

Source: Restaurants & Institutions (2008, http://www.rimag.com/article/CA6554059.html?nid=4137).

employees at chain restaurant locations typically are employees of the parent company.

Chain operations have many advantages, generally related to size. The chain can afford to hire talented specialists to oversee individual departments

TABLE 6.2 2008 "Consumers' Choice in Chains" Top 10 Winners

Rank	Name	Score (out of 100)
1.	Carrabba's Italian Grill	76.3
2.	The Cheesecake Factory	75.9
3.	Mimi's Café	75.7
4.	Olive Garden	74.7
5.	Papa Murphy's	72.8
6.	P.F. Chang's China Bistro	72.7
7.	Cracker Barrel	72.5
8.	Bonefish Grill	72.3
9.	Panera Bread	70.8
10.	LongHorn Steakhouse	70.6

Source: Restaurants & Institutions (October 15, 2008, http://www.rimag.com/article/CA6554059.html?nid=4137).

and operations. The chain usually has greater buying power and credit resources than do individual operations. Usually the chain offers national marketing campaigns, centralized purchasing, and customer loyalty programming. Sometimes it is more financially feasible for a chain to experiment with new menu items, operational procedures, or facility designs than it would be for an independent, because a chain can try out its new ideas on a small scale before committing to company-wide change. A chain is not as flexible as an independent and cannot respond as quickly to changes in customer demand or economic conditions. Nevertheless, its greater size may allow it to ride out business cycles more easily than an independent.

A chain requires numerous standardized operating procedures and specifications for everything from minimum pricing to menu graphics, ingredients, inventory levels, portion sizes, promotional specials, uniforms, and hours of operation. Typically, chain restaurants are more costly to start up, but over time they are a more stable investment, and offer a more significant opportunity for success, than independent or even franchise operations.

Franchises

A franchise is a form of restaurant ownership commonly utilized by chains. Franchises are business arrangements between the individual business operator, called the **franchisee**, and the franchise company, called the **franchisor**. The franchisor sells the franchisee the right to use its name and logo (the symbol that identifies the company), its products, and its concept. An individual, partnership, or corporation puts up a certain amount of money to buy a franchise. The franchise company then gives the franchisee licensing rights to an established identity, along with training, advertising support, start-up assistance, and tested operating procedures. The franchisee is the actual owner of the business, but does not operate with total independence, because it must agree to meet specific conditions and operating standards set by the franchisor. These conditions usually establish the location for the restaurant, and may also specify the equipment, products, procedures, menu specifications, and facility designs that must be used.

The franchise owner typically pays the franchisor an annual fee based on sales plus a marketing co-op fee, also based on sales. This allows the franchisee to benefit from national marketing campaigns designed to strenghten the brand image and build customer loyalty. Owning a franchise of a popular chain can enable a restaurateur to reap considerable profits. However, the initial purchase fee for successful franchise chains is well beyond the means of most start-up entrepreneurs. The most successful franchise companies tend to charge higher purchase prices, sometimes more than half a million dollars.

Many restaurant chains combine elements of both franchise and chain operation, with some of a restaurant's units being company-owned and others franchised. Franchises allow chain restaurant firms to expand far more rapidly

Business Profile

HOWARD JOHNSON'S

A Franchise Built on Twenty-Eight Flavors

Photo courtesy of Franchise Associates

Although the Howard Johnson Company has changed over the years, for many it still conjures the image of orange roofs, Tendersweet™ fried clams, and twenty-eight flavors of ice cream. The company began when Howard Dearing Johnson bought a small drugstore and decided to sell his own brand of very rich, high-quality ice cream. The ice cream was a hit. Wanting to expand, he built stands at many area beaches along the Atlantic and hired boys to sell ice cream cones and hot dogs to bathers.

In the 1930s Howard Johnson saw the opportunities franchising offered and became a franchise pioneer. Unfortunately, World War II and subsequent rationing of gas and tires led to the closing of nearly every Howard Johnson's restaurant—people just were not traveling. The ever-enterprising Mr. Johnson kept his manufacturing plants busy by providing food to defense plants. After the war, he reopened his restaurants and expansion began again.

The basis of the success of Howard Johnson's restaurants in the 1950s and 1960s was threefold: highway locations, high-quality food and ice cream, and clean, attractive, easily identifiable orange-roofed buildings. During that time, Howard Johnson's began to cook and freeze many of its menu items in manufacturing plants or commissaries and then transport the frozen food to the restaurants. This meant short-order cooks could replace expensive chefs, allowing the company to offer its high-quality, standardized menu items at reasonable prices.

The addition of a motor lodge component to the Howard Johnson's restaurant operation came in 1954 at the urging of Mr. Johnson's son, Howard Brennan Johnson. In 1959, the son became president of the company until it was sold. In the 1970s, the Howard Johnson's empire consisted of over one thousand restaurants and more than five hundred motor lodges.

Unfortunately, Howard Johnson's, whose sales once exceeded the combined sales of McDonald's, Burger King, and KFC, met with fierce competition from fast-food restaurants in the 1980s, and has never been able to recapture the success of its glory days. Still, it will forever remain an important part of restaurant history.

Source: http://www.roadsidefans.com

than would be possible with only company-owned units. This is because franchising is a strategy for financing. The chain acquires the capital it needs for growth through the franchisees, who put up the money required for the investment from their own resources.

Multiunit Foodservice Firms

The most common kind of multiunit foodservice firm is a single firm that owns and operates a number of restaurants, each with a different concept, menu, and target market. Other multiunit firms do not own restaurants but are completely responsible for their management and operation.

One of the better-known multiunit restaurant firms is Lettuce Entertain You, Inc., based in Chicago. Lettuce operates over sixty restaurants, many of which have independent themes. Papagus Greek Taverna is a Greek restaurant, Café Ba-Ba-Reeba serves Spanish tapas, Ben Pao offers Asian dishes, Scoozi is a boisterous Italian trattoria, and Tru is a dynamic fine-dining restaurant with dramatic design flair. The firm also operates "Food Life," a food court in an upscale shopping mall.

Multiunit foodservice operations enjoy some of the economies of chain restaurants such as centralized staff functions and the benefits of experience. However, they are risky to the extent that each concept, being unique, must prove itself in the marketplace.

Commercial Restaurants Within Other Businesses

Historically, restaurants have often been connected to other businesses. Early inns and taverns offered rooms and meals. Department stores operated informal coffee shops and elegant tea rooms. Drugstores featured counters that sold sandwiches, ice cream, and sodas. Today, these trends not only continue, but are expanding. Movie theaters cook up pizza, fries, and nachos and deliver them to the customer's seat. Laundromats sell hot dogs, chips, and beverages to customers while they watch big-screen TVs and wait for their clothes to dry. And foodservice remains an important feature for most hotels and motels. Full-service hotel operators often have extensive restaurant and catering operations. The hotel sector also offers opportunities for third-party independent or chain operators to operate restaurants in leased space on hotel premises. This can be a win-win situation in the event that a hotel has little experience or no interest in operating its own food and beverage component. Retail stores still operate a variety of restaurants. And food courts, found in many large shopping malls, attract the hungry with today's most popular sandwiches, sweets, and soft drinks.

Hotel/Motel Foodservice

From time to time hoteliers have considered their restaurants to be of secondary importance to their primary task of providing lodging. Doug Fountain, a hotel owner from Pascagoula, Mississippi, summarizes this sentiment: "I view the restaurant as a necessary evil. We do manage to make a profit, but it's always been tough."[14] This view is understandable insofar as food and beverage departments have substantially smaller operating margins than the rooms departments in most hotels. However, food and beverage services are an integral part of most lodging concepts and are therefore necessary to fulfill the needs and expectations of guests.

Brought on by overexpansion, the hotel industry recession during the early 1990s caused many hotel and motel operators to look to their food and beverage operations as a new profit source. The emphasis on quality, creativity, and a more casual atmosphere enabled many hotels to attract hotel guests to their restaurants. This trend continued through the decade. In Chicago, Le Meridien hotel changed its formal French dining room into a casual bistro and moved it from the second floor to a street-level location, With its own entrance and floor-to-ceiling windows facing the street, the restaurant now attracts diners from the surrounding area, as well as hotel guests. Other hotels have leased their restaurants to third parties, as discussed above.

Many hotels have begun to aggressively market their banquet facilities. This enables hotels to increase both restaurant and guest room sales. Holding a wedding reception at a particular hotel typically generates the rental of several guest rooms, in addition to the food and beverage sales associated with the banquet. Catering and convention service operations in full-service hotels are a strong profit center in food and beverage sales. Significant competition exists among major hotel brands to capture the high-dollar, high-volume, high-profit catering market. Some hotels have begun catering food and beverages for

Business Profile

KIMPTON HOTELS

Trend-setting Boutique Hotels and Restaurants

Kimpton Hotel and Restaurant Group positions its enterprise as a stylish and hip boutique hotel and restaurant company. Kimpton hotels are designed in different styles, each creating a distinctive environment for travelers. Most properties offer smaller, European-style accommodations, some in renovated historic buildings. Upscale destination restaurants are located next to most hotels. In 1981, Bill Kimpton founded the company's first hotel, the Bedford, in San Francisco. Their featured restaurants and bars in locations throughout the Western United States are always sought-after destinations. Kimpton has now expanded the company's operations into the Pacific Northwest and as far eastward as Boston.[1]

What makes Kimpton's business model unusual is that its properties are organized into separate operating divisions, each of which has its own reporting relationship to the parent organization. The restaurant division relies solely on food and beverage operations to produce return on investment. The end result is that Kimpton properties offer highly creative, trendy food and beverage operations that function as destination restaurants, attracting a greater than average share of in-house hotel guests while also generating a strong local following.

[1] http://www.kimptonhotels.com

off-site functions, enabling the hotel restaurant to maximize use of its large kitchen and waitstaff, as well as its cooking facilities.

Food Courts

Food courts are an enhancement of the store-based restaurant concept that provide a variety of convenient fast-food choices. Food courts are most commonly located inside self-enclosed malls, but are also found in airports, sports stadiums, resort venues, convention centers, and municipal facilities Individual restaurants within a food court need to do little advertising in order to attract customers, because most food courts are built so that shoppers can readily view the menu choices as they pass through the area. Just as the presence of retail stores attracts diners to a mall, and thus to its food court restaurants, a successful food court will attract shoppers to a mall and increase retail store traffic.

One recent trend in food courts is the mini–food court, which combines kiosks and limited-menu operations. These mini–food courts may offer only three or four different restaurant choices, but can be profitably run in locations that receive considerably less traffic than is needed to support a free-standing restaurant. Mini–food courts featuring ethnic cuisine and themed dining are being added to school and university campuses, hospitals, airports, and supermarkets.

Retail Operations

Restaurants that are located inside other retail operations are directly influenced by the fortunes of the host store's sales. When a store's retail sales are

Courtesy of EklecCo

Shoppers can get a bite to eat and ride the Ferris wheel at this food court.

Restaurant food is now sold in grocery stores.

Photo by Kaye (Kye-Sung) Chon

high, restaurants within it tend to do well. When fewer shoppers enter a store, it is likely that fewer shoppers will eat at the store's restaurant. Restaurants have long been fixtures in large upscale department stores. But large department stores are less dominant now, and specialty shops claim a much larger share of the retail market. On the other hand, restaurants are being added to many large discount stores such as Target and Wal-Mart, which are experiencing tremendous growth. Name-brand franchises are expanding into retail outlets. In another example, supermarkets throughout the country are offering coffee houses, delis, health-conscious dining options, pizza shops, and other foodservice operations under their roofs.

Convenience Stores

Convenience stores and gas stations have also added take-out restaurant operations specializing in frozen drinks, coffee and doughnuts, soup, hot dogs, and other quick items that can be heated by the customer in the store's microwave. Taco John's, Subway, Arby's, and other brand-name restaurant chains are testing limited-menu operations in convenience stores.

Retail-based restaurants quickly adopt the trends affecting the restaurant industry as a whole. Good value for the price, superior service, and a variety of interesting food choices are key in this market. Healthful and ethnic foods, along with regional specialties, are strong attractions.

Contemporary On-Site (Institutional) Foodservice

One of the principal ways to divide the foodservice industry is to distinguish between commercial and institutional foodservice operations. Often the term "non-commercial" is used in place of "institutional" because the latter sounds so, well—institutional. The term on-site foodservice has become the accepted name for these operations.

On-site and commercial foodservices are distinguished by the markets each serves. **On-site foodservice** operations serve people who are associated with particular societal institutions, such as hospitals, colleges, schools, nursing homes, the military, and industry. These institutions provide foodservice not as their primary mission, but as an auxiliary service to their members and constituents. **Commercial foodservice** operations, on the other hand, do not serve markets defined by institutional affiliation. Instead, they compete for customers in the open market. This means that commercial foodservices face a risk of failure that institutional foodservices do not have to contend with.

The Blurring Boundaries Between On-site and Commercial Foodservice

In the mid-twentieth century, the distinction between on-site and commercial foodservices was clear. Not only did each serve different markets, but the two went about their business with distinct concepts. Institutional food became associated with casseroles and starches, stainless-steel steam tables and soggy vegetables, and drab dining rooms where patrons ate from fiberglass trays under harsh fluorescent lights. Commercial foodservice, on the other hand, was where excitement, innovation, and quality were to be found. Restaurateurs developed new menus to cater to changing tastes, dining areas were more and more visually exciting, and the food was appealing. Restaurants were places where food was good; in institutions, it was "good for you."

Institutions offered inexpensive and nutritious, if not very exciting, food, because there was neither expectation nor incentive to do otherwise. Their reason for being was to provide sustenance for the body, economically and efficiently. School foodservice, for example, began in Boston in the early decades of the 1900s to offset what social reformers thought were the non-nutritious eating practices and preferences of immigrant families.[15]

Today, the boundaries between on-site and commercial foodservice have become blurred, with several trends bringing the two operations closer together. Academic dining operations are as varied and quality oriented as commercial foodservice operations found in the community at large. Some large institutional foodservice companies specialize in universities and other large institutional venues. Major players in the institutional foodservice arena include Sodexho and Marriott. Historically, institutional foodservice, in its various forms, has served what is called a "captive market." Here the term

Industry Insights

BUSINESS INNOVATION

Zagat Survey

Deciding where to eat when dining out can be a perplexing task. A critique by a restaurant reviewer in a local paper may offer some guidance. But a review based on the opinion of hundreds of people promises to be one you can sink your teeth into. So when people hear that Tim Zagat, once an attorney with political aspirations, engages thousands of independent volunteer restaurant reviewers for the Zagat Survey, they put down their forks and listen. Zagat and his wife Nina (also a former practicing attorney) co-publish the nationally acclaimed Zagat Survey, a series of major metropolitan and regional restaurant reviews. Cuisine, ambiance, and service are rated on a 30-point scale, with 0 being poor and 30 being perfect. Meal costs are estimated based on dinner, one drink, and gratuity.

For the one million people who purchase the reviews, the Zagat Survey is the reference book for dining out all over the United States. According to the Zagats, the survey formula is more reliable than individual critiques because each Zagat restaurant review is based on an average of one thousand meals. Therefore, a greater number of menus, seasonal items, and serving idiosyncrasies can be sampled, critiqued, and distilled into an accurate and succinct description of what diners can expect at restaurants in more than twenty different cities and regions across the country.

captive means that members of a given institution cannot choose to eat elsewhere, or their choice to eat elsewhere does not have a negative economic impact on the foodservice operation. For example, a patient recovering from surgery in a hospital is expected to eat what is brought to her on a tray. Food serves both dietary and treatment purposes. In this scenario, where nutritional intake is highly critical, the patient will be billed for the meal, whether or not she eats it. Similarly, a college student on a meal plan that includes nineteen meals per week can skip breakfast and eat lunch in town every day, but there is no negative economic impact on the college's foodservice operation. The student has bought and paid for every breakfast and every lunch she misses.

Changing Expectations of Institutional Members and Constituents

Institutional members and constituents are becoming more and more discriminating in their expectations for foodservice. They demand the same high levels of quality, service, health consciousness, and variety that they encounter in commercial foodservice operations.

Here are some examples of the effects of changing expectations in institutional foodservices.

- A large financial institution replaces its vending machines with a foodservice operation that offers deli sandwiches made to order, fresh-baked breads, homemade soups, and a salad bar.
- A museum eliminates its old snack shop and leases the space to a commercial quick-service food franchise.
- A university replaces the cafeteria in its student union with a food court and opens a late-night pizza delivery service.

In many cases institutions transform the "institutional" character of their foodservice operations in response to an eroding captive market. But other institutions create foodservices every bit as dynamic and attractive as their commercial counterparts for other reasons. Improved facilities and commercial-quality food and service may maintain employee loyalty, increase participation, and generate greater operating surpluses (profits). However, in recent years, perhaps the strongest reason for making changes in foodservice operations is the downsizing or belt-tightening that institutions have undergone. With fewer dollars to go around, hospitals, schools, and other institutions have had to restructure their foodservice operations to accommodate shrinking budgets. Institutions no longer are willing to subsidize their foodservices; instead, on-site operations are expected to break even or show a surplus.

Segments in the On-Site Foodservice Industry

The segments that make up the on-site foodservice industry have made some striking changes in recent years. Some of these changes are detailed below.

Health-Care Organizations

To remain competitive, hospitals and other health-care facilities have improved their menu selections for patients. In fact, in some health-care facilities, the menus offered to patients can barely be distinguished from the menus offered to customers in commercial restaurants. Gourmet meals are available. And, to accommodate those who have dietary restrictions (no salt, no sugar, no milk, and so on), multiple versions of menu items are prepared.

Food is prepared in a central kitchen and transported to patient floors. For the sake of both food safety and patient satisfaction, hospitals and other health-care facilities use technology to keep hot foods hot and cold foods cold. Hospitals have taken the lead in using advanced food production technologies such as **cook-chill** systems that permit bulk production ahead of time without sacrificing food quality. Also, they use computers to keep track of inventories, analyze the nutritional content of foods and menu items, and assess possible food/drug interactions.

Although of vital importance in all foodservice operations, sanitary food preparation in health-care facilities is exceptionally critical because ill patients can be especially vulnerable to food-borne diseases. Health regulations outline specific measures for food handling, which must be followed meticulously.

Strict sanitary procedures are essential for all on-site food preparation.

Courtesy of Photodisc

Patients are not the only target of the health-care foodservice operation. Increasingly, hospital cafeterias are enticing employees and visitors with a wide selection of food in settings refurbished to resemble restaurants. Some hospitals offer brand-name foods such as TCBY Yogurt and Dunkin' Donuts.

Schools

Brand-name foods are carving out a widening niche not just in hospitals, but also in secondary schools and even in some elementary schools. In schools that have an open-lunch policy, cafeterias that sell Pizza Hut, Taco Bell, and other quick-service foods are finding satisfied customers who choose the cafeteria over nearby fast-food restaurants. Another innovation is the à la carte program, which offers students a much greater variety of food from which to choose than was available in the past.

Some public schools receive federal subsidies to help fund their school lunch program. This means that certain students are eligible for free and reduced-price meals. Along with providing funding, the government imposes standards for nutrition and menu variety. However, in recent years, as a result of federal cutbacks, fewer schools and students participate in the program.

Colleges and Universities

College and university foodservices range from very small to very large operations, depending on the school's size and whether it is primarily a commuter or a residential facility. While snack bars and vending machines may adequately meet the needs of students in a commuter college, larger residential colleges must offer multiple foodservice outlets, including both residential dining (meal plans) and cash operations such as snack bars, food courts, concessions, vending machines, convenience stores, and dorm deliveries.

Changes in residential dining began as long as thirty years ago, when contemporary food items (for example, pizza) began to make their way onto menus. Current menu offerings today include ethnic foods, extensive salad bars, omelette stations, wok cooking, and made-to-order pasta, plus a wide selection of healthy cuisine options. A more recent trend, a switch to à la carte items, is gaining popularity because it presents more choices and therefore helps reduce waste. The use of debit cards instead of traditional meal plans has furthered this trend because the cards allow students to pay only for what they eat. The à la carte system lets foodservice managers keep careful track of what students eat—and don't eat. This enables the managers to take a more market-driven approach to meeting students' needs and retaining their business.

Like many changes, a switch from traditional meal plans to the à la carte system usually takes time and adjustment before the new system turns a profit. Managers can no longer rely on the "missed-meal" factor. That means that when ordering and preparing the food they need, they can no longer take into account the number of meals students are likely to miss. Instead, managers now have to learn to base what and how much they order on precisely what and how much students are really buying. The result, though, is well worth the effort. Those foodservices that have adopted the à la carte/debit card system have seen an increase in sales of 10 to 15 percent.

Business and Industry

Like foodservices in colleges and universities, foodservices in business and industry run the gamut from very small—a bank of vending machines—to large, multiunit operations with food courts, executive dining rooms, catering, and kiosks. The menu varies with the type of operation—from gum (vending machines) to four-star cuisine (executive dining). In most company cafeterias, the traditional hot lunch has been completely displaced by deli sandwiches, a salad bar, pizza, and similar items with contemporary appeal.

Because of growing concern for the bottom line, most businesses are reluctant to subsidize their foodservice operations, forcing foodservice managers to take a more market-driven approach to successfully compete with nearby operations. In addition, in light of the health-and-fitness mood of the times, some firms are offering health foods to employees—the idea being the healthier the employee, the lower the cost of medical benefits. Moreover, changing workforce demographics have recently pressured corporations to reevaluate their employee dining options. Today, employee meals are one more way for a company to attract and retain quality workers.

Vending

In recent decades, vending operations have grown rapidly. Success in the vending industry can be attributed to several developments. Perhaps the most important is the microwave oven, which provides hot food in minutes. Second, advances have been made in the variety and quality of items available through machines. Vending machines now offer a wide variety of food options, from snacks to full-course dinners. Third, as companies reduce spending, vending services, with their lower labor price tag, provide a cost-effective alternative to full-service dining operations. Using vending machines to supplement other foodservice operations is also becoming increasingly popular.

Particularly in factories and colleges and universities, the fact that vending machines offer food around the clock is a big advantage. And in colleges and universities where vending machines accept debit cards, vending sales have doubled.[16]

Airlines

In general, airline food is produced at a facility that is a cross between a traditional kitchen and a food processing plant. For the sake of efficiency, most facilities are located adjacent to major hub areas. The menu offered to travelers is limited by transportation and storage constraints.

Airlines are meeting modern challenges in several ways. They have cut back on food on short flights and during off-hours (nonmealtimes). They have changed their menus to include low-fat, low-salt, and other more nutritious items. Finally, for those flying first class, the airlines offer gourmet meals, complete with vintage wines. Today, most airlines have stopped serving free meals and now offer snack boxes or full meals for sale during long-haul domestic flights. In fact, most regional communter airlines only offer complimentary beverages and a small snack. At the time of writing, International flights still come included with complimentary meal service.

Military

Foodservice operations in the military vary widely in size, type, and location, ranging from ships' galleys to open mess halls, officers' clubs, and field operations. As a result, military foodservice operations face some unusual and large-scale challenges. For instance, large bases situated far from major urban centers need extensive warehousing capacity. Field and shipboard operations require ingenious solutions to overcome the many constraints involved.

Recent expansion of military spending and overseas operations have brought about changes in all military foodservice operations. Some of the changes include consolidating mess hall operations and contracting private foodservice operations to run officers' clubs. Other changes involve carefully monitoring food purchases to obtain the best buys and establishing on-base fast-food restaurants such as Burger King and McDonald's.[17] Supplemental dining options are now offered to those serving overseas in war operations in order to alleviate otherwise dismal conditions far away from home. In this instance, meals and dining are a perk that helps to build morale. Such meals are more upscale and flavorful than ever before.

Correctional Institutions

Typically, foodservice operations in correctional institutions involve large production kitchens, storage areas, and dining rooms. Kitchens are designed to keep lines of sight open, and equipment contains security features to ensure the safety of guards and inmates.

Compared with the other institutions discussed, menu choice is quite limited. Some prisons do offer contemporary food items such as pizza. An increase in new prison construction has resulted in a decrease in the amount of capital available to make needed improvements to existing foodservice facilities.

Running the Operation

With budget-tightening in the government, service, and business sectors, some institutions are looking to electronic information systems to increase savings and improve productivity. Programs created especially for the on-site foodservice industry, such as those put out by CBORD, determine nutritional values, plan and print menus, produce summary reports, keep food tallies, and analyze vendors' bills. Many institutions, however, no longer want to deal with

Graduate Glimpse

MICHELE POLCI

For Michele Polci, no two days are ever alike. Currently the Director of Catering Sales for the Rio All-Suite Hotel and Casino in Las Vegas, she has to stay flexible all the time and deal with whatever comes in throughout the day. The main challenges usually occur when there are a number of groups to serve at the same time and she needs to keep up with the sales process. Besides taking care of her own clients, she also has a catering team that demands her attention. Although she wears different hats on different days, her love for catering never ceases, because she views the service as a one-stop shop for the venue's clients. "We get to sell the dream and finish it," says Polci, "[so] it is a very fulfilling process."

Polci believes that being flexible and keeping herself humble helped her to reach her current status. A graduate of the William F. Harrah College of Hotel Administration at the University of Nevada, Las Vegas, and an active member of the Las Vegas Chapter of the National Association of Catering Executives since 2001, she has won numerous awards, including "The Caterer of the Year" in 2007. When asked what advice she would provide to students of hospitality, Polci suggests that students get involved with an industry organization. "My involvement with the local chapter has made me stronger, motivated, and a better salesperson." She also advises graduates to be honest and up front throughout the sales and service process, and to work in partnership with their clients. Polci explains, "When the small stuff goes awry, it will be overlooked if you have done a fabulous job on the front end."

running foodservice operations themselves. Increasingly, they are hiring professionals that know how to run a profitable operation. A foodservice company typically pays its client a percentage of sales as a form of rent. In many cases, independent foodservice management companies are entirely responsible for the success or failure of the host institution's foodservice operations. Profits and losses are largely the domain of the foodservice company, not the host institution.

Growing Career Opportunities

The hospitality and foodservice industry offers many growth and career development opportunities. Today, globalization and the popularity of celebrity chefs have created **exponential** opportunities for aspiring graduates within the growing hospitality and foodservice industry.

Career growth in the hospitality and foodservice industry begins with the determination of job fit, either in culinary arts (back-of-the-house) or dining room and bar operations (front-of-the-house).

The front-of-the-house in the foodservice industry offers a wide range of career choices. To understand the many opportunities available, one must first understand the various segments of the industry. Commercial foodservice operations include table-service, quick-service, casual, themed, ethnic, and formal fine dining concepts. Catering foodservice opportunities exist in special events management, hotel catering, banquet and convention operations, stadiums and other sporting event venues, cruise lines, and airline caterers.

The culinary arts (back-of-the-house) industry also offers a wide range of opportunities for career development. Jobs include purchasing agent, pastry chef, executive chef, sous chef, banquet chef, restaurant chef, butcher, kitchen manager, expeditor, line cook, food preparation, and steward. Entry-level positions usually involve apprenticeship programs lasting up to one year. Culinary operations are highly complex. Each discipline within the kitchen should be learned, because career professionals perform best if they have a general working knowledge of all areas, complemented by an area of specialization such as saucier, pastry, or garde manger.

Summary

- Market, concept, and menu all play a part in defining foodservice operations. Each foodservice operation meets the needs of its market through its concept and menu.
- The foodservice industry can be divided into market segments—groups of individuals who share a set of needs and expectations. Geographic location, age, ethnicity, social class, and price are some of the ways the foodservice industry can be segmented.
- Concept includes the size of a foodservice facility, its location, and its hours of operation.

- Celebrity chefs have emerged as branded entities with their own themed eateries.
- Theme and design work together to create a restaurant's "atmosphere."
- The different forms of service used to present food and beverages to guests include table, cafeteria, family, quick counter, and take-out, among others.
- Quality of service is based on the form of service and the concept used. Service scripts are helpful in determining those expectations that lead to quality of service.
- Changing workforce demographics are placing higher demands on training programs, recruitment, and retention strategies.
- The menu represents the foodservice operation's plan for serving its guests. It lists the items the customers will want and is the primary driver of profit or lack thereof.
- Commercial foodservice operations include fine dining, theme dining, casual ethnic, family restaurant, cafeterias/buffets, quick service, and neighborhood/third places.
- Restaurants may be independently owned, owned by a chain company, or franchised. Multiunit foodservice firms resemble independently owned restaurants in some ways and chains in others.
- Some restaurants are located within other commercial enterprises, such as hotels and motels, retail stores, convenience stores, and food courts in malls, schools, and office buildings.
- Foodservice operations are either commercial or on-site (institutional), although the lines between these two operations are less distinct than in earlier years.
- On-site foodservices include health-care organizations, educational institutions, business and industry, airlines, the military, and correctional institutions. All have had to make changes to their operations in recent years to compensate for shrinking budgets.
- Some institutions are turning to independent foodservice management companies to run their operations in order to reduce financial risk and to better focus on their financial objectives.

ENDNOTES

[1] National Restaurant Association, News Resource. 2007, http://www.restaurantnewsresource.com; National Restaurant Association, Pocket Facts, 1999. http://www.restaurant.org.

[2] Harvey A. Levenstein, *Revolution at the Table: The Transformation of the American Diet* (New York: Oxford University Press, 1988), 188.

[3] Oldenburg, *The Great Good Place*, Da Capo Press; 3rd edition (August 17, 1999) 14–19.

[4] Ibid., xvi.

[5] Ibid., 24.

[6] Ibid., 25.

[7] Ibid., 26–31.

[8] Ibid., 32.

[9] Ibid., 37.

[10] Ibid., 41.

[11] "Cashing in on Catering," *Restaurants & Institutions* (October 16, 1991): 14.
[12] Waters, *The Big Picture*, 150.
[13] Deloitte & Touche, *National Restaurant Association Restaurant Industry Operations Report 1992* (Washington, D.C.: National Restaurant Association, 1992), 5.
[14] Feed 'Em or Forget 'Em," *Restaurant Business* (February 10, 1993): 64.
[15] Harvey Levenstein, *Revolution at the Table: The transformation of the American Diet* (University of California Press: Los Angeles, 2003)..
[16] Keeping the Change," *Restaurant Business* (September 20, 1992): 118.
[17] Laurie Freeman, "Fighting Trim," *Restaurant Business* (September 20, 1992): 126–127.

CHECK YOUR KNOWLEDGE

1. How are market, concept, and menu related?
2. List the main characteristics of each of the following kinds of restaurants: fine dining, theme, casual, ethnic, family, and cafeteria/buffet.
3. How do independent, chain, and franchise restaurants differ from one another?
4. What are some differences between commercial and on-site foodservices?
5. Identify the segments of the on-site foodservice market and briefly describe the characteristics of each.
6. Identify a celebrity chef's restaurant concept and indicate which specialty this chef capitalizes on in her restaurant's positioning and market image.

APPLY YOUR SKILLS

1. Table 6.3 shows the changes in sales for quick-service and full-service restaurants. What was the percentage of growth for each segment of the industry from 1998–2008?
2. Table 6.4 provides data about four chain dinnerhouses. What is the average sales per unit for each of the four restaurant organizations?
3. Table 6.4 shows the overall sales for the chain dinnerhouse segment of the restaurant industry. What is the market share for each of the four organizations?
4. Assume that you are qualified for a restaurant manager position in a chain dinnerhouse. Assume (hypothetically) that each of the four chain dinnerhouses in Table 6.4 offers you a base salary of $50,000 plus 1 percent of gross sales of the restaurant you manage. At which firm would you make the most money?

TABLE 6.3 Quick-Service Sales and Growth

Sales	*Quick-Service*	*Full-Service*
2008	$121.8 billion	$123.0 billion
1998	$105.7 billion	$110.0 billion

TABLE 6.4 Sales at Four Chain Dinnerhouses

	Applebee's	*Chili's*	*Red Lobster*	*Olive Garden*
Sales (in millions)	$1,523.0	$1.035.1	$1,774.9	$1,255.0
Units	810	486	650	461
Sales for Chain Dinnerhouses (in millions)	$10,583.8	$6,821.2	$5,817.0	$8,614.1

INTERNET EXERCISES

1. Visit the *Restaurants & Institutions* magazine Web site. Search through the back issues and/or archives for articles that identify a major trend affecting each of the following segments of the foodservice industry:
   a. Fine dining restaurants
   b. On-site (institutional) foodservice
   c. Quick-service restaurants
2. Visit the Web site for the National Restaurant Association. Look at the pages related to governmental issues affecting the restaurant industry. What are three of the major issues that the association believes are likely to have a negative impact on the industry? Explain why the negative impact could occur. Do you agree with the association's position? Why or why not?
3. Visit the Web site for Starbucks. From the material presented on their Web page, do you think Starbucks is a "third place"? Why or why not?
4. Visit the Zagat restaurant review Web site. Read the reviews of the top ten restaurants in a major city of your choice. Then decide how the ratings were determined. Is this the best way to rate restaurants?

WHAT DO YOU THINK?

1. Would you prefer to own a restaurant outright or be a franchisee?
2. This chapter discusses different restaurant concepts—fine dining, theme, and so on. If you were to open a restaurant, what kind would it be? Why?

3. Quick-service food operations make up the largest category in the foodservice industry. Why do you think fast foods have become so popular? How will healthy dining trends impact the quick-service segment?
4. Choose two different popular restaurants in your area. What concepts and forms of service do they use to appeal to customers?
5. Foodservice operations are appearing in some unusual places, such as laundromats. In what kind of place would you add a foodservice operation? Why?

CASE STUDY

Students at a local college have the option of buying a meal plan to eat meals at the college cafeteria. At dinner, the students can choose one of three entrees prepared in advance, plus salad, beverage, and dessert. At no extra cost, students can go back for as many helpings as they want. Lately, fewer people are choosing to buy the meal plan and instead are going off campus to buy their meals at various quick-service restaurants.What advice would you give to the college cafeteria manager to help improve business?

Introduction to Culinary Arts

OVERVIEW

Customers at a well-run restaurant take for granted the menu they receive, the service they get, and the meal set before them. The whole production, from soup to nuts, seems almost effortless—an effect that takes great effort on the part of many people.

In this chapter you will read about those people and what they do. You will learn much about what it takes to run a foodservice operation successfully—from kitchen organization to purchasing, preparation, cleanup, food safety, and environmental issues. Because we will discuss the traditional techniques of food preparation and service, a brief history of cooking and culinary arts is included.

OBJECTIVES

When you have completed this chapter, you should be able to:

1. **Explain how the word *restaurant* came to mean a place to eat meals.**
2. **Define *mise en place*.**
3. **Explain the four factors that influence menu planning and development.**
4. **Identify the components that make up the production cycle.**
5. **Discuss the social and cultural issues involved in foodservice operations.**

KEY TERMS

chef
chef de rang
chef de salle
chef d'étage
chefs de partie
contribution margin
danger zone
databases
demi-chef de rang
entremetier
forecasting
garde manger
grillardin
kitchen brigade
maître d'hôtel
menu engineering
menu mix
pâtissier
poissonier
positioning
saucier
servers
sous chef
spreadsheet
standard purchase specifications

Historical Overview of Cooking and the Culinary Arts

Studying history gives a sense of what the past was like and how things have evolved. The history of cooking began about one and a half million years ago, when people learned to control fire. No doubt early people quickly discovered that fire not only provided warmth, protection, and light; it could also change and enhance the texture and taste of food. With the cultivation of grain, the domestication of animals, and the appearance of pottery among various cultures sometime between 10,000 and 6000 B.C., cooking became easier and more varied. Early Mesopotamian cultures began to harvest grain, figs, and dates, and to domesticate sheep and goats. People in the Americas grew squash, chili peppers, beans, and potatoes.

As various civilizations developed, their ruling classes came to appreciate good food, and reserved for themselves those people with special talents for preparing delectable dishes. Food became central to the cultures of ancient civilizations. For example, in ancient China, the *ting* cauldron, a cooking vessel, was a prime symbol of the state. Records from the time of the Zhou dynasty (1027–221 B.C.) provide a list of those responsible for running the emperor's palace. From among the approximately fourty thousand positions listed, almost 60 percent handled food and wine, including 162 master "dietitians," 256 chefs, and 62 assistant chefs.[1] In ancient Egypt, food played an integral part in burial rituals. Important officials were entombed with a rich assortment of prepared dishes to sustain them until they reached the other world.

European cooking seems to have originated in Athens and subsequently developed in Rome, where professional cooks were called upon to plan social banquets for the well-to-do. Some of the first sauces were served at these feasts, along with the finest wines of the ancient world. Unfortunately, little is known of early culinary developments among many civilizations in Africa, Asia, and the Americas.

The diets of ordinary people were usually plain and unvaried. The commoners of Mesopotamia and Egypt lived on such staples as bread and beer. Most Greeks and Romans ate coarse bread, olives, and goat cheese, while vendors roamed city streets selling roasted meats, fried fish, and sweets. A special preparation of maize provided the people of ancient Mexico with the *tortilla*, the foundation of their diet. The diet of India's ancient culture consisted of a wide variety of vegetable and dairy products and a complex mixture of seasonings known by Westerners today as curry.

Perhaps the first highly sophisticated regional cuisine was that of imperial China. The basic foodstuffs were rice or grain, vegetables, fish, and pork, prepared according to strict principles that reflected deeply held beliefs about food, food preparation, and proper eating habits. In spite of regional variation, the cuisine developed as a distinctive, cohesive mixture of ingredients and seasonings, elegantly prepared and served. Meals had a very important place in Chinese culture. They reflected status and ethnicity; they cemented social transactions and business deals; and they marked special occasions and family events. Food preparation and consumption became a social language.

Industry Insights

CULTURE

Food Sculpting

Photo courtesy of Johnson & Wales University

Dine out at any Hunan-style restaurant or Japanese sushi bar and it is easy to get caught up in the delicate mix of flavors, all the while taking the presentation for granted. But presentation is very important in traditional Asian cooking. Those little radish blooms and other vegetable blossoms are more than just pretty garnishes; they are part of Asian culture and tradition. Such presentation is not usually used for family, but instead is reserved for important and special occasions such as holidays and New Year's celebrations.

Such a craft is not limited to China and Japan. In fact, the elaborate carvings for vegetables and fruits take "root" in the ancient Thai art known as *kaesalak*. *Kaesalak* is a tradition that goes back to the time when Thai girls were sent to the royal palace to learn this painstaking art in which onions, radishes, turnips, pineapples, cucumbers, and even watermelons are delicately carved into elaborate creations.[1]

Modern instruction in this technique can take thirty hours or more when one studies under a great chef, such as those at the Thai Temple in North Hollywood, California. *Kaesalak* represents the state of the art in patience: wielding sharp knives that cut—yet do not bruise—the fruits and vegetables as they take shape as flowers and animals.

---

[1] Dolores Long, "Vicki Thapthimthong, She Slices, She Dices...," *Los Angeles Magazine* (April 1988): 18.

Elements of American and European Fine Dining

Classic French cooking is the most influential and highly esteemed cuisine in the Western world. Its formalized culinary style—which prizes subtlety, order, balance, and elegant presentation—is supported by a broad, specialized vocabulary and a rich body of cooking literature. As food items and cooking techniques are developed and mastered, they are described in meticulous detail and passed on, building a tradition of shared experience. Recipes are communicated in a form of technical shorthand, and identical results can be anticipated with each use.

The French tradition is the standard for many fine dining establishments today. American and European fine dining is firmly rooted in the work of the early French cooks. Their influence, modified over the years, can still be seen in the many stages of dining operations, from the way dishes are prepared, to the way many kitchens and dining rooms are organized, to the way kitchen staff are trained.

Major Figures of the French Culinary Tradition

Numerous figures have made important contributions to the French culinary tradition. Guillaume Tirel (also known as Taillevent), cook to Charles V, sometime before 1380 compiled *Le Viandier*, one of the first cookbooks to establish some fixed rules and principles of cooking. Catherine de Medici (1519–1589) and Anne of Austria (1601–1666) married men who became kings of France. Each woman brought her personal chefs, who introduced foreign (particularly Italian) influences to French cooking. The highly educated and energetic Catherine had a taste for delicacies and refined dishes, and is credited with introducing the use of forks and napkins to French dining practices.

Marie-Antoine Carême (1784–1833) is the founder of classical French cuisine and is considered by many to be the greatest chef who ever lived. He garnered fame for his decorative displays and elaborately sculpted confections. In his writings he stressed the importance of fresh ingredients, kitchen organization, and the relation of individual dishes to the whole meal to create a singular effect.

At first a disciple of Carême's methods and principles, Georges Auguste Escoffier (1846–1935) simplified the excesses of the previous century and brought a system of organization to everything he did. Dinner menus listed courses in a clear and logical progression. In addition, Escoffier devised an efficient system of kitchen organization, the **kitchen brigade** system, that is still used in large upscale restaurants today. Table 7.1 shows a diagram of the system.

The Kitchen Brigade System

Auguste Escoffier founded the kitchen brigade system (brigade de cuisine) on well-defined organizational principles. The kitchen staff was divided into

TABLE 7.1 Kitchen Brigade System

Chef
- Sous-Chef
  - Chefs de Partie:
    - Saucier (Sauté Chef)
    - Poissonier (Fish Chef)
    - Grillardin (Grill Chef)
    - Friturier (Fry Chef)
    - Rotisseur (Roast Chef)
    - Potager (Soup Chef)
    - Garde Manger (Pantry Chef)
    - Legumier (Vegetable Chef)
    - Patissier (Pastry Chef)
    - Tournant (Swing Chef; works in the kitchen where needed)
    - Boucher (Butcher)

specialized departments, and each had defined tasks and responsibilities, whereas previously, a chef was responsible for the total preparation of an entire meal. Escoffier's system resulted in greater efficiency and better, more consistent results. This organization became the standard for the large classical kitchen of European and American fine dining and is found in scaled-down versions in many kitchens today.

Chef

At the top level of authority in the kitchen brigade system, the **chef** is culinary expert, supervisor, financial manager, and personnel director for the team of talented and specialized individuals working at the establishment. In cooperation with management, the chef develops the menu, orders supplies, organizes work schedules, and maintains quality standards for food preparation and service. A chef's work integrates creativity, quality, consistency, and flair, and should also reflect knowledge of current culinary developments and trends. The preparation of a variety of menu items all at once during peak dining periods calls for the precise scheduling, monitoring, and coordination of activities. A chef's duties as kitchen manager require enough business experience to perform basic financial and business decisions, and to oversee the purchase and use of all food, supplies, and equipment, ensuring economy and efficiency. Today, the chef's role has taken on a newly elevated profile, and a chef may participate in restaurant ownership and franchising. Highly talented chefs are often rewarded with lucrative royalty and ownership interests in successful operations built around their talent and fame.

Sous Chef

In many larger organizations the next in command under the chef is the sous chef. The **sous chef** carries out such functions as scheduling, daily supervision, training and development of personnel, assisting other stations as needed, and, if called upon, covering for the chef. In addition to having station

Professional Profile

AUGUSTE ESCOFFIER

Chef Supreme

Courtesy of Corbis

Auguste Escoffier, who as a young boy yearned to be a sculptor, became one of the world's most famous chefs. He elevated the prestige of French cooking and restored dignity to the title of chef.

In 1860, Escoffier got his first taste of the restaurant business when, at the age of twelve, he worked as a cook in his uncle's restaurant, Le Restaurant Français, in Nice, France. At that time, in contrast to just a generation or so earlier, restaurant cooks were not held in high regard. Though pushed into the restaurant business by his father and grandfather, Escoffier decided that if his destiny in life was to be a cook, he would make it his mission to restore honor to the title.

Early—and briefly—in his career, Escoffier emulated the eighteenth century's most illustrious chef, Marie-Antoine Carême. Soon thereafter, he took on the task of modernizing and simplifying Carême's style of cuisine. Carême had been a master chef, but his elaborate style created problems for guests: hot food was rarely hot, and his towering creations were nearly impossible for most guests to eat comfortably. Escoffier soon changed all that. Reflecting both the talent he had for cooking and the gift he had for organization, he felt that cuisine could be artistically inspired yet scientifically executed. He created simple yet elegant dishes and served them with exquisite timing to maintain proper food temperature. It was after 1883, when Escoffier met César Ritz (of Ritz Hotel fame), that his talent for organizing led him to develop the kitchen brigade, a system of organizing the restaurant kitchen that some restaurants still follow today.

As a duo, Escoffier and Ritz worked beautifully. For example, faced with an English-speaking clientele in Monte Carlo (where Escoffier frequently worked in the summers in the 1890s, and where his wife and three children lived), Escoffier and Ritz developed a new menu concept, *prix fixe*, for parties of four or more. With *prix fixe*, a waiter simply informed the chef of the host's name and the number of guests in the party. Escoffier then chose a selection of menu items that he felt complemented the party's tastes. The menu was noted in a special record book so that returning guests could be treated to a new selection of entrees, unless favorites were requested. This system was successful not only in Monte Carlo, but in England as well. Today, most fine dining restaurants still offer a classic *prix fixe* option, often referred to as the *table d'hôte* menu.

As chef at the Savoy Hotel and then the Carlton (both in London), Escoffier created many new dishes. Among the most famous was peach melba, named in honor of the Australian opera star Nellie Melba, who stayed at the Savoy. Among the most interesting was chicken Jeanette, a stuffed chicken breast served atop a carved ice ship, to commemorate the ship *Jeanette*, which had an unfortunate and fateful run-in with an iceberg.

Escoffier was awarded the *Légion d'Honneur* by the French government in 1920, and was honored as an officer of the Légion in 1928. Escoffier retired in his mid-seventies, although he remained very active. He died in Monte Carlo in 1935.

In celebration of Escoffier's life's work, the *Musée de l'Art Culinaire* (the Museum of Culinary Arts) was founded in 1966 by some of the chefs who studied under Escoffier. The museum occupies the house where Escoffier was born, in the little town of Villenueve-Loubet. It has a wonderful library, mementos that belonged to Escoffier and other famous chefs, and a room filled just with Escoffier's menus—a fitting tribute to a man who did much to further the art of French cuisine.

expertise, the modern sous chef must be adept at financial management, understanding the finer points of food cost control, labor productivity and management, menu engineering, and food sanitation requirements.

Chefs De Partie

Under the sous chef come the **chefs de partie**, also called the station chefs or line chefs. A very large establishment with a full, traditional brigade system may have twenty or more chefs de partie. Often, though, one person combines two or more responsibilities in one station. Included in the chefs de partie are the sauté cook, or **saucier**, who prepares all the sautéed items and their individual sauces; the **poissonier**, or fish station chef, who prepares all fish items and their appropriate sauces; the **grillardin**, or grill cook, who prepares all grilled or broiled menu selections; the **entremetier**, or vegetable chef, who prepares all hot appetizers in addition to soups, vegetables, pasta and noodles, and sometimes egg dishes; the **pâtissier**, or pastry chef, who prepares pastries and desserts as well as all other baked items offered on the menu; and the **garde manger**, or pantry chef, who is in charge of the cold stations, preparing a large variety of salads, patés, cold appetizers, desserts, and salad dressings. The garde manger carries out such preparations as marinating, smoking, and brining. This station also prepares all breakfast items.

Dining Room Organization

Dining room workers provide the link between the customers and the kitchen staff. Much as in the kitchen, a traditional chain of authority exists in the dining room. Today, the French-style system of service is most often seen in formal fine dining establishments. Depending on the size and formality of the restaurant, the positions described below may be combined to deal most efficiently with the needs and expectations of the guests. Variations are made to the brigade system depending on the size and market positioning of the restaurant.

Maître D'hôtel

At the top, coordinating service policies and quality expectations with the owners or managers, is the dining room manager or **maître d'hôtel**. This person oversees the entire operation of the dining room, training and supervising the service staff, organizing seating, selecting the restaurant's wine menu, and cooperating with the chef to finalize daily menus.

Chef De Salle

Next in line is the **chef de salle**, or head waiter, who is responsible for the service provided in the dining room. This person organizes and supervises the service staff.

Chef D'ètage

Of all the front-of-the-house staff, the person who has the most direct contact with the diners is the **chef d'ètage**, or captain. This person takes the guests'

Graduate Glimpse

CHEF PROFILE: MARK BAKER

Age: 42

Job Title; Place of Employment: Executive chef, Seasons Restaurant, Four Seasons Hotel, Chicago, Illinois

Education: High school graduate, Quincy, Massachusetts; apprenticeship at Greenbrier resort, White Sulphur Springs, West Virginia

Professional Background: Line cook, Four Seasons Hotel, Washington, D.C.; executive chef, Four Seasons Hotel, Vancouver, Canada; chef, Four Seasons Hotel, Boston, Massachusetts

When did you decide to become a chef? When I was young, I cooked with mom at home. We watched Julia Child together, and I just fell in love with cooking. I originally wanted to be a scientist—a chef was not a high-profile career in the 1970s. Then I thought I could combine chemistry with cooking. I get a lot of satisfaction out of cooking, so I guess it was a good choice.

What was your first job in the industry? In high school, I worked at the 1622 restaurant in Quincy, Mass. It was a big restaurant with basic food. I was really lucky to get a job working in the kitchen, since I had no experience. I worked there two summers in a row.

Did you have a mentor? If so, who and what did he or she teach you? Douglas McNeal, whom I worked with at the Four Seasons in Washington, D.C. He was Scottish and came from a European background that was very structured in the kitchen. He let me see the possibilities in this business. He had the biggest effect in helping me get to this point in my career.

Describe a typical workday. I come into the hotel between 8:30 A.M. and 9:30 A.M. Depending on what's going on, I check in with the sous chef and make a round through the different areas of the kitchen. Then I take a look at the special events we have planned for the day and the day's lunch specials, and review the banquet-room menus with the sous chef. We're always planning a couple of days ahead. I check my e-mail and return phone calls before lunch. Every day I meet with our purchasing person to see what's on the market that may be interesting to us. Then I start planning the evening menu with our sous chef. I also do our wine buying, so I look at the wine list to make sure we have an accurate list at all times. Once our dinner and banquet service starts, I spend a lot of time in both areas. Then before you know it, the day's wrapping up.

What is the most rewarding part of being a chef? One part is the self-satisfaction you get from this kind of work—feeling great when the day is over because of what you've put together. And the other part is working with people to help them develop their careers. I'm now in a position to influence younger people—to share some perspective and help them realize their dreams.

What is your favorite thing to cook, and why? Seafood. There's an incredible variety to be creative with. I enjoy fish and shellfish quite a bit.

What qualities do you look for when you hire employees? I'd say 90 percent of what I look for is a positive attitude. Technical skills are important, but we can always teach people how to do this or that. Attitude is very critical to being successful.

What advice would you give aspiring chefs? You have to work hard in this business, so be prepared for that. Cooking is a growth process. There's so much to learn that's difficult to do at a young age. A lot of people don't realize that the people they see on TV have years and years of training behind them.[1]

[1] http://www.restaurant.org.

orders after explaining the menu, describes the special daily features, and answers questions guests may have. In addition, the captain may carry out appropriate tableside preparations such as finishing salads or adding special sauces to certain dishes as they are served.

Chef De Rang

The **chef de rang**, or front waiter, sees to the service needs of the guests as they dine, making sure that the proper service is set for each course, that water and other beverages are kept fresh, and that used items are promptly removed.

Demi-Chef De Rang

The **demi-chef de rang**, also called a back waiter or busperson, clears all appropriate service items from the table between courses and often freshens water glasses. In addition, the back waiter may assist other service personnel as necessary.

Today's Dining Room

The kitchen brigade system emerged from a particular cultural tradition and, in practice, is found in only a small minority of foodservice operations worldwide today. Rising labor costs and the need for faster service have blurred Escoffier's rigidly defined duties, and responsibilities frequently overlap at the peak of dinner-hour preparations. The modern large kitchen may feature an executive chef, kitchen manager, sous chef, and various line chefs. In many small operations, though, the whole staff could be only one or two people.

Today's dining room staff is usually more streamlined, reflecting changes from the service style of Escoffier's time, when many final preparations were carried out at tableside. Frequently, a dining room manager and host or hostess supervise the waitstaff, who transport pre-portioned food to customers, and the buspersons, who clear the used service items.

Today the complete, traditional kitchen brigade system is most commonly found in fine dining restaurants in Europe. It is less prevalent in the United States. However, it has influenced the organization of the kitchen in many other foodservice concepts. The traditional roles of chef, sous chef, and garde manger, and the workstations associated with these positions, are found in most full-service restaurants. However, it is important also to recognize that the kitchen brigade system was developed by Escoffier prior to the twentieth century. It predated the development of many managerial techniques, such as work design, human factors engineering, and process reengineering, which have led to significant improvements in productivity and efficiency in other industries. In today's fiercely competitive environment, foodservice operators

A Day in the Life of...

A CHEF

Alice Waters, Charlie Trotter, and Paul Prudhomme all have done a great deal to raise the rank of chef in the minds of the public. While these famous chefs have carved out a niche for themselves through cooking, writing cookbooks, making television appearances, and (for two of the three) operating restaurants, the typical day in the life of a chef does not include all these activities. Rather, it is focused on preparing the meals for the day.

An average day begins very early, when the chef purchases the day's seasonal fresh vegetables, fruits, fish, and other foods. Since storage is limited and freshness is a priority, such purchasing is done on a daily basis. The chef then begins the day's food production or supervises the kitchen staff. Later in the morning, the chef may meet with other managers and sometimes clients to consult about menu planning. Menus are planned according to availability, season, and daily market quotations. Throughout the remainder of the day, the chef may take care of paperwork or refine recipes, often taking a few hours off before returning for the evening dinner period.

A chef is officially in charge of preparing all food for the restaurant or hotel dining room. The chef is also head of the cooking staff and, in larger establishments, supervises helpers, assistants, and apprentices. A chef can oversee a staff of specialized chefs such as a pastry chef or salad chef. In addition, the chef sets the style of cooking and originates the recipes. Frequently, a chef who changes jobs takes along the recipes he has originated. Also, the chef

- continually evaluates what is being prepared and how it is being prepared to ensure consistency in menu items' appeal to customers
- is responsible for ensuring a clean and sanitary workplace that is compliant with state and municipal codes and regulations
- manages and develops the workforce, including: training (or overseeing the training of) new kitchen staff

Photo courtesy of Hilton Hotels Corporation

- is responsible for ensuring that all foods and beverages that are to be prepared meet standards of quality, are delivered in the correct amounts, are portioned properly, and are stored properly
- must be able to connect well with people in the workplace.
- must be able to deliver financial results and build loyal customer support.

The work of a chef is demanding, entailing long hours and days, totaling anywhere between forty and seventy hours per week, and usually including evenings, weekends, and holidays. Perhaps that explains the shortage of skilled, trained executive chefs in this country—there are less than seventy-five certified master chefs in the United States.[1] Still, a properly trained chef can earn a very good salary (executive chefs can earn upwards of six figures), plus benefits and meals.

In order to become a chef, most large-scale hotels and restaurants require at least two to three years of apprenticeship plus additional training as an assistant chef. A college or post-secondary degree in culinary arts or hotel/restaurant management is also very helpful.

---

[1] Shepard Henkin, *Opportunities in Hotel and Motel Careers* (NTC Publishing Group, Lincoln, Illonois: 1992), 91, 95–97.

Courtesy of Photodisc

The chef d'étage is sometimes called the *captain* in fine restaurants.

have developed new forms of organization for the kitchen and dining areas. In some instances, classical service techniques and etiquette have been eroded, casualties of foodservice's profit-centered orientation.

Mise en place (literally, "to put in place") is the foundation for many cooking techniques, from basic stocks to the most complex dishes. It means being prepared by having all the necessary ingredients and cooking utensils at hand and ready to use at the moment work on a dish begins. Students must master the basics of mise en place before they can progress to more complex tasks. For example, students need to know what different knives are for and how to use them. Students also must learn to create the classic seasoning combinations, such as *mirepoix* (usually, chopped onions, carrots, and celery) and marinades, and to cook flavorful stocks, the essential component of soups and stews. A primary culinary principle is followed throughout: Learn the basic techniques first. If they are properly understood, basic techniques are versatile enough to produce a variety of products.

The greatest test of a chef's skill is considered to be sauces. Mastery of the grand sauces, such as béchamel or hollandaise, and their variations, is a skill that develops throughout a chef's career. It requires a highly refined understanding of food, and sauces can become a chef's signature.

Today, many executive and celebrity chefs excel at adapting the foundational principles of Escoffier into a post-modern cuisine that mixes ethnic variety with a fusion of flavors. Recent movements within the culinary profession include using locally grown, seasonally fresh ingredients; celebrating indigenous foods; and incorporating environmentally sustainable practices at all levels.

Culinary Education and Apprenticeship

Many cooks and chefs begin their careers with practical experience on the job, in one of the less-skilled kitchen positions. However, it takes a great deal of work, and often formal education as well, to rise to a more skilled level. Both technical and leadership skills are necessary to advance in the culinary field and serve what has now become a highly competitive industry. For example, years of training and experience are required to achieve the position of executive chef. Cooks frequently are trained through vocational programs at the high school or post–high school level, or through programs in an increasing number of two- and four-year colleges. One hospitality industry source lists 126 colleges and universities with programs in the culinary arts, and 260 restaurant and foodservice management programs. In addition, apprenticeship programs organized by professional culinary institutes, industry associations, and some large hotels and restaurants are available in the United States and abroad. Today, rising demand for culinary professionals has placed pressure on these programs to place capable culinarians into the workplace more rapidly. For instance, the California Culinary Academy in San Francisco has a sixteen-month professional chef program. The Culinary Institute of America in Hyde Park, New York grants an associate degree after completion of a twenty-one–month program and an externship.

Although the curricula in these programs vary, students usually learn food preparation procedures through actual practice in working environments. Externships in nearby restaurants are often required. Attention is also given to financial, procedural, and social aspects of the foodservice industry, such as menu planning, cost control, purchasing, personnel management, sanitation, and waste management. Today, those culinarians that demonstrate a mastery of financial issues along with artistry in food handling have better opportunities for hiring and advancement.

Industry Insights

CULINARY INSTITUTE OF AMERICA—GREYSTONE CAMPUS—NAPA VALLEY, CALIFORNIA

The Culinary Institute of America (CIA) campus in Napa Valley offers education in hospitality, culinary, and viticulture in a picturesque rural setting. The Greystone campus sits among beautiful rolling hills and vineyards. In addition to culinary degree programs, the campus offers public programs including cooking demonstrations, cooking lessons, party planning, wine pairing, and wine tasting events. The CIA at Greystone offers culinary excellence in a wine enthusiast's paradise.[1]

[1] http://www.ciachef.org.

Photo courtesy of Johnson & Wales University

Johnson & Wales University is one of over 125 colleges and universities offering culinary arts programs.

Certification from the American Culinary Federation formally recognizes the skill levels of cook, working chef, executive chef, and master chef, as well as pastry professionals and culinary educators. Table 7.2 lists the certification requirements at various levels.

Menu Planning and Development

The menu is the operational plan a restaurant uses to meet the needs and expectations of its guests. Today, the menu is the single most important element in the dining operation, and may destine your dining operation for success or failure. Successful menu design, costing, engineering, and market positioning require careful analysis and planning. Although menu development is ideally part of initial concept planning and occurs before the restaurant is designed, changing the menu is an ongoing part of successful restaurant operations.

Menu composition in most quick-service establishments and in many mid-scale restaurants is often determined by the chain or franchisor. Generally a white-tablecloth restaurant has the greatest freedom in selecting food and beverages. Owners of independent operations, of course, can choose whatever they want to serve. However, success comes only when the menu selections satisfy restaurant patrons and provide a profitable return. A menu that satisfies customers and builds market share is desirable; however, a menu that builds market share at the expense of profit is less likely to sustain a long-term return on investment.

In cooperation with the chef, a restaurant owner usually develops a solid basic menu when opening the business. Adding items or changing the basic

TABLE 7.2 Certification Requirements

1. CC—Certified Culinarian/CPC—Certified Pastry Culinarian Written exam Practical exam (exempt if graduate of ACF accredited program) And one of the following combinations of education and experience: High School Diploma or GED with 2 years entry level culinarian/pastry experience. OR: 100 continuing education hours (CEH) with 2 years entry level culinarian/pastry experience. OR: Culinary Arts Program Certificate (1 yr.) with 1 year entry level culinarian/pastry experience. OR: Associate's Degree in Culinary Arts (no additional experience required). OR: ACFF Apprenticeship program (no additional experience required).
2. CSC—Certified Sous Chef/CWPC—Certified Working Pastry Chef Written exam Practical exam And one of the following combinations of education and experience: High school diploma or GED plus 50 CEH with 5 yrs. entry level culinarian/pastry experience. OR: 150 CEH with 5 yrs. entry level culinarian/pastry experience. OR: Associate's Degree in Culinary Arts with 3 yrs. entry level culinarian/pastry experience. OR: ACFF Apprenticeship Program is acceptable with a minimum of 4000 hrs. on the job training.
3. CCC—Certified Chef de Cuisine Written exam Practical exam 3 yrs. experience as a Sous Chef or chef who supervises a shift or station in a food service operation. And education as follows: High school diploma or GED plus 100 CEH, OR: 200 CEH with the same level of experience described directly above. OR: Associate's Degree in Culinary Arts with the same level of experience described directly above. OR: ACFF Apprenticeship program with the same level of experience directly above.
4. CEC—Certified Executive Chef/CEPC—Certified Executive Pastry Chef Written exam Practical Exam 3 yrs. experience as Chef de Cuisine or Executive Sous Chef/Pastry Chef or chef in charge of food production in a foodservice operation. Must have supervised at least 3 full time people in the preparation of food. And education as follows: High school diploma or GED plus 150 CEH, OR: 250 CEH with the same level of experience described directly above. Associate's Degree in Culinary Arts with the same level of experience described above. OR: ACFF Apprenticeship program plus 50 CEH with the same level of experience described above.
5. CMC—Certified Master Chef/CMPC—Certified Master Pastry Chef High School Diploma plus 150 CEH, OR: GED plus 150 CEH, OR: 250 CEH, OR: Associate's degree in culinary arts, OR: ACFF apprenticeship program plus 50 CEH. See CMC/CMPC Manual for additional experience and requirements.
Comprehensive written exam covering the following areas: 1. Healthy Cooking 2. Buffet Catering 3. Classical Cuisine 4. Freestyle Cooking 5. Global Cuisine 6. Baking and Pastry 7. Continental and Northern Europe Cuisines 8. Market

Source: http://www.acfchefs.org

menu requires additional planning and analysis. **Menu engineering** is an industry term that refers to the review of menu item sales, pricing, cost analysis, and item contribution to profit. Menu engineering is most effective when it can be integrated with the restaurant's point-of-sale system and reviewed daily by key managment personnel. The concept of the operation, the customers' wants and needs, the margin of profitability, and the staff and equipment that are available all influence menu planning and development.

The Concept

To a great degree, an operation's concept determines what will be on the menu and what will not be on it. A French restaurant that serves pizza would be most unusual, as would a Chinese restaurant that offered enchiladas. When a restaurant does add selections to its menu that are not in keeping with its concept, its concept becomes diluted. Today, careful research and market analysis are necessary in order to determine the ideal **positioning** and cuisine selection for a concept or themed restaurant. Advance feasibility studies and a competitive analysis of existing restaurants and concepts must be undertaken in order to determine the demographic profile of the marketplace.

Customers' Wants and Expectations

Within the constraints of an operation's concept, the customers' wants and expectations should govern menu planning and development. Consideration should be given to the food habits specific to the region or neighborhood where the restaurant is located. Also, the opinion of "regulars"—individuals who frequent the establishment—should be taken into account. While formally surveying customers about their wants and expectations is not often feasible, customers will express their views by what they select. Menu engineering is very helpful in this regard, because if it is conducted regularly by management, it will identify patterns and point out emerging trends in both customer preference and profit contributions. With these trends in mind, a chef can supplement the basic menu and offer new and exciting menu alternatives. For example, recent years have witnessed a distinct trend toward healthful eating that deemphasizes salty, fatty, and cholesterol-filled foods—and a number of menus have been changed accordingly. Also, experimenting with a small number of new menu items may quickly tell the operation how to proceed. Today, most successful full-service restaurants offer special health-and-wellness menu items and list calorie and nutrient breakdowns on the menu.

Another feature of today's dining establishments is the daily fresh sheet. The daily fresh sheet enables the establishment to present short-term specials designed to reinforce its core cuisine specialty. It also helps the restaurant manage inventory in order to reduce waste. Sophisticated chefs know how to present creative and innovative menu items that also achieve budget efficiencies. The fresh sheet is often used to upsell customers into higher average check purchases by featuring special promotions like coho salmon during the annual salmon runs, or Beaujolais Nouveau during the annual release of this traditional French red wine.

Staff and Equipment

The capabilities of the staff and the equipment available affect what can be included on the menu. What employees know how to do needs to be considered in relation to the time, labor, and skills required at various stages of food preparation. Specific skills and experience are necessary for making complex or elaborate dishes. Many menu items cannot be prepared and stored ahead of time, while others require last-minute preparation just before service. This imposes certain responsibilities and limitations on employees at peak service times. Items that require lengthy, elaborate preparation or a high level of skill may have to be omitted from the menu.

The equipment available for storage and preparation also influences the type of menu that may be developed. The amount of equipment and its capacity affect the time and labor costs for menu items. Without the right kinds of equipment, some dishes cannot be prepared.

Margins of Profitability

The general price range of the operation is inherent in its concept. A menu item that has to be sold at twice the cost of other entrees is a poor choice. Similarly, low-priced items may have low contribution margins, and their popularity may hurt the sales of higher-margin items. The **contribution margin** is the difference between what it costs to produce an item and the selling price of the item. The contribution margin represents money that is used to pay fixed expenses and taxes, leaving profits. The greater that the overall contribution margin is, the higher the profit potential is. A measure of success in menu development is how well it increases the overall contribution margin. A successful menu makes efficient use of available resources, such as labor and food raw materials, ensuring maximum profitability.

The Benefits of a Limited Menu

The menu limitation concept has clear advantages. A restaurant does not need variety for variety's sake; in fact, too much variety is often a recipe for failure. Menu limitation provides a clear focus for the establishment, defining it in relation to its locale, its clientele, and its suppliers. A restaurant will be "positioned" in customers' minds for a specific taste, atmosphere, or style. (See Figure 7.1). Menu limitation reduces inventory and space requirements, as well as capital expenditure for equipment. Furthermore, it significantly reduces spoilage. All of this leads to greater profits.

Menu Engineering

As discussed earlier in this chapter, menu engineering plays a critical role in successful restaurant operations. For many years foodservice operators controlled ingredient costs and set menu prices by using the "food cost percentage" of each menu item. The food cost percentage is the percentage of the

Hors d'Oeuvre Froids

Salade Tiède de Caneton aux Asperges et Champignons 9.25
warm salad of duckling with asparagus and mushrooms

Terrine de Foie Gras de Canard au Naturel 16.75
pâté of fresh duck liver marinated in Madeira, cognac and spices

Nage d'Huîtres, Moules et Homard au Curry 11.75
cold oysters, mussels and lobster in a light curry broth

Salade Niçoise au Homard et St. Jacques 11.75
yellow fin tuna, lobster and scallops with assorted greens, tomatoes, beans, potato and a light dressing flavored with anchovy

Hors d'Oeuvre Chauds

Lasagne de Langoustines aux Épinards 11.75
lasagne of "Langoustinas" with spinach—basil, chive and tomato, lobster cream sauce

Feuilleté de Petits Légumes à la Tomate Crue 8.75
a small puff pastry of assorted vegetables with fresh raw tomatoes flavored with lemon juice, olive oil and fine herbs

Poivrade d'Escargots aux Champignons 15.75
fresh snails sautéed with black pepper, mushrooms and red wine—served in a nest of cracked wheat

Foie Gras de Canard Chaud aux Reinettes 16.75
fresh duck liver sautéed with apple and "calvados"

Potages

Soupe à l'Oignon Gratinée 4.50

Bisque de Homard 7.50
lobster bisque

Potage du Jour 4.00

Nos Spécialités de Tous Les Jours

Escalope de Veau Sautée au Paprika—Gratin de "Cheveaux d'Ange" aux Piments Rouges et Fine Herbes 32.75
veal steak sautéed with a light paprika sauce—gratin of angel hair pasta with sweet pimentos and fine herbs

Tournedos Sautés aux Échalottes 30.50
a duo of petite filet mignons with two shallot sauces—creamed horseradish and red wine

Côtelettes de Chevreuil au Génevrier 32.75
sautéed red deer chops with juniper berries and gin—lightly creamed venison sauce

Châteaubriand Bouquetière (for two) 30.50 per person
a double center cut filet mignon, broiled and served with a garnish of assorted fresh vegetables—béarnaise sauce

Filet d'Agneau Rôti Niçoise (for two) 32.50 per person
roast rack of lamb served boneless with an assortment of fresh vegetables

Terrine de Ris de Veau "Pompadour" 28.25
braised veal sweetbread with mushroom, tomato, cream, cognac and veal coulis

Poitrine de Volaille au Vinaigre de Framboises 19.75
marinated chicken breast with raspberry vinegar—and small vegetables

Aiguillettes de Caneton aux Endives à la Bourguignonne 28.00
broiled and thinly sliced duck breast with braised Belgian endives—red wine sauce with shallots, bacon and mushrooms

Poitrine de Faisan aux Poireaux et Morilles 30.50
sautéed Scottish pheasant breast with stewed leeks and morels

Filet de Flétan Rôti en Écailles—Beurre Blanc à la Ciboulette et Anneth, Coulis de Veau 28.25
roasted fillet of halibut in "Potato Scales" with a chive and dill butter sauce and a thin veal coulis

Filet de Saumon Grillé au Coulis de Tomates Crues à l'Huile d'Olive et Citron 27.25
broiled Norwegian salmon fillet with a garnish of raw diced tomatoes, olive oil and lemon juice

Filets de Sole de Douvres et Homard sur Risotto—Sauce Bisque 32.75
baked fillets of Dover sole with lobster on risotto—light lobster sauce

Darne d'Espadon Sauté aux Câpres et Crabe 28.25
sautéed swordfish steak with a caper butter sauce with crabmeat

La Sole de Douvre Sautée Meunière 32.75
fresh English sole sautéed in lemon butter

Salades

Laitue du Kentucky 7.00
Kentucky limestone (Bibb) lettuce

Salade Mimosa 8.00
assorted lettuce, green beans, tomato, ripe olives and radishes with chopped egg

Salade Escoffier 7.00
bibb lettuce, avocado and artichokes, with vinaigrette dressing

Salade d'Endives Belges et Champignons (en saison) 7.00
Belgian endive and mushrooms

Salade de Fromage de Chèvre 7.75
goat cheese salad

Salade César (for two) 6.25 per person

Salade Mixte, Sauce "Maisonette" 5.75

When appetizers, salads, vegetables or soups are served as a main course, there will be an additional charge

Légumes

Asperges Vertes Fraîches (en Saison) 7.75
fresh asparagus with butter or sauce hollandaise

Epinards au Beurre ou à la Crème 7.00
fresh leaf spinach with butter or cream

Brocolis Frais, Hollandaise ou Beurre Fondu 7.00
fresh broccoli with hollandaise or butter

Champignons Frais 7.00
fresh mushrooms sautéed with fine herbs

Haricots Verts Frais 7.00
fresh green beans

Pommes Soufflées 6.50

Pois Gourmands 6.00
fresh snow peas

In consideration of others, please refrain from pipe or cigar smoking in the dining room. The bar is available for your smoking pleasure. Thank you.

10/93

FIGURE 7.1 Upscale Menu
Source: Maisonette Restaurant, Cincinnati, Ohio

Industry Insights

BUSINESS INNOVATION

Menu Design

Customers approach food selection in much the same way as the menu is designed—by price or by food. Therefore, careful consideration of menu design can turn a price list into an innovative marketing tool.

Serving up food via a menu is a complicated task involving more than making a price list, says menu consultant Gregg Rapp. Rapp, founder of Seattle's Menu Workshop, contends that highlighting a restaurant's most profitable appetizers, entrees, and desserts is the key to successful menu design.[1]

Since the menu is what sells the food to diners, it should be used as an attractive and appealing marketing tool. Graphics and mouth-watering copy can help sell high-profit items. Placement of menu items is also an important consideration. Research shows that diners tend to look to the upper right of a two-panel menu or to the top of a single-panel menu. By designing the menu with this in mind, a restaurateur can spotlight selected menu items—and increase profitability.

---

[1] Frances Huffman, "Food For Thought," *Entrepreneur* (August 1993): 120.

selling price of an item that must be spent to purchase the raw ingredients. For example, a pizza might sell for $12. If the ingredients (dough, sauce, toppings) cost $3, then the food cost percentage for pizza is 25 percent. By setting the prices of all the menu items so that they average a target food cost percentage, an operation ensures a sufficient contribution margin—the money remaining after the cost of the product has been subtracted—to cover payroll, rent, and other expenses.

Menu engineering is a sophisticated approach to setting prices and controlling costs. Menu engineering operates on the principle that the food cost percentage of each menu item is not as important as the total contribution margin of the menu as a whole. For example, using the traditional food cost percentage approach, a restaurant manager might set the price of pizza at $12 to maintain a cost percentage of 25 percent. If, at $12, customers buy one hundred pizzas, the total contribution margin from pizza would be $900. Suppose, however, that if the price were lowered to $9, guests would buy two hundred pizzas. Although the food cost percentage would rise to 33 percent, the operation would now receive $1,200. Clearly, the restaurant owner would prefer $1,200 in contribution margin over $900—even though the actual cost percentage for the pizza rose 8 percent, from 25 percent to 33 percent. Menu engineering applies this same logic to the entire **menu mix**, enabling the restaurateur to maximize contribution margin regardless of the actual food cost percentage. Through menu engineering, menu items that should be repositioned, dropped, repriced, or simply left alone are identified.

Today, menu engineering has become easier to manage, thanks to technological advances and the restaurant point of sale system. A computer's ability to store and organize large amounts of information and rapidly handle complex calculations has relieved management of countless repetitive, routine tasks. Although menu engineering software packages are available, it also can easily be performed using a simple **spreadsheet**.

The Production Cycle

The most important focus of the kitchen is, of course, the preparation of food items. Menu design and development is more than a marketing tool. The entire production cycle is built around the menu. Careful thought and significant planning are needed to arrive at the ideal balance between optimal market position and profitability.

Standard Recipe File

The more detailed and specified the recipe, the more consistent the product. The more consistent the product, the more efficient the operation, and the higher the customer satisfaction level. The standard recipe file is therefore an important factor in menu planning, forecasting, and purchasing. Restaurants organize the recipes used for basic menu items and specialties in a recipe file. This file is a vital part of the food preparation process. Recipes for every menu item are recorded on a standard form, designated by a title and a category, for easy organization, and a recipe number, which can be used for cross-referencing. Also included are serving standards (i.e., the size of the pan or the number of portions), expected yield, a complete list of ingredients, and the exact amount of ingredients required. Finally, the method of preparation is described in great detail. Even instructions for serving are sometimes added. Today, the recipe file is electronically prepared and illustrated with a full-color picture that can be placed in the kitchen prep and server work stations. It is a form of quality control, a way to guarantee a consistent, high quality item. Since anyone preparing any dish from the menu must consult the standard recipe file and follow the instructions to the letter, results should always be identical. Standardized recipes also act as a quality control tool by listing the expected number of portions, the exact amount of required ingredients, and the serving standards. This cuts down on overproduction and waste.

Forecasting

What menu items are going to be requested next week or next month, and how many will be sold? When must an order be placed with a supplier to ensure a plentiful supply of fresh produce? What seasonal specialties are popular over the Christmas holidays? What long-term sales trends can be identified that will affect the organization of the restaurant staff? All foodservice operations must be prepared to answer these questions. **Forecasting** is the process of estimating future events, often combining intuition with formal statistical models. The reasonably accurate calculation and prediction of future needs is a major factor in the cost-effectiveness of a restaurant. It provides some idea of the expected results, as long as management makes no changes in operation.

Forecasting deals with the future, but relies on the past record of the restaurant's operation. A major assumption in forecasting is that some pattern exists that can be identified and used to prepare for future events. Therefore, well-kept records of sales and production are the basis for forecasting. Three types of patterns in these data can emerge: trends (long-term projections), seasonal patterns, and cyclical patterns. While intuition does play an important part in forecasting, objective models based on either qualitative or quantitative methods have been developed to assist in interpreting the data. These models vary in complexity, and the selection process will depend on the specific forecasting need, the relevance of the data to that need, the length of time into the future that the forecast will cover, and the cost of setting up the model. Today, highly sophisticated forecasting software models exist and are implemented in most high-volume restaurant operations. Forecasting models can be linked to inventory management, labor management, receiving, and menu engineering systems, permitting agile and synergistic reporting. To maximize operating efficiencies, chefs and dining room managers should learn how to use these applications, especially their report writing and interpretation capabilities.

Purchasing

Food items on the menu determine what raw ingredients need to be purchased, what qualities and quantities are necessary, and when they should be made available. The purchaser must buy the necessary goods in the right amount, at the right time, and at the right price. Good purchasing is a critical element of cost control. Purchasing personnel need a variety of skills and experience, including an awareness of the market and how suppliers operate, the ability to forecast needs and respond to fluctuating market conditions, and the ability to negotiate with suppliers for favorable product, delivery, and shipping costs. In order to make good choices, purchasers need a thorough knowledge of the items to be purchased and the way they will be used. In the produce area alone, purchasers must know terminology, specifications, laws, regulations, and processing requirements, and be able to assess produce quality. In addition, they must coordinate storeroom inventory to fit the schedules of the purchasing and receiving areas and the supplier. In short, these duties demand someone with overall experience in a foodservice operation.

In carrying out their jobs, purchasers rely on **standard purchase specifications**, or "specs"—standards of food quality established by the restaurant, custom-made for the facility, and documented in detail on food sample data sheets. Specs should be based on experience, tests, and objective measurements. Clear, technically accurate language should describe each commodity and identify its size, quality, and condition. Information should include the common, trade, or brand name of the product; the recognized trade, federal, or local grade; ranges in weight, thickness, or size; and the degree of maturity or end use date. In effect, specs are statements of management policy on the minimum requirements for purchasing. They communicate to the seller exactly what is needed and thereby eliminate misunderstanding.

For example, standard purchase specifications are used to determine the quantity of produce to buy. These specs include information on the amounts of specific food items to be purchased, stated in commonly used units; the name and size of the basic container; and the count and size of units within this container. Excess purchased produce ties up money unnecessarily in inventory, and monopolizes valuable storage space. Furthermore, the quality of perishable products quickly deteriorates. On the other hand, if too little produce is purchased, the restaurant faces repeated stockouts, emergency rush orders, loss of volume discounts (applicable to large purchase orders), and upset customers.

In selecting suppliers for either raw or processed ingredients, purchasers must take into account food quality while also factoring in quantity, price, delivery time, and service. The quantity of each ingredient ordered is based on forecasting: how many servings of each ingredient of every food item on the menu will be necessary for each meal over an exact period of time? However, purchasing decisions are based on more than just immediate menu needs. Other factors include the general inventory on hand, storage capacity, seasonal fluctuations in availability or cost of produce, the types of suppliers, and their proximity. Often, supplier constraints such as minimum dollar or weight requirements or standard commercial units of packaging also must be considered.

Buying for small operations may be done through informal agreements that are fast, convenient, and require little paperwork. In fact, smaller to mid-sized culinary operations give the chef the ultimate purchasing responsibility. Large operations are more likely to use a formal method of "competitive buying," and staff a substantial purchasing department. The purchasing department is where written sets of specifications and requests for bids are sent to possible vendors (perhaps several at once) and sophisticated purchasing and receiving processess are set up, including requisition procedures and protocols for inventory turnover and management. Formal purchasing procedures create an "audit trail" of records and documents that traces the flow of goods through the operation. These records take the form of requisitions, inventories, purchase orders, and delivery packaging slips and records. Many operations generate purchase orders from computerized systems linked to **databases** that contain ingredient specifications, recipe files, and inventory records.

Receiving

The receiving department makes certain that the products delivered by the vendors are those that were ordered by the purchaser. Therefore, the purchasing and receiving departments must communicate clearly with each other and coordinate schedules. Receiving personnel need a keen awareness of the market and of product quality standards. They must know what produce has been ordered, when it is expected, and how it should be stored. And they must clearly understand receiving procedures and internal receiving records.

When a delivery arrives, receiving personnel check the incoming products against the in-house purchase order, delivery invoice, and standard produce specifications. Equipment such as scales, calculators, rulers, marking and tagging equipment, thermometers, tools, and transport devices like dollies and hand trucks are necessary. Perishable goods (fresh seafood, produce, and raw meats) should be marked and tagged with delivery date and price information as it is checked in; this information is essential to inventory control and stock rotation plans. Items must then be moved to storage immediately, and any additional documentation, such as daily receiving reports, must be completed. If receiving is left to anyone who happens to be handy at the moment, produce of unsuitable quality or improper quantity might be accepted, inventory can be lost or poorly stored, and records may be incomplete or misplaced—all of which can hurt a foodservice operation financially.

Storing and Issuing

All items, whether frozen, refrigerated, or canned, perishable or nonperishable, need to be properly stored in appropriate areas and issued in a definite sequence. Storage areas must be clean, well ventilated, well insulated, and easily accessible from the receiving area as well as the food preparation areas. Uniform stock rotation ensures that items previously purchased are used first. The rule of thumb in food and beverage inventory managment is called FIFO (first in, first out). Careful storing and issuing procedures also protect against theft, spoilage, and waste. For this reason, many operations limit the number of staff members that have access to storage facilities.

Personnel should weigh out, measure, or count each item before distribution. A record of these transactions helps to maintain inventory control, showing the quantities available for use or that need to be ordered, the dollar value of the products used or on hand, the food cost incurred for menu items, and the food cost percentage. In large foodservice operations, requisition forms are also used to monitor and control the flow of inventory, giving management an additional tool for checking expenses and analyzing sales. In most culinary operations today, access to inventory storage is highly restricted and inventory is accounted for in sophisticated inventory management systems tied directly to the point-of-sale system. High-value inventory items such as prime rib of beef, lobster, and sushi ingredients are usually secondarily secured within the storage areas to protect and isolate them, because they are the most expensive ingredients, and therefore are the most susceptible to theft and waste.

Photo by Michael Dzaman

Food and supplies must be easily accessible in a restaurant's storage facility.

Pre-Preparation

Food items can often be cleaned, processed, mixed, seasoned, and otherwise worked with before the actual meal period begins. Pre-preparation ensures that a menu item can be readied for final service to a customer with as little labor as possible. Tasks might include cleaning, peeling, and chopping fresh vegetables; thawing frozen meat and trimming it; adding liquid to dehydrated items; simmering broth; or making salad dressing. However, efficiency must be balanced against the potential for spoilage, waste, and diminished freshness and taste if the menu item is prepared too far in advance.

Final Preparation

Final preparation is the point in the production cycle where heat is applied to food immediately prior to service. Food that needs cooking is brought from the pre-preparation area, made ready for final preparation, and placed in easy reach of the cooks. Typical final preparation processes include frying, sautéing, steaming, and charbroiling. During final preparation food is "plated" and garnished for service to the guest. Final preparation typically occurs in a dedicated work area. In most restaurants, this area is known as the "line," and is the area defined by an aisle with the chef's table on one side and the ranges, fryers, charbroilers, steamers, and similar equipment on the other side. Most culinary operations in the middle to upper scale of the market do less pre-prep work than lower-priced operations and cook all menu items fresh to order on the line.

A number of foodservice operations locate the final preparation area in a special area of the dining room so that customers can watch the chefs at work and the tantalizing smells of broiling meat can increase their sensory enjoyment of the meal. This setup is referred to as a 'demonstration kitchen.' When designing a demonstration kitchen, careful attention must be given to the equipment selection and wall, floor, and lighting finishes because the kitchen will be a focal point of the front-of-the-house.

Service

Chapter 6 described the many forms of service that are used in foodservice operations, such as buffet, table, and counter service. Here it is important to note several trends in table service. Traditionally, **servers** were expected to take guests' orders, deliver them to the kitchen, and, when the food had been prepared by the chefs, bring the food from the kitchen to the guests' tables. This system continues in many table service restaurants. However, technological developments have made it possible to change this system and thus overcome two of its greatest weaknesses. First, when servers are in the kitchen placing orders, checking the progress of the food, or picking up the plates, they cannot be in the dining room attending to the immediate needs of the guests. Second, it is possible for servers to collude with the cooks to feed guests for free.

New technology replaces the traditional server's book of guest checks with a few point-of-sale terminals located strategically in the dining room and monitors and/or printers at the various stations in the kitchen. Servers enter the guests' orders into the point-of-sale terminals. The orders then appear on the monitors above the cooking line or emerge from printers on the chef's table. When the food is ready, a "runner" delivers the food from the kitchen to the guests' table. When the guests have finished their meals, the server obtains a check from the point-of-sale terminal, presents it to the guests, receives payment, and rings it into the terminal. Today, some restaurants provide handheld wireless order takers to the servers so the order goes directly from the guest's table to the kitchen, bypassing the need for the server to enter it into the point-of-sale system at a different location within the dining room. At no point in the process does the server need to leave the dining room, which improves the quality and immediacy of guest service. Because the servers never communicate directly with the cooks, they cannot collude with them to provide free meals to friends.

Chain dinnerhouses and multiunit restaurants were the first to adopt new technologies in table service, perhaps because point-of-sale systems are often bundled with management software that permits the corporate office to obtain up-to-the-minute operating data.

Although quick-service restaurants rarely offer table service, that segment of the market also has been pursuing new technologies in customer service. For example, several chains have experimented with automated order-taking systems that could eventually supplant or replace service from counterpersons.

Cleanup and Warewashing

Cleanup and warewashing involve the pots, pans, and utensils used in food preparation, as well as the kitchen and equipment. Although cleanup and warewashing do not involve food production, they are important parts of the production cycle. Cleanup includes bussing dishes and silverware to the dishroom, while warewashing consists of scrapping, cleaning, and sanitizing.

Cleanup and warewashing are parts of the production cycle that are becoming increasingly important. Concerns about the environmental impact of foodservice focus on these processes. Increasing landfill costs may drive more and more operations to use pulpers and shredders to reduce the volume of waste leaving the kitchen. A continuing difficult labor market for low paying service jobs, particularly for less desirable positions like potwashers or dishwashers, will encourage equipment manufacturers to increase the automation of dishwashing and potwashing processes. Increasing concern about food safety will encourage foodservice operators to incorporate powerwashing and improved sanitizing systems in new and remodeled kitchens.

Social Issues

As public businesses, all foodservice operations must keep up on issues of concern to customers. Five issues that affect foodservice are access for the physically challenged, food safety, the environment, food-labeling laws, and health-conscious dining options.

Equal Access

The Americans with Disabilities Act (ADA) applies to the restaurant industry, just as it does to lodging. All new restaurants and foodservice facilities must comply with ADA guidelines in their design and construction. Ongoing renovations and specific new construction elements added to existing structures must be modified to meet the regulations wherever "readily achievable," unless doing so creates an "undue burden." In terms of actual restaurant layout and design, numerous modifications can make restaurant access more comfortable for individuals with disabilities. Here are some specific accessibility requirements.

- At least 5 percent of parking lot spaces should be accessible, with an eight-foot-wide parking space and a five-foot aisle.
- A ramp with a slope of no more than 1:12 should lead to the front door.
- Entry doors should provide thirty-two inches of clearance.
- Fire exits should be accessible.
- Paths through dining areas, and at least one path leading to the restrooms, should be at least thirty-six inches wide.
- At least 5 percent of a restaurant's tables should be handicap accessible, with leg space that is twenty-seven inches high, thirty inches wide, and nineteen inches deep; these tables should be located within the main dining area so diners will have an equal opportunity to enjoy the atmosphere.

- Self-service areas should be within reach of someone seated in a wheelchair, meaning not higher than thirty-six inches from the floor.
- Wheelchair-accessible restrooms should be available.[2]

The ADA requires that restaurants be accessible to individuals with any disability, including those with visual, hearing, mental, or psychological impairments. For example, a restaurant can provide appropriate service to a visually impaired guest by providing menus in Braille or offering to read menus and item prices. Some venues, such as the restaurants at the Lake Buena Vista Embassy Suites Resort in Florida, offer a audio recording of the menu. Several quick-service chains have developed Braille menus for the visually impaired as well as picture menus for those who are nonreaders or non–English speakers.

Today, many professional organizations have emerged as watchdogs and advocates for ADA compliance. In fact, they often drive by establishments and verify compliance or non-compliance with entry requirements, or even enter the facility and verify compliance with ADA specifications in great detail. If they discover noncompliance, they contact the owner of the establishment and file an administrative compliance complaint warning the owner to remedy the noncompliance or face legal ramifications. Settlements of these issues can have a dollar cost ranging from the cost of fixing existing deficiencies, to several thousands of dollars in claims, fines, and mandated compliance. Noncompliance can also lead to a lawsuit and civil liability.

The ADA applies to employee hiring as well as public access. The guidelines for hiring the disabled that were discussed in Chapter 5 are equally applicable to foodservice. As Steve Zivolich, founder of a consulting firm dedicated to including people with disabilities in the workforce, states, "Complying with the employment portions of ADA generally is not that difficult. And it will lead some operators to find fantastic employees who happen to be disabled."[3]

Food Safety

Food safety is a core part of any foodservice business. It is a health issue with life or death implications, as more than nine thousand people die each year of food poisoning in the United States alone. Most victims are sickly, very young, or very old. In addition, food safety is a big economic issue. A single incident of food poisoning can damage a restaurant's image for years and cost the owners thousands of dollars in settlement or litigation costs.

Some foods are especially hospitable to disease agents that cause food poisoning. Seafood, eggs, cooked pasta or rice, soups, meats, and poultry are common culprits. Chicken, for example, frequently harbors salmonella bacteria, as do turkey, beef, eggs, fish, and milk. Camphylobacter bacteria are found in chicken, cheese, shellfish, and raw milk. Pork and other meats can carry the trichina worm, which causes trichinosis. Numerous persihable foods provide especially fertile ground for the growth of E. coli bacteria, responsible for numerous recent outbreaks of food poisoning. A new and rather nasty strain of

E. coli, discovered long ago has been found in meat, poultry, mayonnaise, potatoes, and apple cider.

Total food safety can never be assured, but the risk of food poisoning can be greatly reduced by practicing cleanliness in the workplace as well as personal cleanliness; preventing contamination; thawing and cooking food safely; and handling cooked food safely. Several government agencies—from the federal to the municipal levels—are charged with the protection of consumer food consumption safety. Today, the regulatory environment for food handling and safety is strict. For example, municipal officials may have the power to close your establishment if it is deemed to be a danger to the consumer. They may require it to get an annual operating permit and conduct frequent inspections to monitor equipment maintenance, food handling, temperature control, and potentially hazardous food management programs. In some cities and towns, local authorities have created a rating system and require eating establishments to post their health inspection score, along with current permit(s), in full view of patrons.

Practicing Cleanliness in the Workplace and Personal Cleanliness

Cleanliness in the workplace means a sanitary workplace—one that discourages food-borne disease. Personal cleanliness means following stringent hygiene practices to discourage food contamination. Workplace cleanliness and personal cleanliness go hand in hand to form the first line of defense in combating food poisoning.

Key elements of maintaining a sanitary workplace include cleaning and sanitizing all utensils, equipment, and work surfaces each time they are used; taking equipment apart to clean it thoroughly; using leak-proof containers, with tight-fitting lids, for trash; frequently removing trash from the food area; and keeping trash cans in an area separate from the food area.

Even before a foodservice facility opens for business, it must take measures to foster a sanitary workplace. Plans for building or remodeling must be reviewed by the health department to ensure that all aspects of the facility promote safe food preparation. For example, health codes typically require

- surfaces (walls, floors, ceilings) made of durable materials that are easily cleaned and sanitized
- proper ventilation of grease-laden vapors over cooking equipment
- hot water or chemical sanitizing in potsinks and dishmachines
- air gaps to prevent sewage from backing up into food in drains connected to ice machines, serving wells, and display units
- hand sinks at various locations
- adequate lighting
- access for cleaning under counters

Key elements to remember in maintaining personal cleanliness include a variety of practices. Employees should wash their hands thoroughly and frequently—especially after touching body parts such as the mouth or nose, after touching food, or when switching from one job function to another. Also, employees need to wear aprons and change them when they get dirty. Wearing hair nets or hats, keeping fingernails short and scrubbed, and not handling food when sick are three other important personal cleanliness habits for employees.

The Culinary Institute of America claims that poor personal hygiene causes more than 90 percent of the sanitation problems in the foodservice industry. Poor handwashing alone accounts for more than 25 percent of all food-borne illnesses.[4]

Preventing Contamination

A sanitary kitchen and hygienic workers both are integral to preventing contamination. However, in addition the food itself needs to be stored, prepared, and handled properly. The refrigerator should be organized so that foods that do not have to be cooked occupy the higher shelves, and meat and other animal foods with natural juices occupy lower shelves. That arrangement helps to prevent contamination, which might occur, for example, if meat juice were to drip on cucumber wedges. All food and food-related products stored in a cooler need to be dated and labeled properly so spoilage and proper use rates can be monitored. Providing separate workstations for raw and cooked foods is another preventive measure. Cross-contamination of cutting boards and utensils is a leading cause of food-borne illnesses. Using tongs and wearing gloves when handling food both reduce the risk of contamination—as long as the tongs are sanitized and the gloves are changed after each task. Finally, installing special hand-washing sinks in the foodservice area is a must because hands should never be cleaned in a sink where food is prepared.

Thawing and Cooking Food Safely

The critical element in preparing food safely is the temperature of the food. Harmful bacteria and other organisms flourish in temperatures between 40° and 140°F. (This temperature range is frequently referred to as the temperature **danger zone**.) This means that the shorter the time that food stands at those temperatures, the safer it will be. For example, the need to keep food at a safe temperature dictates how to thaw it and reheat it. The best way to thaw food is to take it from the freezer and put it directly in the refrigerator. This is the safest method because no part of the food will exceed 40°F as it is thawing. It also is a slow process. Food that has to be thawed more quickly can be put in a waterproof plastic bag and either kept under running water or immersed in cold water in a sink. When the latter is the case, the water needs to be changed about every twenty minutes.

Cooking food to a temperature above 140°F kills most harmful disease agents. It is imperative that the entire food item reaches at least 140°F. The U.S. Department of Agriculture recommends higher temperatures for meat and fish. The only way to know whether the food has reached the desired temperature is to test it with a special thermometer called a chef's thermometer. The chef's thermometer, which looks like a huge tack, can pierce to the

TABLE 7.3 A sample of minimum internal temperatures recommended by the U. S. Department of Agriculture*

Food	*Temperature*	*Food*	*Temperature*
Ground Beef:		Fresh Pork:	
Medium	160° F	Medium	160° F
Well Done	170° F	Well Done	170° F
Other Beef, (Steaks, Roasts and so on)		Chicken	180° F
Rare**	145° F	Turkey	180° F
Medium	160° F	Finfish***[3]	140° F
Well Done	170° F	Shellfish	160° F

Source: U.S.Department of Agriculture,

*Just a reminder: These aren't the temperatures used to cook the foods. They are the temperatures the foods should reach—and register on a thermometer—to be safe to eat.

**In 1993, the FDA added this recommendation; so it's now safe to have a rare steak, but still not safe to have a rare hamburger.

***Fish is so thin that a chef's thermometer would simply not be useful to measure the temperature.

center of the food to sample the temperature at the innermost part. This thermometer needs to be cleaned and sanitized after every use. When cooking or cooling large quantitites of soup or sauce, careful attention must be given to the reheating time. This often requires breaking down the batch into smaller portion sizes to prevent food-borne contamination.

Serving food as soon as possible after it is cooked helps to reduce the chances of food poisoning by reducing the time the food will be in the danger zone. Another benefit is satisfied customers—people like their food to be hot and freshly cooked. The golden rule in foodservice applies: hot food served hot and cold food served cold.

Handling Cooked Food Safely

Bacteria thrive on cooked food that either has not been refrigerated soon enough or was not cooled or reheated properly. Cooked food needs to be refrigerated as soon as possible. If it has been left at room temperature for more than two hours, it should be thrown away.

One of the primary causes of food-borne illness is improper cooling of foods. Commercial and on-site foodservice operations frequently prepare foods such as soups, sauces, roasts, and other products in bulk for later use. When food products are cooked in bulk and then placed in a walk-in refrigerator to cool, the outside of the product cools much more rapidly than the inside. A large roast, such as a steamship round of beef, can take as long as seventeen hours at 40°F in a walk-in cooler for the temperature at the center to fall out of the danger zone. That is more than enough time for bacteria to multiply. If the steamship round were removed from the walk-in cooler and sliced to make cold sandwiches, both the sandwiches and the slicer would be dangerously contaminated.[5]

Food-borne illness due to improper cooling can be prevented in several ways. Roasts and similar solid products should be sliced into smaller pieces so that the cooling process occurs more rapidly. Soups, stocks, and sauces can be chilled by specialized "bottles" that are placed cold directly into the pot with the product. However, the safest technique is to purchase a blast chiller—a refrigerator specifically designed to reduce product temperature quickly and safely—and to strictly follow the manufacturer's instructions for use.

HACCP

The acronym for Hazard Analysis—Critical Control Points is HACCP. It refers to a systematic technique for reducing the possibility of food-borne illness. Originally developed to protect astronauts from food-borne illness while in space, HACCP involves four basic steps. First, the flow of food through a processing or production system is studied to determine those points where contamination and/or the growth of dangerous microorganisms could occur. Such points in the process are called "critical control points." Because contamination is frequently caused by improper handling (such as cross-contamination due to unsanitary work surfaces or lack of handwashing), it is somewhat easier to observe and correct. However, even if food is properly handled, dangerous microorganisms introduced into the product during processing or transportation can multiply if the temperature of the food is allowed to rise (or fall) into the temperature danger zone. Thus, the primary focus in identifying critical control points is evaluating whether and, if so, how long food remains in the danger zone (40°–140°F).

Second, the production processes are redesigned to prevent contamination and to limit the time food spends in the danger zone. Work processes may be changed and refrigeration equipment added or upgraded to maintain product temperatures below the temperature danger zone.

The third step involves continuous monitoring of food handling and temperature at each of the critical control points in the production process. For example, blast chillers used in health-care foodservice to ensure safe cooling of foods use probes to check internal product temperature. The probes are linked to computers, so there is a continuous record of the time required to bring food out of the danger zone.

The fourth step in HACCP involves remedial action to resolve problems discovered through monitoring. For example, if monitoring shows that large pots of stock are not cooling rapidly enough, smaller batches or containers that disperse heat more rapidly may be necessary.

The U.S. government recently mandated the use of HACCP in seafood processing plants. In addition, in some states regulations require health-care facilities to employ some of the HACCP principles and processes in their foodservice operations. Because restaurants and other foodservice operations increasingly use convenience (preprocessed) foods, HACCP should have a significant impact in years to come. Today, it is not uncommon for managers of foodservice and culinary operations to be HACCP certified.

Recycle

Environmental decisions are not always clear cut. The choice between using disposable paper or polystyrene packaging is not as easy as some think. Polystyrene, used to form coffee cups and "clamshell" sandwich boxes, does not degrade in landfills, but neither does paper. The typical landfill does not allow sufficient air and light to reach the paper to enable it to degrade. Polystyrene is recyclable. So are paper food wrappers. Still, many restaurants have chosen to switch from polystyrene to paper whenever possible. Restaurants continually search for ways to efficiently recycle their waste products.

Burger King, KFC, and McDonald's have all tested composting programs that allow used paper, food scraps, and other organic wastes to break down naturally. This compost can then be used for soil enhancement. KFC, for instance, found that up to 80 percent of its waste could be composted.[6]

The item most widely recycled by foodservice operations is corrugated cardboard. Many restaurants recycle hundreds of pounds of corrugated cardboard each month. In addition, chains including Red Lobster, Jack in the Box, McDonald's, and Burger King all recycle used fryer oil. This oil is refined and reused in products such as pet food and cosmetics. Recycling of aluminum, plastic, glass, and tin is more common in back-of-the-house operations than among restaurant customers themselves.

Reduce

Restaurants work hard to reduce the amount of waste they generate. Domino's redesigned its pizza box from a square to an octagon to reduce cardboard use by 10 percent. McDonald's switched to smaller paper napkins. Refillable mugs have been successfully introduced by many restaurants and institutional foodservice operations to replace disposables. And many restaurants have gone back to using cloth tablecloths, napkins, and dish towels to reduce waste. Of course, the volume of water used for washing increases dramatically when cloth items are used. Food suppliers are working to reduce waste by using more efficient product packaging. One manufacturer switched from cans to plastic film pouches for its product, eliminating the use of thousands of cans each day.[7]

Reuse

Restaurants and their suppliers work cooperatively to find ways to reuse and participate in recycling programs for paper, cans, plastic, and cardboard shipping and packing materials. International Dairy Queen and its waffle cone supplier reuse the packaging that protects the delicate waffle cones in transit. Some restaurants offer their customers a small discount if they return a package or box to reuse for their next take-out order.

Food Labeling Laws

In the 1990s Congress passed the Nutrition Labeling and Education Act, which requires food processors to provide consumers with complete nutritional information about their products. The act also established definitions and guidelines for the use of health claims such as "light," "low fat," "low sodium," "high fiber," and "fresh." The section of the law that requires complete nutritional analyses does not apply to the restaurant industry or its menus, except when a restaurant retails a particular product, such as its salad dressing or barbecue sauce.

Health-Conscious Eating

Today's consumers are more educated and aware of the nuritional components of food and food-related products than ever before. Thanks to labeling improvements, consumers can pay more careful attention to the caloric and nutritional content of the foods they eat. Wellness cuisines span all levels of sophistication and visibility. Specific foodservice establishments may serve only health-conscious foods. This may be done as part of a proactive health management or dietary program. Other establishments, including many in the mainstream restaurant industry, offer daily fresh sheets or dedicated menu sections designed to accommodate customers interested in healthy dining. Health-conscious dining is no longer a fad; it has become integrated into the standard offerings of dining establishments. Recent movements have begun to address the obesity crisis in the United States. Trans fats are fast becoming taboo in recipe development and certain product offerings. Legislative pressure has compelled fast-food operators such as McDonald's to cease using trans fats in their French-fry cooking oils. Future legislation promises to extend grocery labeling requirements to menu language. Fairly soon, menus will list all ingredients and their nutritional composition. This will help consumers as they strive to make food choices for the benefit of their health.

Summary

- Every great civilization had its cooks, and as one civilization succeeded another, culinary knowledge and achievements were absorbed and passed on.
- The brigade system of kitchen and dining room organizations increased productiveness and still influences many large modern kitchens and dining rooms.
- *Mise en place* is the state of being prepared for cooking and is the foundation of many cooking techniques.

- Menu planning and development involves having a concept, knowing customers' wants and expectations, employing good staff and equipment, and correctly gauging profit margins. Today, it may also include incorporating healthy dining options.
- The production cycle is the step-by-step process of taking food from its purchase and storage through pre-preparation, final preparation, service, cleanup, and waste management. The segments of this process are interconnected and interdependent. Each of these factors affects the bottom line.
- Social and cultural issues that concern foodservice operations include offering equal access to persons who are physically challenged, food safety, the environment, food-labeling laws, and health-conscious dining.

ENDNOTES

[1] K.C. Chang, ed., *Food in Chinese Culture: Anthropological and Historical Perspectives* (New Haven, Connecticut: Yale University Press, 1977), 11–12.

[2] Adapted from Jeff Weinstein, "The Accessible Restaurant, Part I," *Restaurants & Institutions* (April 8, 1992): 96–117.

[3] Beth Lorenzini, "The Accessible Restaurant, Part II," *Restaurants & Institutions* (May 20, 1992): 154.

[4] Michael Doom, *Fighting Back: How to Protect Yourself Against the "Food Bug" and Report Food Poisoning Hazards* (Los Angeles: M&C Publishing, 1992).

[5] Ray Sparrowe and Marsha Leister, *Food Safety Is No Mystery, Trainer's Manual* (Washington, D.C.: U.S. Department of Agriculture, August 1987).

[6] Brian Quinton and Jeff Weinstein, "Who's Leading the Green Revolution?" *Restaurants & Institutions* (November 27, 1991): 32–54.

[7] Melissa Larson, "Innovative Containers Give Foodservice a Boost," *Packaging* (March 1993): 29.

CHECK YOUR KNOWLEDGE

1. What does *mise en place* mean? How does it provide value to the establishment?
2. How do employees influence what will be offered on the menu?
3. What is the advantage of using a standard recipe?
4. Identify and explain three ways that restaurants can help the environment.
5. Identify current trends in health-conscious dining and indicate how a restaurant can gain a stronger market position as a result of offering healthy dining options.

APPLY YOUR SKILLS

Visit one of your local full-service restaurants for lunch or dinner and answer the following questions about the menu:

1. Identify how many sections and categories exist on the menu.
2. What item do you believe is most popular? Why?
3. What item do you believe is the least popular? Why?
4. What item on the menu do you believe has the highest cost of goods sold to produce? Why?
5. Do you feel the most popular item you selected has the highest contribution margin to profit on the menu? Why?

INTERNET EXCERCISES

1. Visit the Web sites of three major multiunit foodservice firms. At each site, look for information that describes how the firm is supporting the community or society through special programs or support for charities. Answer the following questions for each firm:
   a. Is the firm's community involvement or charitable support related to the interests of its primary market segments?
   b. How do you think the firm's customers feel about the support it provides to the community?
2. Using Internet search engines, locate the Web sites for three celebrity chefs and/or their restaurants. Compare and contrast the three in terms of how effectively the culinary artistry of each chef is presented. Also, identify how each chef incorporates health dining options.
3. Imagine that you manage a large on-site foodservice operation and have been asked to design and develop a food safety training program for your employees. Using Internet search engines, locate information on training materials and programs regarding the use of HACCP in foodservice operations. What materials and/or programs might you select for use in your training program?
4. Visit the website for the American Culinary Federation. Review the requirements for professional certification, and select a level that fits your goals. Develop a written plan of what you would need to do to achieve certification at that level.

WHAT DO YOU THINK?

1. Is there a distinctive American culinary tradition? If so, describe some of its characteristics. Who are the leaders of the current American culinary scene?
2. Customers at your restaurant have repeatedly asked you to offer a new item on your menu that has become trendy at other eating establishments. However, you are satisfied with your menu selection as it stands, and the new item does not seem to fit the character of your restaurant. How would you respond?
3. A food item featured at your restaurant is now available in frozen, preprocessed form. The quality seems good and you are interested because it would eliminate the need for several raw, perishable ingredients. If you decide to start using the new product, what would be the effect on the purchasing and receiving departments? What consideration would need to be given to consumer perceptions?
4. At a time when airlines and other businesses have been deregulated, should regulations regarding equal access to restaurants be relaxed? Why or why not?

5. Smoking in restaurants has become a hot social issue in your town. A group of citizens has petitioned the town council to ban it. As the owner of a popular, white tablecloth restaurant—where about a third of your customers smoke—you have been asked by the town manager to voice your opinion on the ban. What would you say?

CASE STUDY

You own an established, upscale restaurant in the downtown of a midsize American city. Because business has been good in the past, you have had little reason to change your operation or tamper with your menu, which features a selection of classic American dishes. Recently, however, the character of the downtown has changed, becoming less commercial and more service-oriented. Some stores are closing or relocating, while a new state office building and a major banking institution have opened. The clientele now seems different. Also, new restaurants opening nearby are giving you strong competition.

1. What is your first course of action to meet these changes?
2. How might you attract new customers to your establishment?

Beverage Management

OVERVIEW

Beverage sales are a major part of the foodservice industry, and trends in consumption patterns for beverages of all types are followed closely by foodservice operators. In addition, beverage sales and service, particularly of alcoholic drinks such as wine, beer, and mixed drinks, follow a certain etiquette of presentation and service. The fine dining restaurant, for example, is expected to offer beverages that complement its menu and ambiance, and to prepare and serve these beverages as tradition dictates. Today, beverage products have become highly sophisticated. Some are infused with new flavors and ingredients that appeal to the health conscious. Moreover, beverage products are very profitable.

OBJECTIVES

When you have completed this chapter, you should be able to:

1. Name the variety of beverages available in today's foodservice market and describe current trends in nonalcoholic beverage sales and consumption.
2. Examine current trends in alcohol sales and service and relate them to today's emphasis on healthier, more moderate lifestyles.
3. Differentiate between the way wines from Europe, Australia, and the United States are named, and list at least four notable red and white wines.
4. Explain briefly the process of fermentation as it relates to wine making and brewing beer and the process of distillation that is used in the production of liquor.
5. Name two major legal issues related to alcohol sales and tell how restaurants and bars protect against violations in these areas.

KEY TERMS

aging
alcohol
brewpub
call brand
cannibalize
distilled drinks
distilleries
draft
dram shop legislation
dry
electronic cash register
electronic liquor dispenser (ELD)
ethyl alcohol
fermentation
fermented beverages
free pouring
hand-measured pouring
hops
infusion
liquor
maceration
malt
malting
microbreweries
must
point of scale (POS)
proof
solera
sommelier
spirits
split
tannins
taverns
varietal
vintage
VIP
well brand
wort

Trends in Beverage Consumption

Throughout the 1990s and into the 2000s, the nonalcoholic beverage industry has seen relative stability, while the alcoholic beverage industry has undergone considerable change. Public consumption of nonalcoholic beverages, such as milk, tea, coffee, and citrus juices, has remained fairly constant.

Per capita consumption of soft drinks and bottled water in the United States steadily increased between 1992 and 2006, whereas the consumption of other beverages did not change dramatically. Coffee consumption, which had been on the rise, appeared to be approaching a plateau.

Per capita consumption is the most important indicator of the health of each of the segments of the beverage industry because it reflects increases or decreases in the marketplace. Per capita consumption is affected by fundamental business and societal trends. Broad lifestyle issues, such as societal acceptance of alcoholic beverage consumption, affect the consumption of beer, wine, and spirits. Demographic shifts, such as decreases in the number of young people below the age of twenty-one, affect the per capita consumption of milk and soft drinks. However, per capita consumption is not the only important indicator of trends in the beverage industry or the health of each of its segments. Per capita consumption can decrease at the same time that sales and profits increase in a particular segment of the beverage industry. This occurs when consumer preferences shift from low price/low margin brands to premium/high price brands. Put simply, consumers may drink less but spend more. This pattern has been evident in the case of spirits, where declines in consumption have been partially offset by a shift to premium brands. Similarly,

TABLE 8.1 Top Beverage Brands by Market Share

	Soft Drinks		Beer		Bottled Water	
Rank	*Brand*	*Share*	*Brand*	*Share*	*Brand*	*Share*
1.	Coca-Cola Classic	17.7%	Bud Light	20.1%	Aquafina	14.5%
2.	Pepsi-Cola	11.8%	Budweiser	13.3%	Private Label	13.2%
3.	Diet Coke	9.9%	Miller Lite	9.1%	Dasani	11.8%
4.	Mountain Dew	6.6%	Coors Light	7.2%	Poland Spring	6.8%
5.	Diet Pepsi	5.8%	Natural Light	4.2%	Propel	6.3%
6.	Sprite	5.7%	Corona Extra	3.7%	Dannon	5.4%
7.	Dr. Pepper	5.7%	Busch	3.5%	Arrowhead	4.9%
8.	Caffeine-Free Diet Coke	1.6%	Busch Light Draft	2.7%	Deer Park	3.7%
9.	Fanta	1.4%	Heineken	2.4%	Crystal Geyser	2.8%
10.	Sierra Mist	1.4%	Miller High Life	2.3%	Ozarka	2.7%

Source: Beverage World Publication Group, 2006.

although the volume of coffee sold dropped almost 3 percent from 1995 to 2006, overall sales rose 10 percent as consumer preferences shifted toward specialty coffees.

Table 8.1 shows the top ten brands of soft drinks, beer, and bottled water by market share.

Nonalcoholic Beverages

Nearly all restaurants offer a selection of traditional "with-meal" beverages. In the United States these typically include hot coffee and tea, iced tea, soft drinks, lemonade, milk, hot chocolate, fruit juice, and bottled water. Popularity of various beverages changes rapidly. Nearly one-third of the population never orders alcohol, so the nonalcoholic beverage menu is an important one.

Increased awareness of fitness and a trend toward healthier lifestyles influence beverage purchases. In addition, societal emphasis on moderate and responsible alcohol consumption has prompted many to make alternate beverage choices.

The economy can also affect beverage selection and sales, although soft drinks are affected less than more expensive drinks such as fine wines and spirits. During tight economic times, people have less discretionary income and so are less likely to spend money on luxury or higher-priced items. Conversely, during times of economic expansion, exotic and specialty drinks such as those served at trendy nightclubs have become high sellers. During strong ecomomic times premium-brand spirits such as Crown Royal whiskey, Absolut vodka, and single-malt Scotch whiskeys become more popular.

Carbonated Soft Drinks

The per capita consumption of carbonated soft drinks has been rising steadily, despite industry experts' predictions that it would plateau.[1] However, within this market, the popularity of individual brands and types of drinks changes rapidly. The 1980s saw tremendous growth in diet soft drinks, so that by 1993 Diet Coke was the third most popular soft drink, with a 9 percent share of total soft drink sales.[2] Diet Coke remains one of the most popular soft drinks today. Caffeine-free colas, on the other hand, appeared to be losing market share from their 1991 to 1992 highs. Any new product, such as the clear colas that made their first appearance in early 1993, has the potential to do one of two things. Either it can **cannibalize** (eat away at) the market share of existing products, or it can attract new customers who might have chosen another beverage over a soft drink.

International sales of soft drinks are expected to continue to see large volume growth, as market saturation in the United States forces soft drink producers to seek growth opportunities overseas.

Coffee and Tea

In the 1980s, espresso bars in the United States began opening as free-standing specialty shops, kiosks, and within traditional restaurant operations. New trends in coffee and tea products began developing in 1992 and 1993. Specialty coffees made from gourmet beans, as well as espressos flavored with nonalcoholic syrups, became a big new market. Because a commercial-quality bean-grinding and espresso machine could be purchased for a relatively small investment ($2,000–$3,000), many restaurateurs added this popular product.

At the same time, gourmet coffee chains became popular. The classic example is Starbucks, which started in 1971 as a small specialty shop in Seattle, Washington. Today it has over thirteen thousand stores, and its net income in 2006 was $564 million on sales of almost $7,786 million. Starbucks' phenomenal growth is due mainly to two marketing strategies: extending its line into supermarkets to go head-to-head with the traditional brands, and opening European-style cafes where customers can sit, socialize, and enjoy their coffee.

Although per capita consumption of coffee appears to be approaching a plateau, Starbucks and other coffeehouses are likely to prosper because their success depends upon a shift in consumer preferences toward specialty drinks such as latté and cappucino.

Tea consumption has also begun to show the effects of a shift in consumer preferences. Although the per capita consumption of tea fell somewhat during the past decade, specialty teas are growing in popularity at coffee houses, and tea sales are rising at supermarkets.

Bottled Water

Between 1984 and 2003, annual per capita consumption of bottled waters in the United States rose from four gallons to almost twenty-four gallons. The increased consumption of bottled waters is the result of several factors occurring in the marketplace. The first is the growth of the market segment concerned with health, including baby boomers concerned about aging. These consumers believe that drinking six to eight glasses of water each day contributes to general health. Some bottled waters have been marketed as "pure," and therefore seem more healthful than ordinary tap water. Second, the acceptance of bottled waters is part of the broader trend in consumer willingness to purchase specialized or premium products. Bottled water marketers thus have sought to invest their products with a special "cachet" or set of ostensibly unique characteristics. The third factor involves packaging. Spring water bottled in an attractively shaped plastic container with a spiffy label and squirt top is convenient for people to take to an athletic club and drink on the treadmill. Carrying that same container to the office or the mall conveys the impression that the individual lives an active, healthy life.

The challenge faced by the marketers of bottled water is to persuade consumers to pay for a product that they can get for free (or for significantly less) by turning a tap. In the late 1980s, a small number of producers overstated the health-inducing benefits of "pure" bottled waters. Further, in several of these cases, bottled spring water was found to contain significantly more impurities than tap water. Consumers were, in effect, paying a premium for bottled water that was worse for them than what was available from their municipal water supply. In the 1990s, the Food and Drug Administration proposed new labeling standards for bottled waters to prevent misrepresentation. Today, many hotel companies offer "signature" bottled water for sale. Placing it in guest rooms is a suggestive selling technique designed to generate additional incremental profits from room sales.

Juice Drinks

Frozen slushy drinks, many of them nonalcoholic versions of popular drinks like margaritas and strawberry daiquiris, have been restaurant, beach, and nightclub staples for years. In addition to these frozen drinks, many restaurants offer "mocktails," nonalcoholic cocktails based on orange, pineapple, or cranberry juices. Juice bars, operating as specialty restaurants or kiosks, have also gained popularity by offering stylishly served fresh fruit mixtures of pineapple, papaya, melon, and oranges.

Nonalcoholic Beer and Wine

Unlike the other nonalcoholic beverages, nonalcoholic beer and wine are marketed toward a more limited audience—the adult who enjoys the taste of beer or wine, but for health or social reasons prefers to abstain from alcohol. On store shelves and on menus, nonalcoholic beers and wines are grouped with the alcoholic originals.

In the early 1980s only ten nonalcoholic beers were marketed in the United States, but by the early 1990s more than sixty brands were being retailed. Market leaders in nonalcoholic beer sales in the 1990s were Anheuser-Busch's O'Doul's and Miller Brewing Co.'s Sharp's. Industry experts predict that nonalcoholic beers will ultimately account for about 3 percent of all U.S. beer sales.[3]

Nonalcoholic wines have been slower to gain popularity, in part because much of wine's distinctive flavor and aroma comes from the alcohol itself. Sutter Home Winery in the United States made its first shipments of alcohol-free Chardonnay and White Zinfandel in late 1992. Sutter Home uses an alcohol-removal process called the spinning cone, first developed in Australia for fruit juice. The spinning cone breaks the wine down into its constituent parts, which are then recombined without the alcohol.

Nonalcoholic beer and wine consumption depends on a societal and cultural link between certain social activities and the consumption of alcoholic beverages. As long as consumers associate alcoholic beverages with social gatherings, sports events, or restaurant dining, these products will offer a way to participate in such occasions without appearing to abstain.

Alcoholic Beverages

Alcohol is a naturally occurring and easily synthesized compound. Pure alcohol is colorless, volatile, and flammable. Beverage alcohol is **ethyl alcohol**, identified scientifically as C_2H_60, is the agent that induces intoxication when consumed.

The two main groups of alcoholic beverages are fermented and distilled. **Fermented beverages** are those formed by the action of yeast on sugar-containing substances such as grain or fruit. Wine and malt beverages (beer) are the two most common fermented beverages. The alcohol content of fermented

Often, bartenders are responsible for serving alcoholic beverages such as beer, wine, and liquor, as well as nonalcoholic juices and soft drinks.

beverages varies between 2 and 20 percent. Beers typically range from 2 to 7 percent alcohol; most wines contain between 12 and 14 percent alcohol.

Distilled drinks, also called **spirits** or **liquor**, are made from a fermented product which is then put through a distillation process that recovers and adds additional alcohol. Both these processes are discussed in greater detail later in this chapter. Distilled beverages generally contain between 12 and 55 percent ethyl alcohol.

The liquor's alcohol content is represented in a figure called **proof**. In the United States, proof equals twice the percentage of alcohol in the beverage. In other words, a bourbon labeled "90 proof" contains 45 percent ethyl alcohol. In Great Britain and Canada, 100-proof spirits contain 57 percent alcohol.

Alcohol Consumption Today

After a period of significant decline in the 1980s, the drop in overall consumption of alcoholic beverages has slowed. From 2003 to 2004, the per capita consumption increased slightly from 2.22 to 2.23 gallons. Distilled spirits and beer consumption fell, while wine consumption held steady. The broad trend in the consumption of alcoholic beverages is one of no growth or slight decline. However, certain alcoholic beverages are experiencing modest growth, such as tequila, rum, and beers brewed in microbreweries. The consumption of American and imported whiskey fell during this period, but rum, tequila, and brandy/cognac showed marginal increases.

Interestingly, while overall consumption of alcoholic beverages has been flat, the sales of beer and wine in restaurants have risen. As mentioned earlier, consumers continue to associate wine and beer with social occasions such as dining out.

Alcohol and Health

In 2003, the popular CBS newsmagazine *60 Minutes* aired a television story with industry-wide impact. The show highlighted a phenomenon called the "French paradox." The French eat 30 percent more fat than Americans, smoke more, and exercise less, yet they suffer fewer heart attacks—one-third as many as Americans. The French also lead the world in per capita consumption of alcohol, with wine consumption alone a staggering 73.1 liters per person. Numerous medical researchers have investigated this phenomenon. Morley Safer, *60 Minutes* anchor, summarized the research findings this way:

> The wine apparently affects the platelets, the smallest of the blood cells. It is platelets that cause blood to clot. They prevent bleeding. But they also cling to rough, fatty deposits on the artery walls, clogging and finally blocking the artery and causing a heart attack. The wine has a flushing effect. It removes platelets from the artery wall.[4]

In the four weeks immediately following the show, grocery sales of red wines increased 45 percent. Restaurant owners reported increased wine sales in general, and a shift in preference from white wine to red.[5]

Additional studies have continued to point toward possible health benefits of moderate alcohol use, including decreased risk of heart disease, stroke, and certain cancers. The American Heart Association suggests that a glass or two of wine per day may impart long-term health benefits. On the other hand, the health and social costs of excessive alcohol use are all too well known.

Bars and Taverns

The future of bars and **taverns**, establishments that serve some food but specialize in alcoholic beverages, probably offers little real growth. Bar owners lament the difficulty of attracting customers, despite the decrease in the number of bars doing business. Sports bars, complete with multiple big-screen TVs and sports memorabilia, have grown in popularity as bar owners search for new concepts to attract customers. Food sales have taken on more importance. Partly as a means to encourage sensible drinking habits, and partly as a means of retaining customers and increasing sales, bars and lounges offer a wider variety of appetizers, munchies, and casual dinners than ever before.

Beverages and Taxes

No discussion of beverage trends would be complete without some mention of taxation of beverage sales. Taxes on alcohol sales are a major revenue source for the United States government. States also collect tax on alcohol sales. Current taxes make up about one-half the final price of a bottle of liquor, and there is always talk of further increases in these so-called "sin taxes."

Wines

The exact beginnings of alcoholic beverages are lost in time. In fact, our ancestors' first experiences with alcohol were probably accidental, because alcohol is

Business Profile

"PURE"—LAS VEGAS CAESAR'S PALACE HOTEL

Trend-Setting Nightclub

Today, high-end **VIP** nightclubs are prevalent in the Las Vegas marketplace. Destination nightclub venues on the Vegas Strip have fast become the symbol of style, decadence, and innovation. VIP lounges within a nightclub offer high-quality spirits by the bottle only. Each of the VIP lounges offers concierge service and private couch seating areas. The Pure nightclub, home of the infamous "Pussy Cat Doll" show, is located in the Caesar's Palace Hotel. The club alone comprises over 40,000 square feet of space on four levels. Admission to Pure is difficult due to high demand. The decor at Pure and other destination Vegas clubs reflects ultra-modern design elements and state of the art sound, lighting, and video components.[1]

[1] http://www.vegas.com.

Formal hotel/lobby cocktail lounge.

the result of a natural fermentation process. The chemical change that produces wine requires only two simple ingredients: grapes and sunshine. The enzyme that enables this transformation to take place is found in the microscopic buds of yeast that grow naturally on the outer surface of grapes. The yeast transforms the natural sugars in the grape. Thus, an ancient farmer may have discovered wine when he opened a sealed pottery jar containing the fermented juice of grapes he previously had stored. Egyptian hieroglyphics and Mesopotamian pottery both attest to wine's ancient origins.

The Naming of Wines

Wine is categorized and named in several different and sometimes contradictory ways. First, wines are classified as either red or white. Then, at least in the United States, wines are named by the type of grape, or **varietal**, from which they are made. Chardonnay, Sauvignon Blanc, and Riesling are three different grapes, each of which is used to make a particular white wine bearing its same name. By U.S. law, a varietal wine must be composed of at least 75 percent of the grape that names the wine. Most wines easily meet this requirement.

On the other hand, most European wines are called by the name of the region where they originate. The European process of name assignment, the older of the two naming procedures, is partially due to the unique characteristics that wines develop in response to the climate and soil conditions of each grape-growing area. Bordeaux, Champagne, and Burgundy are individual regions of France in which specific wines are produced. A true French Burgundy may be either a white or a red wine. A red French Burgundy is made primarily from Pinot Noir grapes; the white is made from Chardonnay grapes. The wine made in the United States and labeled Burgundy bears little resemblance to its French namesake. It is often an inexpensive red table wine made from a blend of various grapes.

A wine may also be identified by its **vintage**, the year in which its grapes were harvested. The vintage is important because subtle differences exist from year to year in the flavors of grapes and their resulting wines, due to the weather's effect on a harvest.

Winemaking

Many fruits and a few vegetables will yield wine. Apples and pears have been used to produce cider and perry, respectively, for generations. In addition, most berries, as well as carrots and dandelions, are popular for making wine. These wines, however, are normally produced as homemade beverages for small-scale consumption. Grapes continue to be the primary source for commercial wines. The following description is a very general summary of a wide range of winemaking procedures.

At harvest time, grapes are pressed to break the skins and allow the juice to flow. Then, the resulting **must**, a mixture of grape pulp, skins, seeds, and stems, is placed in huge vats where fermentation can begin. **Fermentation** is the chemical process in which yeast acts on sugar to produce alcohol and carbon dioxide. This early fermentation is strikingly active—the must heaves and bubbles as the gas rises through the mass and breaks through the surface. Depending on such factors as temperature and the amount of sugar in the mixture, the fermenting action may continue for a week or more. Finally the young wine is drawn off, usually into large wooden barrels or glass-lined vats where **aging**—the slow, subtle completion of fermentation—begins.

Wine aged in wood acquires additional flavor nuances. A few wines, such as Beaujolais Nouveau, may be bottled after about two months, but hearty red wines may age as long as two years or more before they are bottled. Once bottled, the wine often continues to mature, undergoing subtle changes and improvement in taste and quality.

During both the fermentation and the aging processes, wines absorb **tannins**, substances drawn from the grape skins and the wooden barrels used for aging. Tannins contribute astringency to wine. In their undiluted form, tannins taste somewhat like bitter tea. In addition to contributing a special taste, tannins are key elements in promoting a wine's longevity. To a certain degree, a tannin's strength in wine can be controlled by changing the containers in which the wine is fermented, stored, and aged. Tannin strength also differs according to grape variety.

Although the general principles of fermentation and aging remain the same, there are numerous variables that the vintner can change in order to alter the taste and quality of the wine.

Red Wines

Red wines are one of the two basic categories of wine. They are made from red grapes, following the general procedures summarized earlier. The coloring is derived from pigments in the grape skins. The major grape varieties used to make red wines, and the wine varietals named after them, are Cabernet Sauvignon, Pinot Noir, Merlot, Gamay, Syrah, and Zinfandel.

Some popular and reasonably priced red wines are actually blends of two or more varietals. Chianti, an Italian wine from the region bearing its name, France's Cotes-du-Rhone, and Spain's Rioja are three red blends.

Rosés, sometimes categorized as red wines, are light pink wines made by removing the skins from the must early in the fermentation. The longer the skins are allowed to remain, the deeper the color of the wine. Blush wines, shunned by many serious wine connoisseurs but nevertheless popular, are lighter in color and sweeter in flavor than the rosés. White Zinfandel, a varietal made from red Zinfandel grapes, is made by preventing the juice from having contact with the skins and stopping the wine's fermentation before all the sugar is used. Many feel it has more in common with some of the lighter, sweeter white wines than with red wines.

White Wines

White wines are generally made from white grapes and from nearly any other grape that produces white juice. However, even red and black grapes can be used for making white wine, as long as the skins are removed from the must before fermentation begins. White wines often are lighter and have a lower sugar content than most red wines. In addition, they often age and mature faster than red wines, which may require ten years or more in the bottle before they are ready for consumption. Some of the most common varieties of grapes used to make white wine, and the wine varietals named after them, are Chardonnay, Sauvignon Blanc, Riesling, Chenin Blanc, and Pinot Blanc.

Some popular white wines are actually blends of two or more varietals. The German Liebfraumilch, Italian Soave, and Spanish Rioja are three examples.

Types of Wine

Beyond the color categorization of wine, wine is divided into four different groups based on production methods. These include table, or still, wine; sparkling wine; fortified wine; and flavored wine.

Table Wines

Table wines are the most commonly consumed wines and are made by the basic methods described earlier. Often, wine drinkers evaluate a wine based on its relative sweetness. A wine lacking sweetness is referred to as **dry**. Wines that are relatively dry are more popular than those with very noticeable sweetness. Temperature range for wine service varies according to tradition and

Wines are divided into categories based on the type of crop and production method.

Photo courtesy of Baron Philippe de Rothschild, Inc.

personal preference. In general, reds are served at room temperature, between 63°F and 66°F, and whites are served chilled to between 40°F and 50°F . Most wines are served in balloon-style wine glasses.

Sparkling Wines

Wines that contain carbon dioxide, whether naturally produced or mechanically infused, are known as sparkling wines. The most famous sparkling wine is Champagne, from the French province of the same name. Dom Perignon, a French monk who lived in the late 1600s, is credited with the perfection of the techniques that produce Champagne. Because the amount of carbonation in any batch of wine was unpredictable, it was fairly common for the bottles to explode. Perignon's improvements and his innovation of using natural cork for bottle stoppers enabled more successful transport of Champagne. Demand quickly spread to Great Britain and, ultimately, the entire wine-drinking world.

Making quality French Champagne is a time-consuming process. Although generally following the typical winemaking stages, Champagne-making involves additional steps to clear it of all sediment and to maintain its fizziness. To clear the sediment, the bottles of young wine must be placed horizontally and shaken daily in a special way. Gradually the tilt at which the bottles are stored is increased until they are vertical and the residue has been shaken and settled in the neck of the now-inverted bottles. Conveyor belts and mechanization complete the next steps most efficiently. To remove the sediment and protect the carbonization, the necks of the bottles are quick-frozen in a special solution. Flipped right side up, the corks are removed, and the natural carbonization spews out the frozen plug of residue. Another machine adds wine to top off what was lost and then recorks the bottle. From harvest to table, making French Champagne may require as long as four years.

A less complicated system of making sparkling wine is often used in wineries in the United States and many other countries. The second fermentation is carried out in huge vats, and the wine is then filtered and bottled under pressure to maintain the fizz. Experts feel the resulting product is somewhat inferior to the French product, but the mass production serves a large market that enjoys a good but less expensive beverage. Asti Spumante is a famous Italian sparkling wine produced by this method.

According to French law, only those sparkling wines made in the Champagne region of France can be labeled as Champagne. This law was passed in 1911 after a devastating crop disease hit vineyards in the Champagne region. In order to maintain production of their sparkling wine, some vintners imported grapes from outside the Champagne region. The sparkling wine they produced and bottled was different from the traditional one, yet they still called their wine "Champagne." The French government stepped in to establish a legal definition of the boundaries of Champagne, and declared that this name could be used only on wines whose entire product was grown in the region. In later years, additional French laws were written to define other regional boundaries, stipulate regional wine names, and identify the grape varieties that could be used in a particular regional wine.

The United States does not restrict the use of the name Champagne or the use of other European regional wine names; consequently, many American-made sparkling wines are called Champagne if they are made in the French fashion.

Fortified Wines

Fortified wines are those that have had brandy or wine alcohol added to them, making the resulting wine higher in alcohol content. Natural fermentation usually yields a wine with an alcohol content of between 12 and 14 percent. Alcohol of this concentration kills the yeast, and thus ends the fermenting action. Brandy added to the wine, however, raises the alcohol content to as high as 20 percent. Because fermentation has been halted, the additional sugar remains suspended in the wine, increasing its sweetness. Brandy, made by distilling any fermented fruit juice, such as that from the grape, apple, pear, apricot, or blackberry, adds a distinctive flavor and sweetness to the wine. Port, Sherry, Marsala, and Madeira are fortified wines.

Flavored Wines

Flavored wines are those with added flavoring substances. Usually the flavoring substance is from a fruit or herb. Vermouth is a white wine flavored with herbs. Many of the heavily fruit-flavored wines are inexpensive, sweet, and unacceptable to the serious wine drinker.

Professional Profile

DOM PERIGNON

"Father" of Champagne

Photo by Corbis

Known as the single most famous person in the history of wine and its making, Dom Pierre Perignon is often regarded as the inventor of Champagne. While Perignon was not, in fact, Champagne's inventor, he was one of its catalysts.

Dom Perignon was born to a middle-class family in Lorraine, France, in 1639. At the age of twenty-nine, Perignon was sent to Hautvillers, perhaps the most well-known winemaking abbey in the region. Within a short time Perignon was named procurator (administrator) of the abbey, and became responsible for running the estate and supervising its winemaking. Since he could never aspire to the position of abbot because he was not a nobleman, Perignon remained in the position of procurator for nearly fifty years. During that time he vastly increased the size of the abbey's vineyards and the quality of the wines it produced.

It was during this time that the monk Perignon began his lifelong journey of discovering and perfecting winemaking, including the transformation of black grapes into fine white wine. As French writer Fernand Woutaz says of him,

> If Dom Perignon did not "invent" champagne, all the same he was its "inventor" in the legal sense of someone who uncovers buried treasure… Perignon lifted to the highest possible level all the stages of making white wine, from the cultivation of the vine to bottling the wine…[1]

In those days, white wine made from white grapes often turned yellow by the spring following its vintage. Red wine, less popular and consequently less profitable than white wine, tended to last an average of five or six years. Perignon, however, made white wine from black grapes (called *vin gris*), creating a white wine with the lifespan of a red wine.

Perignon also spent a number of years developing a fine white sparkling wine from black grapes. Even though sparkling Champagnes were made and sold before Perignon came on the scene, it took almost a century after his death to truly perfect the process of creating a fine Champagne. While today Champagne is considered a luxury beverage, in Perignon's time any sort of sparkling wine was considered inferior to other wines.

After his death in 1715, Perignon became somewhat of a legend. It has been claimed that Perignon went blind and in spite of the handicap became a master grape taster—so much so that he could tell the source of the grape simply by its taste. This, however, has been refuted, largely because his blindness was never mentioned by his contemporaries.

The most famous modern Champagne, Dom Perignon, was named after the monk by the Moet family in 1936, when they introduced the region's first luxury brand. The Moets laid claim to Perignon's "secrets" for winemaking when, after nearly two centuries, they uncovered Perignon's memoirs, which disclosed his winemaking techniques. Ironically, Perignon probably was not much of a wine drinker, it was said that he subsisted primarily on fruit and dairy products. Still, it was his influence on the process that even today sustains his reputation as the inventor of Champagne.

---

[1] Nicholas Faith, *The Story of Champagne* (New York: Facts on File, 1989). 22.

Wine-Producing Regions

Viticulture, the cultivation of grapes, probably had its origin in the Middle East several thousand years ago. Harvesting grapes and making wine may have gone hand in hand with the development of farming as groups of people made the transition from nomadic life to a sedentary one. Early Egyptians learned to make wine, although the best wines were undoubtedly reserved for the priests and the very wealthy. The Greeks adopted and improved these winemaking techniques, which in turn were adopted and adapted by the Romans. The Greeks may have been the first to introduce viticulture to the Gauls in what is now southern France, but the Romans continued and expanded the practice nearly everywhere they went, in Europe as well as in northern Africa.

Because prolonged exposure to heat and air encourages wine to turn to vinegar, it did not travel well to the outposts of the Roman empire. Military officers and civilian officials, expecting something better than the rations provided to the troops, wished to maintain their "civilized" habits even in frontier areas, but they could not depend on wine from Rome reaching them in palatable condition. By taking vine cuttings with them, they could establish new fields, sometimes even including some of the wild varieties that already grew in the area. In this way, the beginnings of the modern wine industry were established, and remained after the soldiers and officials departed. Today, flourishing vineyards are found throughout most temperate regions around the world.

France

Climate, soil, and the personal dedication of the French people combine to make French wines the height of quality and set the standard for nearly all other wine-producing areas. Today, France's wines are strictly regulated by the government to ensure certain standards of quality and consistency.

The finest French wines are identified as *Appellation d'Origine Contrôlée.* French law dictates that these wines be made from specific grapes grown on specially pruned and tended vines in a certain area. They must contain a specified minimum content of alcohol, and the yield per hectare, or 107,639 sq. ft., must fall within a set amount. Following similar guidelines, others of France's better wines are identified as *VinsDélimités de Qualité Supérierure* (V.D.Q.S.). Another group of good but less expensive wines are called *Vins de Pays. Vins Ordinaires* are unclassified wines that often are blended from wines from different areas. These and the Vins de Pays are the most common French table wines, easily available and reasonably priced.

The wines traditionally produced in France include red, rosé, and white—both still and sparkling—and range from wines with little or no remaining sugar to those that are very sweet. Historically, the most famous wine-growing regions are Bordeaux, Burgundy, and Champagne. Famous subdivisions include Medoc, Sauterne, Barsac, St. Emilon, Chablis, and Beaujolais. As you may have recognized, each of these regions and subregions has a wine unique to that particular area.

Italy

Some people have described Italy as one gigantic vineyard. The climate and soil of Italy have combined to make the area an ideal place for growing grapes ever since viticulture was first introduced. Although French wines have been regarded as the standard against which the quality of other wines is measured, Italy nevertheless produces excellent wines. Italian wines cover the spectrum of traditional varietals. Except for those in Greece, Italy's vineyards are older than any others in Europe.

The Italian government has tried to develop a system of labeling, somewhat like the French system, but it is not well organized and applies to only some of Italy's vineyards. The system does, however, offer some guidance as to the quality of the wines it governs. The finest wines are labeled *denominazione di origine controllata e guarantita*, or controlled and guaranteed. The next category is *denominazione diorigine controllata*, or controlled wines. Although there are variations and exceptions among the wines in the groupings, they still are of consistently good quality. The simple, everyday table wines are labeled *denominazione di origine simplice*.

Apart from government regulation, many wine-producing areas have local organizations, or consortia, that issue their own quality standards and protect the reputation of specific wines. Well-known, popular Italian wines include Barolo, Gattinara, Barbaresco, Chianti, Lambrusco, and Spumante.

Germany

Many experts as well as connoisseurs rate Germany as the producer of the world's greatest white wines. Germans have worked hard over the years to grow grapes in a climate somewhat harsh for viticulture, and have created some extraordinary beverages.

The most renowned German vine, the Riesling, produces wines of varied sweetness. It is this natural sweetness that German lawmakers were protecting when they decreed that the label had to state if additional sugar had been added. In addition, labeling identifies whether the wine is a table wine, a quality wine from a specific region, or a quality wine "with attributes." This category is subdivided to indicate cabinet *(Kabinett)* wines with no sugar added, late harvest wines, wines from selectively picked grapes, wines from berry grapes, or wines from raisinized grapes. Well-known German wines include Moselle, Rhine, Sekt (a sparkling wine), Liebfraumilch, Spätlese, and the tongue-twisting but tasty Trockenbeerenauslese (often called "T.B.A." by people who don't speak German).

Spain and Portugal

Grape vines were growing in Spain and Portugal long before the coming of the Romans. Spanish sherry and Portuguese ports and Madeiras have been exported and enjoyed for years. Both countries have product and labeling laws that, as in other countries, endeavor to protect both wine producers and consumers.

Much of Spain's wine is not even bottled at home. It is shipped in bulk, often in tankers, to other wine producers who use it in making their own blended wines or as a base for vermouth and other beverages.

Many other winemaking regions produce sherries, but the only authentic sherry comes from the Andalusian region of Spain. There, the wine is made mainly according to standard procedures, but the fermenting is stopped at about 12 percent alcohol by the addition of grape brandy that kills the fermentation.

The young wine is then placed in oaken barrels called butts, where it begins to age. The butts are stored in tiers, with the newest vintage on top and the oldest at the bottom. To ensure consistency, sherries are blended from a mixture of several vintages. This system of blending is called a **solera** system.

Genuine port is produced only in the Douro region of Portugal. After aging about two years in wooden casks, the port is bottled, and aging continues. It is not unusual for a port to age in bottles as long as fifteen to twenty years before it reaches its fullest flavor.

Madeira, a Portuguese island in the Atlantic Ocean off the west coast of Africa, is the source of authentic Madeira wine. Legend has it that the Portuguese who discovered the island set afire its immense forests, which burned for seven years. The resulting thick layers of ashes provided fertile soil for the vineyards that were later planted there. At any rate, the vintners make Madeira in a process similar to port. At a certain stage brandy is added to the fermenting wine, stopping the fermentation and raising the level of alcohol to as much as 20 percent. Then, using a solera process, the vintners blend wines of different ages to produce a consistent Madeira. Like sherry and port, Madeira has a special market in England. Other widely enjoyed Portuguese wines include Dio, Lancer's, and Mateus—especially Mateus Rosé.

Australia

Australia began its entry into the wine business with vineyards planted in Sydney Harbor in 1788. Today there are over sixty-three wine regions across the country totaling over 170,000 hectares. Australia ranks fourth in the world in terms of wine exportation, selling to over one hundred countries and generating close to $5.5 billion dollars in sales annually. Australian wine makers are respected viticulture leaders that combine tradition with new ideas and technical innovation. The result is a diversity of wine styles, making Australia known throughout the world for distinctive wines.[6]

United States

Much of the climate in California is so similar to that of the Mediterranean area that it is called a Mediterranean climate. It is not surprising, then, that the early Spanish settlers were the first to introduce viticulture to California. Winemaking in California continues to the present, although it has experienced interruptions by disease and almost total destruction by Prohibition, when alcohol production was generally illegal. Since the burst of renewed interest in wine drinking,

Business Profile

ROTHSCHILD'S WINERY

Fine Wines of Bordeaux, France

Photo courtesy of Baron Philippe de Rothschild, Inc.

The name of Rothschild is synonymous with tradition, excellence, and fame. The Rothschild family today is one of the most famous wine producers in the world, laying claim to some of the world's greatest estate-produced wines: Chateau Mouton-Rothschild and Mouton-Cadet. The family-owned enterprise of Château Lafitte Rothschild has evolved over five generations, and the Rothschild family has owned its Bordeaux vineyard since 1868. As a young adult, Baron Philippe de Rothschild was given control of the management of the family vineyards, continuing an empire in the wine industry. He died in 1988.

Today the Rothschild wine company, officially known as Baron Philippe de Rothschild SA, produces 12 million cases of Mouton alone each year, selling at $100 per bottle.[1] Baron Philippe, who once said "Wine is a woman—uncertain, coy, and hard to please"[2] would be pleased.

---

[1] James Suckling, *Wine Spectator* (March 15, 1993): 22.

[2] Joan Littlewood and the Baron Philippe de Rothschild, *Baron Philippe: A Very Candid Autobiography of Baron Philippe de Rothschild* (New York: Crown Publishers, Inc., 1984), 140.

California wineries have expanded, and exceptionally fine wines as well as inexpensive table wines abound. The most prominent wine regions in California include Napa, Sonoma, Monterey, Santa Clara, and Mendocino.

Because soil conditions vary among these regions, many different kinds of grapes grow in California, enabling it to produce about as many different wines as do all the major growing areas in Europe. Vineyards are found in Napa Valley and throughout Sonoma County, in the Monterey area, along the southern coast, and in Santa Barbara County. Large wineries, such as Robert Mondavi, bottle wines made from grapes grown in different parts of the state under different labels such as Mondavi, La Famiglia di Robert Mondavi, Byron Vineyard & Winery, and Vichon Mediterranean. Other operations are more intimate in scale. Grgich Hills Cellars is a relatively small operation that produces a few high-quality wines each year under the supervision of vintner Miljenko Grgich. Grgich established his reputation when a California

Chardonnay he produced for Chateau Montelena bested the field of French wines in a famous challenge match in Paris.

The history of California wines would not be complete without a discussion of one of America's winemaking pioneers. Robert Mondavi and the Robert Mondavi Winery are recognized nationally and internationally as leaders in the wine industry. From introducing cold fermentation in stainless steel tanks and aging in French oak barrels, to collaborating with NASA on the use of aerial imaging to understand the health and vigor of their vines, the Robert Mondavi Winery has always been at the forefront of winemaking technology. Its innovations, such as gentle winemaking techniques to increase wine quality and natural farming to protect people and the environment, have led to fundamental changes in the industry's approach to viticulture. With more than fifty-five years of Napa Valley viticultural experience, the Mondavi family has played an instrumental role in developing and promoting the quality of wines from the Napa Valley. In the mid-1980s, Tim Mondavi helped establish a clear and logical system of appellations, or American Viticultural Areas (AVAs), for wines from the Napa Valley. He integrated the valley's most fundamental geographic features with the region's history to help vintners create a meaningful appellation structure.

Robert Mondavi Winery harvests a majority of the fruit for its wines from its own vineyards within the Napa Valley. Each of these vineyards lies in a different sub-appellation, giving the winery a wide variety of soils and climatic conditions in which to plant different grape varieties.[7]

Another large wine-producing state is New York. Its output is much smaller than California's, but New York's wines are distributed and enjoyed all over the world. Although other New York wines are produced and are well received, New York's sparkling wine from Taylor is its most famous.

The Pacific Northwest has gained prominence as a top wine-producing region in the United States. Most of the wineries in Oregon, Washington, and Idaho have been in operation only since the 1960s and 1970s, but they have quickly become major producers of white wines. All three states specialize in Chardonnay, Johannisberg Riesling, and Gewurztraminer. In addition, Oregon produces a world-class Pinot Noir, while Washington makes top quality varietals among various boutique wineries.

A few other states, such as Virginia, Missouri, Michigan, Ohio, and Texas, also produce quality wines. With wine's popularity continuing to increase, new wineries continue to open each year. Some of the wines being produced are excellent, rivaling old-world excellence. Many are average, but these ordinary, inexpensive wines have introduced many to the wine-tasting adventure.

South American Countries

In South America, the oldest wine-producing country is Peru, where vineyards were established during the time of the Spanish conqueror Pizarro. Peru still produces large quantities of wine, but most is for local consumption. Today,

Argentina is the largest producer of South American wines. Mendoza, a city in the foothills of the Andes, has grown abundant harvests for several years. The highest quality wine, however, comes from the Central Valley in Chile. Chilean wines, many exhibiting French influences in techniques and flavors, have received growing acceptance in the world market.

Other countries gaining increasing recognition in the wine market include Canada and South Africa. The major wine centers, however, continue to be the traditional European giants—France, Italy, Germany, Spain, and Portugal—plus Australia and the United States.

Food and Wine Pairing

No one can predict or prescribe another person's tastes or preferences in food or in drink. An experienced wine taster can detect subtle flavors and distinctions among a large variety of wines that completely elude the novice. Nevertheless, a long history of experimentation has yielded some dependable traditions for the optimum appreciation of beverages. Today, the combination of food and wine has taken on a new level of simplicity. Simplicity means almost anything goes: if a guest prefers a white wine with red meat, it is not an issue. If a guest wants to pair an extraordinary first-growth Bordeaux with a prime-grade filet mignon, that is fine, too. However, the following general guidelines apply to selection of wines with foods.

White Wines

White wines typically accompany the lighter fare of fish, fowl, and egg entrees as well as those with light sauces. Dry or slightly sweet white wines are traditional choices. With chicken and turkey, however, the choice may rest in part on cooking and serving styles. A chicken dish with a light cream sauce would probably call for a white wine. A heartier dish of roast stuffed turkey, on the other hand, may blend better with a light red wine. Obviously, there is room for variation. Personal choice and taste are still the best guidelines.

Red Wines

For the heartier dish, a richer and fuller-flavored wine will generally be recommended for the greatest dining enhancement. The adage "red meat, red wine" is still worthy of consideration. The stronger flavors of game and red meat overpower a light wine. These meats call for the heartiness of the reds. Typical choices include Burgundy, Bordeaux, Merlot, and Cabernet.

Sparkling Wines

Sparkling wines can fit well with nearly any course and any occasion, depending again on individual preferences and tastes. Sparkling wines range from the driest (*brut*) to the sweetest (*doux*). French champagnes are the most traditional of the sparkling wines, but Asti Spumante—the "champagne" of Italy—is a favorite of many wine lovers. American wineries, especially those in California and New York, produce quality sparkling wines.

Appetizers and Dessert Wines

Appetizers stimulate the appetite and freshen the palate to enhance a diner's appreciation and enjoyment of the foods to come. Appetizer wines, or *aperitifs*, tend to be light and fairly sweet. Popular aperitifs include Madeira, vermouth, sherry, Moselle, dry white Burgundy, or any chilled, light, white wine. Dessert wines are sweet wines served after a meal. The popularity of dessert wines seems to have declined somewhat in recent years.

Tasting and Rating

Competitions held regionally, nationally, and internationally allow wine tasters to evaluate new wines. These competitions are important to vintners and restaurateurs alike, since award-winning wines increase sales for both industries.

In the United States two scales are used in wine tasting and rating. The first is the 100-point scale, used in most academic judging of wine as well as in such publications as the *Wine Spectator*. In this system, wines are evaluated based on five categories: color, clarity, nose, taste, and impression. See Table 8.2 for an example of the 100-point scale.

The second and more widely used rating system is the twenty-point scale developed by researchers at the University of California at Davis. Ten criteria are involved: clarity, color, aroma, bouquet, total acidity, tannin, body, sugar, general flavor, and overall impression.

In both systems the aroma of a wine is one of the most important factors, because the human nose is the most sensitive organ involved in wine evaluation. In order to describe aromas in specific terms recognizable by all wine tasters, a standardized system was developed, again at the University of California at Davis. This Wine Aroma Wheel uses three tiers of definitions to accurately describe the aroma of a particular wine. For example, Gewurztraminer is considered "spicy," Chardonnay may be "buttery" or "fruity," and Cabernet Sauvignon may have a "bell pepper" aroma. This system allows wine tasters to communicate effectively the nuances of a particular wine.

Selection and Pricing

Restaurants select wines based on the type and cost of the food the wines will accompany. For example, Mexican restaurants might opt for ethnic table wines like Los Reyes or Terratola, while Italian restaurants might serve such standards as Valpolicella or Chianti. Restaurants with limited menus might offer a limited selection of wines, since many restaurants do not have the space to store a variety of wines for very long. Restaurants with wine cellars have a broader and deeper range of wines. These fine dining restaurants often buy wines that will be stored for three to seven years, allowing the wines to age to their full maturity.

Although wines can be expensive items for restaurants to buy and serve, the price markups can be substantial. It is fairly common in a restaurant for a

TABLE 8.2 The 100-point Scale for Wine Evaluation

Examination Segment	Wine No. 1	Wine No. 2	Wine No. 3	Wine No. 4	Wine No. 5	Wine No. 6
COLOR (20)						
Hue (5)						
Intensity (5)						
RTV*(10)						
CLARITY (20)						
Suspension (10)						
Precipitate (10)						
NOSE (25)						
Acescense**(10)						
Bouquet (8)						
RTV (7)						
TASTE (25)						
Tartness (3)						
Astringency (3)						
Sweetness (3)						
Balance (3)						
Body (3)						
Flavor						
Taste (3)						
Aftertaste (2)						
RTV (5)						
IMPRESSION (10)						
TOTAL (100)						

Source: Richard P. Vine, Wine Appreciation: A Comprehensive User's Guide to the World's Wines and Vineyards (New York: Facts on File, 1988).

*Representative of Type or Variety
**Acetic acid formation

bottle of wine to sell for twice its retail price, even though the restaurant probably paid only one-half of the retail cost. Wines bought and then stored in restaurant wine cellars are even more profitable.

Wines are most frequently sold by the bottle, but increasing numbers of restaurants have expanded their range of wines sold by the glass or by the **split**, or half bottle. Technological innovations like the Cruvinet and the Vacu-Vin have helped to make selling wine sold by the glass, since they preserve wines from the effects of oxygen exposure. The Cruvinet is a temperature-controlled machine that pumps the oxygen from an open wine bottle and pressurizes it

A Day in the Life of...

A SOMMELIER

Sommelier is a derivative of the French word *saumalier*, meaning pack animal driver, which later became used to identify a court official responsible for the transportation of supplies.[1] Fortunately for the sommelier in the hotel industry, the term has come to mean simply *wine steward*. In other words, a sommelier is an expert in wine selection and service and directs guests to appropriate wine choices.

A sommelier, who is also called a *chef de vin*, can be likened to a chef: both are in charge of selection and purchasing, oversee a staff, and must turn a profit for the hotel or restaurant. The sommelier is an expert in the field whose duties include:

- supervising the ordering process and the storage of wines
- preparing a wine list
- overseeing the staff
- maintaining a cost-control methodology
- assisting guests in their wine selections
- properly serving a wine

All of these responsibilities are done in conjunction with satisfying customer demands.

In addition to these duties, sommeliers increasingly are educating their waitstaff about proper wine selection and service. This includes having servers become familiar with at least two red wines and two white wines as well as being able to recommend dishes to complement these wines, according to wine consultant and educator Kevin Zraly.[2] For more complicated situations, the waitstaff can call upon the sommelier for advice.

It is standard for a sommelier to be well versed in wines and liquors, including knowing good and bad vintage years, the proper care of wines and liquors, and the history of the profession and its products. Not only must a sommelier be familiar with types of wines and liquors; she must also work closely with the chef to prepare a list of wines suitable for serving in the restaurant. This list should relate well to the restaurant's menu and style of presentation. Such knowledge takes many years of training, often through an apprenticeship at a large hotel.

Like a chef, the sommelier is a high-prestige position, requiring not only tremendous training but a keen sense of taste to distinguish among different wines. Historically, a sommelier's honored position was handed down from generation to generation or given after a long apprenticeship as a wine steward's assistant. Now, however, proper training and years of hard work can gain entry to the position.

Every three years the International Association of Sommeliers sponsors a competition to determine the finest sommelier in the world. Taste tests, a written examination, and each candidate's suggestions for wine and food pairing are all considered in the selection of the winner.

---

1 Frederick C. Mish, ed., *Webster's Ninth New Collegiate Dictionary* (Springfield, Mass.: Merriam-Webster, Inc., 1987), 1124.

2 "Winning Ways with Wine: Tips from the Experts," *Lodging Hospitality* (October 1989), 151.

Photo courtesy of Johnson & Wales University

with nitrogen instead. The Vacu-Vin is a much simpler and more affordable device that purges the oxygen from the bottle through a rubber cap. These innovations have allowed customers the luxury of sampling an expensive wine in a restaurant without purchasing an entire bottle.

Liquors

A liquor is an alcoholic beverage made by distillation. The process of distillation is possible because water evaporates at 212°F (100°C) at sea level, while the evaporation point of alcohol is 176°F (78.3°C) at sea level. When a liquid that contains alcohol is heated, the alcohol begins to evaporate before the water in the liquid starts to boil. This alcohol can be collected and condensed to become a distillate. Distilled beverages, known as spirits, have a higher concentration of alcohol than either wine or beer.

Types of Distilled Liquors

The two main categories of distillates are aged products and products that are compounded with other ingredients. Aged products include grain whiskeys, rums, vodka, gin, and brandies. Products that are compounded with other ingredients include liqueurs.

Whiskey

Whiskey is one of the most popular alcoholic beverages in the United States, following beer and wine. The four main types of grain whiskeys are Scotch, Irish, rye, and bourbon. Each has its own unique flavor, and all are known worldwide. Whiskeys may be consumed neat, meaning straight and unmixed, or on the rocks, meaning over ice. Some prefer to mix their whiskey with water, either bottled or tap, or with club soda.

Scotch Whiskey The first large-scale production of whiskey was carried out in Scotland, nearly a thousand years ago. To make Scotch whiskey, the distiller starts with barley. Wet barley is smoothed over a special floor to begin germination (sprouting). The germinated barley, now called green **malt**, is then dried in special kilns heated with peat, a kind of very soft coal common in Scotland that gives the malt a smoky flavor. Next the malt is mashed, or crushed, and mixed with water in special ways that extract the starch from the grain and convert it to sugar. This liquid is then transferred to huge tanks where certain yeasts are added and fermentation takes place.

The raw whiskey is now ready to be distilled in a special device called a copper pot still, which draws off the main alcohol-containing part of the liquid, separating from the water other elements such as yeast residues. The young whiskey is transferred to barrels for storage in warehouses until it ages, sometimes for two or three years. When this aging is complete, the whiskey is bottled as a straight malt whiskey, or blended with other batches of whiskey in certain proportions. The blended whiskeys must be aged another few months before being bottled. Most liquors labeled as Scotch are blends, some from as many as forty to fifty different single-malt liquors. Scotland is the only place in the world where this whiskey is produced. One producer, the Macallan-Glenlivet Distillery, has been making Scotch whiskey since the late 1800s. This distillery employs only about fifty people, yet it is the fourth-largest producer of Scotch in the world.

Irish Whiskey Irish whiskey is made from small grains such as barley, corn, and rye. The process is very similar to the production of Scotch whiskey, but Irish whiskey malt is not exposed to smoke and thus lacks the smoky flavor of Scotch. Irish whiskey is usually distilled three times in a columnar still and is sometimes blended with neutral grain whiskeys to produce a lighter-bodied product.

Rye Whiskey Canada is the primary producer of rye whiskey, which is mainly made from rye and corn, although small amounts of other cereal grains may be included. Rye whiskey is usually lighter in body and flavor than other whiskeys. It is made in a similar way to Irish whiskey and then aged in barrels six years or longer. Just before bottling, several batches of rye whiskey are blended in certain proportions, colored slightly with caramelized sugar, and sweetened with a small amount of sherry.

Bourbon Whiskey Whiskey has been distilled in the eastern part of the United States for at least two hundred years. Tradition has it that Bourbon County was the first place in Kentucky where bourbon whiskey was produced. Bourbon whiskey is made mostly from corn, but other grains, such as rye or wheat, may be mixed with it as well. Bourbon whiskey is distilled in a similar way to Irish and rye whiskeys; however, the charred oak barrels used for aging the liquor provide bourbon with its unique flavor and color. The United States is the largest producer and consumer of bourbon whiskey. The largest family-owned American distillery is the Heaven Hill Distillery in Kentucky.

Rum

Made from sugar cane, rum was first produced in the West Indies in the 1600s. Historically known as "kill-devil," "rumbullion," and "blackstrap," rum is made from molasses, a by-product of sugar production. The molasses is fermented and then distilled to make rum. Since molasses already contains sugar, no malting or mashing is required. Otherwise, the rum-making process is similar to that which produces whiskey. Rum is generally categorized as either light (pale in color) or dark (with an amber color). Rum serves as the basis for numerous mixed drinks, many of them on the sweet side. It is rarely consumed without a mixer of some kind.

Vodka

Vodka, another distilled alcoholic beverage, can be made from many different grains or starches, including barley, corn, rye, wheat, and potatoes. Originating in fourteenth-century Russia, vodka is odorless, colorless, and almost entirely lacking in flavor. It is because of vodka's lack of flavor that it is so widely used in mixed drinks, where it is combined with other juices or alcohols that have assertive flavors of their own.

Gin

Gin was first developed in the seventeenth century by a Dutch doctor as a medicinal treatment for kidney complaints. It derives its distinctive flavor from the mixture of juniper berries and alcohol. The alcohol in gin is made primarily from corn and barley. In addition to juniper berries, gins may contain a variety of other "botanicals," such as coriander seed, fennel, calamus root, almond, ginger, cinnamon, licorice, and caraway. Various **distilleries**, companies that make distilled alcoholic beverages, closely guard the recipe for their gin's particular flavor. Gin's most famous use is in the martini, where it is paired with dry vermouth. It is mixed with various citrus juices to form other popular cocktails.

Brandy

Brandy is made from distilled wine or a distillate of fermented fruit. The word brandy comes from the Dutch word *brandewign*, which means "burnt wine." This refers to the fact that wine is heated in the distillation process. There are

Industry Insights

CULTURE

Tequila

Formerly known only by margarita lovers and worm chasers, tequila has gone mainstream. With tequila sales consistently on the rise, this Mexican spirit is growing in popularity and losing its "ethnic" aura.

Tequila is made from the fermented and distilled agave plant, usually blue agave. A member of the amaryllis family that is grown only in Mexico, the blue agave has been likened to a 100-plus–pound pineapple. Mexican law dictates that tequila be at least 51 percent agave juice; with the rest comprising sugarcane spirits or other distillates.

Lesser known brands of minimum-standard tequila mix well with citrus juices, which mellow its bite. This type of tequila is known as white or silver. Gold is a smoother tequila, made so by short-term cask aging. *Anejos*, or aged tequilas, are cask aged from one to three years and are the mellowest in taste. Of these *anejos*, super premiums are tequilas made from 100 percent blue agave juice and are usually double distilled for added smoothness.

Some experts attribute tequila's popularity to an increase in the consumption of Southwestern and Mexican fare. Still other experts contend that tequila appeals to the adventurous drinker because of its mystique and novelty. The availability of tequila drinks in all types of restaurants and the popularity of the margarita have no doubt contributed to the increase. Whatever the reason, tequila has now earned its place among the more traditional liquors.

many wine-producing countries that also produce brandy. Some of them include France (Cognac), Greece (Mextaxa and Ouzo), Spain, Portugal, the United States, and Peru (Pisco). Brandies are traditionally served alone as an after-dinner drink or used to fuel flaming desserts, such as bananas Foster or cherries jubilee.

Liqueurs

Liqueurs, some of which are called cordials, were first developed by monks in Europe during the Middle Ages. Long familiar with the medicinal qualities of alcohol and many herbs, the monks began to combine these elements to create a wide variety of flavors. Many of the recipes and exact production techniques continue to be held in secret by the producers of various liqueurs.

Two methods of making liqueurs and cordials are maceration and infusion. **Maceration** is accomplished by immersing heat-sensitive ingredients such as fruits in a cold alcohol base. The mixture is allowed to steep until the flavor of the ingredient has been absorbed by the alcohol, often as long as a year. This flavored alcohol is then sweetened with sugar and colored with coloring additives. The beverage is now ready for bottling. Raspberry, peach, and wild strawberry liqueurs are produced by this method.

Other liqueurs, such as hazelnut and vanilla liqueurs, are usually produced using **infusion**. This method is very much like maceration except that the base alcohol is hot instead of cold. The hot liquid is poured over such ingredients as seeds, spices, herbs, and nuts, steeping until the water-soluble flavor elements have been extracted by the alcohol. After filtering, sweetening, and coloring, the beverage is ready to be bottled. All liqueurs contain at least 2 1/2 percent sugar; many contain 30 to 40 percent sugar. Liqueurs are usually served as after-dinner drinks, and are widely used in dessert recipes.

Bartenders

Bars and restaurants employ bartenders to mix alcoholic beverages for customers. Many fine bartenders have professional training, as well as extensive experience. In addition to the techniques and recipes for various drinks, a bartender knows how each drink is traditionally served. For instance, the martini is served in a distinctive glass called the cocktail or martini glass; the whiskey sour in a sour glass; and a bourbon and water in an old-fashioned glass, unless the guest has requested a tall glass (a highball). Alcohol may be measured out in a jigger or shot glass, which may hold anywhere between one and two ounces of liquor.

Some bartenders, particularly those in fast-paced operations, use an **electronic liquor dispenser (ELD)**, a device that dispenses an exact measure of liquor into each glass. The ELD looks and operates much like the soda gun used to dispense soft drinks and carbonated water. It offers speed and convenience, as well as strict portion control. Since liquor is a high-cost item, restaurant and bar owners are anxious to ensure the use of accurate pouring methods—a task easily performed by the ELD.

Disadvantages of using an ELD include its initial expense and maintenance costs and its lack of customer acceptance. Bar customers like to see bartenders pour their drinks to be sure that the correct amount and brand of alcohol were used in the proper order. ELDs do not allow this to occur. A bartender who does not use an ELD uses either **hand-measured pouring**, using a jigger or shot glass, or **free pouring**, where she visually estimates the amount of liquor dispensed.

Bars stock a variety of brands of each major type of liquor. To prepare drink orders, most bars use a generic or **well brand**—a lesser-quality product with a label or name that is not familiar to customers.

A variety of call brands of each liquor type are also stocked. A **call brand** is one called for by name by the customer. For instance, instead of ordering bourbon and water, a customer may ask for a "Maker's Mark and water." Many upscale bars now use call brands as their standard pour for all beverages served. They usually also offer a selection of super-premium liquors.

The quality and wholesale price of the liquor used in each drink's preparation are factors affecting the price charged to the customer. A computerized **point of sale (POS)** system can allow the bar to set every drink price according to the specific ingredients served. The server keys in the ingredients used, including call liquors, and the POS system figures the rest. The POS system differs from an electronic cash register in its degree of sophistication.

Industry Insights

BUSINESS INNOVATION

Microbreweries

The Germans call it liquid bread. American commercials say it livens up any occasion. Comedians say it's good for what "ales" you. Microbreweries, however, are calling it money in the bank. "It" is beer.

In approximately fourteen microbreweries across the country, boilers, liquid mash, and fermentation tanks are processing water, barley, yeast, and hops into local brews with such names as Sierra Nevada, Abita Amber Lager, and Catamount Porter. Microbrewery proprietors claim that their beers are more flavorful, and that a more flavorful beer means moderate consumption. The major advantage, however, seems to be freshness: a microbrewery pub takes a beer directly from tank to table.

While a microbrewery's annual output is small—perhaps 15,000 gallons, a mere drop compared to the 70 million gallons put out by, say, an Anheuser-Busch—the impact of microbreweries has been phenomenal.

The microbrewery process is quick, simple, and cost-efficient, taking anywhere from four to eight weeks for a lager beer and two weeks for a regular beer. The western half of the United States, particularly California and Washington, was the first region to catch on to the concept, forging the way for the proliferation of microbreweries and spreading the gospel of locally brewed beer.

An **electronic cash register** can record the volume of drinks sold, the price per unit, the time of service, the particular type of drink, and the name of the server. The POS system can record all of this data plus more, calculating changes in inventory given the daily sales and capturing various other details.

Malt Beverages

Malt beverages, generically called beer, have been around about as long as wine. History indicates that the ancient Babylonians, Egyptians, and Greeks all brewed various kinds of beer. After the Romans adopted brewing techniques, they helped spread beer throughout many parts of the empire, especially the northern regions. Beer is the antecedent to whiskey, which is in essence a distilled beer.

Beer Making

Whether produced in small amounts as a home-brewed beverage or in massive quantities in a modern mass-production facility, beer is made by a similar process. The brewing of beer begins with water. Mineral content and purity are key to the quality of the finished beer. Next comes the grain—preferably good barley that has been malted. **Malting** is a process where the grain is germinated to produce an enzyme that can convert starch into fermentable sugar. The water and malt are mixed together in a huge mash tub where the grain softens and separates. While this is happening, other small grains such as corn or rice are boiled in water. Then the two mixtures are combined, and special enzymes from the malt act on the starches in the grain, turning them into maltose sugar.

When this process is complete, the mash is strained and filtered. The remaining liquid, now called **wort**, is transferred into a giant copper kettle where hops are added. **Hops** are the dried, conical fruit of a special vine. It is hops that impart to beer its special bitterness. After the hops infusion, the wort is again filtered into a fermenting tank where certain yeasts are added to induce fermentation and effervescence. Some strains of yeast carry out fermentation at the bottom of the tank, so carbon dioxide bubbles rise and disperse throughout the liquid. Bottom fermentation produces the beers called lagers. Other yeasts are top fermenting; the bubbles of carbon dioxide gradually spread downward. Most ales are top fermented.

After fermentation the young beer is then drawn off into glass-lined aging vats, the heavier ales for one to three weeks and the lighter lagers for as long as four months. Ales are generally considered to have a full-bodied taste and a strong hops flavor. They usually have a higher alcohol content than lagers. Two different styles of ales are stout and porter. Stout can be either dry or sweet, while porter is dry, and usually is lighter in body and less creamy than stout.

Once matured, the beer is filtered to give it a sparkling clarity, given a final carbonation, and placed in bottles or cans or in barrels to be served as draft beer.

The Brewery

During the early years of the United States, beer was common, and many inns and taverns as well as families produced their own brews. Over time, as businesses grew larger and as greater quantities were demanded, larger breweries began to develop. The first large commercial brewery was owned by William Penn, founder of Pennsylvania.

When refrigeration became available in the late 1800s, beer could be shipped greater distances without loss of quality. Large breweries began producing beer for a growing market. Milwaukee saw the growth of Miller, Pabst, and Schlitz. Anheuser-Busch dominated St. Louis. Hudepohl grew in Cincinnati. Philadelphia and St. Paul each had a Schmidt's brewery, and Stroh's in Detroit became Michigan's largest brewery.

Microbreweries

The United States is by far the world's largest producer of malt beverages. The early 1990s saw more than two hundred breweries produce 200 million barrels annually. Although Anheuser-Busch was still the largest single brewer in the United States, the 1980s witnessed a boom in small, local breweries called

Photo by Michael Dzaman

The microbrewery process is relatively simple, taking about two weeks to brew beer.

microbreweries. At the beginning of the decade, there were fewer than a hundred breweries—large or small—in the United States. In 1983, there were only seven microbreweries in the United States. By the end of the 1980s, microbreweries, or craft breweries, as many preferred to be called, were springing up everywhere. By 2002, there were over 1,400 specialty brewers operating in the United States. While they are not able to compete against the giants in quantity produced, these small, local operations focus on producing high-quality, distinctive beverages that compete with higher-priced imports. Some microbreweries operate in tandem with a bar or restaurant as a **brewpub**. Although each of these breweries is in itself a small operation, added together their total production and sales are worthy of financial as well as social recognition.

The rapid growth of microbreweries has led some industry experts to raise the possibility of a shakeout. Robert Weinberg, of Weinberg and Associates, an industry consultancy, argues that the supply of microbreweries has now surpassed the demand. Further pressures come from large distributors who seek to squeeze microbrews off precious retail display shelves as well as from large brewing firms who have entered the market with their own specialty brands.

Imported Beers

Imported malt beverages come in many styles, such as lagers and ales. Such names as Heineken, Molson, Moosehead, Modelo, and Dos Equis have become well known and popular in the American market. Current interest in imported beers correlates with a similar interest in ethnic, regional, and international cuisine.

Trends in Beer Sales

Beer is the most popular alcoholic beverage in this country, and in many others as well. Beer's lighter alcohol content appeals to many. Then, too, beer has shed its negative image and is now viewed as an upscale beverage worthy of serious consideration. Beer tastings are a regular means of introducing customers to the wide taste variations of beers. Extensive beer lists featuring imported, national brand, premium brand, and microbrewery products are common. Beer consumption, once dominated by males, has risen sharply among females as well. Beer consumption may be up, in part, because beer is seen as a good accompaniment to many popular foods. Pizza, as well as Mexican food and other full-bodied ethnic cuisines, pair well with beer.

In bars and restaurants beers are often available on tap, as well as in bottles. **Draft** beer is not pasteurized and consequently must be held at 36°–38°F. Beer can spoil; when it does, it appears cloudy and tastes sour. Traditionally, draft beers are served with a one-inch head of foam. Draft beers are typically sold by both the pitcher and the glass. Bottled beers are best when sipped from a glass rather than from the bottle, since drinking directly from the bottle does not allow for release of excess carbonation. American beer drinkers usually prefer to drink their beer very cold, as opposed to the custom in many other countries, where beer is served at a moderately cool temperature.

Industry Insights

TRENDS IN BEER CONSUMPTION

The beer industry saw moderate growth in consumption in 2007, comprising 1.4 percent. Of this total, domestic beers and international imports grew 1.5 percent while the craft-brewed segment reflected over 12 percent growth.

Beer consumption has regained some ground against the wine and spirits segment. According to William Brand of the Brewers Association, based in Boulder, Colorado, "Craft beers are the darlings of the beer business." Brand points out that fourteen of the top fifteen craft products showed increased sales through food, drug, and mass merchandise outlets in 2007. Recent price increases on nearly every raw material, from aluminum to hops, and especially fuel costs, may hit small brewers particularly hard. But Brand says, "I still expect the craft segment to grow in the high single digits to low double digits in 2008."

Source: www.bevindustry.com

Risk Management and Liquor Liability

Liquor Liability and Legislation

Two areas of major concern for modern lawmakers are the minimum legal age for drinking, and drivers who operate motor vehicles while under the influence of alcohol. When Congress threatened to shut off federal highway funds to states that did not raise their legal minimum age for drinking to twenty-one, every state that had not already done so promptly adjusted its laws. Today most restaurants and bars carefully check patrons' identification cards, such as driver's licenses, in order to verify legal drinking age. A popular promotional tool distributed by a major brewery was a booklet showing the authentic design and layout of each state's driver's license. This manual was designed to curb the use of fake identification by underage drinkers.

Every state also has strict laws forbidding people to drive motor vehicles or to operate heavy machinery if they have been drinking. Many of these laws carry mandatory sentences for people who drive when they have been drinking, including jail sentences, heavy fines, and loss of driving privileges.

Dram shop is a legal term in the United States that refers to a bar, tavern, or other establishment where measured alcoholic beverages are sold. Traditionally, it referred to a shop where spirits were sold by the dram (a small unit of liquid). Depending on the state or the locality, there may be regulations governing the hours a store or restaurant may be open, whether it may be open on Sunday, and even whether alcoholic beverages may be sold there at all. In addition, many states have stepped up their attack on drunk driving by passing laws that make selling or even serving drinks to an inebriated person illegal. **Dram shop legislation** refers to laws that impose legal liability on an establishment if it sells alcoholic beverages to knowingly intoxicated patrons who then cause death or bodily injury to third parties unaffiliated with the bar as a result of alcohol-related car crashes and other accidents. These laws are intended to protect the general public from the hazards of irresponsibly serving alcohol to minors and intoxicated patrons. Such "third-party" liability has been the major cause of soaring liability insurance rates for people and establishments in the business.

In the 1990s a court case held a bartender liable for the death of a twenty-one-year-old Florida man. Within hours after drinking twenty-three drinks, all served by the same bartender, the man died of alcohol poisoning. While a few judges have recently begun to limit the amounts awarded in court settlements and de-emphasize the legal duty of bar owners and hosts to keep people sober, insurance rates continue to be a problem for many businesses.

Risk Management

To combat the soaring costs of liability insurance and the legal repercussions of third-party liability, the beverage industry and retailers in particular have initiated a variety of risk management procedures and techniques. These include encouraging designated drivers and responsible drinking, as well as emphasizing alcohol management and server training. Today, an establishment may have to offer a server training program in order for its owners to obtain liability insurance. Offering a responsible alcohol service program can reduce an operator's liability insurance premiums.

Perhaps the most useful alcohol service training in the industry is the Training for Intervention Procedures by Servers (TIPS) program. This is a program designed to teach participants to prevent intoxication, drunk driving, and underage drinking among the people to whom they sell or serve alcohol. This program addresses concerns specific to restaurants, hotels, bars, nightclubs and other on-premise liquor license holders.

The following topics are covered in the program:

Legal Information: Presents the legal responsibilities for servers of alcohol, explains the types of illegal sales, and provides extensive information about checking IDs and documenting incidents.

Assess Your Guest—Legal: Allows establishments to apply the legal information to real-life scenarios through practical application exercises using short video scenes.

Alcohol Information: Describes how alcohol affects people, signs of intoxication to look for, and relevant information about alcohol that the server can use to serve more responsibly.

Assess Your Guest—Alcohol: Shows how to apply the alcohol information to real-life scenarios through practical application exercises using short video scenes.

Intervention Information: Gives the establishment numerous guidelines for providing customer-friendly, responsible alcohol service. Frames the server's role in a three-step, easy-to-follow model.

Decide and Implement: Shows the server how to apply the intervention information to real-life scenarios through practical application exercises using short video scenes.

Certification Exam: Certifies servers as TIPS-trained for insurance and liability purposes.

Designated Driver Programs

A common practice that many groups and numerous establishments encourage is the use of a designated driver. One or more people in a group agree to remain alcohol free in order to safely drive the other group members home after socializing. Businesses that support the practice may provide free nonalcoholic drinks to the designated driver. Often food items are offered free or at reduced prices. Today, major wine, spirits, and beer manufacturers are using high-profile TV ads and mission statements to reflect their commitment to safe consumption of alcohol. Their messages are framed in the form of public service announcements and can also be used as evidence in support of their opposition to unsafe and illegal consumption of alcohol.

Responsible Drinking

Another concept that can help a business owner decrease the risk of legal liability is the active encouragement of responsible drinking. Discontinuing promotions that encourage people to over-imbibe may indicate to a court that a business is acting responsibly toward its patrons. Many businesses now have de-emphasized or discontinued such promotions as happy hour, two-for-the-price-of-one drinks, and oversized drinks. The trend now is to

Industry Insights

LAW & ETHICS

Dram Shop Laws

Orginally enacted in the mid-1850s, dram shop laws or civil damage acts dictated that owners and operators of drinking establishments were liable for injuries caused by intoxicated customers.[1] In other words, the act of providing alcohol was said to be the cause if injury or death occurred.

Prior to this time, tavern owners and bartenders were exempt from such liability. It was commonly believed that the consumption of alcohol, not the serving of it, made customers (not innkeepers) liable. The dram shop laws changed all of that.

The first dram shop act—which served as a model for other such laws that would follow—was established in Indiana in 1853 amid the growing temperance movement. The law stipulated that anyone injured by an intoxicated person could file suit against the third-party server.

Today many states in the U.S. have traditional dram shop acts on the books.

---

[1] Gerald D. Robin, "Alcohol Service Liability: What the Courts Are Saying," *Cornell Hotel and Restaurant Administration Quarterly* (February 1991): 102.

provide free or low-priced food and to offer nonalcoholic substitutes such as flavored waters and fruit juice beverages. Bars and lounges that operate in or near a restaurant often offer small-portion servings of items from the restaurant's hors d'oeuvre menu, thus enticing customers to order food.

Alcohol Management and Server Training

With emphasis shifting from quantity drinking to quality drinking, declining liquor sales can often be offset by lower liability insurance premiums and increases in food receipts. The challenge now becomes how to increase sales without encouraging patrons to drink too much.

Requiring the service staff to participate in training programs such as TIPS (discussed above) or Responsible Alcohol Service, sponsored by the National Restaurant Association, is helpful. Servers who obtain this type of certification learn about alcohol and how it affects people, the common signs of intoxication, and how to help patrons avoid overdrinking. This training benefits servers, patrons, and businesses alike.

In another strategy, instead of asking "What would you like from the bar?" a trained server might suggest a specific house drink that is not only an interesting choice for the customer but also a profitable sale for the bar. The server also might encourage an order from the appetizer or dinner menu by suggesting high-interest items.

Profitability is also increased by prompt, consistent, high-quality service. Patrons who are pleased with both their selections and how these selections are served will be most likely to return, ensuring future business. Well-trained servers are friendly and efficient. This efficiency goes hand-in-hand with well-planned physical layouts and serving procedures. Efficiency and effective planning and preparation promote guest satisfaction.

Another vital concern for beverage managers is maintaining revenues and increasing profits by protecting against losses. Good planning helps avoid waste. Careful control of portions assures consistency, protects against drinks being made too strong, and avoids loss of money through spillage, as well as affording more accurate inventory control. Controlled portions also help servers monitor overdrinking. Finally, controlled portions and careful inventory help deter theft, which can pose a real threat to revenues and profit.

Summary

- Public consumption of most nonalcoholic beverages remained stable throughout the 1980s and 1990s. In the 21st century, sales of soft drinks and other specialty, energy, and health conscious, flavor-infused drinks have grown by more than 100.
- Although there has been a trend toward greater beer and wine sales, the decrease in liquor sales has resulted in an overall decrease in alcohol consumption.

- The main steps in making wine including crushing, fermenting, aging, and bottling.
- Although French wines have long been the standard, vintners in the United States, Australia, Italy, Germany, Spain, Portugal, and several South American regions also produce excellent wines.
- Distilled spirits are made by the process of distillation. The major distilled beverages are grain whiskeys, rums, vodkas, gins, and brandies.
- The most important ingredients in beers, or malt beverages, are water and grain. Hops give beer its special bitterness.
- The increase of modern microbreweries or craft breweries has made them a force in the beverage industry.
- The encouragement of moderation and responsible drinking, as well as required staff training programs, are changing the market but also bringing new opportunities to creative businesses.

ENDNOTES

[1] "Diet Decade' Spurs Industry to New Heights," *Beverage Industry Supplement* (March 1993): 10.
[2] "Big Three Continue Hold in Beverage Industry's Top 10," *Beverage Industry Supplement* (March 1993): 8–9.
[3] Greg W. Prince, "Middle of the Road," *Beverage World* (September 1992): 46.
[4] Ibid., 41–42.
[5] James Scarpa, "Just a Taste," *Restaurant Business* (April 10, 1992): 10.
[6] http://www.wineaustralia.com.
[7] Source: Robert Mondavi Wineries

CHECK YOUR KNOWLEDGE

1. Name some of the beverages available at restaurants. What are the current trends in specialty drinks and flavor-infused products?
2. How are wines named in the United States? In Europe? Name four kinds of red wines and four kinds of white wines.
3. How is today's emphasis on healthier lifestyles reflected in alcohol sales and service?
4. Compare the processes for making wine, beer, and liquor.
5. What are two major legal issues relating to alcohol sales? How do restaurants and bars protect against violations in these areas?

APPLY YOUR SKILLS

1. With growing trends in beer consumption indicating interest in craft beers and specialty beer products, how would you recommend that a full-service bar operation incorporate more craft beers than traditional tap products while still retaining marketing support from major brands?
2. A sports bar generates 1 million dollars in annual sales. The segmentation, or mix of business, reflects 50% wine, 25% spirits, and 25% specialty beer. Is it likely the cost of goods sold for each category is equal? What impact does the mix of cost of sales have on the overall profit of a beverage business enterprise?

INTERNET EXERCISES

1. Visit the Web site of a major beverage magazine such as *Beverage World*. Read the current statistics section. What are the current top five soft drinks? Beer brands?
2. Visit the Wine Institute Web site. Search for information about the current harvest of California grapes. Will it be a good harvest? Are there any threats to the harvest this year, such as weather or insects?
3. Visit the Web site of *Wine Spectator* magazine. Examine the results in the "Top Ten Wines" by category (reds and whites). Compare the prices with the ratings. How can less expensive wines be as good as much more expensive wines?

WHAT DO YOU THINK?

1. You are a server in a fine restaurant. A customer orders a glass of sherry to be served with her prime rib of beef. The sherry she has selected is extremely sweet and, you feel, an inappropriate wine choice. Should you say something to the customer about her choice?
2. A group of four young adults has been seated at the bar for two hours now, drinking steadily. They are getting progressively louder and sillier. You think they may be inebriated. What would you do?
3. You are in charge of selecting three different nonalcoholic beverage categories to stock in your family-oriented restaurant. What would you select and why?
4. Your bar sells draft beer by the pitcher. Your bar is most heavily used by college and near-college-age individuals. How would you ensure that only those of legal drinking age receive beer?
5. Your bar is being renovated, and your budget allows you to choose one piece of new equipment. What would you choose, and why?

CASE STUDY

A neighborhood bar, owned and managed by a seventy-year-old, comes up for sale. The price is very reasonable, but the entire facility will require remodeling. The existing clientele comes primarily from the immediate neighborhood. You notice many of the same people there day after day. The average customer age is mid-fifties. The bar has been a traditional full-line bar, with a heavy emphasis on beer and distilled liquor sales. A gallon jug of red wine is available if you ask. You have decided to purchase the bar and completely remodel it as a casual tavern/restaurant. What beverage products would you carry, and why?

NEW YORK
NEW YORK

PART 4

Specialized Segments of the Hospitality Industry

Picture the hospitality industry as a faceted sphere made up of pieces of mirror, each piece shining in its own right but very much a part of the whole. The bits and pieces of the looking glass let you peer at the industry from a number of different angles. Some pieces—the meetings industry, for example—reflect the side of the industry that caters to business. Those people who plan and organize meetings and expositions, who arrange conventions and attend to the comfort and welfare of meeting attendees and visitors, are an integral part of the hospitality industry. Another business facet looks to the well-being of long-term guests, especially the elderly, who frequently require assisted-living facilities. Still, other facets, such as the recreation segment, reflect and cater to the leisure activities of guests. Cozy bed and breakfast places, grand chateaux, country clubs, theme parks, casinos, and cruises—each radiates a specialized view from a sociable perspective. Spas and fitness clubs illuminate two others. Even though each offers a different image of the hospitality industry, each also reflects the basic mission of the hospitality and tourism industry—offering food and lodging to people away from home.

ch9

Meetings, Conventions, and Special Events

OVERVIEW

The meetings, conventions, and expositions (MICE) business and the long-term health-care industry have both become increasingly important in recent years. The meetings, conventions, and expositions business has grown to keep up with the demands of businesses and associations, and the long-term health-care industry has expanded to meet the needs of a population that is growing older. Just as specific sectors of the hospitality industry focus on, for instance, restaurants and hotels, other sectors specialize in meetings, conventions, and expositions and in long-term health care.

In this chapter, you'll read about the meetings, conventions, and expositions business—why it has grown, what effect it has on local economies, and who works in it. And you'll learn about different kinds of residential health-care facilities, mainly for older people, which depend heavily on hospitality services. Although meetings and residential health care are not necessarily related to each other, foodservice and lodging play a vital role in both types of operations.

OBJECTIVES

When you have completed this chapter, you should be able to:

1 **Identify two factors that distinguish meetings, conventions, and expositions from other hospitality industry segments.**

2 **Discuss the role of the meeting planner with respect to the planning, organization, and execution of an event.**

3 **Tell how a working relationship with the local convention and visitors bureau can enhance a meeting, convention, or exposition.**

4 **Explain how the hospitality industry relates to long-term residential health care.**

KEY TERMS

- assisted-living
- blog
- convention
- convention and visitors bureau
- CVB
- exposition
- extended-care centers
- intermediate-care centers
- life-care communities
- meeting
- residential-care centers

Meetings, Conventions, and Expositions

Just three short decades ago, the business of meetings, conventions, and expositions was not much of a business at all. In fact most meetings were secondary aspects, almost afterthoughts, of the hospitality industry. The meetings business, however, has come into its own. Today, meetings, conventions, and expositions are serious business and provide significant economic stimulus to host destinations, generating about $75.6 billion in 2004.

How Meetings, Conventions, and Expositions Differ from One Another

This chapter will frequently use the term *meetings business* (or *meetings industry*) as shorthand for "the meetings, conventions, and expositions business." However, sometimes it is necessary to refer to meetings, conventions, and expositions separately, so it is important to know how they differ from one another. The differences are subtle but distinct.

Providing appropriate service and space is based on the size and needs of the meeting.

- A **meeting** is a gathering of people for a common purpose. Meetings come in all sizes and varieties and include training sessions for employees, required business meetings, events at social/fraternal organizations, motivational seminars, and religious gatherings.
- A convention differs from a meeting, not in size, but in the objective of the group. A **convention** is a group of delegates or members who assemble to accomplish a specific goal. The goal may be civil, social, political, or economic. Probably the best known examples of conventions with political goals are the Democratic and Republican conventions that occur every four years to nominate the parties' candidates for president. Conventions are also held for the purpose of exchanging ideas, views, and information of mutual interest within the group. Convention gatherings can range in size from 200 to 100,000 attendees.
- An **exposition** is a large exhibition or special event in which the presentation is the main attraction as well as a source of revenue for exhibitors. Trade shows, which are special events geared to a certain industry, fall into the category of expositions. So do auto and home improvement shows, which, unlike most trade shows, are open to the public.

How Meetings, Conventions, and Events Differ from Other Hospitality Areas

Two major distinctions give the meetings business its own classification within the hospitality industry. One is the size of the group. The second is the function of the group.

Although attendance at a meeting, convention, or exposition can vary—from a handful of delegates to thousands of registrants—the exact number of attendees (whether two or two hundred thousand) is not the primary distinguishing factor. As a whole, meetings, conventions, and expositions are groups utilizing convention hotels and facilities. They often reserve space months, even years, in advance and negotiate package deals that may include rooms, meals, events, local tours, and entertainment. Therefore, in addition to the number of participants, the group's needs, its length of stay, and the number of meetings and conventions scheduled are all determinants of "size."

What distinguishes meetings, conventions, and expositions from other aspects of the industry is that each of these groups has a function. These groups have very defined purposes and agendas (for example, planning policy, exchanging ideas, or presenting services) and have outcomes in mind. Business, leisure, and other hospitality travelers and guests have more general purposes (for example, sightseeing or finding a place to stay between business appointments).

Event Management

Event management is the application of the techniques of project management to the creation and development of festivals and events. Event management involves studying the customer, identifying the target audience, devising the event concept, planning the logistics, and coordinating the technical aspects before—sometimes long before—actually presenting the event.

The recent growth of festivals and events as an industry around the world means that their management can no longer be *ad hoc*. Events and festivals, such as the Asian Games or the Dubai Shopping Festival, have a large impact on their communities and, in some cases, their whole country. The industry now includes events of all sizes, from the Olympics to a breakfast meeting for ten businesspeople. Every industry, charity, society, and group holds events of some type and size in order to market themselves, raise money, or celebrate. Celebrities and socialites often attend gala celebrations and award shows that feature elaborate staging, decor, menus, and entertainment. Outdoor and exotic locations are common venues for special events. A growing trend is for weddings to be held at exotic locations ranging from secluded islands to mountain retreats, castles, museums, and art galleries.

Event management companies offer services in a variety of areas including corporate events (product launches, press conferences, and corporate meetings and conferences); marketing programs (road shows and grand opening events); special events like concerts, award ceremonies, film premieres, launch/release parties, fashion shows, and other commercial events; and private events such as weddings.

Clients hire event management companies to handle a specific scope of services for the given event, which at its maximum may include all creative, technical, and logistical elements of the event. Alternatively, the company may handle just a subset of these, depending on the client's needs, expertise, and budget.

Specific Factors Affecting Event Planning

The event planning industry offers both creative opportunities and an array of challenges in operational delivery and production management. There is no typical special event—events can be very large (ten thousand guests) or small quaint affairs for twenty-five or fifty. Each special event involves specific details and execution requirements that must be taken into account. Variables affecting event planning include but are not limited to weather, permitting, governmental oversight, budgetary constraints, privacy, security, risk management/insurance, food preparation and delivery, decorations, lighting, theme and concept development, power requirements, tenting, environmental controls (e.g., air conditioning), and staffing.

When producing or managing a special event, exceptional customer service and logistical skills are essential. A special events coordinator or manager needs to be calm under pressure and be capable of multitasking and making quick decisions on the fly. Working knowledge of service etiquette, culinary production, site decor, and transportation logistics, as well as overall creativity, are the attributes most sought after in event planning job candidates.

Careers in the Event Planning Segment

The event planning industry offers a well-paying career track that combines imagination and creativity with organization. An event planner is someone responsible for organizing business and social events. Today, professional event planners organize award shows, ancillary activities at professional sporting venues, parades, charity fundraisers, business conferences, trade shows, holiday events, grand openings, fashion shows, new product launches, fairs and festivals, political functions, and a host of other events.

The event manager is the person who executes the event. Event managers and their teams are often behind the scenes running the event. Event managers may also be involved in other facets of the event, such as brand building, marketing, and communication strategy. The event manager is expert at the creative, technical, and logistical activities that help an event succeed. This includes event design, audiovisual production, scriptwriting, logistics, budgeting, negotiation and, of course, client service. It is a multi-dimensional profession.

Event planners also work on a myriad of other smaller events, such as weddings. Any time a group of people gathers together for a singular purpose, there is a need for someone to be responsible for all the details. Obviously, event planners must be creative and very organized. But they must also have exceptional interpersonal skills. Any planned event is about people, so the successful event planner needs to be able to fulfill the desires of the client by listening effectively to what she wants. Additionally, event planners need to develop business relationships with, and negotiate with, a host of suppliers.

A Major and Growing Source of Hospitality Revenue

Conventions, meetings, and events are a major and growing enterprise, not just for the people who work in the business, but also for the communities that reap the economic benefits of such meetings. Up to now, however, there has been no way to measure the exact size of the convention business. Some estimates indicate that meetings and conventions increased fourfold in the years between 1980 and 1989, and experienced a full 43 percent increase from 1987 to 1990.[1] In 1992, Destination Marketing Association International (formerly the International Association of Convention & Visitor Bureaus-IACVB-employed Deloitte & Touche, a multinational public accounting and consulting firm, to determine a straightforward and statistically valid measure of the economic impact that conventions have on the average city.

In a study examining the various types of meetings conducted (see Figure 9.1 for a breakdown of the different types of meetings), Deloitte & Touche analyzed responses from more than 17,000 meeting delegates, associations, exhibitors, and exposition service contractors before it reached its final conclusions. According to the survey:[2]

- Professional and trade associations held 45 percent of conventions.
- Sixty-one percent of the events were international, national, or regional.

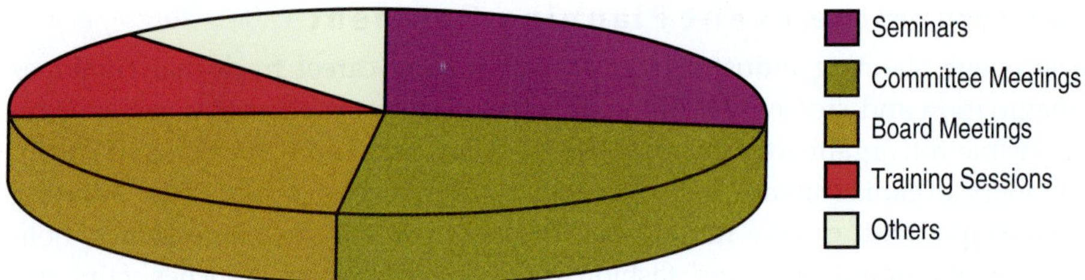

FIGURE 9.1 Breakdown of events by type

- Delegates spent an average of $638 during an average stay of 3.48 days.
- Out-of-town delegates spent an average of $763, eight times more than local delegates, who spent an average of $93.
- Forty-six percent of delegate expenditure went to overnight lodging.
- Spending increased 52 percent from 1985 to 1993.

Certainly, no one who works within the industry would argue with the proposition that the growth in significance of this portion of the hospitality industry has been remarkable. Joseph R. McGrath, former chairman of the IACVB, sums it up nicely: "The results of this year-long study clearly reflect the substantial economic impact of these events."[3]

Primary Reasons for Growth

No one factor caused the growth of the meetings industry. A number of factors are responsible, but explosive growth in information and easy availability of airline travel head the list, supplemented by expansion of municipal facilities and robust economic activity worldwide.

Perhaps the primary reason for growth in the industry is also the major reason people hold meetings, conventions, and expositions: a need to communicate information. People attend meetings, conventions, and expositions to exchange ideas, sell products, reward exceptional performance, and create knowledge. In the last thirty years, the availability of information has exploded. Computers have made it possible to gather, manipulate, and disseminate a wealth of information on every conceivable subject. Certainly, no one can keep up with all that information. In fact, most people cannot keep up with the information in their own field. They attend meetings, conventions, and expositions to learn what is happening in their field, describe what they are doing, align resources, and trade ideas. This is as true for the hair stylist as it is for the scientist. As more information has become available over the years, it has become necessary to hold more meetings, conventions, and expositions to keep pace.

Airlines

Another major reason for growth in the meetings business is accessibility to air travel. With the airlines' introduction of jumbo jets, and the entry of low-cost carriers into the market, for the first time large numbers of people could travel from one point to another—no matter how far—quickly, affordably and efficiently. Since that time, no destination has been considered "off limits" for the meetings industry, which, in turn, has made national and even international meetings, conventions, and expositions possible.

At about the same time, one of the biggest alliances between the airlines and the meetings business took place—the formation of a trade association called Meeting Planners International (MPI). MPI formed a task force to attempt to obtain similar travel privileges for meeting planners that the major carriers offered travel agents.[4] In the wake of rising fuel costs, the airlines were more than willing to accommodate this new and growing business as a way to increase their passenger load—and their profits.

Besides the introduction of the jumbo jet, the deregulation of the airline industry also directly affected the meetings business. Deregulation stimulated price wars between airlines, and airfares plummeted, making travel to and from meetings, conventions, and expositions more affordable. As a result, the airlines began catering specifically to the meetings business by offering package deals and negotiated fares.

Other Influences

As the meetings business grew, other businesses, organizations, and jobs grew to meet its needs, and in turn they made it easier for the meetings business to grow. Specifically, the growth of the lodging industry, convention centers, convention bureaus, conference centers, and meetings technology, and the new influence of meeting planners and ground suppliers,[5] spurred and were spurred by the expanding meetings business.

Lodging Expansion

How has the meetings business affected the lodging industry? To answer that question, it is important to understand the lodging industry in a "before and after" context. "In 1966, group business was a tiny percentage of the total picture for hotels, motels, and resorts," says Mike Leven, at that time president of Days Inns of America (and former president of the Holiday Inn Franchise Group). "In some hotels, group business [now] may account for as much as 80 or 90 percent of bookings."[6]

As a result of the exceptional increase in the number of meetings and in the tremendous growth in the size of meetings, hotels have had to become physically larger. Hoteliers of all sizes have adapted their services to meet the needs of a varied clientele, while increasing their profits on this growing segment. Chains such as Sheraton, Hilton, and Hyatt, and later, Radisson, Omni, and Marriott, cornered the meetings market. Today, these large facilities continue to book the majority of the hotel meetings business. However, select service brands such as Hilton Garden Inn, Courtyard by Marriott, and Holiday Inn Express, whose properties do not include large conference areas, still benefit from increased convention and association travel because of the increase in stand-alone convention facilities capable of accommodating meetings of all sizes.

Convention Centers

There is another growing niche serving the changing needs of the industry: the convention center. During the past twenty-five years, convention centers have driven lodging industry expansion. Space, accessibility, and storage capabilities have made convention centers a one-stop arena for meetings, conventions, and expositions. Many cities finance convention centers with tax-exempt bonds and alternative funding mechanisms designed to revive economic vitality within the community or metropolitan center.

"The days are over when a meeting planner was handed a key to the exhibit hall and told to turn out the lights when he left," says Dan Graveline, director of the Georgia World Congress Center in Atlanta.[7] Convention centers and convention hotels (hotels that include lodging plus exhibit and meeting facilities) are now all-inclusive places that have moved beyond the old four walls, a floor, and a ceiling concept of accommodation.

The Coliseum in New York City was probably the first convention center built to accommodate groups of varying size. Completed in 1958, the Coliseum offered flexibility: soundproof movable walls to subdivide large areas, designated registration areas, a variety of lighting options, and truck ramps to the lower exposition floors. Now, hundreds of cities around the world boast their own convention centers.

Because of the convention center boom of the last decade or so, many have argued that the market has reached total saturation. Just the same, building continued into the mid-1990s. In the Midwest, existing convention centers in Columbus, Ohio, and Indianapolis, Indiana added space to expand their facilities. The Greater Columbus Convention Center doubled in size, adding 216,000 square feet of exhibit space and a 31,000-square-foot lobby area. The Indiana Convention Center and Hoosier Dome in Indianapolis added a 36,000-square-foot ballroom and 22,050 square feet of flexible meeting space. In 1997, McCormick Place in Chicago dedicated a $675 million addition, expanding the facility to a total area of 2.2 million square feet.

Convention and Visitors Bureaus

Yet another factor affecting the meeting business is the relationship between meeting planners and convention and visitors bureaus (**CVB**s). According to the IACVB, a **convention and visitors bureau** is a not-for-profit umbrella organization that represents a city or urban area in soliciting and serving all types of travelers to that city or area—whether they visit for business, pleasure, or both. In other words, a CVB has three primary purposes:

- to encourage groups to hold meetings, conventions, and expositions in the city or area the CVB represents

- to assist groups with meeting preparations and offer services during the course of the convention, exposition, or meeting
- to encourage tourists to visit and enjoy the historical, cultural, and recreational opportunities that the city has to offer

In the late nineteenth century, a group of Detroit businessmen sent a full-time salesman on the road to bring conventions to their city. They unknowingly launched a phenomenon that has resulted in billions of dollars of revenue for convention-holding cities. In 1896, after pounding the pavement alone for a year, the Detroit salesman became so successful that he was able to hire a secretary, which marked the birth of the first CVB. By the early 1900s, convention bureaus began popping up all across the United States in such cities as Cleveland, Atlantic City, St. Louis, Denver, and Louisville. By 1914, the convention bureaus had teamed up to form the International Association of Convention Bureaus (IACB). (It was not until 1974 that "& Visitors" was added to the association's name to reflect the expanded scope of member activity in the leisure and travel industry and the promotion of tourism.) Still, even with the presence of CVBs, far fewer than 100,000 meetings were being held nationwide in 1980. By 1990, though, that number jumped to more than 350,000.[8]

Today, the IACVB has 418 member bureaus in thirty countries and offers association and corporate meeting planners a wide variety of advisory and administrative services. CVBs worldwide orient visitors to host cities, act as liaisons between suppliers and meeting planners, and offer convention and meeting management services. CVBs are indispensable in that they attract meetings, conventions, and expositions that might otherwise never be interested in a particular city or region. The following case study illustrates just how valuable a local CVB's input was for a convention held in Kerrville, Texas.

Each year the Regional Publishers Association (RPA) holds an annual convention for its members. Seminars, nationally known speakers, roundtable discussions, information exchange, and, of course, sightseeing are on the agenda for the week-long conference, which travels from host city to host city across the country.

In 1991, RPA member publications *Texas Highways* and *Texas Parks & Wildlife* teamed up to host the annual convention. Although *Texas Highways* and *Texas Parks & Wildlife* are located in Austin, both magazines focus on the entire state of Texas. The challenge was to host an informative, fun-filled conference while proudly showcasing their diverse, and very large, state.

The designated conference planner began by noting some nearby tourist attractions, namely the Alamo and the River Walk in San Antonio. Then, the planner contacted the local CVBs. In conjunction with the meeting planner, the CVB in Kerrville, Texas, developed an itinerary that included sightseeing, shopping, theme dinners, and recreation.

From the beginning, the CVB made its presence known to the group. A representative of the CVB was on hand to welcome the one hundred international guests and to offer assistance to the group. Later in the week, CVB staffers served a fried chicken lunch at one of the local parks, wrangled a "Texas lobster" (a crayfish) for a practical joke, and arranged for a group of singing cowboys to perform at a sunrise breakfast. The conference was a huge hit, in no small part due to the local CVB.

The task of the CVB is not an easy one. There are unusual requests to fulfill, demands to be met, and schedules to adhere to. Like other segments of the hospitality industry, convention and visitors bureaus face much competition within their segment of the hospitality industry. They, too, must compete regionally, nationally, and internationally for hospitality dollars.

This competition can be a distinct advantage for the meeting planner. While most CVBs can recommend suppliers, secure hotels, and act as a liaison between a group and the community, they also can provide the meeting planner with materials, tour arrangements, and on-site assistance.

Simply put, CVBs work for the visitors and meeting planners, as well as for the city—at no cost. Some are funded solely by membership fees, and others are funded through varying combinations of membership fees, state taxes, and local taxes. It is important to remember that the meeting planner is the "organizer" and the CVB is the "assistant." CVBs help visitors learn more about the host city and its area attractions. At the same time, they help the planner make the best possible use of all the services and facilities the city has to offer.

Conference Centers

The continued evolution of conference centers has also been greatly influenced by the incredible growth of the meetings business. Formerly, conference centers were usually sparse rooms, barren of everything except chairs and necessary audiovisual equipment. The fitness boom in the 1970s, however, hit even this part of the industry. No longer were conference participants content to sit for hours and hours with no diversion. Conference centers jumped on the fitness bandwagon and began designing their centers to be more resort-oriented. With recreational and physical exercise facilities available, conference centers now cater to even broader audiences.

And they no longer cater to them just on land. Floating conference centers—conference centers aboard ships—are a recent development. Ships are fitted with meeting rooms and auditoriums and offer such technical amenities as closed-circuit television and videoconferencing. Airport meeting rooms are another variation on the theme. American Airlines, for example, provides nineteen conference rooms at O'Hare International Airport.

Not all conference centers are available to the public. Some are owned by corporations and are used only by these corporations. Others are owned by corporations that use the facilities but also rent them out. And still others, owned by universities, are accessible to the public. In fact, Columbia University established the first conference center, Arden House, in Harriman, New York, in 1950.

Industry Insights

ENVIRONMENT

Environmentally Friendly Meetings

Protecting the environment is everybody's business. So it's not surprising that it is part of the meetings business, too. The people who plan meetings are introducing small changes that can make a big difference in the world.

Here are a few things meeting planners are doing:

- checking with convention centers and hotels when choosing a convention site to see if they have a recycling program
- putting recycling bins in areas, such as lobbies and meeting rooms, where people are likely to be drinking or eating
- printing handouts and other written material on recycled paper
- making sure that foodservice operators use ceramic dishes and metal utensils instead of paper and plastic dinnerware
- arranging for meeting-goers who travel by plane to share rides to and from the airport
- using energy-efficient lighting and thermostatic control devices

Meeting planners are even giving thought to the foods that will be served. David Phillips, former director of operations for the Virginia Association of Realtors, underscores this point: "At our last conference, we served Ben and Jerry's Rainforest Crunch ice cream for dessert. It contains nuts from Brazil, and is part of Ben and Jerry's effort to help save the rain forest by showing that trees can be used for nuts, not lumber. Part of the proceeds from the sale of the ice cream goes to this cause."[1]

[1] "Green to the Extreme," *Meetings & Conventions* (March 1, 1993): 1126.

Increased Use of Technology

The electronics revolution of the late twentieth century has given the meetings and convention industry new flexibility with respect to group presentations. Videos, 360-degree projection techniques, multi-image presentations, Webcasts, and digital sound systems have all become commonplace. Technological advancements within the industry have opened up a world of different ways to communicate that make meetings, conferences, and conventions more interesting to attend and easier to arrange. Today, technology is an indispensable part of the meetings business. Its use of videoconferencing, computer applications, and other technology will continue to keep pace with with technological innovation.

Video Technology Before the mid-1970s, the term "video" was virtually nonexistent. With the advent of such technology as the video projector, video has now become integral to the meetings business. Current capabilities include video-enhanced speakers, multi-image video walls, instant replay, and "live projection." (Live projection is similar to what is now commonly seen at concerts. A close-up of the speaker is projected onto a large screen, bringing the audience "closer" to the speaker and facilitating a more personal interaction.)

Photo courtesy of Hilton Hotels Corporation

Teleconferencing has become an important aspect of today's business meeting as a link between cities.

Teleconferencing In the 1980s, technology advanced beyond video into teleconferencing. Satellites, commonly used to beam news coverage worldwide, made it possible to link separate groups and speakers. Today large convention centers and major hotels often broadcast national teleconferences, linking thousands of participants at multiple meeting sites. Many feared that teleconferencing would replace the need for meeting and convention services altogether. Fortunately for the industry, however, this fear has not been realized—people still feel the need to meet in person in order to exchange ideas, create relationships, and collaborate with one another.

Computers Computers are used in virtually every aspect of the meetings business: reservations, workshops, PowerPoint presentations, interactive Webcasts, animation, video-streamed marketing messages, and virtual demonstrations. For example, a computerized information network enables CVBs to exchange important demographic and historical information about potential meeting sites with other CVBs worldwide. The IACVB utilizes a system called Convention Information Network (CINET). The system contains information on nearly 20,000 meetings and more than 9,400 organizations. Nearly 24,000 future bookings are recorded in the system, as well as approximately 38,000 meeting histories, half of which are for groups that use fewer than 200 rooms on a peak night. Each year IACVB subscribers add over 1,500 meetings to the database.

Meeting Planners

The role of the meeting planner (which will be discussed in detail later in the chapter) began to evolve about twenty-five years ago and has progressed as the meetings industry has grown. As the name suggests, a meeting planner plans events, and also assists with execution by organizing details that link

Courtesy of Photodisc

The role of the meeting planner has expanded in recent years to include many details of conference preparation.

the client with the facility, thereby making the meeting, convention, or exposition operate smoothly.

Certainly no event is produced singlehandedly. But without the support of the many planners within the industry, the growth and success experienced by the meetings industry would have come more slowly. Today, it is essential for hotel and convention center operators to welcome meeting planners as partners, because meeting planners are critical to operators' ability to satisfy client needs.

Ground Suppliers

The role of ground suppliers (vendors who handle details of tours, transportation, sightseeing, banquets, and hotel registration) should not be underestimated. Although in the past ground suppliers were primarily "shuttle operators," their role has grown. Today they are also program planners, offering special events for spouses of meeting participants, on-site sports tournaments, and motivational speakers. (Meeting planners also can perform these functions.)

Economic Impact: An Example

Obviously, each of the factors just discussed plays an important part in the meetings industry. The best way to determine their cumulative effect is by looking at the economic impact of conventions, meetings, and expositions on a city or region.

The Minneapolis Convention Center serves as an example of how conventions, meetings, and expositions generate revenue, as well as goodwill, for a community. The Minneapolis Convention Center can host more than 27,000 visitors and serves various domestic and international clients. Visitors to conventions there,

Industry Insights

LAW AND ETHICS

Disclosing Destination Health Risks

Reports about problems like SARS, a hepatitis outbreak, a mysterious virus, or a health hazard transmitted by contaminated drinking water appear in the news frequently. Do meeting professionals and other authorities in the hospitality industry have an ethical, if not legal, obligation to inform visitors about such health risks?

Financial losses could be great if people chose to cancel their trip after they were informed of a health risk. Such losses would be felt deeply by hotels, restaurants, airlines, cruise lines and meeting places and by all the people who work with them. Add to these losses the cost of informing potential visitors and the stigma associated with the disease (a stigma the city may have to endure for months), and the losses compound. Should such costs determine whether or not to warn people of the potential risks? On one hand, it is likely that the problem will be successfully dealt with by the time the event takes place. Informing visitors would create an unnecessary scare.

On the other hand, shouldn't people have the right to make their own decisions about the health risks they will face? Being informed about a disease allows a person to take precautions such as getting appropriate vaccines; using bottled water, even for toothbrushing; or refraining from feeding a cute little prairie dog whose bite could be harmful.

who come from all over the United States and abroad, directly affect the economy of the local community and surrounding areas by generating revenue from lodging, food and beverage, shopping, and transportation services.

Industry experts agree that the meetings business can open doors for all segments of local and state economies. A convention center gives its host city a springboard into the regional and national marketplace, rich with opportunities to draw tradespeople from around the world, showcase its amenities, and, of course, generate revenue for itself and local businesses.

In addition, such centers create hundreds of jobs and generate billions of dollars in tax revenues. For this reason, convention centers have been called "economic machines." In Minneapolis, as a result of the bookings and commitments of its convention center, tax revenues can easily exceed $47.6 million in one year. The hospitality and tourism industry (including meetings and conventions) is second only to health care as Minnesota's top industry, and in some parts of the state, such as Bloomington, hospitality is the top revenue source. In Washington, D.C., another popular convention and vacation area, tourism and hospitality are second only to the federal government as a revenue source.

The Regional Connection

Many existing convention centers have expanded to accommodate bigger groups and tap into the regional marketplace. For example, in 1991, Kansas

City, Missouri, expanded its H. Roe Bartle Hall Convention Center. The $130 million expansion created the largest contiguous column-free exhibition space in the nation and brought the center's total square footage to nearly 400,000 square feet. There are now fifty-five meeting rooms, a 2,400-seat performing arts theatre, and an arena that seats more than one thousand people.[9]

Regional convention centers have the advantage of being able to cater easily to smaller groups, and their proximity to clients' sites means travel expenses can be limited. This is good news to many corporations, since 80 percent of the meetings business consists of corporate conferences that involve fewer than one hundred people.[10]

The International Meetings Business

People hold meetings, conventions, and expositions in foreign countries for a number of reasons. Airplanes have made it easy to get to meetings in other countries. The locations are usually interesting and sometimes exotic. Many businesses are multinational and may choose to host a meeting in one of any number of countries in which they do business. And international meetings sometimes cost much less than comparable national meetings.[11]

> In general, the meetings business is big business worldwide, with huge, elaborate meeting centers in Paris, Birmingham (England), Amsterdam, Singapore, Macau, Frankfurt, and other places. In fact, the Equip' Hotel Trade Show in Paris is about twice as big as the National Restaurant Show in Chicago, which is currently the largest trade show in the United States. This show, presented by the National Restaurant Association, hosts more than 74,000 industry professionals from 115 countries. There are more than forty different foodservice segments represented, and buyers from the top two hundred restaurant chains participate.
>
> *Source:* http://www.restaurant.org

Opportunities in the Meetings Industry

The meetings, convention, and exhibition industry has a far-reaching effect on the global economy. Through its affiliation with industry and related organizations, it touches almost all facets of the economy. The players in the MICE marketplace offer various job opportunities for future graduates on both the host and supplier sides of the industry.

The MICE host industry includes the following types of employers:

- Corporate travel agencies
- Conference, event, and exhibition organizers
- Hotels and resorts, including their sales divisions
- Destination management companies
- Incentive houses

- Airlines and aircraft operations businesses
- CVBs and trade associations
- Convention and exhibition centers

Competition Within the Industry

National, regional, and international meetings have made the business of conventions, meetings, and expositions an increasingly competitive environment. Formerly, the limited number of sites and accommodations meant that competition was limited to a few major players. Now, however, competitors flood the field. According to some experts, competition has increased an average of 300 percent in the past several years. This is good news for meeting planners, because increased competition means that venues offer better service and more amenities to their meeting or convention clients. Some argue that without such offerings, convention centers will have a difficult time luring groups to their facilities. Joseph Psuik, former acting executive director of Denver's Colorado Convention Center, said, "These amenities are really becoming necessities to those of us in the business. Without them, we're just another face in the crowd."[12] According to a recent study, the average convention center loses $2 million a year.[13] Because stakes in the millions of dollars are involved, it becomes crucial for convention centers to compete actively.

Planning, Organization, and Execution

In its early years, the meetings business suffered growing pains. Many people had no idea of the amount of effort and knowledge required to plan, organize, and execute events. The perception was, and often still is, that meeting planners are "party-givers." Not so. In one short generation, the job has transformed itself into a profession.

The Role of the Meeting Planner

The expanded role of the meeting planner has been one of the most significant developments within the hospitality industry. In the beginning, meeting planners merely set dates and picked site locations, leaving the rest of the conference details up to the hotel or other meeting place. As the industry matured, the role of the meeting planner expanded. Meeting planners now

- select the site for the meeting, convention, or exposition
- reserve meeting space
- reserve hotel rooms
- reserve audiovisual and other equipment
- arrange for food and beverages
- organize guest registration
- arrange for name tags and handouts
- plan programs for participants and their guests
- work with exhibitors and lecturers
- make floor plans
- arrange for security

A Day in the Life of...

A MEETING PLANNER

Image copyright Demid, 2009. Used under license from Shutterstock.com

In a small café in a quaint Midwestern town, two young women stand, briefcases in hand, talking animatedly, leaving change for their cups of tea. As they leave, they are interrupted by an older man who bids them good morning and wishes them luck planning their party. "Actually," they respond, "we are planning a week-long international conference for two hundred people."

Not surprisingly, many people, like the gentleman in the scenario above, mistake meeting planning for "party giving," but the meeting planner has a clearly defined and very important purpose. She takes total responsibility for planning and conducting the meeting, as well as coordinating and directing all activities necessary to the successful operation of the meeting.[1]

From Los Angeles to Chicago and from Peoria to Baton Rouge, meeting planners across the country invest thousands of hours each year doing just that—planning meetings. No single day is like any other in this position. Meetings are planned months, even years, in advance, making the life of a meeting planner a hectic, albeit exciting, one.

Needless to say, to be able to plan meetings years ahead, meeting planners must be extremely well organized. Meeting planners must also be innovative and confident, and able to handle the emergencies that inevitably arise without worrying anyone else. Lastly, they must be people-oriented and willing to "go the extra mile." For example, one meeting planner overseeing a conference in Ohio overheard a conference visitor who hailed from Arizona wishing aloud for a particular fast-food hamburger not found in the western part of the United States. While the visitor was in a seminar, the meeting planner secretly made a trip to a drive-through restaurant and left a sackful of the burgers for the guest. A good meeting planner will do everything possible to ensure a guest's enjoyment of an event.

On a typical day, a meeting planner is likely to negotiate with hotels, meet with caterers, arrange for speakers, and deal with other suppliers, getting the best service at the least cost.[2] She also may look after other details such as room arrangements, audiovisual needs, decorations, exhibitions, transportation—the list is endless.

The position of meeting planner is relatively new and is, therefore, still evolving. In the twenty-first century, thanks to ever-changing market needs and increasing technology, the field of meeting planning is expected to explode. This means that opportunities abound for meeting planners, making this one of the most exciting, available positions in the industry.

---

1 David R. Jedziewski, *The Complete Guide for the Meeting Planner* (Cincinnati: South-Western Publishing Co., 1991), 318.

2 Lola Butcher, "Hold Tight to Your Yellow Legal Pads! It's Time Again to Meet About Meetings," *Kansas City Business Journal* (February 15, 1991): 19.

- arrange for transportation
- troubleshoot unforeseen problems
- review vendor contracts
- secure final payment for services
- troubleshoot operational issues and assist with their resolution
- evaluate the meeting, convention, or exposition after it is over

Each of these duties can entail dozens of tasks or action steps. And each requires maintaining careful records, adhering to a schedule, and working within a budget. Indeed, because meeting planners do so much, some people believe a more appropriate job title would be "meeting manager."

Meeting planners can work directly for hotels, associations, or corporations, or they can be independent, hiring their services out to different organizations. Their responsibilities may vary somewhat from the list above, depending on the organization they work for. In general, though, the job of all meeting planners is to make and oversee the execution of arrangements to ensure that things run smoothly.

Planners' Associations

Meeting Planners International (MPI) boasts more than 22,000 members. Another major industry organization, the Professional Convention Management Association (PCMA), began as an association of medical meeting planners. PCMA has grown into an industry-wide association similar to MPI. Such associations provide a vehicle for their members to share information and help each other, and also offer educational programs. Many hotels and convention and visitors bureaus join these trade organizations. This helps their management secure future business by networking with decision makers in the meeting planning industry.

Education and Certification

Hundreds of colleges across the country offer programs in hospitality, tourism, and meeting planning. Individual associations such as MPI, PCMA, and ASAE (American Society of Association Executives), as well as such organizations as the IACVB, offer advanced management certification courses. Taking courses in the hospitality field and getting practical experience through summer or after-school jobs are probably the best ways to prepare for getting a job as a meeting planner. Taking postgraduate courses is another excellent way to keep up with new trends and innovations and move up in the field.

Others Move into the Field

Studying to become a meeting planner is the most direct way to become one, but not the only way. In search of new career opportunities, sales and operations professionals at all levels of the hospitality business who have experience arranging meetings, conventions, and expositions are entering the field. The transition to the job of meeting planner is a fairly natural one for them because they already have knowledge of the business and are familiar with the customer service element of meeting and special event planning.

In addition, because of the growth in Web-based travel intermediaries and the introduction of low-cost carriers, travel planners have had to find other ways to compete in the marketplace, and many are expanding their existing jobs by adding meeting planning. This allows travel planners to collect commissions not only on airfares, but also on hotel reservations and other hospitality services.

Working with Exhibitors

Next to convention and visitors bureaus, exhibitors are probably the most important organizations meeting planners work with. Exhibitors are businesses that promote goods or services in a particular setting. Exhibitors use meetings, conventions, and especially expositions to showcase their products, often utilizing booth space, sponsorship opportunities, and networking to achieve their goals. Expositions, which are major exhibit venues, are thriving. More than 10,000 expositions a year attract more than 77 million visitors and generate billions of dollars.[14] As underwriters of receptions, banquets, and other costly events, exhibitors are an integral part of the planning process.

Special Considerations: Meeting the Needs of the Physically Challenged

The passage of the Americans with Disabilities Act brought the special needs of the physically challenged to the industry's attention. Arranging for needs such as interpreters, translators, and readers is now a common task for meeting planners and other hospitality professionals. In addition, elevators with Braille floor numbers on the buttons, Braille guest room and restroom signage, elevators with buttons set low so that people in wheelchairs can reach them, ramps for wheelchairs, and phone access for the hearing impaired make the facilities themselves easier to negotiate.

Hospitality and Sports Management

Sports management offers a myriad of opportunities for hospitality career development. Sports management includes jobs with professional sports teams and leagues, college athletic departments, national and international amateur athletic associations, and public and private recreational agencies, as well as club and facility management, marketing, and event promotion.

The sports management industry now is a significant segment of the hospitality industry. Sports franchises and institutions have significant travel, lodging, dining, and entertainment needs. In addition to these hospitality production elements, sports management has a professional services component that includes public relations, ticket sales and marketing, travel planning, logistics, sports governance, and sports information.

Business Profile

LOEWS ANATOLE HOTEL

City within a City

Photo courtesy of Loews Anatole Hotel

Billed as the largest, most complete convention hotel in America's Southwest, the Loews Anatole Hotel in Dallas boasts 1,620 guest rooms, eighteen restaurants and lounges, thirteen shops, fifty-eight meeting rooms, four major ballrooms, a state-of-the-art health and fitness facility, and a seven-acre park. World-class easily describes the Loews Anatole Hotel.

Even more impressive than its size is the hotel's extensive private art collection comprising more than one thousand pieces, some of which date back to the second century B.C. Known as the Anatole Collection, it is the largest private collection of fine art ever permanently displayed in a hotel and includes nine original Picasso lithographs and one of the largest known pieces of Wedgwood china.

A city within a city, the Loews Anatole Hotel is situated on a forty-five–acre site. Guest rooms and suites, which vary in amenities and accommodations, are decorated in eighteenth-century style. Seven presidential suites occupy 3,400 square feet per unit and offer the ultimate in comfort and privacy.

The Loews Anatole Hotel is a superlative convention hotel. Its $12 million world-class health and fitness club was ranked as one of the top ten fitness facilities in the United States by FITNESS magazine. Covering 82,000 square feet, the Verandah Club includes:

- six outdoor tennis courts
- eight racquetball courts
- indoor and outdoor swimming pools
- indoor and outdoor jogging tracks
- an aerobics studio
- a gymnasium with a full basketball court
- steam, sauna, and massage rooms
- a full-service salon with tanning rooms

If that weren't enough, guests are treated to an exciting array of shops and restaurants. The shops at the Loews Anatole Hotel offer everything from Texas souvenirs to Italian ceramics to Western apparel. Dining facilities offer a variety of cuisines, including Tex-Mex, heart-healthy cooking, Mediterranean fare, and a Chinese restaurant that requires coat and tie.

The Loews Anatole Hotel has also been consistently recognized as one of *Corporate Meetings and Incentives* magazine's ten best hotels for excellence in meeting services. It has received awards from numerous other magazines, including *Meetings and Conventions*, *Successful Meetings*, and *Medical Meetings*.

Perhaps the most significant component of sports managment in the hospitality sector is facility management. Sports facilities are multi-million-dollar operations. Often one facility will simultaneously host multiple sports and non-sports events. The manager of the facility must understand the business of sport and also be able to run a large-volume complex with its associated staffing, production, and profit considerations. Responsibilities may include scheduling, supervision, payroll, reporting, budget development and administration, supervision of maintenance personnel, customer service, product sales, security, and overseeing compliance with food and beverage safety requirements. In the event facility rental is required, facility managers must also be skilled in contract negotiations, traffic and security management, risk management, and contingency planning.

Concession management is another significant component of sports management that falls within the hospitaltiy sector. Concessions can vary in size, handling anywhere from 50 to 50,000 customers per event. Venues may be either indoor or outdoor and may sell any combination of food, beverages, souvenirs, and logo materials. Concession management services involve personnel supervision, product inventory and procurement, trash and waste management, customer service, monetary controls, and overseeing responsible alcohol service.

Sports Management Career Opportunities

There are several opportunities for career advancement within the sports managment sector of the hospitality industry. Career opportunities include both event-related and professional administrative roles in subdisciplines including sports marketing, ticket sales, public relations, event management, facility management, agency, concessions, and sports governance.

Hospitality and Long Term Residential Health Care

Just as the needs of people with disabilities must be met, so must the needs of the elderly population, who make up approximately 12.5 percent of the total population of the United States. Retirement communities and health-care facilities for older people are a specialized segment of the hospitality industry and offer careers such as management, food preparation, housekeeping, and engineering.

Long-Term Health Care

Because of the increase in average life expectancy as well as the aging of the baby boom generation, long-term health-care management is gaining importance. Although long-term health-care management has existed since the late nineteenth century, the passage of the Social Security Act in 1935 began a new era for this aspect of the industry. Small for-profit nursing homes began operating in this country, and a number of federally funded grant and loan programs began offering aid to long-term care facilities. When the Medicare

Growth in assisted-living and extended-care centers is a result of increased life expectancy.

Photo by Michael Dzaman

program (a federal program that pays certain medical expenses for people age 65 and older and for some disabled people) and the Medicaid program (a joint state/federal program that helps pay medical expenses for those who earn less than a specified amount of money) were created by the 1965 amendments to the Social Security Act, inspection standards, licensing, and other regulations were imposed upon this industry. These two changes dramatically affected the hospitality professional's role. As the legal and regulatory environment for health care evolves, it will continue to affect this subspecialty of the hospitality profession.

Types of Health-Care Facilities

Long-term health-care facilities include extended-care centers, intermediate-care centers, residential-care centers, and life-care communities. **Extended-care centers** offer intensive, round-the-clock nursing care under a physician's direction and may include the services of registered nurses, licensed practical nurses, aides, and orderlies. Such facilities are entitled to Medicare and Medicaid payments and are subject to regulations and guidelines that govern those programs. **Intermediate-care centers** offer assistance to persons incapable of living independently. They provide only basic nursing care combined with social and lodging services. Medicaid support is available for this type of care, but Medicare is not. **Residential-care centers** provide regular nursing care and some social services, primarily to mentally challenged individuals of any age, in a residential environment.

Industry Insights

BUSINESS INNOVATION

Assisted-Living Centers

In the area of business innovations, few ideas seem to show as much promise as **assisted-living** housing, a relatively common concept in Europe that is now catching on in the United States. Assisted living offers a much-needed bridge between retirement communities and full-service nursing homes. For those individuals who do not yet require round-the-clock skilled nursing care, but who cannot maintain wholly independent lives, assisted-living facilities offer a comfortable and cost-effective alternative.

In most assisted-living facilities, residents are offered either a private or semiprivate room, which includes refrigerator and sink, in a residential setting. Community areas include living rooms, a cafeteria, and a full kitchen for those who wish to prepare their own meals. Most assisted-living facilities offer limited nursing care but maintain a staff that is licensed to bathe residents and to dispense medications as needed. Activity directors are usually on staff and are responsible for arranging and promoting engaging social activities, day trips, and other excursions and serving as a staff point of contact for residents. Many assisted living facilities offer on-site culinary services. These vary in food quality and menu offerings.

DevelopMed Associates, an Ohio-based assisted-living provider, operates several assisted-living facilities. One of DevelopMed's principals, Richard Slager, noted, "We saw [that] at the (conventional nursing) homes...30 percent to 50 percent of the residents...were inappropriately placed." William Eggbeer, vice president of marketing for Manor Healthcare Corp. of Maryland, one of the nation's largest nursing home companies, states, "Our sense is [that] assisted living is growing 8 percent a year versus 1 percent or 2 percent a year for skilled nursing homes."[1]

With lower staffing costs and increased interest in the assisted-living concept, assisted-living facilities will most likely continue to flourish. This will present new challenges for the hospitality industry, which will be called upon to provide a variety of services to these facilities.

---

1 Christopher Amatos, "Assisted Living Offers Options," *Columbus Dispatch*, May 17 1993.

Life-care communities are long-term health-care facilities that cater to both dependent and independent older adults. Residents in life-care communities most often pay a substantial entry fee and a monthly maintenance or rental fee for nursing, social, and lodging services. They may begin living at the community in a totally independent setting and then move to an assisted-living arrangement if needed. Finally, if health concerns necessitate it, they are able to move into a skilled nursing facility within the community.

Life-care communities are a new segment of the health-care industry. Today, thousands of people (most over seventy-five) live in more than eight hundred such settings in the United States. The term *life-care* has become a catch-all phrase for independent living for the senior set. The independence that life-care communities offer is, perhaps, the most important factor contributing to the growth of this industry segment.[15]

Professional Profile

J. WILLARD "BILL" MARRIOTT

Marketing Genius

Photo by Corbis

The founder of Marriott International, J. Willard "Bill" Marriott, began his hospitality career at a root beer stand in Washington, D.C. That root beer stand was the beginning of his ascent in the lodging and foodservice business, an ascent that eventually led to pre-eminence as a hospitality industry leader.

As a young man, in 1927 Marriott and a business partner, Hugh W. Colton, used savings and borrowed money to purchase the A & W Root Beer franchise for Washington, D.C., Baltimore, Maryland, and Richmond, Virginia. Marriott opened his first nine-seat root beer stand the day Charles Lindbergh successfully flew the Atlantic.

After developing the root beer business, Marriott turned his attention to institutional foodservice and hotels. By the mid-1980s the Marriott Corporation boasted annual sales in excess of $3 billion and had expanded into many arenas including resorts, cruise ships, fast food, and senior living communities.

Today, the Marriott legacy lives on with over 2,900 lodging properties located in the United States and sixty-seven other countries and territories. However, its heritage can be traced to a root beer stand opened in Washington, D.C., in 1927 by J. Willard Marriott. Many family members, including J. Willard's son Bill, are still active in day-to-day operations of the corporation. In fact, you can visit Bill Marriott's daily **blog** and learn more about the company and his personal commitment to leadership in the hospitality industry.

Source: http://www.blogs.marriott.com

Hospitality Corporations and Life-care Communities

The growth of the hospitality industry's role in senior care, the expansion of life-care alliances, and the increasing population of seniors will yield many new opportunities for hospitality professionals. Life-care facilities require the services of foodservice and lodging personnel. Large hospitality corporations such as Hyatt Hotels, Marriott Corporation, Food Dimensions, Inc., and Morrison Custom Management are developing and contracting for the management of life-care communities.[16] Senior Living Services is a rapidly expanding division of the Marriott company with approximately 150 such communities. If the growth rate of this Marriott division continues, it soon will own the largest group of life-care communities in the United States. With the continued expansion of large corporations into the health-care field, the dynamics of the hospitality industry could dramatically shift. This could mean a decrease in independent operations, because large hotel and hospitality chains have an advantage over independent facilities: they can apply economies of scale to operating and managing health-care centers. For example, chains can buy food in large enough quantities to demand and get a substantial discount in price.

Summary

- A meeting is a gathering of people for a common purpose. A convention is a group of delegates or members who come together to accomplish a specific goal. An exposition is a large exhibit.
- Two distinguishing factors—size and function—make meetings, conventions, and expositions a separate segment of the hospitality industry.
- The meetings business is a significant source of hospitality revenues and contributes a high margin of profit.
- Innovations that have enhanced the meetings business include video technology, teleconferencing, Webcasts, wireless technology, and computer capabilities.
- Meeting planners plan, organize, and execute events.
- The most important organizations meeting planners work with are convention and visitors bureaus, travel agencies, and exhibitors.
- Long-term health care is a specialized segment of the hospitality industry. It offers career opportunities such as manager, food preparer, and housekeeper.
- Extended-care centers offer intensive, round-the-clock nursing care; intermediate-care centers offer social and lodging services, but provide only basic nursing care for individuals who cannot maintain wholly independent lives; and residential-care centers offer basic medical and nursing services in a residential setting to individuals of any age.
- Life-care communities allow residents to move from living arrangements offering a totally independent lifestyle to arrangements offering twenty-four–hour skilled nursing care.

ENDNOTES

[1] International Association of Convention & Visitor Bureaus, "Delegate Meeting Survey History," *Supplement to International Association of Convention & Visitor Bureaus Information Packet* (December 1993).

[2] 1993 Convention Income Survey (Champaign, Ill.: International Association of Convention & Visitor Bureaus, 1993).

[3] International Association of Convention & Visitor Bureaus, http://www.iacvb.org, 1998.

[4] Mike Maynard, "An Industry Comes of Age: Airlines," *Meetings & Conventions* (June 1986): 53.

[5] Mel Hosansky, "An Industry Comes of Age: Associations," *Meetings & Conventions* (June 1986): 50–52.

[6] Linn Varney, "An Industry Comes of Age: Hotels," *Meetings & Conventions* (June 1986): 54.

[7] Barbara Korth, "An Industry Comes of Age: Convention Bureaus," *Meetings & Conventions* (June 1986): 56–57.

[8] Edwin McDowell, "Shorter Meetings on Short Notice Are the Rule," *New York Times*, February 9, 1992, F-10.

[9] Kansas City Convention and Visitors Bureau, http://kcmo.org, 1997.

[10] McDowell, F-10.

[11] Susan Crystal, "China: The Next Great Destination?" *Meetings & Conventions* (October 1992): 67–75.
[12] Meeting News, October 6, 1997.
[13] David Migdal, "From Dining to Day Care," *Meetings & Conventions* (June 1986): 73.
[14] Exposition Industry Economic Report, 1993.
[15] Bosselman, "Long-Term Health Care Management," 514.
[16] Ibid. at 515.

CHECK YOUR KNOWLEDGE

1. How do meetings, conventions, and expositions differ from one another?
2. How have meetings, conventions, and expositions affected state and local economies?
3. What are the two main factors that have affected the growth of the meetings business in the past twenty years?
4. List six things a meeting planner does.
5. How do extended-, intermediate-, and residential-care facilities differ from one another?

APPLY YOUR SKILLS

Use the following information to fill in the worksheet below.

1. You are arranging a four-day meeting (three nights of lodging) for three hundred people.
2. One hundred people are bringing spouses, who are not going to the meeting but will be attending the banquet.
3. To save on expenses, fifty participants are sharing rooms (two participants per room).
4. Double rooms cost $105 a day.
5. Single rooms cost $125 a day.
6. Each banquet table can accommodate eighteen guests.
7. The cost of the banquet for meeting participants is $35 per person.
8. The cost of the banquet for spouses is $25 per person.

WORKSHEET

	Number of Rooms	Cost
1. Double rooms: Single rooms:		
2. Total cost of rooms:		
3. Number of tables needed:		
4. Cost of banquet for all meeting-goers: Cost of banquet for all spouses:		
5. Total cost of rooms and banquet:		

WHAT DO YOU THINK?

1. A company that runs a chain of clothing stores has narrowed its choice of meeting places to your hotel and a hotel near the airport. What would you say to the company to convince it that your hotel has a better location? What would you say to the company if you represented the other hotel?
2. Why do you feel the use of teleconferencing has increased substantially? What is causing this increase to occur?
3. Imagine you are a consultant who has been asked to evaluate the need for a convention center in your city. Knowing that the average convention center loses $1.5 million a year, what arguments would you use to advocate construction of a new facility?
4. Meeting planners are finding it more difficult to obtain group discounts for airline tickets. Do you think the airlines should continue to give these discounts?
5. Your career path has taken you into the field of long-term health-care management. What opportunities do you feel exist for your own advancement and interests?

CASE STUDY

You have just opened an independent meeting planning service in your hometown. Your first client is a group of fifty people who are specifically interested in a week-long conference in your area. They have never held an offsite meeting before and are looking to you for guidance. The nearest CVB is located two hundred miles away.

1. How will a CVB two hundred miles away be able to assist you?
2. What local sources of information may be able to assist you with your meeting?
3. How much should you rely on your own judgment in lieu of working strictly within parameters set by your client?
4. A number of people who are coming to your meeting are bringing their families. However, family-oriented activities in your area are limited. What alternatives would you suggest?

ch10

Recreation and Leisure

OVERVIEW

Imagine yourself on the deck of a luxury cruise liner docking at the exotic port of Antigua. Picture yourself in the center of one of the world's most glamorous hotel resorts, overlooking an emerald sea. Indulge yourself in the fantasy world of thrill rides, professional shows, and historic reproductions at a theme park. Are you looking for the excitement of such places? Indeed, many people dream of being whisked away on such adventures. Recreation and leisure have long been a part of society and are becoming increasingly important. Although Americans feel that there are fewer and fewer hours in the day for leisure, the fact is that many enjoy more free time than they did decades ago. This is especially true for middle-aged and older individuals who have sufficient discretionary income to afford club memberships, athletic events, and cruises. Nevertheless, changes in how travelers experience time are transforming what people expect from leisure activities.

This chapter looks at the management of this specialized segment of the industry—one that is driven by the pursuit of leisure. In particular, the chapter views destinations that provide opportunities for social and cultural, recreational, adventure, and health and wellness pursuits.

OBJECTIVES

When you have completed this chapter, you should be able to:

1. **Identify one type of leisure-time activities and explain how it relates to the hospitality industry.**
2. **Compare and contrast four types of social clubs.**
3. **Identify at least two types of specialized hospitality sectors related to recreation.**
4. **Explain the major environmental issues facing the cruise industry.**
5. **Differentiate between the cruise and lodging sectors of the hospitality industry.**

KEY TERMS

amenity spa	cruise	resort spas
baby boomer	leisure	social membership
bed-and-breakfast	recreation	spa
château	recreation management	spa cuisine
club	resort	theme park

Managing Leisure Segments of the Hospitality Industry

A widely held view is that the increased pace of modern living has meant more work and less play. John Robinson and Geoffrey Godbey, who conduct the "Americans' Use of Time" research project, describe Americans' response to this intensifying of the psychological experience as the "deepening of time."[1] To "deepen" time, people speed up their activities, attempt multiple activities at once, or manage their time more precisely.

Time deepening has important implications for marketing and management in leisure-oriented firms. When people expect more activity in less time, they are likely to patronize recreational facilities that pack lots of experiences into short time frames. For example, an amusement park gives patrons a beeper when they enter. If there is a thirty- or forty-minute wait for a ride, a patron can give his or her beeper number to an attendant and wander off to other attractions. When the patron's turn for the ride comes up, the beeper goes off and he or she knows to return.[2] A number of high-volume popular destination restaurants use a similar system when guests must wait for a table. Carrying their beepers, guests are free to visit nearby retail stores until their tables are ready.

Although Americans enjoy more free time than before, they expect more from their leisure activities. Time deepening will continue to affect how the leisure-oriented segment of the hospitality industry designs, markets, and manages its offerings.

Purpose of Leisure Segments of the Industry

Fortunately, an entire industry is devoted to helping define, expand, and offer recreation and leisure services. Without such a niche in the hospitality industry, the pursuit of leisure and recreation would indeed be paradoxical: individuals would spend the better part of leisure working to get away from work. Today, leisure activities are blended among everyday activities and may no longer be blocked out in traditional vacation periods once a year. Changes in travel (low-cost or international carriers) and advances in technology afford travelers the opportunity to communicate and conduct business from almost anywhere in the world. Long-weekend getaways are more readily available. Integrating business activities with leisure activities offers yet another way of carving out more time to experience different recreational activities and destinations.

Leisure is defined as freedom resulting from the cessation of activities, especially time free from work or duties. **Recreation** is defined as refreshment of strength and spirits after work, a means of diversion. This definition of recreation must be broad, for no one activity or pursuit can adequately satisfy everybody. However, some underlying commonalities that motivate individuals do exist.

Recreation and leisure evoke feelings in those who pursue them. For some, the feeling may be amusement; for others, revitalization or enlightenment. It may even be a combination of both, or another feeling entirely. Whatever the motive, there is one key factor to consider: Recreation and leisure serve a purpose, and, as such, are not simply "play." Leisure can be play but it is not limited to the scope of this definition. Health and wellness interests, sightseeing, cultural exchanges, adventure travel, ecotourism, educational and aesthetic experiences, eating, shopping, and sporting events, as well as simply getting away from the pressures of work or home, can all be a part of recreation and leisure. Figure 10.1 shows the kinds of trips longer than 100 miles taken by Americans.

Leisure travel has become increasingly popular with American families.

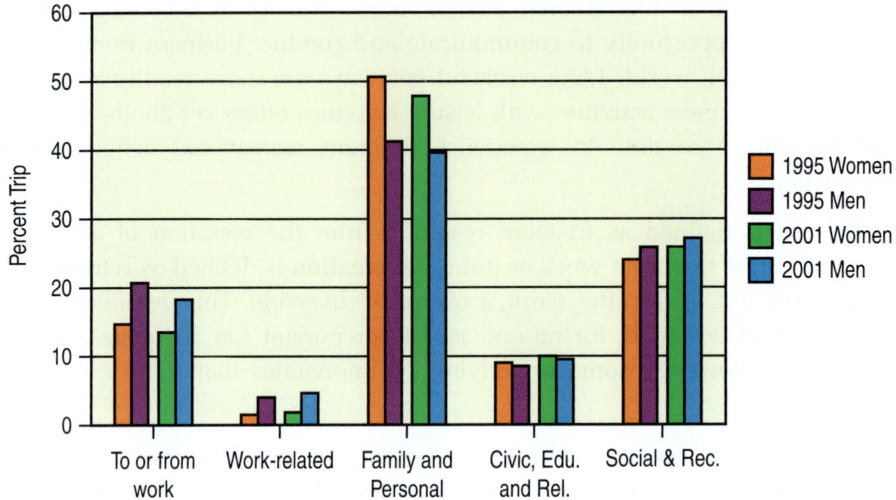

FIGURE 10.1 Travel Patterns Among Americans (Trips of 100 miles or more).
Source: NHTS 2001.

Advent of Hospitality Professionals in the Leisure Segment

For the purposes of this chapter, the management of the social, recreational, and health and wellness segments will be referred to as "recreation management." **Recreation management** is the professional handling of physical facilities where recreation and leisure activities occur.

Recreation management in the United States didn't get its "official" start until the 1920s and 1930s, when recreation and social programs were offered to the public as a form of community service. Some sources of recreation in the 1920s and 1930s—gambling, burlesque, vaudeville shows, and speakeasies—were illegal or not well respected. In the 1930s, a handful of colleges and universities offered parks and recreation management programs as areas of study. Park rangers, guides, and program coordinators are all careers that fall under the heading of recreation management.

World War II took recreation management into the mainstream as the morale and well-being of American troops became a priority. Recreation management grew as more respected forms of entertainment, such as those provided by the USO, became popular.

In the post–World War II era, commercial recreation grew by leaps and bounds with the introduction of such facilities as sports stadiums and Disneyland in California, and the rapid expansion of American parks. At the same time, the creation of the interstate highway system allowed people relatively easy access to these facilities. In the 1970s government cutbacks, inflation, recession, and other social ills gravely affected recreation management programs in government parks and forests. Unfortunately, by the 1980s most recreation management training programs had not fully recovered from the setbacks of the previous decade.

But today recreation management, particularly that of commercial facilities, is among the fastest-growing segments in the industry. With new, state-of-the art sports stadiums either open or under development in major metropolitan locations, recreation management will continue to offer new challenges and opportunities in the future. Andrew Zimbalist, a professor at Smith College, predicted that over $10 billion will be spent in new stadium development between 1990 and 2006.[3]

Novel Lodging Facilities

Some travelers want more than recreation and relaxation when vacationing. They may choose to stay at a bed-and-breakfast house, where people experience travel in a less commercialized atmosphere. If abroad, travelers may opt to stay in historic castles in France or ancient monuments in Spain. Those who want an unusual experience may lodge in a hotel converted from a school or an out-of-service schooner. They may stay in an African game preserve, in and among the wild animals. In any case, guests can find almost any type of lodging to fit their needs.

Bed-and-Breakfasts

A segment of the hospitality industry that has shown a dramatic increase in popularity in the last few years is the **bed-and-breakfast**. Difficult to define, a bed-and-breakfast is generally a private home with a family in residence that offers one to five guest rooms, although some are much larger. Originating from an old European tradition of people opening their homes to travelers, many of today's B & Bs (as they are frequently called) provide as much of that historic charm and personal touch as possible.

Bed-and-breakfasts are flourishing for several reasons. Business travelers are growing weary of the complexity of check-ins and check-outs at some commercial hotels. Also, many leisure-time travelers are looking for lodging on a scale somewhere between that of a large, formal hotel and the private home of a friend or family member. Bed-and-breakfasts offer a friendly, home-like atmosphere. Many guests say that arriving at a B & B at the end of the day is like returning home after a hard day's work. Community breakfasts with hosts and other guests seem to enhance that feeling, as do shared bathrooms (although these are rapidly disappearing). Each B & B is as distinctive as its owner. People might be attracted to a carefully preserved antebellum home in the deep South, a restored Victorian home in the Northeast, or an old seaside cottage restored to perfection.

The increased interest in B & Bs has led to the publishing of several B & B guides and directories. There are now reservation service organizations (RSOs) that enable travelers and B & Bs to connect. Also, hotels are working with B & Bs to form organizations that refer business back and forth for both their mutual benefit and the benefit of their guests. Today, B & Bs are recognized throughout the nation and have created industry-wide marketing associations. They also participate in local and regional visitors' bureaus, much like hotels do.

Although B & Bs are considered a distinct segment of the lodging industry, statistics about them are difficult to assess. Regulations covering B & Bs vary from state to state, so in some states they are licensed as hotels and in others they are not. Also, B & Bs often are organized as sole proprietorships that, unlike publicly held corporations, are not required to make public financial disclosures.

Ron Thomas, a faculty member at Oakton Community College Illinois, whose expertise has earned him the nickname "the B & B Guy," estimates that there are approximately 25,000 bed-and-breakfasts in the United States. This total includes home stay facilities with one to five rooms and shared baths, mainstream B & Bs with five to twenty-five rooms, and larger country inns. The number of B & Bs continues to grow in the Midwest and the Southeast, but has slowed in New England and the Pacific region. The growth in B & Bs is due largely to the personalized nature of the service they offer. Unlike large properties, at a B & B the guest is personally greeted by the owner and served breakfast by the chef (often the same person).

According to Thomas, the B & B industry has pioneered the use of the Internet as a marketing tool. Through the development of websites such as "The B & B Channel," a bed-and-breakfast can make itself known to prospective guests at a cost far below that of advertising in travel magazines. Because the market segment for B & Bs includes a high proportion of educated individuals who are Internet users, this strategy has been very effective. A small B & B located in a leisure travel destination like Charleston, South Carolina, or Kalispell, Montana can compete effectively with a large hotel. The same is true in urban areas where B & Bs offer an alternative to large properties. Surprisingly, occupancy and average room rates of urban B & Bs tend to be higher than those of urban hotels.

Châteaux

A **château** is a castle, manor house, or palace. Located all over the French countryside, some châteaux are privately owned and accept paying guests. Some of these properties, like the Château Hôtel de Rieutort in southern France, may offer all the amenities of a sleek, full-service hotel, complete with swimming pool. On the other hand, guests might opt for châteaux that are private homes offering guest rooms, like the elegant Château de Roussan in Provence. Featuring canopied beds, a country garden, and hosts who make their guests' privacy a priority, this château ensures rest and relaxation.

In either type of château, guests enjoy the opportunity to stay in majestic, centuries-old buildings that offer a special insight into history. Organizations like Relais & Châteaux or Châteaux Accueil often publish catalogs of available châteaux to help guests find a perfect match for their vacations.

Courtesy of Photodisc

Châteaux in France resemble large castles, but often have full-service amenities.

Recreation Management

As the United States continues to move away from its previous emphasis on manufacturing and becomes a more service-oriented society, service will become the hospitality consumer's number-one demand. All functions of hospitality—food and beverage, lodging, tourism, conventions, maintenance, and recreation management—are service-oriented and interrelated. Since the crux of hospitality (particularly recreation management, such as theme parks, resorts, and spas) is repeat business, service and all it entails is essential to fostering a guest's desire to return.

Clubs

Yet another market segment of interest to hospitality professionals is club management. A **club** is an association of persons with some common objective, usually jointly supported and meeting periodically. People join clubs to enjoy the company of friends in comfortable surroundings. As there are more than ten thousand clubs in the United States alone, hospitality career opportunities abound.

Clubs have been around for hundreds of years, but most clubs in existence today are patterned after British ones dating from the seventeenth and eighteenth centuries. The Royal and Ancient Golf Club of St. Andrews, Scotland, founded in 1758 and said to be the birthplace of golf, is the forerunner of the modern country club. Today's city clubs are similarly related to English social clubs, which arose when members met over drinks and dinner in local taverns.

For example, the Mermaid Club, founded by Sir Walter Raleigh and attended by Marlowe and Shakespeare, met at London's Mermaid Tavern.

Private Clubs and Club Membership

Clubs have always restricted their membership, whether to alumni of a particular school, residents of a particular community, members of a particular profession, or believers in a shared religious faith. In fact, membership in some clubs can only be obtained upon the invitation and recommendation of one or more current members. Private clubs, by their very nature, are selective.

Clubs have often been accused of deliberately discriminating against women, minorities, and members of certain religious groups. Private clubs are protected by the First Amendment, which guarantees the right of free assembly; however, local, state, and federal laws continue to evolve to control the degree to which private clubs can limit their membership. Many cities already prohibit private clubs from banning members because of gender, race, or religion. One trend which will no doubt continue is the voluntary amendment of club policy to admit interested members regardless of their gender, race, or religion.

Types of Clubs

All clubs, regardless of size, type, or location, share one characteristic: the guest. The club guest is a dues-paying member who has a financial and possibly an emotional connection to the club. Many clubs charge both an initiation fee and an annual membership fee. The initiation fee for an exclusive country club may run as high as $150,000, although most clubs charge far less.[4]

Country Clubs

About 50 percent of all private clubs are country clubs that provide recreational and social facilities, usually in a suburban setting. The primary recreational activity of the country club is golf, but swimming and tennis are also standard pursuits. In addition, some country clubs may offer bocce courts, horseback riding, billiard rooms, aerobic facilities, saunas or steam baths, and other activities for their members' enjoyment. Most country clubs operate at least one dining room, along with extensive catering and banquet facilities. Members commonly hold weddings, reunions, or other social events there. In recent years some country clubs have been built as part of upscale community development projects. The presence of a neighborhood country club may attract a significant number of new homebuyers to a region.

Country clubs sell both full and partial memberships. The **social membership**, for example, may enable the member to use the dining room, meeting rooms, and pool, but not the golf or tennis facilities. Country clubs offer a full range of food and beverage services, including catering events such as weddings, award banquets, and community gatherings.

City Clubs

City clubs promote trade, business, and friendship among colleagues. As the name implies, city clubs are found in cities or business districts. A tremendous variation exists among city clubs in terms of facilities, size, and purpose, but most offer top-quality food service to members and their guests. Some city clubs rent guest rooms, either for short-term or extended stays. City clubs may be organized around a certain profession, such as the National Press Club in Washington, D.C., and the Lawyers' Club in New York City. They may be associated with a particular college or university and restrict membership to alumni, faculty, and staff of the university. Most city clubs do not restrict membership to such a narrowly defined group, but may attract business leaders and professionals from a variety of fields.

Military Clubs

The U.S. Department of Defense provides clubs for its officers and noncommissioned officers. Located near major military installations, these clubs have dining and meeting room facilities; some also have beaches, recreational facilities, and guest rooms. Designated hotel resorts exist around the world for enlisted personnel who can utilize their services at discounted rates.

Yacht Clubs

Yacht clubs are designed to promote and regulate boating and yachting. Typically, the yacht club owns and operates a marina for its members. The club may also operate a clubhouse with dining and recreation facilities.

Courtesy of Photodisc

Yacht clubs provide docks for members.

Fraternal Clubs

Although less prestigious than many city and country clubs, fraternal clubs such as the Shriners, Elks, Kiwanis, and Veterans of Foreign Wars (VFW) enjoy large memberships in some parts of the country. Usually such clubs own a facility that is available to members for banquets, weddings, and other special events. Food services may be operated by the fraternal club as well. Today, many of these clubs conduct annual international meetings that can have more than 50,000 attendees. They represent a significant economic stimulus to host destinations and nearby tourism-related venues, and are a regular contributor to the MICE circuit.

Service at Clubs

The unique nature of clubs and their membership status raises the service requirements and expectations of guests. Clubs, by their very nature and definition, are selective. Members want to feel like the service they receive is a step above that available in other venues. This raises the demands on all those who work for clubs, but especially on the general manager, who must meet a host of sometimes divergent goals. Club managers must have excellent technical skills. Still more important, though, are their people skills.

The first priority of a club manager is member satisfaction. A club manager must be diplomatic, provide exemplary service, prepare the budget, and oversee the entire operation. Most club managers are not recent graduates; instead, they often come from the ranks of hotel management and are at a later stage in their careers.

The job of assistant manager is usually an entry-level position for a college graduate with a degree in hospitality management. An assistant manager might be in charge of food and beverage operations, and supervise the purchase and service of food and beverages in the dining room and lounges. In this case the assistant manager would work closely with the chef, who is in charge of the kitchen, or the purchaser, who is in charge of the expenditure of club funds. Other areas of responsibility for the assistant manager may include the athletic facilities, as well as the security and maintenance of the clubhouse itself. A large club might have more than one assistant manager to oversee specific areas of the club.

For those interested in club management, the Club Managers Association of America (CMAA) serves as the professional association for club managers. Founded in 1927, CMAA offers educational opportunities for its members, publishes the trade journal *Club Management*, and provides a certification program for participants. This program includes a comprehensive examination, in addition to coursework that enables a successful participant to attain the title "Certified Club Manager." For those who enjoy the challenge of providing the best, the club career may be of interest.

Health and Wellness Facilities

The fitness boom has provided a tremendous opportunity for today's hospitality industry. By catering to this trend, resorts and spas are attempting to capture a share of the extensive fitness market. Clubs and wellness facilities also meet current demands for attractive, convenient exercise and healthy-lifestyle programs.

Spas

Today, we use the word **spa** to refer to any wellness or health-related resort. However, the original meaning referred to those resorts with either thermal or mineral springs. Thermal springs were used for warm-water bathing. Mineral waters were consumed for their supposed medicinal value. The word *spa* is actually the name of a town in Belgium that had a popular mineral spring.

Guests can visit two types of spas: resort spas and amenity spas. **Resort spas** are single-purpose spas, devoid of outside temptations and distractions. Individuals attend resort spas to lose weight, increase fitness, reduce stress, advance energy levels, and relax. The cornerstones of a resort spa are its exercise and diet programs, but a strong emphasis is also placed on beauty services, therapies, and relaxation. The basic definition of an **amenity spa** is a spa within a resort. Amenity spas have some spa facilities available, such as exercise classes, facials, and herbal wraps. They usually offer these services in addition to traditional resort, recreational, and social activities. The key components of the amenity spa are the "feel good" elements, although they can include aspects of diet and fitness.

Hot Springs in Virginia and Saratoga Springs in upstate New York are spas that have been popular relaxation destinations for hundreds of years. In fact, both were used by Native Americans long before they developed into popular

Guests drawing their own mineral water at Saratoga Springs in the 1800s.

An amenity spa is a spa within a resort, like Cliff Spa at Cliff Lodge in Snowbird, Utah.

Courtesy of Snowbird Ski and Summer Resort; photo by Rob Seely

spa resorts in the 1770s.[5] Other famous spas are those at Vichy, France; Baden-Baden, Germany; and White Sulphur Springs, West Virginia, site of the Greenbrier resort.

In Europe and the United States, spas long ago gained the reputation as relaxation spots for the rich and famous. They provided luxury accommodations and fine dining, as well as access to their therapeutic waters. Now, however, people look at spas as places to exercise and become more fit, as well as to unwind from stressful lifestyles and be pampered.

A major component of today's spa operation is its distinctive food service. **Spa cuisine**, as it is called, emphasizes low-calorie, low-fat entrees that feature an abundance of fresh fruits and vegetables and complex carbohydrates. Artful presentation of spa cuisine is all important, and using the freshest, highest-quality ingredients is a must. Spa cuisine has become so popular that spa menu selections have been added to many fine dining restaurants, including the Four Seasons, Le Cirque, and the "21" Club, all in New York City.

Fitness Clubs and Centers

Many private city clubs offer extensive fitness facilities, including a running track, swimming pool, weight room, handball court, and the latest high-tech stationary bikes, treadmills, and stair-climbing machines. Historically, some of the country's finest city clubs were organized to provide opportunities for exercise, as well as access to fine dining and business and social interchange. The Downtown Athletic Club of New York City, which annually sponsors the award of the Heisman Trophy to honor a college football player, is one such old-line city athletic club.

YMCAs were founded in part to provide an alternative to the expensive, private city athletic club. Today, many Ys still run a wide variety of fitness programs, and provide lodging and dining to both long- and short-term guests.

Recreational Facilities

A variety of hospitality facilities offer people a means of diversion from work. In this section we will discuss three principal types of recreation: theme parks, resorts, and cruises.

Theme Parks

Each year, millions of visitors flock to regional, national, and international theme parks. Why? Simply put, to have fun. Although this is the reason theme parks are such sought-after travel destinations, it is their attention to service that brings visitors back year after year.

History of Theme Parks

The historical roots of theme parks originate in the fair. Historians note that fairs have existed for thousands of years, and the earliest fairs were probably agricultural shows. Today the agricultural fair is still the most common type held in the United States and Canada. Fairs also usually offer musical entertainment, sports events, and carnival rides and games. In addition to agricultural fairs, international expositions like the World's Fair highlight scientific, industrial, and artistic contributions from various countries.

From the temporary, seasonal operation of the local fair sprang the idea for the development of permanent amusement parks. One of the earliest known amusement parks was Vauxhall Gardens in England, created in the 1600s. Copenhagen's Tivoli Gardens, which celebrated its 150th anniversary in August 1993, is probably the world's most famous amusement park. Tivoli contains twenty acres of gardens, twenty-five rides, and more than twenty-five restaurants. One roller-coaster ride, called the Flying Trunk, takes travelers through a fairy-tale world of Hans Christian Andersen characters. The Tivoli Gardens, visited by Walt Disney, provided some of the inspiration for his Disneyland development.

Amusement parks were first built in the United States in the 1800s at popular beaches. The major attraction was often a roller coaster, originally called a "sliding hill."[6] The establishment of Coney Island in 1895, however, took amusement parks to a new level. Located in Brooklyn, New York on the Atlantic Ocean, Coney Island was (and still is) a popular tourist attraction known for its amusement facilities, boardwalk, beaches, and the New York Aquarium.

Such amusement parks were, of course, the predecessors to modern-day theme parks. Today's theme parks have exploited the thrills of amusement park rides and combined them with the educational entertainment of fairs.[7] A **theme park** differs from an amusement park in two distinct ways. First, theme parks are based on a particular setting or artistic interpretation such as "Frontierland" or "Old Country." Second, theme parks usually operate on a much larger scale than amusement parks, with hundreds or thousands of acres of parkland and hundreds or thousands of employees running the operation.

The primary purpose of a theme park was best described by the father of theme parks, Walt Disney. He thought that theme parks should be clean, friendly places where people could have a good time. In July 1955, Disney opened the world's first theme park, Disneyland, in Anaheim, California. The face of family recreation has never been the same. Legend has it that Walt Disney conceived his theme park idea while sitting on a park bench watching his daughters ride a merry-go-round. He thought that adults should have the chance to enjoy themselves, too, rather than just pay the tab. Accordingly, Disney found a way to manufacture and market fun for every age. Today, Walt Disney's vision has taken his original theme park concept into the international marketplace with Disney World locations in Paris, France; Toyko, Japan; and Hong Kong.

Today's Theme Parks

While the Disney empire is the prototype for the modern-day theme park, many other parks have found or created their own niche in this segment of the hospitality industry. One of a national chain of theme parks, Six Flags over Texas in Arlington, Texas, has an American history theme; Opryland, USA, in Nashville, Tennessee, has a country music theme; and Busch Gardens in Florida has a section with an African theme.

Other successful theme parks are those related to the entertainment industry. Universal Studios owns two such parks—one in Hollywood, the other in Florida—and is building a third in Japan. Audience participation makes the shows popular, and trade secrets of show business are shared with tourists. At the Hollywood park visitors can experience "Jurassic Park," a ride that cost $110 million to build and takes just over five minutes to complete.

Amusement and theme parks have always tried to meet the demands of a public looking for recreational stimulation. In fact, the 1982 opening of EPCOT Center at Walt Disney World in Florida can be directly attributed to the need for amusement facilities for the senior set. The 1992 opening of EuroDisney (now called Disneyland Resort Paris) in France was due in part to the desire of the European community for a successful theme park. The continued success of regional theme parks such as Dollywood in Pigeon Forge, Tennessee; Six Flags over Georgia; and Knott's Berry Farm in Buena Park, California seems to indicate that specialized theme parks have a place in the future. In Japan, indoor water parks and ski slopes offer leisure sports enthusiasts year-round experiences.

One reason behind the success of regional theme parks is the popularity of shorter, more frequent, close-to-home vacations. Regional theme parks are targeted to specific customer demographics, geographic locations, and seasonal markets, and rely heavily on young people as employees. These theme parks are expected to continue to experience growth and success.

Resorts

At the distance of a strong tee shot off the coast of South Carolina lies a boot-shaped island whose allure draws visitors from around the world. Wide, white beaches stretch unbroken for miles. Narrow fairways and luxuriant greens challenge the best golfers. Bike trails meander through stands of ancient oaks with boughs draped in Spanish moss. On this curve is a swimming pool; on that one is a tennis court. Lingering over the island like a sweet cloud, a wisp of jasmine perfumes the air. At the southern end of the island, in Harbour Town, the fragrance hangs so heavily it's dizzying. Or perhaps it's the ring of million-dollar yachts encircling the harbor that sets heads spinning. Welcome to Hilton Head Island and Sea Pines Plantation.[8]

Photo courtesy of Luxor Corporation

Many resorts provide a variety of entertainment—from gaming for adults to amusements for children—at a single location.

Descriptions such as this are typical of the resort industry. Resorts are as varied in amenities and types as are the people who are attracted to them. A number of resorts specialize in golf or tennis, offering packages that enable guests to golf or play tennis to their hearts' content and still enjoy the other amenities available at the complex. The Balsams Grand Resort Hotel in New Hampshire, the Casa de Campo Resort in the Dominican Republic, and the Pebble Beach Golf Resort in California are three that offer such packages.

Other resorts are farms or ranches that allow city dwellers to experience a whole new lifestyle, and some showcase nature at its best. These guest or "dude" ranches take people back to the days of the Western frontier so they can experience roping calves, eating chuck wagon food, and sleeping under the stars in bedrolls. Some resorts are closely tied to the conventional aspects of the hospitality industry in terms of lodging and food service. Others are connected through travel and tour agencies.

Overview and Definition

A **resort** is a place that provides recreation and entertainment, especially to vacationers. Roman spas of the second century were the sites of some of the first resorts. These resorts were created exclusively for the pleasure, rest, and relaxation of their visitors. Until the mid-twentieth century, however, resorts were used and frequented only by the wealthy.

Many resorts began in remote locations, far from any established communities. The fact that resorts were developed in such locations was a prime indicator of the public's need to "get away from it all." The appeal of remote locations, as well as ideal climate, natural scenic attractions, and recreational activities, helped this segment of the industry succeed in the evolution of its conceptual underpinnings. Resorts rank considerably higher than other industry segments in the areas of average daily rates and occupancy levels, although the costs of operating resorts are substantial. Table 10.1 shows occupancy levels and sales per room of the top ten resorts in the United States.

A Special Emphasis on Personal Service

The behind-the-scenes managers and crew members at resort destinations are in the full-time business of bringing pleasure and relaxation to their guests. Their primary goal is pleasing guests in ways that ensure repeat business. Doing that, however, isn't as glamorous as it might seem. According to Tom Norby, manager of community services for Sea Pines, "From the outside looking in, the resort business looks like a world of leisure. But if you're on the inside working to make sure that those here to enjoy it are happy, you're working hard."[9] Still, the hospitality professional in this specialized area will definitely discover a challenging career position, since it is the nature of resorts to respond to guest demands by showering attention, service, and care at every turn. There are distinct differences between catering to the business traveler at a commercial hotel property and meeting guest service expectations

TABLE 10.1 Top Ten Resorts in the United States

Rank	*Property*
1.	The Ritz-Carlton, Orlando, FL
2.	Post Ranch Inn, Big Sur, CA
3.	Wynn Las Vegas, Las Vegas, NV
4.	Montage, Laguna Beach, CA
5.	The Breakers, Palm Beach, CA
6.	The Greenbrier, White Sulfur Springs, VA
7.	Whiteface Lodge, Lake Placid, NY
8.	Wheatleigh, Lenox, MA
9.	The Cloister, Sea Island, GA
10.	The Four Seasons, Jackson Hole, WY

Source: www.luxist.com (May 2006).

at a resort destination. The resort customer is primarily interested in relaxation, pampering, and exploring local attractions. In contrast, the business traveler is in need of special support services, is on the go, and needs to conduct his or her business in a timely and functional manner.

Personalized service is both the boon and the bane of the resort industry. Offering lavish luxury is most resorts' primary goal, but such luxury not only costs the industry a large share of total revenues, but also causes high turnover in personnel. According to Monika Church, personnel manager for Sea Pines in North Carolina, "Many people want to work at a resort—but not too hard. They don't want to work the long hours you have to during the season. Or they may not recognize that the basis of the business is service."[10] Other factors like the scarcity of affordable employee housing also affect turnover rates.

Still, resorts can be quite profitable, and depending upon relations with the local community, resorts can provide significant employment opportunities for hospitality professionals and generate revenue for local businesses. The Sea Pines personnel manager says, "If you display some professionalism and initiative, there are good promotional opportunities."[11]

Resorts Expand Tourism—and Sometimes Create Problems

The ambivalent relationship between tourists and residents can upset the balance necessary to run a successful resort operation. The traditional dilemma is that local residents are relatively poor people who live in beautiful places. They like the money that tourism brings, but they resent the tourists. It's a problem which needs careful forethought by resort developers and continued attention by resort managers.

Industry Insights

HISTORY

John Muir and Environmental Concerns

Photo courtesy of Colby Memorial Library, Sierra Club

Nearly blinded as a boy in an industrial accident, John Muir soon traded the dismal life of a factory worker for that of a nature adventurer. In his first year as an explorer, Muir trekked about a thousand miles (from Indiana to Florida), and the following year he traveled to the Sierra Nevada and Yosemite Valley in California. It was here that the young naturalist dabbled in odd jobs such as sheepherder, sawmill operator, and guide. He fled to the wilderness for refuge and revitalization.

Although Muir had published many essays during his youth about the Sierra, it wasn't until the late 1800s that Muir became a national figure, urging Congress to establish Yosemite National Park. With his friend Robert Underwood Johnson, Muir formed the Sierra Club, established to defend the wild areas of California. Muir returned to writing and composed two essays that proposed a national park. In 1890, Congress created Yosemite National Park.

In spite of Muir's efforts, Congress radically altered the boundaries of the park in 1906. In that same year the city of San Francisco was given the go-ahead to construct a hydroelectric dam and reservoir that would, thought Muir, kill part of Yosemite. Muir is said to have asked, "Are we so poor...that we must destroy what we should love and protect? To invade a sacred place because such a scheme was cheaper than other ways to advance civilization [is] false philanthropy."[1]

Today, the Sierra Club is a 550,000-member club devoted to global environmental preservation. More than one hundred years later, Muir's ideas live on in this group.

Environmental preservation has also impacted the resort industry. A growing mass of leisure travelers become more defined in their expectations of sustainability and adventurous in their desires. Ecotourism rating systems have now emerged that measure resort property integration of eco-friendly programs such as energy conservation, air quality maintenance, water conservation, use of durable service items, provision of hotel recycling bins, environmental cleaning, towel and sheet reuse programs, composting, serving organic and eco-friendly food, promoting green initiatives, educating guests and staff, using alternative energy, offering non-smoking rooms, and gray-water recycling.

---

[1] "Muir & Yosemite," *Los Angeles* (December 1987): 185.

Throughout its evolution, tourism fueled growth and economic prosperity in Colorado mountain towns such as Aspen and Telluride. However, many residents complained of lack of access to public lands, increased crime, and the changing landscape caused by commercial development. In the 1990s,

Colorado residents voted against a tax that had been used to fund state tourism marketing efforts, including approximately $10–12 million spent annually on national advertising campaigns. Residents' concerns about tourism and resort development are not unique to the state of Colorado. Although resorts often bring positive effects, the social costs of commercial development to small communities and wilderness areas can outweigh the immediate economic benefits. Resort developers must, therefore, carefully consider how economic returns on their investment are affected by environmental and social factors. Today, dialogue surrounding sustainable tourism is reaching the forefront of tourism research. It is not uncommon for global conferences to convene solely to explore the impact of development and expansion on local communities and valuable natural resources.

The Resort Industry Today

Today, the resort industry is highly competitive, and major brand expansion is occurring, perpetuating a more segmented customer marketing effort and acquisition strategy.

Graduate Glimpse

JOE VANDEL HEUVEL

Joe Vandel Heuvel's day of work always starts thirty minutes before everyone else's. As a group sales manager at the Hyatt Regency Dallas at Reunion (Texas), Vandel Heuvel handles large groups (from 251–1,000 rooms during peak periods) in the Association and SMERF (Social, Military, Education, Religious, and Fraternal) markets. Each day he has to prioritize his projects and decide which ones have the most urgency. Arriving thirty minutes early helps him to catch up on events of the day and attend to any e-mails or leads that he was not able to respond to earlier.

Vandel Heuvel's main focus at his job is to develop and maintain strong relationships with his clients and try to discover their needs. In the late afternoon, he participates in a daily business review with other directors and managers to analyze all aspects of the business, from room rates to food and beverage consumption.

Vandel Heuvel feels his alma mater provided him with an excellent stepping-stone to his current status. Graduating from the Kansas State University with a bachelor's degree and a business minor, Heuvel became the president of its hospitality management society during his college years, and had invaluable experiences in leadership and hospitality management. He also worked at several jobs and had a summer internship at the Hyatt's sales division during his junior year. He advises students of hospitality, "Attend as many career fairs as possible to connect with potential employers and colleagues."

Vandel Heuvel views challenges as an opportunity to learn to become more developed on a professional and personal level. He is confident that he will be at the director level in the sales division within the next five years.

The changing society in the United States offers what is perhaps the biggest challenge to the resort industry. Even though resorts are now available to everyone, two primary groups are targeted for intense marketing by the resort industry: the **baby boomer** generation (1940–1964) and the veteran generation (1920–1940). The baby boomer generation is the group which desires either a family vacation or an active, entertaining one with a chance to meet new people. Besides this group, another market segment that smart resort managers cater to is the veteran generation, which represents a growing percentage of the total population. In additon, projections indicate that by 2030 the baby boomer cohort will represent over 57.8 million people still living.[12]

Business Profile

GRAND TETON LODGE COMPANY

Trendy Mountain Park Lodge

Photo courtesy of Grand Teton Lodge Company

The Grand Teton Lodge has been welcoming millions of tourists for over forty years. Located in Wyoming's Grand Teton National Park, the lodge is nestled in the Jackson Hole mountain valley.

The Grand Teton Lodge and operator Grand Teton Lodge Company operate under a concession lease with the U.S. National Park Service as part of the Department of the Interior. Much like the great American lodges in Yosemite and Glacier National Parks, the Grand Teton Lodge boasts a rustic décor and Western motif. As a condition of its concession agreement, the Grand Teton Lodge Company also provides an array of recreational services and amenities for its guests, including golf, fishing, transportation, and hiking.

The Lodge Company began in the early 1930s when the Jackson Hole Preserve, Inc., a nonprofit conservation and educational organization, founded the company then known as the Grand Teton Transportation Company.

Because it is a concessionaire in one of the country's national parks, the Lodge Company has an unusual operating culture. It is important to remember that the concession agreement is a government contract and requires compliance with a full range of regulatory requirements related to access, hazardous materials, diversity, and environmental consciousness. In addition, the business cycle in the Western national parks is seasonal and requires high levels of efficiency in operations in order to achieve acceptable profit levels in a short period of time. Today, the Grand Teton Lodge company embraces sustainable tourism practices while carefully marketing nature's best to over 2.4 million National Park visitors a year.

Economic conditions have caused vacationers to take shorter, more frequent vacations. This, coupled with the fact that more families are dual-income households, means that consumers want more for their money. Vacationers generally want at least one of two things: a vacation that focuses on the family, or an educational vacation that will help the vacationer grow in a personal area such as gourmet cooking, wine tasting, or computers.

Today more than ever before, resort developers and managers must rely on more than location and natural scenic beauty to attract guests. Three essentials help define the success of a resort: the reputation of the resort, the attractions of the area surrounding the resort, and the amenities offered by the resort itself. The development and management of a resort area are directly influenced by these factors as well as changing demographics and consumer demands.

Resorts are also looking at ways to expand their customer base. One way has been through targeting the convention and meetings market. By creating new market segments and expanding services, the future of resort management can remain bright.

The Cruise Ship Industry

Technically speaking, a **cruise** is a tour by ship. Some people think of a cruise ship as a floating resort. Others see it as a lovely mode of transportation, a way to visit faraway places while enjoying all the comforts of home.[13] Whatever the connotation, there can be no disputing that cruising is a popular pastime.

The cruise industry is now competing directly with resorts for leisure travelers as the market for cruises increases.

The Growth of the Industry

Cruise lines are poised for growth in the twenty-first century. New ships are being launched, including several with capacities for over two thousand guests. Today, cruise ships and the cruise ship industry are showing significant growth in customer base and offer viable career oportunities for future graduates. From 2000 to 2005 the North American cruise ship customer base grew from 6.5 million to 9.6 million, while the worldwide cruise ship customer count grew from 7.2 million to 11.1 million customers. The majority of the growth domestically has come in the form of two- to five-day mini-vacations. Over 9 percent of the total North American growth between 2000 and 2005 was attributable to shorter vacation getaways.

The cruise industry is one of the most exciting growth categories in the entire leisure market. The uniqueness of the cruise industry is its customer loyalty and targeted market segments. Since 1980, the industry has had an average annual passenger growth rate of 8.1 percent per annum. The Cruise Lines International Association (CLIA) estimates that 12.6 million people cruised in 2007, a 4.6 percent increase from 2006. The largest cruise company in the world, Carnival Cruise Lines, is putting most of its new ships in its European brands, and Royal Caribbean International (RCI) is also basing more of its fleet in distant ports. Carnival and RCI reported revenues for 2007 at $13.1 billion and $6.1 billion, respectively, building on their 2006 figures of $11.84 billion and $5.2 billion respectively.[14]

The market for cruises is expanding. According to a study sponsored by the Cruise Industry Association of America, the cruise market has the following characteristics:

Age	27 percent are under 40
	45 percent are between 40 and 59
	28 percent are 60 or over
	Median age is 47
Gender	54 percent are females
	46 percent are males
Marital Status	73 percent are married
Income	Median income is $70,000

Source: 2006 Market Profile Study, Cruise Industry Association of America

Facilities and Amenities

Most cruise ships are broadening their guest amenities considerably with extra suites, adults-only zones, and more restaurants. Many of the cruise ship lines offer a wide variety of culinary choices and sophisticated entertainment products. The cruise ship line Cunard, with its 90,000-ton, 2,250-passenger vessels, offers fencing lessons at sea.

Professional Profile

SAMUEL CUNARD

Sailing to Success

Born in Nova Scotia in the winter of 1787, Samuel Cunard would become world famous as the founder of the Cunard Steam Ship Co. Ltd. The line began as a mail carrier service that traveled to and from Newfoundland, Halifax, Boston, and Bermuda. With the success of this enterprise, the 27-year-old Cunard solidly established himself and his reputation in the business world.

Samuel Cunard's father, Abraham, was a carpenter by trade and found employment in the Halifax dockyard. Eventually, Abraham and his son built a growing family shipping enterprise, A. Cunard and Son. Samuel Cunard first dabbled in government service, learning the business of shipbrokering. It was during the early to mid-1800s that Samuel developed his interest in shipping. He purchased a deep-sea ship called the *White Oak*, engaged in the whaling trade, purchased land, and acted as the distributor of China tea for British North America.

Eventually Samuel was appointed commissioner of lighthouses, Nova Scotia and changed the name of his father's firm from A. Cunard & Son to S. Cunard and Company. In 1831, the visionary Cunard and his brothers took a financial interest in a steamship known as the *Royal William*, which sailed across the Atlantic. Cunard went to Great Britain in 1839, "determined to seek out and exploit the possibility of steamship service."[1] Having already negotiated a contract with prominent marine engineer Robert Napier of Glasgow to build three steamships, in May 1839 Cunard secured the first of many government contracts for mail carriage service to and from Liverpool, Halifax, Boston, and Quebec.

In partnership with Sir George Burns of Glasgow and David MacIver of Liverpool, Cunard founded the British and North American Royal Mail Steam Packet Co., later to become the Cunard Steam Ship Co. Because the government modified the size, power, and number of ships needed for its mail service, four ships launched the new company—the *Acadia*, the *Britannica*, the *Caledonia*, and the *Columbia*. Each was about two hundred feet long, had 750-horsepower engines, and could carry up to one hundred passengers.

The *Bothnia* and the *Scythia* were the first of Cunard's Atlantic passenger ships to weigh over 4,000 tons. They could carry three hundred salon and twelve hundred steerage passengers. Because its operational costs rose with this increased capacity, profit margins for the company shrank. Even so, Cunard's entrepreneurial skills aided in the founding of the first regular Atlantic steamship line. The British monarchy recognized his achievements by bestowing a baronetcy upon him in 1859. When Cunard died six years later, he left a shipping and cruise legacy that has dominated the industry for more than a century.

---

[1] Francis E. Hyde, *Cunard and the North Atlantic, 1840–1973* (Atlantic Highlands, NJ: Humanities Press, 1975), 3.

Cruise Ships and Safety/Security

Safety and security is a major element within the cruise ship industry. Threats may come from piracy, physical attack, disease outbreak, and/or unstable political conditions present in exotic destinations. The large number of people aboard a ship, coupled with the variability of international destinations, offer many safety and security challenges. Whether the danger is large or small, if the consequences are potentially severe, cruise lines must be seen to take the appropriate steps to mitigate those risks. The issue of risk and crisis management covers a broad spectrum of potential dangers, but it is essential that operators examine them all and ensure they have the skills, strategy, and awareness to respond appropriately.

Cruise ship operators are now taking an even more serious approach to intelligence, security, and strategy. In planning itineraries, for instance, a clear view of the changing geographical risk pattern is vital. Currently Somalia, where there is no effective government and high levels of civil unrest, is obviously a key area of concern. However, it is not the only part of the world where the potential for injury, loss of life, damage to commercial reputation, and damage to the public perception of cruise safety exists. Evasion and defense are two options available to cruise ships threatened by pirates. Among the technologies on the table for consideration are advanced sonic weapons (long-range acoustical devices) which make it difficult for a pirate ship to approach the vessel it has targeted.

Another threat to passenger safety that surfaced in 2005 is of a very different nature. This threat is disease. Its magnitude was highlighted by numerous outbreaks of viruses and gastrointestinal illnesses on board cruise ships during 2005. Like piracy, such outbreaks can have a negative effect in the eyes of the public, so appropriate countermeasures and control strategies are a priority. Illnesses found on cruise vessels are similar to those that occur in other high-density locations such as university dormitories, day care centers, nursing homes, and summer camps. The common factor is a large number of people sharing the same space for several days at a time.

It seems, therefore, that whether the risk management issues facing the cruise industry involve deploying high-tech sonic weapons to repel pirates or washing hands to limit the spread of infection, the most important piece of advice is to cooperate fully with the relevant authorities and follow their guidance. The processes and systems to protect passengers and control risk are in place, and it is up to industry members to adhere to them.

Cruise Ships and the Environment

Most of the cruise industry follows international protocols for environmentally sound practices. The international regulations governing the environmental management of marine operations place strong emphasis on waste reduction and recycling and using cleaner-burning propulsion technology in new ships.

Technological advancement has found its way into the cruise ship industry in many ways. Ships utilize technological advancements to reduce fuel consumption and air emissions. Recently, some cruise ships have been retrofitted to use shore power at the Port of Seattle. While docked, these ships will buy and use electricity provided by Seattle City Light instead of diesel fuel. Investment in cutting-edge emission reduction technology is being implemented in ships at a cost of $1 million per ship. The new technology is designed to demonstrate the feasibility of using seawater to 'scrub' (reduce) engine emissions of vessels.

- **Ballast water and non-native species** are the bane of ship operators worldwide, but the cruise industry is taking every feasible step to curb the problem. First of all, cruise ships travel to open ocean environments to take on their ballast water, so the chances of taking on non-native species are reduced. In addition, the industry is testing a number of new technologies, including the use of ozone, ultraviolet, filtration, heat, chemical biocides, and deoxygenation, to help reduce this problem.
- **Wastewater** includes both gray water, the most common form of liquid waste, which is the by-product of cleaning, and black water, which is sewage. The industry has agreed to discharge gray water and black water only when ships are underway at a speed of not less than six knots and are more than four miles away from port. In addition, marine sanitation devices with discharge characteristics equivalent to those of land-side treatment plants are used to process black water. Some Cruise Lines International Association (CLIA) members have adopted even stricter rules. Manufacturers continue to develop advanced treatment systems that produce drinking-quality water from effluent that should eventually be permitted to be discharged anywhere.
- **Hazardous waste**. Current standards require the disposal of all hazardous materials by licensed land-side vendors, who must ensure full compliance with laws and environmental regulations. In addition, cruise operators are eliminating the use of products that result in the production of hazardous waste materials. Where use of such products cannot be eliminated, procedures are being put in place to limit their use.
- **Oily bilge water** is the result of minor engine and machinery leaks, as well as residue from maintenance. Management of oily bilge water is a challenge the cruise industry takes very seriously. In addition to the current generation of oily water separators, which result in lower oil content in discharge, new technologies, such as gas turbine engines and the use of plasma energy to treat bilge water, now make it possible to reach environmental goals that were not possible a decade ago.

Career Opportunities in the Cruise Industry

Career opportunities abound in the cruise industry. Opportunities range from maritime-specific positions to the full spectrum of hospitality services. Most seagoing vessels are considered to be floating hotels and gaming venues. These ships require rooms division management, which includes front office, housekeeping, guest services, and executive management positions. Food and beverage career opportunities are significant, and include food and beverage director, restaurant outlets manager, sales and marketing, event planning, purchasing, culinary, beverage management, and showroom management positions. Facilities engineering is a growing field, both in the hospitality industry generally and the cruise ship sector. Therefore, chief engineers and engineering specialists are in high demand.

The New Competition

While the ocean cruise business is just one sector of the industry known as "hospitality," today it is sweeping many of the other sectors of this industry aside. The cruise industry is challenging the resort industry and is giving other aspects of hospitality, including hoteliers, a run for their money.

Some experts insist, however, that cruising's competitive edge is slipping and that the cruise ship market is headed to where resorts have been in the recent past—the point of saturation. However, with smart marketing, competitive pricing, and the creation of new markets, perhaps the cruise industry can avoid the pitfalls experienced by its land counterparts.

Summary

- The social and recreational segment of hospitality is one of the fastest-growing areas of the industry.
- Recreation management has "legitimized" itself into a multimillion-dollar industry.
- Bed-and-breakfasts, châteaux, and other unique lodging facilities offer alternatives to standard hotels.
- The different types of clubs include country clubs, city clubs, yacht clubs, military clubs, and fraternal clubs.
- Spas are fitness or health-related resorts where one can lose weight, increase fitness, or relieve stress. Amenity spas may have some health maintenance facilities, but specialize in recreational and social pampering and wellness programs.
- Regional theme parks expect continued success as people take shorter, closer-to-home vacations serving the family segment. Attention to service has ensured repeat visitors to these theme parks.
- A resort's success depends upon its reputation, the attractions of the surrounding area, and the amenities offered by the resort.
- Resorts are trying to reclaim their share of a saturated market through marketing strategies that include image improvement, aggressive promotion packaging, expansion of services, and creation of new markets.

- Cruise ships are "floating palaces" that are giving the hotel and resort industry new competition. They reach exotic worldwide destinations and offer a complete range of product experiences, complete with amenities often found in hotels and lodging facilities.

ENDNOTES

[1] John P. Robinson and Geoffrey Godbey, *Time for Life: The Surprising Ways Americans Use Their Time* (University Park: Pennsylvania State University Press, 1997).
[2] Ibid.
[3] James Zoltak, "Academician Schools IAAPA Delegates on Leisure Trends," *Amusement Business* (November 30, 1998).
[4] Club Managers Association of America, 1992 Operations and Financial Data Survey (Alexandria, VA: Club Managers Association of America, 1992), 41.
[5] "Taking the Waters: Ancestral American Spas," *Food Arts* (January/February 1991): 44.
[6] Judith Adams and Edwin Perkins, *The American Amusement Park Industry* (Boston: Twayne Publishers, 1991).
[7] Burton Benedict, *The Anthropology of World's Fairs* (Brookfield, Vt.: Ashgate Publishing Company, 1983).
[8] Michael Stanton, "Working on Fantasy Island: A Visit to Hilton Head," *Occupational Outlook Quarterly* (Winter 1990): 2.
[9] Stanton, 3.
[10] Ibid. at 5.
[11] Ibid.
[12] http://www.census.gov.
[13] M. T. Schwartzman, "Lines Add to Roster of Exotic Port Calls Due to Client Demand," *Travel Weekly* (August 5, 1991): C11.
[14] http://www.cruising.org/press/overview%202006/2.cfm.

CHECK YOUR KNOWLEDGE

1. Identify the three major types of leisure activities and explain how they relate to the hospitality industry.
2. Compare and contrast three types of alternative resort products.
3. Identify three specialized hospitality sectors related to recreation.
4. Identify two types of facilities that cater to clients interested in health and fitness.
5. Identify five elements that make a resort eco-friendly.

APPLY YOUR SKILLS

1. The Tara Hill Country Club charges a $15,000 initiation fee for full membership, as well as $3,000 in yearly dues. Those not wanting to take advantage of the golf course can purchase social memberships for $7,500 and have their yearly dues reduced by one-third. If the 280 current members voted to receive 12 new regular members and 8 new social members, what would be the total of the new members' fees? If the club must take in at least $325,000 annually in new member dues, how many more new regular members will the club need to receive in order to make their budget?

2. The Seaspray Cruise Line decides to build a new cruise ship, which will be completed in three years. Anticipated cost to the cruise line is approximately $150,000 per berth for each two-berth cabin. If the ship contains 800 cabins, what will be the cost of the ship? If 200 of these cabins will be reserved for the crew, what percent of rooms will be available for passengers? If 300 crew members sailed with 1,500 passengers aboard, what would be the ratio of crew members to passengers?

INTERNET EXERCISES

1. Imagine that you are planning a vacation trip by car and plan to stay in bed-and-breakfasts along the way. Select your imaginary destination and a minimum of three intermediate stopping points. Using the Internet, identify the B & Bs where you would most like to stay. Print out the relevant information.
2. You plan a cruise along the western coast of Canada and into Alaska. Select a cruise using information provided on the Internet. Print out the relevant information.

WHAT DO YOU THINK?

1. Do you think recreation management will continue to grow? Why or why not?
2. Which of the six interdependent areas of specialization within recreation management do you think has the most income and growth potential? Why?
3. Why do you think hospitality's specialized segments are considered to be growing fast?
4. What are some of the drawbacks of a career in the social and recreation segment of hospitality?

CASE STUDY

Welcome to Desert Sands, New Mexico. You have been hired by a resort manager to do a feasibility study for the development of a new 1,000-acre resort on the outskirts of a small town whose main industry has been the disposal of hazardous waste.

1. What specific areas will you include in your study?
2. Assuming the resort opens, what do you feel are its ethical obligations to guests in regard to informing them of the presence of hazardous wastes?
3. After the resort has been in operation for several years, local residents begin to resent the influx of tourists. What measures do you suggest the resort employ to appease the locals?

ch11

Global Gaming and Casino Operations

OVERVIEW

This chapter begins by looking at and identifying a cycle for the legalization of casinos that transcends time, and then discusses the history of gambling worldwide. Narrowing down the scope, this chapter then examines how American casinos are different from other global ventures and who the major casino companies are today. It discusses the pros and cons of allowing casinos to open as the legalization of new jurisdictions slows down in America following a series of industry mergers. The chapter ends by discussing the details of gaming operations and the career opportunities they offer.

In the industry, the words gaming and gambling are used interchangeably. Many dictionaries also use the terms as synonyms. The word **gaming** actually dates back to 1510, predating the word *gambling* by 265 years. However, *gambling* has often been used as a term of reproach leveled against people who played for money. Nevada regulations refer to casinos as part of the gambling industry. However, in Louisiana, gambling is illegal according to state laws, so casinos practice the art of "gaming." Another word that is used in relation to casinos is *recreation*. Back around 1990, Steve Wynn, a major mover and shaker in the casino industry, said that casinos are only part of the recreation of an area. People

OBJECTIVES

When you have completed this chapter, you should be able to:

1 Identify different aspects of the history of global gambling.

2 List the pros and cons of gambling.

3 Explain the relationship of gambling to other hospitality operations.

4 Identify casino market segments.

5 List the layers of a casino's organizational structure.

KEY TERMS

action
cages
casino host
drop
fill
gaming
high rollers
house
junkets
low rollers
mega-resort
middle rollers
pit
property management system (PMS)

make a decision on Friday night to go to the movies, go out to dinner, or go to the casino. It is all recreational budget money that is being spent.

Many hospitality ventures are looking at adding casinos to their portfolio, so it is important to understand the corporate culture and job responsibilities. There are significant differences between a casino-based hospitality operation and a more traditional one. One of the major differences is that casinos have different levels of service for each customer, so a brief discussion will identify broad casino market segments. Another major difference is that casinos have more layers within their organizational structure than do other hospitality operations. This addresses the primary objective of casino management, which is to protect the money trail. Therefore, although casino resorts employ hospitality professionals to operate hotels, restaurants, and attractions, casinos also employ workers in gaming industry–specific positions. As a result, there are some new career paths available in the casino industry.

History of Gambling and Current Status

To begin, it is important to know a little bit about the infamous history of gambling.

Cycles of Legalized Gambling

Throughout the history of the world, gambling has gone through stages of legalization and regulation. The cycle begins with a government needing money. Governments do not want to increase taxes because the people are already outraged about that prospect. The politicians see gambling dollars as a quick, easy way to make money that their constituents do not mind. As soon as the decision is approved to allow casinos in the jurisdiction, construction begins. Money quickly flows into the economy, stimulating growth and taxes. Casinos then enter the growth stage of the product life cycle and life is good. Casinos make money and enter the maturity stage. However, inevitably a little trouble begins to enter in terms of social problems such as addiction and crime. The public outcry increases as social problems grow. Finally, governments are forced to regulate casinos to appease their constituents. Now that you understand the life cycle, the question is, "Does the cycle always have to prevail? Can casino operators work with social service organizations to prevent or at least slow down the problems?"

Gambling and risk taking have been part of human culture since the beginning of recorded history. Every human civilization seems to have had some type of gambling apparatus. For example, Asians were known to amuse themselves with games of skill and chance as early as 2300 B.C., and ivory dice recovered from Egyptian tombs were made sometime before 1500 B.C. Some say that games of luck originated in Asia and migrated along the trade routes between Asia and Europe.

Even then, casino owners were concerned about employee theft and the ability of their clients to pay their gambling debts. The proprietors had their own network of informers to keep track of their employees. In addition, the owners wanted to know about the private lives and fortunes of their millionaire clients from Hong Kong and Singapore, especially since wealthy gamblers were comped (accommodated free of charge) in some places—a privilege that included rooms, meals, girls, and opium. "The world would not be the world if it did not play fantan."[1] according to one Korean proverb. However, Asian gaming was perceived as fraught with danger. For example, for Americans, Macao represented a "gambling hell." This stereotype originated "in a French film made by Jean Delannoy in 1939. The film depicted an impenetrable jungle where opium dealing, gambling, and prostitution were rife. The stereotyped setting—the hero plunged into a baffling sinister world controlled by inscrutable Orientals—was an ideal way to bring fresh life to the genre of the detective film."[2]

However, the plot was exciting, and American filmmakers began to use this stereotype in their movies. It helped that Macao already had a sinister reputation and gambling had been a way of life there as early as the mid-1700s. For strangers, playing in Macao had interesting differences from Western-style gambling. For example, in blackjack, a perfect stranger could grab a player's shoulder and place his bet on top of the existing bet, effectively raising the stakes. Then, the highest bidder would continue the game and the original gambler would be cut out of the action. Even as late as 2000, people described Macao as seedy and tiny. However, in 2003, Macao embarked on a tourism/gambling economic drive. It wanted to be a global recreation capital with gambling at its heart. Notwithstanding its size of thirty square kilometers, casino developers came flocking to its shores.

Asian Casino History

Currently, Asia is booming with mega-casino projects. According to the International Gaming and Wagering Business (IGWB) trade publication, in August 2007, the Venetian Macao opened with 16,000 employees, which is almost 5 percent of the total labor force. In nearby Singapore, Resorts World at Sentosa, the Singapore recreation island, is in the process of building a complex of six hotels,

Southeast Asia's first Universal Studios theme park, and the world's largest oceanarium. The Las Vegas Sands is building another **mega-resort** in Singapore, located in the city-state's main business district. In Vietnam, Pearl of Asia Development Corp. is building a $9 billion luxury entertainment complex that will include sports facilities, a concert area, a world-class health center, parks, gardens, and of course, a world-class high-stakes casino. Illustrative of the product life cycle described earlier, "Taiwan's economy is slumping and the new President Ma Ying-Jeou is reported to be ready to push for casino legalization."[3] Indonesia is another country rethinking its decision to forbid casinos. While these Asian nations have been considering reinventing themselves with gaming, Australia, which is considered to be geographically Asian, has been developing gaming at a fast pace, and some say the country's industry is now in its maturation stage. The 2008 economic uncertainty felt world-wide may significantly affect on-going global economic activity. Only those enterprises capable of weathering the storm will survive until the next economic cycle occurs.

European Casino History

On the European history side, gambling was always associated with predictions and the aristocracy. In Greek mythology, when a person wanted to make a difficult decision, he or she went to the oracle to ask for guidance. For example, if a maiden wanted to get married, she would pray at the temple of Aphrodite (the goddess of love) for advice. The high priestess would also pray and ask for a sign. A die or two dice would then be tossed, and the gods would express their wishes through the number that came up. Usually, it was the rich and famous that consulted the oracle.

In Rome, gambling occurred more often at the mineral spas and baths where people soaked in the waters to be healed. Betting on cards and dice was prevalent: they were readily available, easy to transport, and helped while the time away. In addition, the possibility of winning a bigger fortune by using one's skills and wits was exciting. A person could get physically well, increase his fortune, and improve his mental facilities simply by going to the baths. The rich, who did not have to work, were constantly looking for distractions from the boredom of their lives. Betting relieved that monotony. As a result, gambling developed as a pastime for the aristocracy. However, the religious authorities took a dim view of such distractions.

Part of the worry about gambling stemmed from the possibility that young aristocrats would gamble away their entire fortunes in a different country. If this happened, foreigners would own the major estates. Therefore, in 1710, the Statute of Anne made gambling debts legally uncollectible under British common law. This was to prevent the British aristocracy from losing its wealth to the "wrong" people. This law applied to all British colonies and was used well into the twentieth century as a way to prevent casinos from collecting their winnings.

In polite French company, casinos had spawned rumors about card sharks and suicides. The theater frequently denounced gambling, presenting dramas about the gambler who ruins his loving spouse and squanders his children's birthright. As a result of the public pressure, France signed a decree banning gambling and casinos on the night of December 31, 1837.

At about the same time, there were twenty-four casinos in Germany. A similar wave of prohibitions and formal notices followed, and Germans were required to close their casinos in 1848. However, a year later, the governors of Baden authorized the reopening of the town's gaming rooms because its economic development depended on the money. As a result, Baden-Baden continued to prosper. Today Casino Baden-Baden in western Germany is known as one of the most beautiful and opulent casinos in the world. Characterized as a "mini–Versailles Palace," it offers morning sightseeing tours so that visitors can see not only the elaborate gaming rooms, but also the magnificent decorations and paintings, which rival any art treasures found in a museum.

Francois Blanc made his fortune owning a series of German casinos. He was so successful at his trade that in the early 1860s, Charles III of Monaco went to him to work out a deal. It seems that Charles III was in financial difficulties and wanted to create a casino monopoly in Monaco, so he made a deal with Francois Blanc to set up a casino in a new town, Monte Carlo. The casino association took full responsibility for the infrastructure of the town and, in exchange, Monaco citizens were forbidden to gamble. Francois maintained his golden touch at running casinos and Monte Carlo became the place for the rich and famous to party and gamble.

Today, gambling halls in Europe are maintaining a relatively stable environment. The Cyprus-based Rizio Entertainment Group operates 160 gaming clubs in Germany and casinos in fifteen other countries, and just added slot

Monte Carlo casino in Monaco.

machine halls in Serbia. "Foreign gaming outlets are showing quite high sales growth and also high profitability,"[4] Chief Executive Oleg Boyko says. On the other hand, in the Netherlands, the state-owned monopoly Holland Casinos is finding that while it has more visitors, its guests are spending less money per visit. Additionally, Russia, once the world's fastest-growing casino market, is going through unstable political times, and as a result gaming companies there are looking to expand into Western and Eastern Europe.

South American Casino History

In South America, gaming is growing, but there are legal concerns. Chile has entered the list of countries allowing gambling, with eight projects opening in 2008 and another six slated to open in 2009. On the other hand, Venezuela has been cracking down on illegal operations by imposing stricter license renewal rules and suspending new license distributions until 2011. Regulations promulgated in Ecuador in 2002 stipulated that casinos could only operate in hotels; however, new regulations promulgated in 2004 did not include this mandate. As of this writing the Gran Casino Guayaquil was under construction and on track for an October 2008 opening, but no one is sure whether the casino is legal. Argentina's Cordoba Province is shutting down its unprofitable government-owned casino in Alta Gracia. "Provincial Secretary Ricardo Sosa said the casino lost US $475,000 in 2007 and started 2008 with a loss of more than $120,000."[5]

North American Casino History

Both Native American and European colonial gambling history and culture shaped early American views and practices. Native Americans, believing that gods determined their luck and chance, developed games and language related to gambling, while the British colonization of America was partly financed through various lottery game proceeds beginning in the early seventeenth century, when the Pilgrims started a lottery to help fund their voyage to the New World. Unfortunately, the organizers became greedy and were run out of town on a rail, but not before the money was used to pay for the supplies.

Lotteries played a very important part in early American life. When the colonies needed infrastructure, such as safer roads and lighting, they funded them with a lottery because they did not have any taxes. Also, the American Revolution was funded in part by lotteries.

In the seventeenth century Louisiana created the largest lottery in America. Originally, it was to help Charity Hospital in New Orleans finance its care of poor citizens who could not afford medical care. The organizers could keep whatever they made over the hospital's needs. As usual, people became greedy as this lottery expanded across the entire North American continent. It took the full weight of the new federal government to break up the operation. That was about the time when gambling fell out of favor again and was banned across most of the East and South. American societal standards of tolerance versus intolerance, and state laws related to gambling, have continued swinging from prohibition to regulation back and forth over time.

In the 1930s, Nevada legalized gambling again. Some say it was to allow Californians a place to play adult games without jeopardizing their social standing back home. Reputed mobster and creator of Murder Inc. Bugsy Siegel allegedly created the first casino in America. Actually, he was about a century too late, because the first casino was started in New Orleans in 1805 by John Davis. However, Siegel offered free lodging, food, and drink to entice his socialite and movie star friends to come and gamble. The rest, as they say, is history. Now, people go to Las Vegas for a weekend or a week's vacation. Las Vegas continually grows and changes to meet the new challenges of its competitive environment. As its competition has grown, Las Vegas casinos have evolved to become mega-resorts that include some of the world's largest hotels, multiple name-brand restaurants, shopping complexes, health spas, and convention centers, the newest attraction. The latest amenity-rich, upscale, expensive casino is Steve Wynn's Wynn Resort.

World-class attractions are no longer available in just one place. Las Vegas boasts that it can recreate any world-class attraction. The art museums of Paris, Amsterdam, and New York are recreated at the Bellagio in its world-class art museum. Broadway-style musicals can be found at New York New York Casino. Renowned restaurants with notable chefs have opened outlets in multiple casinos. The Eiffel Tower, the desert sands, New York's Coney

Wynn hotel and casino, Las Vegas.

Island roller coaster and Stock Exchange, the pyramids of Egypt...if you can name it, it can be found on the Las Vegas Strip.

Las Vegas was so successful that when Atlantic City, New Jersey found itself penniless and without its resort clientele, it asked to be the only city in New Jersey to have casinos. Twelve casinos were allowed to operate by a law passed in 1976, and the first opened in 1978. Atlantic City was an instant hit because it was located in the midst of the densely populated Northeast Corridor. Depending on traffic conditions, the driving time to Atlantic City is up to two hours from Philadelphia, Pennsylvania and New York City, and three to four hours from Hartford and New Haven, Connecticut and Washington, D.C. To attract still more drive-in traffic, Atlantic City created a new market niche: the bus tour. People came from all over the eastern seaboard and the Midwest. A bus could leave Cleveland at 7:00 P.M. with food, drink, and entertainment for everyone. Passengers would then sleep on the bus; when they awoke, the casinos awaited them. They could enjoy the boardwalk and the free lunch buffet and gamble with the free $20 in chips they received when they got off the bus. When they were tired, they climbed back on the bus to sleep until they got home. It was an inexpensive, easy way to relax and enjoy the town. It took a while, but Atlantic City has now begun to improve its image with civic improvements and a new convention center to attract meetings. In 2008, there were eleven casinos operating, with the newest and brightest being the Borgata.

Native American Casino History

By 1988, most of the Native American population in the United States was in a state of poverty. Technically, they were citizens of sovereign nations within the American nation. That meant that they did not pay taxes, but neither did they get any assistance from the state governments of the states where they resided. In 1988, the Indian Gaming Regulatory Act changed everything. It allowed gaming on Indian reservations, provided that each tribe negotiated in good faith with the relevant state government to create a compact (contract). Foxwoods Casino in Ledyard, Connecticut was the first Native American casino to open under the new law. Led by one of the few Native Americans to earn a doctorate in business, Foxwoods became one of the most successful and most profitably run casinos in the world. The Mohegan Sun casino in Uncasville, Connecticut also has found a niche.

While there are many Native American casinos, not all are profitable. Some are glorified bingo parlors and others have gone bankrupt. And, contrary to popular perceptions, not all tribes want a casino. Some believe that it is not right to make money in that fashion. While many jurisdictions are still working on compacts, the largest compact to date is in the state of California. California has always had Native American poker parlors, but extending gaming to include casinos has been disputed for many years. With so many casinos opening up, some forecasters are worried that Las Vegas will lose its place as the Mecca of gambling.

Riverboat Casino History

The last type of gambling in America is the riverboats. In 1812 the first steamboat, the *New Orleans*, made its way up the Mississippi River. By 1860, just before the Civil War, there were over seven hundred steamboats making their way up and down the river. Since the Mississippi River was the main route to get plantation products to the docks in New Orleans, these boats were packed with all kinds of travelers. However, there was not much to do on board other than gamble, so many cheats as well as businessmen frequented the tables. As with many changes, several things happened around the same time. Gold was struck in California; trains became a new, faster mode of transportation; and the Civil War made riverboats an unsafe way to travel. So the riverboat slowly faded from use.

Then, in the late 1980s, economic hardship struck the Midwest. Manufacturers, the backbone of the region's economy, began to move their factories offshore to take advantage of cheaper labor in Asia. Unemployment was in the double digits, state governments needed capital and new revenue sources, and state residents needed jobs. In keeping with the tradition of the gambling life cycle, casinos were identified as the way to revitalize the economy. Therefore, in 1989, the first riverboat casino began to ply the Mississippi River, operated by the state of Iowa. Within a four-year period, the states of Illinois, Mississippi, Louisiana, Missouri, and Indiana all approved riverboat casinos. Riverboats were seen as a way to contain gambling and its negative effects within a small area, while providing a statewide economic benefit.

American Casinos—Current Status

In America, the benefits from casinos have been impressive. There are 467 commercial casinos in twelve states plus 424 Native American casinos in twenty-nine states.[6] As the state governments had hoped, the casinos earned $34.13 billion in gross gaming revenues in 2007, which was a 5.3 percent increase over the previous year. The largest growth in gross gaming revenues occurred in Iowa (16.2 percent) and Mississippi (12.5 percent). Iowa's earnings growth was a result of opening one new operation and the first full year of operations for three others. For Mississippi, this was the first full year of operations since Hurricane Katrina destroyed the Gulf Coast. In the fourth quarter of 2007, growth slowed in some states. This was blamed on the economic slowdown, increased competition, and changes in local smoking laws. Many jurisdictions required non-smoking gaming rooms, in keeping with the social push for non-smoking public facilities.

In 2007, commercial casinos employed over 360,818 people and generated $5.68 billion in direct taxes. This was the first year where national commercial casino wages were tracked for the State of the States survey. There were significant employment increases in Iowa (7.2 percent), Missouri (11.6 percent), and Michigan (9.9 percent). On the other hand, New Jersey, Nevada, and Illinois all experienced decreases in employment in 2007 as the result of a complex set of economic factors. Nationally, casino workers earned $13.8 billion in wages (including benefits and tips). This was a 3.8 percent increase over 2006 and a 26.6 percent increase over 2000 figures.

These increases in taxes, employment, and wages were made possible by the 54.5 million Americans who visited casinos in 2007. These consumers made 376 million casino trips, which was 5 million more than in 2006. To add some perspective to this consumer spending, people spent less on commercial casinos than they did on home remodeling, quick-service meals, cable television, or soft drinks, but more than they did on movie tickets, candy, or computer and video game software.[7]

Casinos are a unique industry because their reputation has been less than socially acceptable, yet despite this perception, the casino business has grown rapidly. As a result, this industry continually requires new employees. Obviously, it needs people for gaming operations, but keep in mind that the employment numbers cited in the preceding few paragraphs do not include workers at the major hospitality operations that are affiliated with casinos, including hotels, restaurants, entertainment, recreation, and meetings/conventions.

Business Profile

WEATHERING THE STORMS: HARRAH'S NEW ORLEANS

In the early 1990s, New Orleans, Louisiana wanted to have one land-based casino. Originally, it was created with a Louisiana-based group and Harrah's Entertainment. From the beginning, the project was a series of storms. Politicians really wanted the casino, and so the feasibility studies for the project estimated that it would generate gaming revenues in a range from $500 million to $1.2 billion.

Residents were afraid that gambling would take over the city and New Orleans would lose its charm, historical values, and fabulous restaurants. The New Orleans Restaurant Association and the Louisiana Hotel/Motel Association, perceiving the casino as a potential threat to local business, banded together to lobby the legislature for a clause that said that the casino could not have its own hotel and could only operate a small restaurant/cafeteria for the casino patrons. They won.

At the insistence of government officials, a temporary casino opened in 1995 in the old Municipal Auditorium. However, it was in an economically depressed area of the city and lasted only seven months before filing for bankruptcy. The permanent downtown casino, at the foot of Canal Street, opened in October 1999 after many delays that more than doubled its cost.

In 2000, gaming revenues (before expenses) totaled $254 million, $100 million of which went to pay the state casino tax. Net revenues were further decreased by $12.5 million rent paid to the city of New Orleans and over $3 million for "social" costs like police details and fees paid to the City of New Orleans Marketing Corporation. By 2001, this casino, too, had declared bankruptcy.

To try to restore the casino's viability, the state casino tax was sliced virtually in half. The original minimum of $100 million was reduced to $50 million or 21.5 percent of gaming revenue in the first year, whichever was higher. The minimum then escalated to $60 million for the

Continues. . .

Continued. . .

next four years. The casino also emerged from bankruptcy with the rights to build a 450-room hotel and add restaurant and entertainment venues, a significant concession.

Harrah's Entertainment Inc. took full control of the casino in late 2002. Harrah's New Orleans prospered. It looked as if the casino would be all right. Then, three years later, on August 29, 2005, another disaster occurred.

Hurricane Katrina was the storm New Orleans residents believed would never happen. There had been plenty of hurricane threats over the years, but none that caused more than a temporary setback to the residents. Therefore, when Hurricane Katrina actually hit New Orleans, it was a total shock. Harrah's New Orleans closed just before the storm, and luckily, its physical plant sustained very little damage. As a result, the building was used by first responders as a base of operations after the storm.

Because rescue people, insurance adjusters, and government officials poured into the area and few entertainment venues had reopened, some opened before Christmas and experienced an amazingly profitable period. However, Harrah's New Orleans waited to open until February 17, 2006, just before Mardi Gras. There was no housing for its employees; there was a lack of tourists; and New Orleans East, where many of the regular gamblers lived, had been decimated.

However, Harrah's Entertainment, in keeping with its "employees first" corporate culture, created makeshift emergency shelters and information centers so that employees had safe places to stay, basic necessities, and resources to help them locate housing and family members. Harrah's employees worldwide offered financial support and the Harrah's Foundation started the Harrah's Employee Recovery Fund with a $1 million contribution. Ultimately, the fund reached $6.6 million thanks to generous employees, customers, business partners, community leaders, and Harrah's entertainers, supplemented by an additional $500,000 gift from the foundation.

Harrah's Entertainment finished what had they started before Hurricane Katrina, building the first completely new hotel project in New Orleans since Hurricane Katrina. The twenty-six–story, 450-room hotel opened on September 21, 2006 and within the year earned AAA's four-diamond rating along with a place in *Condé Nast Traveler*'s listing of the top 100 best hotels on the U.S. mainland.[1] In addition, for the first part of 2007, Harrah's New Orleans casino revenues were 13.6 percent higher than 2005 pre-Katrina revenues.[2]

In August 2008, just before the three-year anniversary of Hurricane Katrina, Hurricane Gustav threatened, causing the evacuation of New Orleans and the temporary closing of Harrah's New Orleans. Gustav had much less impact than Katrina, and Harrah's New Orleans quickly got back to doing business, having weathered another storm.

---

[1] http://www.reuters.com/article/pressRelease/idUS04145+30-Nov-2007+PRN20071130

[2] Rivlin, G., (2008) Casinos Booming in Wake of Katrina Wake As Cash Pours In. New York Times. Retrieved September 8, 2008. http://query.nytimes.com/gst/fullpage.html?res=9C02E1DD1631F935A25754C0A9619C8B63&sec=&spon=&pagewanted=all

Major Players in America

The casino industry came of age in 2005, when several casino companies merged, creating three of the largest gaming companies: Harrah's Entertainment (including Caesar's), MGM Mirage (incorporating Mandalay Bay Group), and Penn National Gaming (which merged with Argosy). These three companies are the current major players in 2008.

The story of Harrah's Entertainment began in 1937, when William F. Harrah opened his first bingo parlor in Reno, Nevada. He believed even then in taking care of his guests and employees. His attention to detail created an environment where the employees worked to create new policies and procedures to protect and serve. In 1971, detailed corporate records proved to Wall Street that he and his business were honest and good corporate citizens, and Harrah's stock was offered to the public. A year later, Harrah's was listed on the American Stock Exchange, and a year after that, it became the first gaming corporation to be listed on the New York Stock Exchange. In June 2005, Harrah's Entertainment completed a $9.3 billion merger with Caesar's, which was the largest merger in gaming history. This made Harrah's the world's largest gaming company, with more than forty casinos in twelve states and three countries. In 2008, their brand names included Harrah's, Caesar's, Horseshoe, Bally's, Flamingo, Grand Biloxi, Harvey's, Imperial Palace, Paris, Rio, and Showboat.[8]

MGM Mirage is a diversified company with interests in gaming, hospitality, and entertainment. It is involved in the operation of twenty-four casinos. In April 2005, it merged with Mandalay Bay Group, its largest competitor, formerly known as Circus Circus. In 2008 MGM Mirage owned and operated seventeen properties in Nevada, Mississippi, and Michigan, and had a 50 percent investment in other properties in Nevada, New Jersey, Illinois, and Macao. Its brand names include MGM Mirage, MGM Grand, Bellagio, Circus Circus, Monte Carlo, New York New York, The Mirage, Treasure Island, Excalibur, Slots-a-fun, Colorado Belle, Edgewater, Gold Strike, Mandalay Bay, MotorCity, Nevada Landing, Grand Victoria, Railroad Pass, and Luxor.[9]

New York New York in Las Vegas.

Penn National Gaming, Inc. began as Penn National Race Course in 1972. In 2005 it merged with Argosy Gaming, whose original property was the Alton Belle Casino. Penn National Gaming's brand names include Argosy, Black Gold, Boomtown, Bullwhackers, Casino Rama, Charlestown, Empress, and Hollywood.

The Pros and Cons of Gambling

Because of the large amounts of money generated, gaming has inherent bonuses and risks. When politicians see the amount of money generated by the gaming industry, everyone wants a piece of the action. From a local perspective, it begins with the construction trade, since a construction company (or companies) will be selected to build the casino. Then, as the hiring begins, people move to the area for the jobs. They need to buy or rent homes, and then they need banks, grocery stores, drugstores, and other retailers to supply their day-to-day living needs. The expansion of the local population increases the need for public facilities like schools and hospitals, infrastructure development like roads, and other public projects. All of these people and businesses pay taxes both directly and indirectly. The government takes the taxes and prospers.

In addition, tourists coming to gamble need hotels, restaurants, shopping complexes, spas, and world-class entertainment venues. In fact, many casino visitors say they come for the food, shows, and other entertainment than come for the gaming alone.[10] This creates jobs for the locals and generates many different tax bases for the government. To meet the needs of the visitors, the new tax revenues are used to improve and further expand local infrastructures that support the traffic. As the commercial base continues to expand, more new businesses open to support the growing number of tourists and locals. As a result, gaming is a very strong economic development tool. Casino development creates an upward spiral that increases jobs, adds more taxes from businesses and tourists, and decreases taxes for the townspeople. When residents see the projected economic impact, they are likely to agree that the positive aspects of gaming are impressive.

However, as with any growth in tourism, this expansion comes with costs. The main problem is rooted in the business itself. Casinos generate millions of dollars a day in hard currency. For example, to convert the customers' paper money to chips and back again, the casinos have many areas called **cages**. They act as mini-banks. At any given moment, the average cage may hold five million dollars in cash. That figure does not even include all the money that is on the tables, in the slot machines, or in the patrons' possession at that moment.

Think about being around that kind of money! Does it make you contemplate some different ideas? It does for everyone. This leads us to the negative aspects of the industry. It is perfectly normal to watch millions of dollars changing hands and think what it would be like to have some of it for your very own. Politicians, employees, customers, and local people are not exempt from this fantasy. This has sometimes led to bribery, graft, money laundering, and other illegal and/or criminal operations, and has given gambling its negative image. In addition, because enormous amounts of money are located in one place, organized crime has always been reputed to be a part of the gambling industry. However, when respected businesspeople like Howard Hughes and Baron Hilton invested their money in casinos, gambling gained social acceptance. Although gambling's criminal background will always be part of the excitement of a casino, strict government regulation of casino employees and owners, as well as the formation of large business conglomerates, have helped to alter the reality.

There are two main problems for casino employees and players: wanting the casino's money and spending too much of their own. Understanding both sides of these issues is important so that you, as an individual, can decide how you stand on each issue.

The first issue is that some people want the cash they see in the casinos. If they cannot win it, they may want to steal it. This is one of the arguments that many anti-gaming advocates use to deter people from voting to allow gaming in their community. They speculate that crime will increase in the areas where casinos operate. On one hand, this is a simple, logical argument. With any increase in population density, problems are going to arise. On the other hand, you can argue that a casino-related crime increase is counterintuitive. Newer longitudinal studies show that crime increases during the introductory phases of casino development, but crime rates actually decrease over the long term. Casino owners understand that the open display of cash is a temptation. The casinos do not want big winners to be robbed, because it is bad for business. People who do not feel secure are not going to come back. Therefore, security and surveillance are a major part of any casino operation. Good security deters people from thinking about theft too long or too seriously.

The second issue is that some people become obsessed with trying to win the jackpot and stay at a casino too long. A select few will become problem gamblers. Problem gamblers tend to follow similar patterns. Usually, they win big early in their careers, and then they chase their losses. This means that if they lose, they double the bet to get the money back. This is a bad strategy and rapidly increases gambling debts. However, less than 2 percent of gambling players are at risk of becoming addicted to gambling. Some researchers have stretched this statistic to 40 or 50 percent of the population.

The key point to remember is that there are many ways to define "problem." Do you become a problem gambler when you spend $10 more than you budgeted, or when you steal to get money to gamble? Keep in mind that problem gamblers are a very small percentage of players overall. On the whole, over 98 percent of the people who come to a casino will not suffer any ill effects from the experience.

10 Questions about Gambling Behavior

1. You have often gambled longer than you had planned.
2. You have often gambled until your last dollar was gone.
3. Thoughts of gambling have caused you to lose sleep.
4. You have used your income or savings to gamble while letting bills go unpaid.
5. You have made repeated, unsuccessful attempts to stop gambling.
6. You have broken the law or considered breaking the law to finance your gambling.
7. You have borrowed money to finance your gambling.
8. You have felt depressed or suicidal because of your gambling losses.
9. You have been remorseful after gambling.
10. You have gambled to get money to meet your financial obligations.

If you or someone you know answers "Yes" to any of these questions, consider seeking assistance from a professional regarding this gambling behavior by calling the National Problem Gambling HelpLine Network (800.522.4700) toll free and confidential throughout the U.S.

Similarities and Differences Between Casinos and Other Hospitality Operations

There are many similarities between casinos and other hospitality operations because many casinos have hospitality operations as amenities. You may not realize that not all casinos are Las Vegas-style. Some are small, plain, buildings that cater to locals, while others are in Las Vegas, with all that entails. Therefore, casinos are all sizes and run from simple to sophisticated and plain to glitzy. But, at the very least, casinos all have food and beverage outlets. However, most casinos are labeled "casino resorts" because they usually have at least three restaurants. A busy buffet in a medium-size casino resort can average 20,000 to 30,000 covers a day. The larger casinos can have twenty to twenty-five restaurants. To accommodate all types of guests, they offer food courts and buffets at the cheaper end and five-star restaurants at the upper end. Many casinos have lured world-famous restaurants like Charlie Trotter's, Emeril's, Commander's Palace, and Spago to be part of their product assortment. Other casino amenities may include room service, catering, meetings and conventions, or any other food and beverage opportunity. Many operations are so large that they employ several ice carvers, personal chefs, and room designers. Personal chefs maintain the high-roller suites. For students interested in working in culinary venues, casino resorts offer a seemingly infinite choice of job opportunities and career paths. Individually, most of these opportunities are available at other restaurants, but casinos have them all in one place.

Lodging at casinos also varies widely. Some have RV campsites, but most have regular hotels. Indeed, some casino resorts have some of the largest hotels in the world, with 3,000 to 5,000 rooms. To accommodate world-class gamblers special penthouse suites are available at some properties. These suites come with their own entrance and concierge, personal chef, butler, and gambling rooms. There are around two hundred whales in the world and their gambling play credit is upwards of one million dollars.

Like other resorts, casinos can have amenities like bowling alleys, swimming pools, tennis courts, and golf. Shopping has become a big investment for casinos because they realize that money can be captured in more places than at the gaming tables. Spas and health clubs are hot commodities at casinos, as they are in most lodging operations.

In order to keep or attract tourists as well as locals, many casinos have entertainment venues with headliners that appeal to their clientele. Therefore, a casino resort can market to tourists from out of state who stay for multiple days, focus on attracting locals who return several times a week for various functions, or strive for a combination of both. There is something for everyone. As with food and beverage, casino resorts offer a wide variety of lodging-related jobs and career paths that can match any regular hotel or resort in terms of employment options.

Why learn about casino operations? Don't all hospitality operations run pretty much the same way? Well, not exactly. Certainly, a good manager can function in many environments. However, this industry has some differences that are important to understand.

Prime Objective: Controlling the Money

Once they have gathered all these people and invited them to spend their cash, the primary focus of casino management becomes tracking the money. With $100 bills and $10,000 chips floating around the floor, controlling and securing the flow of cash is the name of the game. Computers, accounting departments, security, and surveillance are very important in this process. With all this money, there is a serious temptation to walk away with cash that is not yours. Therefore, the organizational structure is set up to accommodate the primary goal: tracking the money.

Casino accountants use computers to access credit information and verify customer accounts. Casino floor people can quickly determine credit lines for vouchers by searching online or calling the credit department. Because money watching is the most important activity in the casino, accounting terminology is important. When casinos talk about profits, they describe them in terms of the process. For example, the **drop** is the total amount of cash plus the value of the markers (credit slips) the casino takes in. Drop, therefore, is similar to gross revenues. The handle is the total amount of money that has continuously changed hands before it is actually won or lost. For example, a person can start with $5, then win $45, and lose $50. The casino counts it as a "handle" of $100. However, the casino win (a figure comparable to net revenues) for this person would be $0.

Why is this terminology important? Because it is part of tracking the money. The money has to be accounted for each time it changes hands. If a casino cannot follow the money trail, it may be losing cash without knowing it. To begin the process, patrons can play with dollars or they can exchange their dollars for chips. Chips are easier to use. For example, $10,000 converts instantly into a single chip. It is definitely less bulky to carry around the casino. Also, the casino would like you to carry around the chips. It makes it easier for it to keep track of its money. Psychologically, chips make sense for the casinos. When a person throws a chip onto the table, the gambler does not perceive it as "money." Spending chips operates on the same psychological principles as buying with credit cards. Signing a piece of paper does not "feel" like spending money. On the other hand, handing over $100 bills to a clerk empties your wallet and you know you have spent your paycheck.

The last step in tracking the money occurs when the gambler leaves the casino. Gamblers must then cash in their remaining chips because one cannot play in one casino with chips from another **house** (casino). This allows the

Casino gambling chips.

casino to track its cash flow from the time money enters the casino to the final moment when it (and the gambler) leaves.

Security and Surveillance

Following the money trail creates a big role for security and surveillance. The temptation to cheat the casino is a strong one, and stealing is not just limited to the players. Think of it. You are a dealer. In front of you are stacks of chips in different denominations, worth a total of $250,000. One chip, the size of a half dollar, is worth $5,000. You are an honest person and you have a code of ethics that says you do not steal from other people. Then you get in a car accident and need a new car, but you have not saved enough money to buy one. If you took just one chip—just a small one, say $5,000—it would be small money for the casino, but it would help you get back on your feet. Would you be tempted? Almost anyone would.

Therefore, the casino has two departments whose mission is to watch everyone. One is the security and surveillance, or "eye in the sky," department. The security people walk the casino floor and make sure everything is above board. Their surveillance counterparts are in an office above the gaming floor. They watch hundreds of cameras embedded in the ceiling of the casino. Every square inch of the casino can be watched, photographed, and recorded on videotape. Surveillance cameras can zoom in on a table and read the face of a coin at that table. If someone is cheating, surveillance staff will make a call to security, who will remove the cheater from the gaming floor. Whenever there is trouble, surveillance can rewind the tape and review what happened on the casino floor.

The second department is customer safety, which helps protect the customers. As we said before, it is very tempting to palm a $50,000 chip, so security and surveillance people design procedures to minimize the risk.

Power Structures

In any organization, a department that directly brings in revenues is considered a profit center. This means that it has more control over everyday operations than do other departments. In a hotel, the rooms division directly generates the money, and therefore is the most influential. What happens when a rooms division manager moves to a casino/hotel? Many casino operations use rooms and food and beverage service as marketing tools or "comps." "Comps" are free items that players can receive as bonuses for playing at the casino. Therefore, in casino/hotels, the rooms division manager does not always have control over how many rooms are in inventory or what price the clients will pay. There must always be a block of rooms available for "comping." One hundred percent occupancy is *not* optimal planning. Most casinos like to have a certain percentage, such as 10 percent, of the room inventory available at all times. As a result, power positions, managerial responsibilities, and goals will change when a manager moves from a traditional hotel to a casino/hotel.

Budgets and Finance

Historically, casinos only wanted hotels and restaurants as amenities. These were considered loss leaders, meaning departments that lost money so that the casino could make more. The casino wanted giveaways or "comps" to attract gamblers to their "house." This made it difficult for hotel and restaurant managers. How do you balance a budget if the casino keeps giving away the inventory? In addition, for high rollers, there were penthouse suites worth thousands of dollars a night that could never be rented out. People could get the suite only if they had a credit line with the casino for over a million dollars. These suites might come with a butler, maid, personal chef, and anything else the party requested. A bottle of Dom Perignon worth $150 was automatically a free part of the wine cellar in the suite.

Luckily, today most casino resorts have altered their thinking. They believe that hotels and restaurants should be profit centers. Therefore, they have given back some power to the rooms division management to make decisions about their inventory. However, there is always that high roller...

Casino Customers

Levels of Service

Have you heard the one about how all guests are created equal? It is true in most places—but not in a casino. A casino provides different customers with different levels of service. It can do this because a casino carefully tracks its money. Each patron is tracked around the casino and the casino documents each of his or her monetary transactions through the use of employees and computers. A casino's large staff of managers and marketing people guarantees that each person will be treated in a way that fits his spending habits. Traditionally, a casino has different levels of service and rewards that depend on how much money one wagers. Like other hospitality operations, casinos treat each patron according to his level of involvement. However, casinos offer a much wider variety of services for free, and the levels of service can be radically different. "Comps" are based on a special formula that each casino generates. To create the information, they have to track a player's **action** or amount of play. When a casino tracks a player, employees and computers watch and record information such as length of time at the casino, amount of money wagered, how often he visits, and credit line. Because this is a time-consuming, labor-intensive process, in the past, **high rollers** (people who bet large sums of money) were the only ones who received ratings and, therefore, were entitled to "comps." However, in the age of computers, the casino generates player information quickly and easily. Therefore, it can track any individual to determine his eligibility for "comps."

With new revenue management software, it is even easier for management to track a customer's spending habits everywhere he goes while visiting a casino/resort. Today's casino manager realizes that every dollar a guest spends on site, whether for food, clothes, spas, or gambling, goes to the resort's bottom line. Therefore, a person's worth may be assessed based on how much money he spends at the casino resort, rather than his gambling alone.

Low Rollers

Low rollers are people who play the nickel, dime, and quarter slots. They only gamble small amounts of money. Bus trip promotions were created to accommodate low rollers. They often include round-trip bus fare, $20 in tokens for the slot machines, and a complimentary lunch at the buffet. While this might seem like an extravagance for the casino, it pays off. On average, each person on the bus will leave approximately $40 to $50 of his or her own money at the casino. This is the McDonald's principle: price low, but sell volume.

Middle Rollers

A relatively new category of player, **middle rollers** (few hundred dollars-to one thousand gamblers), was recognized following the arrival of computers. Previously, casinos ignored middle rollers because there were too many of them, and it was hard to find a way for the casino people to keep track of them all. Now, players can request to be tracked, generally by joining the casino's Players Club. The casino immediately puts the player's personal information into the computer and hands back a Players Club Card. All a gambler has to do is insert the card into each slot machine or table game he plays. Once the card is inserted, the gambler's personal information file is updated with details of his play. Software also keeps track of statistics like playing time, machines used, and amount bet. No matter where the customer goes in the casino, management can follow their action.

High Rollers

As mentioned above, high rollers are people who gamble large amounts of money at the tables. At one casino in Las Vegas, there is a penthouse suite with 10,000 square feet of floor space, a butler, a swimming pool, and a Jacuzzi. A chef is also available upon request. To expedite each high roller's requests, at most casinos there is a special employee called a **casino host**. The sole purpose of the host is to be available for a particular high roller while he or she is in town and make sure that everything is in order. Instant gratification is the name of the game. The host will obtain anything for this guest on demand, no questions asked. Everything is comped. In addition to free room and board, casinos invite high rollers on **junkets**. These are special events and parties. The casinos obtain top seats to heavyweight title fights, Super Bowl games, or professional golf tournaments, and invite high rollers to join them, free, provided that they spend a certain number of hours playing at the casino. So, as you can see, casinos treat high rollers with a great deal of respect and lots of service.

Casino/Resort Organizational Structure

Because everyone is watching everyone else, the hierarchy of power in a casino comprises several layers, which provides additional security. All levels of management are responsible for making sure no one under them is taking money that does not belong to them. At the top are the people who oversee the entire casino operation. Organizational structures differ from casino to casino. In some casinos, a vice president of casino operations reports to a property general manager. The property general manager oversees all aspects of resort operations, from food and beverage to marketing, and from casino operations to finance. The vice president of casino operations oversees all aspects of the gaming experience. Casino operations is likely to include table games, slots, poker, keno, bingo, and a race/sports book. Casino marketing, which includes the resort's team of executive casino hosts, can also report to the vice president of casino operations. Some properties refer to this position as director of casino operations or chief operating officer of casino operations. In other casinos, the role of vice president of casino operations is divided into table game operations and slot operations. In these organizations, a vice president of slots and a vice president of table games each report directly to the property general manager.

Vice President of Casino Operations

The vice president of casino operations has overall responsibility for all gaming departments. The person in this position sets strategy for each department and has a great deal of influence in the organization, as he is ultimately responsible for all the major revenue-generating activities of the business.

Casino Manager

Most casinos divide the tactical and operational responsibilities among three casino shift managers, usually identified by the shifts they work. The managers must work together closely to ensure the department functions consistently across all three shifts, which can be challenging given the nature of the business. While the vice president of casino operations is responsible for setting overall policy for the slot department, it is the casino managers who must figure out how best to execute the ideas. This involves administrative functions, such as writing policies and procedures for the department; scheduling; reviewing financial performance of the department; and hiring and training potential staff members. While these functions are important, the casino manager fulfills equally important roles that include ensuring customer and employee satisfaction, building a strong skill set in the staff, and demonstrating exemplary leadership. Casino managers meet with other department heads to ensure that processes are streamlined and teamwork results where departments overlap. Casino managers, in their day-to-day role, are responsible for paying large jackpot winners, resolving customer and employee complaints, and making sure that the players' needs are being met. Much of a casino manager's day can involve "putting out fires" around the property. However, proper planning and hiring techniques can go a long way in preventing such fires from breaking out.

Assistant Casino Manager

The assistant casino manager takes on the role of the casino manager in his absence. The person in this position tends to spend more time with the supervisory and front line staff. As a result, they are more in touch with direct customer service interaction than the casino manager. This gives the assistant manager particularly good insight into what is going on day to day in the casino. The assistant manager is also responsible for ensuring that the supervisors are performing their jobs satisfactorily. In some organizations, the assistant manager reviews all performance evaluations written by supervisors of front-line employees and writes evaluations of the supervisors as well. Whenever the manager has a question about a staff member, the assistant manager is like a reference book with the answer.

Casino Supervisor

Casino supervisors are some of the hardest-working people in the casino. They have to watch everyone on the gaming floor—both customers and employees—and be ready to pitch in and help when business levels rise. At one moment, a supervisor may be observing an employee performing a task; a moment later he may be paying a jackpot winner, and the following moment he may be speaking with a customer about a complaint.

A casino supervisor who is skilled at employee relations pays for himself in just a few years. The number one reason why people leave a job is that they were treated poorly by their boss. Consider that the cost of recruiting and training a new employee may be as much $4,000. Most estimates say that the cost of an employee leaving is one and one-half times his annual salary—maybe more, because there are also immeasurable costs like goodwill and customer relationships that follow the employee who leaves.

Table Games Positions

Table games are defined as any games played on a table. This encompasses the most prevalent games in casinos, such as blackjack, baccarat (*bah-ka-ra*), roulette, and craps, all of which are played against the house (casino). The front-line personnel for the table games are the dealers, who are responsible for keeping the games moving and for making sure the games are played

A Day in the Life of...

A CASINO MANAGER

David Williams

One of the best parts of being a casino manager is that every day is different. You never know what your day will hold. I learned early on to never say, "Now I've seen it all." Every time I think I've seen it all something happens to remind me that anything is possible. One day you are handling dinner reservations for Rod Stewart. The next day you are explaining to a member of DMX's entourage that "Yes, I know who you are, but customers are simply not allowed to swim in the fountain." The next day you are paying a customer a life-changing jackpot over $1 million. And on Friday you are explaining to one of your best VIP customers that you do not allow dogs to stay in hotel rooms, even if he considers his pit bulls to be like children.

So, I can't give you a description of an average day, but I can tell you what I did today.

Working swing shift, I showed up forty-five minutes before my shift began to spend time with my day shift counterpart and debrief on what had occurred over the past day. Yesterday's poker tournament, sponsored by a local morning radio show, had been an enormous success. Security had only dealt with a couple of intoxicated guests out of the 600 tournament guests. A couple of Pai Gow players had tried to cheat the casino by switching cards in table games. Surveillance had caught them and they were excluded from the casino. This meant I needed to work with our compliance managers and complete the paperwork to permanently exclude these players.

The shift started with a fifteen-minute pre-shift meeting with the slots team, followed by a similar pre-shift meeting with the table games supervisors and dealers. In each meeting, we quickly covered the promotion of the day and what bands were playing in our lounges, and gave an update on a group of VIP guests from Chicago who are here for a baseball game, hosted by two of our executive hosts.

Just as I was starting to check my e-mail, a large jackpot hit on the main casino floor and I headed out to verify the jackpot, sign off on the associated paperwork, and congratulate our latest winner. The jackpot winners were a local couple. They were regular customers and I spent a few minutes catching up with them and celebrating their good fortune.

After walking the floor and catching up with employees from security and the cage, I headed to a meeting with our marketing team. The meeting involved managers from across the property and we discussed next month's marketing calendar, focusing on promotion and events that were likely to drive increased customer levels. I e-mailed the meeting notes to our casino schedulers to ensure we were well staffed on a couple of days that looked to be very busy.

I ate dinner at our steakhouse with a couple of VIP customers who wanted to discuss a recent incident at the casino. They were unhappy about being bumped out of a suite. I knew that the decision to move them out of the suite was related to the VIP group from Chicago. The reality is that the biggest players get the best suites.

Continues. . .

Continued. . .

I tactfully explained the decision, and took care of dinner for my VIPs. Before we could get to dessert, I received a call from the cage. I excused myself from dinner, and wished both players good luck. As always, I let them know that if they needed anything I would be on property until 3 A.M. and my counterpart could handle anything after that time.

I headed to the cage to sign paperwork for a large funds transfer. Once the money was counted, I signed the paperwork and headed to table games to see how business was going. Play was strong and I commended the pit boss on managing the table limits to match our business levels. As the day came to a close, security called with a domestic dispute in our nightclub. When I arrived, our officers had everything in hand. It seemed a husband was unhappy with his wife's choice of dancing partners. Since the shouting match had not escalated into any physical confrontation, I let the security officers finish defusing the event and asking the guests to return to their hotel room for the evening.

I spent the last half hour debriefing the events of the day with my counterpart from night shift. I left knowing that tomorrow would hold a completely new set of surprises that would challenge my leadership, management, and customer skills.

David Williams has worked in the casino industry over the past fifteen years, both in the United States and overseas, and has Native American, riverboat, and large-destination–market experience. He has held positions ranging from marketing analyst to chief operating officer.

according to the rules. They also carefully watch the games for players who cheat. For each two to four tables, there is a floor person, who looks for irregularities and handles most customer conflicts. Several floor people and their respective dealers work in an area called the **pit**. The pit boss is the most senior gaming supervisor in the pit. This person is responsible for maintaining the record of customer activity and handling financial accounting tasks like fills, credits, and closing inventory. A **fill** is when a table needs more chips. Overlooking all the different pits is the shift manager. He does the scheduling, oversees the operations for a specific time, and supervises the floor and dealers. Because of these layers, the games are well protected.

Table Games Shift Manager

The table games shift manager is responsible for operating the casino on a day-in, day-out basis. As the title suggests, a shift manager is responsible for the table games department for one of the three 8-hour shifts in this 24/7 business. The day shift usually runs from 7:00 A.M. until 3:00 P.M.; swing shift is 3:00 to 11:00 P.M.; and night shift is from 11:00 P.M. to 7:00 A.M. Typically, a large casino will have three table games shift managers and three assistant table games shift managers. The assistants take on the role of manager on the manager's days off. The assistant role is important for developing a talent pool of future manager candidates.

Customer relations, employee relations, staffing, scheduling, and talent development are central to the role of a shift manager. However, getting to know your biggest players on a first-name basis is the primary aspect of the shift manager's job. Knowing your customers also sets the example for your pit bosses and supervisors. It is important for managers to be on the floor and aware of everything that is happening. A strong personal tie with employees allows communication to grow and facilitates the exchange of information and opinions about things that are happening around the casino floor. This allows employees to feel that they are a part of the corporation and they have had the chance to express their opinions. This mutual communication allows them to feel that they were part of the decision to implement the new policies. Transitions are smoother when people embrace change because it was "their" idea.

Pit Managers

The pit manager reports directly to the shift manager. As the title suggests, pit managers oversee the supervisors and dealers in a specific pit. A table games pit is a collection of tables grouped together so that customers play on the outside and employees work on the inside. Some casinos design pits based on the type of game, for instance a pit of craps tables. Other casinos include all game types in one pit and replicate this pit design multiple times. The latter design is used to handle non-peak business levels so that the casino can offer at least one of each game type with minimal supervision. Pit managers make the final call on any controversial issues that arise in their pit. As a result, they have to know their employees and the VIP customers playing in their pit in order to make the most effective, fair decisions for all concerned. Over the past decade, a number of casinos have eliminated the pit manager position to cut down on the layers of management and thereby reduce employment costs. These duties are then divided between the shift manager and the supervisors.

Supervisors

Table games supervisors are salaried employees who are responsible for directly watching a section of games. They personally observe how casino table games are played and deal with any customer requests or issues that arise. Depending on the casino and jurisdictional regulations, a supervisor may watch from four to eight tables at a time. At some casinos, supervisors are responsible for dealer annual evaluations, and at other casinos the responsibility for annual employee evaluations falls to pit managers or shift managers.

Most of the time managers are asked to supervise or coach dealers who make more money than they do. Because dealers are primarily compensated based on tokes (tips, also called gratuities), a dealer can earn a significant income over his hourly rate. As a result, dealers may not want to be promoted because a supervisor's salary is quite often less than the hourly compensation plus toke rate for the dealer. However, the other side of the coin is that if they perform well as supervisors, it is possible that at the next level they will be rewarded for their patience, because salaries are much higher. It is a difficult situation.

Dealers

Dealers are a casino's front-line customer service providers. The quality of a casino's dealing team is a direct reflection on the quality of the casino as a whole. As mentioned above, the majority of dealer income is generated by tokes. Therefore, although bound to adhere to departmental and casino procedures, a dealer is an entertainer. It takes one to four weeks to learn to deal blackjack, which is typically the first game a dealer learns. For a long time, in order to work as a dealer in Atlantic City, a dealer had to complete a first-game training that required eight hours a day, five days a week for twelve weeks. This jurisdiction had the strictest regulations because it wanted to ensure that the Mafia was kept at a safe distance. However, it has since eased these training requirements because gambling employment opportunities have become more competitive.

Dealing can be a high-stress job. For every hand you deal, you are surrounded by three people that love you and four that hate you. And who they are changes based on who won the last hand. For example, there was a story in Las Vegas about a woman gambler who was so angry at her cards that she slid under the table and bit the dealer's leg. A dealer's ability to read people

Blackjack table.

and understand what type of service experience they require is central to his daily success. Unlike most service-industry workers, a dealer cannot leave the table and must work through all difficult customer service experiences without taking his eyes off the game. Therefore, between securing the game, complying with a vast number of ever-changing rules, and providing the best service, a dealer's mind must stay focused all the time. Dealers usually deal for sixty minutes and then have a twenty-minute break.

As the hierarchy of the table games department becomes clearer, the responsibilities can be summarized on a continuum of skills from conceptual to perspective. One of the main factors in the success of a business is the effectiveness and productivity of the management team. As employees climb the corporate structure, the skills necessary to perform the job change. Frontline employees such as dealers need to master technical skills to fulfill their responsibilities. On the other hand, senior managers require fewer technical skills and more conceptual and decision-making skills.

Other Table Games Positions

This section discusses positions that exist in some casinos, but may not exist in others. They include such jobs as pit clerk, department trainer, table games analyst, card/dice room coordinator, and dual rate. Some of these positions have been eliminated by advances in technology; others have responsibilities that may be incorporated into other jobs or other departments.

As the name suggests, a pit clerk works in a single pit. His responsibility is to enter information about the customers into the **property management system (PMS)**. For example, supervisors maintain rating cards for players betting in their section of the pit. A rating card lists the customer's name, account number, game played, average bet, and length of play. This information is used to assess a player's worth for comping decisions. The pit clerk receives completed rating cards from the supervisors on duty and enters the information in the property management system. Once the data is entered, all of the information about a guest can be brought up to view instantly. This process allows the table games department to make real-time comping decisions using all the information available at that moment. Recent advances in technology have allowed supervisors to enter the rating card information directly at the table; however, the expense of these tableside rating systems has slowed industrywide adoption.

The department trainer coordinates dealer training on new and existing games. One of the issues faced by casinos opening in new jurisdictions is that dealers and supervisors imported from other jurisdictions have learned their craft under different rules and procedures. The trainer works to develop a standardized training program for each game so that everyone deals the same way. This allows dealers new to the casino to adapt their style to its rules and procedures. A department trainer has the ability to establish a benchmark in dealing procedures for the department as a whole, so it can maintain consistency throughout the table games department. In many operations, one or more supervisors take on the role of department trainer. In exchange, they receive a change in responsibilities to allow them time to do this new role. This allows supervisors to advance more quickly.

The table games analyst interprets table games performance data. He provides timely information on department performance in order to facilitate managerial decisions. Some casinos detail a planning and analysis specialist from the finance department to provide table games metrics for the table games management team. Key performance metrics include drop per table per day (DPTPD), win per table per day (WPTPD), department margins, table occupancy levels, and labor hours, all of which are critical information for the table games management team. For example, the analyst computes drop per table per shift and then compares this information across all blackjack tables on the same shift. This information allows a manager to see whether all the tables earned similar wins. Perhaps one table is significantly lower in the win than all the other tables on that shift. This information can send up a red flag, prompting the manager to check whether that table dealer has had other shifts when the same incident occurred. It could just be a coincidence, or the result of a problem in dealing technique, or it could suggest possible employee theft. It is up to the management team to decide how to proceed.

A protected inventory of cards and dice is central to running a table games department. The card/dice room coordinator maintains and protects the inventory of new cards and dice to be used by the table games department. This is another duty sometimes performed by one or more casino supervisors. As you can imagine, if a person wanted to cheat by marking the cards or altering the dice, this inventory would be critical to their plans. Card and dice storage procedures are normally covered in state or jurisdictional minimum internal control standards. This person is also responsible for destroying cards and dice once they are removed from the casino floor to ensure that used cards and dice do not end up in the hands of unscrupulous players. You may have seen used decks of cards and dice in a casino shop. However, there is a hole all the way through the deck of cards or the dice. This allows the casino to sell key chains made of dice or decks of cards for souvenirs, but the hole is also there to make sure the cards or dice cannot be used in the casino again.

The term dual rate designates a member of one level of the table games department who is qualified to step in for the next level of table games management when the need arises. It refers to the fact that the employee is paid a higher rate when working in the higher management position. This occurs most often at the supervisor level. In this case, an experienced dealer takes on the role of supervisor for a scheduled number of shifts each week. There are also casinos where a supervisor may dual rate as a pit manager or a pit manager may dual rate as a shift manager. The value of the dual rate position is that it allows a casino to cover days off for employees without incurring the full cost of an additional member of the management team. It also offers on-the-job experience for the employee for future promotions. For example, it allows a dealer to learn how to be a supervisor. If a problem arises, the dealer can ask how to handle it by checking with other supervisors when he is a dealer again. Therefore, the time pressure to learn a new job is eliminated and a promising dealer can be mentored into management. The difficulty arises from the fact that one day an employee is a peer and the next day that same employee is a supervisor. Thus, the role of dual rate both benefits and creates issues for the employee and the table games department.

The table games division is very labor intensive and requires people trained in dealing. In order to climb this ladder, casinos want experience in the front of the house, interacting with customers and handling financial transactions.

Mechanicals or Slots

Traditionally, the table games were where the "real" gamblers, usually men, played. Casino operators realized that wives and girlfriends needed something to do while the men gambled. Otherwise, the women would get bored and insist that the men leave the games before they were ready to go. Slot machines were the perfect decoys. The women could sit, chat, and "pretend" to gamble in a ladylike fashion.

Today, slots have been joined by video poker and other computerized games. Because computers have revolutionized the industry, all the table games in the casino usually have a video equivalent. Instead of playing around a table with a dealer, the computer chip is the competition. This is less threatening for novices and it gives them a chance to practice the games. Some machines allow a person to play any table game at a single machine. The screens are user friendly and touch sensitized for game selection.

The quarter slots are the most popular denomination. If you think that's not much, do the math. Four spins per minute translate into 240 spins per hour, and more than one thousand spins in less than five hours. Playing with three coins in a twenty-five-cent machine (seventy-five cents per spin), in less than five hours, a person could wager $750 on a quarter slot machine. In the high-stakes groupings, there are slots in bigger denominations: $5, $25, $100, or $500. Slots have become a bigger profit center than anyone could have imagined. In many casinos, slot machines account for 60–70 percent of the win. (Remember that *win* does not refer to how much the gambler wins.) Casino managers are realizing that this is a gold mine and adding more slots to the casino floor.

Slot departments have several layers of managers. On the floor, the slot attendants supervise an assigned area where they cater to customer needs like change, payouts, and problems with the machines. Slot shift managers are in charge for a specific period. They oversee slot personnel, verify major slot payoffs, and sign major jackpot slips. Finally, the slot manager handles slot operations, verifies authenticity of major payouts, looks for unusual variations in operations, and works on promotional programs. Each manager is responsible for making sure the patrons have gambling change and ensuring the safety and honesty of each machine.

Slot Service Personnel

Different casinos may call the employees who work the slot floor by different names, such as slot host, attendant, key person, or service representative, but the essence of the job remains the same: providing customer service. The people working the slot floor undergo significant emotional swings throughout the course of their shift—one moment they are congratulating winners and the next they must demonstrate empathy for those who did not win. This latter duty can make up a great deal of the slot attendant's day, because the majority of the customers who come into the casino do not win and most want to share their bad luck story with the slot employees. It is the slot attendant's job to convey empathy and yet try to keep each interaction positive in order to coax a return visit from the player. This can be very challenging, because the slot attendant is considered by the slot player to be the face of the casino, and the casino has stacked the odds against the player. Frequently it is hard for the slot attendant to convince the player that he is the players' friend, given that the casino usually takes their money.

At the turn of the present century, a new technology revolutionized the slot machine experience and all the jobs within a slot department. That change was the introduction of coinless ticket printers. Prior to that time, slot employees had to carry heavy bags of coins as a central part of their job. These bags could weigh thirty or forty pounds, and carrying bags all day made slot operations a highly physical task. The ticket-based technology added a printer near the bill acceptor of each slot machine. That ticket could then be redeemed at the cage or a ticket redemption machine, similar to an ATM.

This ticket printer replaced a coin dispenser that had for years made the sound of a winning casino—the sound of coins dropping into slot trays and players carrying buckets of coins they just won across the casino floor. With the new ticket technology, when a player decides to cash out his winnings, the slot machine produces a bar-coded ticket showing the amount due to the player. The machine then plays a simulated sound of dropping coins. The move to ticket printers was a risky one, because the sounds of winning coins generated excitement and inspired players to play more. (Psychologists have done studies that show that people's blood pressure rises with increased levels of noise, which in turn makes them more excitable.) In addition, the noise made them feel that everyone around them was winning, so why not them?

While the goal of improved customer relations has not changed much over the years, the recent advent of coinless casinos has changed the job of the slot attendant in many ways. No longer must the attendant transport bags of coins around the casino floor; now the attendant's primary task is to conduct jackpot payouts. Although the odds are not in the players' favor, the reason they come to the casino is to win, and hitting the jackpot is the aspiration of every single one of them. It is the function of the slot employee, while paying the winner, to build upon the player's positive experience by developing a relationship with the player. Cultivating a player relationship has two positive effects. It may lead to repeat visits to the casino by the player, and it increases a player's inclination to tip the slot employee.

Many people do not realize that slot employees make a very good living because of the tips they receive. In many instances, the front-line employees earn more than their supervisors, because slot employees get both wages and tips. Most slot departments choose to split the gratuities among the entire staff at a per-hour rate. This is because teamwork on the slot floor is critical—one slot employee cannot perform his job effectively without another. This is a difference between slots and most table games, where the dealer has ownership of his game and controls the entire game (except for the luck of the cards). If tips are not split equally among all service personnel, a strong possibility exists that individual employees will circumvent their standards of employment and the culture of the business for personal gain. One way employees could do this is by chasing jackpots. Paying jackpots and filling machines with coins or tickets are the primary responsibilities of front-line slot employees. Employees are more likely to receive tips when paying jackpots. Filling machines typically does not involve a tip. Jackpot chasers search out jackpots to pay on the casino floor, while avoiding machines that need fills. If this happened, it could cause a great deal of conflict and even hostility among the slot service staff, and put the supervisors and managers in very awkward positions. Although there may be better ways to manage the splitting of tips in order to improve production in slots, no one yet has found one.

Slot attendants, in addition to paying jackpots, perform many other functions. They exchange larger bills for smaller ones at the player's request, staff booths where other slot personnel obtain their funds, and handle minor customer disputes. Some casinos may have several levels of front-line slot employees, with such titles as slot host I, slot host II, or team leader, and may separate specific job functions between the levels, providing greater responsibility at each step. This can help those wishing to advance their careers by giving them a chance to develop skill sets for the next available higher position.

Other Slot Employees

As indicated by the organizational chart, there are other positions in the slot department. There will usually be an administrative assistant, who handles obligations for the department such as making sure payroll is met and accurate, purchase orders are completed, and staff attendance is tracked. This person may have additional responsibilities assigned by the casino managers.

Another important position in the slot department is the department trainer. This person works closely with the human resources department to "reel in" new employees after the manager has "hooked" them. Although learning to be a slot attendant is not as difficult as learning some other casino operations areas, it can be overwhelming nonetheless, especially to someone with no casino experience whatsoever. The multitude of policies and procedures that the slot attendant must be aware of, along with the significant amount of cash they must carry on their person during a shift, can cause a great deal of stress to someone with no prior experience. It is the department trainer's job not only to conduct the necessary classroom training (usually lasting up to one week), but to create a positive experience during the training of the new recruit. It begins with trust.

Summary

- Gambling equipment has been found in every human civilization and on each continent, and gambling has flourished to different degrees worldwide.
- Throughout the history of gaming, a general product life cycle has emerged that ultimately predicts the demise of legalized gambling.
- As the product life cycle suggests, casinos create economic growth for the surrounding area but they also bring social problems.
- Quite often, casinos have hotels, restaurants, recreation, and entertainment as part of their scheme to attract guests. Many of these are classified as casino/resort operations because the bulk of their profits is derived from the casino. Because all casinos have at least food and beverage services, many of the same jobs are available at casinos as in traditional hospitality operations.
- Within a casino operation, there are typically more levels of managers than in other hospitality businesses because management's prime directive is to protect the money. Every casino employee has a responsibility to maintain vigilance over their job and over everyone below them in the corporate hierarchy. The security and surveillance department is literally at the top, overseeing everyone else from a high position above the casino floor.
- Casino customers receive different levels of service based on their time played, size of wager, and frequency of visits. Part of this service consists

of "comps" including free or discounted rooms, food, and/or entertainment.

- Casinos offer the same positions as do regular hotels, food and beverage operations, and recreation and entertainment venues. The career paths are similar, but in general casinos pay better wages and have better benefit packages.

ENDNOTES

[1] Tegtmeier, R. (1989) *Casinos*. Vendome Press: New York, NY, 160.
[2] Ibid.
[3] Asia-Pacific. (2008, June) IGWB, 29(6), 8.
[4] Europe/UK. (2008, June.) IGWB, 29(6), 13.
[5] South America. (2008, June) IGWB, 29(6), 19.
[6] American Gaming Association. 2008 State of the States. Retrieved July 4, 2008. http://www.americangaming.org/assets/files/aga_2008_sos.pdf
[7] Ibid.
[8] Harrah's Homepage. Retrieved July 4, 2008. http://www.harrahs.com/harrahs-corporate/about-us.html
[9] MGM Mirage homepage. Retrieved July 4, 2008. http://www.mgmmirage.com/companyoverview.asp.
[10] Ibid.

CHECK YOUR KNOWLEDGE

1. List at least five ways gaming can bring revenue to a region or state.
2. List two reasons why casinos should be part of a locality's recreation options.
3. What is meant by "chase your losses"? Is it an effective strategy?
4. How does a surveillance system work in a casino?
5. List the different personnel in either the table games or slots department.

APPLY YOUR SKILLS

1. Divide the class into two groups, one that is for the building of a new casino in your community, and one that is opposed. Each student should cite two examples from other casino openings to support their position. Have a debate in class.
2. Other hospitality operations like hotels and restaurants provide standard levels of service to everyone who comes to their place of business. The casino industry bases levels of service on the financial worth of each consumer. Which policy do you think should be implemented in your place of business?
3. Traditionally, in hospitality enterprises as well as casinos, the standard is to work your way up the ladder. However, if the responsibilities of management move from skills-based knowledge to conceptual decision making, can a job candidate circumvent the lower management positions

and get hired at the upper levels of management because he has strong abilities in conceptual decision making?

INTERNET EXERCISES

1. Go to <http://casinocareers.com> and search their Web site for current jobs. Find five jobs that are potential career choices for you. Make sure they are with different companies, and include at least one with a foreign company. Be prepared to discuss in class why you chose the companies and jobs.
2. Go to three different casino Web sites.
   a. List three things all the casinos have in common.
   b. List one factor that is unique to each one.
3. Go to three different casino Web sites.
   a. Can you tell what type of market segment each one is trying to attract?
   b. What factors in the Web site's design show you who the casino is trying to attract?

WHAT DO YOU THINK?

1. Now that you have learned about the pros and cons of allowing casinos into a jurisdiction, how would you vote on a casino referendum?
2. Given the cycles of gambling history, do you think that casinos in the United States will continue to thrive? Or do you think that casinos will be more regulated in the next thirty years? What are your reasons?
3. Casino operators have asked that the differences between traditional hospitality operations and casino-based operations be explained to potential employees because they have lost many new hires due to these variations. Would you want to manage a casino hotel or restaurant, knowing the casino management will be able to override your decisions?
4. Dual rate supervisor has been a common job description used by casinos when they want to promote someone to the next level. Do you think this dual rate position should be part of the rest of the hospitality industry?
5. As you read over the ten questions about gambling behavior, did you think of someone who could answer yes to all of these questions? Do you think they should get help?

CASE STUDY

Your state has decided to allow a casino in your town. It will not be located in the city center, but will be on the outskirts so that there will be room to build a large parking lot. It will attract many tourists. The state says that it will bring in new jobs and create economic growth for the community. Another strong group has developed that is opposed to having a casino in the town. They are saying, "Not in our back yard. We like the town the way it is without traffic congestion."

1. What side would you take?
2. What arguments would you use?

The Future and You

Part 5, The Future and You, looks at the impact of the twenty-first century on hospitality and tourism and offers insight into the many nuances of seeking career opportunities in the rapidly changing hospitality and tourism network.

Many factors have helped shape and define the hospitality industry: the global economy, political forces, changing demographics, technological trends, business cycles, guest demands, and government regulations.

Because hospitality firms provide a service rather than sell a manufactured product, it has been said that such companies need to remain "high touch" rather than "high tech." The influences of technological advancement continue to offer alternative ways for service delivery and service transactions to be grounded in technological innovation. The ongoing wave of technological advancement will offer both challenges and opportunities for future leaders in the hospitality and tourism industries.

Building success for the future requires careful planning and execution. Establishing your credentials, forming a network of professional contacts, and preparing yourself for a career in the hospitality and tourism industry will require strategic planning. Understanding the global context of hospitality and tourism related job opportunities is essential. The hospitality and tourism leader of the future will be a leader capable of delivering exceptional service and generating good financial returns in a highly technical and culturally diverse business environment.

ch12

Globalization and the Future of Hospitality

OVERVIEW

This chapter focuses on how forces outside the hospitality network can cause changes within it and discusses the future of the hospitality industry. Global events, such as worldwide economic recession, war, terrorism, rising oil prices, and economic expansion in Asia, also affect the hospitality industry. In this chapter you will become familiar with how the life and well-being of the hospitality industry are affected by (1) economic climate, (2) socioeconomic trends, and (3) technological innovations.

The future of the hospitality industry will reflect the changing face of the population—one that is growing older and becoming more culturally diverse. Technological advances are blazing new trails. Both the increased popularity of gaming and the growing concern for the global environment will make inroads that reshape the recreation segment of the industry. At this crossroads in your journey, it is important to understand the new turns the hospitality industry is likely to take, so that you can choose what path to follow and then work toward your future.

Building a successful future is a deliberate process that begins with acquiring abilities such as good communication skills and computer expertise. Evaluating your strengths and setting a **career objective** are part of the process and pave the way to the next steps: seeking out companies you might like to work for and **networking** with people who can help you find a job. Writing resumés and going on interviews are the final steps in the process. They will bring you face to face with your future—your new job!

OBJECTIVES

When you have completed this chapter, you should be able to:

1. **Identify major factors that affect the hospitality network.**
2. **Discuss the effects a more diversified workforce and workforce shortages will have on the hospitality industry.**
3. **Comprehend the relationship of personal service to technology in the hospitality workplace.**
4. **Define *demographics* and list ways hospitality guests have reacted to economic or cultural trends.**
5. **Name examples of technological innovations and explain how they have affected the hospitality industry.**

KEY TERMS

career objective
contraction
demographics
discretionary spending
economics
ecotourism
expansion
global distribution systems
mega-resorts
networking
peak
return on investment (ROI)
socioeconomic
technology
trough
workers' councils
yield management

Economic Climate

The hospitality and tourism network is no different from any other industry in its relatedness to the global economy. The tourism network usually is impacted quickly by changes in the state of the global economy. Spending on travel and leisure activities is considered to be **discretionary spending** and is often the first item cut from a tight budget. Even business travel declines when money is scarce. In times of a strong economy and bigger budgets, travel and leisure activities expand. In this section you will look at some ways the climate of the economy is analyzed. You will also look at the importance of the international market and some ways hospitality customers respond to economic fluctuations.

Business Cycles

The economy is always in fluctuation, creating cycles of upswings and downturns. These business cycles have four phases—expansion, peak, contraction, and trough. During **expansion**, or growth, economic activity increases. Expansion comprises a rising gross domestic product (GDP), higher levels of employment and job creation, and brisk sales of goods and services. Hospitality developers usually find loans or funding for new sites or renovations of existing sites more readily available during a growth period. The uppermost point in a cycle, following expansion, is called the **peak**. A developer's access to capital is based on expected return on investment. **Return on investment (ROI)** is a performance measure used to evaluate the efficiency of an investment or to compare the efficiency of a number of different investments. To calculate ROI, the benefit (return) of an investment is divided by the cost of the investment, and the result is expressed as a percentage or a ratio. Investment returns vary during growth and retraction periods. High economic returns on investment usually are in the double-digit range, while weaker or more moderate returns are in the middle single digits (6 or 7 percent).

An overall decline in an economy starts the contraction or recession phase. **Contraction** comprises a falling GDP, higher unemployment, creation of fewer new jobs, and sluggish sales of goods and services. The lowermost point, following contraction, is called the **trough**. The economy enters a contraction phase after the peak has been reached and continues through to the trough. The expansion phase begins at the trough and continues through to the peak. The optimal time for an entrepreneur to buy or develop a hotel is at the trough because values may be lower for the real estate portion of the project. However, short-term operational sustainability may require significant cash flow reserves until economic recovery occurs.

International Tourism Trends

At the turn of the twenty-first century, international tourism economic actvity saw a dramatic shift toward the Asia-Pacific and Middle East regions. For example, significant development of hotel and travel-related industries is well underway in China and Dubai. Table 12.1 shows the international distribution of the world's fifty largest hotel chains.

With the wide-open opportunities the growing global marketplace offers, businesses face stiffer competition and more intricate business dealings. They must master differences in culture and language, and complex political and legal issues.

Guest Responses to Economic Fluctuations

Economic fluctuations can positively impact travel and associated travel patterns. Today, low-cost competitive airline fares have stimulated both domestic and international travel. Changing currency rates stimulate travel to one destination at the expense of another. For instance, currently the Canadian exchange rate is at an all-time high against the U.S. dollar. One Canadian dollar is worth about one U.S. dollar today. Only five years ago, the Canadian dollar's worth in the United States was about 60 cents. Conversely, economic downturns can cut into the profits of the hospitality network because customers resort to cost-saving travel strategies. They take vacations closer to home and stay away for shorter periods of time. "Mini-vacations" provide expanded marketing opportunities for resort hotels located near major metropolitan markets. Most "mini-vacations" are for the purpose of visiting friends and relatives. Other popular locations include national parks, oceans, lakes, beaches, and historical sites. Such trips are less costly than extended trips farther from home.

Demographics and Socioeconomic Trends

Fulfilling guests' needs and expectations is key to the service-driven hospitality industry. Sometimes an inventive operator will introduce something so unusual, convenient, or cost-effective that people are motivated to buy it, even though they didn't know they wanted it until they saw it. (See the profile of Ellsworth Statler in this chapter.) But much of the time, fulfilling people's expectations means first finding out what people like. This involves understanding the consumer culture.

What Are Demographics?

The statistical study of the characteristics of human populations used to identify markets is called **demographics**. The characteristics tracked include size and growth of the population, distribution, and vital statistics such as amount of education, size of family, family income, ethnic background, age, and gender. Such research provides **socioeconomic** data—data relating to both sociology (the study of human social behavior or lifestyles) and **economics** (the study of the production, consumption, and distribution of goods and services).

Organizations and universities conduct these statistical studies, but much of what is known about the people of the United States comes from the federal government, which conducts a census every ten years. This massive survey by the Bureau of the Census gathers and analyzes data on who Americans are, what they do, where they live, how they live, and their quality of life. The census has become one of the best sources of information about the nation, providing a fairly complete picture of the population at a given time. Businesses use census reports and other data to predict how fast the population is growing, what the size of the workforce will be, and other socioeconomic trends.

Italian Coastal Resort towns.

Businesses also need to predict cultural shifts in order to spot opportunities or problems. For example, concern for the environment has created a trend called the "greening of business." Quick-service outlets serving hamburgers in recyclable containers and large resorts conserving energy are just two examples of how the cultural shift toward environmental awareness has affected business.

While some businesses may resist change when a trend first takes hold, others jump on the bandwagon to avoid losing customers. Businesses also take advantage of cultural concerns, promoting their corporate efforts in hopes of maintaining a favorable image in the public eye.

Technological Innovations

One of the most dramatic influences on the hospitality network and its guests is **technology**, comprising all the ways people use discoveries and inventions to satisfy needs. The use of technology has enhanced the production of services by making some tasks faster and easier to perform. Computerized property managment systems, restaurant point-of-sale systems, and various food preparation methods are some examples. Technology has also enhanced guest comfort and safety through inventions such as high-speed and wireless Internet connectivity, interactive plasma televisions, automated sensor-based lighting, picture art-mirrors, and kiosk check-in stations. Finally, technology has facilitated people's ability to travel by increasing economic prosperity, leisure time, and the efficiency of transportation systems. Each improvement in transportation—steamboats, railroads, interstate highways, transatlantic flights—has made travel easier and quicker. On-line travel planning and third-party intermediaries have created a more competitive hotel environment that benefits consumers through favorable pricing opportunities.

Technological Management Support

Many technological advances used in the hospitality industry involve computers. Two areas where computers are improving operations in hospitality are reservations and staffing. Most hotels also have sophisticated electronic billing systems that track and record guests' expenses within the hotel, such as those that tally the charges for rooms, restaurants, bars, laundry, and fax use. These systems greatly speed up check-out procedures for guests. Restaurant point-of-sale systems help managers generate greater profits through menu engineering techniques.

Information System Networks

Holiday Inn's Atlanta data center is one example of a hospitality information system network. The $6 million, 42,000-square-foot data center employs 140 people and houses an elaborate computer system to manage the operation of

Professional Profile

ELLSWORTH STATLER

Hospitality Innovator

The story of Ellsworth Milton Statler (1863–1928) is the tale of a man who worked his way up from bellhop to one of the greatest hotel businesspersons of all time. He gave middle-class travelers a standard of convenience and comfort never before available at a reasonable price. His ideas and innovations have since become standard practice throughout the hotel industry.

Statler worked through most of his childhood. At thirteen, he began his career as a bellhop in a prominent hotel in Wheeling, West Virginia, working his way up to bell captain by the age of fifteen. During this time, Statler noticed that the profits generated by the hotel's billiard room and railroad ticket concession were substantial. In the entrepreneurial spirit, he convinced the owner to lease the operations to him, and he began organizing special billiard exhibition games that drew many interested people.

Statler soon applied his business skills to a local bowling alley and then a restaurant called the Pie House. At thirty-one, Statler found new challenges in Buffalo, New York, where he opened a restaurant. At first he had little success; most people in the Buffalo area preferred to eat at home. Many businesspersons would see this as an impossible situation, but Statler decided that if a market for his restaurant did not exist, he would create one by changing the eating habits of downtown businesspeople. He began an advertising campaign, using the slogan "All you can eat for twenty-five cents." He then fired his expensive chef and initiated a series of innovations to turn his business around. He served beans when they were cheaper than peas. He created a service station where servers could pick up napkins, glasses, pats of butter, ice, silverware, and linen without going to the kitchen. He designed octagon-shaped dining tables to seat more people. He is also the first restaurateur on record to have ice water on tap.

In 1904, Statler opened the 2,257–room Inside Inn at the St. Louis World's Fair. This was a temporary structure that tested some of his ideas. But it was the Hotel Statler, which opened in 1908 in Buffalo, that introduced many of the innovations for which he is famous. Back-to-back rooms shared shafts for electrical wiring and plumbing, saving construction costs. These are now referred to as "Statler plumbing shafts." Every room provided ice water on tap. Statler said that 90 percent of bellhop calls were for ice. By making ice water available in the rooms, he cut down on the service staff. Statler also was the first to put a telephone in every room, and his cost accounting methods became standard for the industry. Statler is also credited with being the first hotel businessperson to address employee relations and benefits issues.

Statler soon had a chain of hotels in Great Lake states, Missouri, and New York City. With them he introduced other innovations. He posted rates in the rooms, attached reading lamps to the headboards, and placed radios in every room at no extra cost. He also provided plenty of towels with hooks to hang them on. This last item helped cut down laundry costs.

Statler preached the "Statler Service Code," a formal company policy that each employee had to memorize and carry during work hours. The code is memorialized on a plaque at the Cornell Hotel School, whose founding was made possible by a bequest in Statler's will.

Holidex, the company's reservation system. The centralization of reservation systems and technology has become highly advanced. Such technology is more than a convenience; for Holiday Inn it has become a necessity. The hotel chain receives a deluge of calls every day on rate issues, bills, and service questions. The new system allows the company to provide customers with quick responses on nearly anything—from the number of Priority Club (Holiday Inn's frequent guest program) points they have available to booking a convention for a thousand people. One computer is capable of handling 49 million transactions per second, while the other can handle 70 million. The center is staffed twenty-four hours a day and has become the information hub for Holiday Inn's 1,607 U.S. hotels.[1]

Holiday Inn also introduced the Holiday Inn Rate Optimization (HIRO) database. This application helps Holiday Inn's general managers pinpoint their optimum room rate based on the number of guests, stay statistics, area cost of living, and busiest time of the year. Its major objectives are to maximize revenues and improve revenue management. Holiday Inn also introduced the ENCORE property management system, which provides complete guest histories.[2]

Responding to the increased frequency of business travel, many hotel companies have built significant loyalty programs based on computerized guest history travel patterns. They can then offer reward and redemption benefits that fit their brand and target customer. The sophistication of these loyalty program databases, coupled with high transaction volume, afford certain major brands significant competitive advantages in the marketplace.

Computerized Production Management

In both the lodging and restaurant industries, computerized management systems greatly simplify the inventory, purchasing, preparation, and costing processes. Computerized inventory systems automatically record each time particular cleaning or foodservice products are used and reorder them when appropriate.

Computer-assisted production systems for large foodservice operations maintain and manage ingredient, recipe, menu, and price data. A manager using one of these systems can forecast sales based on previous demand, adjust menu mix for greater margins, adjust recipes, and select the best prices from vendors. The more sophisticated systems will print a "precost" for a period, such as a week, day, or meal. The precost tells the manager just how much the food items for the period will cost before the food is purchased. If the precost exceeds budget, the manager can adjust the menu or prices in advance. Today, restaurant computer applications also monitor credit card payment procedures and are capable of ensuring compliance with the security requirements now imposed by all major credit card processing companies. The restaurant point-of-sale computers also provide sophisticated programming capabilities for training staff on menu knowledge and specifications;

reservation and table management; timed order release for room service; hand-held and pay-at-the-table features; employee sales analysis and coaching in increased selling; kitchen management, including functions to promote speed of service; and wireless cash bar options.

Technology in Guest Service

Customers have grown accustomed to efficient, high-tech amenities in hospitality operations. From services such as automated check-in and check-out to electronic entertainment and in-room Internet access, the use of computer-age technologies contributes to overall guest service and satisfaction.

Automated Check-in and Check-out

Many major hotel companies have kiosk check-in and check-out stations in their lobbies. Hotel kiosk technology is similar to the airline self–check-in kiosks now found in most major airport terminals. Making travel as effortless as possible is a concept that continues to evolve in the hospitality industry. In-room check-out is as easy as switching on the television set and acknowledging charges through a remote control process.

Automated Car Rental

Car rental companies also speed checking in and out with automated systems. An individual who has called ahead to rent a car enters the parking lot to find her name on a large computerized sign. The sign directs the renter to a stall number where the car, key, and rental agreement are waiting. When returning the car, the traveler enters the appropriate mileage information into a wall-mounted computer station. The computer automatically calculates and charges the appropriate fee to the patron's credit card before issuing a receipt. Hurried

Industry Insights

TECHNOLOGY

Revenue Managment Systems

Revenue management as a strategic capability in today's marketplace would not be deliverable without the advanced technology found in most established hotel companies. The typical revenue management technology found in hotels consists of software designed to capture optimal price data. Revenue management systems such as Micros Fidelio let users maximize room inventory management, execute daily and monthly forecasts of demand trends, and benchmark key competitive performance indicators.

In the future, the increasing importance of automated revenue management capability will have a significant impact on a hotel operator's ability to manage customer relationships and maximize total profit per customer.

airport travelers can rent and return their cars without ever standing in line or waiting for a customer service representative. Today, car rental agencies also offer global positioning systems as upgrade features, giving renters advanced mapping and directional capabilities within the car.

Government Regulation and the Hospitality Industry

Some government policies exist to maintain safety and to control international travel; and to generate revenue, governments require licenses, inspections, and certificates, and collect taxes and fees. In-depth research and analysis should be completed when considering international investment and global enterprise.

Taxes and Fees

Most countries throughout the world have health, fire, and safety codes that restaurants and lodging establishments must comply with. Hospitality establishments may be inspected and licensed by the local government, and frequently a fee is charged for the license. In addition, the hospitality establishment may be required to pay tax to the government. Some countries, such as the United States, require that a hospitality corporation pay income tax, based on a percentage of total business profits. Sales tax, sometimes called a value-added tax, is charged by many countries. This tax is charged directly to the customer, based on the price of the service or product purchased. In many countries, a sales tax can be levied at the local, regional, or national level. In addition, many cities have specific travel taxes such as airport taxes and hotel room taxes that pay for the promotion of local tourism.

If taxes become too high, they can discourage travelers from visiting a particular location. Taxes can also discourage the development of new hotels, as was the case with the Tax Reform Act of 1986, which eliminated certain investment tax credits. Alternately, tax incentives and abatements can sometimes spur new development. New hospitality operations throughout Eastern Europe are a result of such incentives. Typically, governments or local entities offer development incentives in order to spur economic growth and expansion activity. In exchange, developers incorporate community improvements such as parks, recreation facilities, walkways, and green spaces.

Human Resources Legislation and Hospitality

In the United States, numerous state and national laws ban discrimination on the basis of sex, national origin, race, religion, age, or disability. These laws prohibit workplace discrimination based on any of these factors, and they prohibit discrimination in access to hospitality services. Now, thanks to the Civil Rights Act of 1991, Americans working for U.S. companies abroad are protected from employment discrimination based on all applicable laws found in the U.S.

Immigration Laws

Political turmoil, war, and economic uncertainty are all factors that increase emigration from affected countries into more stable, industrialized ones. The early 1990s saw tremendous immigration into Western Europe from countries in Africa, Eastern Europe, and Asia. Iimmigration from these countries into Japan, Australia, Canada, and the United States also was very high. Immigration can strain slow economies, since jobs may already be scarce for a country's existing pool of workers.

Most industrialized nations' governments control the numbers of immigrants allowed to enter each year, and require that immigrants receive work permits before being hired. Countries like Japan and the United States try to limit the number of unskilled workers allowed to enter. Yet thousands of immigrants enter these countries illegally every year. Some employers knowingly hire illegal immigrants, particularly for low-paying, low-skill jobs. Illegal immigrants may be deprived of insurance and pension benefits and be paid lower wages, since there is little likelihood that an illegal immigrant will report employer misconduct.

Other Legal Issues in Hospitality

Every country has its own set of laws that affect the conduct of business and in particular the conduct of the hospitality industry. For centuries, innkeepers and restauranteurs have been expected to provide safety and security for their guests. English common law held innkeepers responsible for the loss of a guest's property and obliged an innkeeper to admit as many guests as an inn could accommodate. In the United States, courts have established a duty of care for innkeepers: If a hospitality establishment should be able to foresee danger to any guest, then it is required to take reasonable steps to deal with the danger or be held liable in a court of law.[3]

Unions

Labor unions are a political and legal force in countries around the world, but the degree to which they affect the hospitality industry varies by city and state. Labor unions and workers' associations, sometimes called **workers' councils**, are quite influential in establishing workers' wages, benefits, and hours in European countries. Most countries have strict laws that regulate conduct between employers and the unions or workers' councils representing employees. Unions often make wage and benefit concessions in order to maintain international competition and retain jobs within their industry.

The management of a hospitality business requires knowledge and sensitivity to the political and governmental forces that may shape the business. It is often a manager's familiarity with variations in the community's expectations that enable the business to modify itself proactively to meet these changes, rather than waiting until it is legally forced to comply.

Focus on the Future

Many factors have helped shape and define the hospitality industry: the global economy, political forces, changing demographics, technological trends, business cycles, guest demands, and government regulations. This section examines the effect of current trends on the future of the hospitality industry.

Because they provide a service rather than selling a manufactured product, it has been said that hospitality firms need to remain "high touch" rather than "high tech." But that prediction will be put to the test in the next decade. The next wave of technological innovation will transform how individuals interact with service organizations. Hospitality firms will be at the center of that transformation.

Many factors are shaping the hospitality industry's future: international and multinational influences, globalization, increasing cultural diversity, workforce sourcing challenges, security threats, differing consumer preferences and increasing consumer expectations, as well as changing patterns of leisure. Perhaps the greatest driver of change at the beginning of the twenty-first century is ongoing technological advancement—precisely because it fosters globalization and awareness of diversity, and accelerates transaction activity. The most obvious manifestation of how technology has changed the shape of society is the Internet. Today hospitality consumers can purchase airline tickets, reserve a hotel room, and rent a car using a computer. Desktop videoconferencing, discussed later in this section, now makes some business trips unnecessary.

Yet, in many ways, the Internet is just the tip of a technological iceberg whose size and progress are increasing at a staggering rate. Technological advancement supports international growth by transmitting information quickly, as well as by allowing individuals from most developed countries to stay in constant contact. More importantly, it has sped the pace of commercial activity. Firms no longer have to wait for the delivery of information by traditional mail services; instead they have instant access through e-mail.

Technology has also transformed the relationship between firms and the markets in which they do business. Companies now have access to extraordinarily detailed information about their markets, including what individuals purchase at the grocery store, what they paid for their home, and whether they pay their bills promptly. The mass marketing of goods and services already is being superseded by more tightly defined market segments and lifestyle categories.

Demographics in the Twenty-first Century

Throughout this book, we have referred to hospitality as a service-oriented profession operating on the basis of supply and guest demand. As our society moves even more toward a service-based economy, identifying trends and developing market strategies for the hospitality industry will become increasingly important. More than any other industry, hospitality is a business that caters to people. The more you know about people, the more you can satisfy their needs and demands. For example, let's assume that you are a hotel developer. Digging the foundation of a new hotel would not be practical or cost efficient without first knowing the answers to a few questions. How many potential guests will visit the hotel? Should you build convention and meeting room facilities? Are the likely guests families or business travelers? Will they spend top dollar or are they looking for economy? Should the dining room provide quick-service or comfortable, leisurely dining? Should there even be a dining room? What about entertainment? Without the answers to such questions, your success in meeting the preferences of your guests and providing a return on investment cannot be assured. Given the population's changing age, education, demographics, and cultural traditions, you will need to redefine your role and adapt your career aspirations accordingly.

Attracting a Changing Workforce

Hospitality is a booming industry that offers many career opportunities for trained professionals. As service-oriented businesses edge out manufacturing, the makeup of the labor force will take on a new face.

America's workforce is older, more ethnically and culturally diverse, and more equally divided between men and women than ever before. African Americans, Hispanics, and Asians account for more than one-third of all those currently entering the job market. Figure 12.1 shows trends in demographic changes in the workforce from 2006 to 2007. The U.S. labor force increasingly comprises women—a trend that is expected to continue throughout the twenty-first century (Figure 12.1A). This change is due in part to the fact that more and more women above the age of sixteen are entering the workforce, but it also reflects a steady decline in the number of working men. The racial and ethnic composition of the U.S. labor force also will continue to change throughout the twenty-first century, but at a slower rate than it did during the later decades of the twentieth century (Figure 12.1B). Participation by Hispanics and Asians is growing particularly fast due to immigration. The age

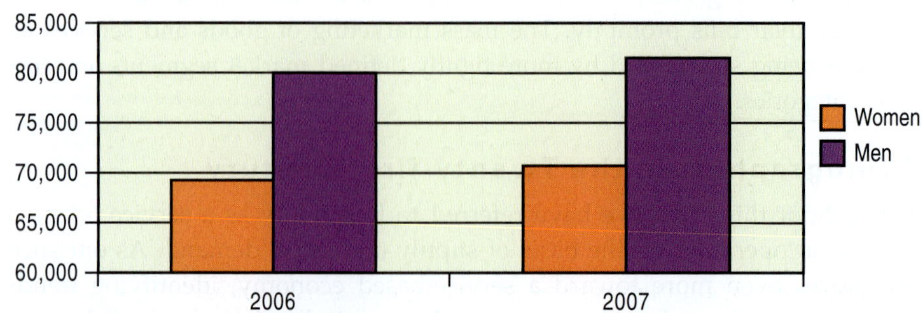

FIGURE 12-1A Women and men in the United States labor force, 2006–2007 (Numbers in thousands)

Source: U.S. Department of Labor, Bureau of Labor Statistics, 2007.

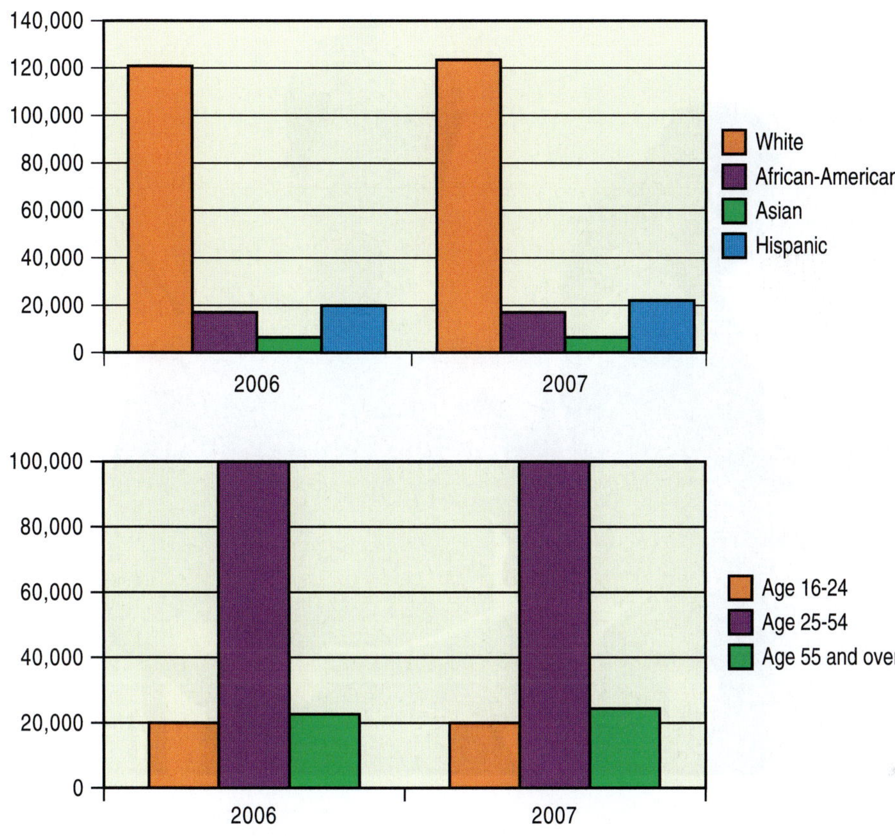

FIGURE 12-1B Labor force participation of minority groups, 2006–2007 (Numbers in thousands).

Source: U.S. Department of Labor, Bureau of Labor Statistics, 2007.

FIGURE 12-1C Labor force participation by age group, 2007–2007 (Numbers in thousands).

Source: U.S. Department of Labor, Bureau of Labor Statistics, 2007.

composition of the U.S. labor force also is changing as baby boomers mature (Figure 12.1C).

Workers with Special Needs

The 1990 Americans with Disabilities Act opened new doors for people with disabilities by requiring employers to accommodate physically or mentally challenged workers. With the shrinking number of young people entering the workforce, the hospitality industry can turn to this often overlooked and underemployed segment of society. As with older workers, the industry is making specific changes in its attitude toward those with physical challenges. Among other things, employers need to:

- Learn how to recognize the work competencies of physically challenged or mentally challenged individuals.
- Become educated about the excellent performance records and the generally low cost of accommodating these workers.
- Hire professionals specifically trained to work with persons with physical or mental challenges to assist in the mainstreaming process.
- Redesign jobs for employees with progressive disabilities.
- Develop awareness programs to educate employees.[4]

Two growing segments of the hospitality industry's workforce are developmentally disabled and minority employees.

Two of the industry's leaders in employing individuals with special needs are Marriott and McDonald's. Marriott operates a foundation that is dedicated to helping individuals with special needs find gainful and rewarding employment. One program, called "Bridges," arranges internships for physically and mentally challenged persons. The "Bridges" program has placed over 2,700 students in paid internships, with over 87 percent receiving offers of full-time employment following their internships.

Minorities

The U.S. Department of Labor expects that 35 percent of all those entering the labor force will be African American, Hispanic, or Asian. Part of this new labor pool will result from immigration into the country. Part is due to the higher birth rate experienced by African Americans and Hispanics relative to other groups. By the year 2050, the Hispanic population will account for 21 percent of the population in the United States, making it the country's largest minority.[5] In short, the future workforce as well as the future customer population will be the most culturally diverse to date.

With such an influx of people into the country, the new workforce will be a blend of many ethnicities. Already, the hospitality field employs more women and minorities than any other industry. The challenge for the industry will be to ensure that this diversity is reflected at all levels of the organization, and not just in entry-level or low-skill jobs.

> Today, the National Restaurant Association reports the restaurant industry employs an estimated 13.1 million people, making it the nation's largest employer outside of government. The number of women employed in the restaurant industry represents more than 55 percent of the workforce.
>
> *Source:* <http://www.restaurant.org>

Women

The size and shape of the American family has changed dramatically over the past fifty years. The average family size is now slightly over three people, the smallest ever recorded in the United States. For the first time in the country's history, the majority of households contain no children living at home. Of the families that do have children at home, one-third are headed by women, and the majority of all women with children work outside the home.[6] These changing family patterns point out yet another source of labor for the hospitality industry—women.

To continue to attract women, the industry must approach staffing needs with greater flexibility and creativity. Flexible work schedules and job sharing will appeal to many working mothers. Providing child-care facilities or financial assistance for child-care expenses will be another employment draw. Offering tuition reimbursement will encourage continuing education. Most important, the hospitality industry needs to aggressively train and promote competent women to positions of higher authority. The industry's multitiered management system makes it an ideal management training ground.

Flexibility is critical to attracting working mothers to management positions in hospitality.

Cultural Diversity

There is no question that the United States is becoming more culturally diverse. The migration of Hispanics, Asians, Africans, and Eastern Europeans into the United States continues at a dramatic pace. However, it is important to recognize that the influx of immigrants is not dispersed evenly across the United States. Instead, it is concentrated in a relatively small proportion of geographic areas. Hispanics tend to migrate to specific metropolitan areas, such as Los Angeles, Miami, New York, and Chicago. Similarly, Asians tend to congregate in "gateway" cities such as Los Angeles, New York City, and San Francisco. In comparison to these metropolitan areas, the influx of immigrants to other parts of the country is relatively insignificant.

Such patterns of immigration as well as migration within the United States have led William Frey, a researcher at the Institute for Social Research at the University of Michigan, to suggest that cultural diversity is far less widespread than the raw numbers would indicate.[7] Interestingly, however, because immigration is concentrated in a small number of cities, those areas are becoming highly diverse. Frey identified twenty-one metropolitan areas characterized by relatively high combined percentages of Hispanics, African Americans, and Asians—all of which, with the exception of New York, Washington/Baltimore, and Chicago, are located in California or Texas. There are, of course, many other U.S. metropolitan areas with high percentages of African Americans, Hispanics, or Asians. However, genuine multicultural environments in which all major groups are represented remain relatively rare.

The fact that immigrant groups tend to cluster in specific metropolitan areas has important implications for the future. When ethnic groups cluster in defined geographical areas, they are able to maintain language, traditions, and cultural practices such as *foodways*, which are the foods, preparation techniques, and eating practices characteristic of a culture. Moreover, geographic concentration can lead to social, political, cultural, and commercial clout. In large metropolitan areas such as Miami, Los Angeles, and Chicago, where Hispanics live in well-defined neighborhoods, they enjoy political power, define social issues, and have the attention of marketers. In Chicago, for example, they also shape the tastes of non-Hispanic groups through the marketing of authentic Mexican food products as well as by opening Mexican restaurants throughout the metropolitan area.

Fulfilling Consumer Expectations of Quality Service

Because the hospitality industry is a service business, it has traditionally taken pride in meeting consumer needs. However, there is some indication that service to guests needs improvement. The American Customer Satisfaction Index (ASCI), reports on survey data gathered by the National Quality Research Center at the University of Michigan.

Table 12.2 presents the results of the ACSI using data gathered in 2007 for selected companies, including major hospitality and tourism firms, which appear in italics. Generally consumers are less satisfied with hotels, airlines, and restaurants than they are with many other goods and services. In fact, consumers appear to be more satisfied with their underwear (Fruit of the Loom) than with many hospitality firms. Other hospitality firms were ranked below the U.S. Postal Service and urban police departments, and were ranked not too far above the Internal Revenue Service. There are, of course, significant problems with comparisons of this kind. The experiences a regular

TABLE 12.2 American Consumer Satisfaction Index Rankings for Selected Firms

Rank	*Company Name*	*2007 Score*	*Previous Year % Change*
1	FedEx Corporation	84	–2.3
2	Southern Company	82	2.5
3	PPL Corporation	81	0.0
4	United Parcel Service, Inc.	81	–2.4
5	Sempra Energy	80	6.7
6	*Olive Garden (Darden Restaurants, Inc.)*	80	N/A
7	Duke Energy Corporation	79	–1.3
8	Allegheny Energy, Inc.	79	–1.3
9	*Outback Steakhouse (OSI Restaurant Partners, Inc.)*	79	N/A
10	*Marriott International, Inc.*	79	5.3
11	*Red Lobster (Darden Restaurants, Inc.)*	78	N/A
12	*Starbucks Corporation*	78	1.3
13	*Wendy's International, Inc.*	78	2.6
14	Papa John's International, Inc.	77	–2.5
15	U.S. Postal Service—Express Mail & Priority Mail	77	2.7
16	Progress Energy, Inc.	77	0.0
17	*Global Hyatt Corporation*	77	2.7
18	*Starwood Hotels & Resorts Worldwide, Inc.*	76	1.3
19	*Hilton Hotels Corporation*	76	–2.6
20	FirstEnergy Corp.	76	1.3

Source: Fortune (2007).

business traveler has with airlines and hotels are more complex and difficult for the organization to control than are the same traveler's experiences with a bottle of beer or a bar of soap. Nevertheless, there clearly appears to be room for improvement. Firms that are successful in strengthening consumer satisfaction will enjoy greater loyalty. Loyalty, in turn, translates into profits, because it is much more expensive to attract a new guest than it is to serve a loyal guest.

Technology and Innovation in Foodservice

In discussing technology and innovation in the foodservice segment of the industry it is helpful to think in terms of three separate areas: the back of the house, the front of the house, and the manager's office.

The Back-of-the-House

The back-of-the-house refers to the food production process. Technological innovation in food production involves how food is stored, prepared, and served. Innovation comes in the form of new or improved foodservice equipment designed to improve operating efficiency, conserve energy, and sustain production over time, and new ways of designing kitchens that make the preparation process more efficient or effective. Technological innovation in foodservice equipment occurs relatively slowly compared to other areas. With few exceptions, improvements are incremental, and are designed to reduce labor and other operating costs. Recent developments include:

- blast chillers that quickly reduce product temperature prior to storage, thus preventing the growth of dangerous bacteria
- induction heating systems for sautéing foods, which replace gas-fired burners and traditional electric heating elements
- French-fryer systems that automatically load frozen fries, then remove them from the oil and dump them at a bagging station
- centralized refrigeration systems that replace multiple compressors in walk-ins, reach-ins, ice machines, and display units
- hot food holding units that control the humidity and rate of evaporation within the cabinet, thus making it possible to hold fried eggs and biscuits for longer periods without loss of quality
- kitchen fire suppression systems that extinguish range fires with water mist, rather than spraying chemicals that are difficult to clean
- pot-washing sinks that remove food by agitating the soiled pots, thus reducing the time spent scrubbing pots

Technological changes in the back-of-the-house are driven by large, multi-unit foodservice operations and introduced by equipment manufacturers rather than by small, single-unit restaurants. This is because the larger firms have the resources to invest in equipment research and development. Similarly, foodservice equipment manufacturers are more willing to invest in research and development if their new products can be sold in large quantities

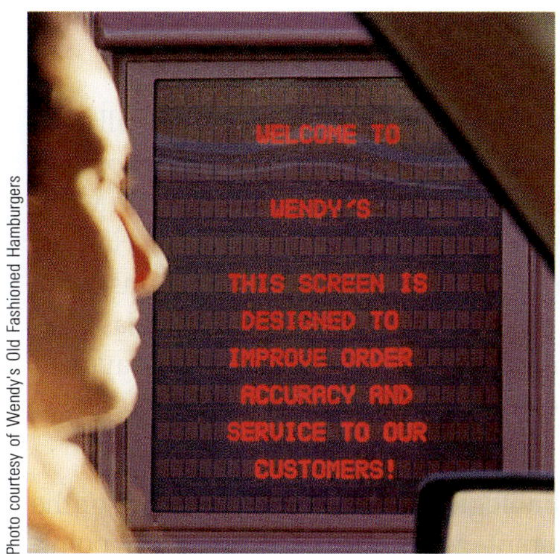

Photo courtesy of Wendy's Old Fashioned Hamburgers

An electronic terminal automates drive-through orders.

to chains. McDonald's, for example, has been responsible for a number of innovations in the production and service of French fries.

The Front-of-the-House

The front-of-the-house refers to all the processes involved in delivering the menu items prepared in the back of the house, including reservations and seating, menus, taking orders, serving food, and collecting payment. Technological innovation in the front of the house often is associated with computerized order-taking systems and point-of-sale terminals. However, technology should not be associated only with computer systems. The different forms of service discussed in Chapter 6, such as table service, cafeteria service, and buffet service, reflect different technologies for delivering food products to guests. The drive-up window used at most quick-service restaurants is a technological innovation, just as is the computerized point-of-sale terminal used to enter the driver's order.

Technological innovation in how consumers interact with foodservice operations to obtain food products is likely to continue in quick-service restaurants for two reasons. First, innovations that increase the speed and convenience of service give a competitive advantage. Second, quick-service restaurants usually compete on the basis of price. Innovations in which customers do work previously performed by employees reduce labor costs and thus strengthen competitive position. Today, it is not uncommon to see quick-service restaurants move their beverage dispensing machines from behind the counter to the customer service area. Self-service beverages save the cost of having employees draw beverages for customers. Similarly, quick-service restaurant firms have been experimenting with technological innovations designed to reduce the involvement of employees in the order-taking and payment process by having customers enter their own orders on touch screens and pay by credit or debit card. (A parallel is found in the airline industry, where customers are now encouraged to print their boarding passes from their own computers or check in at a kiosk in the airport or in selected hotel lobbies.)

Interestingly, many of these technological "innovations" are not all that novel. The drive-through window is a technological descendant of carhop service. Similarly, having the customer select menu items and pay for them without employee involvement was the hallmark of the Horn and Hardart Automat, discussed in an earlier chapter. In the Automat, menu items were displayed behind little glass doors. A customer peered through the glass, selected her food, and deposited coins in a slot next to the glass door. Payment unlocked the door, and the customer removed her food and took it to a table. The last Automat closed in the 1990s.

Computer systems have brought technological innovation to the front of the house by replacing the manual restaurant guest check system with point-of-sale terminals. The manual guest check system requires servers to take orders at guests' tables, carry the checks into the kitchen, and post them on the chef's order wheel. When the orders have been prepared, servers must return to the kitchen to pick them up and deliver them to the table. With point-of-sale systems, servers key in orders at terminals in the dining room. Orders are then transmitted electronically to the various production areas in the kitchen. When an order is complete, a "runner" (rather than the server) delivers it from the kitchen to the table. Point-of-sale systems thus enable servers to stay in the dining area attending to the needs of guests. They also increase management control by preventing collusion between servers and cooks to give away food. Point-of-sale systems have become so advanced and efficient that they are considered an integral part of any successful foodservice operation.

The Internet has had a relatively small impact on the foodservice industry apart from providing ready access to restaurant reviews, customer complaints and recommendations, and, in some cases, actual menus. Large, multiunit restaurant firms, along with fine dining and destination restaurants and city-guide destination services, are leaders in enabling guests to obtain reservations on the Internet. These organizations have benefited the most from the Internet's ability to automate the reservations process because they have the resources to invest in the ongoing development and maintenance of interactive, secure, Web-based customer acquisition methodologies.

The Manager's Office

Technological innovations in the manager's office are driven by developments in computer hardware and software. In cash-based operations such as restaurants, management systems are integrated with point-of-sale terminals and can perform the following functions:

- tracking sales by menu item and menu mix
- estimating production requirements on the basis of sales histories
- calculating inventory replenishment needs

- transmitting sales information to corporate offices
- calculating food cost

In addition, some large noncommercial foodservice operations now use complex production systems that are capable of:

- estimating food costs before products are purchased (pre-costing)
- controlling inventory by interfacing with bar code readers
- forecasting purchasing needs and transmitting orders directly to vendors
- generating daily recipes sized precisely to forecasted needs
- preparing nutritional analyses for recipes and checking for possible allergens
- managing debit card and access systems
- scheduling labor
- preparing real-time revenue forecasts
- financial modeling

Technology and Innovation in Lodging

Technological development in lodging in the twenty-first century will be characterized by increased integration of property management systems and increasing implementation of Internet-based guest services.

Property Management Systems

A property management system (often referred to by the acronym PMS) combines hardware and software into an integrated system that handles many or all of the following functions:

- receiving reservations (often done at a central facility and transmitted to individual properties
- setting prices based on anticipated demand (**yield management**)
- maintaining profiles of guests' preferences and needs
- recording every transaction in the many departments of the property, using point-of-sale terminals
- tracking room availability and checking guests in and out of the property
- activating electronic keys and locks, telephones, and movie services in guest rooms
- tracking guest telephone usage and long-distance charges
- maintaining housekeeping data, such as which rooms have been cleaned
- food and beverage management (see previous section on these systems)
- employee timekeeping and payroll
- bookkeeping and accounting, including performing the night audit and maintaining guest folios
- preparation of financial statements
- monitoring and managing energy usage in building utility systems

Few lodging establishments in developed countries do not use some form of property management system. As a means to manage a large, complex hotel, these systems have proven themselves to be extraordinarily effective. Most major hospitality brands invest significant research dollars in next-generation technology and service enhancements to PMS systems. Typically, a strong PMS will be the backbone of a major brand's attractiveness to potential franchisees and independent hotel owners.

Many property management systems are capable of reducing labor costs by automating the check-out process. Guests can review their folios on the room television using the remote, approve their charges, and authorize payment. However, this type of system is used primarily by business travelers and other guests who are comfortable with electronic technology. Other next-generation technology in guest rooms includes digital-smart thermostat and motion sensor-triggered energy systems; interactive television sets, which may provide Internet access; and high-speed and/or wireless Internet connectivity. When more people become accustomed to making financial transactions electronically, and a standard interface has been developed that is as familiar as a personal check, electronic check-out will surely become more prevalent.

The Internet

Many lodging organizations have established a presence on the Internet, enabling prospective guests to see locations, rooms, amenities, and rates. A much smaller percentage offer on-line reservation capabilities utilizing corporate reservation systems. For large properties that are part of well-known chains, a presence on the Internet provides yet another way to attract guests and handle reservations.

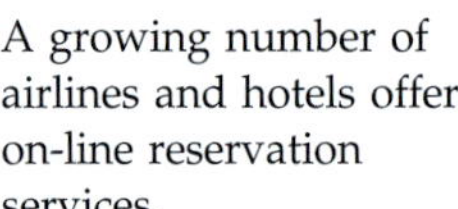

A growing number of airlines and hotels offer on-line reservation services.

However, the marketing opportunities offered by an Internet presence may be even more useful to smaller and/or independent properties that do not have the corporate resources necessary for national advertising. Inns, bed-and-breakfasts, and small hotels can use the Internet to give prospective guests visual information about their special characteristics and amenities. In this way they can overcome any hesitancy leisure travelers might have about staying at an "unknown" property.

Technology and Innovation in Tourism

Perhaps the greatest impact of technology upon tourism is the transformation of the role of the travel agent that has been brought about by the Internet. This is occurring as a result of several interrelated innovations. First, many of the resources and much of the information necessary to plan leisure or business travel are now accessible on the Internet. Hotel and restaurant reviews, city guides, information on attractions and recreational opportunities, as well as airline flight schedules and rates, are available to anyone who logs on. And, although travel agents continue to have far more specialized and detailed information and experience than is available on the Internet, the perception is growing among consumers that on-line information is sufficient to plan a trip. Reliance on travel agents to plan trips is thus decreasing because travelers are obtaining the information they need from the Internet.

Second, the increasing availability of on-line airline, hotel, and car rental reservations, combined with "ticketless travel," mean that travelers no longer need to rely on travel agents to provide tickets. Information on low fares and special rates is readily accessible on the Internet, so travelers are able to evaluate fares, compare routes, select convenient departure times, rent an automobile, and book a room at a hotel on-line with relative convenience and ease. Several airlines reward travelers for booking flights using the Internet with special low fares and/or enhanced frequent flyer benefits.

Decreased consumer reliance on travel agents will, no doubt, reduce employment and future opportunities in the field. These factors suggest that the role of the travel agent in the twenty-first century will be substantially different than it was in the previous century. The independent travel agency will certainly suffer, and the survivors will be those businesses that focus their expertise and provide a high level of service to clients who have neither the time nor the inclination to plan a complex trip on their own. Business travel arrangements will become increasingly centralized. They will handled by in-house travel planners who can demand fare concessions because they book a high volume of business, rather than by travel agents.

Revenue Management and On-Line Distribution

The Internet has created new career opportunities in the field of revenue management. In the American marketplace, by the end of 2007, more than half of all travel in the United States was purchased on-line. Thirty-four million

Americans have made the Internet the primary way they buy their leisure travel. On-line travel sales in 2008 were expected to top $136 billion annually. While third-party intermediary on-line booking sites in the U.S. market account for 20 percent of the overall on-line market, they are expected to top 35 percent in the year 2009. A clear pattern is emerging: on-line traffic is growing in the United States, as is the popularity of travel-specific search engines. Additionally, competition is intensifying between direct travel suppliers and third-party intermediaries. This increased competition favors the consumer and places a greater burden on hotel and lodging operators to enhance their electronic distribution strategies. The on-line travel distribution model of today is made up of inter relationships among consumers, travel intermediaries, **global distribution systems (GDSs)**, and airline suppliers.

Hotel operators need to offer room rates and inventory control mechanisms that accord with anticipated demand. Revenue management is the art and science of predicting customer demand and fine-tuning the price and availability of products to match that demand. Career opportunities exist at all levels of the industry for those managers who can grasp the importance of revenue management and have technical expertise in electronic channel management and strategic room inventory planning.

Videoconferencing and Business Travel

The claim that videoconferencing would eliminate the need for business travel has been proven wrong more than once in the past. Face-to-face communication provides a far richer experience than "talking heads" on a video monitor, and probably never will be totally replaced. Nevertheless, as individuals and firms increasingly are networked with high bandwidth lines, desktop videoconferencing will become more commonplace. Individuals will see one another on display screens as they converse in real time. Because relatively high-quality visual interaction is as convenient as placing a long-distance conference call, the nature of how business is done is changing. Although meetings will continue to be necessary, business people have already discovered that one-to-one videoconferences can be an economical, convenient, and time-saving alternative to face-to-face meetings. As desktop videoconferencing becomes more widely adopted as a meeting substitute, the segments of the hospitality industry that support business travel will need to adapt their product offerings.

Laptop computers, personal digital assistants (PDAs), cellular telephones, and e-mail have freed people from the need to be physically present "in the office," and thus have changed fundamentally the way business is conducted. Salespeople can cover far greater territories now that laptop computers are available, because they can enter orders from a customer's site and send them directly to the home office. Managers can keep in constant contact with key employees. Firms can expand into new geographic markets, both domestic and international, far more economically than before.

International Business Hotel

Individuals have used these same technologies to change the way they arrange their personal lives. Telecommuting has made it possible for individuals to "live anywhere." For example, many individuals who telecommute to computer and software firms in Silicon Valley (the San Jose, California area) have moved hundreds of miles away to live in Washington, Oregon, or Idaho. The money they save in housing prices is far more than the cost of airline tickets to attend meetings at the corporate office on the occasions when their physical presence is absolutely necessary.

In short, recent technological innovations that facilitate contact without face-to-face interaction have spurred corporate expansion as well as individual mobility. Like laptop computers, e-mail, and cellular telephones, desktop videoconferencing will reduce the reliance of individuals and firms on being in a particular place at a particular time and so will decrease the need for travel.

Security Systems

Biometric systems, in which machines recognize personal characteristics of a guest, eventually could replace electronic key cards or metal keys for hotel rooms. Identifying characteristics such as fingerprints or retinas already provide access to some casinos and Middle Eastern hotels.[9] In addition to these measures, electronic guest room safes provide added security for a guest's valuables.

Trends

The trends reflected in the following sections are indicative of the influences on your future and that of the hospitality industry. While this list is not all-inclusive, it represents examples of opportunities and challenges facing the industry. As with other aspects of hospitality, the future of these components is dependent on many factors, including advances in technology, changing lifestyles, consumer demand, and economic changes.

Career opportunities for hospitality professionals abound in these specialized components. Since service is the underlying factor in the hospitality industry, and service is the expected growth pattern for society, new opportunities within the industry will become available. In particular, service-oriented, all-in-one social and recreational opportunities—mini-theme parks and **mega-resorts** consisting of mixed-use hotel, retail, recreation, and entertainment complexes—will be a growing part of the recreation and social component of hospitality.

Foodservice

Historically, the primary engine of growth for foodservice firms has been to increase market penetration by adding new restaurants. This is not to say that increasing sales and profits in single units is unimportant. Nor do we suggest that the owner of a single-unit family restaurant should be looking for expansion opportunities instead of enjoying a successful small business. Nevertheless, growth in the restaurant industry has been primarily attributable to the expansion of multiunit firms.

The overall prospect for the foodservice industry is one of growth in the early decades of the twenty-first century, provided that world economies remain solid. Because the foodservice industry is increasingly dependent on global development for growth opportunities, its prospects are linked to economic trends in all of the world's major economies.

In the United States and Canada, growth opportunities vary depending upon the sector of the industry and the specific market segment. Quick-service restaurants are encountering an increasingly saturated market, thus limiting growth opportunities. In the past, quick-service restaurant chains grew at the expense of family-owned single unit restaurants. Today, however, multiunit chains are the primary players in the quick-service segment. New quick-service concepts will have to gain market share at the expense of established, national firms that have tremendous competitive resources. Real estate prices have increased tremendously—particularly for desirable restaurant sites. Workforce sourcing and labor shortages in certain international marketplaces are driving operating costs upward. Also, other players such as grocery stores have entered the foodservice market, and often compete for the same market segment as quick-service restaurants.

Another changing area is hotel food and beverage service. Once the bane of hoteliers, the hotel restaurant is now thriving in the hands of branded operators, especially celebrity chef operators. Contracting hotel foodservice out to restaurants with name recognition is a trend that seems to be a profitable alternative to hotel-run eateries. Formerly, hotel restaurants were places known for high prices and less-than-desirable food. Now, outside management companies are bringing such well-known restaurants as T.G.I. Friday's, Starbucks, Olive Garden, and Wolfgang Puck's into hotels.

Growth in noncommercial foodservice is likely to be strongest in long-term care, corrections, and educational facilities. These predictions reflect demographic trends—the population will age and require residential care, new prisons will be constructed, and the children of baby boomers will crowd schools, colleges, and universities. Corporate foodservice is also likely to remain strong to the extent that large firms build new facilities. However, should mergers and acquisitions lead to consolidation among larger firms, with economic growth occurring largely at the level of small firms, on-site foodservice will suffer. This is because larger firms are far more likely to invest in employee foodservice facilities than are small firms.

Foodservice is projected to be the fastest- and steadiest-growing component of the business in the United States well into the current century. The U.S. foodservice industry generates $430 billion in annual sales. Like many components of the hospitality industry, foodservice is charting new courses. Developing trends, changing lifestyles, and advancing technology all will affect the future of foodservice. The industry has already seen major changes in areas such as alcohol awareness, smoking/nonsmoking areas, design and architectural innovation, eclectic culinary offerings, and service improvements. However, the future of foodservice is a challenging one. Working with ethnic groups to develop appealing menus for school foodservice, adopting cost-efficient cooking methods, dealing with changing staffing needs and workforce shortages, and improving customer service are some of the challenges that foodservice professionals will have to meet.

Lodging

In lodging, the nature of hotel development means that the supply of rooms and the demand for them rarely are in perfect balance. The wave of hotel development that began in the middle of the 1990s came to a screeching halt as a result of the 9/11 terrorist attacks. Today, the lodging industry has enjoyed strong demand curve, which is reflected more in average rates (price per room per night) than in occupancy levels (number of rooms occupied per night). In the Middle East, for example, year-to-date figures for October 2007 indicated occupancy at 74 percent, with an average rate of $203. In the Asia-Pacific region, occupancy was 82 percent, with an average rate of $182. In the European market, occupancy was 84 percent, with an average rate of $234. In the Caribbean and Latin American nations, occupancy was 75 percent, with an average rate of $137.[10]

Environmental Regulations and Hospitality

For many years, concern for the environment has been growing. Preserving wildlife and forests, conserving natural resources, and cleaning up the air, water, and soil often lead to conflicts with industry. Environmental concerns affect how and where developers can build, and often those concerned must satisfy the wishes of many organizations. Hospitality industry professionals are often in the midst of environmental battles, since the properties they operate may degrade the ecological or cultural environment their facilities were built to highlight.

Concern for the environment directly affected the development of the 400-room Embassy Suites in South Lake Tahoe, California. This project required cooperation among several organizations, including the League to Save Lake Tahoe, the California attorney general's office, the Tahoe Regional Planning Authority, the South Tahoe Redevelopment Agency, and the city of Lake Tahoe. To avoid time-consuming litigation, the builders worked out the following deal under strict environmental parameters:

- Redevelopment regulations called for 1.31 old rooms to be retired for every new room built.
- The new hotel had to reduce the amount of ground the hotel covered by 38 percent.
- The length of the building could not exceed 600 feet.
- The building could rise no more than 95 feet.
- The roof had to be built with a slope of 22 degrees.
- The building exterior had to display minimal color accents and use earth tones.
- All wastewater had to be treated before being returned to the ground.

These and other guidelines added about 10 percent to the cost of construction, for a grand total of $65 million. The water-treatment system alone cost about $250,000.[11]

In some parts of the world, including China, Japan, Latin America, and Eastern Europe, pressure to industrialize rapidly allowed environmental concerns to be ignored for too long. These countries are now beginning to regulate environmental impact more closely, and emphasis on the environment and energy conservation will increasingly affect the construction and operation of hospitality businesses there.

In the United States, hotel guests are responsive to conservation programs. Hotels and restaurants in California and parts of the American Southwest aggressively reduced water consumption during a drought in the early 1990s. Many hotel chains participate in recycling programs that collect aluminum, glass, plastics, and paper. Since some communities are initiating mandatory recycling programs, this will become standard policy in many hotels and restaurants. Today, many hotels are embracing sustainable energy and green program efficiencies in their new construction projects. Solar heating, digital energy conservation programs, and carbon emission reduction equipment is used whenever possible.

Ecotourism and Green Marketing

Ecotourism and "green" tourism is a growing segment of the hospitality industry. It encompasses a number of related travel experiences that focus on nature-related destinations and are designed to have a minimal impact on the environment. The Ecotourism Society defines **ecotourism** as "responsible travel to natural areas that conserves the environment and improves the welfare of local people." However, ecotourism has come to be associated with a relatively broad spectrum of tourism experiences, from those that are specifically focused on improving the local, natural environment to others that emphasize adventurous outdoor activities. Examples of ecotourism experiences include trips to parks and preserves in Costa Rica and Africa, trail-building in Australia, and canoeing on the Amazon River.

Although the number of persons who participate in ecotourism remains relatively small, it has the potential to become a very important segment of the tourism industry in the future. Ecotourism is growing at a more rapid rate than tourism overall, and ecotourists tend to have relatively high personal incomes. This combination of growth potential and participant wealth signals an opportunity for local operators as well as for not-for-profit groups that sponsor ecotourism trips.

Perhaps even more significant is the potential impact of ecotourism on the hospitality industry as a whole. Ecotourism is based on specific values, such as protecting the environment and bettering the lives of local residents. Inasmuch as those values are widely held among baby boomers, they may become increasingly important in other segments of the tourism industry. The traditional pattern of tourism development in the latter half of the twentieth century was to construct large resort hotels along the beachfronts of relatively undeveloped areas. These hotels provided travelers with all the comforts of home and more. The creation of those resort destinations often transformed a local agrarian economy into a wage-earning economy as the native population took jobs in hotels, as taxi drivers, and in other service industries. If a significant percentage of travelers proactively seeks destinations that are developed in harmony with the local environment and indigenous way of life, more traditional resort destinations may suffer financially.

International Development

In the past, U.S. companies dominated the hotel industry. Today, hotel companies are multicultural and global. Regional trade pacts will continue to encourage future business endeavors that span the borders of North America, Europe, South America, and Southeast Asia. Moreover, while the hotel markets in many developed countries are relatively mature, in developing countries opportunities for growth are greater. Hilton Hotels plans to expand in Canada and Mexico. In the late nineties, Hilton International (a separate company) opened ten new properties in the Middle East, and planned to open another fifty hotels around the world between 1998 and 2004. In 2008, Hilton Hotels Corporation was acquired by BlackRock, a global investment company, and is currently evaluating future international growth and strategic options. Marriott has been developing full-service hotels in major cities worldwide, and is taking its Executive Suites and Courtyard concepts international as well. Cendant, currently the world's largest hotel franchising company, owns over 6,500 franchised hotels with 543,000 rooms on six continents. Hyatt International manages over seventy hotels and resorts worldwide, and has an additional thirty properties under development. Wyndham, currently operating hotels in the United States and the Caribbean, plans expansion into Latin America and Europe. Westin has over one hundred properties worldwide, and plans to open another fifteen properties in Asia. Four Seasons is developing hotels in China. Accor plans to add over thirty hotels in Indonesia, Thailand, and Vietnam over the next ten years subject to global economic conditions.

Globalization of hotel firms is also being driven by consolidation and the brand conversion that follows. Wyndham's parent company has acquired the Arcadian hotels in Europe, and will convert them to the Wyndham brand. Marriott is converting Renaissance hotels to its own brand. However, not all mergers or acquisitions are followed by conversions. When Starwood Hotels and Resorts Worldwide acquired both Westin and ITT Sheraton, they expanded internationally under both brand names, carved out the Luxury Collection of Hotels, and expanded its St. Regis Collection, named after the famed St. Regis Hotel in New York City.

The Growth of the Industry

The hospitality industry as a whole—including tourism, foodservice, lodging, and related businesses—is one of the world's largest industries, and is expected to grow even larger. In 1998, the industry generated $3.6 trillion of economic activity and supported over 230 million jobs. In 2010, it is expected to generate $10 trillion dollars of economic activity and employ 328 million individuals.[12] Table 12.3 shows the importance of the tourism industry in each of the major regions of the world, and predicts industry growth between 1998 and 2010.

The hospitality industry will be important in generating and sustaining economic growth, particularly in relatively less industrialized or developed countries. Key areas for significant growth are Southeast and South Asia and Eastern Europe, where the industry is expected to grow at rates exceeding 8 percent annually.

Ethics in Hospitality

- For its grand opening, a casino hires 200 foodservice workers, dealers, and security people, but does not tell its new employees that only 150 of them will be kept on after the first six weeks.

TABLE 12.3 Projected Growth of the Tourism Industry in 2010

	Economy			*Employment*	
Region	*Demand (in millions of dollars)*	*Demand (% real growth)*	*Economy GDP (% of total GDP)*	*Economy Jobs (in millions)*	*Economy Jobs (% of total employment)*
World	7,060,288	3.9	10.4	231,222	8.3
Caribbean	56,077	3.0	16.5	2,447	14.8
Central and Eastern Europe	302,826	4.4	8.3	10,504	7.1
European Union	2,486,881	2.2	10.9	25,712	11.8
Latin America	186,356	7.9	7.3	12,990	6.9
Middle East	172,242	5.9	9.6	5,416	10.0
North Africa	61,985	7.6	13.6	5,744	12.8
North America	2,040,764	3.0	10.5	21,115	11.1
Northeast Asia	1,184,810	6.5	10.6	83,175	9.5
Oceania	151,856	2.8	12.7	1,853	13.7
Other Western Europe	197,855	2.3	12.2	2,823	9.3
South Asia	82,037	8.1	5.5	31,493	5.2
Southeast Asia	196,794	5.1	10.6	21,420	8.4
Sub-Saharan Africa	90,114	4.2	8.1	10,354	5.9

Source: World Travel and Tourism Council, March 2007.

- A female server in a quick-service restaurant complains that the assistant manager (who happens to be the franchise owner's son) is sexually harassing her.
- A wealthy guest asks a reservations manager to "bump" someone else's reservation for the hotel's banquet room. The influential patron, a "regular," threatens to take her company's business elsewhere if this is not done.
- A restaurant refuses to hire a qualified sommelier solely because he is HIV-positive and might make coworkers and guests feel "uncomfortable" if he were hired.

Ethical problems like those just mentioned arise daily for hospitality managers and workers. Besides these issues, questionable practices like offering or accepting bribes, concealing tips or other income from the Internal Revenue Service, condoning unsafe or unsanitary conditions, advertising false claims, or raiding a competitor's staff can cause trouble for both managers and employees alike. Hospitality professionals are now placing more emphasis on ethics. Dealing with problems in an ethical manner involves creating guidelines for an ethical workplace and helping staff make ethical decisions to meet the challenges of the future.

Guidelines for an Ethical Workplace

Many people work in an environment that permits unethical behavior as a means of getting ahead of the competition or as a rationale for unfair hiring and serving practices. However, this type of workplace neither enhances employee satisfaction nor attracts guests, who want to be treated fairly. Since both are important to the service industry, many leaders in the hospitality industry propose that companies create a workplace which emphasizes honesty, integrity, and trust.

Some basic guidelines, according to the Business Roundtable, an association of large corporations across the country, will help create this ethical environment. Its guidelines include the following:[13]

- Managers and top executives need to model expected behavior and be committed to both the company and its employees. Strong leadership is essential in cultivating an ethical environment. If the top management is not committed, it is absurd to believe other employees will be.
- A written code of ethics that clarifies expectations of behavior should be available. Employees need to know exactly what to do in certain situations. Businesses with clearly defined policies that provide company standards to follow regarding ethical issues help employees make difficult decisions when they encounter complex problems.
- A process is needed to implement a code as well as ensure compliance with it. No matter how this is done—through training courses, audits, rewards for exemplary ethical behavior, or other means—managers need to oversee employee adherence with company policy.
- All personnel need to know they have a stake in their company. Being held responsible for certain levels of business as well as feeling a commitment to a corporation's values strengthens the employees' sense of involvement, belonging, and pride in their company. This, in turn, will help to improve the company's ethical atmosphere as coworkers trust each other more and see themselves as part of a team dedicated to living up to company standards.

Once a company establishes an ethical environment, it must constantly improve and refine its code of conduct. No code can possibly cover all problems that might arise, and employees need to know how to face new challenges.

A company that makes ethical awareness a priority finds that its standards give it a competitive edge in the marketplace—perhaps because its staff is committed to the goals and values set by that company.

Summary

- Some common factors that have an impact on the industries in the hospitality network are economic climate, socioeconomic trends, technological innovations, and government regulations.

- Globalization has led nations to change their economic profiles as well as their political systems, and has led to increased international investment worldwide.
- Fulfilling the needs and expectations of guests is key to the service-driven hospitality industry. Research that provides demographic and socioeconomic information on the population is especially helpful to decision makers in the industry.
- Rapid technological advances have greatly influenced the hospitality industry. Advances in transportation, foodservice, and computer information systems have improved industry productivity, enhanced service, and generated greater profits.
- Many government regulations and policies dictate how hospitality organizations operate. Some regulations and policies deal with taxes, human resource legislation, environmental standards, and labor unions.
- Service-oriented businesses like the hospitality industry continue to be more prominent in the overall economic landscape than manufacturing industries.
- In the future the world's population will be older, more culturally diverse, and more equally divided between male and female than ever before.
- The hospitality industry must be at the forefront of technological advancement, because today's educated consumers rely on advanced technology to book their own reservations and communicate through video-conferencing and other social networks on-line to conduct of business.
- Hospitality must maintain a balance between "high-tech" and "high-touch," between the need for service and the need for efficiency, speed, and technology.
- In order to compete in the global economy, the industry will need to market to new segments and to international travelers. Adaptation to the needs of a changing workforce and guest is the key to success.
- Opportunities for hospitality professionals, especially in recreation management and foodservice, continue to grow.
- Dealing with problems in an ethical manner involves creating guidelines for an ethical workplace.
- Companies that emphasize honesty, integrity, and trust find that their standards give them a competitive edge in the marketplace.

ENDNOTES

[1] Larry Chervenak, "Hotel Technology at the Start of the New Millennium."

[2] Ibid.

[3] "DeFacto Security Standards: Operators at Risk," *Cornell Hotel and Restaurant Administration Quarterly* (February 1991): 107–117.

[4] David Jamieson and Julie O'Mara, *Managing Workforce 2000* (San Francisco: Jossey-Bass, 1991): 25–27.

[5] B. Bremner, "A Spicier Stew in the Melting Pot," *Business Week* (December 21, 1992): 29–30.

[6] "All-women excursions fill a niche," *Columbus Dispatch* (April 12, 1993): 54.
[7] William H. Frey, "The Diversity Myth," American Demographics (June 1998): 38f.
[8] "DeFacto Security Standards: Operators at Risk," *Cornell Hotel and Restaurant Administration Quarterly* (February 1991): 107–117.
[9] World Travel and Tourism Council, Travel and Tourism Satellite Account World Economic Impact (London, U.K.: Author, 1998).
[10] John Jesitus and Glenn Hasek, "Design Dilemia: Environmental Regulations, Slow development of Two California Hotel Properties," *Hotel and Motel Management* (July 27, 1992).
[11] Deloitte (2007) International Hotel Benchmark Survey.
[12] Christine O'Dwyer, "Opening Doors and Minds." Lodging (May 1992): 12.

CHECK YOUR KNOWLEDGE

1. List four external forces that affect the hospitality industry.
2. What are the two main parts of a business cycle? What are the extremes called?
3. Name one way in which technology has improved methods of service in the hospitality industry.
4. Identify three types of political forces that affect the hospitality industry. Explain how the labor force is changing.
5. Outline the areas of growth expected in the industry. What regions of the world will see the most dynamic changes?
6. Identify areas of technological advancement and explain their effect on the hospitality industry.

APPLY YOUR SKILLS

1. Refer to Table 12.2, "American Consumer Satisfaction Index Rankings."
   a. What factors might explain why hospitality companies did not do very well in comparison to other firms on this survey?
   b. Think back over the last few weeks, then make a list of twenty-five firms with which you had some form of business contact (e.g., grocery store, gas station, restaurant, school or college, clothing store, telephone company, bike shop, copy shop, etc.). Rank the firms in terms of your satisfaction with their products and services. Share your re-
1. sults with other class members.
2. Which phase of a business cycle would be the best time to launch a trend-setting new hospitality business? Why?
3. How might an economic downturn affect the implementation of technological innovation?

INTERNET EXERCISES

1. Visit the Web site of the National Restaurant Association. Find the projections for food and beverage sales for the coming year. Download the information. Identify what segment of the foodservice industry will enjoy the greatest level of sales increases, and which will have the lowest level of growth.
2. Using the Web, locate articles published in *American Demographics* magazine. Read several articles and prepare a one- to two-page summary of demographic trends likely to affect some segment of the hospitality industry.
3. Compare and contrast the "user friendliness" of three Web sites that allow consumers to book airline travel.
4. Imagine that you are traveling to New Orleans, Louisiana. Using the Internet, select three hotels and three restaurants that you would consider. (If you live in New Orleans, do the same exercise for San Francisco, California.)

WHAT DO YOU THINK?

1. What effect do you think a more diversified workforce will have on the hospitality industry? How will workforce shortages affect the industry?
2. What technological innovation do you think will be most important in the future? Why?
3. Should the federal government invest more money in promoting the hospitality industry? Give the reasons for your answer.
4. Why will ecotourism be important to the hospitality industry in the future?

CASE STUDY

In the 1960s, the Federal Trade Commission banned cigarette ads from television. In the 1980s, the Federal Aviation Administration banned smoking on most domestic flights. Some cities have banned smoking in government buildings. The U.S. Environmental Protection Agency has declared secondhand smoke a Class A carcinogen, like asbestos and benzene. In the 1990s, restaurants became the target for groups such as Action on Smoking and Health (ASH), which want to rid the restaurant industry of secondhand smoke. Opponents to ASH say that their businesses will be unfairly penalized. They argue that their ventilation systems eliminate the smoke and that designating nonsmoking sections should be enough to serve nonsmokers.

Today, as the owner of a small family restaurant in a jurisdiction that still permits limited smoking in restaurants, you are aware of the societal forces at work to change the way people think about health and smoking. You are approached by a representative of ASH and asked to ban smoking from your restaurant completely. The representative explains that although you will probably suffer a temporary loss of customers, in the long run society will shun smokers and most of your customers will appreciate the cleaner atmosphere. Currently, about 25 percent of your customers smoke.

1. Would you ban smoking from your restaurant, even though smokers represent one-fourth of your business?
2. Other than changing social attitudes about health and smoking, what forces are at work here?
3. Do you believe your restaurant should follow cultural trends or be part of the force that changes cultural attitudes?

ch13

Building for Success

OVERVIEW

Your personal definition of success might be to obtain a career position that allows you to serve the public directly. Maybe your idea of success is to become part of a management team. Your definition might even be to secure a 9-to-5 job. Your definition of success may be an ideal work–should life balance. Whatever your definition, you can take certain steps to achieve success and execute a successful career development strategy. This chapter outlines those steps.

Later in the chapter, you will learn specific answers to common questions and advice from a professional who has been where you are now and who has forged his own successful path within the hospitality industry. And you will follow the steps that will take you from student to career professional—from taking a realistic, practical look at yourself, to carefully evaluating the needs of companies you want to work for, to preparing for the interview—steps that will help you to build a future filled with success.

OBJECTIVES

When you have completed this chapter, you should be able to:

1 **Identify eight communication skills needed for a successful hospitality career.**

2 **Evaluate your skills to determine what kind of job you want and what you have to offer an employer.**

3 **Formulate a career strategy.**

4 **Explain how to develop a network.**

5 **Describe how to prepare for an interview.**

KEY TERMS

career objective
communication
databases
employee assistance programs (EAPs)
informational interview
networking
professional development
receiver
resumé
screening interview
sender
spreadsheet
word processors

Some Basic Business Skills

To succeed in today's and tomorrow's world, certain skills are essential. Some, such as communication, are time-honored. People have always needed good communication skills to succeed. Others are newer, the result of advances in technology.

Communication

The process of sending and receiving messages is **communication**. At least two people are required for communication to take place—the sender of the message and the receiver. Communication is always a two-way process. The terms sender and receiver are relative, depending on what a person is doing at a certain moment. If you are speaking to a friend, you are the **sender**, and your friend is the receiver. When your friend speaks, you become the **receiver**, and your friend becomes the sender. These roles change quickly and often.

Although many kinds of communication exist, in hospitality you will be mostly concerned with business communication. The function of business communication is to make your ideas clear to the people you work with and to the public.

To communicate effectively, it is important to follow these guidelines:

- Have a clear message.
- Speak clearly.
- Speak at a moderate rate.
- Be enthusiastic.
- Be sure your listeners understand.
- Keep your message short and simple.
- Project a positive demeanor and tone.
- Encourage open communication.

Have a Clear Message

Whenever possible, prepare your message ahead of time. Ask yourself, "What is my point?" Write down the facts and organize them logically. You should also know exactly what you want your listener(s) to do with your information.

If you are going to address a group on dishwashing procedures, write down the steps in sequence. If you must discipline an employee, specifically define what was done wrong, what changes should be made, and what the consequences will be if the employee repeats the violation. Try to anticipate what the receiver may say or how he may react to your message.

Speak Clearly

Carefully pronounce your words and use proper grammar to help relay your message; refrain from casual diction. Speech that is slurred or ungrammatical is difficult to understand. Pay particular attention to those for whom English is a second language. For them, contractions, slang, and vague language can be impossible to comprehend. And avoid trying to be "one of the guys" by using street language. This can lead to unclear communications or even a breakdown in your authority, which will erode credibility.

Speak at a Moderate Rate

Take time to think before you speak, then speak at a moderate rate. It is true that most people can take in information about twice as fast as they can speak. This should not lead you to speak quickly, however. Besides being easier to understand, words that are spoken at a moderate rate let your audience focus more easily on your message. While speaking, pay attention to the mannerisms and body language of the receiver and adjust your message accordingly.

Be Enthusiastic

If you want others to care about what you are saying, show that you care. Enthusiasm is difficult to fake, so you are better off if you really care about your subject and project genuineness. Don't try to fill every sentence with emotion, but do not try to hide your emotions either. Your feelings are part of your message, and it is important to let people know when you are pleased, concerned, or upset. Always keep your emotions within the bounds of professional conduct. Never yell, cry, or laugh in a way that would indicate you might be out of control.

Be Sure Your Listeners Understand

When possible, ask listeners to restate what you have said. Do not assume people will ask questions when they do not understand something they hear. They rarely do. Most often they will nod and walk away confused rather than ask for clarification. Have them repeat your message in their own words. And if some of your listeners do not understand, do not blame them. Apologize for not being clear, and then repeat your message. Use different words and examples, or approach your topic from another angle. Generally, if someone does not get it the first time, repeating yourself verbatim will not help. You may have to wait and ask for feedback once the receiver has had the opportunity to digest your conversation.

Keep Your Message Short and Simple

Forget about impressing people with big words. They frequently get in the way of your message. Words, phrases, sentences, and paragraphs should be short and to the point. Avoid jargon or technical terms, unless you are sure your audience will understand. Always be precise and give details, but do not get sidetracked by nonessential facts. Strike a balance between giving too little information and too much. When unsure of a topic or answer, do not be afraid to say "I'm not sure." It is better to admit you do not know than try and make excuses or provide inaccurate responses.

Encourage Open Communication

Never assume that you know it all. A professional always encourages thoughtful input from employees. Why rely only on your ideas when you can have dozens of others available? Successful managers see their employees as resources, not just workers.

Becoming a good communicator takes practice and patience. At every point in your career, you should take advantage of opportunities to improve your communication skills. Setting the stage and providing a trustful environment can go a long way toward open communication.

Skills for Today's Technology: Working with Computers

Computers are a significant part of daily life and a normal part of the business day. Your life and interactions on a daily basis involve some form of technology and computerization—in cars, houses, libraries, watches, jets, grocery stores, answering machines, banks, hotels, and restaurants. Hospitality workers are no exception: they use computers to order supplies, send daily e-mail messages to co-workers and guests, book guest accommodations, confirm airline tickets, transmit food orders, and perform hundreds of other tasks. Thus, an important skill to develop while in school is the use of electronic mail (e-mail). While you may never have to be a computer expert, you will need to be familiar with a few basic functions. In addition to e-mail, three important ones are word processing, spreadsheets, and database management.

Word Processing

Just as typewritten correspondence replaced longhand as the standard in business communications, **word processors**—software used to create documents on a computer—have replaced typewriters as the writing tool of choice. Word processors make creating, storing, editing, and printing documents simple and efficient. In hospitality, word processing generally involves the production of letters, reports, memos, and business proposals.

Spreadsheets

A **spreadsheet** is a computerized version of an accountant's ledger book that not only records numeric information, but performs calculations with that information as well. (See a sample spreadsheet in Table 13.1.) A spreadsheet helps answer the question, "What if?" For example, suppose a spreadsheet is set up with a restaurant's operating costs, such as rent, salaries, taxes, and supplies. If one cost goes up, how will this affect the others? Will the operation show a profit if two jobs are eliminated? If the cost of flour is cut, what does it do to the profit from pastries? If taxes increase by 2 percent, how much will prices have to rise to show the same profit? A well-designed spreadsheet will calculate the answers. It will take much of the guesswork out of money management. And while hospitality concerns itself with satisfying guests, it is most definitely a bottom-line business. Spreadsheet use is commonplace in the hospitality industry. Most supervisory and management positions require at least a basic level of understanding of and experience using, compiling, and interpreting spreadsheets. The more advanced your skill in spreadsheet management, the more opportunities you will have for career growth.

Databases

A database is useful tool capable of storing massive amounts of information. **Databases** are organized collections of information, such as names, addresses, prices, and dates. Databases are useful for billing, direct mail, reservations,

TABLE 13.1 Part of a Restaurant Spreadsheet

	Budget	*Actual*	*Variance*
REVENUES			
Food Sales	$845,000	$885,217	$40,217
Beverage Sales	125,000	118,000	(7,000)
Total Revenue	970,000	1,003,217	33,217
Cost of Goods Sold			
Food	270,400	309,826	39,426
Beverages	18,750	14,160	(4,590)
Total Cost of Goods Sold	289,150	323,986	34,836
Income	680,850	679,231	(1,619)
EXPENSES			
Payroll and Benefits			
Wages and Salaries	271,600	239,009	32,591
Benefits	48,888	43,022	5,866
Employee Meals	54,320	47,802	6,518
Total Payroll and Benefits	374,808	329,832	44,976

payroll, guest history information, and other functions that require analysis of large quantities of like data. More and more businesses are using databases to market and manage their services, target their key customers, and show their product offerings. For example, in Chapter 12, you read about Holiday Inn's Atlanta data center, a huge database system that handles the company's reservation system, payroll, expenses, and travel agent commission programs. With this system Holiday Inn is able to respond to hundreds of calls every day regarding rates, bills, and service complaints. Such database systems can also assist in tracking employee hours, overtime, tips, and dozens of other management concerns. Again, you won't be expected to become a database expert, but you will have to understand their importance and use in day-to-day operations.

Prepare yourself by taking a few computer classes. Many systems present little difficulty, as they are now graphically based, and some require nothing more than touching a computer screen to book a guest or confirm a reservation. Still, you need to be computer literate to operate in a modern business environment. Take every opportunity to hone your computer skills and create a competitive advantage through your skill set and technological expertise.

For those of you with an interest in or aptitude for computers or database management, career opportunities exist within the industry for information technology professionals. Many of the established chain hotel brands have significant infrastructures to serve their information technology and data management needs.

How to Acquire the Skills and Knowledge You Need

There are two ways to learn basic business skills, along with the specialized knowledge you need to succeed in the hospitality industry. One way is to learn them on the job. The other is to study them in classes. Ideally, combining both practical and educational elements will provide the most dynamic skill set.

Increasingly, postsecondary education is required to obtain a job in the hospitality industry. For example, most experts and industry professionals agree that a bachelor of arts in hotel and restaurant administration (or a liberal arts degree coupled with hotel experience) is a must for hospitality managers. A degree earned by taking courses in administration, accounting, economics, data processing, hotel maintenance and engineering, foodservice management, and catering is often the first stepping-stone to a management career.[1]

Many graduates begin their careers as trainee assistant managers and are promoted more quickly than those who work their way up through the ranks. Large operations typically cultivate management talent with on-the-job training programs and tuition reimbursement. Although not required, certification programs offered by several associations, such as the American Hotel and Motel Association and the Educational Foundation of the National Restaurant Association, also can enhance a person's credibility as a qualified manager. Many industry professionals are certified in their particular discipline.

Certification may be obtained in the following areas from the American Hotel and Lodging Association's educational institute: general manager, rooms manager, manager, trainer, educator, food and beverage professional, wine programming, housekeeping, and technology.

A broad array of postsecondary hospitality programs are available, offering instruction in everything from hotel and restaurant management to travel and tourism, food preparation (from meat cutting to fine French cooking), foodservice management, beverages, nutrition, catering, club management, meeting planning, institutional management, and elder care.

Not everyone who enrolls in a hospitality program does so directly after graduating from high school. Sometimes people first enter the world of work and then decide they want to go on with their education. It is not unusual for someone to start out, say, washing dishes, move on to making salads, and then decide on cooking as a career and enroll in a culinary institute to become a chef.

Because of the globalized economy and the international tourism marketplace, gaining international experience by studying abroad or working in an overseas internship program can give hospitality students an advantage. You can find out more about these programs by contacting organizations, such as the Association of International Practical Training, that promote international student exchanges and internships. Whatever training route you choose, however, you must follow some specific steps to find a job.

Steps to a Career in Hospitality

To have a satisfying, rewarding position, your interests, your likes and dislikes, and your skills, values, and goals must match your employer's. Finding the right job starts with you: you need to determine what you want and what you have to offer.

Self-Evaluation of Skills and Career Alignment

The simplest way to ascertain what you have to offer is to make a list of your experience and your assets. Begin with an honest assessment of your education, skills, previous jobs, strengths, and values. List each job you have had. Include dates of employment and contact names, but more importantly, write down your achievements—not only what you have done, but also what the long-range effects of your accomplishments have been. Business is, after all, about getting things done, and results are proof of your labor. Learn to quantify your achievements—translate them into statistics and create a compelling story of your capabilities and potential contributions to an organization. For example, if you were a fast-food cashier for two years and excelled at French fry sales, you might write "led the organization in incentive selling programs by 15 percent over a two-year period."

On your list include information about school, offices you have held in organizations or clubs, sports activities, awards, interests, hobbies, and anything else you can come up with that is relevant to the position and the organization you are marketing yourself to. You can edit the list later when you begin to write your resumé. Remember to focus on the results of your actions. If you were president of a club, did you increase membership? By how much? In your summer job, were you given a service award? Did you advance into positions with more responsibility? What ideas did you come up that benefited your employer? Don't overlook the seemingly small things.

This list will help you pinpoint what you like to do and what you have accomplished. It will help you not only when you write your resumé, but also when you formulate your career objectives. Remember to be flexible about how you tell your story; you may end up preparing more than one resumé, modifying the content to recast it in a way that aligns with the industry and organization you're seeking to join.

Career Objectives

A **career objective** describes the kind of job you hope to get. For example, a career objective might be "To obtain an entry-level management position that offers the opportunity for training in foodservice presentation." As you can see from the example, a career objective states a purpose. Formulating a career objective starts you on your career path.

Define your objective by asking yourself such questions as:

- Am I better qualified for a management trainee position or an entry-level job?
- Do I want to be involved in a position that requires skill in human relations?
- Do I want to work with computers?
- Do I want to work with finance?
- In what direction do I expect this position to take me? What has been the experience of others? How fast and how far have they risen within the organization?
- What are my expectations with regard to advancement and training?

For example, if your objective is "To obtain a position in foodservice management," asking yourself questions such as those above will help you zero in on a specific position in the foodservice industry. It will also help you clarify your expectations and requirements. Inteview those in the industry to determine if there is a good fit between your ideals and the practical realities of the position or career path.

You can have more than one career objective. And you will probably change your objectives as you progress in your career. Don't worry about how things might change. Just define what you want now and would strive for in the near term. A career objective is just a tool that will take you one step further along in a career in hospitality. Setting a career goal enables you to examine your own values and determine what courses of action to take as you explore the opportunities available in the hospitality industry.

Discover Your Opportunities

When you have set your career objective, the next step is to look for companies that fit your objective and for whom you might like to work. There are two ways to do this. One is to target companies, and the other is to develop networks and become involved in professional organizations.

Targeting Companies

To develop a list of possible companies to approach for a position, you will need to gather information. There are three sources you should use.

School Career Placement Services Don't wait until you are about to graduate before getting to know your school's career placement services office. The staff can help you identify your skills, prepare your resumé, and refine your job search. Many career centers also offer assessment services in which you complete a survey that identifies and compares your interests with those of people working in the field. Investing time in an assessment will help you prevent a wrong career decision.

The Internet The Internet is integral to hospitality industry enterprises as both an external vehicle to reach and attract customers and an internal platform for organizational communication and information processing. Many firms provide information through the Internet. Some provide special information for prospective employees, such as job listings, locations, contact information, and application instructions. Many companies also maintain Web pages that feature recent press releases, customer feedback, investor relations, employment and career opportunities, environmental vision statements, and company mission statements. Current news about a company can be especially helpful if you are invited for an interview. By checking the latest news about the organization, you will gain a background from which to ask informed questions. You also can find current information about hospitality firms on the Web sites of major industry periodicals, such as *Nation's Restaurant News*. And do not forget to check career pages on the Internet that list opportunities directly.

The Library Many college libraries maintain collections of company annual reports. They also are likely to have information about geographic areas where you might want to work, such as housing costs, weather, and transportation.

If you begin with a general idea of what you are looking for, targeting a company is easier. Ask yourself such questions as:

- Where do I want to work? In the United States? Overseas? In a specific region?
- Do I prefer large cities or small towns?
- Do I want to travel frequently or stay near home?

- What is the lowest starting salary I will accept?
- What benefits are important for me?
- What training do I want the company to provide?
- Is the organizational culture compatible with my values?
- How stable is the company and what are its long-term prospects?

Keep Asking Questions From your answers, you will see a profile begin to emerge of a company that offers what you need. Eliminate companies that do not meet your requirements or share your values, and spend more time researching those that do.

For specific information about the research process, look at sources like *How to Find Information about Companies*. You can research company history on-line; the Web offers easy access to company information. (This information will also help you prepare for interviews.)

Professional Profile

ADRIAN ZECHA

Innovative Resort Developer

Amanresorts Founder

Adrian Zecha is a product of the turbulence and opportunity of postwar Asia. He was born in 1933 to a family of Czech-Indonesian plantation owners, was raised in Indonesia, and was educated in the United States. In 1956, the Zecha family lost its landholdings when then-President Sukarno nationalized the country's businesses. The family fled to Singapore. Zecha, then in his early twenties, was already in New York working for *Time* magazine. His first stab at business came at age twenty-seven when he launched *Asia* magazine, the first regional newspaper color supplement on that continent. The $750,000 venture involved negotiations in thirteen countries, censorship problems, and logistical nightmares. But its successful debut in 1961 established the young Zecha as a resourceful and persuasive deal maker.

In the seventies and eighties, after working with U.S. hotelier Bill Marriott, Zecha teamed up with two other hospitality entrepreneurs, Robert Burns and Georg Rafael, to establish the Regent Hotel chain, Asia's first five-star network. The trio built twelve hotels. He then bought London's Dorchester Hotel and sold it shortly thereafter to the Sultan of Brunei for an undisclosed profit.

When Zecha unveiled the first Amanresort, he reinvented the high-end holiday. Instead of the 400-room compound of manufactured, marbleized opulence required by resort-business convention, he built Amanpuri ("place of peace"), a 40-room designer park in Phuket, Thailand. Instead of shielding visitors from the "untidy" environment, Zecha left things as pristine as possible and invited guests to merge with the natural surroundings.

Aman is Sanskrit for "peace," and Amanwana ("peaceful forest") is the most extreme manifestation of Zecha's resort-hotel ethos—a back-to-nature concept that the rest of the industry found bizarre when he opened his first property in 1988. Zecha calls Amanwana a "campsite," but "tent" is hardly a suitable term for the twenty palatial, canvas-roofed, air-conditioned pavilions erected on Moyo Island, Indonesia's national reserve jungle.

Source: http://www.pathfinder.com

A trip to the library or bookstore will reveal many sources of practical information for job hunting and career building. Here are a few books that can help you achieve your career goals.

For the names and addresses of various professional and trade associations, see the *National Trade and Professional Associations of the United States*. For specific information on corporations, try Dun and Bradstreet's *Million Dollar Directory*, Standard & Poor's *Register of Corporations, Directors, and Executives*, or Ward's *Business Directory*. All of these directories should be located in the reference section of your local or college library. For a list of additional resources, see Table 13.2.

Networking and Professional Development

Job search specialists say that 80 percent of jobs never appear in the classified ads, the source most people use to hunt for a job. Most jobs, the specialists say, are in the "hidden job market." If ads represent only 20 percent of jobs and the majority of people apply for them, competition for those jobs is bound to be stiff. However, if only a few people apply for the remaining 80 percent of jobs, the field is more open and employment prospects are more likely. Check the classified ads, but use them as a supplement to your other efforts. Most of your time should be spent on **networking**—the process of meeting with and gathering information from an ever-expanding channel of acquaintances—and on **professional development**—the process of becoming involved with trade-related activities, including meetings, seminars, and committees. Today, headhunters and professional search firms play a major role in recruitment of middle management and executive-level positions in the hospitality industry. Typically, the company pays the recruitment commission.

You can begin your networking and professional development ventures now. Many trade associations have special chapters that allow students to become members at a reduced cost. Sign up to serve on committees and boards. Don't worry about lack of experience; many associations encourage committee work as a forum for learning. For example, when a professional organization was in need of a newsletter editor, a new associate member was interested, but

TABLE 13.2 Recommended Reading for Job Hunters about Travel and Hospitality-Related Jobs/Careers

1. *Careers in Travel, Tourism, & Hospitality*, by Marjorie Eberts, Linda Brothers, and Ann Gisler (McGraw-Hill)
2. *Jobs for Travel Lovers*, by Ron Krannich, Ph.D. (Impact)
3. *Opportunities in Hotel and Motel Management Careers*, by Shepard Henkin, Darryl Hartley-Leonard, and Marguerite Duffy (McGraw-Hill)
4. U.S. Department of Labor, *Occupational Outlook Handbook* (U.S. Government Printing Office; revised every two years).

Source: http://www.quintcareers.com

The library is an excellent source for researching companies.

didn't have the experience. She volunteered her time, and the group, grateful to have a fresh perspective, walked her through the process until she learned to produce the newsletter by herself. Volunteerism is a critical element in networking and relationship-building activities. Make the best of the opportunity to interact with industry professionals and participate in industry-related events. You will learn more about the business and establish valuable connections.

Trade organizations offer great networking opportunities. In addition, trade publications such as *Nation's Restaurant News*, *Restaurant Hospitality*, and *Hotel and Motel Management* provide a wealth of industry information. Getting involved through trade-related reading and activities will help you get a feel for what is going on in different segments of the hospitality industry. It will also prepare you for networking and interviews later on, where you will be expected to discuss business knowledgeably.

Several words of advice on networking. Networks are as critical for finding your first position as for your subsequent career progression. Some networks are more effective than others, though. When looking for a position, the best contacts to have in your network are the people who meet the following criteria:

- They are working in the industry. Otherwise they are not likely to be in a position to hear about job opportunities to pass your way.
- They hold positions of responsibility. Although information about opportunities can come from anyone in the industry, people in positions of responsibility are likely to have more effective networks of their own that they can use to help you.
- They are not people whom you know very well, such as friends or relatives. You need contacts that reach beyond your social circle to get the broadest information about opportunities.
- They know someone who thinks highly of you. Having someone else promote your abilities is always better than doing it yourself!

- They are not close friends, coworkers, or relatives of any of your other contacts. Why invest the time in maintaining a network relationship with two people who share the same contacts when one will do the job?

Common advice about networking says, "the more contacts the better." This is not necessarily good advice because it can put you in the position of having to maintain a number of relationships that are not strategically important for your career.

Soon you will find people who possess so much knowledge about the job you are interested in that you will want to set up an **informational interview** with them. This type of interview is different from a job interview in that you are the interviewer. Informational interviews allow you to gather specific information about a job, company, or industry. The best ones will be with people already doing what you want to do, and although you are not (or should not be) pitching for a job, you just may find out about one or be remembered if a future opportunity does arise. When conducting informational interviews, remember that the people you are talking to are valuable resources. It is important not to waste their time or abuse their hospitality. Even though you thank the person personally when the interview ends, it is still necessary to write a thank-you letter. It is also a good idea to stay in touch—even after you have secured a position.

Don't be afraid of the networking process. Hospitality is a people business, and you will find that most people are glad to help. (If talking to people seems unpleasant, you might want to rethink your decision to get into hospitality in the first place.) Most people like to be asked for advice, if approached from the informational standpoint, and rarely will refuse to help. As well, the people you talk to will probably want to make you part of their network, in the hope that you may one day return the favor.

If done properly, networking will eventually provide you with an effective group of contacts. Since you may not be able to remember much of the information you will receive, start a record-keeping system. A notebook, file folder, or computer database will help you organize the names, addresses, and phone numbers of the people you contact. Record contact dates and any information given to you, and follow up on this information. Sophisticated personal information management software is available that lets you convert a collection of paper business cards to a readily available database on your computer. Periodically call, write, or send clippings from articles to people you have met. It is important to stay in touch with your network, so that people remember you and speak highly of you.

Internship Programs An internship is an effective way to "get your foot in the door" and evaluate your fit with a firm where you would like to be employed on a full-time, permanent basis. Many hospitality firms use their internship programs to identify candidates for future opportunities and introduce them to their cultural environment. Even if you do not end up working for the firm where you had an internship, you still will have gained the benefit of solid experience and established invaluable contacts.

A successful internship experience depends on several factors. First, you should evaluate whether you need breadth or depth in an internship. If an internship is your first experience working in the hospitality industry, then breadth is important. That is, you should look for an internship that will give you exposure to as many different positions and learning opportunities as possible. For example, a summer position at a hotel in which you spend several weeks each in housekeeping, front desk, and food and beverage offers the opportunity for you to experience the major departments. If you already have broad exposure to the industry, then you should seek depth in your internship and build potential industry contacts. That is, you should look for an internship that will deepen your experience and develop your expertise while establishing important and valuable relationships. Especially valuable are internship opportunities where you have major responsibility for a project, so that at the conclusion of the experience you can list your accomplishments on your resumé.

A second factor in determining the value of an internship is the level of commitment of the organization offering the internship. Although the percentage of firms that employ interns simply as short-term labor is small, it is nevertheless important that you ask thorough questions about the kind of work you will be doing, how you will be trained and supervised, how the internship program will be structured, and what the employer's expectations are. Just as a good internship experience benefits both you and your employer, so also can a bad experience be damaging for both parties. Be sure that you understand who your supervisor will be and how much time he or she will devote to working with you each week. Be wary of an internship where the supervisor cannot make time to work with you regularly. Do not be afraid to pass up an opportunity that does not meet your needs. You can gracefully withdraw your interest and still retain a congenial relationship with the organization.

The third factor that is critical to the success of an internship is you and your commitment to professional development. Treating the internship simply as a "part-time" or "summer" job will guarantee that that is all it will be for you. Be intentional about your internship. Decide in advance what you need to learn. Prepare a written proposal detailing what your learning and professional development objectives are for your internship. Share that proposal with the organizations that are considering you as an intern. Select an internship where your professional development needs are a good fit with what the organization offers. Then, during the internship, persist in pursuing your learning objectives, because your internship can be overlooked in the day-to-day pressures of running a business. Especially in small firms, it may be unrealistic to expect your supervisor to prioritize your professional development over his immediate responsibilities to the business. Take the lead and persist!

Courtesy of Photodisc

Internships require strong commitments from the employer and the student.

Getting the Job

Students dream of the day when they can hear those four little words—"You have the job." The next steps in making that dream a reality are preparing a resumé and going for a job interview.

Letters and Resumés

A **resumé** is a brief, written account of a job applicant's work experience, education, and other qualifications. The purpose of the resumé is not to get the job, but to get an employer's attention and secure an interview. (The interview will give you the opportunity to clinch the job.) The resumé should include enough detail to arouse curiosity, but not so much that an interview would be redundant. Because most employers spend only a few moments glancing at a resumé before deciding whether to call for an interview, it's important for the resumé to be properly written.

Hundreds of books and articles on resumé writing are available, so the focus here is on some dos and don'ts of letters and resumés:

- Do tell the truth. Be proud of your accomplishments and portray yourself in the best light, but stick to facts. Employers have seen it all and know a snow job when they see one. Besides, should you be hired, lying on a resumé is often grounds for dismissal.

- Don't send a resumé by itself. In the direct-mail business, it's been said, "The letter sells; the brochure tells." Your complete sales package generally should consist of a cover letter and a resumé. (In some circumstances, sending a letter by itself is appropriate—see the next bullet.)
- Do write the cover letter in a way that directs attention to your resumé and sells your qualifications. A well-written letter can convince the reader to call for an interview. Some job consultants suggest sending only a letter and then sending a resumé later when asked. This approach lets you do more selling and eliminates the possibility that some detail (or lack of it) on your resumé will prevent the employer from calling. When fishing for a job, your letter is bait, meant to hook the prospective employer's interest.
- Don't worry whether your resumé is set up in chronological (by date) or functional (by experience) order; the format is really a matter of preference. Be sure to stress your capabilities, and remember to quantify your achievements, as mentioned in the section on self-evaluation. Link your talents to the company's needs and create a compelling story to gain an opportunity to meet in person with the key company decision makers.
- Do limit your resumé to one or two pages. One page is standard; two is fine if you have enough experience. Otherwise, using more than one page means you probably are including too many details. A resumé is not a biography; it is a sales tool.
- Don't include personal information. Height, sex, age, marital status, and other items are irrelevant. You may include hobbies, but only if they are closely related to the job. References and salary history should be provided only on request.
- Do state the facts in the fewest possible words. Use powerful words and phrases that emphasize actions rather than tasks. For example, say "formulated" instead of "came up with." Write "organized" rather than "put together." Try "initiated" for "started up." Avoid overstating facts and exaggerating achievements.
- Don't address your letter "To Whom It May Concern." If you do not have a name, look up the company's phone number and call to ask for a name. In addition, in the first sentence of your letter, make it clear why you are writing. (Use phrases like "I'm responding to your ad…"; "I'm writing to ask about job openings…"; and "I'm writing to thank you….")
- Do customize your letter. If you are applying for a job, summarize relevant experience and show how this will benefit the employer. Keep the letter brief and to the point. Most executives are presssed for time and will look more closely at the work history and experience than the rest of the letter.
- End your letter by telling the reader that you will call on a certain date. Then make sure you do call on that date.
- Don't use attention-getting tricks. Brightly colored paper and clever resumés may seem like a good way to get attention, but they give the appearance of unprofessionalism. The resumé is your calling card and is the

first impression an employer has of you. You must appear dependable, not offbeat.

- Do invest in high-quality paper and matching envelopes. Laser printing is best. Never send poor-quality photocopies of your resumé. If you do need to use photocopies, a print shop can make quality duplicates quickly and cheaply.

Interviewing

The purpose of an interview is for you and a prospective employer to formally meet, exchange information, and evaluate the chemistry or fit between the two of you. Interviewing can be a stressful situation—after all, how you perform in the interview can determine whether you get the job. The interviewer will ask you a number of questions to find out about you and decide if you are right for the job. Likewise, you will want to be prepared for the interview and have questions ready for the interviewer. You want to make sure this company is right for you, so it is appropriate for you to ask questions, too. You may want to ask about management style, company policy, responsibilities of the position, and why the position is open, if the interviewer has not already told you.

Often, the first interview you will have is a **screening interview**. The purpose of this type of interview is to eliminate applicants from consideration when too many people apply. Although this process might sound cold, when hundreds of people apply for a handful of jobs, a human resources department has to quickly narrow the choices by finding reasons not to consider many of the applicants. This is done by checking off *yes* or *no* on a predetermined list of qualifications. Sometimes a screening interview is conducted over the phone, so be prepared if a company calls you about your application. If you begin with a phone interview, remember to project positiveness over the phone. It even helps to smile when answering questions over the phone. Phone interviews have one advantage: you have the opportunity to prepare a written "cheat sheet" to use during the interview that outlines the key points you desire to articulate to the interviewer.

Generally, if a company eliminates you from consideration without a screening interview, you will receive a letter thanking you for your application and indicating that your resumé will be kept on file. While this is usually the last you will hear from the company, some employers do look to their files up to a year later to fill job openings. When you are rejected (and you probably will be—more than once), do not take it personally. It just means you do not fit a specified profile. Don't worry; you will find a good fit sooner or later.

When you do secure an interview, take time beforehand to prepare yourself. Don't wait until the last minute to decide how you will answer questions or what you will wear. Perhaps the best way to approach it is to look at the interview as a two-part process, consisting of first impressions and answering/asking questions.

First Impressions

It's been said that you never get a second chance to make a first impression. Certainly the first few moments of an interview can have a lasting impact. The three keys to making a good first impression are appearance, courtesy, and preparation.

Appearance

Throw out the idea that a book should not be judged by its cover. You will be judged by how you look, so dress conservatively. A suit and tie or a pant or skirt suit with blouse and jacket is recomended. Be sure to keep attire low key and professional.

Courtesy

Courtesy begins before the interview. Arrive ten to fifteen minutes early. Take time to pay attention to personal grooming, calm down, go to the bathroom, etc. Also, use the extra time to ask the receptionist about the pronunciation of the interviewer's name. Administrative personnel and receptionists are known as "gatekeepers" because they control access to managers and decision makers. Treat them as courteously and professionally as you would a manager; they can be an invaluable source of information before and after the interview.

Begin the interview by greeting the interviewer, introducing yourself if necessary, and offering a firm handshake. Then you and the interviewer will probably engage in small talk. You may be asked if you had trouble finding the office or if the weather is nice. Be polite but do not talk too much about these things.

During the interview, watch your body language. Maintain eye contact with your interviewer, but do not stare. Sit forward to show your interest, and smile. Never look at your watch. This indicates impatience and can distract the interviewer. At all times keep good eye contact with the interviewer.

Also, do not smoke. Whether you are a smoker or not is not the issue. Many workplaces are smoke-free, and many people take offense at others lighting up cigarettes or cigars in their office. The best course of action is not even to ask if the interviewer minds—but simply not to smoke.

Preparation

Preparation involves many things—from being knowledgeable about the industry and the company, to having a list of references handy, to knowing how to answer a question. Begin your preparation by learning all you can about the company interviewing you. This includes history, financial condition, training programs, salaries, recent developments, size, structure, and management philosophy. Use many of the same sources you did for targeting a company, but also read company brochures, newspaper articles, and annual reports. If possible, learn what you can about the person who will interview

A Day in the Life of...

A HUMAN RESOURCES DIRECTOR

One area of employment students of hospitality often overlook is that of personnel management, also called human resources. Because of the nature of the hospitality profession and its high turnover rate, the job of human resources director is a vital one in making an entire operation run properly.

Above all, a human resources director should like people. "Human resources" is just another way of saying "people," and dealing with people is at the core of the human resources director's job. Probably the next most important qualification is being able to communicate well, since good communication is key to everything human resources directors do. The basic duties of a human resources director include:

- helping potential employees fill out applications
- maintaining employee records
- interviewing applicants
- corresponding with applicants
- placing want ads in newspapers, in other pertinent publications, and on-line
- maintaining time records
- checking applicants' references and screening resumés
- updating data on current employees, such as changes in hours, wages, personal information, education, and training
- collecting data on absenteeism and analyzing the data to see what can be done to reduce it
- analyzing employee performance evaluations to make sure they are fair
- logging disciplinary actions and merit notices
- supplying references on outgoing and prior employees
- analyzing job descriptions
- participating in labor negotiations
- informing employees about benefits, job classifications, and company policies
- developing training and in-service programs that support the company's mission
- ensuring that all equal opportunity laws and regulations are followed scrupulously[1]
- locating rehabilitation programs for employees who have a problem with drugs or alcohol, or engaging third-party vendors to provide **employee assistance programs (EAPs)**

Generally, in large hotels, the human resources director does not perform all these duties single-handedly; instead, the director supervises a staff of people who frequently specialize in just a few tasks each.

Human resources directors must be highly trained with a strong educational background in human resources or labor management. A degree from a four-year college or university is almost always required, and a master's degree is becoming increasingly necessary.

[1]Shepard Henkin, *Opportunities in Hotel and Motel Careers* (Lincolnwood, IL: NTC Publishing Group, 1992), 65–66.

you. A company administrator or members of professional associations may be able to provide you with some information. But be careful; you do not want it to look as if you are investigating the interviewer.

At the time of the interview, it is a good idea to bring an extra copy of your resumé. (If you have more than one version of your resumé, make sure you bring the same version you sent to this employer.) Many interviewers read through the resumé during the interview and ask questions as they go, so it's helpful to have one in your lap for reference. In addition, bring a list of references. These should be people who can vouch for your abilities in the kind of job you are seeking. (Friends and family members do not count.) Never volunteer the list; wait to be asked. If you have impressive college transcripts, marketing materials you have written, certificates, or newspaper write-ups about your accomplishments, bring them too. Spend much of your preparation time on questions. (This is discussed in detail in the next section.) When answering questions it's best to be brief. Your answers should last about thirty seconds.

Advice from the Expert

Bob Hunter is executive vice president of operations and client services for the stadium corporation Maple Leaf Sports and Entertainment (MLSE), the company that operates the SkyDome in Toronto, Ontario. A native of Hamilton, Ontario, Hunter majored in kinesiology at the University of Waterloo and then studied sports medicine in graduate school at the University of Washington. His advice for students interested in pursuing a career in hospitality management: "Start as early as possible, probably through part-time work. This may be either by volunteering or by attempting to get into facilities via work placement programs."

Hunter has spent his career managing and operating sports and entertainment facilities in Canada. Hunter notes, "The day-to-day operations of a major sports and entertainment facility are ever changing and challenging because of the need to run a very busy and profitable facility. The majority of my time is spent on ongoing negotiations and planning with event tenants and suppliers who are putting on events in the building. As well, a good deal of focus is directed toward our quality, service, and presentation to all the guests. Equally important is the people management of a department that includes six management staff and approximately one hundred employees."

He goes on to say, "There is absolutely no doubt that education is critical to the long-term potential of an employee. The business background and understanding of management that are delivered to students during their university years are required in the long run if they hope to be successful and work their way up to senior management positions."

Hunter strongly advises that job seekers take "an honest and sincere approach to interviewing and job hunting, highlighting why they believe this industry is for them. They should also have done some prior research on the hospitality industry. Understand that although it may appear glamorous, the industry involves a lot of hard work and great attention to detail. It is extremely important to be well prepared for interviews in order to maximize the communication between the employer and the candidate."

However, do not feel you need to rush into your answers. Taking a few seconds to collect your thoughts enables you to organize your answer.

Be sure to summarize your qualifications. At the end of the interview, briefly remind the interviewer why you want the job, why you are qualified, and what you have to offer. Ask what the next step in the selection process is, but do not force the issue. If you still want the job, ask for it directly.

Finally, remember to be yourself. Trying to put on an act will just make you more nervous. The best interviews are those in which you present yourself genuinely. This will also ensure that when you are offered a job, it will be with a company that wants you rather than the person you were trying to be during an interview. And remember this is your interview. Eliminating companies that do not fit your personality or style is part of the process.

Answering/Asking Questions

The interview is a question-and-answer process. Approach it in your mind from the interviewer's point of view, and think of questions you might ask if you were the interviewer. Then think about how you would answer those questions. Prepare answers to as many questions as you can think of, especially hard questions. Most likely, the interviewer will begin with a series of questions to find out who you are, what experience you have, and why you are right for the position. Prepare responses to typical questions such as:

- Why do you want to work for us?
- What are your strengths and weaknesses?
- Where do you see yourself in five years?

Industry Insights

LAW & ETHICS

Equal Employment Opportunity

Because our society believes in giving every citizen an equal chance to succeed, equal opportunity laws prohibit employers from discriminating against applicants or employees with respect to hiring, firing, promotion, or compensation. Decisions about these matters cannot be made on the basis of race, color, religion, sex, national origin, disabilities, or age. A number of federal laws and executive orders affect the way employers staff their operations, and any manager in the position to hire or fire should become familiar with them.

According to these regulations, job qualifications and selection procedures must be job-related. Interviews, for example, must follow strict guidelines about appropriate and inappropriate questions. As an interviewer, you cannot ask: "What is your date of birth?" since this would reveal a person's age, which is not relevant except if the person is under eighteen. You should instead ask: "Are you eighteen years of age or older?" You also cannot ask about maiden names, marital status, health, or religious affiliation.

Today, most interviewers structure conversations to place you at ease and lay the groundwork for a dialogue in which they will learn more about your interests, personality, values, and lifestyle. Often an interviewer will begin with something vague, such as "Tell me about yourself," to get you to talk. Don't memorize responses, but do think them through ahead of time.

If the interviewer brings up the question of salary, try to turn it around by asking "What is your salary range?" or "What are you offering?" You should know the average salary and competitive market value for the job before your interview. During the interview process salary expectations are best stated in general ranges. If at all possible, have the interviewer state the position's pay range rather than the other way around. Salary negotiation can take place later in the process.

You do not have to answer certain questions. Marital status, age, race, religion, and other personal information are irrelevant to the job, and questions about them violate the law. If you are asked questions such as these, do not get upset or tell the interviewer that he or she is violating the law. Just say that you do not believe such information is relevant or important to your performance.

Finally, because this is your interview, prepare questions to ask, such as:

- Why is this position vacant?
- Why do you work for this company?
- What are the best and worst things about working here?
- What is the company's management philosophy?
- What is a typical day like for someone in this position?

Have a pen and pad handy to write down information, but do not bury your head in a notebook. Your questions should cover information you can easily get from other sources. Most importantly, do not be too aggressive in your questions. Interviewers like questions, but nobody likes to be put on the spot.

Again, be sure to write a thank-you note to the interviewer soon after you have completed the interview. It is a common courtesy and a reminder that you want the job.

Summary

- Communication is the process of sending and receiving messages. It takes at least two people for communication—one to be the sender of the message, the other to be the receiver.
- To communicate effectively, have a clear message, speak clearly, speak at a moderate pace, be positive and enthusiastic, be sure your listeners understand, keep your message short and simple, and encourage open communication.

- Computers are becoming increasingly important to the hospitality industry. Basic knowledge of e-mail, word processing, spreadsheets, and databases is a must.
- The first step toward a career in hospitality is to know yourself. You can do this by evaluating your skills.
- The next step is to formulate a career objective—a statement that describes what you want to achieve.
- You can discover your opportunities by targeting companies and by developing networks and actively participating in professional organizations.
- The final steps in getting a job are preparing a resumé and going for a job interview.

ENDNOTES

[1] U.S. Department of Labor, *Occupational Outlook Handbook* (Washington, D.C.: U.S. Government Printing Office), 41.

CHECK YOUR KNOWLEDGE

1. List five ways to communicate effectively.
2. What kind of questions can spreadsheets answer?
3. Define a career objective and write a sample one.
4. List two dos and don'ts for resumé writing.
5. What is the difference between a screening interview and a job interview?

APPLY YOUR SKILLS

Table 13.3 shows the projected growth in six managerial positions, including managers of foodservice and lodging operations.

TABLE 13.3 Projected Growth in Selected Managerial Occupations

Occupation	*Projected Growth, 2006–2016*
Foodservice and lodging managers	+28% or 1.4 million jobs
Leisure and hospitality	+14.3% or 600,000 jobs
Professional and managerial	+14.9% or 270,000 jobs
Scientific and technical	+28.8% or 2.1 million jobs
Administrative support	+20.3% or 4.1 million jobs
Education and health services	+18% or 5.5 million jobs

1. Which managerial occupation has the highest projected growth rate? Why do you think this is so?

2. Which managerial occupation has the lowest projected growth rate? Why do you think this is so?
3. How would you evaluate the opportunities for foodservice and lodging managers in comparison to other managerial occupations?

INTERNET EXERCISES

The federal government provides information about job prospects in a publication entitled *Occupational Outlook Handbook*. Visit the U.S. Department of Labor's Web site and search for data on three hospitality-related positions. Answer the following questions for each of the three positions you selected.

1. What are the typical working conditions for the position?
2. What are the primary qualifications for the position?
3. What is the job outlook for the position?
4. What are the average earnings for the position?

WHAT DO YOU THINK?

1. If you had to choose just one of these two career skills to develop, which would it be: communicating or using computers?
2. You have the choice of starting in a hospitality job right now or spending the next four years studying hotel and restaurant management. Which do you think would be more beneficial?
3. You are at a job interview, and the interviewer asks you if you are married. What do you say?
4. As you network for information about a hospitality job, you discover that a certain hotel manager is looking for a front desk clerk. You also find out that this manager likes aggressive people who are into sports. You do not like sports, but you want the job. What do you do?
5. Some people believe that when you write a thank-you note for a job interview, you should recap the reasons why you think you want the job and why you are qualified for it. Do you think this is a good idea? Why or why not?

CASE STUDY

Imagine that you have been working as an assistant manager at a medium-size hotel for two years. Because of your good communication skills, the hotel manager gives you responsibility for leading the group training sessions for new employees. You are excited about the prospect of sharing your knowledge and enthusiasm with the group, and you prepare a five-page list of duties and responsibilities to go over with the group. You also prepare a detailed job description for each job type.

When the day comes to deliver your talk to the group, you find the group less enthusiastic than you expected—not like how you felt on your first day on the job—but they quietly listen as you go through the five pages of notes and hand out the job descriptions. Afterwards, you ask if there are any questions. One woman asks where she should park her car. Apart from that, no one asks anything.

You assume the meeting went well, and you continue your day. That afternoon you are called to the hotel manager's office, where you find several of the people who were at the training session earlier. They have been confused all day about what they are supposed to do. They are asking questions about all the things you went over.

1. What went wrong at the training session?
2. What should you do to correct the problem?
3. How might you conduct the next training session to prevent such problems?

APPENDIX **A**

Commonly Used Acronyms

AAA	American Automobile Association
AARP	American Association of Retired Persons
ABA	American Bus Association
ABBA	American Bed and Breakfast Association
ACF	American Culinary Federation
ACFEI	American Culinary Federation Educational Institute
ACTE	Association of Corporate Travel Executives
ADA	Americans with Disabilities Act; also American Dietetic Association
ADEA	Age Discrimination in Employment Act
AFA	American Franchise Association
AGTE	Association of Group Travel Executives
AH&LA	American Hotel & Lodging Association
APEC	Asia-Pacific Economic Cooperation
APTA	Asia Pacific Tourism Association
ARTA	Association of Retail Travel Agents
ASAE	American Society of Association Executives
ASBE	American Society of Bakery Engineers
ASEAN	Association of South-East Asian Nations
ASFSA	American School Food Service Association
ASH	Action on Smoking and Health
ASHFSA	American Society for Hospital Food Service Administrators
ASHRAE	American Society of Heating, Refrigerating, and Air-Conditioning Engineers
ASSE	American Society of Sanitary Engineers
ASTA	American Society of Travel Agents
ATI	American Travel Inns
ATM	Automatic Teller Machine
BBL	Bed and Breakfast League/Sweet Dreams and Toast
CARA	Chinese American Restaurant Association
CATS	Customer Attendance Tracking System
CEO	Chief Executive Officer
CHA	Certified Hotel Administrator

CHART Council of Hotel and Restaurant Trainers
CHE Certified Hospitality Educator
CHRIE Council on Hotel, Restaurant, and Institutional Education
CHRS Center for Hospitality Research and Services
CINET Convention Information Network
CLIA Cruise Lines International Association
CMAA Club Managers Association of America
CPA Certified Public Accountant
CRS Computerized Reservation System
CTP Certified Tour Professional
CVB Convention and Visitors Bureau
DMO Destination Marketing Organization
EAP Employee Assistance Program
EC European Community
ECU European Currency Unit
EDS Electronic Distribution System
EEOC Equal Employment Opportunity Commission
EFNRA Educational Foundation of the National Restaurant Association
ELD Electronic Liquid Dispenser
EPCOT Experimental Prototype Community of Tomorrow
FABULOUS Food and Beverage Undergraduate Learning on a Unix System
FCIA Franchise Consultants International Association
FCSI Foodservice Consultants Society International
FISA Food Industry Suppliers Association
FORCE Family of Responsible and Caring Employees
GAO General Accounting Office
GATT General Agreement on Tariffs and Trade
GDP Gross Domestic Product
GITHE General Indicator to Hotel Efficiency
HFTP Hospitality Financial and Technology Professionals
HII Heritage Interpretation International
HLTRF Hospitality Lodging and Travel Research Foundation
HMGI Hotel-Motel Greeters International
HSMAI Hospitality Sales and Marketing Association
IACB International Association of Convention Bureaus
IACVB International Association of Convention and Visitor Bureaus
IAHA International Association of Hospitality Accountants
ICTA Institute of Certified Travel Agents
IFA International Franchise Association
IIA Independent Innkeepers Association
IMO International Maritime Office
IoH Institute of Hospitality
ISHAE International Society of Hotel Association Executives
ISTTE International Society of Travel & Tourism Educators
MFBB Mexican Food and Beverage Board
MICA Mobile Industrial Caterers' Association
MICE Meetings, Incentive, Conventions and Exhibitions Industry
MPI Meeting Planners International
NABHP National Association of Black Hospitality Professionals
NAC National Association of Concessionaires
NACE National Association of Catering Executives
NAFTA North American Free Trade Agreement
NAILM National Association of Institutional Linen Management

NAPO National Association of Pizza Operators

NARM National Association of Restaurant Managers

NB&BA National Bed-and-Breakfast Association

NBMOA National Black McDonald's Operators Association

NCCR National Council of Chain Restaurants

NEPA National Environmental Policy Act

NFSA National Food Service Association

NRA National Restaurant Association

NSMH National Society of Minority Hoteliers

NSSFFA National Soft Serve and Fast Food Association

NTA National Tour Association

NTO National Tourism Organization

OECD Organization for Economic Cooperation and Development

PATA Pacific Asia Travel Association

PCMA Professional Convention Managers Association

PHA Preferred Hotels Association

PMS Property Management System

POS Point of Sale

RPA Regional Publishers Association

RWFBH Roundtable for Women Food-Beverage-Hospitality

SABRE®* Semi-Automated Business Research Environment

SAFSR Society for the Advancement of Food Service Research

SCANS Secretary's Commission on Achieving Necessary Skills

SFM Society for Foodservice Management

SLHOTW Small Luxury Hotels of the World

SMERF Social, Military, Educational, Religious, and Fraternal

STTE Society of Travel and Tourism Educators

THAA Tourist House Association of America

TIA Travel Industry Association of America

TIPS Training for Intervention Procedures by Servers

TO Tourism Office

TTRA Travel and Tourism Research Association

UNWTO United Nations World Tourism Organization

USTC United States Tourist Council

USTTA United States Travel and Tourism Administration

VDQS Vins Délimités de Qualité Supérieure

VFW Veterans of Foreign Wars

WES Washington Ethical Society

YTP Young Tourism Professionals

*A registered trademark of American Airlines, Inc.

APPENDIX **B**

Hospitality Industry Associations and Organizations

Please note that Internet resources are of a time-sensitive nature, and may often be modified or deleted.

American Association for Leisure and Recreation
1900 Association Dr.
Reston, VA 20191
703-476-3472
800-213-7193

American Association of Retired Persons (AARP)
601 E St. NW
Washington, DC 20049
202-434-2277
<http://www.aarp.org>

American Automobile Association (AAA)
1000 AAA Dr.
Heathrow, FL 32746-5063
407-444-7000
<http://www.aaa.com>

American Bus Association (ABA)
400 NY Ave., Suite 1050
Washington, DC 20005-3934
202-842-1645
<http://www.buses.org>

American Culinary Federation (ACF)
10 San Bartola Dr.
P.O. Box 3466
St. Augustine, FL 32085
904-824-4468
<http://www.acfchefs.org>

American Dietetic Association
216 W. Jackson Blvd.,
Suite 800
Chicago, IL 60606
312-899-0040
<http://www.eatright.org>

American Franchise Association (AFA)
10850 Wilshire Blvd., Suite 700
Santa Monica, CA 90025

American Hotel and Lodging Association (AH&LA)
1201 New York Ave. NW,
Suite 600
Washington, DC 20005
202-289-3100
<http://www.ahma.com>

American Recreation Coalition
1331 Pennsylvania Ave. NW,
Suite 726
Washington, DC 20004
202-662-7420

American School Food Service Association (ASFSA)
700 S. Washington St., Suite 300
Alexandria, VA 22314-4287
800-877-8822
<http://www.asfsa.org>

American Society of Association Executives
1575 Eye St. NW
Washington, DC 20005
202-626-2723
<http://www.asaenet.org>

American Society of Bakery Engineers (ASBE)
2 North Riverside Plaza,
Suite 1733
Chicago, IL 60606
312-332-2246
<http://www.asbe.org>

American Society of Heating, Refrigerating, and Air-Conditioning Engineers (ASHRAE)
1791 Tullie Circle NE
Atlanta, GA 30329
404-636-8400
<http://www.ashac.org>

American Society of Sanitary Engineering (ASSE)
28901 Clemens Rd.
Suite 100
West Lake, OH 44145
440-835-3040
<http://www.asse.plumbing.org>

American Society of Travel Agents (ASTA)
1101 King St.
Alexandria, VA 22314
703-739-2782
<http://www.astanet.com>

Association of Group Travel Executives (AGTE)
c/o The Light Group, Inc.
424 Madison Ave., Suite 705
New York, NY 10017
212-486-4300
<http://www.incentivesmotivate.com>

Bed and Breakfast League/Sweet Dreams and Toast (BBL)
P.O. Box 9490
Washington, DC 20016
202-363-7767

Broker Management Council (Foodservice Brokers)
P.O. Box 150229
Arlington, TX 76015
817-465-5511

Center for Hospitality Research and Service (CHRS)
c/o Dept. of Hotel, Restaurant, and Institutional Management
Virginia Polytechnic Institution and State University
Blacksburg, VA 24061
703-231-5515

Chinese American Restaurant Association (CARA)
173 Canal St.
New York, NY 10013
212-966-5747

Convention Liaison Council
1575 Eye St. NW, Suite 1190
Washington, DC 20005
202-626-2764

Council of Hotel and Restaurant Trainers (CHART)
8341 North 400 East
Bryant, IN 47326
219-997-6823

Council on Hotel, Restaurant, and Institutional Education (CHRIE)
1200 17th St. NW
Washington, DC 20036-3097
202-331-5990
<http://www.chrie.org>

Cruise Lines International Association (CLIA)
500 5th Ave., Suite 1407
New York, NY 10110
212-921-0066
<http://www.cruising.org>

Educational Foundation of the National Restaurant Association (EFNRA)
250 S. Wacker Dr., Suite 1400
Chicago, IL 60606
312-715-1010

Educational Institute of the AH&MA
1407 S. Harrison Rd.
East Lansing, MI 48823

Foodservice Consultants Society International (FCSI)
304 W. Liberty Street, Suite 201
Louisville, KY 40202
502-583-3783

Hospitality Financial & Technology Association
11709 Boulder Lane, Suite 110
Austin, TX 78726-1832
512-249-5333

Hospitality Lodging and Travel Research Foundation (HLTRF)
c/o American Hotel and Motel Association
1201 New York Ave. NW, Suite 600
Washington, DC 20005
202-289-3117

Hospitality Sales and Marketing Association International (HSMAI)
1300 L St. NW, Suite 1020
Washington, DC 20005
202-789-0089
<http://www.hsmai.org>

Hotel Employees and Restaurant Employees International Union
1219 28th St. NW
Washington, DC 20007
202-393-4373
<http://www.hereunion.org>

Independent Innkeepers Association (IIA)
P.O. Box 150
Marshall, MI 49068
616-789-0393
<http://www.innbook.com>

Institute of Certified Travel Agents (ICTA)
P.O. Box 812059
148 Linden St.
Wellesley, MA 12482
781-237-0280
<http://www.icta.com>

International Association of Amusement Parks and Attractions
1448 Duke St.
Alexandria, VA 22314
703-836-4800
<http://www.iaapa.org>

International Association of Fairs and Expositions
P.O. Box 985
Springfield, MO 65801
417-862-5771
<http://www.iafnet.org>

International Executive Housekeepers Association
1001 Eastwind Drive, Suite 301
Westerville, OH 43081
614-895-7166

International Food Information Council
1100 Connecticut Ave. NW, Suite 430
Washington, DC 20036
202-296-6540
<http://http://ificinfo.health.org>

International Franchise Association (IFA)
1350 New York Ave. NW, Suite 900
Washington, DC 20005
202-628-8000
<http://www.franchise.org>

International Society of Travel & Tourism Educators (ISTTE)
23220 Edgewater St.
St. Clair Shores, MI 48082
586-294-0208

Les Clefs d'Or USA
c/o John Neary
The Carlyle Hotel
35 E. 76th St.
New York, NY 10021
212-744-1600

National Association of Catering Executives (NACE)
304 W. Liberty St., Suite 201
Louisville, KY 40202
502-583-3783

National Association of Concessionaires (NAC)
35 E. Wacker Dr., Suite 1816
Chicago, IL 60601
312-236-3858

National Association of Institutional Linen Management (NAILM)
2130 Lexington Rd., Suite H
Richmond, KY 40475
606-624-0177
<http://www.nailm.com>

National Association of Pizza Operators (NAPO)
P.O. Box 1347
New Albany, IN 47151
812-949-0909
<http://www.pizzatoday.com>

National Bed-and-Breakfast Association (NB&BA)
P.O. Box 332
Norwalk, CT 06852
203-847-6196
<http://www.nbba.com>

National Black McDonald's Operators Association (NBMOA)
6363 W. Sunset Blvd., Suite 809
Hollywood, CA 90028-7330
323-933-2070

National Council of Chain Restaurants (NCCR)
1101 Connecticut Ave. NW, Suite 700
Washington, DC 20036
202-626-8183

National Frozen Dessert and Fast Food Association
P.O. Box 1116
Millbrook, NY 12545
800-535-7748

National Restaurant Association (NRA)
1200 17th St. NW
Washington, DC 20036
202-331-5900
<http://www.restaurant.org>

Professional Convention Management Association
100 Vestaria Office Park, Suite 220
Birmingham, AL 35216
205-823-7262
<http://www.pcma.org>

Roundtable for Women Food-Beverage-Hospitality (RWFBH)
145 W. 1st St., Suite A
Tustin, CA 92680

Society for Foodservice Management (SFM)
304 W. Liberty St., Suite 201
Louisville, KY 40202
502-583-3783

Society for Foodservice Systems Hospitality Institute of Technology and Management
670 Transfer Rd., Suite 21A
St. Paul, MN 55114
651-646-7077
<http://www.hi-tm.com>

Society for the Advancement of Travel for the Handicapped
347 5th Ave., Suite 610
New York, NY 10016
212-447-7284
<http://www.sats.org>

Trade Show Exhibitors Association
5501 Backlick Rd., Suite 105
Springfield, VA 22151-3940
703-941-3725
<http://www.tsea.org>

Travel Industry Association of America (TIA)
2 Lafayette Centre
1133 21st St. NW
Washington, DC 20036
202-293-1433

United Nations World Tourism Organization
Calle Capitan Haya 42
E-28020 Madrid
Spain

United States Tourist Council (USTC)
Drawer 1875
Washington, DC 20013-1875
301-565-5155

United States Travel Data Center
2 Lafayette Centre
1133 21st St. NW
Washington, D.C. 20036
202-293-1040

Washington Ethical Society (WES)
7750 16th St. NW
Washington, DC 20012
202-882-6650
<http://www.ethicalsociety.org>

Glossary

aging the slow, subtle completion of fermentation, usually in large wooden barrels or glass-lined vats

Alaska Airlines gold member a designation for elite travelers that have attained predetermined thresholds of air miles flown, entitling them to upgrades and preferential services

alcohol naturally occurring and easily synthesized compound that induces intoxication when consumed

all-suite hotels hotels that only rent suites

ambiance a hotel's or restaurant's atmosphere and setting, or the overall impression and mood it creates

amenities features that add material comfort, convenience, or smoothness to social interactions

amenity spa spa within a resort

assistant housekeepers staff members that supervise the day-to-day work of room attendants in larger hotels; also called floor supervisors

assisted living residential option that bridges retirement home and full-service nursing home

baby boomer individual born between 1946 and 1964

back of the house the support areas behind the scenes in a hotel or motel, including housekeeping, laundry, engineering, and foodservice; individuals who operate behind the scenes to make a guest's stay pleasant and safe

base fee arrangement determined by the gross operating revenue that ensures a management company a profit

bed-and-breakfast private home with a family in residence, offering one to five guest rooms; also called B & B

bell captain staff member who greets guests and trains and supervises all bellhops, door attendants, and valet parking crew

bellhops individuals who usher arriving guests to their rooms and carry their luggage

blog Internet publication vehicle

break-even point point at which costs equal revenue

brewpub microbrewery that operates in tandem with a bar or restaurant

call brand alcohol product called for by name by a customer

cannibalize eat away at the market share of existing products

career objective statement of the kind of job one hopes to get

carrying capacity the maximum number of people who can use a destination without causing the environment to deteriorate and the quality of the visitor's experience to decrease

catastrophe plan plan developed by the security staff to ensure staff and guest safety and to minimize direct and indirect costs from disaster by reviewing insurance policies, analyzing physical facilities, and evaluating possible disaster scenarios

charter operator tour wholesaler who assembles a package tour and sells it to the public or to tour operators

château castle, manor house, or palace

chef the top level of authority in the kitchen

chef d'etage captain of waiters; individual who has the most direct contact with diners

chef de rang front waiter; sees to the service needs of guests as they dine

chef de partie line chef or station chef

chef de salle head waiter; responsible for the service provided in the dining room

chief engineer supervises the engineering department, also called the plant manager

chief of security heads the security department

club association of persons with common objectives, usually jointly supported and meeting periodically

coaching inns developed after stagecoach routes were established in the 1600s, these inns fed and lodged travelers overnight and exchanged tired horses for rested ones

collectively bargains negotiates to establish conditions and wages acceptable to both union members and management

commercial foodservice operations that compete for customers in the open market

communication the process of sending and receiving messages

computerized reservation system (CRS) a complex computer database that provides information about many travel options

concept elements of a foodservice operation that contribute to its function as a complete and organized system serving the guests' needs and expectations

concierge staff member who answers questions, solves problems, and performs the services of a private secretary for a hotel's guests

congress term often used outside the United States for convention

contraction recession phase in a business cycle

contribution margin key indicator in menu engineering, determined by subtracting food cost from selling price; used as a measure of profitability

controller head accountant who manages the accounting department and all financial dealings of the hotel

convention generic term referring to any size of business or professional meeting held in one specific location; a group of delegates or members who assemble to accomplish a specific goal

convention and visitors bureau (CVBs) organization responsible for promoting tourism at the regional and local level; a not-for-profit umbrella organization that represents a city or urban area in soliciting all types of travelers to that city or area, whether for business, pleasure, or both

cook-chill technology used in large institutional foodservice operations to increase efficiency and maintain food quality

corporate travel manager staff member who handles all aspects of travel arrangements for a corporation's employees

credit manager responsible for validating and authorizing guest credits and collecting overdue accounts

cruise tour by ship

cuisine food cooked and served in styles from around the world

CVB convention and visitors bureau

danger zone temperature range between 40° and 140° Fahrenheit at which bacteria flourishes on food

database organized collection of information, such as names, addresses, prices, and dates

debt service interest on loans

demi-chef de rang back waiter or busperson; clears all appropriate service items from the table between courses

demographics statistical study of the characteristics of human populations

demonstration effect adoption by local people of practices learned from tourists

destination location where travelers choose to visit and spend time

destination marketing organizations (DMOs) organizations in charge of developing and implementing tourism programs for individual states

direct spending money that goes directly from the traveler into the economy

discretionary spending spending on items such as entertainment, food away from home, alcoholic beverages, and personal care products and services

distilled drinks beverages made from a fermented product which is then put through a process that recovers and adds additional alcohol; also called liquor or spirits

distilleries companies that make distilled alcoholic beverages

diversity training programs educational programs that teach hotel management and staff about ways to provide access, inclusion, and opportunity for all people, regardless of age, sex, race, or disability

draft beer that is not pasteurized

dram shop legislation laws that govern the legal operation of establishments that sell measured alcoholic beverages

dry wine term; refers to lack of sweetness

economics social science relating to the production, distribution, and use of goods and services

ecotourism balance between tourism development and preservation of natural and cultural heritages ; new segment of the industry in which travelers learn about or advance the environment and its causes

elastic demand that changes with economic conditions

electronic cash register device that records the volume of drinks sold, the price per unit, the time of service, the particular type of drink, and the name of the server

electronic liquor dispenser (ELD) device that dispenses an exact measure of liquor into a glass

electronic voice mail systems technology that allows a caller to leave a message keyed to a guest room phone

employee assistance programs (EAPs) services offered to employees for the management of personal problems

entremetier vegetable chef

entrepreneur individual who creates, organizes, manages, and assumes the risk of an enterprise or business

equity club a not-for-profit club typically owned and organized by its members for their own enjoyment

ethyl alcohol beverage alcohol, identified scientifically as C_2H_6O

excursionists people who travel to a site or destination and return home the same day

executive assistant manager hotel staff member who manages the functions that deal directly with room rental

executive housekeeper head of the housekeeping department

expansion a phase of growth in a business cycle, during which time there is an increase or upswing in economic activity

exposition event held mainly for informational exchanges among tradespeople; large exhibition in which the presentation is the main attraction as well as a source of revenue for the exhibitors

exponential describes growth of revenue after baseline steadily increases

extended-care centers health-care facilities that offer intensive, round-the-clock nursing care under a physician's direction; may include the services of registered nurses, licensed practical nurses, aides, and orderlies

familiarization trip free or reduced-price trip given to travel agents, travel writers, or other middlemen to promote destinations; also called a fam trip

fermentation chemical process in which yeast acts on sugar or sugar-containing substances such as grain or fruit to produce alcohol and carbon dioxide

fermented beverage liquid formed by yeast acting on sugar-containing substances

floor supervisor staff member who supervises day-to-day work of room attendants at larger motels; also called an assistant housekeeper

forecasting process of estimating future events

franchise agreements contracts in which the franchisor grants the franchisee the right to use the franchisor's name and proven method of doing business

franchisee franchise buyer; individual business operator

franchisor franchise seller; brand owner

free pouring dispensing of liquor where the bartender estimates the amount of liquor needed for a drink

frequent flyer promotional program whereby traveler earns free trips based on miles flown

frequent guest promotional program whereby traveler earns free or upgraded lodging

front-desk manager handles all functions of the front office and often supervises a team of workers

front of the house comprises all areas the guests will contact, including the lobby, corridors, elevators, guest rooms, restaurants and bars, meeting rooms, and restrooms; employees who staff these areas

functional image impression of a destination associated with specific activities and attractions

fusion cuisine blending of ingredients and cooking techniques from different cultures

gaming wagering of money or other valuables on the outcome of a game or other event

garde manger pantry chef who prepares all cold appetizers, desserts, and salads

Gestalt evaluation holistic evaluation of a service encounter, as in "everything went right"

glass ceiling invisible barriers preventing women and minorities promotion to top management positions

green card Permanent Resident or Alien Register Receipt Card visa given to immigrants and refugees who enter the United States legally

Gen-Xer individual born between 1965 and 1980

grievance complaint filed by an employee against the employer

grillardin grill cook

gross domestic product (GDP) total value of goods and services produced within a country, minus the net payments on foreign investments

gross operating profit revenues minus operating costs before taxes

hand-measured pouring the dispensing of liquor using a jigger or shot glass

hops the dried, conical fruit of a special vine that gives beer its special bitterness

hospitality and tourism network group of separate and competitive, closely interrelated industries

hospitality industry wide range of businesses, each of which is dedicated to the service of people away from home; businesses that emphasize personnel's responsibility to be hospitable hosts and managers of services offered

hotelier keeper, owner, or manager of a hospitality property

hot rock massage a spa treatment that involves heated rocks strategically placed on the body

human resources manager staff member who manages the hotel's employee benefits program and monitors compliance with laws that relate to equal opportunity in hiring and promotion

illegal aliens individuals who move to another country illegally, without permission to enter as immigrants or refugees; also called undocumented workers

immigrants individuals who move from their country of origin to live and work in another country

inbound operators agencies that specialize in providing tour packages to international travelers visiting the United States

incentive fees income generated above the normal management fee; based on exceeding budgeted profit targets

incentive-fee arrangement requiring that the management company take some risk in the hotel's operation

incentive travel marketing and management tool used to motivate people by offering travel rewards for achieving a specific goal

indirect spending respending of tourist dollars within an economy

informational interview interview that allows a person to gather specific information about a job, company, or industry

infrastructure underlying economic foundation, including transportation and communication systems, power facilities, and other public services

infusion immersion of heat-sensitive ingredients such as fruits into a hot alcohol base

intermediate-care centers health-care facilities that offer assistance to persons incapable of living independently; provide only basic nursing care combined with social and lodging services

job coach professional who trains and supervises a mentally or physically challenged worker

iPod digital audio device used to play and store large amounts of music and video

kitchen brigade system of kitchen organization in which the staff is divided into specialized departments, all contributing collectively to the preparation of a meal

kiosk stand-alone electronic station designed to check guests in and out of a hotel through an automated process

labor-intensive relying on a large workforce to meet the needs of guests

laundry manager staff member who supervises laundry room attendants

laundry room attendants individuals who wash, dry, iron, and fold laundry

leakage money that flows out of the economy to purchase outside resources

leisure freedom resulting from the cessation of activities, especially freedom from work or duties

lifecare communities long-term health-care facilities that cater to both dependent and independent older adults

liquor an alcoholic beverage made by distillation

maceration immersion of heat-sensitive ingredients such as fruits into a cold base alcohol

maître d'hôtel dining room manager who oversees the entire operation of the dining room

malt germinated barley

malting process in which grain is germinated to produce an enzyme that can convert starch into fermentable sugar

management contract agreement under which owner maintains financial responsibility for a property and management company is responsible for operating the property using the owner's money

market price levels general classification system of lodging facilities whose price definitions depend on the city or geographic region

market segments smaller, identifiable groups that can be defined using any set of characteristics, such as those found in geographic, demographic, or psychographic information ; subgroups of customers who share a specific set of needs and expectations

marketing related group of business activities that have the purpose of satisfying demand for goods and services; process of planning a hotel's concept (type of facility, services offered, location), rates to charge, and how to reach potential customers, all in a way that satisfies individual and organizational objectives

meeting gathering of people for a common purpose

meeting planner professional who coordinates every detail of meetings and conventions

mega-resorts hotel and resort complexes that encompass thousands of acres of land, with self-contained services and activities

menu engineering tool in menu planning that uses the menu as a whole, not individual items that make up the menu, as a measure of profitability

menu mix indicator in menu engineering; a detailed record of customer preferences based on menu selections

microbreweries small, local breweries

middlemen business firms that distribute products from producers to consumers

millennial individual born between 1981 and 1999

mise en place state of overall preparedness; having all the necessary ingredients and cooking utensils at hand and ready to use at the moment work on a dish begins

mixed-use development a real estate project that incorporates hotel, restaurant, retail, and entertainment components

multiplier effect respending that expands the economy

must a mixture of grape pulp, skins, seeds, and stems

national tourism organizations (NTOs) organizations national governments use to promote their countries

necessary leakage cost of promoting a destination abroad

networking process of meeting with and gathering information from an ever-expanding channel of acquaintances

occupancy rate percentage derived by dividing the total number of rooms occupied during a given period (night, week, year) by the total number of rooms available for occupancy during that period

on-line distribution Internet-based reservation sytem for lodging properties

on-site foodservice operations that serve people who are members of particular societal institutions, such as hospitals, colleges, schools, nursing homes, the military, and industry; formerly known as institutional foodservice

opportunity cost opportunities lost by excluding the development of one industry in order to develop a different industry

ordinaries public houses in Colonial America

overbooking lodging practice of booking 10 to 15 percent more reservations than available to combat the loss of revenue

patissier pastry chef; also responsible for breads and rolls

paymaster staff member who heads a large payroll division within a hotel

peak uppermost point in a business cycle

plant manager supervises the engineering department, also called the chief engineer

point of sale (POS) computerized system that allows bars to set drink prices according to the specific ingredients served

poissionier fish station chef

positioning process of establishing a distinctive place in the market (and in the minds of potential guests)

preopening expenses expenses incurred during the development process of a hotel, including advertising, office equipment, and payroll for the preopening team

price-value relationship cost in relation to the value received

professional development process of becoming involved with trade-related activities, including meetings, seminars, and committees

profit-sharing lease agreement between two or more parties to share expenses and profits

proof figure representing liquor's alcohol content

property management system (PMS) computerized system for storing information about reservations, room availability and room rate; allows integration of all the systems utilized by a lodging property—reservations, front desk, housekeeping, food and beverage control, and accounting

plasma TV type of flat-panel display commonly used for large TV displays (typically above 37-inch or 940 mm diagonal)

quid pro quo situation in which a supervisor demands sexual favors in exchange for tangible job benefits, like a promotion or raise

receiver in the communication process, the audience the message is aimed at

recreation refreshment of strength and spirits after work, a means of diversion

recreation management professional handling of the physical facilities where recreation and leisure activities occur

refugees individuals escaping persecution in their home country because of ethnic group, race, religion, belief, or or other group membership

reservations manager staff member who oversees reservation functions

resident manager staff member who supervises front-office operations and reservations, as well as housekeeping

residential-care centers health-care facilities that provide regular nursing care and some social services, primarily to mentally challenged individuals (of any age), in a residential environment

resort place providing recreation and entertainment, especially to vacationers

resort spas single-purpose spas, devoid of outside temptations and distractions

resumé short, written account of a job applicant's work experience, education, and other qualifications

retail travel agent seller of travel services who receives income directly from suppliers and other intermediaries in the form of commissions

return on investment A performance measure used to evaluate the efficiency of an investment or to compare the efficiency of a number of different investments

rethermalized thawed and heated

room attendants staff members who perform the daily room cleaning at a hotel

room clerk individual at the front desk who greets and registers hotel guests

room rack cards posted at small hotels showing the status of all guest rooms

room service manager staff member that heads the room service department

room service operators staff members that take reservation orders over the telephone

saucier sauté cook

screening interview interview used to eliminate applicants from consideration when too many people apply for a job

securitization process of issuing bonds to finance or refinance a loan

sender in the communication process, the person delivering the message

servers staff members that transport the food from the kitchen to the guest room

service encounter period of time in which a customer directly interacts with either the personnel or the physical facilities and other visible elements of a hospitality business

sexual harassment occurs whenever any unwanted sexually oriented behavior changes an employee's working conditions and/or creates a hostile or abusive work environment

sexually offensive or hostile work environment situation in which an employee might be subjected to sexual comments, pictures, or actions that are deemed offensive, even though they may not threaten the person's job or possibilities for promotion

social membership a partial membership that enables the member to use specific aspects of a club, but not others

socioeconomic relating to both sociology and economics

solera system of blending sherries or ports from a mixture of several vintages to ensure consistency

sommelier an expert in wine selection and service

sous chef next in command to the chef

spa any fitness or health-related resort

spa cuisine emphasizes the preparation of low-calorie, low-fat entrees that feature an abundance of fresh fruits and vegetables and complex carbohydrates

spirits another name for distilled drinks

split half bottle of wine

spreadsheet electronic version of an accountant's ledger book that not only records numeric information, but can also perform calculations with that information

standard purchase specifications food standards established by a restaurant; also called "specs"

stipend allowance provided for child care

suite combined living space with kitchen facilities, or a bedroom section with an attached parlor

symbolic image relationship between one's self concept and the destination's image

tannins substances drawn from grapeskins and wooden barrels used for aging wine, which contribute an astringency to wine

taverns establishments that serve some food but specialize in alcoholic beverages

technology all the ways people use discoveries and inventions to satisfy needs; generally refers to industrial technology

theme park recreational venue that is based on a particular setting or artistic interpretation; may comprise hundreds or thousands of acres of parkland and employ hundreds or thousands of workers in its operation

total yearly expenses record of all costs for the year

tour operators agencies that sell (usually escorted) tour packages to groups of tourists

tour package composite of related services offered at a single price

tour wholesaler company or individual that designs and packages tours

tourism travel for recreation, or the promotion and arrangement of such travel

tourism industry industry concerned with attractions and events that draw people to an area

tourism offices organizations in charge of developing and implementing tourism programs for individual states; also referred to as destination marketing organizations

tourists people who take trips of one hundred miles or more and who spend at least one night away from home

trade show event held for informational exchanges among tradespeople, also called an exposition

trading blocs associations, usually between or among governments, that encourage, regulate, and/or restrict elements of trade

travel intermediaries travel middlemen or business firms that distribute travel products

trends prevailing tendencies or general movements

trough lowermost point in a business cycle

turnover rate statistic calculated by dividing the number of workers replaced in any given time period by the average number of employees needed to run the business

undocumented workers individuals who move from another country illegally, without permission to enter as either immigrants or refugees; also called illegal aliens

vacation ownership a fractional interest in a condominium or hotel room or suite that is designated for weekly usage by the owner and then offered in a booking pool to tourists on a year-round basis

varietal the type of grape from which wines are made and for which they are named

vintage year in which a wine's grapes were harvested

VIP very important person, usually a dignitary or other high-ranking official or regular customer that frequents an establishment

wake-up call computer or manually placed call to a guest's room to wake him or her at a set time

walk-ins people who do not have reservations

well brand a lesser-quality product used to prepare drink orders at a bar

wireless Internet local area network (LAN) that uses radio waves rather than wires

word processor software that has replaced typewriters as the writing tool of choice

workers' councils labor unions and worker's associations in Europe

wort in beer-making, the liquid remaining after the mash is strained and filtered

yield management practice of analyzing past reservation patterns, room rates, cancellations, and no-shows in an attempt to maximize profits and occupancy rates and set competitive room rates

yuan Chinese currency

Index

Page numbers in *italic* indicate figures or tables.

K

L

M